FIFTH EDITION

Persuasion

and

Social Movements

FIFTH EDITION

Persuasion
and
Social Movements

Charles J. Stewart
Purdue University

Craig Allen Smith
North Carolina State University

Robert E. Denton, Jr.
Virginia Polytechnic Institute and State University

WAVELAND

PRESS, INC.

Long Grove, Illinois

For information about this book, contact:
Waveland Press, Inc.
4180 IL Route 83, Suite 101
Long Grove, IL 60047-9580
(847) 634-0081
info@waveland.com
www.waveland.com

Contents

12   Justifying Violence through Good Reasons   273

13   The Use of Terrorism by Social Movements   299

Preface

The United States has a long history of social movements. A social movement precipitated the Revolutionary War for independence in the eighteenth century. The nineteenth century witnessed movements to free the slaves, end child labor, improve working conditions for industrial workers and farmers, gain rights for women, abolish alcoholic beverages, and improve animal welfare. The twentieth century saw the continuation of many of these movements as well as those for peace, the environment, abortion rights, changes in U.S. culture, suffrage for women, and the rights of African Americans, Native Americans, Hispanic Americans, Asian Americans, the elderly, gays and lesbians, students, and animals. The twenty-first century appears to be a continuation of these movements—for instance, third wave feminism and third wave environmentalism—while experiencing growing conflicts over globalization and the timeless struggles between those on the social, political, and religious left and right.

The fifth edition of *Persuasion and Social Movements* continues to reflect the growing sophistication with which the study of social movements is being approached in the fields of communication, sociology, and social psychology. The ever expanding body of research not only looks to the past, particularly nineteenth century movements opposing slavery and espousing women's rights and labor reform, but to the present and future with studies of global conflicts generated by attempts to change and sustain economic, social, religious, and political cultures, practices, and beliefs. A growing number of people around the globe see themselves as being in a state of siege. As of this writing, many countries are experiencing outrage and violence over a series of cartoons in a Danish newspaper that portrayed the Prophet Mohammed in an insulting manner.

Our purpose in writing this book since it was conceived in the late 1970s (the first edition appeared in 1984) has been fourfold: to synthesize, apply, extend, and develop findings, theories, and approaches to the persuasive efforts of social movements. The book has continued to evolve as new movements have appeared, research has offered new insights, and new technologies have transformed how social movement organizations communicate with their audiences. For instance, the role of the Internet is an integral part of many chapters as we have turned increasingly to Web sites to discover and understand the persuasive efforts of contemporary social movements and their organizations. The roles of music and obscenity appear to be less important in current protest, so we have focused less on these persuasive tactics and more on violence and terrorism that appear to dominate our experience and thinking in the twenty-first century.

Chapters 1, 2, and 3 of this fifth edition address the role of persuasion in social movements and include topics that explore the characteristics of social movements, the social movement from an interpretive systems perspective, and the persuasive functions of social movements. Chapters 4, 5, and 6 address the stages through which social movements tend to progress or retreat, the personal needs of members of social movements (focusing on authoritarian and democratic personalities), and the nature of leadership and how it is attained and maintained. Chapter 7 consolidates and refines three previous chapters into a single chapter that addresses languaging strategies and tactics in social movements—symbolism and symbolic acts—including identification, polarization, slogans, music, obscenity, and ridicule. Chapters 8, 9, 10, and 11 address argument in social movement persuasion, including types of political argument, argument from narrative vision, argument from transcendence, and argument from conspiracy. Chapter 12 is a new chapter that identifies, explains, and illustrates the "good reasons" social movement organizations provide to justify the use of violence to bring about or resist change. Chapter 13 is a new chapter that focuses on the uses of terrorism by social movement organizations and how it is an interactive process dependent on the actions and reactions of both institutions and terrorists. Chapter 14 addresses the strategies and tactics institutions and countermovements use to resist social movements.

While this fifth edition contains new chapters on violence and terrorism, all other chapters are updated, including research cited, examples offered, new insights into social movement persuasion, and the use of the Internet. For instance, more than half of messages cited in the chapter on argument from transcendence are now from Web sites of pro-life and pro-choice organizations. Considerable attention is devoted to recent movements such as animal rights, militias, the religious right, workers' rights in sweatshops, and the rising resistance to the globalization of the economy and production. The selected bibliography is reorganized and updated to the spring of 2006.

We have approached this book once again with five fundamental assumptions. First, since persuasion is inherently practical, we can study it most profitably by examining the functions of persuasive acts. Second, even apparently irrational acts make sense to the actor; the trick is discovering the reasoning behind the act. Third, people create and comprehend their world through symbols, and it is people who create, use, ignore, or act upon these symbolic creations. Fourth, public speeches are an important form of social movement persuasion, but they are neither the most prevalent nor necessarily the most effective form. The Internet is rapidly becoming a major resource for protest activities of all sorts. And fifth, social movements are rarely mere instances of orneriness, perversion, or ignorance. Someone once wryly observed that a rebel who loses is a traitor, while a rebel who wins is a patriot and founder. These assumptions may strike some readers as heresy and still others as old-hat. We hope this revised, restructured, and updated edition strikes a useful balance.

Charles J. Stewart
Craig Allen Smith
Robert E. Denton, Jr.

CHAPTER

1

The Essential Characteristics of a Social Movement

The history of the United States has arguably been a history of social movements striving for a more perfect social order in which freedom, justice, and morality will reign.[1] Many colonists came to America to escape persecution for their religious, political, and social beliefs. The American Revolution began as a social movement in which our first "radicals"—Samuel Adams, Benjamin Franklin, John Dickinson, and Patrick Henry among others—protested unfair laws and treatment by the king and parliament and demanded unqualified justice. Only later did it turn into a full-scale military conflict to attain independence and freedom from tyranny.

The nineteenth century witnessed social movements to free the slaves, end child labor, improve the plight of industrial workers and farmers, gain rights for women, and temper or abolish the use of alcoholic beverages. But for every social movement formed to bring about change, countermovements and institutions confronted and sometimes suppressed the dissatisfied to sustain the social order already in place. Inevitably the nineteenth century passed along unfulfilled dreams and agendas to their twentieth-century counterparts.

The twentieth century could be called the age of the social movement because of the changes social movements initiated, aided, or achieved. There were nationalistic movements throughout the world and the collapse of the Soviet Union and communism in Europe. In the United States, African, Hispanic, Asian, and Native Americans, women, gays and lesbians, college students, prison inmates, and workers from the vineyard to the university campus struggled for constitutional and human rights, equality, justice, identity, and a share of the American dream. Social movements formed to end military conflicts, to protect the environment, to prevent the construction of nuclear power plants, to limit violence and sex on television and the Internet, to end apartheid in South Africa, to gain rights for animals, to halt legalized abortion, and to reduce the power of corporate, governmental, religious, and educational bureaucracies. The growing conflict over moral, religious, social, political, and economic values, beliefs, and attitudes fueled social movements on the left and the right.

But just as the nineteenth century passed along unfulfilled dreams and agendas, the twentieth century passed to the twenty-first century struggles for justice and equality, protection and prohibition, values and attitudes. At this writing, a former Ku Klux Klansman has just been tried and sentenced for his part in the 1964 killings of three young civil rights workers in Mississippi.[2] War, the environment, abortion, and equal rights for women, minorities, and animals continue to be contentious issues. We now study third wave feminism and third wave environmentalism. At the same time, ever-increasing institutional bureaucracies, the shrinking of our world through inexpensive and fast air travel, the widespread availability of electronic means of communication, and the rise of multi-national corporations have spawned social movements to counter perceived threats to identity, values, culture—our way of life—from the "new world order" and globalization.

Even though scholars have studied the persuasive efforts of social movements for decades, there continues to be some confusion and disagreement about what constitutes a social movement. This is due in part to the widespread use of the ambiguous label *movement* to identify any effort to bring about or resist change. These efforts include internal changes within established institutions, isolated acts of protest, protest organizations, campaigns, uprisings, revolutions, civil wars, trends, and fads. To recognize differences among movement phenomena, we attach modifiers such as social, political, religious, historical, rhetorical, reform, nationalistic, and individualistic. When suspicious or fearful of movements we call them radical, violent, revolutionary, repressive, and fanatical. Some groups compound confusion by calling themselves "movements" to inflate their egos, add "saliency" to a cause, and enhance perceptions of their size and influence.[3] Social movements add to this confusion because they may quickly change forms, strategies, tactics, and some goals. As Wim van de Donk, Brian Loader, Paul Nixon, and Dieter Rucht conclude, "A social movement is a 'moving target,' difficult to observe."[4]

This book focuses on the persuasive efforts of one type of movement formed to bring about or resist change—the *social* movement. If we seek insights into the persuasive efforts of a social movement or portions of a social movement—social movement organizations (SMOs), campaigns, or strategies—it is essential to determine if the phenomenon under investigation is in fact a *social* movement. This chapter identifies the essential characteristics of social movements and contrasts social movements with other collective phenomena such as political parties, established institutions, campaigns, lobbies, special interest groups, civil wars, and revolutions.

AN ORGANIZED COLLECTIVITY

A social movement is at least minimally organized. If we cannot identify leaders or spokespersons, members or followers, and organizations or coalitions, the phenomenon under investigation is a trend, fad, riot, or spontaneous protest, not a social movement. As Sidney Tarrow writes, "the presence of even a large number of protest events does not, in itself, constitute a social movement." For a social movement to come into existence,

> Challengers must frame their demands in ways that will attract followers and build on social networks, and connective structures must link them to one another with a shared definition of reality, of "us" and "them," and of fundamental goals through changing seasons of opportunities and constraints."[5]

While a number of seemingly similar protests—such as protests on college campuses to end racism or protests against illegal immigration along the Mexico-United States border—may be a social movement in the making, the presence of a few demonstrators or bloggers does not constitute a social movement. Without some identifiable organizing characteristics the claims or dreams of a group that has not organized to attract members and to create connections are insufficient to constitute a movement.

A phenomenon of the early 1990s called the men's movement (in which groups of men attended weekend retreats, sweated around fires in teepees, poured out their hearts, and sought comfort in brotherhood) never developed into an *organized* social movement. There were no organizations, no recognizable leaders (other than poets and writers), and no identifiable membership. The "men's movement" faded away after a few years. On the other hand, the concern over clothing made in sweatshop conditions surfaced in the late 1990s in labor union literature, within human rights organizations, and on television talk shows. It remained beneath the consciousness of most U.S. citizens until the winter and spring of 2000. Students and faculty on college campuses around the country formed local organizations and demanded that their institutions become members of the Worker Rights Consortium (WRC), a coalition of universities, labor unions, and human rights groups created to investigate and take actions against human rights abuses. A major target was the profits universities received from the sale of university apparel produced in sweatshops. Student-led groups brought pressure on administrations to create codes of conduct for manufacturers and to join the WRC. They employed Web sites, leaflets, symbolic actions, demonstrations, sit-ins, tent cities, and hunger strikes. Although the sweatshop movement is seldom in the news today, it continues to monitor possible sweatshops around the world, to maintain active Web sites, and to inform college and university administrations and students when violations of agreements are detected.

Degree of Organization

The number of organizations, visibility of leaders, and nature of membership varies from social movement to social movement, but none consist of a single organization or leader. For instance, Martin Luther King, Jr., of the Southern Christian Leadership Conference (SCLC), Roy Wilkins of the National Association for the Advancement of Colored People (NAACP), and Stokely Carmichael of the Student Nonviolent Coordinating Committee (SNCC) were highly visible leaders of well-known organizations within the civil rights movement. No social movement is a single-minded, cohesive unit because each generates factions and internal conflicts over philosophical, ideological, and strategic differences.

Although it might be difficult for most of us to name a leader or organization of the gay rights, animal rights, militia, or pro-choice movements, there are many. All the movements have sizable memberships, which are essential for the continuing existence and progress of each social movement. Leaders, members, and organizations that stage frequent public demonstrations and media events—such as pro-life's Operation Rescue or PETA (People for the Ethical Treatment of Animals)—are more visible than ones that operate primarily through the Internet, courts, in small groups, or within the social movement community such as the National Right to Life Committee or Trans-Species Unlimited. Regardless of their visibility, all social movements must have at least minimal organization.

On the other hand, if we are studying the persuasive efforts of a highly structured protest phenomenon with a clear hierarchy of leadership, a charter or constitution that delimits ideology and the means to achieve it, membership requirements, a membership list, Web site, and headquarters location, we are most likely studying a social movement organization (SMO), not a social movement. Some writers have identified "new social movements" of the past decade or so as different from "old social movements" in their absence of a defining ideology (such as the Communist Manifesto), membership roles, and well-known and powerful leaders. In fact, few social movements have ever exhibited these highly structured characteristics, but many SMOs do. As Karlyn Campbell writes, the women's liberation movement (second wave feminism) was never a cohesive, carefully organized effort to bring about "well-defined social changes." She tries to give her students "a sense of the diversity of its discourse, of the aims of its many organizations, the varied audiences that were targeted, and the many conflicts among activists and groups."[6] These are the characteristics of minimally organized social movements.

The mass media may create the illusion of a social movement by labeling and treating "relatively isolated, but similar, rhetorical situations throughout the nation . . . as a single, dynamic, and interrelated phenomenon."[7] For example, the "death of God theology" received substantial media coverage and the attention of religious leaders in the 1970s and 1980s and appeared to be a thriving social movement when no leadership, membership, or organization existed.[8] A similar phenomenon, the "secular humanist conspiracy," attracted a great deal of attention in the 1980s and 1990s from Christian fundamentalists and political conservatives who saw it as a powerful, demonic social movement responsible for moral decline. However, the secular changes occurring in the United States and elsewhere were the results of decades-old *trends* rather than the work of a well-organized secular humanist social movement. There is no evidence of organizations, leaders, or demonstrations beyond the "Humanist Manifesto I" that first appeared in 1933 and was endorsed by thirty-four "liberal humanists" and an expanded "Humanist Manifesto II" that appeared in 1973 and was signed by one hundred and fourteen "individuals of prominence and distinction."[9] There is no evidence the signers and fellow humanists who endorsed the manifestos conducted campaigns urging teenagers to have sex, athletes to use steroids, husbands and wives to divorce, women to substitute the workplace for the home and to have abortions, or God-fearing people to stop attending churches, temples, and mosques. A trend indicating significant alterations of norms and values at least since the end of World War II is readily apparent, but this unorganized trend is not the equivalent of an organized social movement.

Social Movement Campaigns

Social movements are often confused with campaigns because social movements conduct numerous campaigns to achieve specific goals. For instance, Operation Rescue conducted campaigns to close down abortion clinics in targeted cities around the country and to clog the jails with arrested demonstrators so police would be unable to disrupt their sit-ins and blockades. Earth First! conducted campaigns to stop the logging of redwoods in the northwest, often by sitting in the tops of giant trees, lying in front of bulldozers, driving spike nails into trees, or sabotaging equipment. Although campaigns and social movements share similarities, they have significant differences.

Social movements tend to be organized from the bottom up and consist primarily of "ordinary people" with limited and tenuous commitments to the cause, while campaigns tend to be highly organized from the top down.[10] A social movement leader usually rises from within a protest group as it develops and sees the need for leadership. It is an *evolutionary process* in which an effective spokesperson who can articulate the fundamentals of the cause emerges as a leader. On the other hand, a *campaign* leader is usually selected by an organization prior to the start of the campaign and then selects and organizes a staff to run the campaign. Campaigns typically have managers with assigned roles, organizational charts, chiefs of staff, schedules of operations, specific goals, budgets, time tables, and known end points such as Election Day, an anniversary celebration, or a projected date when a fund or membership drive is to "go over the top" of the predetermined goal.

Native Americans have organized protest campaigns when the Atlanta Braves or Washington Redskins played in the World Series or football league championship games. The demonstrators demand that these teams stop employing what they see as offensive, racist nicknames, "sham rituals and ridiculous impersonations."[11] Similarly, during the Christmas holiday season when sales are robust, animal rights activists organize campaigns to picket Macy's and other department stores that sell fur coats and stores that sell pets. But these protest campaigns end when the sports event or the holiday season ends. By contrast, the Native-American and animal rights social movements have lasted for decades, changed as circumstances have changed, rarely maintained tight control over memberships, and altered or added goals as they have evolved. No social movement knows when or if it will achieve its ends, and some have been with us in various forms for more than a century.

Impressive, media-generating campaigns and rallies often remain just that. In the late 1990s, the Promise Keepers held well attended rallies for men in sports stadiums, where attendees promised to be strong heads of their households and good fathers and husbands. The rallies ended after a few years, and no organized social movement resulted. The same is true of the "Million Man March" held in Washington, D.C., on October 16, 1995, that asked those in attendance to pledge to be better persons, sons, fathers, and husbands when they returned home, and the "Million Mom March" held in Washington, D.C., on Mother's Day, May 14, 2000, that demanded "sensible gun laws" and an end to gun violence.[12] We might call them "movements" for a better society, but neither flowered into lasting *social* movements. "It is only by sustaining collective action against antagonists that a contentious episode becomes a social movement."[13]

Social Movement Organizations

Social movement *organizations* are often confused with social *movements*. The National Organization for Women (NOW), the American Indian Movement (AIM), People for the Ethical Treatment of Animals (PETA), and White Aryan Resistance (WAR) are organizations within social movements; they are not themselves social movements. Each is *one* organization striving for equality for women, Native-American rights and dignity, humane treatment of wild and domestic animals, and preservation of a way of life and the so-called Aryan race.

To understand fully the persuasive efforts of the animal rights movement, for example, we would need to study the messages and symbolic actions of several organizations within the movement, including Friends for Animals, the Animal Protection Institute of America, Beauty Without Cruelty International, Trans-Species Unlimited, the Animal Welfare Institute, Humans Against Rabbit Exploitation (HARE), the Animal Liberation Front (ALF), and PETA. These differing factions within the movement often compete with and attack one another. Coalitions, when possible, tend to be fragile and short-lived. When Denise Bostdorff studied the Internet rhetoric of the Ku Klux Klan to see how it appealed to women and children, she had to analyze the Web sites of twenty-three different Klan organizations, including The Alabama White Knights of the Ku Klux Klan, The Imperial Klans of America, The Kalifornia Knights of the KKK, The North Georgia Knights, and the Northwest Knights of the Ku Klux Klan.[14]

Multiple organizations are an essential characteristic of social movements, and no single organization is synonymous with the whole movement. Many social movements never evolve to high levels of organization. Unlike campaigns, they do *not* proceed in orderly step-by-step fashion, contain one supreme leader who controls the movement, appeal to a single target audience, have a carefully defined and identifiable membership, or strive to attain a single, well-defined goal through the employment of one persuasive strategy.

AN UNINSTITUTIONALIZED COLLECTIVITY

A social movement is an *uninstitutionalized* collectivity. No social movement or social movement organization is part of an established order that governs, maintains, or changes social, political, religious, or economic norms and values.[15] When people within the Southern Baptist Convention or the Presbyterian church recommit their denominations to the inerrancy of the Bible, or Republican members of the Senate work to eliminate filibusters, or Democratic members of the Senate block the nominations of pro-life conservatives to the Supreme Court, or banks consolidate with other banks, or players or owners of the National Basketball Association agitate to change rules, these efforts are not social movements. Rather, members and elements of established institutions are attempting to change their organizations through institutionalized means and procedures. The primary impetus for change comes from within rather than from without, and only recognized members (usually elected or appointed) play roles in bringing about or stifling change.

To understand the persuasive efforts of complex social movements, observers have often presumed that they differ little from the activities of political parties, political action committees (PACs), legislatures, lobbies, religious organizations, and corporations. But two essential differences are that social movements exist and operate primarily from *outside* established institutions, and they are populated primarily with *ordinary* people. Although they do attempt to persuade members of established institutions (legislators, governors, judges, bishops, trustees, industrialists, college presidents) to join or support their causes and activities, these relationships may insert "them into complex policy networks," such as the relationship of Christian Evangelicals to the Republican Party and pro-lifers with the Roman Catholic Church. However, they cease to be social movements if they become parts of institutions.[16] For instance, the Lutheran Church was once a social movement in Germany, but it later became the official church of Germany and a recognized religious denomination around the world. The American Federation of Labor was one organization within the American labor movement for decades until it attained the legal right to represent workers in grievances and collective bargaining through the Wagner-Connery or National Labor Relations Act in 1935.

Social Movements as Out-Groups

The *outsider* or *uninstitutionalized* status of social movements, according to Herbert Simons and others, presents leaders with "extraordinary rhetorical dilemmas" in the rhetorical requirements they must fulfill, the problems they will face, and the available strategies they may use to meet these requirements.[17] Although success is never assured in any persuasive undertaking, a comparison of the persuasive situations faced by uninstitutionalized social movements with those faced by institutionalized organizations suggests that social movements encounter unique requirements and handicaps.

Social movements are always *out-groups* that society views as illegitimate. They are criticized for not handling conflicts and controversies through normal, proper channels and procedures, even when those channels and procedures are systematically denied them. Social movements have virtually no powers of reward and punishment beyond disruptions and personal recognition or expulsion, and expulsion often leads the exiled or disillusioned to create conflicting organizations. They have neither legislative nor enforcement powers—nor any assured means of financial support. Monetary funds are mere fractions of those available to government agencies, churches, political parties, PACs, and corporations.

Uninstitutionalized leaders survive only as long as they perform necessary tasks well. When new tasks, abilities, or strategies are required, movement organizations may unceremoniously discard the old. Leaders have minimal control over single factions or fragile coalitions of movement organizations and none over important institutions such as courts, investigative agencies, boards of trustees, and media. Rarely can they bring more than a single SMO's resources to bear on an event, let alone a lengthy campaign.

The mass media generally cater to conservative viewers and readers, government agencies, advertisers, and owners—supporters of the status quo—so they devote little space or airtime to social movements. News reports are rarely favorable toward movements (unless success appears inevitable or an element is becoming institutionalized), are rarely controlled by social movements (although some movement organizations and leaders become adept at manipulating the media to attain coverage), and provide exposure only when a social movement does something spectacular or stupid. Marlene Sanders of ABC noted that "in the initial phase of the women's movement, reporting on it was done primarily by men, and it was snide or hostile. Women's lib was treated with humor at best, and contempt at worst." The movement "evolved only slightly, from invisibility to trivialization."[18] The need for media attention may drive organizations to ever more extreme proclamations and actions (including violence) to gain attention, and the media "are quick to give priority to their violent and bizarre aspects."[19] Social movement organizations rarely have the money to purchase or the power to attract significant space or airtime to present their cases directly to the people. In contrast, a single presidential candidate may generate and spend more money in a few months than a social movement will in decades. The Sunday morning talk shows are populated by members of Congress, government agency employees, and cabinet members who expend nothing for the media exposure. Representatives of social movements are rarely invited.

Persuasion is the sole means available to social movements to accomplish such functions as transforming perceptions of reality, attaining a modicum of legitimacy, and mobilizing the discontented. Limited funds and power relegate this persuasion to speeches, leaflets, pamphlets and, increasingly, the Internet.

Institutions as In-Groups

Institutionalized groups and leaders, on the other hand, are always the *in-group*, and society views them as legitimate agents for sustaining the social order and tinkering with change when warranted. Leaders strive to maintain the appearance of dealing with conflicts and controversies through normal, proper channels. Institutions have immense powers of reward and punishment because they control the procedures and select those who populate the agencies that enforce the law, investigate crime and misbehavior, regulate the media and commerce, create and discard laws, levy and collect taxes, conduct trials, operate the prisons, and appoint persons to lucrative bureaucratic, corporate, church, and governmental positions. They may keep the disgruntled in line by enhancing or diminishing their economic well-being, threatening their membership status, amending or burying pieces of legislation, withholding contracts and licenses, or withholding sacraments and endorsements.

Institutional leaders may serve guaranteed terms (ranging from two years to life), enjoy the support of organized and well-financed groups, and advance within corporate, political, educational, and church hierarchies. Funding is far less of a problem for institutionalized groups and individuals. Legislatures have access to billions of tax dollars. PACs can raise millions of dollars through sophisticated computerized mailings. Lobbies such as the National Rifle Association fund the increasingly expensive political campaigns of sympathetic legislators and executives. Large corporations such as Mobil Oil and Georgia Pacific have vast financial resources and influence to counter the efforts of environmentalists. Political candidates, challengers, and incumbents generate enormous campaign chests, often collecting millions of dollars at a single fund-raiser.

Institutionalized groups and leaders are newsworthy and demand media attention. They command network, cable, and front-page coverage for trivial as well as consequential speeches, press conferences, conventions, announcements, stockholder meetings, ceremonies, or events. C-SPAN channels give continuous coverage of Congress, press conferences, speeches by institutional leaders, and interviews with those who aspire to become institutional leaders. For instance, a group called ANSWER (Act Now to Stop War & End Racism) gathered on the National Mall on January 18, 2003, to express opposition to potential military action in Iraq. They gave speeches, sang traditional antiwar songs, and provided entertainment, hoping to gain national attention for the antiwar effort. C-SPAN recorded the protest for a later showing, while other media barely mentioned it in their newscasts. On the other hand, high profile television interview and talk shows such as *Meet the Press*, *Face the Nation*, and *Larry King Live*, 24-hour news channels, and evening news broadcasts provided the president, members of his cabinet, members of Congress, and military officers with opportunities to defend the pending war, attack the opposition, present plans, interpret information, and build their images as authoritative and trusted voices for protecting the United States from terrorism. Few social movement leaders ever appear on such programs. The president's cat or dog may attract more news coverage than thousands of people at a social movement demonstration. The president may gain international attention by strolling through the White House rose garden, attending the annual Easter egg hunt on the south lawn, or traveling to a foreign country.

Institutions have the means to stifle uncooperative or unfriendly media outlets by threatening not to provide their representatives with seats on campaign planes, access to leaders, entry into restricted areas, or opportunities to ask questions at press conferences. Advertisers may threaten or be threatened by powerful religious and political groups to withhold advertising dollars from programs that appear sympathetic toward social movements. All major networks, cable channels, newspapers, and magazines are owned by institutional groups and individuals devoted, with few exceptions, to maintaining their versions of social norms and values and making a profit. Support of social movements is likely to be minimal and implicit rather than publicly explicit.

LARGE IN SCOPE

Social movements are large in terms of the geographical area covered, length of time advancing beliefs, and the number of events, organizations, participants, goals, strategies, and critical adaptations. Scope distinguishes them from pressure groups, religious cults, lobbies, PACs, campaigns, and isolated protests, which tend to be of relatively short duration with limited goals and small memberships. A few hundred high school students protesting the firing of a popular teacher and basketball coach is not a social movement.

Although campaigns may follow rhetorical careers *similar* to social movements, it is not accurate to conclude that "whatever differences that exist between movements and campaigns may not be rhetorically significant."[20] A campaign is to a social movement as a battle is to a war. They are similar in some ways but very different in others. Conducting the battle of Gettysburg was not the same as conducting the Civil War. Understanding a single battle does not fully inform us about the war. Unlike campaigns, social movements typically assume national or international scope, sustain efforts for decades, select many leaders, create many organizations, conduct continuous membership drives, carry out many campaigns, expand and constrict ideologies, set and alter many goals, and employ a wide variety of strategies.

It is difficult to imagine a "campaign" that would pose the same rhetorical challenges to leaders and members as does a social movement. Martin Luther King, Jr., for example, discovered that conducting limited and highly focused campaigns in Montgomery, Selma, and Atlanta was not the same as attempting to maintain attention, cohesion, commitment, control, and excitement within a large social movement consisting of many organizations, factions, leaders, and belief systems over many years and beyond the regional borders of southern states. He had to adjust rhetorically to temporal and societal changes, new generations of protestors, internal and external challenges, regional differences, the need for and appearance of new strategies, a rising militancy within the movement, and growing frustrations by younger, more militant members over the lack of what they perceived as meaningful victories and changes. As social movements evolve over time, leaders and members must evolve rhetorically or face division and inconsequentiality.

Size

In order to persuade others to join, to establish legitimacy, and to pressure institutions and adversaries to take demands seriously, social movements must work to increase the size of their memberships and the scope of their activities. Social movements in the United States cannot thrive if they are perceived to be *small* because people tend to see small ventures as either inconsequential (likely to be ignored or ridiculed) or dangerous (and therefore requiring suppression for the safety of the people and the good of the nation).

Pamela Oliver and Gerald Marwell note that "one person marching for a thousand hours is not the same as a thousand people marching for one hour."[21] Institutions and their supporters went to great lengths in the 1960s and 1970s to characterize the antiwar, women's rights, student rights, and black power movements as small groups of radicals, sex perverts, traitors, cowards, racists, and degenerates—people not representative of the great "silent majority" of citizens, women, students, and African Americans. Bonnie Dow notes that television coverage of the 1970 women's Strike for Equality divided the movement into legitimate and illegitimate feminists—separating a small number of activists from millions of so-called "ordinary women" who were dedicated to preserving the traditional masculine-feminine balance in U.S. society.[22] In all three major network stories, "the only interviews with women are for the purpose of demonstrating opposition to the Strike or to the movement itself." Conservative talk show personality Rush Limbaugh coined the epithet "feminazi" to characterize women's rights advocates as a small group of radicals out of step with the vast majority of women in the United States. Similarly, political cartoonists portrayed armed militia organizations formed in the 1990s as small cells of uneducated, unintelligent, overweight, unshaven, paranoid trailer-park residents who played soldier on the weekends and assumed exalted military ranks.

The Native-American movement—relatively small in number, mostly isolated in scattered, remote regions of the country, and ideologically split between urban and reservation residents—experienced difficulty in attracting attention, maintaining media and governmental interest, and persuading audiences to take it seriously. It resorted to takeovers of Alcatraz Island in San Francisco Bay, Wounded Knee in South Dakota, and the Bureau of Indian Affairs in Washington, D.C., to gain attention for its cause. The media and the public soon grew tired of the occupations and ignored them, while the *Wall Street Journal* dismissed the occupation of the Bureau of Indian Affairs as "an exercise in playacting—an effort by a relative handful of militants to speak for the broader Indian community."[23] The establishment of lucrative gambling casinos on reservations in such states as Wisconsin and New York, successful court cases to reclaim land lost a century or more ago, and a whale hunt off the West Coast captured more media and public attention than years of protest and demonstrations.

Forces on both sides of the abortion conflict have portrayed the other as a vocal minority, little more than a handful of radicals wishing to force their will on the majority. Virtually every social movement claims to be a "great grassroots movement." Whenever social movements stage "mass demonstrations," institutional and movement estimates of turnout vary drastically because each side has a stake in the size game. When a survey found that only 1 percent of men considered themselves to be exclusively homosexual (contrary to the long-standing claim of 10 percent) *Time* magazine published a story entitled, "The Shrinking Ten Percent: A New Survey Claiming that Only 1 percent of Men Are Gay Put the Movement Off Stride."[24]

Time

Most significant changes in social structures, norms, and values take decades, if not centuries, to bring about, so institutions have time on their side. They may wait until a social, economic, or political crisis passes; a war ends; protestors graduate or become disillusioned by lack of progress; or the impact of a movement campaign lessens. For instance, in the early 1990s, the animal rights campaign against wearing fur had persuaded or forced many women to stop wearing and purchasing fur and resulted in a sharp decline in sales and profits. Many furriers closed for lack of business. By 2000, however, fur was making a comeback with brisk sales, and new furriers opened for business. Women no longer feared that animal rights activists might harass them and were not deterred by efforts to shame them for wearing the skins of slaughtered animals in order to appear stylish or to demonstrate that they could afford expensive garments.

Institutional leadership changes occurring through normal processes such as election, retirement, resignation, or discharge may remove favorite targets of agitators. President Johnson's decision not to run for reelection in 1968 and the end of President Clinton's second term in 2001 deprived antiwar and Christian right enthusiasts of favorite nemeses. The public may become disenchanted with and intolerant of protest and disorder, particularly if their travel, shopping, entertainment, and work routines are affected. The mass media and their audiences become bored with issues, events, and strategies (particularly boycotts and takeovers) that seem to drag on endlessly. A person may refrain for a while from buying lettuce to support the farm workers movement, from taking children to Disney World to oppose gay and lesbian rights, or from crossing a picket line to avoid a confrontation with environmental protesters, but desires and convenience may later overcome commitment or reluctance.

Time directly affects social movements. Changes in movement leadership resulting from power struggles, deaths, or assassinations may weaken social movements or lead to the dissolution of social movement organizations. Leaders and followers may grow weary of the struggle or become disillusioned by lack of real progress. A great victory for one generation of protestors, such as the Montgomery bus boycott that energized the civil rights movement and brought a young Rev. Martin Luther King, Jr., to national prominence, may mean little to the next generation that wants true equality in all aspects of life. If social movement leaders and followers do not tire of the struggle, they or some factions of the movement may become desperate for victory and resort to extreme methods, including violence and terrorism, that allow institutions and countermovements to suppress or discredit them as fanatical and dangerous. Tarrow writes that "where violence occurs or is even likely, this gives authorities a mandate for repression and turns nonviolent sympathizers away."[25]

Events

A few victories, campaigns, or events do not guarantee success. Even spectacular events such as the 1963 civil rights march on Washington, D.C., that drew over 250,000 persons and concluded with Martin Luther King's "I Have a Dream" speech can be forgotten. What happened to the men's fledgling movement after the "million man" rally in Washington? Friend and foe ask "What's next?" Social movements and the media have insatiable appetites for "happenings," but few social movements have sufficient leaders, members, funds, or energy to satisfy these appetites over long periods of time while fending off the counterefforts of other movements and institutions.

The radical environmental group Earth First! employed every tactic it could copy and invent during the 1980s and 1990s to defend Mother Earth from the logging industry and those who would pollute her streams and eliminate her wildlife. Earth Firsters! used "guerrilla" theater, nonviolent civil disobedience, confrontations, destruction of property and machinery (called monkeywrenching, ecotage, or ecodefense), cemented themselves into roadblocks, chained themselves to trees and logging equipment, sat in the top of trees for months at a time, dropped a three-hundred-foot roll of black plastic from the top of the Glen Canyon Dam to simulate a catastrophic crack in the dam, and draped a huge banner across the face of George Washington on Mount Rushmore reading, "We The People Say No to Acid Rain."[26] Several protesters were seriously injured or killed in accidents with trucks and bull-dozers during confrontations. Yet its efforts and name have largely disap-peared from the media. Logging, development, and pollution in the Northwest have continued. Julia Hill, a member of Earth First!, took resi-dence on a six-by-eight foot wooden platform at the top of a 180-foot red-wood tree she called Luna in December 1997. A year later her protest, largely ignored except for Pacific Lumber that wanted to cut down the tree, garnered a picture and a single column in *People* magazine.[27] This is little attention for the personal sacrifice made for the movement, but it is more than most pro-longed protests get in the media. When Hill finally descended from her tree-top platform in late 1999 after an agreement to save Luna and some other trees, few took notice and the logging went on.

PROMOTES OR OPPOSES CHANGE IN SOCIETAL NORMS AND VALUES

A social movement promotes or opposes a program for change in soci-etal norms and values. Its rhetoric includes prescriptions for what must be done, who must do it, and how it must be done.

Basic Types of Social Movements

Three types of social movements are distinguishable by the nature of the changes they advocate or oppose. An *innovative social movement* seeks to replace existing norms and values with *new* ones. Innovative movements include women's liberation, civil rights for African Americans, socialism, gay liberation, and animal rights. A *revivalistic social movement* seeks to replace existing norms and values with ones from a *venerable, idealized past*. Revivalis-tic social movements include the Native-American, Back to Africa, pro-life, environmental, and Christian evangelical movements. A *resistance social move-ment* seeks to block changes in norms and values because it perceives *nothing wrong with the status quo*, at least nothing that cannot or will not be resolved in due time through established means and institutions. Resistance social move-ments include antiwomen's liberation, anti-civil rights, antigay rights, white supremacy, and pro-choice movements.

Social movements tend to be both valuistic and normative because changes in values alter norms, and changes in norms alter values. For instance, movements espousing the values of equality, fairness, and justice led to normative changes through court decisions and laws. These normative changes guaranteed equal pay, benefits, and employment opportunities for African Americans, women, and senior citizens. In turn, these changes affected how Americans perceived the values of equality, fairness, and justice. Unfortunately, they also generated opposition from those who saw such changes as threatening traditional values that had shaped their identities and ways of life.

Reform and Revolutionary Movements

Many social movements have reform-oriented (demanding partial change) and revolutionary-oriented (demanding total change) elements. Their ideologies, leaders, members, and organizations develop and change over time. The student movement, for example, began in the 1950s as a reform-oriented free speech movement at U.S. universities that had traditionally restricted who could speak, to whom they could speak, when they could speak, and where they could speak on campuses. The movement evolved into demands not only for removal of strictures on speech but also the elimination of restrictions on where students could live, the hours they could stay out at night, and the clothes they could wear. Students wanted to serve on important committees that affected their education and well-being. They argued for the creation of grievance, grade appeal, and student affairs committees that would empower them to address unfair treatment. Eventually, on some campuses, the movement became revolutionary with demands that students determine courses offered, course content, course requirements, graduation standards, appointments of administrators, and investment of endowments.

Efforts to place a social movement along a reform-to-revolution continuum depend on time, perceptions, and elements ascendant within the movement. For instance, many Americans viewed Martin Luther King, Jr., as a revolutionary until Stokely Carmichael and H. Rap Brown became leaders of the Student Nonviolent Coordinating Committee and preached black power. Suddenly, Rev. King appeared to be a reformer. Some view the animal rights movement as merely a reform movement aimed at assuring the humane treatment of animals, a simple extension of the animal welfare movement of the nineteenth century from which the American Society for the Prevention of Cruelty to Animals (ASPCA) emerged. Others see this movement as a revolutionary attempt to alter the relationships between animals and humans and thus between humans and God, to restrict the rights of hunters and those who raise animals for food, to stifle lifesaving medical experimentation, or to increase the intrusion of big government into American lives.

Moderate and Radical Movements

Labeling a movement as moderate or radical may be as misleading as labeling it reform or revolutionary. While one person's moderate is another's radical, most social movements contain both radical and moderate factions. Organizations within the women's liberation movement included the National Organization for Women, the Women's International Terrorist Conspiracy from Hell (WITCH), and the Society for Cutting Up Men (SCUM). Elements within the pro-life movement include those who believe change must come about through prayer and peaceful protest and those who believe violence and assassination are essential to ending legal abortion and stopping the slaughter of innocents. Terms such as moderate and radical best describe types of strategies and arguments rather than types of social movements, a point we will emphasize in later chapters.

Ideologies and Belief-Systems

The natures of social movement ideologies or systems of belief preclude precise classification. They tend to be strange mixtures of vagueness and precision, parts of old and parts of new systems, static and ever changing, consistent and contradictory. Some social movements have one ideology for true believers and a somewhat different one for public consumption. As Hans Toch writes, "Each person joins a somewhat different social movement, often for reasons far removed from the central concerns of the movement."[28]

People perceive a social movement's demands, goals, strategies, and potential outcomes from their unique personal perspectives and needs. A campaign to protest the development of a large resort at the edge of a national park may attract those who want to save the environment, those who desire to protect a pristine wilderness for their children or future generations, those who seek protection of their nearby ranches or a favorite hunting area, those who oppose development by large corporations, and/or those who want the fellowship of the protest group.

The diversity, flexibility, and fluid nature of social movement belief systems or programs for change set them apart from other collectives. Most religious, political, social, and pressure groups have a single set of principles that remain relatively constant and goals that are fairly precise: convert unbelievers, elect a party's candidate, maintain subsidies for milk producers, institute prayer in the public schools, or prevent gun control legislation. In contrast, even a fairly focused social movement such as pro-life has a wide variety of organizations that espouse positions ranging from no abortions under any circumstances to some abortions in particular situations (incest, rape, danger to mother's health). Strategies range from prayer and legal action to violence, and goals range from protection of the unborn to protection of the unborn, disabled, infirm, and aged. Kristy Maddux argues that once the antiwomen's suffrage movement shifted from a narrow orientation against suffrage to "a conservative defense of the status quo and a fear of radical global social revolution," it ceased being a social movement and became a "counterpublic."[29] But merely expanding or contracting an orientation or focus does not alter the fundamental nature of the collectivity unless it also becomes devoid of organization, members, and commitment to proposing or opposing societal change. Most social movements alter their belief systems significantly during their lives to meet new exigencies and societal changes.

Local issues, what Steven Goldzwig calls "critical localism," may dominate the concerns, rhetoric, and demonstrations in a community or on a college campus.[30] For example, a large tuition increase and the firing of the student editor of the campus daily newspaper for printing editorials that included expletives fueled large demonstrations, fiery rhetoric, and arrests on the Purdue University campus in the 1960s and 1970s. The press reported these as countercultural and anti-Vietnam War movement incidents even though these issues played insignificant parts in each incident. However, it is unlikely either incident would have come about without a climate conducive to protest—the result of social movement activities on and off college campuses. As Goldzwig and Patricia Sullivan write, "In these local discursive performances cultural history and local experience help shape beliefs and attitudes; they meld together an epistemological outlook that authorizes an additional move."[31]

ENCOUNTERS OPPOSITION IN A MORAL STRUGGLE

Whether a social movement's leaders and members are striving to bring about or resist change in norms and values and whether these changes pertain to people (right to life or right to die), things (nuclear weapons or alcoholic beverages), or animals (medical experiments or fur coats), they assume the power to distinguish right from wrong, good from evil, and ethical from unethical motives, purposes, characters, choices, strategies, and actions. Each social movement believes that it alone constitutes an ethical, virtuous, principled, and righteous force with a moral obligation it cannot ignore. The movement must raise the consciousness of the people by revealing the moral, intellectual, and coercive bankruptcy of the targeted institution, its actions, and its motives. Kenneth Burke and Leland Griffin conclude that "all social movements are essentially moral strivings for salvation, perfection, the good."[32]

Claim to Legitimacy

The moral stance and tone of social movement rhetoric is of critical importance to claims of legitimacy as *uninstitutionalized* forces. Simons notes that a movement establishes its legitimacy by representing its cause as one that any virtuous individual may endorse.[33] A PETA leaflet states the case for its claim to the moral high ground.

> All species fear injury and death, and all species fight for life and freedom. How can one species, ours, consider it has the right to deny others their basic interests of liberty and life? Just as we denied these rights to other human beings in the past for arbitrary reasons, such as skin color, we now deny these basic rights to others because they happen not to be of our own species.
>
> We do not need animals' fur, skin or flesh to survive. But we have come to like the feel, look and taste of these pieces of animals and we are loathe to give them up, even though to do so means a healthier existence for us all.
>
> What gives human beings the right to kill other animals who have lives of their own to live?
>
> Truly, history will judge the worth of our "civilization" less by our technological accomplishments than by the way we treat our fellow beings.[34]

The social movement rhetoric of collectives that place themselves on a moral pedestal (particularly those striving for the mantle of legitimacy), often magnifies the righteousness of members. Delegates to the 1900 American Federation of Labor convention were welcomed with these words:

> Upon you rests the dawn of a new century, and may the record made here shine forth during the years to come as does now the Declaration of Independence. Your work is a noble and holy one, and when accomplished will be but the realization of the Savior's mission on earth—the uplifting and elevation morally and socially of all humanity.[35]

Herbert Simons, Elizabeth Mechling, and Howard Schreier note that "most ideological messages" of social movements "tend to exaggerate the strength, unity, and intellectual and moral legitimacy of the movement."[36]

Disaffection and Confrontation

As a social movement promotes or resists a program for change from a moral perspective and lays claim to legitimacy, members become frustrated to the point of disaffection with established institutions and institutional means of change and control. They become willing to devote their lives, and on occasion to give their lives, to attain victory in the moral struggle between good and evil. Innovative and revivalistic social movements see institutions as unaware of, disinterested in, or openly resistant to necessary changes to resolve moral issues. Resistance movements see institutions as unwilling or unable to respond to grievous threats to social norms and values. Some, such as contemporary militias and the Christian right, claim that institutions actively compromise norms and values.

Robert Cathcart writes that social movements must create a "drama or agonistic ritual which forces response from the establishment commensurate with the moral evil perceived by movement members."[37] Tarrow claims that "it is only by sustaining collective action against antagonists that a contentious episode becomes a social movement."[38] It seldom takes long for a social movement to pose a threat that an institution cannot ignore, and some theorists claim that a social movement at the national level spawns immediate organized opposition. Perceived threat and increasing use of confrontational strategies produce, according to Cathcart, a "dialectical tension growing out of moral conflict," and provokes a clash between the social movement and the threatened institution. The struggle between institutional and uninstitutional forces becomes a "true moral battle for power and for the legitimate right to define the true order."[39]

During the 1980s, students and faculty on hundreds of U.S. college campuses launched protests against the brutal apartheid policies of South Africa. They created shantytowns on campuses that resembled those in South Africa, distributed facsimiles of the passbooks blacks were required to carry in South Africa, and gave speeches emphasizing the reality of life for the black residents of South Africa. A common demand was that universities eliminate from their endowments all investments in South African corporations and in U.S. corporations doing business in South Africa. At first, university administrations distributed press releases explaining why they could not or would not divest, made modest changes in their investment policies, and met with protesting groups. As protestors gained media attention, began to embarrass administrations with claims to the moral high ground, and refused to stop demonstrations or to remove their shantytowns at prescribed deadlines, university administrators came to see the antiapartheid demonstrations as threats to their powers of moral suasion and their legitimate right to enforce university rules and to determine investment policies. They could not cede the moral high ground to students and faculty and sometimes resorted to destroying the shanties and arresting the protestors to maintain authority.

A "social conflict," Simons writes, is "a clash over incompatible interests in which one party's relative gain is another's relative loss."[40] If the Gray Panthers representing millions of senior citizens pressure legislatures into allocating more money for Social Security, Medicare, Medicaid, and long-term care facilities, younger persons and taxpayers will pay higher taxes. If the logging industry or tourist industry accedes to demands of environmentalists opposing removal of redwood trees or the building of a ski lodge and slopes in a pristine mountain area, the environmentalists win and the industries lose lucrative money-making ventures. Social movements are always players in zero-sum games of social control and change, and institutions do not like to lose. Institutions, no matter how tolerant and understanding they may seem or want to be, can accept only minor challenges to norms, values, and their legitimacy. They cannot sustain a loss to uninstitutionalized forces and still maintain their authority, credibility, and control over constituencies. They must retain the moral high ground at all cost.

Institutions often portray themselves as goaded into action by violent acts that pose dangerous, irresponsible, and unreasonable threats to legitimate— and therefore moral—social order. They counter social movements directly and indirectly through agencies, agents, and beneficiaries. *Agencies* include legislative bodies, executive and administrative groups, courts, police, armed forces, councils, task forces, regulatory bodies, tax authorities, communication media, and investigative groups. *Agents* include legislators, presidents, governors, mayors, bishops, judges, police officers, soldiers, owners of communication media, editors, reporters, commentators, and investigators such as special prosecutors. *Beneficiaries* include most of the above plus corporations, business owners and operators (including farmers and ranchers), colleges and universities, churches, patriotic and civic groups, and the "silent majority" of citizens.

PERSUASION IS PERVASIVE

Social movements must satisfy a number of requirements if they are to *become* and *remain* significant forces for and against change. For instance, they must transform perceptions of reality, enhance the egos of protestors, attain a degree of legitimacy, prescribe and sell courses of action, mobilize the disaffected, and sustain the movement over time. Theoretically, social movements may attempt to satisfy such requirements through coercion, bargaining, and persuasion.

Coercion and Bargaining

Coercion is the "manipulation of the target group's situation in such fashion that the pursuit of any course of action other than that sought by the movement will be met with considerable cost or punishment."[41] White Citizens Councils and the Ku Klux Klan in the South relied heavily on coercion in their efforts to counter the civil rights movement. *Bargaining* may occur when the "movement has control of some exchangeable value that the target group wants and offers some of that value in return for compliance with demands."[42] The United Farm Workers offered productive, reliable, and loyal workers to California growers in exchange for recognition, collective bargaining, and contracts.

The typical uninstitutionalized, minimally organized social movement enjoys few means of reward or punishment necessary either to coerce people to join or to remain loyal to a cause or to coerce institutions to capitulate to demands. Institutions, with little to gain and much to lose, resist bargaining with social movements whose leaders and followers they have stigmatized as dangerous and inferior social degenerates. Michael Lipsky notes, "People in power do not like to sit down with rogues."[43] Mere association with a social movement's leaders may grant an undesired degree of legitimacy to the social movement and its cause. In addition, as Lipsky writes, institutions doubt the capability of movements to bargain effectively: "Protest oriented groups, whose primary talents are in dramatizing issues, cannot credibly attempt to present data considered 'objective' or suggestions considered 'responsible' by public officials. Few can be convincing as both advocate and arbitrator at the same time."

Social movements often have little or nothing to exchange in bargaining sessions. Ralph Turner and Lewis Killian comment, for instance, that "the difficulty that constantly besets black movements is that they have nothing to offer whites in a bargaining exchange to match their disruptive potential."[44] The same can be said for most minorities. Institutions pressure one another not to "give in" to demands of protestors. When students and faculties were protesting the apartheid policies in South Africa, the *Wall Street Journal* commented:

> A surprising number of colleges have caved in to protest and announced divestment. This cowardice, too, promotes the kind of disruption going on this week on campuses across the nation, and undermines the institutions the administrations and trustees are supposed to protect.[45]

Social movements are equally loath to bargain with the "devil" they have vilified in their portrayals of reality and demands for change. They have suffered grievous mental, economic, social, and physical abuse for their beliefs and protests. Talking to, let alone compromising with, corrupt and oppressive institutions may be deemed a moral outrage by a movement's true believers. For example, Terence Powderly, the longtime leader of the Knights of Labor in the 1880s and 1890s, complained that he should be "permitted to exercise his own judgment" and "permitted to think for the Order" and not be subjected to the "demagogue's cry" that "he is selling out the labor movement" if he is seen "talking to a capitalist or entering the office of a man of wealth."[46] Thus, the constituencies of both parties are likely to perceive offers to bargain as signs of weakness, desperation, deception, and "selling out."

Social movements can satisfy only a few major requirements through bargaining and coercion. For example, bargaining may help mobilization for action by uniting disparate movement elements into coalitions, and it may exert pressure on institutions to meet with moderate collectives operating from a position of strength that are willing to discuss potential compromises. The Christian evangelicals exhibited their fund-raising and voter turnout powers in the 2004 election and were able to bargain effectively with the Bush administration and conservative elements in Congress. Coercion is limited mainly to pressuring the opposition or transforming perceptions of society by goading institutions into excessive repression, thus undermining their credibility. The Ruby Ridge incident in Idaho during which an FBI agent shot and killed the wife of white separatist Randy Weaver and the Branch Davidian standoff in Waco, Texas, instigated by agents of the Bureau of Alcohol, Tobacco, and Firearms that ended with a fiery inferno that claimed the lives of David Koresh and his followers were two examples of damaged credibility. After those incidents, some people believed that the federal government blew up the Murrah Federal Building in Oklahoma City in which 168 people died (including 19 children) to provoke public outrage against militias and other groups opposing intrusive government.

Although a social movement may unmask an institution and gain some sympathy by provoking violent suppression, the public may just as easily condemn the movement and perceive the suppression as an "unfortunate but inevitable" result of dangerous radicalism.[47] Social movements often splinter into factions over the issue of employing coercion (particularly violent acts such as bombings, assassinations, destruction of property, and disruptions) to achieve their ends.

Persuasion

Because of the many constraints under which uninstitutionalized social movements must operate, persuasion is the primary agency for satisfying requirements and meeting obstacles. Persuasion is the use of verbal and nonverbal symbols to affect audience perceptions and thus to bring about changes in thinking, feeling, and/or acting. The pro-life and pro-choice movements, for example, have employed speeches, videos, publications, the Internet, mass mailings, local organizations, and interpersonal contacts to sell their views on abortion since the Supreme Court decision in 1973 that legalized abortion.

Persuasion is pervasive in social movements. Bargaining, for instance, includes elements of persuasion. A social movement attempting to bargain must *convince* both supporters and the opposition inside and outside of the movement that it is serious in desiring to bargain, is a worthy participant for bargaining interactions, and has something of value to exchange for concessions. On the other hand, persuasion may preclude bargaining as a strategy. Lipsky writes that "admission to policy making councils is frequently barred because of the angry, militant rhetorical style adopted by protest leaders."[48]

Coercion also includes elements of persuasion. Turner and Killian observe that "nonviolence always couples persuasive strategy to coercion."[49] For example, sit-ins, mass demonstrations, marches, hunger strikes, and disobedience of laws perceived as unjust all have persuasive elements such as language, arguments, and symbolic acts—but they also threaten institutions. Simons uses the phrase "coercive persuasion" to emphasize that "all acts of influence are rhetorical in at least some respects." He argues:

> The trouble with the persuasion-coercion dichotomy it that it cannot be applied reliably to the real world, and especially to most conflict situations. Although the criteria used to distinguish persuasion and coercion enable us to identify different elements within a given act, and although there are a great many cases of "pure" persuasion which are free of coercive elements, by these same criteria, acts conventionally labeled as "coercive" are almost never free of persuasive elements.[50]

Are any acts devoid of symbolic value and thus instances of pure coercion? The Supreme Court has ruled that coercive acts such as marches, sit-ins, boycotts, demonstrations, and articles of clothing such as armbands and uniforms constitute "symbolic speech" and are entitled to First Amendment protection. The Berrigan brothers' destruction of draft records from the Selective Service Office in Catonsville, Maryland, was a coercive and yet highly symbolic act of protest during the Vietnam War. Pro-life's "sidewalk counseling" (during which protestors scream "Don't kill your baby!" at women attempting to enter abortion clinics) and the throwing of blood or red paint by animal rights activists on women wearing fur coats are also examples of coercive symbolic protests. The occasional burning of an American flag by protestors is a highly symbolic act that expresses their anger, even hatred, of certain governmental actions or policies. Each burning, particularly when the appearance of protestors makes them look "radical" or different, inevitably produces outrage in many Americans and political leaders who see this as a direct attack on the nation's highest symbol and therefore on the nation itself. Legislation is immediately proposed that would amend the Constitution to make flag burning a crime and to prevent the Supreme Court from declaring the legislation unconstitutional. Parke Burgess argues that persuasion is essential when social movements *threaten* to use coercive tactics:

The Victim must be convinced that dire consequences are likely, not to say certain, *before* he can feel forced to comply, just as he must become convinced of the coercer's probable capacity and intent to commit the act of violence *before* he can conclude that the act is likely to follow noncompliance.[51]

Are any acts pure bargaining and devoid of persuasion and coercion? When two antagonists sit down to bargain, they attempt to convince (an act of persuasion) one another that they are sincere, have something of value to offer, are operating from a position of strength, and can and will break off negotiations (and resort to force, introducing the coercive element) if all does not proceed as desired. Neither party can be or appear to be in a situation where it must accept an offer.

Are any acts pure persuasion and devoid of bargaining or any hint of the carrot or the stick? Malcolm X's famous persuasive speech "The Ballot or the Bullet" opens with attempts to appease the followers of Elijah Muhammad (founder of the Black Muslims), Christians, and followers of Martin Luther King, Jr. (thus bargaining or negotiating differences).[52] The speech proceeds with a lengthy appeal for black capitalism (pure persuasion). And the speech ends with thinly veiled threats to resort to the bullet if the ballot is unavailable or fails to produce results (coercive persuasion). Robert Doolittle reveals that some people perceived the race riots of the 1960s as inherently symbolic, others conceded that the riots were potentially symbolic, and some viewed them as lawless and totally lacking in symbolism.[53] News reports of the 1992 riot in Los Angeles following the acquittal of the white police officers who had attacked Rodney King indicate that people interpreted this event much the same as they had the riots of the 1960s. James Andrews suggests that persuasion may be most effective when institutions "accept the harsh reality that they may be coerced."[54]

Clearly, persuasion permeates the efforts of social movements to promote or resist change and is the primary agency available for satisfying essential requirements. The role of persuasion distinguishes social movements from two, often closely related, collective actions: civil wars and revolutions. In social movements, *persuasion is pervasive* while *violence is incidental* and often employed for symbolic purposes. In civil wars and revolutions, *violence is pervasive* and rarely symbolic while *persuasion is incidental.*

To say that persuasion is pervasive in social movements and that it is the primary means for satisfying major requirements and overcoming obstacles is not to suggest that persuasion *alone* can bring ultimate success to social movements. Social movements must have skilled leaders, dedicated followers, effective organizations and coalitions, a social system that permits or at least tolerates protest while confronting it, a climate conducive to change, and luck. Pivotal incidents such as the nuclear power accidents at Three Mile Island in Pennsylvania and Chernobyl in the Ukraine, the advent of AIDS in the United States, *Brown v. Board of Education* that overturned the separate but equal court interpretations that had made separation of the races legal, the Great Depression of the 1930s, and withdrawal of U.S. troops from Vietnam were critical to the progress and dissolution of antinuclear power, civil rights, labor, and the anti-Vietnam War movements. However, such events would disappear into the pages of history if social movements did not employ persuasion to interpret them, focus media attention on them, and keep the images fresh for audiences through demonstrations, anniversary celebrations, ceremonies, monuments, speeches, songs, the Internet, and books. Persuasion grows stale without the urgency that events inject into protest.

CONCLUSIONS

A social movement, then, is an organized, uninstitutionalized, and large collectivity that emerges to promote or resist change in societal norms and values, operating primarily through persuasion encountering opposition (in its moral struggle). This definition addresses *what* a social movement is and *how* it attempts to achieve its program for change or resistance to change. Persuasion is pervasive and is not restricted to a particular audience, purpose, requirement, strategy, or stage of a movement's life. No other phenomenon shares all of these characteristics. A trend or fad, for example, is unorganized and contains no program for change. A revolution relies primarily upon violence rather than persuasion. A PAC or lobby group tends to be institutionalized (licensed and incorporated), small in size, and created for limited, pragmatic ends (elect a candidate, maintain a subsidy for rice farmers, prevent gun legislation) rather than a moral struggle for change or maintenance of societal norms and values. A campaign is typically organized from the top down, includes managers with assigned roles, has specific and narrow goals, is relatively short in duration, and often has a known end point.

Our attempt to define the social movement as a unique collective phenomenon is designed to provide a clear focus for the chapters that follow and to inform readers of the underlying premises on which this book is based. This definition is not designed to place rigid limitations on *movement* or *campaign* studies, and we recognize that movements occur within established institutions, describe changes in academic fields of study and voting trends, and determine our personal dress, appearance, habits, actions, and tastes. The continuing discussion about the uniqueness of *social* movements is analogous to the study of other common phenomena. For instance, researchers who analyze political, health, sales, advertising, and recruiting campaigns recognize that all campaigns share *some* common persuasive characteristics. They do not claim, however, that the sharing of some characteristics means they have no significant differences. Institutional movements share many persuasive characteristics with social movements. These shared characteristics, however, do not make them identical twins. We are using the term *social movement* to identify a specific type of movement for study and research.

Notes

[1] Leland M. Griffin, "A Dramatistic Theory of the Rhetoric of Movements," *Critical Responses to Kenneth Burke*, William Rueckert, ed. (Minneapolis: University of Minnesota Press, 1969): 460–461.

[2] Ellen Barry, "Klansman, 80, gets 60 years," Lafayette, Indiana, *Journal and Courier*, 24 June 2005, A3.

[3] Michael C. McGee, "A Social Movement: Phenomenon or Meaning," *Central States Speech Journal* 31 (Winter 1980): 233–244; Charles J. G. Griffin, "Movement as Memory: Significant Forms in *Eyes on the Prize*," *Communication Studies* 54 (Summer 2003): 196–210.

[4] Wim van de Donk, Brian D. Loader, Paul G. Nixon, and Dieter Rucht, *Cyberprotest: New Media, Citizens and Social Movements* (London: Routledge, 2004): 3.

[5] Sidney Tarrow, *Power in Movement: Social Movements and Contentious Politics* (Cambridge, United Kingdom: Cambridge University Press, 1998): 105.

[6] Karlyn Kohrs Campbell, " 'The Rhetoric of Women's Liberation: An Oxymoron' Revisited," *Communication Studies* 50 (Summer 1999): 138–142.

[7] James W. Chesebro, "Cultures in Conflict: A Generic and Axiological View," *Today's Speech* 21 (Spring 1973): 12.

[8] Roger W. Howe, "The Rhetoric of the Death of God Theology," *Southern Speech Communication Journal* 37 (Winter 1971): 150.

[9] Paul Kurtz, ed., *Humanist Manifestos I and II* (Buffalo, NY: Prometheus Books, 1973).

[10] Herbert W. Simons, Elizabeth W. Mechling, and Howard N. Schreier, "The Functions of Human Communication in Mobilizing from the Bottom Up: The Rhetoric of Social Movements," *Handbook of Rhetorical and Communication Theory*, Carroll C. Arnold and John W. Bowers, eds. (Boston: Allyn & Bacon, 1984): 792–867.

[11] Jackson B. Miller, " 'Indians,' 'Braves,' and 'Redskins': A Performative Struggle for Control of an Image," *Quarterly Journal of Speech* 85 (May 1999): 189.

[12] "A New Awakening," *U.S. News & Report*, 30 October 1995, 32–34; "And Now What?" *Newsweek*, 30 October 1995, 28–36; "To the Beat of His Drum," *Time*, 23 October 1995, 34–36; "High Noon on the Hustings," *Newsweek*, 22 May 2000, 30–31.

[13] Tarrow, 6.

[14] Denise M. Bostdorff, "The Internet Rhetoric of the Ku Klux Klan: A Case Study in Web Site Community Building Run Amok," *Communication Studies* 55 (Summer 2004): 340–361.

[15] At one time labor organizations such as the United Auto Workers, Teamsters, and the AFL-CIO were movement organizations within the American labor social movement. Today, however, they are institutions that control millions of workers, bargain collectively with giant corporations, have direct roles in grievance processes, and have attained (in many situations) profit sharing for members. The Teamsters and other unions have attempted to thwart the efforts of new unions such as the United Farm Workers in California.

[16] Tarrow, 25.

[17] Herbert W. Simons, "Requirements, Problems, and Strategies: A Theory of Persuasion for Social Movements," *Quarterly Journal of Speech* 56 (February 1970): 11.

[18] Bonnie J. Dow, "Fixing Feminism: Women's Liberation and the Rhetoric of Television Documentary," *Quarterly Journal of Speech* 90 (February 2004): 54.

[19] Tarrow, 116.

[20] Donald Fishman, "Reform Judaism and the Anti-Zionist Persuasive Campaign, 1897–1915," *Communication Quarterly* 46 (Fall 1998): 376.

[21] Pamela E. Oliver and Gerald Marwell, "Mobilizing Technologies for Collective Action," *Frontiers in Social Movement Theory*, Aldon D. Morris and Carol McClurg Mueller, eds. (New Haven, CT: Yale University Press, 1992): 258.

[22] Bonnie J. Dow, "Spectacle, Spectatorship, and Gender Anxiety in Television Coverage of the 1970 Women's Strike for Equality," *Communication Studies* 50 (Summer 1999): 146–149, 152, 155.

[23] *Wall Street Journal*, 16 November 1972, 26.

[24] *Time*, 26 April 1993, 27.

[25] Tarrow, 96.

[26] Jonathan I. Lange, "A Refusal to Compromise: The Case of Earth First!" *Western Journal of Speech Communication* 54 (Fall 1990): 473–494.

[27] *People*, 28 December 1998–4 January 1999, 145.

[28] Hans Toch, *The Social Psychology of Social Movements* (Indianapolis: Bobbs-Merrill, 1965): 21–26.

[29] Kristy Maddux, "When Patriots Protest: The Anti-Suffrage Discursive Transformation of 1917," *Rhetoric & Public Affairs* 7 (Fall 2004): 284.

[30] Steven R. Goldzwig, "Multiculturalism, Rhetoric and the Twentieth-First Century," *Southern Communication Journal* 63 (1998): 276.

[31] Steven R. Goldzwig and Patricia A. Sullivan, "Reconfiguring the Rhetoric of Social Movements: Concepts and Approaches in Transition," unpublished paper presented at the 1999 annual convention of the National Communication Association.

[32] Leland M. Griffin, 456.

[33] Herbert W. Simons, "Persuasion in Social Conflicts: A Critique of Prevailing Concepts and a Framework for Future Research," *Speech Monographs* 39 (November 1972): 235.

[34] PETA, *Animal Rights*, n.d.

[35] William H. Higgins, "Welcoming Address," *Report of the Proceedings of the American Federation of Labor* (1900), 13.

[36] Simons, Mechling, and Schreier, 797.

[37] Robert S. Cathcart, "Movements: Confrontation as Rhetorical Form," *Southern Speech Communication Journal* 43 (Spring 1978): 242.

[38] Tarrow, 61.

[39] Cathcart, "Movements," 242, 246; Robert S. Cathcart, "New Approaches to the Study of Movements: Defining Movements Rhetorically," *Western Speech* 36 (Spring 1972); 87.

[40] Herbert W. Simons, *Persuasion: Understanding, Practice and Analysis* (Reading, MA: Addison-Wesley, 1976): 18.

[41] Ralph H. Turner and Lewis M. Killian, *Collective Behavior* (Englewood Cliffs, NJ: Prentice-Hall, 1972): 291.

[42] Turner and Killian, 291.

[43] Michael Lipsky, "Protest as Political Resource," *The American Political Science Review* 52 (December 1968): 1154.

[44] Turner and Killian, 421.

[45] *Wall Street Journal*, 9 April 1986, 32.

[46] Terence V. Powderly, "Address of the General Master Workman," *Proceedings of the General Assembly of the Knights of Labor*, October 1887, 1539.

[47] Kurt W. Ritter, "Confrontation as Moral Drama: The Boston Massacre in Rhetorical Perspective," *Southern Speech Communication Journal* 42 (Winter 1977): 114–136.

[48] Lipsky, 1154.

[49] Turner and Killian, 298.

[50] Simons, "Persuasion in Social Conflict," 232.

[51] Parke G. Burgess, "Crisis Rhetoric: Coercion vs. Force," *Quarterly Journal of Speech* 59 (February 1973): 69.

[52] Malcolm X, "The Ballot or the Bullet," *The Sixties Papers: Documents of a Rebellious Age* (New York: Praeger, 1984): 126–132.

[53] Robert J. Doolittle, "Riots as Symbolic: Criticism and Approach," *Central States Speech Journal* 27 (Winter 1976): 310–317.

[54] James R. Andrews, "The Rhetoric of Coercion and Persuasion: The Reform Bill of 1812," *Quarterly Journal of Speech* 56 (April 1970): 195.

CHAPTER

2

Social Movements as Interpretive Systems

Chapter 1 defined social movements and explained their dependence on persuasion to bring about or resist change. This chapter sets forth a theoretical orientation for studying social movements from a communication perspective.

Basically, communication is the process through which "you" and "I" become an "us" (and sometimes the process through which "we" realize that "you" and "I" are drifting apart). It is the fundamental social process through which individuals create and sustain relationships (some would say "relational units") such as "The Smiths" or "The Black Panthers" and "la Raza." If we seek to understand the social movement, we need to understand the communication process through which it comes into being, interacts with other relational units (such as institutions and countermovements), and tries to sustain itself.

Students of human communication since Aristotle's day have suggested a variety of models (sometimes called paradigms) to explain communication. Theorist Leonard Hawes wrote: "Developing analogues lies at the heart of the social scientist's activity. An analogue (or analogy) is the use of a familiar object to understand more completely an unfamiliar object or idea."[1] For example, communication is sometimes presented as though it were a mechanical process ("We weren't on the same wavelength" or "I need your feedback").

As communication theorists used models to explain communication, they posed interesting and important questions, such as: Is communication a matter of *transmitting meaning* to receivers, or is it a matter of *constructing meaning* from all the stimuli in their environment? Over time the sophistication of theorizing and search techniques grew, and we realized that some approaches to communication work well in particular settings (such as advertising or arguing) and others are more overarching ways of understanding human communication.

One of the most widely used analogues is the "systems model." The late communication theorist B. Aubrey Fisher identified four characteristics of the systems view of communication: the nonsummativity of its components; the importance of structure, function, and evolution; hierarchical organization; and the principle of openness.[2]

SYSTEMS THEORY AND COMMUNICATION

Characteristic 1: Nonsummativity

Any system is comprised of interdependent components. The *principle of nonsummativity* describes the whole of this interdependence as something other than a simple sum of the individual parts. Consider the difference between a pile and a system: one item can be removed from the pile without altering the other pieces, but any change in a system's components will produce changes in other components in the overall system. For example, the removal of a kidney requires the other kidney to work harder, and a dirty fuel injector causes your car to run inefficiently and unreliably.

As individuals interact they become a group, usually with its own identity such as MADD (Mothers Against Drunk Driving), the National Gay and Lesbian Task Force, and PETA (People for the Ethical Treatment of Animals). Thus, just as auto parts can be put together to form a Model T Ford, Dodge, or a Mercedes, similar people interacting differently can create noticeably different human groups—each with its own identity, behavioral tendencies, needs, and energies. The interdependent relationships among a system's components foster the creation of a whole that behaves differently from its individual members. We may enjoy a rally against mistreatment of research animals more (or less) than we enjoy the company of individual rally members.

This principle of nonsummativity is important to understanding social movements because a movement collectivity is something more or less than the sum of its parts. Fisher illustrates nonsummativity by contrasting labor unions with "all left-handed people":

> There is simply little or no consistent effect of one left-handed person on another because of their left-handedness. But the labor union does function as a whole in many significant ways. Its members go on strike as a whole. They all go to work, perform assigned jobs, and in other ways honor the labor contract as a whole. In short, the actions of one affect the actions of others.[3]

The interaction between individual union members—their communication— was the catalyst for the creation of something other than an aggregate or heap of individuals.

Thus, students of social movement persuasion need to pay close attention to the communication opportunities and activities that transform individuals into groups. Fisher's left-handed people exemplified the heap for him only because they had not, to his knowledge, begun to interact on the basis of their shared concerns about left-handedness. But in 1995, Stephen Mack created a Web site, "The Left Hander: Living in the Mirror" (now defunct), to do just that. The site provided accounts of living left-handed in a right-handed world, links to scientific studies of laterality, links to left-handed poetry, humor, and fiction and links to a variety of resources. Web sites and blogs make it much easier for individuals to express themselves, and search engines such as Google make it increasingly likely that someone, some day will read those expressions (even if it is only a right-handed textbook author).

Conversely, Fisher cited the labor union as a system because individual workers interacted over the years to develop a sense of "usness." In his autobiography, American Federation of Labor founder Samuel Gompers reflected on the opportunities for interaction among his fellow cigar makers:

> It gave education in such a way as to develop personality, for in no other place were we so wholly natural. The nature of our work developed a camaraderie of the shop such as few workers enjoy. It was a world in itself—a cosmopolitan world. Shipmates came from everywhere—some had been nearly everywhere. When they told us of strange lands and peoples, we listened eagerly.[4]

Other social movement organizations come into being because of shared concerns over abortion, nuclear power plants, and the environment. Some of these interactions have developed into the consciousness-raising sessions of the women's liberation, gay rights, and environmental movements. In each case, individuals discover common experiences, aspirations, problems, and solutions through communication.

Characteristic 2: Function-Structure-Evolution

The second axiom of systems theory is that interdependent relationships can be explained in terms of function, structure, and evolution. Human behaviors and actions are purposeful because they fulfill needs or "functions" for individuals and collectivities. When a function regularly recurs (e.g., seasonal greetings, monthly bill payments, and the selection of government representatives), we develop behavioral "structures" that assure their performance (e.g., Christmas cards, household budgets, and elections). Most of these structures perform the function imperfectly, and we continue to tinker to enhance the performance of the function. Sometimes we create a structure that performs the function so nicely that needs and functions previously obscured from view become apparent. At this point, we "evolve" into a new phase guided by these new functional necessities, and we search for fresh behavioral structures. Thus, the interplay of functional behaviors leads to evolutionary change as the system moves from the performance of one hierarchy of functions to another.

The structure of a social movement can refer to its membership profile, its organizational structure, or its pattern of strategic efforts. The anti-Vietnam War movement needed dedicated workers during its early phases, but in

1968 and 1972 it needed a plurality of voters that it could not attract. The American Federation of Labor organized skilled tradesmen and excluded unskilled industrial workers, a tactic that worked until the increasing industrialization of the United States led to the formation of the Industrial Workers of the World (IWW) and later the Congress of Industrial Organizations (CIO). David Duke's branch of the Ku Klux Klan moved from the old Klan's tactics of cross-burning and lynching to the recruitment of Catholic and women members and the use of television and radio talk shows. The pro-life movement began with emphasis on elections and the passage of a constitutional amendment but turned toward direct actions such as Operation Rescue's blockades of abortion clinics and civil disobedience when elections and legislative efforts failed to stop abortions.

Chapter 3 will identify and illustrate the persuasive functions of social movements and the ways in which persuasive communication fulfills these needs. For now, the point is that social movements continuously create structures to perform functions, thereby altering the pattern of functions remaining to be performed. This process is continuous—every aspect of a system has evolved from, and will evolve into, something else; hence beginnings and endings are basically punctuation marks between phases or stages. We rarely know when a social movement begins or ends, only that it has evolved.

Characteristic 3: Hierarchical Organization

The third axiom is that all systems have hierarchical organization. It is possible to locate each system (a social movement) within an encompassing "supra-system" (the society) and to ascertain "subsystems" (such as individual organizations and persons) within each system. All systems are influenced both by their subsystems and by their supra-systems. However, the precise distinction between subsystem, system, and supra-system is generally a matter of the observer's perspective. One could just as easily consider the movement as the supra-system, an organization as the system, and individuals as the subsystems. Once we have identified the hierarchical structure of systems, the level of analysis is largely a matter of choice.

This "nesting" of systems in other systems is important for understanding social movements. It is common for social movements to fail, even if they are led by major figures and/or have widespread support. The American Railway Union won several major victories in 1893, leading to vast increases in membership. Although rapid growth may seem like a good thing, the union's leader, Eugene V. Debs, lacked the communication structures necessary to control, discipline, and organize these new members. The union was promptly and permanently demolished only months later in the Pullman Strike of 1894.

An energetic social movement may change the behavior of the supra-system by altering the supra-system's functional needs. The civil rights movement raised society's concerns about discrimination, poverty, and voting rights by demonstrating that all was not well in the United States. The War on Poverty, the Civil Rights Act of 1964, the Voting Rights Act of 1965, and other changes were responses to a restructured set of functional priorities derived from the movement's demands for justice and white Americans' discomfort over these demands. In the aftermath of the Kennedy assassination, the 1964 Democratic Party did not need African-American votes to defeat Barry Goldwater and the Republicans. As a consequence, the party convention voted against minority challenges to several segregationist delegations. But by 1988, the Democrats sorely needed Jesse Jackson and his multitude of new voters to contest the presidential election, and Jackson's historic convention address signaled the end of the civil rights movement as challengers at the convention gate. The African-American voting bloc had taken its rhetorical place alongside the labor and women's movements as institutionalized pillars of the Democratic Party.

Characteristic 4: The Degree of Openness

Fisher's fourth axiom is that any system can be described on the basis of its *openness*—the permeability of its boundaries. We can assess a system with respect to the freedom of exchange between the system and its environment and thereby classify it as "open" or "closed." Open systems have boundaries that permit the interaction of system and environment, whereas closed systems are entirely self-contained. The degree of openness is important because open and closed systems are governed by different principles.

Closed systems are governed by the principle of equilibrium—the final state of the closed system is determined by its initial state because a self-contained system must sustain balance without any input from the outside. Thus, a closed system must eventually return to its initial starting point. Open systems are governed by the principle of "equifinality," which states that "the same final state may be reached from different initial conditions and in different ways . . . [and] different open systems with the same initial condition could well achieve different final states."[5] Put differently, you can get anywhere in an open system from anywhere, and you can get there by a variety of paths.

The difference between the equilibrium of closed systems and the equifinality of open systems derives from the principle of entropy, an irreversible process of disintegration. Closed systems can only respond to entropy by exerting a counterforce (negentropy) to slow disintegration, but the disintegration is not reversed. As Fisher observes, "The balanced state of homeostasis . . . does not suggest an increase in order or structure, only a slowing down or stoppage of the disintegrative process."[6] The rights of African Americans, women, gays, and animals have expanded in spite of Herculean efforts by institutions and resistance movements.

Open systems, capable of exchange with their environment, can combat entropy either by adding new information from the environment or by generating their own original or novel information. In this sense, open systems take stock of their environment and adjust to it. The net result is that open systems can increase order over the original state and grow stronger because of a more equal sharing of rights, duties, and rewards.

There are few truly closed systems, even in the natural sciences, and all human and social systems are considered open. To summarize, all systems models of communication emphasize that: the whole is more than the sum of its parts because of the interaction of persons; communication systems evolve as structures perform various functions; each system is comprised of sub-systems while itself constituting part of a supra-system, both of which influence and are influenced by it; and each system is to some degree capable of exchange with its environment. With this foundation, we turn to the differences between "mechanical" and "social" systems as models of human communication.

MECHANICAL VS. SOCIAL SYSTEMS

As mentioned at the beginning of the chapter, people often evoke a mechanical systems model to describe communication, using concepts such as transmission, reception, feedback, noise, barriers, breakdowns, leverage, being pushed around, or being on the same wavelength. They tend to think of com-munication as a process of mechanical adjustment. This thesis pervades works that emphasize the similarities between human communication and mechani-cal systems.[7] Indeed, a *closed system* does measure its environment and adjust to it. But a thermostat has only one pattern of reaction; it heats or cools until the preset temperature is reached. Unlike a person, the thermostat cannot decide to offer you a sweater, close the windows, or build a fire; it simply per-forms its specified function for the system. The thermostat cannot choose; it can only execute. Even the most sophisticated computer can only execute pro-grams provided—at some point and in some form—by a human programmer.

Dennis Smith challenges the mechanical view of human communication when he notes that our study of communication is too heavily influenced by the engineering sciences. He argues that the differences between human com-munication and mechanical systems are more important than the similarities. Smith specifically challenges the concept of "communication breakdown" on the grounds that it teaches four fallacies about communication:

- *The fallacy of linearity* presumes communication is a straight line from one person to another, rather than an interdependent process in which people anticipate and build on one another's (and even outsiders') behaviors to create meaning.

- *The fallacy of mechanism* mistakenly treats persons as machines rather than humans, thereby omitting consideration of biological, psychologi-cal, and sociological influences.

- *The fallacy of noncommunication* presumes that communication involves purely what is said or written and overlooks the communicative signif-icance of interpretation.

- *The fallacy of reification* presumes that unsatisfactory communication results from a "thing" (breakdown) that can be removed or fixed, rather than from interpretive behavior.[8]

We would add a fifth fallacy to Smith's list. *The fallacy of success* presumes that communication will be satisfactory and effective unless something goes wrong (i.e., the breakdown). Much communication is fairly difficult, and effective or satisfying communication is more often the exception than the rule. It is more productive to approach communication as a constructive, adaptive process at which people sometimes succeed and often fail. All of our conflicts are not due to "failures to communicate" or communication breakdowns; many derive from deep-seated, irreconcilable differences between subsystems. Too often references to "ineffective communication" or a "breakdown in communication" distract us from more important issues.

Smith's critique of communication breakdowns illustrates the implications of choosing inappropriate metaphoric models for explaining human communication. Like Smith and Fisher, we find mechanical models inappropriate for the explanation of human communication in general and social movement persuasion in particular because they omit human choice and creativity from the process. However, the concept of system need not be discarded simply because mechanical metaphors are inappropriate to social systems.

Brent D. Ruben summarizes the four propositions of a social or living systems approach as: (1) People, like other animals, are instances of living systems. (2) Living systems are structural and functional units (individual and social) that maintain themselves (and grow, change, and deteriorate) only through interactions with their environment. (3) Environmental interaction(s) are of two types: (a) transactions that involve the transformation of matter-energy, which may be termed biophysical metabolism; and (b) transactions that involve the transformation of data information, which may be termed informational-metabolism or communication. (4) The functional goal (of the behavior) of all living systems is adaptation with the environment.[9]

First, Ruben differentiates living systems that grow and change only through interaction with their environments from both mechanical systems (which only deteriorate) and closed systems (which cannot interact with their environments). Elaborating upon the characteristics of living systems, Ruben says that there are no "breakdowns" in communication because communication with the environment is constant so long as the system is alive. Indeed, silence itself is a means of adapting to the environment.

Second, Ruben observes that an organism adapts to its environment and adapts its environment to it. It is not a question of how a persuader responds to a rhetorical situation *or* how the persuader creates the rhetorical situation through language.[10] Rather, we should search for both in the mutual adaptation of system with environment.

Third, adaptation occurs as "discrepancies between the needs and capacities of the system and those of the environment emerge, and the system, acting on the discrepancy, strives to close the gap." From a social systems perspective, the natural, healthy state of affairs involves people actively adapting to their environment by creating alternatives and choosing among them. This creative choosing leads us into new eras of human progress.

Conceptions of Human Influence

Influence in mechanical systems is highly manipulative. A persuader examines the persuasive landscape and ascertains (1) the audience's susceptibility to influence and (2) the persuader's resources for influence, so that (3) the persuader can construct or apply a formula or equation that creates the necessary and sufficient stimuli for the auditor to respond in accordance with the persuader's intent. Mechanical conceptions of influence suggest that we can structure message variables to produce consistently the desired audience behavior. The key to mechanistic persuasion would be knowing the right equation for a particular target audience.

But influence in social systems is adaptive behavior. An organism can adapt to its environment in a variety of ways (the principle of equifinality): by attempting to change its environment, attempting to change itself, or attempting to escape from the environment through selective attention, selective perception, and selective retention. For example, drivers choose to ignore or obey speed limits or road conditions, to drive faster or slower, to take dubious shortcuts, or to maintain the car's mechanical operation. Drivers regularly ignore speed limit signs, no matter how many they see. Some drivers choose to pay the cost of a radar detector for a few additional miles per hour.

Adaptive humans have often confounded mechanical systems theorists. Sensing that someone has concocted a formula to influence them, auditors can feel that their essential human ability to choose is endangered. These concerned humans may refuse to comply by imposing new conditions, misunderstanding the message, and/or reconstructing the relationship and its ground rules. While mechanistic theorists revise their equation to account for this erratic behavior, social systems theorists recognize it as the kind of adaptive behavior that is central to communication studies.

Mechanical systems models are particularly ill-suited to the study of persuasion and social movements because movements need to be creative and unusual. Any social movement that responds predictably to institutions will not long survive, since institutions create and enforce all of the rules. Saul Alinsky, a lifelong social activist and creator of a training institute for would-be activists, recommends that:

> radicals must be resilient, adaptable to shifting political circumstances, and sensitive enough to the process of action and reaction to avoid being trapped by their own tactics and forced to travel a road not of their own choosing. In short, radicals must have a degree of control over the flow of events.[11]

A social movement must adapt in a manner that retains its freedom and independence from institutions, which would seem to render institutional equations for influence almost useless.

Additionally, it is very difficult to predict the effectiveness of a tactic. An assassination may end a movement or perpetuate it by creating a martyr. Nonviolence worked well for Gandhi in India and Martin Luther King, Jr., in America, but failed horribly for Jews in Nazi Germany. Human influence in social movements, then, is by necessity highly adaptive and does not conform to manipulative mechanical laws.

Conceptions of Human Conflict

Mechanistic systems view conflict as imbalances that should be prevented or repaired. At best, imbalance is prevented and the system hums along, quietly disintegrating under the law of entropy. When imbalance does occur, balance can only be restored after considerable upheaval (negentropy). When a car breaks down, it is out of commission until the mechanic pronounces it "as good as new." Equilibrium is attained only through financial setback, after the upheaval of children waiting at school, the cat stranded at the vet's, and a strong sense of frustration. In systems terminology, negentropy has been introduced to restore equilibrium. Because nothing can ever be *gained* in mechanical systems, we must engage in preventive maintenance of our mechanical systems lest they "break down."

But social systems theorists see conflict as creating the opportunity for growth and progress. Discrepancies between the needs and capacities of the system and the needs and capacities of the environment challenge the organism. If the organism fails to resolve the discrepancy, it dies; but if it meets the challenge adequately, it survives and evolves into a new phase of life. As Alinsky observes, "in the politics of human life, consistency is not a virtue. To be consistent means, according to the Oxford Universal Dictionary, 'standing still or not moving.' Men [women] must change with the times or die."[12] Of course, this discrepancy simultaneously creates an opportunity for destruction that is the nature of equifinality. The important fact is that unlike the mechanical systems model, the social systems model views conflict and controversy as *potentially* constructive or creative. The difference is that upheaval can lead to an enhanced state of order rather than simply slowed disintegration and temporarily restored order.

Thus, while mechanical conflict is purely disruptive, social systems conflict leads to evolutionary change. Because institutions function to maintain systemic order, no study rooted in mechanical premises should sanction the creation of conflict. Rhetorical studies of agitation reflected this institutional bias until Herbert Simons attacked it and suggested a "dual perspective" (institution and social movement). In so doing, Simons revealed this weakness in mechanistic assumptions.[13]

If human conflict is more nearly social than mechanical, then controversy and conflict are our only paths toward progress. If this is the case, then we should employ models that encourage consideration of multiple conflicting viewpoints and focus on the process of ongoing adaptation. No model based on mechanical assumptions can admit the equivalence of both agitator and institutional perspectives, since mechanical systems models assume that (1) no good can come from imbalance, (2) the institution is empowered to maintain balance, and (3) agitators and social movements function to create imbalance.

The subsystems of a social system attempt to close the discrepancy in various ways. Institutions usually minimize the discrepancy in favor of the prior state of affairs (in which they gained their authority), while one or more parts of the system strive to resolve it in other directions. For example, the Supreme Court's ruling in 1954 that segregation was unconstitutional (*Brown v. Board of Education*) prompted a number of different reactions. Civil rights activists highlighted the discrepancy between the law and our practices; southern politicians such as Mississippi Governor Ross Barnett raised the possibility that states could ignore the federal law; and the federal government wrestled with the problem of satisfying all of its constituent subsystems. The important point is that all parts work in their own ways to adjust their system with the environment. Therefore, all of their efforts deserve comparable attention. Conversely, it would be counterproductive to favor an institution's effort to maintain balance, because that effort could or would restrain the system's adaptive capabilities.

Conceptions of Human Relationships

Another consideration in the mechanical versus social systems discussion is systemic maturation. Mechanical systems are at their prime when new or almost new. All mechanical systems experience friction, deterioration, and general wear. With proper maintenance, this process of deterioration (entropy) can be slowed but never be reversed; even if a Rolls Royce appreciates in value with age, its mechanical system nevertheless deteriorates. Such an approach to human communication is depressing at best and frightening at worst. It implies that relationships begin at or near their peak and can only be slowed in their deterioration—a view that hardly squares with friendship or dating relationships.

In contrast, the social systems approach presumes that relationships develop from initial encounters. Whether we choose to nurture or to ignore them, past experiences influence future conversations. From this perspective, experience and practice become important. The social systems view suggests that one is likely to find the more successful relationships among the longer ones, while admitting that some develop quickly and others may persist unhappily. While the mechanical systems observer of social movement persuasion is concerned with stability, the social systems theorist is concerned with change. Because social systems (governed by equifinality) can develop from any state into any other state through any means, the study of social systems emphasizes the process by which the subsystems emerge and adapt by creating alternatives and choosing among them. Our country is very different in the twenty-first century from what it was in the eighteenth century. While not all of these changes have been improvements, neither have they all been disintegrative. These changes have been adaptive efforts by humans not yet born in 1776 to adapt to environments not yet existing in 1776. In this light, the American Revolution, the Civil War, women's suffrage, agrarianism, labor and civil rights, and environmental movements have led us into new eras of life in the United States that could not be satisfactorily explained as a return to equilibrium, because each movement created novel alternatives. Just as we study U.S. history developmentally, a social systems approach to social movement persuasion views the relationship between the movement and society developmentally. The frequent intransigence of some labor unions today, for example, can be better understood in terms of management's parental behavior during labor's infancy and adolescence.

While many people will undoubtedly continue to use the jargon of mechanical systems to describe human communication, we hope you will become aware of the implications of these metaphors. To conceptualize communication mechanically is to conceive of conflict and change as disruptive, influence as manipulative, and relationships as disintegrative. It is more accurate, realistic, and productive to conceive of conflict as adaptive and evolutionary, influence as accommodative, and relationships as integrative. Chapter 1 discussed the pervasiveness of persuasion in social movements, and this chapter has stressed the importance of thinking about human activities as growing and changing social systems. We will now explore the interpretive systems model and then offer a framework for analyzing social movements.

THE INTERPRETIVE SYSTEMS MODEL

Having said that we should study social movements as communication systems, it is time to see how communication variables are arranged into social systems. The interpretive systems model is an integrative framework that can help us see that controversies arise because people have different needs, preferences, and verbal constructions of reality. Moreover, it helps us to see that these interpretive structures are created and learned through communication and how these structures affect our communicative choices. Thus, the interpretive systems model helps us understand social movements as communication.

The interpretive systems model begins with four "Personal Interpretive Processes": needing, symbolizing, reasoning, and preferencing.[14] *Needing* is the process through which individuals formulate and reformulate their needs and goals. *Symbolizing* is the process of formulating and reformulating semantic relationships among meanings and images. *Reasoning* is the process of formulating and reformulating explanatory accounts that "make sense" out of the needs and symbols. *Preferencing* is the process of formulating and reformulating a hierarchy of values in relation to needs, symbols, and reasons so that some become more important than others. These processes are independent. We learn new words when we need them and forget them when we do not. We sometimes reason our way to a preference, but we often muster reasons to rationalize an existing preference. We are often attracted to persons who think as we do, but we often learn to think like those persons to whom we are attracted.

Parents, teachers, clergy, and others teach and reinforce the "right" ways of needing, symbolizing, reasoning, and preferencing. Because each of us has different parents, teachers, and clergy, we develop personal ways of interpreting life. At home, in school, and through public discourse, each of us is exposed to multiple ways of interpreting life's ebb and flow. We soon discover that things that make sense to us sometimes make little sense to others.

Because we cannot isolate ourselves from other people, we need to coordinate our behavior with theirs. We do this by developing "social interpretive structures" as ways to coordinate our personal needing, symbolizing, reasoning, and preferencing processes with those of others. People adopt or construct "languages" to coordinate their symbolizing, "logics" to coordinate their reasoning, and "ideologies" to coordinate their preferencing. We use languages, logics, and ideologies to guide our daily behavior.

People who share a social interpretive structure are an "interpretive community." They are bound together, and separated from others, by their agreement to coordinate their personal interpretive behaviors. People who speak the same language are a linguistic community; those who share rules of reasoning are a logical community (such as creationists or evolutionists); those who share ways of establishing their preferences are an ideological community (such as socialists or capitalists); and those who agree to conform behavior to a set of laws are a legal community.

Each of us is born into an array of interpretive communities, and we soon learn to use the structures developed by those communities. Sometimes we merge multiple interpretive structures into one, perhaps by blending the economic logic of capitalism, the ideology of Christianity, and the laws of popular sovereignty. Social movements often try to separate these fused structures. As we go through life, we encounter other people and their interpretive structures. We window shop, trying on new and old needs, words, reasons, and preferences to see how they fit. Over time we change the importance of our interpretive communities, and sometimes we change communities.

Interpretive communities are not congruent, and among all of these various communities small and large there exists a struggle for interpretive dominance. We see it most clearly during presidential election campaigns when the candidates for the major parties' nominations seek to build interpretive coalitions sufficient to win nomination and election. During these campaigns, liberals and conservatives disagree about many things, but they share a commitment to institutions and elections that distinguish them from revolutionaries. Institutions, by definition, legitimize a dominant language, logic, ideology, and law (such as the Constitution). They emphasize the importance of "working within the system," "following proper procedures," and "not rocking the boat," and, indeed, that is how most changes come about.

But sooner or later some of these incongruent interpretive communities come into conflict. As elections, appointments, and rulings empower interpretive communities, they also empower their languages, logics, and ideologies. The language of the interpretive community in power necessarily disadvantages members of competing communities, as when they define words such as "patriotic," "right," and "America." The temporarily dominant ideology frames society's problems and solutions, such that the outgoing community's solutions become the incoming community's problems. The logic of the temporarily dominant interpretive community defines the rationality of policies, as when they tackle deficits by cutting taxes and spending, by increasing taxes and spending, or by increasing one and cutting the other.

The establishing of one interpretive structure as legitimate necessarily disadvantages those people who do not share it. Moreover, it poorly equips people who use the dominant interpretive structure to coordinate their perceptions with all those people who use one of the other logics, languages, or ideologies. Thus, the people with the most severe grievances are generally least able to voice them in the ways that institutions either understand or recognize as legitimate. The movements toward and against bilingual education are examples of conflicting linguistic communities struggling over laws, while the pro-life and pro-choice movements are examples of conflicting languages, logics, and ideologies.

Politics consists of the struggle among interpretive communities to establish their own interpretive structures as legitimate so as to define social and political realities for everybody else. When an interpretive community feels that it can be effective within the system, it plays by the rules because those rules provide them with advantages. But when individuals or communities lose confidence in the responsiveness of institutions they begin to mobilize from the bottom up. They step outside existing laws, language, logic, and ideology to challenge them. They regard the institutions that provide legitimacy for the dominant interpretive structures as part of the problem, and they begin to become social movements.

The interpretive systems approach to social movements enables us to see that individuals form relationships and groups on the basis of their needs, symbols, reasons, and preferences. Agitators use language to articulate their potential followers' needs and to critique institutions. They frequently must avoid the dominant language and ideology because the figures of speech, derived from that perspective, can trap the protestor in the web of established modes of thinking. Later chapters will explore some of the ways in which social movements use nontraditional rhetorical forms such as music, slogans, ridicule, and obscenities to introduce new ways of thinking about persistent sources of dissatisfaction.

STUDYING SOCIAL MOVEMENTS AS INTERPRETIVE SYSTEMS: "THE QUESTION"

Those who study the persuasive efforts of social movements can use the interpretive or social systems perspective by pursuing the question: *Which individuals, conceiving themselves to be what "people" in what environment, use what relational patterns and what adaptive strategies with what evolutionary results?* The remainder of the chapter examines each part of this question.[15]

Which Individuals?

A first step in studying a social movement is to ascertain which persons create and lead the movement's adaptive effort and how they persuade others to share their perspective. This means locating prominent individuals, their demographic traits, and their personality or character traits and discovering similarities and differences among the people who come to share rhetorical visions or self-conceptions. Discovering that a social movement is largely comprised of people with a low tolerance of ambiguity, a familiarity with crime and violence, and/or a common regional, racial, or religious experience may help understand their embrace of one characterization of the environment and rejection of other perspectives. Thus, biological, sociological, and psychological information help us to understand the movement, the hierarchy, and their interdependence.

Information about leaders is found in biographies, autobiographies, movement studies, journalistic accounts, histories, and single-speaker rhetorical studies. The social systems approach does not equate a leader's background or behavior with the movement; rather, it seeks to understand the leadership subsystem as a means of understanding the social movement system. It helps, for example, to study the theological development of Martin Luther King, Jr., and Malcolm X before studying their persuasion. It is also helpful to know that John Birch Society founder Robert Welch wrote a primer on salesmanship, that socialist labor leader Debs originally opposed strikes, and that neighborhood organizer Saul Alinsky held a Ph.D. in psychology.

If studying the leadership subsystem requires biographical materials, studying the membership subsystem requires social-psychological data. This kind of scientific research is rare in communication literature. One exception is J. Michael Hogan's study of the people participating in rallies for former Alabama Governor George Wallace.[17] The social systems researcher may draw on surveys and studies from other disciplines, such as political scientist Fred Grupp's survey of John Birch Society members in 1964. His data suggested that Birchers were unrepresentative of the American population in several respects, and he identified types of Birch Society members based on their reasons for joining: the "informed" who joined for educational benefits, the "like minded" who wanted to associate with people who "thought like them," the "politically committed" who wanted an outlet for their political activities, and the "ideological" who wanted something in which to believe.[18] Chapter 5 explores further the role of personality in the adaptive behavior of John Birch Society members, and chapter 10 explores the logic of conspiracy argument. Diane McWhorter's study of the unusually violent Birmingham civil rights clashes found that the local steel industry's prior use of bombings to fight unionization had created a network of bombers available to help segregationists terrorize blacks.[19]

Our first task, then, is to identify the influential leaders and their followers: who are they? What are their demographic, experiential, sociological, psychological, and political traits? This first step tells us something about the people from whom the social movement develops. With this information we can better predict and explain the leaders' and members' adaptive choices.

Conceiving Themselves to Be What "People"?

Having ascertained who people are and what they are like, we can then try to discover who they think they are. Michael C. McGee, Aaron Gresson, and others have described the processes by which "peoples" arise through their shared myths and pasts.[20] In the final analysis, real people, not rhetorical creations, take action. In this sense, we need to be concerned with the movement's and the institutional hierarchy's self-conceptions. We should ascertain who they think they are, the degree to which this self-image corresponds with our appraisal of who they really are, and the psychological/sociological reasons for their rhetorical susceptibility to these characterizations. For example, many segregationists thought of themselves as protecting rather than disadvantaging African Americans.

When "you" and "I" create an "us," we begin to see something beyond our individuality (an example of nonsummativity). This "us" is the relational system created as you and I adapt to our environments (including each other's). The self-conceptions of movement leaders and members are not always consistent with the demographic or experiential profiles. The rationale of a pro-life supporter who kills an abortionist to prevent the killing of unborn babies will not be widely shared by others. The interpretive or social systems analyst wants to know how these people see themselves and how they develop this conception through communication.

In What Environment?

"In what environment" draws our attention to the world in which the movement must survive. Just as an organism develops, so does the environment, partly in response to the organism's adaptive behavior. But the environment contains other social and mechanical systems as well as the movement, all of which mitigate an organism's ability to adapt effectively to its environment. The social systems analyst must pursue factual materials about, for example, labor conditions or discriminatory practices against which to compare complaints of women, African Americans, and gays.

Because humans perceive or interpret their environments, we must also consider characterizations or depictions of the environment. Our experiences (both direct and vicarious) and our relationships help us construct vocabularies and logical frameworks that we use to "make sense" of the world. We interpret people and events through these frameworks whenever possible and reformulate the interpretive frameworks whenever they prove dysfunctional. See, for example, the frameworks of authoritarian and democratic personalities discussed in chapter 5. The discrepancies that concern people most are instances of "relative deprivation": being denied something to which they feel entitled. These deprivations may be as blatant and specific as a wage cut, denial of the right to vote, expulsion from the armed forces for being gay, or imprisonment. The perceived deprivation may be more subtle. The important point, as sociologist John Wilson notes, is that "the individuals involved come to feel that their expectations are reasonable" and are being denied.[21] A frequent complaint of protestors is that they are losing their status or self-respect. In testimony before the Senate in 1883, a machinist emphasized dehumanization and limited horizons:

> Well, the trade has been subdivided . . . so that a man never learns the machinist's trade now. . . . It has a very demoralizing effect upon the mind. . . . When I first went to learn the trade a machinist considered himself more than the average workingman; in fact he did not like to be called a workingman. Today he recognizes that he is simply a laborer the same as the others.[22]

The Native-American movement addresses the lost status of tribes that were well-developed and established centuries before Europeans arrived to take their lands and lives and subject them to meager existences on barren "reservations." Women, African Americans, Hispanics, and gays demand status and to be able to rise above the "glass ceiling" that permits them to view but not assume significant leadership roles in U.S. society.

Persuasion is important to the development of a sense of relative deprivation because people must realize that they have been shortchanged. How do both the social movement and institutional hierarchy perceive the environment? Real things happen to real people that constitute an objective reality (a bloodied nose, a picket line, a limit on how high they can rise on the corporate ladder, and a wage cut are not "tricks of the mind").

These real events are perceived, experienced, and understood in diverse ways, leading to diverse realities. Some individuals are inclined to perceive events as interconnected parts of a conscious conspiracy. The Federal Emergency Management Agency (FEMA) received a great deal of criticism in 2005 for the inefficiency and inadequacy of its response to Hurricane Katrina's devastation of New Orleans and the Gulf Coast. But a decade earlier Mark Westion warned readers of *Paranoia* magazine that FEMA was established by a fascist conspiracy to take control of the U.S. government. He claimed that FEMA's computers and specially equipped vehicles are all designed for that purpose, and that the conspirators wait in secure locations for the signal. Westion's warning challenged readers to accept a surprising and dramatic account of the environment in which they lived. Thus, we should focus on the competing characterizations of the environment and the discrepancies among them.

Use What Relational Patterns?

Who establishes and maintains communicative systems with whom, and how do people connect with one another? Not all that long ago the only alternatives people had were written messages and face-to-face communication. Aggrieved people could write petitions or print fliers, but that limited form of communication was to people who could read and write—a real constraint on communication with unskilled workers and people denied education by institutions. Face-to-face communication was inefficient, because the range of listeners was limited. Loudspeakers did not come into common use until the 1920s, and the expenditure of scarce resources on amplifiers remained unusual during the Depression. Union organizers talked to their fellow workers on the job, at campfires, and at impromptu meetings. But it was difficult for them to gain access to management because management could simply refuse to meet with protestors. When protest meetings could be characterized as threatening, private security forces and police were on call to use force to disperse the gathering.

But the twentieth century was the century of technological change. Louisiana Governor and Senator Huey Long of the "Share Our Wealth" movement was the first to exploit the potential of loudspeakers by introducing the sound truck into political campaigns. Father Charles E. Coughlin of Detroit became known as "The Radio Priest" because of the widespread popularity of his sermons on social justice. Bob Dylan and other folksingers of the early 1960s used the popularity of records among young people to critique U.S. social practices. When the eventual popularity of counterculture music became a potential radio market that profit-oriented programmers could no longer ignore, "underground" FM radio stations quickly emerged. These developments produced indirect communication. For example, you could listen to a radio station for its music, but you would also get its news reports; you could buy an album because your friends recommended it or because you liked the singer's voice, but repeated exposure to the lyrics alters the verbal environment in which you live.

By the 1980s the growth of satellite communication, cable television, and FM radio were drastically altering the mass communication environment. Religious groups who had long criticized the moral decay in popular television began their own television networks. Rev. Pat Robertson established the Christian Broadcasting Network. Potential followers could add it to their cable menu and delete the "immoral" networks, and Robertson and his associates could present news and talk shows to an audience with common interests. As popular music broadcasting shifted from AM stations to FM stereo,

AM stations switched formats to talk shows and telephone callers. Few people call radio shows because they are happy with things as they are, so these call-in shows began to provide modern day equivalents of the old face-to-face meetings, but with much wider distribution. Indeed, many of these stations were small enough that groups with an antiestablishment political agenda could purchase them.

The 1990s saw the development of the Internet. Software has made Web site development user friendly, and antiestablishment groups could easily publish home pages that carried their critiques of the establishment, provided links to allied organizations, and sold books or subscriptions to periodicals. Because the Internet is unregulated, some sites provided information about how to make bombs and how to use firearms and other weapons. Search engines such as Google and Yahoo! have made it easy to find related sites in cyberspace. It is now easier for aggrieved people to share their views than at any time in history. Increasingly, individuals who had never met found one another through chat groups, Web sites, and e-mail. At the same time, it is more difficult for establishment forces to harass or destroy these cyber radicals. Today, as we increasingly listen to our iPods and watch DVDs or premium cable channel movies, we insulate ourselves from traditional newscasts. In short, social movements today have a variety of communication channels (the mechanistic theorist's conveyor belts for meaning) available to them.

But the important point is how relational patterns include and exclude potential supporters and critics, foster or preclude the sense of transformation from individuals to group, and reinforce or contradict adaptive efforts. It is much less threatening for today's potential radical to surf the Web, call a talk show, or watch cable television than it was for anarchists of the 1880s to attend a rally, for an orator like Debs to tell his followers not to fight in World War I, or for Freedom Riders to ride buses into Birmingham in the 1960s. On the one hand, this means that aggrieved persons can interact more freely. On the other hand, these same possibilities provide fewer disincentives for irresponsible communication.

"Use what relational patterns" reminds us that social movement persuasion is not simply the work of the soapbox orator or street corner pamphleteer. Relationships are important for several reasons. First, they indicate the audiences that persuaders consider capable of resolving the problem. Second, relational patterns suggest the persuader's conception of the auditor's importance to both the social movement (system) and to the larger society (supra-system). Third, relational choices suggest the persuader's working assumption that auditors either are, or should be, involved in the process of systemic adaptation.

Attention to relationships, then, can help us discern the functional differences between, for example, animal rights demonstrations (1) at a meat packing plant to influence local regulations, (2) on the steps of the Capitol to influence national legislation by drawing national media attention, and (3) on Main Street to enhance solidarity and recruiting while separating the demonstrators from their opponents. Similarly, attention to relationships can focus our attention on the established order's response to acts of protest, particularly to the differences between meetings with demonstrators, meetings with representatives of demonstrators, arrests of demonstrators, and press conferences that reassure the public and the press that the demonstrators are "simply a handful of troublemakers."

In "The Rhetorical Situation," Lloyd Bitzer defines an audience as one or more people capable of resolving an exigency or problem. Rarely do we take the time to ascertain the relationships between persuader and audience, or audience and exigency. Thus, relational systems and their evolution are important elements of a social systems approach to social movement persuasion that deserve careful study.

And What Adaptive Strategies?

"And what adaptive strategies" directs our attention to the ongoing, thoughtful process of adjustment as individuals and groups, perceiving a discrepancy between their experienced and preferred environments, create instrumental techniques to minimize that discrepancy. Again, we should look for links between individual characteristics, self-conceptions, relationships, and environment. Immigrant workers at the turn of the century who shared no common language marched rather than spoke; reactionary groups with a fundamentalist strain preached; and African Americans in the South, expecting to be brutalized by white authorities, opted for a Gandhian approach to dramatize the system's inhumanity.

We should search for the evolutionary patterns in which choices reflect the attempts of individuals to change the system. This should produce a richer understanding of social movements and their strategies. "What adaptive strategies" leads us to the classic Aristotelian focus of "discovering the available means of persuasion." Rather than simply cataloguing strategies, we must view these strategies from the larger perspective of unfolding adaptations—what others have done and what they may be expected to do in response to one's own adaptive efforts.

With What Evolutionary Results?

"With what evolutionary results" measures movement growth. Because the social systems approach is developmental, it disdains the notion that adaptations are permanent (the environment and other organisms are themselves constantly adapting). We can therefore look for evolutionary phases such as the stages of social movements presented in chapter 4. These evolutionary results might be changes in the movement's people or changes in their self-conceptions, changes in the environment or their characterizations of it, or changes in their relational patterns. Did an attempted adaptation exacerbate the initial discrepancy? Did the organism appear to enter a new evolutionary phase? We can compare any social movement to the normative life cycle. The answers to such questions will enable us to understand more the rhetorical (adaptive, accommodative) functions of movements in society.

Emphasizing evolutionary results requires an examination of the system-environment fit at a minimum of two points in the adaptive process. These points are a matter of critical judgment and may be chosen in either of two ways. The more traditional of these methods identifies historic transitions in the social movement's life cycle and then investigates the role of persuasion in that transition. Although this is a reasonable historical approach, it raises the possibility that persuasive evolution and historical evolution may be "out of synch." The second approach is closer to Fisher and Hawes' approach to interpersonal and small group communication.[24] It involves the careful analysis of persuasion over time for the purpose of ascertaining shifts in recurrent patterns. This is an effective method for finding shifts in argument (such as segregationists' shift from white supremacy to states' rights), changes in audience (the Communist party's shift from workers to intellectuals), changes in relational patterns (the John Birch Society's shift from study sessions to the Goldwater campaign and back again), changes in self-conceptions (the emergence of the notion of Black Power and Black Is Beautiful), or changes in exigencies (pro-life's shift from opposing the legalization of abortion to supporting an antiabortion amendment to the Constitution).

Watch for signs that the social movement and its environment are entering a qualitatively different evolutionary phase. Because change is unavoidable, we are looking for empirically discernible changes in the system-environment fit, not mere changes in the movement, the hierarchy, the environment, or in rhetorical strategy. To the disappointment of many anti-Vietnam War protestors, replacing Lyndon Johnson as president with Richard Nixon changed only marginally the system-environment fit. Despite the change in personnel, both the anti-Vietnam War movement's argument and the government's response remained essentially the same.

Many parts of our question (Which individuals, conceiving themselves to be what "people" in what environment, use what relational patterns and what adaptive strategies with what evolutionary results?) are asked in similar ways. Analysis should deemphasize the parts in favor of their interrelationship. It is not sufficient to know only which people were active in a social movement or which symbols pervaded the movement's rhetoric. We need to know why certain symbolic behaviors proved useful (or futile) for certain people in a particular environment—how all aspects of a movement worked together to arrive at a particular stage.

Conclusions

Stemming from Aristotle's attention to speaker, audience, message, and occasion, the elements of communication have often been emphasized rather than the interdependence and interaction of these variables. In recent years, we have increasingly noticed that an understanding of the pieces fails to explain the whole of human communication. At the same time, we have seen a growth in social systems models that approach communication as the efforts of parties in a relationship to adapt with one another in their environment.

This chapter has developed an interpretive systems approach to the persuasive activities of social movements that provides a framework for bringing analysis of societal communication into line with our knowledge of interpersonal communication. This perspective not only permits but encourages us to examine people and events not always classified as "social movements" and to incorporate insights from interpersonal and organizational communication as well as individual orator, event, and media studies.

Notes

[1] Leonard C. Hawes, *Pragmatics of Analoguing: Theory and Model Construction in Communication.* (Reading, MA: Addison-Wesley, 1975): viii.

[2] Unless otherwise noted, all references to the axioms of systems theory are taken from B. Aubrey Fisher, *Perspectives on Human Communication* (New York: Macmillan, 1978): 196–204.

[3] Fisher, 197–198.

[4] Samuel Gompers, *Seventy Years of Life and Labor,* vol. I (New York: Augustus M. Kelly, 1967): 69–70.

[5] Ludwig von Bertalanffy, *General Systems Theory: Foundations, Development, Applications* (New York: George Braziller, 1968): 40, cited by Fisher, 201.

[6] Fisher, 201.

[7] Norbert Wiener, *The Human Use of Human Beings: Cybernetics and Society* (Boston: Houghton Mifflin, 1954); and Claude Shannon and Warren Weaver, *The Mathematical Theory of Communication* (Urbana: University of Illinois Press, 1949).

[8] Dennis R. Smith, "The Fallacy of the Communication Breakdown," *Quarterly Journal of Speech* 56 (December 1970): 343–346.

[9] Brent D. Ruben, "Communication and Conflict: A Systems-Theoretic Perspective," *Quarterly Journal of Speech* 64 (April 1978): 205.

[10] Lloyd Bitzer argues that rhetorical acts are responses to the situation, while Richard Vatz argues that the persuader defines that situation through language. See Lloyd Bitzer, "The Rhetorical Situation," *Philosophy and Rhetoric* 1 (Winter 1968): 1–14; and Richard E.Vatz, "The Myth of the Rhetorical Situation," *Philosophy and Rhetoric* 6 (Summer 1973): 154–161.

[11] Saul D. Alinsky, *Rules for Radicals: A Practical Primer for Realistic Radicals* (New York: Vintage, 1971): 6–7.

[12] Alinsky, 21–32.

[13] Herbert W. Simons, "Persuasion in Social Conflicts: A Critique of Prevailing Conceptions and a Framework for Future Research," *Speech Monographs* 39 (November 1972): 239.

[14] This chapter is based on a significant revision of the interpretive systems model published in Craig Allen Smith and Kathy B. Smith, *The White House Speaks: Presidential Leadership as Persuasion* (Westport, CT: Praeger, 1994). The model was first presented in Craig Allen Smith, *Political Communication* (San Diego: Harcourt Brace Jovanovich, 1990): 1–77. It was later used to suggest an approach to the college course in political communication and to using C-SPAN materials in the classroom, respectively, "Interpretive Communities in Conflict: A Master Syllabus for Political Communication," *Communication Education* 41 (October 1992): 415–428; and "The Interpretive Systems Approach to Teaching Political Communication," *C-SPAN in the Classroom: Theory and Applications,* Janette K. Muir, ed. (Annandale, VA: Speech Communication Association, 1992): 21–34.

[15] For an example of social systems criticism see Craig Allen Smith, "An Organic Systems Analysis of John Birch Society Discourse, 1958–1966," *Southern Speech Communication Journal* 50 (Winter 1984): 155–176.

[16] Information about major movement figures and their rhetoric can be found in two reference books: *American Orators of the Twentieth Century*, Bernard K. Duffy and Halford Ross Ryan,

eds. (Westport, CT: Greenwood, 1987); and Fred Powledge, *Free at Last? The Civil Rights Movement and the People Who Made It* (Boston: Little, Brown and Company, 1991).

[17] J. Michael Hogan, "Wallace and the Wallaceites: A Reexamination," *Southern Speech Communication Journal* 50 (Fall 1984): 24–48.

[18] Birchers responding to the survey were younger, better educated, and better off financially than the American norm of that period. Most were white-collar Republicans whose education was disproportionately in the natural sciences and engineering, who became politically aware during or after World War II, and lived in states with rapidly fluctuating populations. Fred W. Grupp, Jr., "The Political Perspectives of John Birch Society Members," *The American Right Wing*, Robert A. Schoenberger, ed. (Atlantic: Holt, Rinehart, and Winston, 1969): 83–118.

[19] Diane McWhorter, *Carry Me Home: Birmingham, Alabama: The Climactic Battle of the Civil Rights Revolution* (New York: Simon and Schuster, 2001).

[20] Michael C. McGee, "In Search of 'The People': A Rhetorical Alternative," *Quarterly Journal of Speech* 61 (October 1975): 235–249; and Aaron D. Gresson, III, "Phenomenology and the Rhetoric of Identification: A Neglected Dimension of Communication Inquiry," *Communication Quarterly* 26 (Fall 1978): 14–23.

[21] John Wilson, *Introduction to Social Movements* (New York: Basic Books, 1973): 70.

[22] "Testimony of John Morrison" (excerpted), *The American Labor Movement*, Leon Litwack, ed. (Englewood Cliffs, NJ: Prentice-Hall, 1962): 10–12.

[23] Mark Westion, "FEMA: Fascist Entity Manipulating America," *Paranoia* (Winter, 1994). Reprinted in *The Conspiracy Reader: From the Deaths of JFK and John Lennon to Government-Sponsored Alien Cover-Ups*, Al Hiddell and Joan d'Are, eds. (Secaucus, NJ: Carol Publishing Group, Citadel Press, 1999): 140–144.

[24] Aubrey Fisher and Leonard C. Hawes, "An Interact System Model: Generating a Grounded Theory of Small Groups," *Quarterly Journal of Speech* 57 (1971): 444–453.

CHAPTER

3

The Persuasive Functions of Social Movements

Persuasion is the primary *agency* through which social movements perform essential *functions* that enable them to come into existence, to satisfy requirements, to meet oppositions, and, perhaps, to succeed in bringing about or resisting change. Theorists for thirty-five years have identified and discussed a variety of functions or requirements—indispensable processes—that contribute to the success or maintenance of social movements. Building from these theories, this chapter focuses on six interrelated functions: transforming perceptions of social reality, altering self-perceptions, legitimizing the social movement, prescribing courses of action, mobilizing for action, and sustaining the social movement.[1] Understanding how social movements perform these functions will enable us to begin answering the question central to the interpretive systems perspective developed in chapter 2: "Which individuals, conceiving themselves to be what 'people' in what environment, use what relational patterns and what adaptive strategies with what evolutionary results?"

Before explaining and illustrating each of the six persuasive functions, several caveats are in order. First, although these functions are essential to the existence and success of social movements, they are not unique to social movements. Social movements differ from other collectivities not principally in terms of the functions their persuasive efforts must perform but in terms of the constraints placed on the fulfillment of these functions. The uninstitutionalized nature of movements greatly limits their powers and access to the mass media and hence strategic options.

Second, while social movements must perform all six functions, their fundamental programs for change (innovative, revivalistic, or resistance), the degree of change desired (reform to revolutionary), the exigencies of the rhetorical situation, and the stage of the movement will determine which functions assume greater prominence at a particular time. This functional scheme is not intended to be chronological or related to a series of progressive stages.

49

No social movement will perform a function once and then proceed to another. Although some functions may dominate the persuasion of a social movement at a given time (transforming perceptions of reality during an early stage or pressuring the opposition and gaining support of legitimizers during a later stage), most functions demand attention on a continual basis.

Third, a focus on functions enables us to study the persuasive efforts of whole social movements, a portion of a social movement in time, a social movement organization, or a social movement campaign. We may focus on one or more functions such as transforming perceptions of reality and altering self-perceptions of protestors. Let us turn now to a discussion and illustration of each of the six interrelated persuasive functions.

TRANSFORMING PERCEPTIONS OF SOCIAL REALITY

William Gamson contends that social movements are essentially struggles "over the definition and construction of social reality."[2] Every social movement must make a significant number of people aware that the generally accepted view of social reality fostered by political, social, religious, educational, legal, literary, and mass media institutions is false and that something must be done about it. Wil Linkugel, R. R. Allen, and Richard Johannesen write:

> A problem is not really a problem to an audience until they perceive it as such. A situation may exist, and the audience may know that it does, but in their eyes it remains nothing more than a lifeless fact until they view it as something that threatens or violates their interests and values.[3]

Thus, social movement persuaders must transform how people see their environment—the past, the present, and the future—to convince them that an intolerable situation exists that warrants urgent attention and action.

The Past

Although social movement persuasion tends to dwell on the here and now rather than focusing on times gone by, it is often necessary to transform how people perceive the past if protestors are to succeed in bringing about or stifling change.

The past may be generally unknown to current audiences, so messages may include references to a time of misery, suffering, privation, anguish, and despair—a past no one wants to repeat. For instance, the civil rights song "Freedom Is a Constant Struggle" exclaims that "we've struggled so long," "cried so long," "sorrowed so long," and "died so long." The pro-choice movement refers to the horrors of the illegal and self-induced abortions prevalent prior to safe, legalized abortions following *Roe v. Wade* in 1973. A leaflet entitled "Do you want to return to the butchery of back-alley abortion?" shows police photographs of dead women on bathroom and bedroom floors and abandoned or grossly deformed babies prior to 1973.[4]

On the other hand, revivalistic and resistance movements such as pro-life, the evangelical religious right, and white supremacy portray a glorious past, a time when sex was confined to marriage, everyone went to church, all marriages were wonderful, no abortions took place, homosexuality did not exist, and there were no constraints of integration. During the heat of the civil rights struggle in the 1950s and 1960s, a pro-segregation song declared, "Our southland got along just fine until those integrators came down here stirring up the mess with outside agitators." A women's rights song entitled "Don't I Wish I Was a Single Girl Again" contrasted happy single life with miserable married life, the past with the present.

The past may be well known and ugly, and social movements must transform this perception. For instance, the American Nazi Party (later known as the National Socialist White People's Party) had to address the horrors of World War II and the holocaust in which their hero, Adolf Hitler, killed millions of allied troops, citizens in occupied countries, and Jewish inmates in concentration camps. The Party produced "facts" to prove that the "alleged" holocaust in Europe was a clever creation of the Jews through untruths, fantastic exaggerations, twisted words, confessions extracted under torture, falsified evidence, a best-seller hoax in the diary of Anne Frank, and fake photographs. The alleged purpose of this fraud was to spread the world communist conspiracy. In a pamphlet entitled *The Big Lie: Who Told It?*, Nazi writers identify who was responsible for spreading lies about Hitler, the German Nazi party, and events during World War II.[5]

The past may be more fiction than reality. The Native-American movement, for instance, has had to overcome the Hollywood-inspired vision of "injuns" and "redskins" as bloodthirsty savages who killed and mutilated innocent settlers and peace-loving cavalry led by John Wayne look-alikes. This version of the past has been fostered not only in film but in classrooms, history books, drama, and hallowed historical sites. Until recently, for example, visitors to the Custer Memorial at the Little Bighorn Battlefield received guided tours complete with a rousing story of how the gallant and brave General Custer made his last stand, outnumbered but defiant until the evil Sioux under Sitting Bull shot him down in cold blood. The Native-American movement has attempted to change fiction into fact through historical accounts such as Dee Brown's *Bury My Heart at Wounded Knee: An Indian History of the American West*, novels such as the Pulitzer Prize winning *House Made of Dawn* by N. Scott Momaday, and analyses of social interactions such as Vine Deloria's *Custer Died for Your Sins*. Commercially produced movies such as *Little Big Man* starring Dustin Hoffman and *Dances with Wolves* starring Kevin Costner gave millions a different view of Native-American history.

Social movements may offer historical revelations to transform audiences' perceptions of the past. For example, Rev. Billy James Hargis, founder and leader of the Christian Crusade against communism, often made startling revelations in his radio addresses about President Franklin Roosevelt's deals with Stalin and how the United Nations was a creation by and for the atheistic, communist Soviet Union to further its quest for world domination.[6] Robert Welch, founder and leader of the John Birch Society, searched for explanations for the rise of communism that threatened the United States and its way of life. In 1966, he presented an unbroken chain of events beginning in 1776 with the founding of the Illuminati in Bavaria and ending with the cold war in the last half of the twentieth century.[7] The National Abortion Rights Action League has produced statistics to show that abortions have existed since ancient times and that, prior to the Supreme Court decision, a million illegal and self-induced abortions took place each year in the United States in back alleys and on bathroom floors.

The Present

Social movements devote a large portion of their persuasive efforts toward transforming perceptions of the present. They understand that target audiences, even those most affected by issues such as war, the environment, the economy, equality, and justice, may be unaware of the problem, refuse to believe that it exists, believe the problem is not severe enough to require drastic action, believe the problem does not or will not affect them, or believe the problem should be and will be handled by appropriate institutions through normal channels and procedures. Nearly all institutions (from schools and churches to political parties and the mass media) foster and reinforce these perceptions. After all, a problem that appears briefly on a few evening newscasts and then disappears, occurs on the plains of South Dakota far from most citizens, is apparently sanctioned by the Bible, or is being looked at in congressional committees and pondered by the president does not require a mass movement or uncivil and inconvenient protests and boycotts.

When the antislavery movement emerged in the 1830s and 1840s, U.S. institutions did not see slavery as a degradation of the slave but rather as the slave's (a savage child) salvation as a civilized, Christianized human being.[8] The Bible, according to pro-slavery clergy, supported slavery as God's wonderful and mysterious way to save the black savage-child. When the women's liberation movement emerged during the 1960s, institutions championed the status of women as housewives and mothers who raised children and supported the careers of their husbands. A woman was not to compete in a man's world (not a place for ladies and girls), and a man was not to compete in a woman's world (not a place for a real man). Demands by the gay and lesbian rights movement in the 1990s to add sexual orientation clauses to human rights ordinances and laws were countered, on the one hand, with denials that any discrimination existed and, on the other, that discrimination was necessary because homosexuality was a sin condemned by the Bible and homosexuals were responsible for AIDS, child molestation, and the destruction of the family.

Social movement persuaders search for words to communicate the urgency of the problem and the need to take action. The ability to describe the relevance to the lives of listeners is a critical necessity in transforming perceptions of the present. Gary Woodward writes, "We commit ourselves to different realities through the act of naming because words are devices for telling others *how they should see the world.*"[9] Animal rights activists, for instance, use such words as brutality, invasion, ruthless slaughter, oppression, exploitation, and speciesism. A series of pictures in an animal rights leaflet showing a little ermine trying to gnaw its way out of a trap is accompanied by this emotion-laden caption: "Blood-spattered snow provides a nightmare setting for the terror, pain, and despair which the implacable trap elicits from its small victim—a barbaric drama of suffering which has been compared to crucifixion."[10]

Storytelling is a primary means of altering perceptions of the present. For example, former slaves such as Frederick Douglass, Henry Highland Garnet, and Sojourner Truth delivered speeches throughout the North prior to the Civil War relating the horrors they had experienced as slaves and their harrowing escapes to freedom in the North. Animal rights pamphlets and leaflets contain gruesome stories of leghold entrapments. A leaflet entitled *Say No to Torture* includes this bit of testimony: "One day, I saw a large beaver, a front paw caught in a leghold trap. The front paw was no longer covered with skin or flesh, the bone was visible, naked and white. At my approach, the beaver struggled desperately to free itself; the bone broke with a sickening sound."[11] Pro-life persuasion is replete with testimony from nurses and doctors who give heartrending accounts of aborted fetuses being bashed and smothered to death because they would not die.

Other stories are mythical but no less effective in portraying reality to sympathetic audiences. A letter from Cleveland Amory, president of The Fund for Animals, included the detailed story of a bear hunt complete with a "snarling, yapping pack" of dogs, a "terror stricken black bear," and a "hunt" that ends when a smiling "high-tech" hunter who has been tracking all of this drama through his radio "walks to the base of the tree when the bear is trapped . . . takes aim and shoots her at point blank range."[12] The imagery, emotions, and values appealed to in fictional and nonfictional stories such as these make them a powerful means of portraying a reality—an environment—different from the institutional version.

When feasible, social movements intensify their stories and claims with gory pictures. Animal rights literature shows animals caught in traps or being subjected to horrible scientific experiments. Pro-life publications and Web sites show tiny bodies of aborted fetuses in trash cans or tiny body pieces in buckets, and a video entitled "The Silent Scream" purportedly shows a fetus undergoing the agony of abortion. A click on www.abort73.com (also accessible as abortionismurder.org) opens a title page and video that begins with the warning, "If ignorance is bliss, turn back now. But if you're ready to lift the curtain on one of the greatest injustices history has ever known [quick photos of human carnage], you've come to the right place." This is followed by the number of abortions performed per day, week, month, and year in the United States, and this challenge to the viewer: "We dare you to know." If the viewer dares, another click will provide "photographic evidence" the site warns is "incredibly disturbing." The United Farm Workers distributed videos entitled "The Wrath of Grapes" that showed deformed children and children suffering from cancer, both attributed to the use of unnecessary and excessive pesticides in grape vineyards.

Most social movements use songs to transform perceptions of the present. Their titles reflect bleak states of existence: "Hard Is the Fortune of All Woman Kind" (women's rights), "Cotton Farmer Blues" (farm), "Cold Iron Shackles" (black rights), "Father's a Drunkard, and Mother Is Dead" (temperance), and "Only a Pawn in Their Game" (counterculture). The satirical anti-Vietnam War song "Kill for Peace" exclaims that when Americans do not like the way people walk, talk, or threaten their status, they "kill, kill, kill, burn, burn, burn."

Institutions have long utilized music for a variety of persuasive purposes, and they are leery of its use in the hands of social agitators. Plato warned in *The Republic*, written in the fourth century BC, that "any musical innovation is full of danger to the whole state, and ought to be prohibited."[13] Jeremy Collier, famous for his controversial pamphlets and moral essays that demanded social reforms in seventeenth-century England, wrote that music is "as dangerous as gunpowder."[14] It is little wonder, then, that near panic set in when "The Eve of Destruction," sung by Barry McGuire, reached the number one position on popular music charts in 1965 and remained there for weeks. The lyrics, voice, and instrumentation painted a world filled with hatred, prejudice, destruction, and hopelessness in which institutions were incapable of meaningful reform. Institutions feared that millions of young Americans would drop out of schools, churches, and society; nothing less than the future of the United States was at stake. Decca Records countered immediately with "The Dawn of Correction" and "Better Days Are Yet to Come," sung by the Spokesmen. Each portrayed only the good in society and how the system was creating a better world. Atomic bombs, for instance, assured the peace and would not destroy the world because no one was crazy enough to use them, and the Peace Corps was making the world a better place in which to live. The American Broadcasting Company warned its affiliates that they could lose sponsorship if they insisted on playing music that was a danger to society, while the Federal Communications Commission reminded radio and televisions stations that they could lose their broadcasting licenses if they played the wrong kind of music. The feared impact of "The Eve of Destruction" was greatly exaggerated, however. Sociologist R. Serge Denisoff discovered that only 36 percent of young listeners interpreted the song in the composer's terms, while 23 percent totally misconstrued the lyrics. Of the 73 percent that assimilated all or part of the song's doleful message, only 44 percent approved while 39 percent disapproved.[15]

Some movements use theatre to "tell it like it is." Plays by black authors such as *The Militant Preacher* and *The Job* by Ben Caldwell, *The Bronx Is Next* by Sonia Sanchez, *And We Own the Night* by Jimmy Garrett, and *The Monster* by Ronald Milner portray ministers as Uncle Toms, indict the welfare system, emphasize bad housing, show the detrimental effects of a dominant black mother on her sons and husband, and attack a black college dean who wants to be accepted by whites. Anti-Vietnam War protestors used street theatre to dramatize the horror and death of U.S. soldiers in Vietnam.

Social movement persuaders may emphasize glaring paradoxes or inconsistencies in the rhetoric and practices of institutions or social movements they oppose. John L. Lewis, founder of the United Mine Workers, pointed out in speeches that Illinois had 16 mine inspectors and 147 game wardens while Kentucky, the leading coal mining state, budgeted $220,000 for game wardens and only $37,000 for mine safety. Clearly these states valued wild game over coal miners.[16] Similarly, an advertisement placed in college newspapers by Americans for Medical Progress Educational Foundation challenged the animal rights movement's preference for animals over people. A headline entitled "How Many More Will Die Before You Say 'No!' To The Animal Rights Movement?" introduced an advertisement that read in part:

> The Cure for AIDS will come like every cure before it, through animal research. And yet, there is a growing movement of animal rights activists who oppose any use of animals in biomedical research. As one of their leaders, Ingrid Newkirk, stated: *Even if animal research resulted in a cure for AIDS . . . we'd be against it.*"[17]

Both movements, one innovative and one resistance, emphasize that an institution's or movement's values are the opposite of what they should be.

The Future

Social movement persuaders portray a vision of the future that instills a sense of urgency in audiences to organize and do something *now* before it is too late. Audiences, however, tend to be preoccupied with day-to-day needs and desires. If they look ahead at all, they tend to think things will work out as they always have or that institutions will take care of the future. As Hans Toch writes,

> For a person to be led to join a social movement, he [she] must not only sense a problem, but must also (1) feel that something can be done about it and (2) want to do something about it himself [herself]. At the very least, he [she] must feel that the status quo is not inevitable, and that change is conceivable.[18]

Social movement persuaders try to transform perceptions of the future by showing it as bright and full of hope or dark and full of despair. Which future ultimately comes about, they proclaim, will depend upon the "people" and their collective actions.

A rhetoric of hope relies on one of two appeals or a combination. *Utopian appeals* present a perfect space (often a promised land), while *millennium appeals* present a perfect time (an era when peace, love, and happiness will abound). Eugene V. Debs, a five-time presidential candidate from the 1880s to the 1920s, often spoke of a future when socialism would triumph and life would be wonderful for everyone. In a speech in Girard, Kansas, in 1908, Debs described a socialist utopia and millennium

> Every man and every woman will then be economically free. . . . Then society will improve its institutions in proportion to the progress of invention. Whether in the city or on the farm, all things productive will be carried forward on a gigantic scale. All industry will be completely organized. Society for the first time will have a scientific foundation. Every man, by being economically free, will have some time for himself. He can then take a full and perfect breath. He can enjoy life with his wife and children, because then he will have a home. . . . We will reduce the workday, and give every man a chance. We will go to parks, and we will have music, because we will have time to play music and desire to hear it.[19]

Notice Debs' careful selection of words, concepts, and values likely to motivate his midwestern audience to strive for the future he is portraying: freedom, progress, invention, science, fairness, family, and home. Similarly, the eight-hour work day movement song entitled "Divide the Day" envisioned a day when there would be work for all, plenty of food, and joy in the homes of workers. The pro-life Web site www.abort73.com follows its descriptions of the horrors of abortion with a message of hope and optimism:

> But a new day is dawning [picture of a sunrise over beautiful buildings]. Today the cover-up [by the mainstream media] ends. Today the complacency of ignorance gives way to the responsibility of knowledge. Welcome to the future of abortion history. Welcome to abort73.com. We dare you to know.

The viewer may click on a number of sidebars that provide "The Case against Abortion," the clear message being that the tide is turning against abortion.

Martin Luther King's "I Have a Dream" speech carefully blended utopian and millennium appeals to instill hope in the future if his audience would have faith and continue to support the civil rights movement's crusade for change.

> I have a dream that one day on the red hills of Georgia the sons of former slaves and the sons of former slave owners will be able to sit down together at the table of brotherhood.
>
> I have a dream that one day even the state of Mississippi, a state sweltering with the heat of injustice, sweltering with the heat of oppression, will be transformed into an oasis of freedom and justice.
>
> I have a dream that my four little children will one day live in a nation where they will not be judged by the color of their skin but by the content of their character.[20]

The rhetoric of religious social movements and clergy includes oft-repeated descriptions of a heavenly paradise, a time and place of eternal happiness for which all must strive.

A rhetoric of dread and despair, particularly prevalent in resistance and revivalistic social movements, warns that the current state of affairs can only get worse unless the people act immediately to change the course of events. The *domino theory* predicts that one right, power, possession, place, value, or virtue will fall after another, like dominos, until all is lost. Robert Welch, founder of the John Birch Society, warned in his speech that launched the Society in Indianapolis on December 9, 1958:

> Unless we can reverse the forces which now seem inexorable in their movement, you have only a few more years before the country in which you live will become four separate provinces in a worldwide Communist dominion. . . . We are living, in America today, in such a fool's paradise as the people of China lived in twenty years ago, as the people of Czecho-slovakia lived in a dozen years ago, as the people of North Vietnam lived in five years ago, and as the people of Iraq lived in only yesterday.[21]

Anti-animal rights forces launched a campaign with the warning, "Today fur. Tomorrow leather. Then wool. Then meat."[22] A related appeal, the *slippery slope*, claims society is sliding inexorably down a slope into oblivion. Randall Lake writes about the "moral landscape" presented in pro-life rhetoric and how it warns of a society sliding into total immorality because it no longer protects its unborn.[23] Christian fundamentalists point to the escalating results of a morally bankrupt country that commenced with the outlawing of school prayer in public schools—premarital sex, abortion, divorce, scandals in the highest office in the land, killings in our schools, pornography on the Internet and throughout the mass media, drug use, and acceptance of homosexuality. The environmental movement warns of the greenhouse effect and the end of life as we know it if destruction of the world's rain forests, release of fluoro-carbons into the atmosphere, widespread use of fossil fuels, uncontrolled toxic wastes, and water pollution continue at present levels.

Religious social movements or religious elements of movements often use *apocalyptic appeals* when resisting other movements or trying to revive the past. Persuaders warn state legislatures, city councils, and universities consid-ering sexual orientation clauses in human rights documents or recognition of gay marriages that God destroyed Sodom in ancient Palestine because of its wickedness, particularly homosexuality and perverse sexual preferences, and will destroy the United States if homosexuality is accepted as normal. Some cite the assassination of President Kennedy as the first installment of God's punishment for our sinful ways, and succeeding installments have included the Vietnam War, natural disasters, and the AIDS epidemic.

Inherent in many social movement messages is the notion that society is in the final battle between good and evil, *Armageddon*, merely *one step away* from disaster. For example, during the 1980s, the Clamshell Alliance in New England staged mock nuclear disasters on the ocean beaches a short distance from the Seabrook nuclear power plant, then under construction, to show the impossibil-ity of evacuation and massive deaths that would result from an accident if the plant came on line. Nuclear plants, they warned, were always moments away from disasters like the one in the Ukraine: "Chernobyl has made it crystal clear that nuclear power means nuclear death."[24] Musical instruments accompanying protest songs can create haunting, apocalyptic moods in audiences.

Although we can identify techniques social movements use to transform perceptions of reality, we do not know when movements are most likely to use them and how they might change over time. James Darsey has shown, for example, how "catalytic events," particularly the "scourge of AIDS," greatly altered the rhetoric of the gay rights movement from 1977 to 1990.[25] Studies indicate that revivalistic social movements view the past as a paradise lost that is worth resurrecting at any cost. Resistance movements view the present as a paradise achieved and see social movements and institutions as threats to this way of life, a return to a primitive past or journey to a future devoid of all that is sacred. Innovative movements portray a defective present resulting from an intolerable past and argue that the future can be bright only if the social movement is successful.

ALTERING SELF-PERCEPTIONS OF PROTESTORS

Enhancing the self-concepts of protestors is an essential rhetorical function of social movements; protestors must have strong, healthy egos when they take on powerful institutions and entrenched cultural norms and values.[26] They must see themselves as substantive human beings with the power to change the world.

Some social movements are *self-directed* in that (1) they are created, led, and populated primarily by those who perceive themselves to be dispossessed and (2) are struggling primarily for personal freedom, equality, justice, and rights. These movements include those fighting on behalf of women, African Americans, Native Americans, Hispanic Americans, Asian Americans, and gays and lesbians. Other movements are *other-directed* in that (1) they are created, led, and populated primarily by those who do not perceive themselves to be dispossessed and (2) are struggling for the freedom, equality, justice, and rights of others rather than selves. These movements include animal rights, pro-life, and students opposed to sweatshop and slave labor working conditions and segments of self-directed social movements such as white leaders and members of the antislavery movement, white freedom riders in the civil rights movement, and faculty in the student rights movement. The ego function of self-directed and other-directed social movements is similar but also differs in significant ways.

The Ego Function in Self-Directed Social Movements

The rhetoric of self-directed social movements addresses members as *innocent, blameless victims of oppression*. For example, Hispanic rhetoric claims Chicanos are "united by desire for equality and escape from oppression."[27] Richard Gregg theorizes "If one feels oppressed, he [she] implies that there is an oppressor—someone responsible for the oppression."[28] Targeted oppressors of self-directed movements include men, women, whites, Anglos, straights, the system, corporations, and industrialists. Persuaders in these movements emphasize that they are oppressed because of their sex, race, ethnic origin, sexual orientation, labor class, or student group. As innocent victims of powers beyond their control, oppressed groups are exploited as cheap labor, sex objects, servants, and tourist attractions, and they demand an end to what oppresses them: injustice, inequality, segregation, discrimination, reverse discrimination, racism, and tyranny. It is not surprising that the rhetoric of self-directed protestors exhibits a siege mentality.

The rhetoric of self-directed social movements addresses *self-esteem and self-worth*—and often precedes this theme with terms such as inferior, low, poor, negative, and fragile. Society has taught the oppressed to stay in their place and reduced them to the status of things. Victims of this oppression have often suffered from self-hatred and guilt for allowing themselves to be stripped of their dignity, degraded, humiliated, and dehumanized. An essential ingredient in self-directed rhetoric is to establish the selfhood of members and target audiences by refurbishing, repairing, restoring, and enhancing self-esteem and confidence. Persuaders preach messages of self-worth, respect, dignity, and confidence. Michael Sedano writes that the poetry of the Chicano movement saw "tomorrow's transformation of identity from a quiet, polite, patronized, domesticated pet to a fiercely self-assured Chicano who is in control of his or her destiny."[29] Protest songs often cry out: we are somebody, we are important, we make contributions. For example, the socialist "Hymn of the Proletariat" popular in the first half of the twentieth century asks:

> Who hammers brass and stone?
> Who raiseth from the mine?
> Who weaveth cloth and silk?
> Who tilleth wheat and vine?
> It is the men who toil, the Proletariat.

Ego is also enhanced in self-directed social movements through searches for *new self-identities* and *self-definitions* that will result in identification with groups according to sex, race, ethnic origin, age, sexual preference, and student or labor status. Individual status is affirmed through group identity that provides members with a critical sense of unity, togetherness, solidarity, and community. They often see themselves as brothers and sisters. They are no longer isolated victims standing alone to face powerful oppressors but comrades united through their unique identities and working within organizations populated with people like themselves who are part of powerful, ever-growing social movements with meaningful relational patterns. Self-naming is often a critical step toward self-identity and mobilizing the oppressed. They are now African Americans rather than Negroes, Native Americans rather than Indians, women rather than girls, and Hispanics or Chicanos rather than Mexicans or Mexican Americans. This function dominates protest songs such as "I Am Woman" that exclaim "I am strong, I am invincible."

The rhetoric of self-directed social movements addresses the *status of the oppressed in society.* Gregg writes that the oppressed find themselves in "symbolically defensive positions from which they must extricate themselves before they can realize positive identities."[30] Protestors must locate their proper places in the symbolic and social hierarchy if they are to overcome their oppression and realize equality and justice. They see themselves as marginalized, disenfranchised, and ignored, and claim they are stereotyped and bracketed with children and the lowest elements of society, such as criminals, idiots, and the insane. Their contributions to society and accomplishments cry out for recognition and a place equal to or above others within the social hierarchy. For instance, Jose Angel Gutierrez asked audiences:

> Ever see a Mexican buck private? Obviously you have. How about a general? Chicanos are seldom given positions of authority. . . . Chicanos are hired at the bottom rungs of the corporate structure. This way the Gringos can continue in positions of power and control.[31]

Huey P. Newton, a leader of the Black Panthers, appealed to audiences "to view themselves as special people with unique ability to bring about social change through the pursuit of social alternatives."[32] In his famous "Letter from Birmingham Jail," Martin Luther King depicted the cause of civil rights so his followers became "extremists in the cause of liberty."[33]

The Ego Function in Other-Directed Social Movements

The rhetoric of other-directed social movements is not aimed at restoring, refurbishing, or establishing the selfhood of movement members but at *affirming a positive self-esteem.* Members do not see themselves as members of oppressed or exploited groups but as saviors of the oppressed and exploited. There are no signs of despair, insecurity, or inferiority. Rhetoric affirms and enhances an already exalted self-esteem by celebrating and recognizing the protestor's moral principles, commitment, compassion, humanitarianism, and victories in great moral struggles. There is no siege mentality, no fortifying of walls against attacks because of who or what they are. Persuaders are on the offense rather than the defense. The mentality is one of the moral, righteous crusader on a sacred quest to stop the suffering and oppression of others.

There is little evidence of seeking a higher place in the social hierarchy in the rhetoric of other-directed social movements. Activists appear to believe that they are already at the top of the social and moral hierarchy because they are committed to a struggle for the oppressed and against evils. There is status seeking, but it is *locating a proper status within the social movement and among social movement organizations.* Members implicitly and explicitly contrast social movement organizations according to longevity, size, activities, effectiveness, and victories. Messages for members and sympathizers emphasize that they are supporting and working for excellent organizations struggling for the oppressed. People should feel pride in being part of the very best organization of like-minded crusaders. For example, Trans-Species Unlimited, PETA, and

Greenpeace extol their national and international reputations and campaigns on behalf of animal rights and welfare.

Self-identity in the rhetoric of other-directed social movements, like societal status, comes not through identity with a sexual, ethnic, racial, or age group, but through *identity with a movement and specific social movement organization*. The emphasis is not on what or who a person is individually but on a person's collective association with an organization working for the welfare of others. A meaningful relational pattern comes through the movement.

Persuaders celebrate unification through struggle. The rhetoric of other-directed movements does not attempt to create a new self-identity or to redefine an old self-identity; self-naming and self-discovery are unnecessary. It attaches an identity to other positive self-identities, an addition rather than a transformation. Activists are now heroes as well as college students, rescuers as well as Christians. Self-identity emanates from association with moral crusades and courageous organizations at the forefront of social movements, not from identification with other brothers, sisters, Asian Americans, or senior citizens. They are pro-life, animal rights, or environmental crusaders, protectors, rescuers, and heroes.

Victimage permeates the rhetoric of other-directed social movements, but it dwells on the oppression and exploitation of others, not selves. Typical messages portray the brutality of abortion, apartheid in South Africa, or treatment of animals and how activists are struggling in their selfless, moral crusades to end this brutality. Occasionally, rhetoric addresses movement members as victims of countermovements and/or institutions determined to maintain things as they are. This victimage enhances ego because no institution would bother with a weak or ineffective protest group. Activists are innocent victims because they are willing to sacrifice their security, dignity, and social status for other innocent victims. Pro-life literature, for instance, claims protestors have been victims of police brutality, savage radical feminists, cold-blooded abortion-mill guards, and the media, all because they dare to speak out and try to save lives of the unborn. Ego-enhancement appears to be a major by-product, if not the aim, of such rhetoric.

LEGITIMIZING THE SOCIAL MOVEMENT

Theorists have claimed that legitimizing the social movement is the principal goal or demand of social movements, the primal challenge of movements to institutions, and the most central obstacle leaders of movements must overcome. Gaston Rimlinger and Joseph Gusfield, for example, argue that for a social movement to be successful, its demands and methods must somehow become legitimate in the eyes of institutions, government, the public, and potential members.[34] A major struggle, then, is to attain positive relational patterns with the larger society. Protestors have in their favor only the somewhat mythical American tolerance of dissent, a tolerance most evident when the dissent is nonthreatening or ineffective.

Conferring and Maintaining Legitimacy

The notion of legitimacy contains two inherently rhetorical elements. The first element is the act of conferring, by one person or group to another person or group, the "right to exercise authoritative influence in a given area or to issue binding directives."[35] The second element is the act of retaining legitimacy once it is conferred. Robert Francesconi writes, "Rhetoric bridges the gap between legitimacy as claimed and legitimacy as believed."[36] All societies and their institutions have prevalent ideologies that explicitly and implicitly support and are supported by the prevailing social structure. William Garrison observes that social movement persuaders:

> Face a field of combat that is already occupied by a competing legitimate frame that is established and quiescent rather than emergent and action-oriented. When truly hegemonic, the legitimating frame is taken for granted. Would-be challengers face the problem of overcoming a definition of the situation that they themselves may take as a part of the natural order.[37]

When a people or social order confers such legitimacy on a person or institution, it also confers five powers that, in combination, sustain the original grant. *The power to reward*, perhaps the most important retentive power, allows legitimate institutions to reward those who conform and obey and to coerce or punish those who strive to be different or challenge approved norms, values, and institutional arrangements. Institutional leaders urge protestors and reformers to consider the consequences of their actions, typically by granting or denying tangible benefits and rewards such as diplomas, jobs, advancements, incomes, research and development grants, and tax exemptions. If the disaffected refuse to take the carrot, an institution may resort to the stick to maintain compliance, justifying its use of coercive persuasion in the name of God, the founding fathers, the people, the Constitution, the law, or national security.

The power of control enables legitimate institutions to regulate the flow of information and persuasion to members of organizations and the populace. Thus, they determine if, how, when, where, under what circumstances, and with whom communication will occur. Frances Piven and Richard Cloward contend, "The ideology of democratic political rights, by emphasizing the availability of legitimate avenues for the redress of grievances, delegitimizes protest; and the dense relationships generated by electoral politics also divert people from protest."[38] Institutional leaders often brand reformers and agitators as well-meaning but ignorant of the facts known to established authorities. In the information age, control of information and information flow may be more important than military and police forces. The global availability of the Internet is seriously challenging institutional control of information.

The power of identification accrues to institutions because they are the keepers, protectors, and proselytizers of the sacred symbols, emblems, places, offices, documents, codes, values, and myths of the social order. Institutions and their leaders are seen as the legitimate heirs or successors of the order's founding fathers, patriots, revered leaders, prophets, and martyrs. Identification with the sacred is frequent in the secular courts, legislatures, and schools and at religious and national observances and sporting events. As Anthony Oberschall writes, their positions allow institutional leaders to invoke "elaborate systems of beliefs and moral ideas upon which legitimacy rests."[39]

The power of terministic control allows institutions to control language and thereby the "legitimated meanings for such politically sensitive terms as order, violence, repression, deviance, protest, persuasion, coercion, and symbolic speech."[40] Thus institutional violence is the legitimate maintenance of law and order, never terrorism. Overzealous supporters of the social order are patriots, never fanatics. National security—particularly during time of war—justifies withholding information, infiltration of protest groups, spying on citizens, amassing secret files on social movement organizations, leaders, members, and sympathizers, and making arrests and detentions without formal charges or hearings. When Martin Luther King was jailed during a civil rights campaign in Birmingham, clergy in the city released a statement that labeled him as an "outside agitator" that cast "him in the role of an unneeded external complication for the advance of civil rights in Birmingham." John Patton claims, "This argument went to King's very legitimacy as a voice for civil rights."[41]

The power of moral suasion allows institutions to exert control by operating in the realms of attitudes and emotional attachments. R. R. McGuire claims that people often come to see obedience or deference to legitimate authority as a moral obligation.[42] Thus, institutions persuade people that they have a duty to honor institutional decisions even when those decisions have "unpleasant consequences."[43] Louis Kriesberg, for example, contends that "people learn rules and if they accept them they may become so internalized that violation would be shunned in order to avoid the feelings of guilt or shame which would follow violation."[44]

When uninstitutional forces collide with institutional forces, the rhetorical deck is heavily stacked in favor of the legitimate institutions and their leaders. People tend to maintain the faith even in the face of massive economic and social breakdowns. How, then, can social movements use persuasion to establish legitimate relational patterns? A rhetoric of legitimation must be a combination of coactive and confrontational strategies. *Coactive* or *common ground strategies* emphasize similarities, shared experiences, and a common cause with target audiences. *Confrontational* or *conflict strategies* emphasize dissimilarities, diverse experiences, and conflict with target audiences.

Legitimacy through Coactive Strategies

If, as Francesconi claims, "an implicit requirement" of legitimacy is a "rationality of good reasons," then social movements must identify with fundamental societal norms and values if they are to transport themselves from the margins of society to the centers where legitimacy resides.[45] They must access the sources institutions claim as their rightful domains.

Social movements may identify with what Max Weber refers to as the "sanctity of immemorial traditions."[46] Molefi Asante and others note that social movements usually link themselves with the traditional rights and values of equality, justice, and dignity.[47] While most Americans saw Malcolm X as a dangerous radical, a cursory review of his speeches reveals that he appealed continually to the fundamental American values of a virtuous life dedicated to family, community, religious beliefs, hard work, ingenuity, and the free enterprise system—hardly radical or revolutionary beliefs. Social movements are wise to identify with the moral symbols, sacred emblems, heroes, founding fathers, and revered documents of society rather than to attack or disparage them. Many protest songs are modeled after or sung to the tune of traditional religious hymns such as "The Old Rugged Cross." Denisoff writes that this practice enables social movements to establish important links to institutions:

> The use of religious music adds an appeal to tradition which social movements generally require. Movements, by their very nature of advocating social change, are generally not tied to tradition. Hymns, in part, appear to tie the movement to a national heritage, regardless of the programs they advocate.[48]

Other protest songs use the patterns or melody of well known, popular, and perhaps patriotic songs to identify with tradition and values. These include "Battle Hymn of the Republic," "Yankee Doodle," "Marching through Georgia," "Casey Jones," "Dixie," and "Swanee." Cheryl Thomas, James Irvine, and Walter Kirkpatrick claim that such songs can transfer legitimacy to the social movement from religious, social, and political institutions."[49] Resistance or countermovements may maintain close identification with institutions by singing institutional songs. For instance, Roman Catholic protestors have marched to pro-life Operation Rescue sites singing "Ave Maria," while others have sung "America" or the national anthem during demonstrations.

Social activists may rework the pieces of tradition into new stories that befit their ideologies. Thus, to avoid being stigmatized as a mere fad, a "people going crazy together," or an evil force in society, protestors may emphasize the hallowed tradition of protest in U.S. history, showing for instance what our founding fathers really were—revolutionaries.[50] Carl Oglesby, president of the SDS (Students for a Democratic Society), asked an audience during the antiwar march in Washington, D.C., on October 27, 1965, what would happen if Thomas Jefferson and Thomas Paine were to sit down with President Johnson to discuss the war in Vietnam:

> They might say: "What fools and bandits, sirs, you make then of us? Outside help? Do you remember Lafayette? Or the 3,000 British freighters the French navy sank for our side? Or the arms and men we got from France and Spain? And what's this about terror? Did you never hear what we did to our own loyalists? Or about the thousands of rich American Tories who fled for their lives to Canada? And as for popular sup-

port, do you not know that we had less than one-third of our people with us? That, in fact, the colony of New York recruited more troops for the British than for the revolution? Should we give it all back?"[51]

Martin Luther King employed the same tactic with a more encompassing religious and secular history in his "Letter from Birmingham Jail." Clergy and others had challenged the legitimacy of his actions.

> Of course there is nothing new about this kind of civil disobedience. It was evidenced sublimely in the refusal of Shadrach, Meshach, and Abednego to obey the laws of Nebuchadnezzar, on the ground that a higher moral law was at stake. It was practiced superbly by the early Christians, who were willing to face hungry lions and the excruciating pain of chopping blocks rather than submit to certain unjust laws of the Roman Empire. To a degree, academic freedom is a reality today because Socrates practiced civil disobedience. In our own nation, the Boston Tea Party represented a massive act of civil disobedience.[53]

Reconstructing history can alter perceptions of social reality and show the social movement as not only legitimate but more legitimate than institutions because it alone is telling it like it really is and practicing the hallowed tradition of social protest.

Social movements may strive to establish their actions as those of legitimate organizations by incorporating into legal organizations and operating openly to avoid fears of secretive societies. They may identify with the legal status of protest in the United States by conforming to rules and accepted procedures the populace perceives to be formally correct and by avoiding direct attacks on basic institutions and authorities. Most emphasize the importance of the ballot box rather than violence or coercion in bringing about or resisting change. Endorsements of a social movement by legitimate organizations may produce a "rub-off" effect because social movements, like individuals in society, are judged by their associations. They strive to attract legitimizers—organizations, speakers, writers, senators, clergy, entertainers, scientists, military leaders, war veterans, ex-presidents, and medical professionals—who are respectable, safe, and beyond reproach.

Similarly, social movements may attempt to gain legitimacy by identifying with movements that have gained a degree of legitimacy with the public and institutions. For example, Bonnie Dow claims that a major goal of a documentary on women's liberation "was to confer legitimacy, to 'fix' feminism by analogizing it to civil rights, by emphasizing the benefits for men, and by highlighting its possibilities for individual opportunity and self-improvement."[53] The women's movement might be seen as less threatening with reformers triumphing over revolutionaries, just like the civil rights movement. Some movements employ altered versions of famous songs used by successful social movements. For instance, "We Will Overcome," a southern labor song of the 1920s and 1930s, was revised slightly as "We Shall Overcome" for the civil rights movement in the 1950s and 1960s and became an important song for black nationalist movements in Africa. Black slaves wrote "Oh Freedom" prior to the Civil War, and black regiments marched to it during the Civil War. In the 1960s, SNCC (the Student Nonviolent Coordinating Committee) resurrected "Oh Freedom" with revised verses that included references to segregation, shooting, burning churches, and Jim Crow.

Social movements may employ a strategy of transcendence by identifying themselves with what is large, good, important, and of the highest order in society. *The Gray Panther Manual* relates how the Panthers grew rapidly into a powerful, national organization:

> Throughout 1973 the Gray Panthers grew tenfold again. . . . The ABC-TV network did a documentary entitled: "Gray Panthers," with nation-wide viewing. Local Gray Panther Networks were convening in Philadelphia, Tucson, Dayton, D.C., Chicago, Los Angeles, San Francisco, Charlotte, New York, Denver, Decatur, Kansas City, Portland, and Baltimore. Panthers were on the prowl all over.[54]

Signs of large-scale disaffection may shake confidence in institutions and thus undermine the legitimacy of institutional leaders.[55] Social movements, particularly religious ones, stress a sense of mission and claim to operate in accordance with a predetermined divine plan. They identify with the belief that divine plans transcend the temporal ones of human institutions, argue that "expressive" values (symbols, reflections, meanings) rather than "instrumental" values (means, instruments, tools) are the truly universal ones, and try to locate the movement within what Irving Zaretsky and Mark Leone call a "sacred cosmos."[56] Moral obligations to the state, agitators claim, are limited by moral obligations to humanity and a higher authority.

A coactive rhetoric is essential, then, for a social movement in its struggle for legitimacy because it chips away at three powers enjoyed by institutions: identification, terministic control, and moral suasion. Coactive rhetoric obviously serves more than the "managerial" and "reinforcement" functions ascribed to it, for it demonstrates that a social movement deserves legitimacy by *worth and right*. With worth and right established, institutions can no longer call into question the fundamental legitimacy of a social movement but, as Rhodri Jeffreys-Jones explains, must attack its tactics instead.[57] John Bowers, Donovan Ochs, and Richard Jensen address the importance of a coactive rhetorical approach in establishing legitimacy when they argue that the early employment of a strategy of "petition" (asking authorities to address an urgent concern) is crucial because:

> If the establishment can show that the petition stage was not attempted by the dissenters, it can discredit the agitators as irresponsible firebrands who reject normal decision-making processes in favor of disturbances and disruption. Unless they first attempt petition, activists are unlikely to win support through more drastic strategies.[58]

Thus, coactive strategies tend to dominate the rhetoric of social movements during the early stages of protest when persuaders are attempting to make the people and institutions aware of an urgent, unaddressed problem and to gain entry to the playing field where such problems are debated and resolved. They are essential for establishing legitimate relational patterns.

A coactive rhetoric by itself, however, cannot attain legitimacy for a social movement because it merely establishes the movement as *similar* to the social order in important ways—legal, law-abiding, supporter of traditions, moral—and therefore worthy of a degree of legitimacy. There is always the danger that some people may see the social movement as so similar to the social order that there is no need to join, while others may become estranged from the movement because it fails to differentiate itself significantly from evil or impotent institutions. Thus, a coactive rhetoric may produce a rhetorical stalemate between institutional and uninstitutional forces that leaves institutions with their powers diminished or shared but intact.

Legitimacy through Confrontational Strategies

A confrontational rhetoric is necessary to break the rhetorical stalemate by bringing institutional legitimacy into question and enabling the social movement to transcend the social order in perceived legitimacy. If a confrontational rhetoric is to raise the social movement to a transcendent position in society, it must make a significant number of people see the social order as illegitimate or at least less legitimate than the social movement. As Carol Jablonski argues, a "rhetoric of discontinuity" is necessary to "establish the legitimacy of the collective's grievances as well as the need to induce changes from the outside."[59]

Movements employ a variety of confrontational strategies to show that institutional leaders and organizations systematically distort communication, create barriers, and constrain and distort an alleged "reciprocal accountability." McGuire writes that social movements hope to demonstrate that the order is "irrational and hence illegitimate—involving no moral obligation."[60] The goal is to raise doubts in the minds of the people about their relationships with institutions.

Activists try to exploit societal restrictions on institutional actions. The civil rights, Hispanic, animal rights, and pro-life movements, for example, have employed strategies of nonviolent resistance and civil disobedience, including strikes, boycotts, sit-ins, demonstrations, symbolic acts, and violations of ordinances and laws to reveal the inconsistency (and therefore illegitimacy) of values and established procedures, customs, and laws. Social movements take advantage of outdated laws or quasi-legal practices of authorities by demanding that authorities stick to the letter of the law—actions that might make authorities look ridiculous, unfair, or heavy-handed. Saul Alinsky urges would-be radicals to "*Make the enemy live up to their own book of rules.* You can kill them with this, for they can no more obey their own rules than the Christian church can live up to Christianity."[61] If an institution represses peaceful, nonviolent dissent and refuses to enforce or obey the laws, it may seriously undermine its legitimacy in the eyes of the people and other institutions.

Militant confrontational strategies (disruptions, verbal violence, and assaults on property, symbols, and the police) are designed to provoke institutions into overreactions and violent suppression. As Robert Cathcart claims, "The establishment, when confronted, must respond not to the particular enactment but to the challenge to its legitimacy."[62] If an institution "responds with full fury and might to crush the confronters, it violates the mystery and reveals the secret that it maintains power, not through moral righteousness but through its power to kill." Activists have learned the value of mass arrests and real or apparent police brutality, particularly when television and video cameras are present. Stephen Oates writes that Martin Luther King changed his views on nonviolence after the Albany, Georgia, demonstrations during which the authorities showed remarkable restraint. King became determined to "force his oppressor to commit his brutality openly—in the light of day—with the rest of the world looking on. In short, provocation was now a crucial aspect of King's nonviolent strategy."[63] Televised images of police dragging men and women, some of them members of the clergy, to police vans during Operation Rescue campaigns, for instance, may outrage significant numbers of an institution's constituency and be counterproductive to control efforts. Police explanations that their lines had been "assaulted" by pro-life protestors crawling on their hands and knees appeared laughable at best and brutal at worst.

Activists charge that the "civility and decorum" of authorities "serve as masks for the preservation of injustice" and constitute a thin veneer that hides a vicious, repressive social order.[64] Robert Scott and Donald Smith write that social movements prod institutions to "show us how ugly you really are."[65] And Cathcart writes that a "Confrontational rhetoric shouts 'Stop!' at the system, saying, 'You cannot go on assuming you are the true and correct order; you must see yourself as the evil thing you are.'"[66] Authorities often discredit and humiliate themselves when they lose control and thereby become collaborators with protestors determined to strip them of legitimacy. Violent acts against white supremacists at Ruby Ridge in Idaho, a religious cult in Waco, Texas, and those protesting the World Trade Organization (WTO) meetings in Seattle and Washington, D.C., were viewed on television by millions of people around the world and aided the efforts of protesting groups to reveal the ugly sides of institutions.

There may be two significant by-products of ugly and sometimes violent confrontations between protestors and institutions. First, violent suppression allows the social movement to claim that it acted in self-defense (a noble and legal act cherished in U.S. society) to institutional force and violence that was both unwarranted and violated sacred national principles and traditions. Second, verbal and nonverbal violence by institutions and militant elements of movements may confer legitimacy upon moderate leaders and organizations because they appear to be rational and safe in comparison.

A confrontational rhetoric is essential for a social movement to gain legitimacy because it chips away at four powers institutions enjoy: reward, control, identification, and moral suasion. A confrontational rhetoric breaks the rhetorical stalemate between institutional and noninstitutional forces by demonstrating that the institution deserves neither its claim of legitimacy nor its high place in the social hierarchy. It challenges the normal relational patterns of society while offering new ones.

Although a confrontational rhetoric is essential for a social movement in its struggle for legitimacy, it alone cannot attain legitimacy for the movement. Destruction or reduction of Order A's legitimacy does not automatically bestow legitimacy on Order B, even when Order B was instrumental in revealing the evil and unworthiness of Order A. Social movements must effectively present themselves as the *innocent victims* of institutions out of control. This is why nonviolent civil disobedience as taught by Gandhi in India and Martin Luther King, Jr., in the United States can be effective if institutions resort to violence and lawlessness that shatters relational bonds.

Prescribing Courses of Action

Prescribing courses of action constitutes selling the social movement's ideology. According to John Wilson, ideology "is the generic name given to those beliefs which mobilize people into action in social movements"; an ideology is "a set of beliefs about the social world and how it operates, containing statements about the rightness of certain social arrangements and what action should be taken in the light of these statements."[67] This set of beliefs addresses what must be done, who must do it, and how it must be done.

The What

In explaining *what* must be done, a social movement presents demands and solutions that will alleviate a grave condition, prevent catastrophic changes, or bring on the utopia or millennium. It is a course of action designed to produce positive evolutionary results. Each movement must explain, defend, and sell its program or product. Kenneth Dolbeare and Patricia Dolbeare write,

> each ideology is attached to some values, such as equality or justice, in preference to others. The crucial questions are *the way in which such values are understood or defined* by the ideology, and *how they are ranked in priority* when they conflict with each other.[68]

For example, when environmentalists strive to protect wetlands from commercial development or the spotted owl from extinction if forests are cut in the northwest, they place values of preservation over progress, free enterprise, and property rights. Steven Goldzwig notes, "a value or set of values *denied* helps to determine what is valued. Thus, a negative reaction to a rhetorical effort is just as clear a mirror of a culture's values as the approval of an act."[69]

Michael McGee claims that *ideographs* link rhetoric and ideology, ideographs being "one-term sums of an orientation, the species of 'God' or 'Ultimate' term that will be used to symbolize the line of argument" an "individual would pursue."[70] Thus, we should be able to detect a social movement's ideology by identifying key words and phrases in its rhetoric because they are "the basic structural elements, the building blocks, of ideology." Words such as freedom, equality, justice, liberty, progress, private property, free enterprise, free speech, right of privacy, right to vote, and right to life have dominated U.S. social movements and distinguished one from another for more than two centuries.

Problems develop not only when institutions say no to demands and solutions but also when organizations within social movements prescribe diverse and perhaps conflicting demands and solutions. In the civil rights movement, for example, Martin Luther King, Jr., saw integration as the way to achieve freedom and equal rights, while Malcolm X advocated black nationalism and black capitalism. In the temperance movement, some factions desired to limit the use of alcoholic beverages and other factions would settle for nothing less than banning the sale of all alcoholic beverages. In today's pro-life movement, there are those who would allow abortions under a few circumstances such as saving a woman's life and those who will settle for nothing less than the elimination of all abortions, including birth control methods that prevent conception. Intra-movement conflicts are inevitable because each SMO comes into existence when it claims to have created the *perfect* doctrine and set of principles, and there can be no compromise with perfection.

Changing social situations, efforts of institutions to negate or to co-opt a movement's demands and solutions, and the necessity to address a variety of target audiences require adaptive strategies. Adaptations can include additions or deletions of ideographs, alterations in the content of demands and solutions, and changes in explanations. As Wilson writes, "When new sensitivities are created by social events and collectives, ideologies, to be accepted, must cater to these new sensitivities."[71] Kristy Maddux explores how the NAOWS (National Association Opposing Woman Suffrage) altered its ideology after 1917 from one focused narrowly on resisting suffrage for women to one resisting all radical movements, including socialism, bolshevism, pacifism, and feminism.[72]

Efforts to adapt to new sensitivities and events always expose social movement leaders and organizations to charges of revisionism by movement purists, the true believers who will brook no changes in sacred doctrine. William Cameron notes, "Sometimes the zeal for 'purity' produces isolation from the general public, or even schisms within the movement."[73] Leaders face charges of going too fast or too slow, of being too rigid or too flexible. If situations seem no better as time passes and crises occur, "Illusions are often offered as solutions, to *solve* problems by predicting a rapid transition to a better world." "The person, faced with an intolerable situation," Hans Toch observes, "searches for and finds a miracle."[74]

The Who

Social movements must prescribe *who* must to do the job. Their answer, seemingly without exception, is *the ordinary people*, a *great grassroots* movement for change or resistance to change. All serious social movement adherents understand, however, that the movement needs organization and leaders of some sort.

First, they must convince enough people that only an *uninstitutional collectivity* is both willing and able to bring about or resist change; all others are part of or a cause of the problem. Struggles develop within social movements over how far the movement must distance itself from established institutions. Some elements within the women's liberation movement, for instance, wanted to use the system (Congress, courts, state legislators) to achieve changes. Others argued the only way women could achieve their true identities and power was to break all ties with men, male-dominated organizations, and male tactics.

Second, social movements must espouse types of organization and leadership or organizations and leaders best suited to solving urgent problems. This leads inevitably to a striving for perfection that splinters the movement into competing factions and organizations. Fred Powledge, in his book entitled *Free at Last? The Civil Rights Movement and the People Who Made It*, provides extensive documentation of the competition, jealousy, and hostility among the leaders and organizations of the civil rights movement—the National Association for the Advancement of Colored People (NAACP), the Southern Christian Leadership Conference (SCLC), the Student Nonviolent Coordinating Committee (SNCC), and the Congress on Racial Equality (CORE)—that often hampered campaigns and movement progress.[75]

One movement faction may declare open warfare against another it deems ideologically deviant or inferior. For instance, Tom Metzger, founder of WAR (White Aryan Resistance) espouses a strongly conservative ideology but condemns "right wingers" as "golf course revolutionaries" and "intellectual cowards" and chides militia groups for folding like a "cheap umbrella in a typhoon" after the bombing of the Murrah Federal Building in Oklahoma City.[76] In the early labor movement, the American Federation of Labor and the competing Knights of Labor each claimed to be the perfect labor organization based on a perfect set of principles that made it the historical, natural, and moral leader of the movement and cited the other as an unnatural, unscientific, immoral, and obsolete failure that should either be abandoned or absorbed into the one true union. The struggle ended when the Knights ceased to exist. Thus, persuasion creates *we-they* distinctions within social movements as sharp as those between social movements and institutions. These elements engage in struggles to determine what people they are or want to be.

Third, social movements may establish membership limitations to create elites capable of dealing with unsolvable conditions and the omnipotent forces that produced them. The Ku Klux Klan restricted membership to white, Anglo-Saxon Protestants; some African-American groups restricted membership to African Americans; some women's groups restricted membership to females; some student rights groups restricted membership to people under thirty; and the American Federation of Labor restricted membership to workers from skilled trades, excluding unskilled laborers and factory workers. Chapter 4 reveals how the John Birch Society used an authoritarian rhetoric that effectively limited its membership to an elite deemed capable of defeating the communist conspiracy in the United States. While some movements limit membership to those who can truly understand the plight of the victims, others do so because they see the excluded as the enemy. The Manifesto for New York Radical Feminists declared:

> As radical feminists we recognize that we are engaged in a power struggle with men, and that the agent for our oppression is man insofar as he identifies with and carries out the supremacy privileges of the male role. For while we realize that the liberation of women will ultimately mean the liberation of men from their destructive role as oppressor, we have no illusion that men will welcome this liberation without a struggle.[77]

Other social movements freely admit anyone who espouses their causes, believing that success can come only from mass movements able to exert pressure on institutions.

The How

Social movements must determine how the job must be done and the adaptive strategies most appropriate and effective for their causes. A revolutionary, innovative movement organization may have a wide range of tactical choices (boycotts, strikes, symbolic takeovers) because that is what a revolutionary group does. The range of available channels may be limited to leaflets and the Internet because the group is considered too radical for radio and television. A reform-oriented revivalistic organization may have access to many channels (including radio and/or television talk shows and features in magazines) but a narrow range of moderate, socially acceptable tactics because it does not want to offend its many target audiences. A resistance movement may have ready access to institutions and channels because institutional leaders favor or use it when opposing a social movement but must abide by rules, expectations, and decorum of institutions to maintain these advantages.

No social movement can rely on the same means of change for long. Movement followers, the general public, and the mass media become bored with them, and institutions learn quickly how to deal with specific strategies and tactics. Alinsky advises would-be social movement persuaders, "*Wherever possible go outside of the experience of the enemy.* Here you want to cause confusion, fear, and retreat." He also advises that "a tactic that drags on too long becomes a drag. Man [woman] can sustain militant interest in any issue for only a limited time, after which it becomes a ritualistic commitment like going to church on Sunday mornings."[78] Social movements must search continually for new and different strategies to keep the movement fresh, alive, and moving forward and institutions off balance. So-called "hacktivists" threatened in the summer of 2004 to disrupt the Republican National Convention electronically by taking down Web sites, e-mail servers, phone and fax lines, and electronic billboards.

Social movements often splinter into factions over differing views on how the job must be done, and some movement members may be more committed to means than to ends. Nearly all movements have radical and moderate factions, and the differences are often more pronounced in strategies than ideologies. This is readily apparent in the current militia movement in which basic beliefs are similar but tactics range from information campaigns and military-like maneuvers to violent acts. Roxanne Dunbar, a leader of the Southern Female Rights Union, reported that her original group had seriously considered assassinating a man to make their presence known but decided the victim "would become such an important person because we'd chosen him over all these other guys."[79] This plan and one in which they would "get shotguns and go to the Boston Common to deal with the men who ogle the secretaries" seemed to "horrify" moderate members. The environmental movement has moderate elements such as the Sierra Club that believes in working through the system and radical groups such as Earth First! (eco-guerrillas) that sabotage machinery, equipment, and power lines when they are not conducting blockades and chaining themselves to cranes and trees and ELF (Environmental Liberation Front) that uses arson to destroy threats to the environment: homes, recreational facilities, and Hummers. Organizations and leaders of the civil rights movement disagreed strongly over strategies. The NAACP advocated working through the courts. The SCLC under Martin Luther King, Jr., advocated nonviolent civil disobedience. Malcolm X advocated "black nationalism" and "action."

Social movements must continually search for new tactics and adapt strategies to keep the movements alive and progressing, but each new selection or change may lead to conflicts within and between organizations.

MOBILIZING FOR ACTION

Persuaders must convince large numbers of people to join in the cause, to organize into effective groups, and to unify through coalitions to carry the movement's message to target audiences to bring about desired evolutionary results. Ralph Smith and Russell Windes contend that "the presence of mobilizational exigencies distinguishes, and assists in defining, the rhetorical situation of movements. The rhetorical situation of a movement [its environment] requires discourse to organize support for united action to reach a shared goal of social change."[80]

Organizing and Uniting the Discontented

Social movements expend great persuasive effort trying to educate audiences about the cause and to convince them of the urgency to *join together* to bring about or to resist change. Mailings, newsletters, newspapers, pamphlets, leaflets, books, videos, the Internet, interpersonal contacts, and speeches are devoted to organizing and uniting the discontented. While the Internet has great potential for serving a variety of functions for social movements and most employ Web sites and have e-mail addresses, Wim van de Donk and his associates discovered "only a few provide online discussion forums, and communication is still a one-way street, the SMO providing the visitor with information."[81]

Getting Americans to join uninstitutional organizations is no easy task. Traditions of rugged individualism, belief in the capacity and determination of U.S. institutions to deal with problems effectively once they are identified, and suspicion of movements and agitators prevent most Americans from protesting, let alone joining and becoming active in what they see as strange or dangerous organizations. Even the largest and most successful social movements recruit only a fraction of victims and socially conscious citizens. Very few women, African Americans, Hispanic Americans, gays, workers, and supporters of the environment ever contribute to or join movements on their behalf. Recruiting never ends. Some movements appeal to self-identity or self-worth to activate audiences. Pete Seeger's labor song written for the labor movements of the 1930s, "Which Side Are You On?," asked: "Will you be a lousy scab, Or will you be a man?" Other songs relate conversion experiences, such as this verse from the gay liberation song "Second Chance":

> You know once I was something like you,
> I was scared to try anything new.
> Well then love it conquered,
> Let's see what it can do for you.

Social movement members differ markedly in their commitment to the movement and its cause. Wilson illustrates this commitment as the rings of an onion.[82] At the center are a small number of full-time, paid professionals who are totally committed to the cause and willing to sacrifice everything. The first ring around this center consists of full-time, nonpaid professionals who can be counted on to populate the front lines in marches and demonstrations and remain committed when the movement is under attack or struggling to bring about meaningful change.

The second ring consists of the rank and file where total commitment is rare because the movement plays a small role in their lives. The third ring consists of sympathizers and legitimizers who are neither fully inside nor fully outside the movement. Fear of institutional suppression and distrust of followers and sympathizers has led many extremist organizations to avoid formal membership lists. Tom Metzger of WAR warns his readers on resist.com, "Remain aloof and very slowly seek out a small group of people you can trust; joining an organized group is dangerous because most are infiltrated or contain some head cases." They must not "form a group or go public. If you do they [institutions] will ruin your life and others who join you."[83] He and others espouse a philosophy of "lone wolfism" in which secretive individuals will perpetrate acts that will bring about change. The Internet is ready-made for such paranoid, minimally unorganized groups.

Once people join a social movement, they may splinter into numerous factions because of differences over tactics, ideology, leaders, personalities, organizational structures, and real or imagined grievances. An institution may aid this splintering by favoring one organization or leader over another, playing the game of divide and conquer. Bostdorff suggests that the Internet may be a way of enhancing cooperation among diverse social movement organizations and thus reduce the fragmentation of protest efforts.[84]

Energizing the Discontented

Social movements must persuade significant numbers of people that only collective *action* by uninstitutionalized groups using *unconventional methods* can bring about or resist change. They must create a collective identity, a people, so individuals come to identify themselves as a group through "shared views of the social environment, shared goals, and shared opinions about the possibilities and limits of collective action."[85] In her study of Ku Klux Klan Web sites, Bostdorff identifies a number of unique mobilization functions the Internet may serve for social movements. It can reach a wide audience with ease and at low cost, disseminate information and messages quickly, be accessed from almost anywhere, reach "those who might never attend a Klan meeting but view messages from the privacy of their homes," avoid the "moral dictates from a physical community that might constrain their actions," enhance community building, and "link groups with one another and cross-fertilize ideas."[86]

The discontented must be energized into acting on behalf of the cause. Persuaders call on audiences to march, demonstrate, picket, vote, strike, sign petitions, boycott, and agitate. Songs are employed in most movements to energize the discontented. They urge followers to "stand up and be counted," "go tell it on the mountain," "give your hands to the struggle," "join the union," and "dump the bosses off your back." Some messages aim to arouse feelings of guilt or shame for not acting on behalf of the cause. The antinuclear power song, "Radiation Blues," has a child asking his father:

> Tell me Papa why you didn't say no,
> To nuclear power years ago.
> Tell me Papa why you didn't say no,
> You let it slip away.

Members and sympathizers are fully aware that actions can be socially and physically dangerous. Some use coded messages to mask their intentions and requests. The antislavery song, "Follow the Drinking Gourd," was written so that slave owners would think the singing slaves were speaking of dying, going to heaven, and meeting God. The message for slaves was very different.

Follow the drinking gourd! [the big dipper]
For the old man is a-waitin' to carry you to freedom. [underground railroad]
The riverbank will make a very good road. [Ohio River and others]
The dead trees show you the way. [instructions for escaping North]

Another song, "Steal Away," contained very important but disguised instructions of when to escape—during a storm when few people were out and tracks could not be seen or followed.

My Lord calls me.
He calls me by thunder,
The trumpet sounds within my soul,
I ain't got long to stay here.
My Lord calls me.
He calls me by the lightning.

Musical rhythm may "reduce the inhibitions and defense mechanisms" of singers and listeners and make them more willing to lie down in front of an abortion clinic, sit-in a restaurant, be dragged to a police van, or face the taunting jeers and threats of those unsympathetic to the cause.[87] Singing can also give protestors courage to demonstrate and remain nonviolent in the face of violence and arrests. A Georgia NAACP member comments that "the people were cold with fear until music [broke] the ice."[88] Martin Luther King commented in a television interview that "the [civil rights] movement has also been carried on by these songs ["We Shall Overcome" and "We Shall Not Be Moved"] because they have a tendency to give courage and vigor to carry on."[89] Those struggling for women's liberation sang "I Am Woman" and "I've Got a Fury."

Pressuring the Opposition

Although social movements are to a greater or lesser degree self-change oriented (believing that followers must change themselves before they can change others), they all engage the opposition in symbolic combat. The weapons may be verbal, such as mass mailings, name-calling, ridicule, obscenity, and threats; or nonverbal, such as mass demonstrations, sit-ins, walkouts, boycotts, strikes, obscene acts, and disruptions. They may attempt to gain control of influential agencies such as the courts, executive offices, boards of trustees, and school boards by voting officials in or out of office, purchasing or creating mass media, or gaining control of corporations through stock proxies. Malcolm X urged audiences to use the ballot effectively to take control of their neighborhoods and lives; the bullet was a last resort for self-defense.

One first step in gaining recognition, concessions, and compromises is to induce an institution to admit there is a serious problem. For example, in the 1980s thousands of farm owners descended on Washington, D.C., to protest government policies they believed kept crop prices too low and were causing many of them to lose their farms. Hundreds drove tractors or transported farm machinery to demonstrations near the Capitol, and a few burned obsolete equipment to demonstrate their frustrations and to pressure members of Congress. Pressure tactics may produce negative results. When Native Americans put on war paint and took over Wounded Knee, South Dakota, and Alcatraz Island in San Francisco Bay and held off encircling federal marshals for weeks, they succeeded in pressuring institutions and gaining national attention. Unfortunately, their symbolic actions reinforced the Hollywood stereotype of the painted savage they were trying to erase from the public mind.

Social movements are wise to confine persuasive efforts to symbols and symbolic actions that are lawful or protected by the Constitution. As Bowers, Ochs, and Jensen write, violent acts void of symbolism, or that appear to be so, are likely to cost the movement the support of sympathizers and legitimizers and invite outright suppression under the rubrics of law and order, public safety, and national security.[90] Violent acts may negate much that has been gained through years of persuasive efforts on behalf of the unborn, the environment, civil rights, and prison reform.

Gaining Sympathy and Support of Legitimizers

Legitimizers are social opinion leaders such as judges, politicians, business executives, clergy, sports figures, and entertainers who can help legitimize a movement in the eyes of the public by appearing at rallies, marching in demonstrations, speaking in favor of the cause, donating money, and so on. Contemporary movements have capitalized on the support of actors such as Robert Redford, Alan Alda, and George Clooney; actresses such as Jane Fonda, Joanne Woodward, Barbra Streisand, and Daryl Hannah; singers such as Bono and Bruce Springsteen; former presidents such as Bill Clinton and Jimmy Carter; senators such as Ted Kennedy and William Frist; and clergy such as Jerry Falwell and Jesse Jackson.

Some legitimizers offer more than their names, presence, and money. For example, pro-life sympathizer President George H. W. Bush supported the movement not only by speaking in its favor and advocating legal and constitutional changes but also by outlawing abortion counseling at federally funded clinics, research on fetal tissue, abortions at military hospitals, funding for international population control programs, and withholding approval of the French abortion pill RU-486. His successor, pro-choice sympathizer President Bill Clinton, overturned the first three actions within two days of his inauguration and announced reconsideration of the fourth. RU-486 was approved for sale in the U.S. in 2000. He infuriated pro-life forces when he opposed laws that would prohibit so-called "partial birth" abortions. When President George W. Bush succeeded Clinton in 2000, he overturned Clinton's actions and threw his full support behind a "culture of life."

Movements attempt to provoke institutions or other movements into excessive or repressive acts that reveal the ugliness of the opposition and gain sympathy and legitimacy for the movement and its demands. History has shown that the civil rights movement used these tactics to great advantage. Operation Rescue members have been arrested for blockading abortion clinics around the country and have provoked police officers into acts that appeared to harm protestors and thus to gain the sympathy of television viewers.

SUSTAINING THE SOCIAL MOVEMENT

Social movements last for years or decades and experience changing environments, so persuasion is critical to sustaining lengthy crusades.

Justifying Setbacks and Delays

Every social movement attempts to establish we-they distinctions (relational patterns), to instill strong convictions about accomplishing goals (evolutionary results), and to preach or imply that its ends justify any means necessary (adaptive strategies) to bring about or to resist change. Inevitably, these convictions, distinctions, and ends lead to impatience with moderate leadership, strategies, and slow progress toward goals and to suggestions that radical leadership and actions are necessary. Malcolm X exclaimed that speeches, sit-ins, singing "We Shall Overcome," the 1963 march on Washington, and integration had failed to bring about real change. It was time for the ballot or the bullet, a time to "stop singing and start swinging."[91] Demands for results and effective strategies may result in leadership changes or violent acts such as assassinations and bombings that discredit the movement. The violent Weather Underground faction of the counterculture movement successfully took over the leadership of the moderate SDS to further its radical agenda and to bring about a revolution in the United States.

Leaders use persuasion to maintain order and discipline and to respond to actions that embarrass the movement and threaten its support inside and outside the movement. They offer believable explanations for setbacks or the lack of meaningful gains or victories. They explain why agreements with institutions remain unfulfilled or ineffective, and they justify target dates that come and go without results. The many audiences social movements address may perceive progress, victories, agreements, and priority of goals quite differently. For instance, while some members see all change as too little too late, others become too satisfied with achievements made. Internal and external opposition may capitalize on delays and setbacks to undermine leadership and organizations and to proclaim superiority.

Whatever its goals, a social movement needs years of untiring efforts from significant numbers of people to gain or to prevent change. It must convince followers that victory is near or inevitable if all is done correctly and members remain steadfast in their commitment and true to sacred principles. Leaders attempt to create and sustain Eric Hoffer's "extravagant hope."[92]

Songs reinforce commitment for the long haul by assuring members that "perseverance conquers all," "the union makes us strong," and "our hearts and hands in union strong, not fear or threats can swerve." Others urge members to remain committed to the cause, to "stick together," "to hold the fort," and to "fight on undaunted." Some, such as Seeger's "Which Side Are You On?," express personal commitment:

> My daddy was a miner
> And I'm a miner's son,
> And I'll stick with the union,
> 'Til the battle's won.

Thirty years later, James Farmer of CORE (Congress on Racial Equality) rewrote Seeger's song for the civil rights movement. It read in part:

> Which side are you on, boys,
> Which side are you on?
> My daddy was a freedom fighter and I'm a freedom son
> I'll stick right with the struggle until the battle's won.

Richard Jensen, Thomas Burkholder, and John Hammerback studied how Cesar Chavez of the United Farm Workers used the deaths of "accidental martyrs" (those killed on the job) to "cement" members of the organization together and to turn an individual into "a mythical martyred hero." "Their deaths and funerals provided Chavez with powerful rhetorical opportunities to transform them into martyrs who personified the ideal union member and to call upon audience members to emulate their dedication to the cause."[93]

Maintaining Viability of the Movement

Social movements wage continual battles to remain viable. More rhetorical energy may be expended on fund-raising, membership drives, acquisition of materials and property, and maintenance of movement communication than on selling ideologies to target audiences and pressuring the opposition. Reinforcing the commitment of members limits a movement's ability to perform other functions. Annual meetings are devoted more to internal squabbles, ferreting out traitors and internal conspiracies, and defending movement administrations than to planning offensive campaigns and attacking external foes.

Ironically, a social movement may become either too successful or successful too soon. When African Americans, Hispanics, women, and gays achieved some rights and when environmentalists and animal rights advocates helped to forge some laws, each movement lost membership and drive because the need seemed less urgent. Growth in membership and geographical sphere of influence and creeping institutionalization may seriously reduce the informality of structure and feeling of crisis that initially attracted people to the movement. Thus, a serious decline in membership and commitment may occur when success seems near.

To counteract declines in membership and commitment, movements may turn to memories (past campaigns, victories, heroes, martyrs) to keep the struggle alive. They may strive to create new heroes to breathe life into the aging cause. New, more vibrant organizations may arise to challenge or to replace older, established ones. Leaflets, mailings, speeches, and songs reflect personal commitments. Audiences are continually assured, even when an organization or movement is in rapid free fall, that it is growing stronger every day and victory is near or inevitable.

Maintaining Visibility of the Movement

Social movements are haunted by the adage "out of sight, out of mind." Members, the media, and target audiences have insatiable appetites for persuasive happenings, but few movements have adequate leadership, membership, energy, and funds to satisfy these appetites over long periods while fending off opposition. They try to remain visible through every means imaginable: billboards, bumper stickers, stickerettes, buttons, tee shirts, jewelry, uniforms and items of clothing, famous women paper dolls, playing cards, Christmas cards, dial-a-message, and coloring books. They may select new symbols. They may use street newspapers, journals, and Internet Web sites to communicate directly with members because commercial media ignore the movement or are perceived to treat it unfairly.

Social movements use rhetorical events and happenings such as ceremonies, funerals, annual conventions, and anniversary or birthday celebrations to remain visible and to stoke the agitational fire. Often with the help of institutional sympathizers, movements create memorials to former leaders by turning plots of ground where historical events occurred into hallowed ground and buildings into museums. Bernard Armada writes, for example, that the National Civil Rights Museum in the former Lorraine Motel in Memphis where Martin Luther King, Jr., was assassinated, "teaches about the black American struggle for equality while also inviting visitors to identify themselves as sympathizers for that cause; visitors are invited to join a community of civil rights sympathizers and activists."[94] He claims that the design of the museum not only invites visitors to join a community but "attempts to forge a subculture of civil rights advocates equipped with the disposition needed to carry their political power beyond the institutionalized walls of the museum." Memorials are a key means of sustaining a movement.

CONCLUSIONS

Social movements rely on persuasion as the primary agency through which they attempt to perform critical persuasive functions that enable them to come into existence, satisfy requirements, grow in size and influence, meet opposition from within and without, and effectively bring about or resist change. These essential functions are closely related to the several parts of the social systems question posed in chapter 2. Functions include transforming perceptions of reality (the environment in which they must operate), altering self-perceptions of protestors (which individuals conceiving themselves to be what people), attaining legitimacy (using what relational patterns), prescribing courses of action and mobilizing the discontented (with what adaptive strategies), and sustaining the movement until victory is achieved (with what evolutionary results).

Unfortunately for social movements, their uninstitutional status greatly limits their powers, options, and legitimacy and, therefore, their abilities to perform these persuasive functions effectively on a continual basis over long periods. They compete with other movements, countermovements, and institutions that are attempting to enable individuals to see themselves as a particular people, interpret the environment, further or assign relational patterns, adapt strategies to changing circumstances, and produce evolutionary results that make the future different from today.

Notes

[1] See for example, Herbert W. Simons, Elizabeth W. Mechling, and Howard N. Schreier, "The Functions of Human Communication in Mobilizing for Action from the Bottom Up: The Rhetoric of Social Movements," *Handbook of Rhetorical and Communication Theory,* Carroll C. Arnold and John W. Bowers, eds. (Boston: Allyn & Bacon, 1984): 807–808; Bruce E. Gronbeck, "The Rhetoric of Social-Institutional Change: Black Action at Michigan," *Explorations in Rhetorical Criticism,* Gerald Mohrmann, Charles Stewart, and Donovan Ochs, eds. (University Park: Pennsylvania State University Press, 1973): 96–113; Charles J. Stewart, "A Functional Approach to the Rhetoric of Social Movements," *Central States Speech Journal* 31 (Winter 1980): 298–305.

[2] William A. Gamson, "The Social Psychology of Collective Action," *Frontiers in Social Movement Theory,* Aldon D. Morris and Carol McClurg Mueller, eds. (New Haven, CT: Yale University Press, 1992): 71.

[3] Wil A. Linkugel, R. R. Allen, and Richard L. Johannesen, *Contemporary American Speeches,* 5th ed. (Dubuque, IA: Kendall/Hunt, 1982): 208.

[4] *Do You Want to Return to the Butchery of Back-Alley Abortion?* (New York: National Association for Repeal of Abortion Laws, n.d.).

[5] *The Big Lie: Who Really Told It?* (Arlington, VA: National Socialist White People's Party, n.d.).

[6] From tapes of radio addresses by Billy James Hargis on March 11 and 12, 1963, and others that are undated.

[7] Robert Welch, "The Truth in Time," *The New American,* 17 August 1987, 25–33 (reprinted from *American Opinion,* November 1966).

[8] Philip C. Wander, "The Savage Child: The Image of the Negro in the Pro-Slavery Movement," *Southern Speech Communication Journal* 37 (Summer 1972): 335–360.

[9] Gary C. Woodward, "Mystifications in the Rhetoric of Cultural Dominance and Colonial Control," *Central States Speech Journal* 26 (Winter 1975): 301.

[10] *Say No to Torture* (Washington, DC: Animal Welfare Institute, n.d.).

[11] *Say No to Torture.*

[12] Letter from Cleveland Amory, Fund for Animals, February 1995.

[13] Plato, *The Republic,* Book IV, B. Jowett, trans. (New York: Modern Library, n.d.): 424, 135.

[14] R. Serge Denisoff, *Sing a Song of Social Significance* (Bowling Green, OH: Bowling Green University Popular Press, 1972): 19.

[15] Denisoff, 137–145.

[16] Mary Brigid Gallagher, "John L. Lewis: The Oratory of Pity and Indignation," *Today's Speech* 9 (September 1961): 15–16.

[17] *The Purdue Exponent,* 31 March 1992, 7.

[18] Hans Toch, *The Social Psychology of Social Movements* (New York: Bobbs-Merrill, 1965): 11.

[19] Eugene V. Debs, "The Issue," *Debs: His Life, Writings and Speeches* (Chicago: Charles H. Keff, 1908): 489.

[20] Clayborne Carson, ed. *The Autobiography of Martin Luther King, Jr.* (New York: Warner Books, 1998): 226.

[21] Robert Welch, *The Blue Book of the John Birch Society* (Boston: Western Islands Publishers, 1961): 1.

[22] Mary Ellen Barrett, "Fur Fight," *USA Weekend,* 9–11 February 1990, 4.

[23] Randall A. Lake, "Order and Disorder in Anti-Abortion Rhetoric: A Logological View," *Quarterly Journal of Speech* 70 (November 1984): 425–443.

[24] *Seabrook Alert,* 1981; *Seabrook Clamshell* letter, May 1986; *Seabrook Clamshell* letter, August 1986.

[25] James Darsey, "From 'Gay Is Good' to the Scourge of AIDS: The Evolution of Gay Liberation Rhetoric, 1977–1990," *Communication Studies* 42 (Spring 1991): 43–66.

[26] Unless otherwise noted, this treatment of the ego function of protest rhetoric is taken from Charles J. Stewart, "Championing the Rights of Others and Challenging Evil: The Ego Function in the Rhetoric of Other-Directed Social Movements," *Southern Communication Journal* 64 (Winter 1999): 91–105.

[27] Fernando Pedro Delgado, "Chicano Movement Rhetoric: An Ideographic Interpretation," *Communication Quarterly* 43 (Fall 1995): 451.

[28] Richard B. Gregg, "The Ego-Function of the Rhetoric of Protest," *Philosophy and Rhetoric* 4 (Spring 1971): 79.

[29] Michael Victor Sedano, "Chicanismo: A Rhetorical Analysis of Themes and Images of Selected Poetry from the Chicano Movement," *Western Journal of Speech Communication* 44 (Summer 1980): 179.

[30] Gregg, 81.

[31] Richard J. Jensen and John C. Hammerback, "Radical Nationalism among Chicanos: The Rhetoric of Jose Angel Gutierrez," *Western Journal of Speech Communication* 44 (Summer1980): 198.

[32] Davi Johnson, "The Rhetoric of Huey P. Newton," *Southern Communication Journal* 70 (Fall 2004): 19.

[33] Martha Solomon Watson, "The Issue of Justice: Martin Luther King's Response to the Birmingham Clergy," *Rhetoric & Public Affairs* 7 (Spring 2004): 18.

[34] Gaston V. Rimlinger, "The Legitimation of Protest: A Comparative Study in Labor History," in Joseph R. Gusfield, *Protest, Reform, and Revolt: A Reader in Social Movements* (New York: John Wiley & Sons, 1970): 363.

[35] Herbert W. Simons, *Persuasion: Understanding, Practice and Analysis* (Reading, MA: Addison-Wesley, 1976): 234.

[36] Robert A. Francesconi, "James Hunt, The Wilmington 10, and Institutional Legitimacy," *Quarterly Journal of Speech* 68 (February 1982): 49.

[37] William A. Garrison, "The Social Psychology of Collective Action," *Frontiers in Social Movement Theory,* Aldon D. Morris and Carol McClurg Mueller, eds. (New Haven, CT: Yale University Press, 1992): 68.

[38] Frances Fox Piven and Richard A. Cloward, "Normalizing Collective Protest," *Frontiers in Social Movement Theory,* Aldon D. Morris and Carol McClurg Mueller, eds. (New Haven, CT: Yale University Press, 1992): 303.

[39] Anthony Oberschall, *Social Conflict and Social Movements* (Englewood Cliffs, NJ: Prentice-Hall, 1973): 188.

[40] Simons, Mechling, and Schreier, 810.

[41] John H. Patton, "A Transforming Response: Martin Luther King Jr.'s 'Letter from Birmingham Jail,'" *Rhetoric & Public Affairs* 7 (Spring 2004): 57.

[42] R. R. McGuire, "Speech Acts, Communicative Competence and the Paradox of Authority," *Philosophy and Rhetoric* 10 (Winter 1977): 31, 33.

[43] William A. Gamson, *Power and Discontent* (Homewood, IL: Dorsey Press, 1968): 127.

[44] Louis Kriesberg, *The Sociology of Social Conflicts* (Englewood Cliffs, NJ: Prentice-Hall, 1973): 111.

[45] Francesconi, 50.

[46] Max Weber, *The Theory of Social and Economic Organization*, A. M. Henderson and Talcott Parsons, trans. (New York: The Free Press, 1964): 328.

[47] Arthur L. Smith (Molefi Asante), *Rhetoric of Black Revolution* (Boston: Allyn & Bacon, 1969): 1.

[48] Denisoff, 57.

[49] Cheryl Irvin Thomas, " 'Look What They've Done to My Song, Ma': The Persuasiveness of Song," *Southern Speech Communication Journal* 39 (Spring 1974): 263; James R. Irvine and Walter G. Kirkpatrick, "The Musical Form in Rhetorical Exchange: Theoretical Considerations," *Quarterly Journal of Speech* 58 (October 1971): 279.

[50] Gusfield, 310; Richard L. Johannesen, "The Jeremiad and Jenkin Lloyd Jones," *Communication Monographs* 52 (June 1985): 156–172.

[51] Contained in a collection of SDS papers compiled by James F. Walsh.

[52] Carson, 194.

[53] Bonnie J. Dow, "Fixing Feminism: Women's Liberation and the Rhetoric of Television Documentary," *Quarterly Journal of Speech* 90 (February 2004): 74.

[54] *The Gray Panther Manual* (Philadelphia: The Gray Panthers, 1978): 8.

[55] Oberschall, 308.

[56] Irving Zaretsky and Mark P. Leone, eds. *Religious Movements in Contemporary America* (Princeton, NJ: Princeton University Press): 500, 510.

[57] Rhodri Jeffreys-Jones, *Violence and Reform in American History* (New York: New Viewpoints, 1978): 16, 30, 38.

[58] John Waite Bowers, Donovan J. Ochs, and Richard L. Jensen, *The Rhetoric of Agitation and Control*, 2nd ed. (Long Grove, IL: Waveland Press, 1993): 20.

[59] Carol J. Jablonski, "Promoting Radical Change in the Roman Catholic Church: Rhetorical Requirements, Problems, and Strategies of the American Bishops," *Central States Speech Journal* 31 (Winter 1980): 289.

[60] McGuire, 44.

[61] Saul Alinsky, *Rules for Radicals: A Pragmatic Primer for Realistic Radicals* (New York: Vintage Books, 1971): 128.

[62] Robert S. Cathcart, "Movements: Confrontation as Rhetorical Form," *Southern Speech Communication Journal* 43 (Spring 1978): 246.

[63] Watson, 5.

[64] Simons, "Persuasion in Social Conflicts," 243.

[65] Robert L. Scott and Donald K. Smith, "The Rhetoric of Confrontation," *Quarterly Journal of Speech* 55 (February 1969): 8.

[66] Cathcart, 243.

[67] John Wilson, *Introduction to Social Movements* (New York: Basic Books, 1969): 71.

[68] Kenneth M. Dolbeare and Patricia M. Dolbeare, *American Ideologies: The Competing Political Beliefs of the 1970s* (Long Grove, IL: Waveland Press, 1971): 3, as cited in Steven Goldzwig, "James Watt's Subversion of Values: An Analysis of Rhetorical Failure," *The Southern Speech Communication Journal* 50 (Summer 1985): 307.

[69] Goldzwig, 323.

[70] Michael C. McGee, "The 'Ideograph': A Link between Rhetoric and Ideology," *Quarterly Journal of Speech* 66 (February 1980): 7.

[71] Wilson, 91–97.

[72] Kristy Maddux, "When Patriots Protest: The Anti-Suffrage Discursive Transformation of 1917," *Rhetoric & Public Affairs* 7 (Fall 2004): 292.

[73] William Bruce Cameron, *Modern Social Movements* (New York: Random House, 1966): 15.

[74] Toch, 30.

[75] Fred Powledge, *Free at Last? The Civil Rights Movement and the People Who Made It* (Boston: Little, Brown and Company, 1991).

[76] *Resist.com,* accessed 14 November 1999, 28 November 1999, 26 February 2000.

[77] "Manifesto of the New York Radical Feminists," unpublished paper, n.d.

[78] Alinsky, 127–128.

[79] Roxanne Dunbar, "Women's Liberation: Where the Movement Is Today and Where It's Going," *Handbook of Women's Liberation,* Joan Robbins, ed. (Los Angeles: NOW Library Press, 1970), as reprinted in Charles J. Stewart, *On Speech Communication* (New York: Holt, Rinehart and Winston, 1972): 312–313.

[80] Ralph R. Smith and Russel R. Windes, "The Rhetoric of Mobilization: Implications for the Study of Movements," *The Southern Speech Communication Journal* 42 (Fall 1976): 1.

[81] Wim van de Donk, Brian D. Loader, Paul G. Nixon, and Dieter Rucht, eds. *Cyberprotest: New Media, Citizens and Social Movements* (London: Routledge, 2004): 17.

[82] Wilson, 306.

[83] *Resist.com,* accessed 7 November 1999, 1 January 2000.

[84] Denise M. Bostdorff, "The Internet Rhetoric of the Ku Klux Klan: A Case Study in Web Site Community Building Run Amok," *Communication Studies* 55 (Summer 2004): 349.

[85] Verta Taylor and Nancy Whittier, "Collective Identity in Social Movement Communities," *Frontiers in Social Movement Theory,* Aldon D. Morris and Carol McClurg Mueller, eds. (New Haven, CT: Yale University Press, 1992): 105.

[86] Bostdorff, 342.

[87] Irvine and Kirkpatrick, 277.

[88] Denisoff, 57.

[89] Denisoff, 76.

[90] Bowers, Ochs, and Jensen, 77–78.

[91] Malcolm X, "The Ballot or the Bullet," Detroit 1964, from an audio recording.

[92] Eric Hoffer, *The True Believer* (New York: Harper and Row, 1951): 18.

[93] Richard J. Jensen, Thomas R. Burkholder, and John C. Hammerback, "Martyrs for a Just Cause: The Eulogies of Cesar Chavez," *Western Journal of Communication* 67 (Fall 2003): 336–337.

[94] Bernard J. Armada, "Memorial Agon: An Interpretive Tour of the National Civil Rights Museum," *Southern Communication Journal* 63 (Spring 1998): 236.

4

The Stages of Social Movements

Social movements are intricate social dramas involving multiple scenes, acts, agents, agencies, and purposes.[1] They include heroes and heroines, fools and geniuses, victims and villains, evil and good, successes and failures, hope and disillusionment.

Any effort to prescribe stages of all social movements is fraught with dangers. Social movements differ, change, develop to varying degrees of sophistication, and proceed at varying speeds—rushing forward at times, stalling for long periods at particular stages, retrenching to earlier stages, or dying premature deaths before completing all stages. Social movements (such as women's rights, environmentalism, and animal welfare) and social movement organizations (such as the Moral Majority and labor unions) seemingly appear, disappear, and reappear with altered purposes, ideologies, leaders, structures, and persuasive strategies. We speak of third wave feminism, for example, to indicate as Bonnie Dow argues that "U.S. feminism never really disappeared since its initial emergence in the nineteenth century; it has simply gone through periods of ascendance and decline."[2] William Cameron writes that each "social movement is determined by so many variables that its success or failure, the speed of its growth or decline, the consistency or inconsistency of its operations will not fit any a priori formula."[3] Social movements never follow a neat, linear pattern from birth to death.

To understand complex communicative events, theorists have found it useful to try to detect cycles and phases of human interactions. For example, those studying interpersonal communication have discovered phases of conflict in small group development, interaction stages within relationships, and "how communication functions at each stage" of human relationships "to contribute to the building or dissolution of a relational culture."[4] Most closely related to our concerns is the theory of Richard Crable and Steven Vibbert that issues pass through five status levels: potential status, imminent status, current status, critical status, and dormant status.[5]

We can better understand social movements by looking at the communication processes through which they came into being, interacted with other elements such as institutions and countermovements, and tried to sustain themselves. Attempts to portray each stage in the lives of *typical* social movements can help us understand the ever-changing persuasive requirements, problems, and functions of social movements and the interaction of social-psychological, political-institutional, philosophical-ideological, and rhetorical forces.[6]

The stages discussed in this chapter include: genesis, social unrest, enthusiastic mobilization, maintenance, and termination.[7] They enable us to search for adaptive, evolutionary patterns in which choices reflect the attempts of individuals and organizations to adapt to the constantly changing environment and understand more fully who the "people" of the movement are, why they are as they are, and how they got that way. Unlike campaigns, however, there is never an identifiable moment when a social movement moves from one stage to another. It is an evolutionary process fraught with uncertainty.

STAGE 1: GENESIS

We rarely know when a social movement begins—only that it has evolved in particular ways. It usually begins during relatively quiet times, quiet at least with respect to the issue that the new movement will address. The people and institutions are unaware of the problem or perceive it to be insignificant or of low priority. Other elements of the environment—economic, political, social, military, or religious—dominate the attention of the people, their leaders and institutions, and the mass media. Individuals, often scattered geographically and unknown to one another at first, perceive an "imperfection" in the existing order.[8] The imperfection may be institutional or individual corruption; abuse of power; inequality (in rights, status, power, income, opportunities, possessions, recognition); threats to one's status; an identity crisis; unfilled "legitimate" expectations (all expectations *perceived* to be legitimate); or a threat to the social order, values, or environment. Lisa Gring-Pemble labels this a "pre-genesis process wherein lies the birth, growth and affirmation of consciousness."[9] She claims, for instance, that the 1848 convention at Seneca Falls, New York, that brought women's rights advocates together for the first time "necessarily indicates an antecedent 'pre-genesis' phase, a transitional phase between private and public expression." Obviously, something had to take place prior to a number of activists calling for an organizational meeting, but in what form, when, by whom, and with what effects did they bring like-minded people together for a cause?

Whether this period is labeled pre-genesis or early genesis, it is clear that restless individuals view an imperfection as a serious problem that is likely to grow more severe unless appropriate institutions address it quickly and earnestly. For instance, in the 1960s, growing numbers of clergy became alarmed at the decline in public morals resulting from the anti-Vietnam War and counterculture movements. They felt something needed to be done to reverse the frightening increase in premarital sex, divorce, drug use, alcoholism, and pornography. Warnings of a dangerous moral decline emanated from pulpits and in leaflets and books. In the 1990s, legislation, laws, government actions, and taxation viewed as very similar to the burdens that spurred the American Revolution frightened thousands of citizens. As James Johnson, leader of the Ohio Unorganized Militia and founder of other militias, testified before Senate Judiciary Committee hearings in June 1995 following the Oklahoma City bombing, "the only thing standing between legislation being contemplated and armed conflict is time"—time for citizens to get involved before it is too late.[10]

A social movement's early leaders are sometimes called intellectuals or prophets because they lead through their words, strive for perfection, and work for the good for society. Although they strive to expose the failings of institutional leaders and the status quo, they meet little opposition in the genesis stage because few people take them seriously or are even aware of their efforts. These prophets and intellectuals produce essays, editorials, songs, poems, pamphlets, books, sermons, lectures, and Web sites designed to transform perceptions of reality (the environment) and self (what people). Above all, the social movement's initial leaders believe, often with remarkable naïveté, that appropriate institutions will act if the movement can make them aware of the urgent problem and its solution. The early leader is more of a thinker and educator than an activist, rabble-rouser, agitator, or fanatic. Thus, as Eric Hoffer informs us, "imperceptibly the man [woman] of words undermines established institutions, discredits those in power, weakens prevailing beliefs and loyalties, and sets the stage for the rise of the mass movement—by intention or by accident."[11]

In Lloyd Bitzer's words, the prophet not only apprehends an exigence (something that needs correcting) but attempts to create interest among readers and listeners for perceiving and solving the problem. The prophet, however, often differs little from Bitzer's "man alone in a boat and adrift at sea" who "shouts for help although he knows his words will be unheard." But prophets persist because they believe that "interest will increase insofar as the factual condition" becomes "known directly and sensibly, or through vivid representation."[12] David Snow and Robert Benford call these representations "collective action frames" and contend that they "serve as accenting devices that either underscore and embellish the seriousness and injustice of a social condition or redefine as unjust and immoral what was previously seen as unfortunate but perhaps tolerable."[13]

The genesis stage may last for months, years, or decades. Harold Mixon studied the sermons delivered from 1672 to 1774 on the first Monday in June at the election and installation of new officers into the Ancient and Honorable Artillery Company of Boston. He concluded that "decades before the agitation for independence developed," these artillery election sermons "were, perhaps quite without notice, additional parts of a large stream of discourse promoting patterns of thought which prepared the colonies for the ideas of the revolutionists" resulting in the Declaration of Independence in 1776.[14] Folk songs by Bob Dylan, Pete Seeger, Barry McGuire, and others addressed war and peace before the Gulf of Tonkin incident thrust the United States into the Vietnam conflict in the 1960s. Only later did many of us come to realize that the popular folk songs of the day were calling our attention to a variety of long neglected, social ills.

If comparable social movements are active, a fledgling social movement may take shape rapidly. For example, white students involved in the black civil rights movement created the student free-speech movement. The editor of the *Crimson* wrote to fellow Harvard students, many fresh from freedom rides in the South, "But the realization that lies just around the corner is that we too are an oppressed people. Any radical movement at Harvard should base itself on our own needs—the needs of the oppressed student class."[15] Students then created the peace movement opposing the war in Vietnam, and finally the counterculture movement that rejected most of the American value structure. Female members of these movements, who became painfully aware of their second-class status in organizations fighting for the rights of others, were instrumental in establishing the women's liberation movement. And the women's liberation movement served as a model and inspiration for movements striving for the rights of Hispanics, Asian Americans, Native Americans, and the elderly.

The genesis stage, Leland Griffin's "period of inception," is a "time when the roots of preexisting sentiment, nourished by interested rhetoricians, begins to flower into public notice."[16] A triggering incident is often necessary to move the generally unorganized, ideologically uncertain, and barely visible social movement from the genesis stage to the social unrest stage. The triggering event may be a Supreme Court decision, a nuclear power plant accident, a new law, an economic recession, a police action, the appearance of a movement-oriented book on the best-seller list, or a violent act. For instance, the comment by a North Dakota legislator to a farm delegation in 1915, "Go home and slop your hogs," infuriated farmers and gave rise to the Nonpartisan League in the Midwest.[17] Betty Friedan's *The Feminine Mystique* helped to launch the women's liberation movement, and Rachel Carson's *The Silent Spring* served as the impetus for the environmental movement. J. Michael Hogan and Glen Williams note that prior to the publication of Thomas Paine's pamphlet entitled *Common Sense* in early 1776, "few in the colonies talked of separating from England. . . . Within a matter of months, however, a virtual consensus had been achieved."[18]

A violent act often jars people into action, many of whom seem unlikely social movement activists. For example, a peace movement began in violence-ridden Northern Ireland on August 10, 1976, when an IRA (Irish Republican Army) getaway car, its driver killed by a British soldier, jumped a curb in West Belfast and killed three of Ann Corrigan's children aged six weeks, two, and eight. Their aunt Mairead Corrigan, a Catholic, went on television and condemned the IRA, something no Catholic had dared to do.

At the same time, Betty Williams, who had witnessed the accident, went house to house that evening asking Catholic and Protestant residents to sign a petition for peace and to take part in a rally that Saturday. The two outraged women, one a secretary and one a mother and homemaker, joined forces and were soon holding rallies throughout Northern Ireland with numbers ranging from hundreds to 20,000. They won the Nobel Peace Prize for 1976. The initial result of a triggering or catalytic event may be the first real signs of organizations with titles that begin Citizens for . . ., Concerned Parents against . . ., or Workers United to . . . Williams and Corrigan formed the Community of Peace People to carry on the fledgling peace movement in Northern Ireland.

Some social movements have difficulty advancing without an event or impetus. After more than a decade, the men's movement remained in the genesis stage into the twenty-first century awaiting some event, person, or organization to propel it into the next stage. The movement began in the 1980s with small groups of men (similar to the consciousness-raising groups during the early stage of the women's liberation movement) meeting to share their pains, hurts, and frustrations that resulted from experiences with drunken fathers, emasculating bosses, stifling jobs, divorce laws, child custody fights, or advertisements and television programs that portrayed men as fools. It received national attention in 1990 with a PBS special, *A Gathering of Men*. The documentary narrated by Bill Moyers discussed poet Robert Bly and his book *Iron John: A Book About Men*. Hundreds of men's groups sprang up around the country, many conducting weekend retreats during which men looked inward and experienced a rebirth through sharing their stories and by acting out primitive masculinity through drum beating and sweating around mounds of steaming rocks in teepees. These strivings were an effort to discover what people they were to be. This embryonic movement created no ideology spotlighting how men are abused and oppressed, but it gained attention from intellectuals. A 1993 issue of the *Chronicle of Higher Education* listed 28 books published since 1990 with titles such as *The Adventurous Male, American Manhood, Running Scared, The First Sexual Revolution*, and *The Inward Gaze*. In spite of large rallies of men organized by the Promise Keepers and the Million Man March on Washington, D.C., the movement stalled. Most intellectuals appear reluctant to associate with the "mythopoetic" men's movement because they see Bly's *Iron John* and Sam Keen's *Fire in the Belly: On Being a Man* primarily as a backlash against the feminist movement and as an effort to reclaim turf. R. W. Connell, a sociologist at the University of California at Santa Cruz, writes that

> in the final analysis, *Iron John* and the "mythopoetic men's movement"
> are a massive evasion of reality. Bly is selling simplified fantasy solutions
> to real problems. In the process, he distorts men's lives and distracts men
> from practical work on gender inequalities.[19]

No organization has yet emerged or critical event happened to bring together a significant number of men for purposes other than consciousness-raising, so the movement slumbers in the genesis stage.

The most important contributions of the genesis stage are the apprehension of an exigence and the cultivation of interest in the exigence within a concerned people motivated to do something about it. Without a genesis stage, there will be no movement. However, if the movement cannot go forward, it will eventually wither and die. Snow and Benford contend that the "failure of mass mobilization" to occur when the time seems ripe "may be accounted for in part by the absence of a resonant master frame"—an altered vision of reality centered on objects, situations, events, experiences, actions, and relationships.[20]

STAGE 2: SOCIAL UNREST

As growing numbers of people rise up and express their concerns and frustrations over an issue, the social movement evolves from the genesis to the social unrest stage and may become visible in the media for the first time as a "movement." The prophets and intellectuals of the genesis stage turn into, or join, agitators—literally ones who stir things up. Together they begin to organize the disparate elements of the movement and take it beyond living rooms, talk shows, study groups, churches, and lecture halls. An initial act may be the calling of a convention or conference of like-minded people to form an organization. Rev. Jerry Falwell founded the Moral Majority in 1979 to unite those

> who are deeply concerned about the moral decline of our nation, and who are sick and tired of the way many amoral and secular humanists and other liberals are destroying the traditional family and moral values on which our nation was built.[21]

This was the beginning of the organized Christian right movement in the United States.

An important purpose of gatherings to form organizations is the framing of a manifesto, proclamation, or declaration. For instance, student leaders from a wide variety of organizations (Students for a Democratic Society, National Student Christian Federation, National Student Association, the Young Democrats, Student Peace Union, and SNCC) met in June 1963 at Michigan's AFL-CIO camp at Port Huron, Michigan, to work out a manifesto. The product of these deliberations, the *Port Huron Statement*, served as the essential statement of principles for the student movement and later the anti-Vietnam War and counterculture movements.

A manifesto or body of writings sets forth the social movement's ideology, an "elaboration of rationalizations and stereotypes into a consistent pattern."[22] It serves four essential functions: to describe an exigence; to identify the devils and/or scapegoats, and faulty principles that have caused and sustained the exigence; to list principles, beliefs, and stands on critical issues; and to prescribe the solution and the gods, principles, and procedures that will bring it about. The ideology identifies the social movement with *the peo-ple*, a great grassroots movement in the mainstream of U.S. society. For exam-ple, Ken Adams of the Michigan Militia told those at Senate hearings on terrorism that militia members were "everyday Americans," a "cross-section of Americans" who represented all professions.[23]

Ideologies also identify movements with established norms and values. The effort is to identify with what is good and holy in society and to disasso-ciate from all that is evil. The *Port Huron Statement* begins with these words:

> We are people of this generation, bred in at least modest comfort, housed now in universities, looking uncomfortably to the world we inherit. When we were kids the United States was the wealthiest and strongest country in the world; the only one with the atom bomb, the least scarred by modern war, an initiator of the United Nations that we thought would distribute Western influence throughout the world. Freedom and equal-ity for each individual, government of, by, and for the people—these American values we found good, principles by which we could live as men. Many of us began maturing in complacency.[24]

The next paragraph begins "As we grew, however, our comfort was pene-trated by events too troubling to dismiss," and introduces a litany of problems and disillusionments with society: racial bigotry, the Cold War, the common peril of "the Bomb," politics, the economy, the military-industrial complex, poverty, and communism. This sentence summarizes the concerns of the stu-dents at Port Huron:

> Not only did tarnish appear on our image of American virtue, not only did disillusion occur when the hypocrisy of American ideals was discov-ered, but we began to sense that what we had originally seen as the American Golden Age was actually the decline of an era.

Theorists note that a social movement's ideology is "considerably more potent" and "strikes a responsive chord" if it identifies successfully with "extant beliefs, myths, folk tales, and the like."[25] The Moral Majority's "stands on today's vital issues" clearly linked it with the conservative Catho-lics, Protestants, Jews, Mormons, and fundamentalists it wished to activate. These stands included "We believe in the separation of church and state," "We are pro-life," "We are pro-traditional family," "We oppose pornogra-phy," and "We support the state of Israel and Jewish people everywhere."[26] An ideology contains a set of devil terms (i.e., liberalism, segregation, wage slavery, commercial development, conformity, or welfare state) and a corre-sponding set of god terms (i.e., conservativism, integration, employee-owned cooperatives, natural environment, individualism, or free enterprise).

An overarching principle or slogan may unify the movement, such as "An injury to one is an injury to all" (Knights of Labor), "Never to laugh or love" (pro-life), "Keep abortion legal" (pro-choice), "All power to the people" (Black Power and new left), "Building a Better Tomorrow" (Liberty Federa-tion), "We trust Women" (National Coalition of Abortion Providers), and

"That Freedom Shall Not Perish" (John Birch Society). For the first time, there is a feeling of standing together as concerned individuals.

The act of joining or forming an organization sets members apart from nonmembers and established institutions and fosters a we-they division that becomes more pronounced as the social movement enters succeeding stages. Members increasingly see themselves as an elite with a mission, and they devise strategies for fulfilling their moral crusade. Movement persuaders attempt to instill new feelings of self-identity, self-respect, and power within members that was absent when they were mere individuals. For example, Black Panther leader Huey P. Newton appealed to his audience "to view themselves as a special people with unique ability to bring about social change through the pursuit of social alternatives to the existing political-economic structure."[27] Members now begin to experience an ego boost as Hispanic Americans, evangelical Christians, crusaders for animal rights, and militia members in the tradition of America's Revolutionary War heroes. As a "people" they now have new, meaningful relational patterns.

Although the social movement pays increasing attention to transforming perceptions of society by creating we-they distinctions and to prescribing courses of action (listing beliefs, citing demands, prescribing solutions, and identifying who must bring about or stifle change and through which strategies), the major persuasive effort is aimed at transforming perceptions of reality (the environment). Persuaders continue to believe that if they can raise the consciousness of institutional leaders and followers (make them aware of the facts through words, pictures, exposés, symbolic acts, and theatre), institutions will take appropriate actions to resolve the exigence. Faith in progress through the social chain of command remains strong. Thus, gay rights advocates portray how they are discriminated against in U.S. society; antiwar advocates portray the horrors of war; animal rights advocates portray the horrors of leghold traps and animal experimentation; and the Christian right portrays the moral decadence of society. Movements expend rhetorical energies during the social unrest stage in petitioning courts, city councils, university boards of trustees, corporate boards of directors, state legislatures, Congress, the president of the United States, scientific organizations, and religious synods and hierarchies.

Spokespersons for institutions may openly deny the severity or existence of the problem (exigence) and, often for the first time, take official notice of the fledgling social movement. They may stigmatize the so-called movement as naive, ill informed, laughable, or unpatriotic. The opposition's strategy is to stall the social movement by ignoring or discrediting it in hopes that it will succumb to ridicule or inattention—that it will simply go away. The mass media may note with interest, amusement, or mild foreboding the claims or overtures of the infant social movement. When protestors on college campuses constructed shantytowns to make people aware of conditions of blacks in South Africa under apartheid, the *Wall Street Journal* ridiculed these activities as "the latest fad" in an article entitled "Shanty Raids" (a play on words referring to panty raids common on college campuses decades earlier). "In spring a young student's fancy turns to political protest. This year's fashion is shantytowns, and from Yale to North Carolina to Purdue to Michigan to Wisconsin to Berkeley police are confronting student demonstrators."[28] Cartoonists have portrayed members of militias as dim-witted, overweight, unshaven, heavily armed weekend warriors who work as gas station attendants and live in dilapidated mobile homes.

The duration of the social unrest stage depends on the numbers of people who are attracted to the movement, reactions of institutional agents, and new triggering or catalytic events that may greatly exacerbate the social situation or exigence. The nuclear power plant accidents at Three Mile Island (Pennsylvania) and Chernobyl (Ukraine) and the arrest of Rosa Parks in Montgomery, Alabama, because she would not surrender her seat on a city bus to a white male passenger boosted the antinuclear and civil rights movements from the social unrest stage to the enthusiastic mobilization stage. The accident at Three Mile Island graphically conveyed the real dangers of nuclear power, far beyond what words and symbolic actions could demonstrate. The refusal by Rosa Parks precipitated the Montgomery bus boycott that catapulted a young, relatively unknown local minister, Martin Luther King, Jr., to national prominence and leadership of the movement. Triggering events, such as the loss of an election, failure of Congress to pass legislation, or reluctance of the courts and law enforcement agencies to enforce laws, cause significant numbers of people to lose faith in the ability and willingness of institutions to solve exigencies and in the effectiveness of normal persuasive means to bring about or to resist change. James Darsey argues that triggering or "catalytic" events are essential for moving social movements from one state to another.[29]

Members and sympathizers may begin to see the institution as the problem or as part of a conspiracy to sustain power and to defeat all legitimate and reasonable efforts to bring about urgently needed actions. Members of the Moral Majority, for instance, came to see the "liberalized" mainline Protestant denominations (Methodists, Presbyterians, Lutherans, Episcopalians) as part of the problem rather than as part of the solution. When frustration leads to *disaffection* with institutions and their ability or desire to resolve problems, the social movement enters the stage of enthusiastic mobilization. The growth of social unrest culminates in the development of a dominant exigence, an audience, and constraints.

STAGE 3: ENTHUSIASTIC MOBILIZATION

The social movement in the enthusiastic mobilization stage is populated with true believers who have experienced conversion to the cause. They have grown "tired of being sick and tired."[30] Gone is the old naïveté that institutions—churches, legislatures, universities, corporations—will act if they are made aware of the problem through rational appeals. The converted see the social movement as the only way to bring about urgently needed change and believe firmly that the movement's time has come. Optimism is rampant. Important legitimizers such as entertainers, senators, clergy, physicians, labor leaders, scientists, and educators lend an air of excitement and inevitability to the cause.

The Internet enables social movement organizations to keep members informed, involved, committed, and ready for action. For example, immediately after President George W. Bush nominated John G. Roberts to fill a vacancy in the U.S. Supreme Court in the summer of 2005, the Religious Coalition for Reproductive Choice urged members to "Take Action Now!" by calling their senators in a statement titled "Supreme Court Nominee Roberts: The Next Step toward Overturning *Roe v. Wade*." [31] Nothing less than abortion rights were at stake. On the other side of the conflict, The National Right to Life Committee proclaimed to its members, "You can help us defeat pro-abortion attacks" and warned that misleading ads and unfair attacks were beginning in "earnest against Judge John Roberts."[32] Within hours of President Bush's nomination of Roberts to succeed William Rehnquist as Chief Justice of the Supreme Court, Nancy Keenan, president of NARAL Pro-Choice America, included a press release on its Web site warning that this nomination "raises the stakes for the protection of fundamental freedoms, including the right to privacy."[33]

Institutions and resistance movements are keenly aware of the movement's growth, change in attitude, altered persuasive strategies, perceived legitimation, and potential for success. For the first time, they see the movement as a clear and present danger to institutional power and authority. They, too, mobilize during the enthusiastic mobilization stage. The greater the threat from a social movement (particularly if it is perceived to seek revolutionary changes), the greater are the counterefforts of institutional agents, agencies, and surrogates. Institutions may encourage the creation of countermovements and provide them with resources and an aura of legitimacy. The aim is to stifle the social movement through actions of "the people" or the "silent majority" (often persons the movement claims it is fighting for) and thus avoid the appearance of institutional involvement. If these actions fail and institutions see the movement as a radical, revolutionary force, it may suppress the perceived threat to society.

Institutional counterefforts may produce unanticipated results. For instance, Birmingham police arrested Martin Luther King, Jr., on Good Friday, April 12, 1963, when he refused to discontinue demonstrations for civil rights and, for twenty-four hours, held him incommunicado in solitary confinement. As noted in chapter 3, a group of white Birmingham ministers sent King a letter asking him to call off demonstrations, labeling him an "outside agitator," and accusing him of complicating the advance of civil rights in their city. John Patton writes that "both King and movement leaders were able to recognize the urgency of the moment." They formulated King's famous "Letter from Birmingham Jail" at this "pivotal rhetorical moment" that replied directly to each of the charges in the ministers' letter and took the moral high ground. It was not delivered to the clergy but addressed a national audience and "transformed both King and the movement from a relatively regionalized action into a national and international cause."[34] Institutional attempts to suppress and silence the movement served as a critical catalyst leading to King's "I Have a Dream Speech" delivered in front of the Lincoln Memorial a few months later.

As social movements expand, evolve, and confront serious opposition from institutional forces and surrogates, they may abandon judicial and legislative chambers for the streets, marketplaces, forests, vineyards, and the open seas. They have lost faith in institutions and institutional means to bring about or resist change. Mass meetings, marches, demonstrations, hunger strikes, symbolic actions, and acts of civil disobedience replace sedate conventions, conferences, and testimony at hearings. For example, Kathryn and Clark Olson write that during the 1970s and 1980s, "the Immigration and Naturalization Service (INS) routinely denied even the most well documented refugee appeals from Guatemalans and Salvadorans," even for those facing impending torture and death squads. After years of "helping these Central Americans negotiate the U.S. legal system and being stymied at every turn, sanctuary workers realized that the legal channels for asylum protection were closed to these people."[35] They abandoned the legal system and resorted to smuggling and hiding refugees, not unlike the underground railroad that smuggled slaves to the North and Canada prior to the Civil War. They asserted the centuries-old right of sanctuary in which the church sanctuary, a place of refuge and protection, is immune to civil law.

Coercive persuasion may replace the rhetoric of speeches, leaflets, pamphlets, and newsletters. Protestors burn tractors in front of the Capitol to protest farm prices, bury school buses to protest forced busing to integrate schools, burn flags to protest military actions, blockade clinics to stop abortions, shadow police on their rounds to let them know they are being watched, and appear in public with handguns and rifles to pressure police officers and the courts. They boycott table grapes, corporations doing business with South Africa, department stores selling furs, and hospitals and clinics where abortions are performed. They set up picket lines, declare strikes, defy laws and court injunctions, and welcome mass arrests that attract television cameras and news coverage and clog the jails. They stage sit-ins, sit-downs, sleep-ins, and die-ins.

Protestors harass institutional agents and persons who do not comply with their demands. Threats work. For example, a woman who fears that wearing a fur coat in public will provoke a protestor to yell at her, throw red paint on her coat, or cut it with a sharp knife, will not buy a fur coat or wear one she purchased earlier. Protestors have learned that picketing the homes of the mayor, a physician who performs abortions, the owner of a video rental store that rents X-rated videos, or the manager of a supermarket that sells table grapes boycotted by the movement is more effective than picketing city hall, clinics, video rental stores, or supermarkets. Targets sense greater threats to their persons and families—not to mention reactions of irate neighbors who do not want "radicals" in their neighborhoods.

New organizations arise to compete with or overshadow earlier organizations. When Rev. Jerry Falwell decided in 1986 to step back from his political activities, he created the Liberty Federation to take on a broader political agenda, but others were ready to join the Christian right movement, including James Dobson's Focus on the Family, Citizens for Excellence in Education, Traditional Values Coalition, Free Congress Foundation/National Empowerment Television, American Family Association, and Concerned Women of America.

Charismatic leaders, adept at countering and taking advantage of growing opposition to the movement, replace intellectuals and prophets, although they may pay homage to both. They control the movement by forming strong organizations and coalitions. They stir up great excitement within the membership, stage symbolic actions, and confront institutions and resistance movements. Increasingly, leaders such as Thomas Metzger (founder of White Aryan Resistance—WAR) are adept at using technology to raise money, attract followers through databases, reach out to thousands through sophisticated Web sites, and generate mailings to members of Congress and state legislatures urging them to vote for or against legislation. Leaders and followers may become literal or figurative martyrs for the cause by suffering physical injury, imprisonment, banishment, or death. They not only accept but may readily seek suffering because the cause has become the true believer's reason for being. Charismatic leaders employ the deaths of martyrs, including accidental ones, to "*shape* a sense of unity and determination to fulfill those aims in which all members of the movement can *share*—all in the name of the fallen heroes."[36]

The persuasive goal of the enthusiastic mobilization stage is to raise the consciousness level of the people so significant numbers will pressure institutions. The movement presents simplified *if-only* images of social processes, problems, and solutions: if women are given the right to vote, women will achieve equal rights; if abortion is outlawed, there will be no abortions; if sexual orientation clauses are added to human rights ordinances, there will be no discrimination against homosexuals; if we have prayer and Bible reading in the public schools, student achievement will rise, violence will end, and the decline in morals will be reversed.

Leaders during the enthusiastic mobilization stage face severe persuasive crises both inside and outside the social movement. Externally, persuaders must employ harsh rhetoric and stage symbolic acts designed to pressure institutions into capitulation or compromise, to polarize the movement and its opposition (all who are not actively supporting the movement), and to provoke repressive acts that reveal the true ugliness of institutions and their counterefforts. Persuasion during this stage is replete with name-calling against the devils and conspirators who have perpetrated and prolonged the evil the social movement alone has the will and strength to fight. James Johnson of the Ohio Unorganized Militia claimed that alarmed Americans "began to form themselves in units for their own self-defense and self-preservation" when they realized that, as individuals, they could do nothing to stem the tide of government actions that were undermining the republic.[37]

If leaders are inept at adapting and changing persuasive strategies and judging how far to push for positive results and images, they may provoke institutional and public outrage. At the very least, the movement may lose essential support and sympathy from the public, media, and legitimizers. A few violent acts such as the killing of a physician who performs abortions, firebombing meat wholesaler trucks, and sabotaging logging equipment may doom years of protest, even if the acts are by fanatical, minuscule, splinter groups. The public and institutions do not make fine distinctions: an act *in the name of* the social movement and its cause is an act *by* the movement.

Internally, movement persuaders must deal with competing and often antagonistic organizations, each with its own leaders, followers, and strategies. For instance, prior to World War I, the suffrage movement "saw a distinct split between pacifists and supporters of preparedness and eventually war." The AFL refused to allow suffragist and antiwar advocate Jane Addams to speak because its leadership was concerned "with the 'sinister influences' behind the peace movement."[38] The rise of fanatical elements who propose violence instead of symbolism or who make demands unacceptable to either the movement at large or to institutions splinter the movement and drain persuasive resources from the cause. Militia leaders, for instance, have tried to distance the movement's mainstream from dangerous "fringe elements" to attain legitimacy and credibility.

Leaders may decide that alterations in ideology or persuasive strategies are necessary to keep the movement fresh, to counter resistance forces, or to meet changing circumstances. Jennifer Borda claims that the women's suffrage parades from 1910–1913 took the "message boldly to public spaces," elevated the cause to the national level, reenergized the aging women's movement, attracted the attention of the press, and impressed "upon members of government the extent of the women's determination to continue their equal rights protest as long as necessary."[39] Leaders must sell each change to movement factions or face devastating charges of *revisionism* and *selling out*. A movement's goals may expand or contract with changes in membership and/or situations. For example, the pro-life movement came into existence to make abortion illegal but widened its focus to include all human life—the aged, infirm, mentally retarded, and minorities as well as the unborn. Likewise, Amy Slagell writes that "by 1894, the National WCTU [Women's Christian Temperance Union] endorsement of suffrage was no longer couched only in terms of expediency or home protection, but also in terms of natural rights, asserting 'women are wronged who are governed without their consent.'"[40]

When confrontations between the social movement and resistance forces become severe, persuaders draw sharp and often bitter *we-they* distinctions.

Persons who do not join the movement and former members are labeled traitors. Leaders may look within and decide that some members (whites, males, non-skilled workers, religious liberals) are incapable of true understanding or involvement in the cause, so they purge memberships to purify their movements to prepare for final struggles with the evil forces arrayed against them. Leaders must explain and justify the new elites and relational patterns to internal and external audiences. For example, the Student Nonviolent Coordinating Committee (SNCC) was originally populated and led by a diverse membership, including white students, faculty, and clergy. During the 1964 summer campaign in Mississippi, however, Stokely Carmichael and others "saw the most articulate, powerful, and self-assured young white people coming to work with the poorest of the Negro people—and simply overwhelming them."[41] They concluded this was not good for the African Americans they were trying to help, nor could the young, well-educated, and financially well-off white members understand the cause. SNCC soon became an all-black organization.

Social movements may achieve notable goals and victories during the enthusiastic mobilization stage, but earlier visions of sweeping and meaningful changes—the evolutionary results central to movement dreams—remain unfulfilled. Instant success is elusive. Leaders are unable to satisfy the insatiable appetites of members and the mass media for new and more spectacular events and achievements. New leaders and members ridicule what were once viewed as imaginative and potent persuasive strategies or revolutionary victories, such as the Montgomery bus boycott and civil rights legislation. John Wilson notes, "It is easier for the disgruntled to agree on what is wrong with the old than on what is right with the new."[42] Leaders devote increasing attention to explaining and justifying setbacks, delays, lack of meaningful gains, and failures of old successes to fulfill exaggerated expectations. The extravagant hopes and unrealistic dreams that once energized the movement begin to fade and with them the enthusiasm of the movement.

In some movements, frustration may build within a new generation of activists who become increasingly disaffected with the social movement establishment preaching an *uninstitutionalized* version of patience and gradualism—the rhetorical staple of the institutional establishment they loathe. A revolution within a revolution awaits events and a leader who can "address members' frustrations, recreate and redefine social reality, offer new dreams, and identify with a new generation of true believers."[43] Carmichael played this role in the civil rights movement with his "black power" rhetoric that criticized the aging leaders of the movement, rejected the philosophy of integration, and opposed the strategy of passive, nonviolent, civil disobedience that had produced little change and a great deal of suffering. He denied that he was a "Negro leader" and charged that the old generation of leaders "had nothing to offer that they [audiences] could see, except to go out and be beaten again."[44] Carmichael identified with the younger generation of civil rights activists in age, appearance, dress, speaking style, and militant message.

He appealed to cultural pride and heritage, attacked the war in Vietnam, and created a symbolic realignment by replacing words such as Negro, ghetto, segregation, and integration with black, colony, colonialism, and liberation. For a time, Carmichael's rhetoric of black power gave the civil rights movement a renewed vigor and purpose and involved a new generation of activists who cheered, shouted, laughed, clapped, and danced during his rousing and animated speeches. But then he organized the All African People Revolutionary Party in 1967 and moved to the People's Republic of Guinea in 1968. Without Carmichael's rousing oratory and presence, the black power phase ended, and the civil rights movement proceeded to the maintenance stage.

Neither social movement members nor those in the larger society can accept harsh rhetoric and confrontation for long. Fatigue, fears of anarchy, and boredom inevitably set in. The persuasive efforts necessary for mobilizing the social movement may carry the seeds of its own destruction so that when the boiling point is reached, the movement must revert to an earlier posture to sustain its existence. The movement enters the maintenance stage.

STAGE 4: MAINTENANCE

The maturing social movement needs new leadership and a less impassioned and strident rhetoric as it enters the maintenance stage. The loss of a charismatic leader such as Martin Luther King, Jr., Malcolm X, and American Nazi leader George Lincoln Rockwell to assassins may hasten the movement into the maintenance stage because no one else is capable of sustaining mobilization or reenergizing the movement. The remnants of the old enthusiasm may die with the movement's martyr.

The onset of the maintenance stage is a critical turning point for a social movement because one direction is toward victory of some sort and the other is toward oblivion. Unfortunately, the odds are against victory for, as John Wilson writes, "frustration is the fate of all social movements."[45] The movement undergoes change, which is inevitable in all organizations. Lloyd Bitzer notes, "a situation deteriorates when any constituent or relation changes in ways that make modification of the exigence significantly more difficult."[46]

The social movement returns to more quiet times during the maintenance stage as institutions, media, and the public turn to other, more pressing concerns. Both movement and society are ready for a respite from unnerving, disruptive, and often destructive confrontations. Movement persuasion once again emanates from the pen, computer, printer, and the Internet and from legislative, judicial, conference, convention, and lecture halls. It is time to retain what has been gained and to consolidate movement organization for the duration. Radical organizations such as WITCH (Women's International Terrorist Conspiracy from Hell), and Earth First! disappear and moderate groups such as NOW (National Organization for Women) and the Sierra Club remain to carry the movement forward.

The agitator has no place in the maintenance stage, which requires an administrator skilled at shaping outcomes. A pragmatist who can appeal to disparate elements, maintain organizations, and deal more directly and rationally with institutional leaders is essential in this stage. The agitator is a superb street fighter but a poor bureaucrat unsuited for diplomatic and administrative roles. The harsh and uncompromising rhetoric of polarization and confrontation creates too many enemies within and without.

The pragmatist, a pastor of sorts, must perfect organization, sustain the movement's forward progress as it emerges from its trial by fire, and work with established institutions. Herbert Simons claims that the militant strategies of the agitator may make the moderate strategies of the pragmatist more acceptable to institutions.[47] This clearly happened with Martin Luther King before he was assassinated in 1968. Long reviled as a dangerous, communist radical who fomented violence wherever he campaigned, the public and institutional leaders came to see him as a moderate compared to Malcolm X, Stokely Carmichael, and Eldridge Cleaver. Davi Johnson claims that Black Panther leader Huey P. Newton's mastery of a conservative rhetorical form such as the jeremiad failed because "Newton was already considered an outsider, a militant revolutionary, who posed a threat to traditional values."[48] Dow's study of the documentary *Fixing Feminism* revealed that its goal was "to confer legitimacy, to 'fix' feminism by analogizing it to civil rights. . . . The movement is seen as less threatening with reformers triumphing over revolutionaries— just like the civil rights movement."[49]

While leaders continue efforts to transform perceptions of reality and society, prescribe courses of action, and mobilize believers and sympathizers, the primary persuasive function is to sustain the social movement. Both membership and commitment decline during the maintenance stage, so leaders must recruit new members and reinforce belief in the movement's ideology and potential for ultimate rather than immediate success. They must sustain or resuscitate hope and optimism. Stacey Sowards and Valerie Renegar write that third wave feminists see themselves building upon the legacy and achievements of the second wave while needing to prove that less recognizable inequalities still exist that only a movement can overcome.[50] Unfortunately, leaders become more distant from members during the maintenance stage because there are fewer opportunities to see, hear, and talk with them. Dominant communication channels are newsletters, movement newspapers, and the Internet rather than interpersonal exchanges and speeches before live audiences. While the Internet is readily available, few beyond the truest true believers are likely to access Web sites on a regular basis to see what is going on with the movement and the issue. Sympathizers and those who answer yes for supporting the cause in opinion polls have more pressing things to do.

Incessant fund-raising is necessary to support organizations, property, and publications. Any maintenance task—fund-raising, recruiting, mailings, publications, Web pages—may become an end in itself, and the leader becomes more of an entrepreneur than a reformer or revolutionary. Routinization of dues, meetings, leadership, decision making, and rituals is essential to maintain a highly structured and disciplined movement organization that will survive to carry the cause forward. These bureaucratic necessities, however, siphon off much of the old spontaneity, excitement, and *esprit de corps* that made the movement vibrant and attractive and set it apart from institutions. What was improvised during an emergency or passionate moment in an earlier, exciting stage now becomes a sacred precedent and wisdom of the past. Spontaneity is unacceptable in the maintenance stage because rigid adherence to organization is the norm.

Visibility becomes a major preoccupation. The movement is rarely newsworthy during the maintenance stage, and the mass media begin to address the social movement and its leaders in editorials and columns that begin with phrases such as "What ever happened to" and "Where is . . . now?" The adage "out of sight, out of mind" haunts leaders, but their persuasive options are few. Paradoxically, neither members nor the public will support mass demonstrations at this stage, yet quiet behavior suggests satisfaction with things as they are. There are no charismatic leaders to fire up the membership, and there may be too few active members to be fired up. The Ku Klux Klan, for instance, continues efforts to arrange mass gatherings and cross burnings in cities throughout the United States, but the fewer than fifty members who usually show up are far outnumbered by police, reporters, the curious, and counterdemonstrators. The Internet enables sympathizers to visit Web sites who would never attend a Klan rally, even if they knew how to find one, but their commitment and involvement may be little more that accessing a Web site.

Institutions may not tolerate (or may have learned how to deal quietly with) persuasive tactics such as sit-ins, civil disobedience, boycotts, and hunger strikes. Worst of all, institutions may simply ignore outdated symbolic acts and revolutionary rhetoric. Rhetoric is increasingly internal—directed toward maintenance functions—rather than external—directed toward pressuring the opposition and gaining legitimizers. Leaders resort to ceremonies, rituals, annual meetings, and anniversary celebrations during which martyrs, tragedies, events, and victories are recounted and memorialized, but the rhetoric may be more melancholy than energizing. In June 1999 President Clinton presented Rosa Parks, "the mother of the civil rights movement," the nation's highest honor, the Congressional Gold Medal. The House had voted 424–1 and the Senate 86–0 to award the honor. President Clinton commented, "In so many ways, Rosa Parks brought America home. We should all remember the power of this one citizen."[51] A few days later, there was a celebration in her honor in Indianapolis that included religious and civil rights songs and tributes from the governor, clergy, members of Congress, and the mayor of Indianapolis. For a few days at least, the civil rights movement was once again front-page news, and the actions of its eighty-six-year-old heroine were recalled and honored for their significance. Then it was back to defending the movement's hard-fought gains and planning new battles for freedom, equality, and justice.

The social movement looks desperately for a triggering event to return the cause to the enthusiastic mobilization stage, make the struggle fun and exciting again, and to counteract the gradual hardening of the arteries that aging movement organizations experience. As opposed to a rejuvenating triggering event, the movement may just as likely suffer a severe blow from a debilitating or disintegrating event. For instance, the coming on line of the Seabrook nuclear power plant in New Hampshire and the economic-based decision to stop construction on the Marble Hill plant in Indiana were devastating events for the antinuclear power movement. They failed in their prolonged efforts to stop the first and lost a primary target in the second. The issue no longer seemed urgent. On the other hand, events may greatly alter the life and activities of a social movement. For instance, the onset of AIDS significantly affected the gay rights movement:

> AIDS became the obsessive concern of gay rights activists, coloring all activity concerning the welfare of gay men and lesbians in the United States. AIDS presented the gay community with not only a public health crisis, but crises in the social, legal, and psychological spheres as well. AIDS catalyzed a shift in the rhetoric of the gay movement.[52]

The gay rights movement would never be the same.

Rejuvenation of the movement may come from unlikely and unexpected sources. When President George W. Bush began threatening Iraq and its leader Saddam Hussein with military invasion following September 11, 2001, the peace movement surfaced once again, and Act Now to Stop War & End Racism (ANSWER) and United for Peace and Justice held rallies in Washington, D.C., to stop the war before it started. Once the war in Iraq commenced, however, the movement faded in numbers, activities, and visibility. Then in early August 2005, Cindy Sheehan from Vacaville, California, whose son died in Iraq in 2004, appeared a short distance from President Bush's ranch near Crawford, Texas, demanding to meet with the President and learn why U.S. soldiers were still dying in Iraq. She vowed to maintain her vigil until the President met with her during his month-long vacation and even to follow him to Washington after his vacation ended if necessary. She drew immediate media attention, and, within days, peace activists from around the country descended upon tiny Crawford, joined Sheehan in her vigil, and helped her arrange a field of crosses (at Fort Casey in her son's honor) while other activists (Democracy for America, MoveOn, True Majority, and Peace Coalitions) held candlelight vigils throughout the country. A mother had resurrected the peace movement. It achieved a public relations and media coup on August 12 when the President's motorcade of black Chevrolet Suburbans raced past Camp Casey on it way to a Republican fund-raiser at a neighboring ranch. The necessary counterdemonstrations arrived soon, set up Fort Qualls (in honor of Louis Qualls who died in Iraq in 2004), expressed their support for the President, and declared that leaving Iraq now would mean U.S. soldiers had died in vain. The peace movement was energized and highly visible once again. When President Bush returned to the White House, the movement organized a bus caravan to Washington with their rejuvenator, Cindy Sheehan, on board. The "Bring Them Home Now" campaign was underway. Although the peace movement had not initiated the event on the plains of Texas, it knew how to take advantage of it.

The maintenance stage is not merely a time to hold onto past accomplishments, however, because the movement continues the struggle (with or without cataclysmic events) and little by little may achieve results. For instance, the Native-American movement demonstrated for years against offensive mascots, logos, and names at sporting events with seemingly few results. Then, in the summer of 2005, the National Collegiate Athletic Association (NCAA) informed its member schools that it would ban the use of nicknames or mascots deemed "hostile or abusive" to Native Americans from its tournaments after February 1, 2006.[53] A few days later, college football's Bowl Championship Series announced it would soon review this issue. Persistence was producing results, but at a glacial pace.

The hoped-for rebirth of an enthusiastic mobilization stage eludes most social movement organizations and leaders or arrives too late. For example, when the ideals of women's rights, industrial unionism, social security, and temperance were once again high on the public agenda, original leaders and organizations were history.

As the movement shrinks or faces a long stalemate, it may focus its rhetorical energies on a single issue or solution. Movements claim all will be well once people get the right to vote, a prohibition amendment, the eight-hour day, equal rights legislation, integration of public places, an antiabortion amendment, or prayer in the public schools. The single goal is attractive because it is simple and more attainable than a panacea of hopes and dreams. The shrunken movement can focus its limited resources on a less divisive target. Both the movement and institutions have grown weary of confrontations, and legitimizers are more likely to support a non-radical goal that is handled through normal means and channels.

The social movement is on the threshold of the final stage, termination, during which it will cease to be a social movement. The only question is whether it will die or become another form of collectivity.

STAGE 5: TERMINATION

If a social movement is successful, it may celebrate its victory and disband. The antislavery movement did just that in 1865 after passage of the Thirteenth Amendment to the Constitution: "Neither Slavery nor involuntary servitude, except as a punishment for crime whereof the party shall have been duly convicted, shall exist within the United States, or any place subject to their jurisdiction." The movement no longer had a cause for which to fight. The same happened to the women's suffrage struggle with the passage of the Nineteenth Amendment in 1920: "The right of citizens of the United States to vote shall not be denied or abridged by the United States or by any State on account of sex."

Often movements or phases of movements seem to fade away. The anti-Vietnam War movement gradually dissolved as U.S. involvement in the war came to an end in the 1970s. Total disbandment of a social movement is unlikely, however, because the social movement's ideology may be so broad or idealistic (such as peace, equality, environment, or moral perfection of society) that all of its tasks are rarely attainable. In addition, elements of every social movement make the cause their reason for being, even their livelihood, and trust no one else with its principles or their jobs.

If a social movement maintains an effective organization and its principles come to match current conventions and practices, it may become the new order—as communist and Nazi movements did in Russia and Germany and the democratic-independence movements did in the American colonies, Africa, and Eastern Europe. The movement may become a new institution such as the Lutheran Church in Germany, the Methodist Church in the United States, and the American Federation of Labor.

Leaders of transformed social movements face new and old persuasive challenges. They must strive for obedience among the membership and the people, bring an end to tensions, and establish a perfecting myth in which the social movement organization is believed to have reached a state of absolute perfection and morality. Leaders must purge elements that will not accept the transformation of the social movement or who pose threats to the leadership's attempts to achieve peace and harmony among societal elements.

Rhetorical confrontations do not end with the transformation of a social movement into an institution. As Elizabeth Nelson points out in her study of Mussolini's rise to power in Italy, former social movements may have to continue their "perpetual struggles" to sustain their new positions and the support of followers.[54] The reformers and revolutionaries of movement days become the priests of the new order or institution and must perform pastoral functions. Inevitably, the movement-turned-institution will face a new generation of reformers and revolutionaries who become disaffected with the new order.

Few social movements are totally successful, however. Some shrink into pressure groups (Ralph Nader's consumer-protection organizations), philanthropic associations (the Salvation Army), political parties (the Socialist party), lobbying groups (for milk, rice, or tobacco producers), or social watchdog roles (the Women's Christian Temperance Union). Others are absorbed or co-opted by established institutions such as political parties, religious denominations, and labor unions. Many principles espoused by populists, progressives, and socialists such as banking regulations, voting rights and reforms, social security, and unemployment insurance are adopted into the U.S. system with no recognition of the social movements that championed them for years. Occasionally, an institution will crush a social movement organization such as the Black Panther party, the Communist party, or the Weather Underground if the institution and a significant portion of the public comes to view it as a grave danger to society. Many organizations merely fade away.

Social movements shrink and die for many reasons. Leaders and members may despair of ever changing anything or of achieving permanent and meaningful goals equal to the sacrifices made. They may become overwhelmed by the magnitude or multiplicity of the problems they must solve, or they may lose faith in society's capacity for reform. The social movement may become merely a job, or the new lifestyle may become boring and meaningless as years pass. This happened to the many rural communes settled in the 1960s and early 1970s. Leaders and followers experience fatigue because they cannot continue to endure the dangers, thrills, and privations movements demand. Often they merely grow old. Violent actions by radical groups such as the Weather Underground and "lone wolves" such as Timothy McVeigh (the Oklahoma City Bomber) and Eric Rudolph (the bomber of the Atlanta Olympics, abortion clinics, and gay bars) may frighten movement members, institutions, and the public into seeking normalcy and demanding action from institutions.

During the termination stage, leaders and followers may become as disaffected with social movements as they once were with established institutions. They may opt for military rather than symbolic warfare and wage a civil war or revolution to achieve change. More likely, however, members and sympathizers drop back into the institutions from which they came and go on to live "normal" lives as the "ordinary people" they always were. Sam Riddle, a former Michigan State University rebel, became an oil company lawyer and remarked, "I can do a lot more with a base of capital than with a pocketful of rhetoric. I'm no longer interested in standing on my soapbox and shouting into the wind. Now I'm more interested in producing the soapboxes."[55] Some leaders such as Eldridge Cleaver, a founder and officer of the Black Panther Party, have conversion experiences and become born-again Christians, capitalists, or government bureaucrats.

Many former leaders and members continue to work for change. Black Panther founder Bobby Seale spent much the "turbulent decade [of the 1960s] in the streets and on the barricades, leading a struggle against what he saw as social injustice and 'structured racism.'"[56] By the late 1980s, he was a graduate student and assistant to the dean of the college of arts and sciences at Temple University. He looked to the past and to the future of social change:

> A university . . . is a framework where people can take the time and analyze what is good for the world. . . . There is still a revolution going on . . . and I'm still part of it. In the 1960s and 1970s, the revolution was at high tide. After the mid '70s, it hit low tide, and it's still there. Whether or not it will hit another high in the 90s, I don't know, but wherever the revolution is, I'm involved in it.

Notre Dame Magazine in 1975 included an article entitled, "Yesterday's Activists: Still Marching to a Different Drummer." It discovered the campus activists had gone on to become teachers, workers with inner-city school children, a farmer trying to "put the 'culture' back into agriculture," a rabbinical student striving to "practice being as sarcastic and cynical as possible," and an organizer for senior citizens who was confronting "the issues of crime and community control."[57] Other movement disciples turn inward, toward "privatism," in an effort to protect or to change themselves or their inner circles of family and friends. They give up trying to change society at large.

CONCLUSIONS

Social movements are intricate and evolving social dramas; each stage is marked by changes in acts, scenes, agents, agencies, and purposes. Structures evolve to perform persuasive functions—a continuous process in which every aspect of a system evolves from and into something else.

Each stage (genesis, social unrest, enthusiastic mobilization, maintenance, and termination) requires certain persuasive skills and personalities. Genesis, for instance, demands an intellectual or prophet who excels at defining and visualizing, at using words. Social unrest needs an agitator who can initiate organization, help formulate an ideology, and transform perceptions of the past, present, and future. Enthusiastic mobilization requires a charismatic agitator who confronts and polarizes, excites and insults, unites and fragments. Maintenance requires a pragmatic diplomat who is capable of healing, sustaining, administering, and bargaining. Termination needs a leader who can bring the movement to an end, transform it successfully into an institution, help it evolve into a pressure group, or enable its principles to become part of the institutional beliefs, attitudes, and values. Although we may not be able to determine when a social movement begins or ends until we have time to observe the flow of history, we can discover why and how it evolved.

Each stage poses unique dilemmas and requires persuasion to serve one or more functions. For example, transforming perceptions of reality dominates the genesis stage—a critical function and stage if the movement is to evolve into something other than individual expressions of concern and isolated events. Transforming perceptions of reality, enhancing the egos of protestors, and prescribing courses of action dominate the social unrest stage as the movement becomes publicly visible and members strive to discover what "people" they are or want to be. Transforming perceptions of the other and self, legitimizing the movement, and mobilizing for action dominate the enthusiastic mobilization stage as the movement, institutions, and countermovements struggle to bring about or stifle change. Sustaining dominates the maintenance stage when the movement settles in for a long struggle and hopes for a new awakening.

For social movements that reach the final stage, termination, the results are usually disappointing and disillusioning. Early goals, even when partially reached, rarely bring about the perfection creators of the movement envisioned. Some members condemn society, institutions, and human beings as incapable of reform, unable to attain perfection. Others see the means (social movements, persuasion, coercive persuasion) as impotent tools for achieving meaningful and lasting change. Ultimately, all social movements come to an end or experience frustration, such as when hard-fought gains for gay rights or affirmative action are dismantled in whole or in part. But this does not mean that social movements have little effect or that their causes die with them. As Leland Griffin writes:

> And if the wheel forever turns, it is man [woman] who does the turning—forever striving, in an "imperfect world," for a world of perfection. And hence man [woman], the rhetorical animal, is saved: for salvation lies in the striving, the struggle itself.[58]

The study of the stages of social movements is important because it emphasizes the evolutionary nature of social movements and that they are more than the sum of their parts. While it is important to study parts (campaigns, leaders, members, events, functions, messages, channels, or strategies), true understanding of a movement requires an eventual holistic study to allow us to see conflict as adaptive and evolutionary, influence as accommodative, and relationships as integrative.

Notes

[1] Kenneth Burke, *A Grammar of Motives* (Englewood Cliffs, NJ: Prentice-Hall, 1950).

[2] Bonnie J. Dow, "Spectacle, Spectatorship, and Gender Anxiety in Television Coverage of the 1970 Women's Strike for Equality," *Communication Studies* 50 (Summer 1999): 143.

[3] William Bruce Cameron, *Modern Social Movements* (New York: Random House, 1966): 27–29.

[4] Donald G. Ellis and B. Aubrey Fisher, "Phases of Conflict in Small Group Development: A Markov Analysis," *Human Communication Research* 1 (Spring 1975): 195–212; Mark L. Knapp, *Interpersonal Communication and Human Relationships* (Boston: Allyn & Bacon, 1984): 32–54; Julia T. Wood, "Communication and Relational Culture: Bases for the Study of Human Relationships," *Communication Quarterly* 30 (Spring 1982): 75–84.

[5] Richard E. Crable and Steven L. Vibbert, "Managing Issues and Influencing Public Policy," *Public Relations Review* 11 (1985): 6–7.

[6] Bruce E. Gronbeck, "The Rhetoric of Social-Institutional Change: Black Action at Michigan," *Explorations in Rhetorical Criticism*, Gerald Mohrmann, Charles Stewart, and Donovan Ochs, eds. (University Park: Pennsylvania State University Press, 1973): 98–101.

[7] John Wilson, *An Introduction to Social Movements* (New York: Basic Books, 1973); and Leland M. Griffin, "A Dramatistic Theory of the Rhetoric of Movements," *Critical Responses to Kenneth Burke*, William Rueckert, ed. (Minneapolis: University of Minnesota Press, 1969): 462–472.

[8] Griffin, 457–462.

[9] Lisa Gring-Pemble, "Writing Themselves into Consciousness: Creating a Rhetorical Bridge Between the Public and Private Spheres," *Quarterly Journal of Speech* 84 (February 1998): 42–44.

[10] James Johnson, Public Affairs Video Archives of the C-SPAN Networks, June 15, 1995. Referred to hereafter as Senate Hearings.

[11] Eric Hoffer, *The True Believer* (New York: Harper and Row, 1951): 20.

[12] Lloyd F. Bitzer, "Functional Communication: A Situational Perspective," *Rhetoric in Transition: Studies in the Nature and Uses of Rhetoric*, Eugene E. White, ed. (University Park: Pennsylvania State University, 1980): 23, 26–29, 32.

[13] David A. Snow and Robert D. Benford, "Master Frames and Cycles of Protest," *Frontiers in Social Movement Theory*, Aldon D. Morris and Carol McClurg Mueller, eds. (New Haven, CT: Yale University Press, 1992): 137.

[14] Harold D. Mixon, "Boston's Artillery Election Sermons and the American Revolution," *Speech Monographs* 34 (March 1967): 43, 50.

[15] Richard B. Gregg, "The Ego-Function of the Rhetoric of Protest," *Philosophy and Rhetoric* 4 (Spring 1971): 79.

[16] Leland M. Griffin, "The Rhetoric of Historical Movements," *Quarterly Journal of Speech* 38 (April 1952): 186.

[17] Leslie G. Rude, "The Rhetoric of Farmer-Labor Agitators," *Central States Speech Journal* 20 (Winter 1969): 281.

[18] J. Michael Hogan and Glen Williams, "Republican Charisma and the American Revolution: The Textual Persona of Thomas Paine's *Common Sense*," *Quarterly Journal of Speech* 86 (February 2000): 5–6.

[19] Scott Heller, "Scholars Debunk the Marlboro Man: Examining Stereotypes of Masculinity," *The Chronicle of Higher Education*, 3 February 1993, A6B, A8.

[20] Snow and Benford, 143–144.

[21] *What Is the MORAL MAJORITY?* (Washington, DC: Moral Majority Incorporated, n.d.): n.p.

[22] S. Judson Crandell, "The Beginnings of a Methodology for Social Control Studies," *Quarterly Journal of Speech* 33 (February 1947): 37; Griffin, "A Dramatistic Theory," 462–463.

[23] Senate Hearings.

[24] James Miller, *Democracy in the Streets: From Port Huron to the Siege of Chicago* (New York: Simon & Schuster, 1987): 329–330.

[25] Snow and Benford, 141.

[26] *What Is the MORAL MAJORITY?*

[27] Davi Johnson, "The Rhetoric of Huey P. Newton," *Southern Communication Journal* 70 (Fall 2004): 19.

[28] *Wall Street Journal,* 9 April 1986, 32.

[29] James Darsey, "From 'Gay Is Good' to the Scourge of AIDS: The Evolution of Gay Liberation Rhetoric, 1977–1990," *Communication Studies* 42 (Spring 1991): 43–66.

[30] Wilson, 89–90.

[31] "Take Action Now! Contact Your Senators," www.rcrc.org/get_involved/clergy_choice/index.htm, accessed 11 August 2005.

[32] http://www.nrlc.org/news/2005/NRL08/UnfairAttacks.html, accessed 8 August 2006.

[33] http://www.prochoiceamerica.org/news/pressreleases/2005/pr09052005_chiefjustice.html, accessed 8 August 2006.

[34] John H. Patton, "A Transforming Response: Martin Luther King Jr.'s 'Letter from Birmingham Jail,'" *Rhetoric and Public Affairs* 7 (Spring 2004): 63, 57, 54.

[35] Kathryn Olson and Clark D. Olson, "Beyond Strategy: A Reader-Centered Analysis of Irony's Dual Persuasive Purposes," *Quarterly Journal of Speech* 90 (February 2004): 34.

[36] Richard J. Jensen, Thomas R. Burkholder, and John C. Hammerback, "Martyrs for a Just Cause: The Eulogies of Cesar Chavez," *Western Journal of Communication* 67 (Fall 2003): 354.

[37] Senate Hearings.

[38] Sherry R. Shepler and Anne F. Mattina, "'The Revolt Against War': Jane Addams' Rhetorical Challenge to the Patriarchy," *Communication Quarterly* 47 (Spring 1999): 155.

[39] Jennifer L. Borda, "The Woman Suffrage Parades of 1910–1913: Possibilities and Limitations of an Early Feminist Rhetorical Strategy," *Western Journal of Communication* 66 (Winter 2002): 25–52.

[40] Amy R. Slagell, "The Rhetorical Structure of Frances E. Willard's Campaign for Woman Suffrage, 1876–1896," *Rhetoric & Public Affairs* 4 (Spring 2001): 8.

[41] Clayborne Carson, ed. *The Autobiography of Martin Luther King, Jr.* (New York: Warner Books, 1998): 318.

[42] Wilson, 109–110.

[43] Charles J. Stewart, "The Evolution of a Revolution: Stokely Carmichael and the Rhetoric of Black Power," *Quarterly Journal of Speech* 83 (November 1997): 430.

[44] Stewart, 440.

[45] Wilson, 360.

[46] Bitzer, 35.

[47] Herbert W. Simons, "Requirements, Problems, and Strategies: A Theory of Persuasion for Social Movements," *Quarterly Journal of Speech* 56 (February 1970): 10–11.

[48] Johnson, 27.

[49] Bonnie J. Dow, "Fixing Feminism: Women's Liberation and the Rhetoric of Television Documentary," *Quarterly Journal of Speech* 90 (February 2004): 74.

[50] Stacey K. Sowards and Valerie R. Renegar, "The Rhetorical Functions of Consciousness-Raising in Third Wave Feminism," *Communication Studies* 55 (Winter 2004): 538–539.

[51] Press release, "NEWS from CONGRESSWOMAN JULIA CARSON," June 15, 1999.

[52] Darsey, 55.

[53] Lafayette, Indiana, *Journal and Courier*, 6 August 2005, A1.

[54] Elizabeth Jean Nelson, "'Nothing Ever Goes Well Enough': Mussolini and the Rhetoric of Perpetual Struggle," *Communication Studies* 42 (Spring 1991): 22–42.

[55] "Yesterday's Radicals Put on Gray Flannel," *U.S. News and World Report,* 19 January 1981, 41.

[56] "Bobby Seale: 'Wherever the Revolution Is, I'm in It,'" *The Chronicle of Higher Education*, 2 December 1987, A3.

[57] "Yesterday's Activists: Still Marching to a Different Drummer," *Notre Dame Magazine*, October 1975, 10–19.

[58] Griffin, "A Dramatistic Theory," 472.

CHAPTER

5

Leaders in Social Movements

The public's perceptions of social movement leaders are seldom favorable. It brands people who claim an urgent problem is being ignored, hidden, or promoted by cherished institutions as irrational agitators, losers, misfits, degenerates, extremists, social schemers, or rabble-rousers.[1] A new epithet became popular in the electronic age, "social engineer." If these perverse, un-American "troublemakers" or "do-gooders" persist, organize, and generate mass protests, the public may attach new labels to those perceived as destroying society: demagogues, communists, fascists, terrorists, fanatics, or zealots.

The public's view of social movement leadership is heavily influenced by its faith in *individualism*, in the *sanctity* and *perfection* of U.S. institutions, and the ability of both individuals and institutions to cope with *real* or *serious* problems. Roberta Ash writes, "Only in America is the belief that individualism and collectivism are necessarily in conflict so widely held."[2] After decades of persuasive efforts to organize farmers, farm workers, women, African Americans, gays and lesbians, and Asian Americans, only small percentages of each group ever became active members of organizations created to resolve their plights. John Wilson discovered that during the farm income decline of the 1950s,

> Most farmers had come to feel that the American public was paying too little for its food or else the middle man was taking too large a slice of the cake, and hence believed there was something drastically wrong with the marketing system.[3]

Despite this widespread belief, only six percent of farmers actually joined the National Farmers Organization (NFO).

Strange-looking and strange-acting movement members and leaders reinforce public characterizations when they appear to be "foreign," under the spell of sinister forces such as demagogues, revolutionaries, the devil, or socialists. Examples include the hippies and yippies of the counterculture movement of the 1960s who looked disheveled, wore scraggly beards and long hair, and dressed in old clothes and parts of discarded military uniforms. Others included the Moonies and Symbionese Liberation Army of the 1970s;

111

the leathermen and drag queens of the gay rights movement; and zealous religious cult members of the 1980s and 1990s. Americans see Dave Foreman's Earth First! and its self-styled eco-guerrillas as both outrageous and dangerous.[4] They do not look and act like "ordinary people."

Perceptions of social movements and their leaders are molded by reports, pictures, and interpretations in the mass media, few of which are favorable. Most often movements and leaders are portrayed as disruptive, radical, dangerous, or laughable. For example, nearly all stories about Malcolm X refer to his prison record and apparent calls for violence. An ABC *20/20* report on Operation Rescue of the pro-life movement noted that its founder and "unlikely" leader, Randall Terry, was a former used-car salesman. Bonnie Dow claims the media saw the women's Strike for Equality as entertainment for amused and bemused male spectators and emphasized alleged bra burning and strikers as "braless bubbleheads."[5] They became fixated on physical attractiveness, or lack of it. Media rarely report social movement activities unless they are action oriented (marches, sit-ins, boycotts, strikes, and large gatherings) or violent (bombings, vandalism, arson, and shootings), and media reports have profound effects on how the public views social movements and their leaders.

Institutions such as government agencies and agents, schools and teachers, churches and clergy, labor unions and officers, corporations and executives reinforce attitudes toward social movement leaders. Not many U.S. students learn about social movement leaders in their history and social studies classes. Martin Luther King, Jr., a rare exception, remains controversial in many locales where he is still considered a communist agent. Eric Hoffer claims that social movement leaders desire to divest themselves of an "unwanted self":

> The revulsion from an unwanted self, and the impulse to forget it, mask
> it, slough it off, and lose it produce both a readiness to sacrifice the self
> and a willingness to dissolve it by losing one's individual distinctness in a
> compact collective whole.[6]

Bill Yousman writes that many of Malcolm X's biographers have attempted to show that his frustrations came not from white supremacy but from "his inability to grapple with his own and his family's inadequacies," a rejection of dysfunctional parents, not an unjust society.[7] They reframed Malcolm X's ideological positions into a purely personal struggle against internal demons rather than external oppressors.

Social theorists also reflect and influence public perceptions. Herbert Simons writes that, in spite of the fact that social movements are systematically deprived of the normal channels of communication and influence, "rhetoricians and other scholars have tended to assume that methods of influence appropriate for drawing room controversies are also effective for social conflicts, including struggles against established authorities."[8] Because scholars "have failed to suggest viable strategies for those engaged in rough-and-tumble conflicts," some "have dismissed militant protestors" and leaders "as pathological." A number of studies by Crane Brinton (the American, French, English, and Russian revolutions), Ming T. Lee (the Communist revolution in China), and Seymour Lipset (the socialist movement in Saskatchewan) provide substantial evidence that social movement leaders (and members) do not come from the marginal areas or "lunatic fringe" of society but from the higher strata of groups and subcultures: teachers, students, editors, farmers, civil servants, business leaders, clergy, and lawyers.[9] They are more affluent, better educated, and less anxious and disoriented than their nonactivist counterparts. Writing about the leaders of the French and American revolutions, Brinton notes that they "were not in general afflicted with anything the psychiatrist could be called about. They were certainly not riffraff, scoundrels, scum of the earth."[10] Myra Ferree concludes her study of U.S. social movement organizations with the comment, "Social movement participants are as rational as those who study them."[11]

"The six who dared" to found the Gray Panthers in 1970 did not fit the stereotypes of bewhiskered, disillusioned, radical revolutionaries. Maggie Kuhn instigated the first meeting because they all faced—upon turning 65 years of age—loss of jobs, income, contacts with associates, and opportunities to continue social commitments and active participation in their communities.[12]

Institutions and the public stigmatize social movement leaders as "demagogues" who lie, oversimplify, exaggerate, and make false accusations; who purposely misuse facts, offer insufficient evidence, and employ logical fallacies; who resort to invective, name-calling, and ridicule; and who rely on emotional appeals. The demagogue will use any means to attain personal power and gain. As Steven Goldzwig points out, "the use of the term 'demagogue' generally denotes a rhetor who employs highly suspect means in the pursuit of equally suspect ends."[13] There is no evidence, however, that the typical social movement leader lies, cheats, misuses facts, and makes false accusations intentionally or to a greater degree than institutional leaders. Similarly, no evidence exists that leaders join the movement for personal gain and power, even though the FBI and other government agencies tried desperately to prove otherwise during the 1950s, 1960s, and 1970s.[14] Most leaders could attain greater powers and material wealth through institutional means than through noninstitutional organizations. Movement leaders are guilty of using emotional appeals, invective, oversimplification, exaggeration, and insufficient evidence, but so are political, religious, business, educational, and charity leaders. The label "demagogue" accurately describes few social movement leaders.

The mass media, institutional authorities, and the public too often assume that any person who appears to *act* in behalf of a social movement or cause or *looks like* a movement member (African American, Native American, Hispanic American, woman, student, elderly person, worker) is a movement *leader.* Joanne Woodward (actress) and Gloria Steinem (feminist) wrote letters for the National Abortion Rights Action League (NARAL), but this

did not make them leaders of the pro-choice movement. Minimally organized social movements with few identifiable leaders are particularly susceptible to the problem of mistaken leadership. Dow notes that "commercial
media generally found the [women's liberation] movement a difficult story to
cover because it did not, initially, . . . have clearly delineated leaders or easily
accessed organizational sources."[15] In his study of the Watts Riot in Los
Angeles in 1965 (not unlike the riot of 1992 following the Rodney King ver-
dict), Anthony Oberschall notes that those who assaulted police, threw rocks,
set fire to buildings, and harangued crowds "were neither leaders prior to
these incidents nor do they subsequently play a leader role in other incidents."[16] This distinction, however, escaped the media. Social movements
are often blamed for the words and actions of persons who are at best
bystanders or misfits and who may see opportunities to act under the guise of
the movement. The Internet and Web sites are open to anyone who wishes to
espouse a cause.

Students of social movements should look at the rhetorical-social situation leaders face rather than at pathological traits or early childhood experiences. Simons observes that "unless it is understood that the leader is
subjected to incompatible demands, a great many of his [her] rhetorical acts
must seem counterproductive."[17] The typical leader of a typical social movement has no sanctioned position, no sanctioned authority to implement decisions, no regular salary, no orderly personal life, and no job security. At the
same time, the leader encounters threats, harassment, denial of access to the
mass media, persecution, arrest, jail terms, exile, and the necessity of going
into hiding. Oberschall concludes:

> Put any ordinary, stable individual into a similar position and he [she],
> too, would probably exhibit what some observers consider confused or
> arbitrary behavior as a result of the pressures and dilemmas that one is
> continually faced with as a leader in an uninstitutionalized and emergent
> organizational setting.[18]

This chapter examines the *nature* of leadership in social movements and
how it is *attained* and *maintained* as social movements adapt to an ever-changing environment. One caveat is in order. Our focus on leadership in this chapter does not suggest that leaders can bring about or resist change alone. As
Susan Zaeske writes, "Social movements are more than their leaders, and we
cannot fully understand the rhetoric of a given social movement and its consequences by examining only the discourse of its leaders."[19]

THE NATURE OF LEADERSHIP IN SOCIAL MOVEMENTS

Leadership in social movements, Wilson notes, is more structured than a
naked power relationship and less structured than an authority relationship
associated with an organizational position.[20] Simons claims the leader, at
best, "controls an organized core of the movement (frequently mistaken for

the movement itself) but exerts relatively little influence over a relatively larger number of sympathizers on its periphery."[21] Essentially, the leader gains the right (the legitimacy) to exercise specific skills within a specific social movement organization or coalition through leadership traits, insights into a problem, bravery, and communication skills. These skills are often learned through costly trial and error as the social movement evolves. For example, women's rights leader Elizabeth Cady Stanton discovered that she could use the popular lyceum lecture circuit to deliver a speech entitled "Our Boys" in which she espoused nontraditional approaches to raising children and controversial educational reforms, by speaking "not as a famous suffrage activist, but simply as a mother" of five sons.[22]

Leaders as Organizers

Leaders must have organizational skills, particularly the ability to attract individuals to the idea of collective action and to draw people together into meaningful relationships and organizations. For example, Maggie Kuhn was instrumental in attracting people from all ages and fields of endeavor to join the Gray Panthers, a movement that would primarily benefit elderly Americans. She and her colleagues began with contacts among friends and former associates, attracted young people who were also fighting for basic rights, and then organized all ages to form effective coalitions. According to the *Gray Panther Manual,* "The group was built on the network principle, involving individuals and groups: a network of human relationships each of them has stockpiled."[23]

Saul Alinsky identified a number of essential attributes for successful organizers.[24] An organizer must have *curiosity* that becomes contagious. Samuel Adams in colonial America, Maggie Kuhn of the Gray Panthers, Frank Kameny of the gay rights movement, and Betty Friedan of the women's liberation movement questioned traditional relationships, norms, values, and ways of doing things. They asked questions such as "Why?" and "Why not?" that agitated both victims and victimizers.

An organizer must be *irreverent.* Malcolm X of the Black Muslims, Stokely Carmichael of the SNCC, and Eldridge Cleaver of the Black Panthers detested accepted dogma, defied finite definitions of morality, and challenged and insulted established institutions and social movement organizations and tactics to gain freedom, equality, and justice for black Americans. The counterculture and student movements of the 1960s and 1970s took delight in rejecting all that older generations held sacred. Women became sick and tired of "staying in their place" as wives and mothers. The Christian Right rejected all aspects of what they considered to be liberal dogma forced on God-fearing Christians.

An organizer must have *imagination* to create new ideas, tactics, and organizational structures to function in an ever-changing environment. Martin Luther King, Jr., decided that action, such as the historic Montgomery bus boycott and marches, should replace the slow, behind-the-scenes court actions the NAACP had pursued for decades. Black student leaders in North Carolina were the first to stage sit-ins at lunch counters. The imagination of each leader or group of leaders changed the movement. Maggie Kuhn's group began as the Consultation of Older and Younger Adults, a rather unimaginative title. It took the name Gray Panthers and a unique panther logo at the suggestion of a television talk show producer following a lively and controversial appearance by Kuhn and a group of young people. They adopted it as a "fun name" and more expressive of the group's "quick minds, ready humor, radical and action orientation that characterized the members."[25] Ralph Reed of the Christian Coalition recognized early on the potential of the Internet to disseminate information, create communities of believers, raise funds, and pressure institutional leaders.

An organizer must have a *sense of humor* to relieve tensions within the movement, allay fears members have over imminent nonviolent actions, and make fun of the opposition through satire and ridicule. For instance, organizers of pro-life's Operation Rescue campaigns joke at training sessions about which religious groups are better at kneeling and crawling when confronting police lines and laugh at the oddity of their nonviolent tactics. During its campaign against abortion clinics in Atlanta, its leader Randall Terry answered his cellular phone, "Maxwell Smart," an allusion to the classic television comedy *Get Smart*.[26] Stokely Carmichael's college audiences cheered, shouted, and laughed when, for instance, he would imitate "the sound of horses' hoofs, straddling an imaginary steed, bouncing up and down in a simulated gallop" to recreate the scene of historic conflicts between red men and white men.[27]

An organizer must have an *organized personality* to maintain order within the movement organization and to deal with the uncertainties and disorder of movements. When all else seems irrational, the organizer must remain rational and in control. Alinsky writes that "the organizer recognizes that each person or bloc has a hierarchy of values" and is able to work out coalitions in which all blocs or organizations gain something and maintain critical beliefs, attitudes, and values.[28] One of Martin Luther King, Jr.'s most important leadership traits was his ability to bring disparate civil rights organizations together for campaigns.

An organizer must also have a *strong ego* but not egotism. Leaders believe in themselves and their abilities to achieve goals if they are to instill confidence and belief in others. At the same time, they must have a realistic notion of the odds against them to accept minimal gains or failures, make the best of each, and know when to retire from the field of battle. Rev. Jerry Falwell sensed it was time to disband the Moral Majority in 1986 and to leave the political fight to others in the Christian right. Martin Luther King, Jr., sensed when it was time to call off the unproductive campaign in Albany, Georgia, in 1962 and admitted they had made mistakes: "Our protest was so vague that we got nothing, and the people were left very depressed and in despair."[29] In many movements, moderate elements and leaders seem more capable than radical elements of deciding when it is time to back off and a tactic is getting out of hand.

Leaders as Decision Makers

The social movement leader is a *decision maker* but rarely has the powers of reward and punishment or the claim to legitimacy of an established authority. Joseph Gusfield notes that although the leader is the head of a decision-making hierarchy within a social movement organization, the leader operates within an environment of clients, enemies, adherents, and potential recruits in which he or she has no authority but merely represents the movement.[30] This environment is fraught with repressive uncertainty, complex conditions, conflicting demands, pressures from inside and outside the movement, power struggles among movement elements, disagreements over philosophies and strategies, financial crises, and competition among leaders. The result is a fracturing of movements. The National Right to Life Committee once dominated the pro-life movement, but today a click of the Internet reveals dozens of organizations, including American Life League, Human Life International, Birthright International, Pro-Life Action League, Pro-Life Alliance of Gays and Lesbians, Baptists for Life, and National Campus Life Network.

Herbert Simons summarizes perceptively the plight of those who would lead a single social movement organization, let alone a whole social movement.

> Shorn of the controls that characterize formal organizations, yet required to perform the same internal functions, harassed from without, yet obligated to adapt to the external system, the leader of a social movement must constantly balance inherently conflicting demands on his [her] position and on the movement he [she] represents.[31]

A reading of the annual *Proceedings of the General Assembly of the Knights of Labor* supports Simons' observations. Leaders of the Knights spent most of their time fending off charges from members, attacking "traitors" who had left the organization but were continuing efforts to undermine it or to start competing organizations, answering negative reports in the media, denying associations with anarchists and socialists, explaining strains or ruptures in relationships with other labor movement organizations, reporting on conflicts with institutions such as the Catholic Church, explaining failed actions such as strikes or boycotts, and attacking or negotiating with employers.[32]

The many difficulties social movement leaders encounter and the severe limitations placed on them are exemplified in the civil rights movement. Images of Martin Luther King, Jr., come from memories and pictures shown on the national holiday honoring him in January. We see him delivering his famous "I Have a Dream" speech on the steps of the Lincoln Memorial, walking arm-in-arm with other civil rights leaders through southern towns, and meeting with the press. These are mere highlights of a leader in action. Most of King's time was spent trying to keep or to make peace among fellow clergymen with giant-sized egos or among competing civil rights organizations such as the NAACP, CORE, SNCC, and his own SCLC. He preferred to be on the front lines of the movement, particularly during major campaigns such as Selma, but he frequently was in New York or Washington raising the funds necessary to keep campaigns alive. Bail for hundreds of protestors arrested during demonstrations and fines levied for breaking local and state ordinances were a fraction of the expenses incurred in the operations of a large and diverse organization and movement. Only Martin Luther King, Jr., could perform these essential fund-raising activities effectively, but friends of the movement often grumbled about his absence at critical moments in the streets of the South. Enemies accused him of cowardice, of running away when things got rough, of accepting bail while others remained in jail. Friends and enemies alike resented King's fame and the accolades that went with it.

Leaders as Symbols

Although social movement leaders do not have the powers and legitimacy of institutional authorities, they lead because their skills enable them to function as the symbols of their movements. Leaders become totally identified with their causes, and the causes may become totally identified with them. There would not have been a United Farm Workers movement without the persistence and organizing skills of Cesar Chavez or a Native-American movement without Russell Means. Both were willing to demonstrate, picket, lobby, go to jail, and sacrifice their lives. Successful leaders inspire absolute devotion, love, trust, and dependence.

Eugene V. Debs serves as an illustration from the early labor movement. In April 1894, he led his American Railway Union in a victorious strike against the powerful James J. Hill and his Great Northern Railroad, a remarkable victory for a union that was barely two years old. As Debs left by train from St. Paul, Minnesota, to return to his home in Terre Haute, Indiana, railroad workers lined both sides of the tracks with their hats in their hands in homage to their leader.[34] Some social movements take their leaders' names: Martin Luther (the Lutheran Church), John Wesley (the Wesleyan movement among British and American protestants), and Karl Marx (the Marxist-communist movement that began in Europe and spread around the world), to name a few.

The leader is the "face" of the social movement for members, the public, and the mass media. Gusfield writes:

> It is with leadership that the public identifies in describing and judging a movement. The leader personifies the movement in cartoon, picture, story, and legend. For much of the public, the leader becomes synonymous with the movement and its adherents.[34]

For instance, more than one generation of Americans viewed the labor movement among coal miners as synonymous with John L. Lewis. The fiery, bushy-eyebrowed founder and leader of the United Mine Workers was featured during newsreels in theaters, on front pages of newspapers and magazines, and in numerous cartoons on editorial pages. Phyllis Schlafly, through her Eagle Forum, was the most recognized leader of the antiwomen's liberation movement, particularly for opposing its campaign for the Equal Rights Amendment, and was a frequent subject of cartoons. One cartoon depicted a scene at the Capitol in Washington, D.C., with one member of Congress commenting to another, "Any reaction to the possible extension for ERA?" The second replied, "Well, I understand the Phyllis Schlafly group is flying in." Above the Capitol dome can be seen a flock of witches descending on broomsticks. A multiple panel cartoon depicted a woman in a dress and high heels running up to a cave man, grabbing his club, and beating herself senseless. The cave man turned to another cave man and explained simply, "Phyllis Schlafly."[35]

As we become an increasingly visual society through the proliferation of television, the Internet, videotapes, and DVDs, visual depictions of leaders and their activities dominate our visions of social movements. The words and images of leaders of the white supremacy movement such as Matt Hale of the World Church of the Creator, Thomas Metzger of White Aryan Resistance, Richard Butler of Aryan Nations and Christian Identity, and William L. Pierce of the National Alliance are readily available on Web sites to those who support or sympathize with their cause. Pat Robertson's "Family Channel" on cable television with his "700 Club" provides a continual visual link to the religious right movement.

Herbert Simons concludes his treatment of social movement leadership with the comment that "the primary rhetorical test of the leader and, indirectly, of the strategies he [she] employs is his [her] capacity to fulfill the requirements of his [her] movement by resolving or reducing rhetorical problems."[36] In a very real sense the leader is a *rhetorical* leader of a *social* movement who enables individuals to see themselves as a people, establish lasting relational patterns, and adapt strategies to an ever-evolving social environment.

HOW LEADERSHIP IS ATTAINED IN SOCIAL MOVEMENTS

A leadership position is attained in a social movement when members perceive a person to possess two or more of three attributes: charisma, prophecy, and pragmatism.[37] Creating a Web site, writing a book, composing songs, or taking part in demonstrations does not make one a leader.

Charisma

The charismatic leader's source of legitimacy lies in his or her apparent access to a higher source or divine inspiration. According to William Cameron, an "awe-inspiring" personality leads social movement members to see "truth" in the charismatic leader's utterances.[38] Richard Jensen and John Hammerback write that Cesar Chavez:

Embodied his message in many ways in his first persona [the communicated picture of oneself] by expressing his ideas in a form, style, and manner fitting for the ideas he advocated, for his discourse subtly and overtly depicted him as a teacher of truth, even as he called for listeners and readers to become organizers whose message must be presented clearly in an effort to carry out God's will.[39]

His former secretary described him as a "charismatic hero," the "Mexican Martin Luther King; America's Gandhi."

The charismatic leader is a show person with a sense of timing and the rhetorical skills necessary to articulate what "others can as yet only feel, strive towards, and imagine but cannot put into words or translate explicitly into action."[40] For instance, Jose Angel Gutierrez of the Hispanic movement "argued that Chicanos had a history of dissent, were not inferior due to their color, had not lost their heritage, and possessed a significant history."[41] Chicanos were a people with a proud heritage. On the other hand, he applied negative terms to the Anglo (a devil term for Chicanos), including bigoted, racist, exploiter, barbarian, and white supremacist. The clear we-they distinction instilled self-respect, dignity, and unity among fellow Chicanos. Such rhetoric leads J. Michael Hogan and Glen Williams to approach "charisma not as a product of personality traits nor of sociological conditions, but rather as a *textual* creation—a phenomenon manifested in *rhetorical* artifacts."[42] William L. Pierce wrote *The Turner Diaries*, an account of a future race war in the United States, under the pen name Andrew Macdonald. He achieved charismatic status among white supremacists and those opposing tyrannical government. Oklahoma City bomber Timothy McVeigh had a copy of *The Turner Diaries* with him when he was arrested and reportedly had handed out copies of the book to fellow soldiers when he was in the army. Pierce was not impressive in appearance or as a speaker, but his text has been called the movement's bible and the equivalent of Hitler's *Mein Kampf*.[43]

The person with charisma leads followers in direct actions that stir things up, supply vigor to social movements, and make people believe in the impossible. Examples include Randall Terry (leader of Operation Rescue for the pro-life movement in the 1980s and 1990s), Phyllis Schlafly (president of the Eagle Forum that resisted the women's liberation movement), Samuel Gompers (a founder and leader of the American Federation of Labor from 1886–1924), Frederick Douglass (an escaped slave who became an internationally known leader of the antislavery movement), and Martin Luther King, Jr. Susan B. Anthony coined the slogan "failure is impossible" for the women's rights movement in which she served as a leader from the first Women's Rights convention at Seneca Falls, New York, in 1848 to her resignation in 1900 as president of the National Woman's Suffrage Association.

The charismatic leader feels a duty, not merely an obligation or opportunity, to lead the movement and may exhibit exceptional heroism, bravery, and endurance to the point of martyrdom for the cause. The civil rights movement included famous martyrs (Medgar Evers, Martin Luther King, Jr., Malcolm

X) and little-known martyrs, both black and white (James Chaney, Michael Schwerner, and Andrew Goodman murdered in Mississippi, and a Detroit homemaker named Viola Liuzzo who was shot and killed while ferrying Selma-to-Montgomery marchers in Alabama). The intense, unwavering support of followers (even when the charismatic leader blunders in selecting targets, strategies, and times to act) maintains unity and prevents a shifting of the power structure so common within minimally organized organizations. Speeches about fallen martyrs enhance not only the charisma of the martyrs but that of their leader who appears to be equally fearless and dedicated to the cause and principles for which the martyrs sacrificed their lives.

Perhaps there is no better example of a charismatic leader than Mahatma Gandhi who, for over thirty years, led India's fight for independence from Great Britain. His philosophy and program called satyagraha (literally "truth-force") embodied a method of persuasion that used moral means to achieve moral ends. Gandhi understood the need for showmanship when leading a mass movement and took actions that gained international attention but required few resources and identified himself with the Indian people. He dressed in simple sandals and a loincloth that represented the daily attire of male laborers in India. As a protest against British textile laws, Gandhi wove his own simple clothing and made the spinning wheel a symbol of independence from British rule and influence. He underwent fifteen fasts, his "fiery weapon," to protest low wages and poor working conditions, to restore peace after riots had erupted during a visit by British royalty, to end violence (particularly among Hindus and Muslims), to protest his own imprisonment, and to pressure British prime ministers into altering actions and decisions.

Gandhi spent nearly a third of his life as a social movement leader conducting walking propaganda tours that often covered hundreds of miles and lasted for months. Each walk took him among the people most sympathetic with the movement and gained attention and followers. As "sacred pilgrimages," these walks identified Gandhi and the movement with the religious traditions of India. He literally became a "holy man" for millions of Indians. Allen Merriam writes, "The primacy of symbolic behavior in extending Gandhi's influence corresponded to the traditional pattern of Indian gurus, who are identified more by their lifestyle than by their pronouncements."[44] Gandhi understood the need to create strategies adapted to the environment that would bring about evolutionary results for the movement.

Prophecy

The prophet's source of legitimacy lies in his or her proximity to the writings of the social movement, its ideology. The person may have written all or important segments of the movement's doctrine, may be considered the most knowledgeable authority on the doctrine, or may be seen as nearest in spirit to the doctrine. As a spokesperson for the movement's god—capitalism, socialism, freedom, equality, fundamental religious truths, or the American way of life—the leader with the gift of prophecy elaborates, justifies, and explains the movement's values, myths, beliefs, and methods. After writing *The Turner Diaries*, Pierce wrote *Hunter*, in which he attempted to carry his "readers through a process of development." He termed his work an "educational novel" about a white supremacist who traveled the country killing people.[45]

The prophet knows the "truth" and sets a moral tone for the social movement. Rev. Jerry Falwell, leader of the Moral Majority, crusaded against liberals, secular humanism, and those who would compromise the great truths of the Bible and the Constitution. The prophet alone has the ability to perceive the true nature of the urgent problem, its causes, and its solution. Because the prophet is a person of vision, has a psychological commitment to principles, and perceives the writings of the movement to be sacred, he or she is unlikely to be a reconciler between movement factions or between movement and institutions. The truth cannot be compromised. When Dr. Robert Parker, pastor of the Kosmosdale Baptist Church in Louisville accepted the position of State Chairman of the Moral Majority in Kentucky, he and other leaders had no desire to mix "politics and the pulpit" but sensed that many of our national and state problems were due to moral default and failure to unite under God's standards. They accepted their burden of awakening the republic to national sin and joined together to call this nation to a real moral referendum, turning the United States back toward the path of morality.[46]

The prophet judges the legitimacy of decisions by reference to ideology—to truth—not by ends achieved. When Robert Welch called eleven men together for a two-day meeting in Indianapolis on December 8 and 9, 1958, to found the John Birch Society, he launched his effort to become the undisputed prophet for the anticommunist resistance movement in the United States. Welch opened his two-day speech to these eleven like-minded businessmen by establishing his qualifications to lead the movement:

> I personally have been studying the problem increasingly for about nine years, and practically full-time for the past three years. And entirely without pride, but in simple thankfulness, let me point out that a lifetime of business experience should have made it easier for me to see the falsity of the economic theories upon which Communism is supposedly based, more readily, than might some scholar coming into that study from the academic cloisters; while a lifetime of interest in things academic, especially world history, should have given me an advantage over many businessmen, in more readily seeing the sophistries in dialectical materialism.[47]

Welch's speech became *The Blue Book of the John Birch Society*, the organization's bible, and the new anticommunist force named after the first U.S. martyr in the struggle, John Birch, an army officer apparently killed by communist troops in China shortly before communist forces took over. The John Birch Society designed advertisements to look exactly like Sunday supplements in major conservative newspapers such as the *Chicago Tribune* and the *Arizona Republic* to introduce the John Birch Society to millions in the fall of 1964. An item entitled "He Has Stirred the Slumbering Spirit" presented Robert Welch as a person of vision, wisdom, and commitment in the struggle against the communist menace, a person whose words were gaining scores of converts:

> Mr. Welch's writings have created widespread comment—some critical. Few were ready to believe him when he warned of the impending Communist takeovers by Castro in Cuba, Ben Bella in Algeria, and Sukarno in Indonesia. But with events proving him correct again and again, his writings are now closely scrutinized by all serious students of anti-Communism.[48]

Welch created a monthly periodical for the movement entitled *American Opinion* and remained its editor and frequent contributor until his death in 1985. In an open letter to readers in the October 1978 issue, Welch wrote of the periodical's reason for being:

> You were to read *American Opinion* in order to learn the truth; the plain unmistakable truth about what was really happening. We set out twenty-two [sic] years ago to make this monthly compendium the most accurate, most penetrating, and most widely accepted authority in the world on the nature and the menace of the revolutionary cabal that was steadily undermining our whole civilization.[49]

Welch was never a reconciler in the struggle between good and evil. As a prophet for the anticommunist movement, he structured the John Birch Society to build a "rededication to God, to family, to country, and to strong moral principles."[50]

Pragmatism

The pragmatist's source of legitimacy lies in organizational expertise, efficiency, and tact. As a person who believes that the social movement must have a secure and stable foundation for growth, the pragmatic leader brings common sense and a healthy skepticism to the movement, seeks to reconcile diverse interests, desires communication rather than excommunication, and replaces unattainable goals with diffuse goals and targets. The pragmatist believes that ideals and principles are useless without organization and implementation. John C. Willke, president of the National Right to Life Committee for decades, was not a charismatic leader, but he was effective at disseminating the pro-life message, assisting the creation of National Right to Life Committee organizations in all fifty states, recruiting dues-paying members, raising funds to support the committee's campaigns, and making the cause more than a Roman Catholic crusade.

The pragmatic leader seeks inclusiveness by making the movement acceptable to outsiders (including important legitimizers from the established order) and devotes energies to fund-raising, recruitment, and organization. This leader is more likely to compromise the sacredness of the movement's writings than the integrity of the organization and to see maintenance of the organization as an end in itself. Without the organization, there can be no movement. Leaders such as Maggie Kuhn, Martin Luther King, Jr., Ralph Reed, Russell Means, and Robert Welch see clearly that successful short-term campaigns and long-term social movements require organization, planning, recruiting, training, discipline, funds, and guidance.

With the exception of one year, Samuel Gompers led the American Federation of Labor from its founding in 1886 to his death in 1924; he was a pragmatist. He was aware of the labor movement's history, of labor organizations that had blossomed and wilted, of U.S. opposition to labor radicals, and of the needs and desires of workers. Above all, he understood the need for a strong organization with a central focus (trade unionism) and a sound financial base.[51] Although Gompers was sympathetic with all elements of the labor movement, he refused, for example, to aid the Knights of Labor when it became embroiled in the aftermath of the Haymarket Riot in Chicago and the trial of the accused anarchists.

The violent events "left a bitterly divided memory as its legacy."[52] To many people, the anarchists were murderers, but for others, especially immigrant workers, they were martyrs willing to die for working-class emancipation. The Haymarket Riot occurred on May 4, 1886, during a labor protest rally. The purpose of the rally was to protest the police shootings of two workers the previous day in a confrontation between locked-out union members and the workers who replaced them at the McCormick Reaper Works. Seven police officers dispersing the crowd in Haymarket Square died from wounds suffered when a bomb was thrown and the subsequent hail of bullets. Sixty-eight civilians were wounded. Eight members of the anarchist movement were convicted, and four were hanged. Despite disagreeing with the tactics, Gompers and other union leaders "could not forget that the revolutionaries put to death in Chicago were union organizers and leaders of the crusade for the eight-hour day—the cause that mobilized America's first national labor movement in 1886."[53]

The AFL was too young, could not afford to become identified with the Knights of Labor or the anarchists, and was in direct competition with industrial unionism (open to all workers regardless of skill) championed by the Knights.

> Gompers and other union leaders expressed strong regrets that the explosion in the Haymarket, so closely linked in the public mind with the eight-hour campaign, halted its progress. Wary of being associated with anarchism, they avoided political ideology and critiques of the capitalist system, focusing on bread-and-butter issues such as wages, hours, and working conditions.[54]

Gompers understood the U.S. value system and the inherent conservatism of workers and industrialists. He struggled to make the AFL the accepted umbrella organization for all trade unions. While he tried to avoid unnecessary confrontations within the movement, Gompers was not reluctant to attack elements that posed dangers to his organization. At the AFL convention in 1903, Gompers attacked socialist members head-on:

> And I want to say that I am entirely at variance with your philosophy. I declare it to you. I am not only at variance with your doctrines, but with

your philosophy. Economically, you are unsound; socially, you are wrong; industrially, you are an impossibility.[55]

Gompers built and maintained an organization that withstood the onslaught of industrialists, competing labor organizations, economic depressions, and world wars to become an institutionalized force in U.S. society.

HOW LEADERSHIP IS MAINTAINED IN SOCIAL MOVEMENTS

Social movement leaders maintain their positions as long as they hold the confidence of followers, seem to have solutions to problems, meet the exigencies of new and unexpected situations, and perform rhetorical functions necessary for the stage the movement is in at the moment. As Cameron notes, all leaders "do something exceedingly well," and "when they stop doing it well, they often cease to lead."[56]

A Mix of Leadership Attributes

Theorists agree that every successful social movement leader must display two or more of the three essential leadership attributes—charisma, prophecy, and pragmatism—although not necessarily in the same context. Gusfield, for example, argues that leadership can be conceived as a set of simultaneous roles. As mobilizer, the leader must "breathe the fire and brimstone of enthusiastic mission," and as articulator, the leader "pours the oil of bargaining, compromise, and common culture."[57] Wilson claims that leaders gain the esteem of fellow movement members because of the peculiar mix of their rhetorical abilities, and Oberschall concludes, "Leaders, in sum, are the architects of organization, ideology, and mobilization for the movement."[58]

While single-dimensional institutional leaders can function and survive because they have a multitude of institutional resources at their disposal, social movement leaders rarely have such resources. Unfortunately for social movements, a great many leaders are one-dimensional. Randall Terry is effective at organizing and leading Operation Rescue blockades of abortion clinics throughout the United States, partly because he organizes limited actions well and partly because of his personal enthusiasm, bravery, and commitment. He has been arrested dozens of times but returns to the action as soon as he is released. It is doubtful, however, that he could lead a large national organization, be content with behind-the-scenes organizing and fund-raising, or sit down with other social movement organizations or institutions to reach compromises.

Few spokespersons for black rights during the 1960s were more charismatic, particularly among young black Americans who were becoming disillusioned with the civil rights movement, than Stokely Carmichael. He was attractive, intelligent, articulate, and understood the importance of timing and showmanship. During the famous Meredith March in Mississippi in June

1966, Carmichael cooperated with the leaders of the NAACP and SCLC until the march reached Greenwood, SNCC territory, and Martin Luther King, Jr., left for meetings in Chicago. The sheriff arrested Carmichael and others briefly on June 16 for pitching tents in a school yard. Carmichael used the occasion to escalate his confrontational rhetoric at an evening rally, declaring: "This is the 27th time I've been arrested, I ain't gonna be arrested no more. . . . Every courthouse in Mississippi should be burnt down tomorrow so we can get rid of the dirt."[59] The next evening Carmichael delivered more of the same confrontational message and then, on cue, Willie Ricks shouted, "What do you want?" Carmichael responded, "Black power!" and the crowd was soon enthusiastically echoing this new battle cry. He had seized the moment beautifully, and, during the next several months, traveled throughout the country explaining and extolling "Black Power."

> The civil rights movement would never be the same in tone, demands, tactics, and relationships. A new generation of activists, goaded by frustration with the lack of progress for black Americans in the rural south and the urban north and the perceived failure of established movement organizations and leaders to bring about real and lasting changes, was taking center stage and challenging the heart and soul of the movement.[60]

While Carmichael became a hero among the growing number of young black nationalists within the movement, his much misunderstood and maligned theme of black power and confrontational rhetorical style shattered the fragile coalition of black rights organizations and polarized white liberal legitimizers and blacks. He lacked the attributes of the prophet in failing to develop a clear doctrine of black power meaningful to all elements of the movement, nor was he a pragmatist because he attacked other leaders in his speeches to black audiences. On July 30, 1966, in Detroit, Carmichael remarked:

> I'm very concerned, because you see we have a lot of Negro leaders, and I want to make it clear I'm no leader. I represent the Student Nonviolent Coordinating Committee. That's the sole source of my power, and that's Black Power. I'm no Negro leader, but I think we have to speak out about the war in Vietnam.[61]

By 1968 Carmichael had left the SNCC, reestablished his relationship with Martin Luther King, Jr., and formed a new organization called the Black United Front, an organization that experienced a brief life span. He remained an eloquent spokesperson for black power, pride, and independence, but he failed as a leader. Cameron's declaration, "Many a stirring evangelist makes a poor pastor," could be applied to Carmichael.[62]

Handling Diverse, Conflicting Roles

Few social movement leaders are capable of handling the diverse and often conflicting roles thrust on them or the many rhetorical dilemmas social movements encounter daily. The leader must (1) adapt to different audiences at once but not appear to be a political chameleon, (2) produce short-run victories but not preclude meaningful evolutionary results, (3) use militant tactics to gain visibility for the movement but use moderate tactics to gain entry into decision-making centers, (4) foster strong convictions in the movement's principles but control the implication that their attainment justifies any necessary means, (5) strive for organizational efficiency without dampening the enthusiasm and spontaneity generated during the early, less-structured days of the movement, (6) understand that militants are effective with power-vulnerables such as elected and appointed officials and moderates are more effective with power-invulnerables such as judges, business owners, and much of the "silent majority," (7) vilify established orders but be willing and able to work with them when it is to the movement's advantage, and (8) grasp at opportunities to deal with an institution on its own turf without appearing to be selling out or going soft.[63] The difficulty of meeting and adapting to role demands that require different rhetorical skills and tactics results in a proliferation of leaders that cause conflict within and among movement organizations and the rise of factions.

The civil rights movement of the 1950s and 1960s produced a variety of leaders who performed specific roles skillfully but could not meet all the rhetorical demands of the movement. Roy Wilkins of the NAACP, for instance, believed in working through the system (particularly through the courts) to bring about change, and he feared both the tactics and the results of direct actions such as sit-ins, marches, and demonstrations. Andrew Young was highly successful as a conciliator and diplomat within the SCLC, particularly among its younger members and elements. However, his soft-spoken style and devotion to Martin Luther King, Jr., prevented him from speaking out on his views and becoming visible beyond the SCLC. Ralph Abernathy was highly visible but usually silent during the movement (seemingly always at King's side in marches, jails, meetings, and press conferences). His loyalty, dedication, and bravery were not sufficient to prepare him to take over the leadership of the SCLC in 1968 following King's assassination. Fred Shuttlesworth founded the Alabama Christian Movement for Human Rights in 1956 and later allied this group with the SCLC. He was highly respected within the movement and feared by the southern establishment for his reckless courage and ability to organize and lead demonstrations, but his efforts to become a major leader were plagued by autocratic, egocentric, and tactless personality traits.

Changing as the Movement Changes

Perhaps the greatest obstacle for leadership tenure in social movements is the necessity for change. As movements evolve, leaders and followers must evolve. Wars, economic depressions, the resignation or replacement of institutional leaders, inventions, and political, religious, and social trends greatly affect the nature and progress of social movements. For example, in the conflict over legalized abortion, pro-life faces the possible effects of widespread use of the morning-after pill and recent advances in surgical procedures that would enable women to prevent or terminate pregnancies without going to abortion clinics or finding physicians to perform abortions. They could have an "abortion" within weeks instead of months following conception, long before an identifiable human being is present. The morning-after pill, for instance, could deprive the pro-life movement of data, stories, and pictures showing the extent and barbarism of abortions. New surgical techniques would preclude the powerful, emotional argument against late-term abortions ("partial-birth abortions"). On the other hand, pro-choice faces imminent changes in the makeup of the Supreme Court that would tilt against *Roe v. Wade*, and growing disillusionment among Democratic pro-choice members of Congress who link recent election losses to support of legalized abortion. Given these problems, some pro-choice groups are beginning to question the word "choice" (a consumerist word compared to the moral word "life"), and are suggesting "personal freedom," "a phrase intended to evoke unpopular government intrusion into matters such as the Terri Schiavo case"[64] in which Congress attempted to override several court decisions upholding removal of life-support mechanisms. Advances in medicine have made life "viable" much earlier than when *Roe v. Wade* was determined and has increased public concern about abortions early in the second term of pregnancy. Gusfield observes: "The disjuncture between ideology and the adaptive problems of the movement constantly raises the issue of too much or too little accommodation; of renunciation of the mission or overrighteous inflexibility."[65]

Jerry Rubin was an archetypal leader of the student, anti-Vietnam War, and counterculture movements of the 1960s and 1970s. He was intelligent, articulate, imaginative, brave and outrageous in manner, actions, and dress. He effectively organized civil disobedience at Berkeley, demonstrations against trains carrying troops to fight in Vietnam, the October 1967 march on the Pentagon, and the Yippie protests that created chaos at the 1968 Democratic Convention in Chicago. He was a brilliant manipulator of the media and created put-ons (such as threatening to levitate the Pentagon) that led to both humorous and violent reactions from institutions. He polarized society along age lines with the slogan, "Don't trust anyone over thirty." As one of the famous Chicago Seven, he was charged with conspiracy for actions during the Democratic Convention and stood trial for almost five months.

By the early 1970s, however, Rubin knew "the movement" was rapidly dwindling in numbers and fervor. Society was changing, old methods would no longer be effective, and leaders (including himself) were nearing or had passed their thirtieth birthdays. Many members of the movement, particularly younger ones, resisted change and loved and hated Rubin as a symbol of the sixties. They longed for another 1968-style confrontation during the 1972 Republican and Democratic conventions and called Rubin a "sellout" because he stayed in a hotel instead of a park as he had in Chicago. On July 14, Rubin's 34th birthday, a group calling itself Zippies ("put zip back into yip") marched on his hotel in Miami armed with a cake to throw in his face to celebrate his retirement from the movement. Later in the year, a band of Zippies "trashed" Rubin's car in New York to demonstrate their independence from older Yippies. Rubin came to realize that "changes cannot be made on the political level alone, or that society we are changing will be repeated. We must examine our own process."[66]

Adapting to Events

Events may thrust the social movement and its leaders in new directions, and leaders may appear to be mere puppets controlled by events or by the whims of some members. For example, Jane Addams, characterized as the "Grand Lady of Social Reforms" for her leadership in the women's suffrage movement and for causes such as child labor, prison reform, and world peace, became increasingly concerned about the war in Europe in 1915 and the likelihood that the United States would become involved. On July 9 of that year, Addams delivered a speech in Carnegie Hall in which she questioned the morality of war, the desire of soldiers to fight in the war, military censorship of news about the war, the controlling forces that were encouraging the war, and nationalism that fueled the passions of nations and made war possible.[67] Her speech not only incurred the wrath of those supporting the military and the war in Europe but it also reduced her credibility with the American public and split the suffrage movement between pacifists and supporters of military preparedness (as noted in chapter 4).

Leaders must appear to be at the forefront of necessary change and wise adaptation, while not appearing to abandon norms, beliefs, attitudes, and values of their movements to meet situational exigencies. Terence Powderly became General Master Workman (president) of the Order of the Knights of Labor in 1880 and helped make it the largest and most powerful labor union in the history of the United States, reaching over 700,000 members in 1886.[68] But strikes that year by the eight-hour movement and newly enrolled members of the Knights proved disastrous, and Powderly and the Order were blamed although they had authorized no strikes. Although the Knights and the Anarchists were bitter enemies in the struggle for labor and the Order had played no role in the Haymarket Square rally, the government, newspapers, clergy, and the public identified the Knights of Labor with the anarchists and blamed them for the bloody bombing at Haymarket Square. Membership and influence plummeted in spite of Powderly's charisma, persuasive skills, and considerable organizational abilities. In 1893 with the country in the midst of a terrible depression, Powderly decided that only drastic actions could save the Knights and organized labor, so he approached Samuel Gompers with the notion of merging with the AFL, its major competitor. Other Knights were incensed at his willingness to compromise the Order's "fundamental and vital" principle of industrial unionism open to the "laboring masses" by merging with a "mere trade union" limited to a few skilled workers and headed by archenemy Gompers. Powderly and his lieutenants were "retired from office," and new General Master Workman James R. Sovereign declared to the assembled Knights at the 1894 convention that "any action by members of this Order inimical to or in contravention to this principle [industrial unionism] and this policy is *treason* to the Order and the best interests of labor."[69] Powderly was expelled from the Knights as a traitor and never forgiven for his "treachery."

Leading by Not Getting Too Far Ahead or Behind

Cameron cautions:

> The leader must seem to lead. In order to lead, he must be a little ahead of his followers, a little wiser, a little more informed. But if he gets too far ahead, contact is broken, and he may be a "leader" without followers.[70]

In a study of Malcolm X's autobiography, Thomas Benson focuses on the final year of Malcolm X's life in which he broke with Elijah Muhammad (founder of the Black Muslims). Following a trip to Africa and Mecca during which he had seen blond-haired, blue-eyed Muslims, Malcolm X realized he could call whites brothers. He shifted positions on integration and participation in civil rights demonstrations, no longer saw Uncle Toms and whites as devils, and exacerbated his break with Elijah Muhammed.[71] Many of Malcolm X's supporters and enemies viewed these changes as signs of weakness, inconsistency, softening of commitment, or evidence of the hustler element resurfacing. Yusuf Shah, a former chief assistant to Malcolm X, commented on Malcolm X's conflict with the Nation of Islam and changes during 1964 and 1965 in a CBS news program on Malcolm X. Shah called Malcolm X a Benedict Arnold and concluded that if you create a Frankenstein, you have to live with it.[72] Criticism of changes and adaptations are not limited to true believers. Yousman writes that even today, "Historians and biographers . . . seem uncomfortable with Malcolm X's constant movement and metamorphosis."[73] Benson argues that a careful reading of *The Autobiography of Malcolm X*, published a few months after his assassination, reveals that Malcolm X "contained a principle of change within himself," that his changes can be "seen as consistent steps forward rather than as random and untrustworthy conversions by faith" and that his growing "sense of brotherhood with all men is not the weakening of militancy or a softening of commitment, but an extension of potency."[74] In the months before his assassination when he was facing growing opposition and harassment, Malcolm X opposed "straitjacketed thinking, and strait-jacketed societies."

While some leaders streak ahead of their movements and lose contact, others lag behind or are unwilling or incapable of adapting to new circumstances or new stages in their social movements. A person with strong charisma and prophecy may be unable to abandon unattainable goals or to reconcile diverse elements for the harmony of the larger movement. On the other hand, events may revitalize a social movement that has settled into a comfortable bureaucratic state with a pragmatist who is task oriented and thrives on the routine and mundane. This skilled bureaucrat, unable to instill vigor, set a moral tone, and make followers believe in the impossible, is likely to be thrust aside by a charismatic leader with strong traits of the prophet who can put into words and actions what others can only feel or imagine.

Gusfield's study of the Women's Christian Temperance Union (WCTU) leadership following repeal of the prohibition of alcoholic beverages amendment in 1933 illustrates a leader who refused to move with the movement.[75] The president of the WCTU was determined to uphold the centrality of total abstinence even though the public, many Protestant churches, a significant number of members, and other movement organizations such as Alcoholics Anonymous (AA) argued for lesser restrictions on drinking. In her annual report to the WCTU in 1952, Mrs. Z declared:

> In order not to be considered narrow or unable to see both sides some of the Drys have allowed themselves to be maneuvered into accepting the idea that [total abstinence and prohibition] is an old fashioned approach. . . . Between right and wrong there is only one ground and that is a battleground.[76]

Mrs. Z's refusal to modify her stance on principle brought ridicule on the organization and on herself. Movement members and the press described her as being "too rigid," a "one-woman drought," a "fire-eating leader," and a "diehard." When Mrs. A assumed the presidency of the WCTU in the 1960s, she emphasized the necessity of finding common ground and common goals within the WCTU and between the WCTU and other temperance organizations. Mrs. A was chosen because she was astride of the movement instead of lagging behind in defense of a principle no longer accepted by much of society or the temperance movement itself.

CONCLUSIONS

Social movement leaders face a daunting social environment. The public views them as foreign, radical, dangerous, disruptive, and inimical to individualism and to cherished traditions and institutions. Confidence in the ability and determination of institutions to handle crises and issues ranging from race relations to the environment has persisted for two centuries. The mass media focus on social movement actions, particularly violent ones, reinforcing the public's attitudes that collective action is unnecessary and dangerous.

Contrary to common impressions, social movement leaders are much like the rest of us rather than fire-breathing misfits, demagogues, fanatics, or perverts. Unlike many of us, however, they become committed to a cause and are willing to devote their lives to convincing others to support that cause. Social movements attract their share of losers, extremists, and the pathological. The public, institutions, and the media often mistakenly identify the actions of a single member with the movement as a whole—often assuming the rogue member is a leader whose actions represent the entire movement.

This chapter has focused on the nature of leadership in social movements and how it is attained and maintained. Typical leaders of social movements are organizers who must foster and maintain unity, or at least cooperation, within organizations and coalitions. Leaders must recognize that competing organizations have their own beliefs about what must be done, who must do it, and how it must be done. Leaders are decision makers with limited legitimacy and limited powers to reward and punish while constantly facing conflicting demands from within and without. They are the symbols, the faces, of their movements in the eyes of members, sympathizers, legitimizers, countermovements, and institutions.

Leaders lead because they possess one or more of three critical attributes—charisma, prophecy, and pragmatism. Charisma allows leaders to inspire by leading followers to see the truth, to imagine what might be, to see themselves as a people, and to dare to demand change in the face of real danger. Prophecy allows leaders to lead because of their connection to the writings of the movement, their knowledge of movement truths, and their ability to set a moral tone. Pragmatism allows a leader to lead through organizational expertise, efficiency, and tact. Effective social movement leaders possess two or more of these critical attributes through which they enable followers to see themselves not as individuals but as a people, to form relational patterns, to employ adaptive strategies, and to achieve evolutionary results.

Attaining leadership positions within social movements is easier than maintaining positions in a constantly changing environment. Leaders must sustain an appropriate blend of the three critical attributes (charisma, prophecy, and pragmatism), handle diverse and conflicting roles, change as the movement changes, adapt to events, and lead without getting too far ahead or too far behind their followers. Although a few leaders have led social movement organizations for decades, most lead for a few years and then fade away because they cannot sustain organizations over time or adapt to changes demanded by the movement and the environment.

Notes

[1] Eric Hoffer, *The True Believer* (New York: Mentor, 1951): 119–138; Sherry R. Shepler and Anne F. Mattina, "'Revolt Against War': Jane Addams' Rhetorical Challenge to the Patriarchy," *Communication Quarterly* 47 (Spring 1999): 151–165.

[2] Roberta Ash, *Social Movements in America* (Chicago: Markham, 1972): 40.

[3] John Wilson, *Introduction to Social Movements* (New York: Basic Books, 1973): 78.

[4] "Trying to Take Back the Planet," *Newsweek,* 5 February 1990, 24.

[5] Bonnie J. Dow, "Spectacle, Spectatorship, and Gender Anxiety in Television Coverage of the 1970 Women's Strike for Equality," *Communication Studies* 50 (Summer 1999): 152-153.

[6] Hoffer, 58.

[7] Bill Yousman, "Who Owns Identity: Malcolm X, Representation, and the Struggle Over Meaning," *Communication Quarterly* 49 (Winter 2001): 5, 8.

[8] Herbert W. Simons, "Persuasion in Social Conflicts: A Critique of Prevailing Conceptions and a Framework for Future Research," *Speech Monographs* 39 (November 1972): 236.

[9] Crane Brinton, *The Anatomy of Revolution* (New York: Vintage Books, 1952): 107; Ming T. Lee, "The Founders of the Chinese Communist Party," *Civilisations* 18 (1968): 115; Seymour Lipset, "Leadership and New Social Movements," *Studies in Leadership,* Alvin Gouldner, ed. (New York: Harper and Row, 1950): 360.

[10] Brinton, 127.

[11] Myra Marx Ferree, "The Political Context of Reality: Rational Choice Theory and Resource Mobilization," *Frontiers in Social Movement Theory,* Aldon D. Morris and Carol McClurg Mueller, eds. (New Haven, CT: Yale University Press, 1992): 48.

[12] *The Gray Panther Manual* (Philadelphia: The Gray Panthers, 1978): 3–4; *Maggie Kuhn on Aging*, Dieter Hessel, ed. (Philadelphia: Westminster Press, 1977): 9–12.

[13] Steven R. Goldzwig, "A Social Movement Perspective on Demagoguery: Achieving Symbolic Realignment," *Communication Studies* 40 (Fall 1989): 202–228.

[14] Kirkpatrick Sale, *SDS* (New York: Vintage Books, 1974): 499–500, 541–544, 551–557, 643–645.

[15] Bonnie J. Dow, "Fixing Feminism: Women's Liberation and the Rhetoric of Television Documentary," *Quarterly Journal of Speech* 90 (February 2004): 56.

[16] Anthony Oberschall, "The Los Angeles Riot," *Social Problems* 15 (Winter 1965): 324–326.

[17] Herbert W. Simons, "Requirements, Problems, and Strategies: A Theory of Persuasion for Social Movements," *Quarterly Journal of Speech* 56 (February 1970): 4.

[18] Anthony Oberschall, *Social Conflict and Social Movements* (Englewood Cliffs, NJ: Prentice-Hall, 1973): 148–149. See also William A. Gamson, "The Social Psychology of Collective Action," *Frontiers in Social Movement Theory*, Aldon D. Morris and Carol McClurg Mueller, eds. (New Haven, CT: Yale University Press, 1992): 53–60; Ferree, 38–43.

[19] Susan Zaeske, "Signatures of Citizenship: The Rhetoric of Women's Antislavery Petitions," *Quarterly Journal of Speech* 88 (May 2002): 161.

[20] Wilson, 198.

[21] Simons, "Requirements, Problems, and Strategies," 4.

[22] Lisa S. Hogan and Michael Hogan, "Feminine Virtue and Practical Wisdom: Elizabeth Cady Stanton's 'Our Boys,'" *Rhetoric & Public Affairs* 6 (Fall 2003): 416, 425.

[23] *The Gray Panther Manual*, 5.

[24] Saul D. Alinsky, *Rules for Radicals: A Pragmatic Primer for Realistic Radicals* (New York: Vintage Books, 1972): 72–79.

[25] *The Gray Panther Manual*, 6.

[26] "Operation Rescue," on ABC's *20/20*.

[27] Pat Jefferson, "The Magnificent Barbarian at Nashville," *Southern Speech Journal* 33 (Winter 1967): 81; Dencil R. Taylor, "Carmichael in Tallahassee," *Southern Speech Journal* 33 (Winter 1967): 92.

[28] Alinsky, 76.

[29] Clayborne Carson, ed. *The Autobiography of Martin Luther King, Jr.* (New York: Warner Books, 1998): 168.

[30] Joseph R. Gusfield, "Functional Areas of Leadership in Social Movements," *Sociological Quarterly* 7 (1966): 137.

[31] Simons, "Requirements, Problems, and Strategies," 4.

[32] Charles J. Stewart, "The Internal Rhetoric of the Knights of Labor," *Communication Studies* 42 (Spring 1991): 67–82.

[33] Ray Ginger, *The Bending Cross* (New Brunswick, NJ: Rutgers University Press, 1949): 106.

[34] Gusfield, 141.

[35] Cartoons Mike Peters.

[36] Simons, "Requirements, Problems, and Strategies," 2–3.

[37] Max Weber, *The Theory of Social and Economic Organizations*, A.M. Henderson and Talcott Parsons, trans. (New York: Free Press, 1964): 328–329; Wilson, 201.

[38] William Bruce Cameron, *Modern Social Movements* (New York: Random House, 1966): 73.

[39] Richard J. Jensen and John C. Hammerback, eds. *The Words of Cesar Chavez* (College Station: Texas A & M University Press, 2002): xxvi–xxvii.

[40] Kenelm Burridge, *New Heaven New Earth: A Study of Millenarian Activities* (Oxford: Basil Blackwell, 1969): 155.

[41] Richard J. Jensen and John C. Hammerback, "Radical Nationalism among Chicanos: The Rhetoric of Jose Angel Gutierrez," *Western Journal of Speech Communication* 44 (Summer 1980): 202.

[42] J. Michael Hogan and Glen Williams, "Republican Charisma and the American Revolution: The Textual Persona of Thomas Paine's *Common Sense*," *Quarterly Journal of Speech* 86 (February 2000): 2.

[43] [William L. Pierce] Andrew Macdonald, *The Turner Diaries,* 2nd ed. (New York: Barricade Books, 1978).

[44] Allen H. Merriam, "Symbolic Action in India: Gandhi's Nonverbal Persuasion," *Quarterly Journal of Speech* 61 (October 1975): 290–306.

[45] [William L. Pierce] Andrew Macdonald, *The Turner Diaries.*

[46] *Moral Majority of Kentucky Fighting For a Moral America In the Decade of Destiny* (Louisville: Moral Majority of Kentucky, n.d.): n.p.

[47] *The Blue Book of the John Birch Society* (Belmont, MA: Western Islands, 1961): xiv–xv.

[48] "The John Birch Society: A Report," *Arizona Republic,* advertising supplement, 25 October 1964, 6.

[49] *American Opinion* (October 1978): 56.

[50] "The John Birch Society: A Report," *Chicago Tribune,* advertising supplement, 15 November 1964, 16.

[51] Walter B. Emery, "Samuel Gompers," *A History and Criticism of American Public Address,* Vol. II, William Norwood Brigance, ed. (New York: Russell and Russell, 1960): 557–559.

[52] James Green, *Death in the Haymarket: A Story of Chicago, the First Labor Movement and the Bombing that Divided Gilded Age America* (New York: Pantheon Books, 2006), p. 11.

[53] Green, 11.

[54] http://www.chicagohistory.org/dramas/epilogue/epilogue.htm, accessed 7 August 2006.

[55] Samuel Gompers, *American Federation of Labor Proceedings,* 1903, 198.

[56] Cameron, 164.

[57] Gusfield, 139, 141.

[58] Wilson, 198, 201; Oberschall, 146.

[59] Adam Fairclough, *To Redeem the Soul of America: The Southern Christian Leadership Conference and Martin Luther King, Jr.* (Athens: University of Georgia Press, 1987): 316.

[60] Charles J. Stewart, "The Evolution of a Revolution: Stokely Carmichael and the Rhetoric of Black Power," *Quarterly Journal of Speech* 83 (November 1997): 434.

[61] From an audio recording; and Robert L. Scott and Wayne Brockriede, *The Rhetoric of Black Power* (New York: Harper and Row, 1969): 88–89.

[62] Cameron, 93.

[63] Simons, "Requirements, Problems, and Strategies," 1–11.

[64] "Roe's Army Reloads," *Newsweek,* 8 August 2005, 27.

[65] Gusfield, 152.

[66] Jerry Rubin, "Growing Up Again," *Human Behavior,* March 1976, 17–23.

[67] Shepler and Mattina, 151–165.

[68] Charles J. Stewart, "Labor Agitation in America: 1865–1915," *America in Controversy: History of American Public Address,* DeWitte T. Holland, ed. (Dubuque, IA: W.C. Brown, 1973): 153–169.

[69] James R. Sovereign, "Annual Address of the General Master Workman," *Proceedings of the General Assembly: Knights of Labor,* 1894, 71.

[70] Cameron, 107.

[71] Thomas W. Benson, "Rhetoric and Autobiography: The Case of Malcolm X," *Quarterly Journal of Speech* 60 (February 1974): 1–13.

[72] "The Real Malcolm X," CBS Video, 1992.

[73] Yousman, 11.

[74] Benson, 7, 9, 10, 12. See also Robert E. Terrill, "Colonizing the Borderlands: Shifting Circumference in the Rhetoric of Malcolm X," *Quarterly Journal of Speech* 86 (February 2000): 67–85.

[75] Gusfield, 142–145.

[76] *Annual Report of the National Women's Christian Temperance Union,* 1952, 85.

CHAPTER 6

Personal Needs and Social Movements
John Birchers and Gray Panthers

Although social movements are characterized by minimal organization, they are the products of collaborative individual behaviors. Like universities, corporations, and political campaigns, movements are always recruiting and consolidating. Without recruitment there are no members, and without consolidation individuals do not constitute a group or social movement. But all potential members are not equally attractive to recruiters. For example, different parts of different universities are attracted to seven-foot rebounders, concert violinists, and National Merit Scholars; and each of those recruits will find university life differentially appealing.

The interpretive systems approach presented in chapter 2 discussed the relationships among personal needs, preferences, symbols and reasoning and their social counterparts: laws, ideologies, languages, and logics. This chapter extends that discussion to demonstrate how John Birch Society and Gray Panther rhetoric spoke to potential recruits in ways that appealed to the kinds of people the movements could most easily consolidate while alienating those who would not "fit in." The gratifications offered were primarily psychological rather than political, social, or philosophical. More specifically, John Birch Society materials spoke directly to the needs of a classic authoritarian character structure and Gray Panther materials spoke to a democratic character structure.

AUTHORITARIAN AND DEMOCRATIC PERSONALITIES

The Nazi era in Germany spurred many social psychologists to explore the sources of Hitler's appeal. One of their earliest hypotheses centered on authoritarian personality types. Clinical studies of persons deemed to exhibit tendencies of this authoritarian character structure led Theodor Adorno and his colleagues to introduce their California F-Scale for the measurement of fascist tendencies in 1950. This early work was directed at understanding rightist authoritarianism, and they concentrated on the study of followers' beliefs about authority and those who exercise it. In the 1960s, Milton Rokeach steered psychological research toward the study of "topic free" open- and closed-mindedness, and interest in ideological authoritarianism waned.[1]

One of the earliest studies of authoritarian personality remains especially helpful for understanding how messages provide audiences with psychological gratifications. Abraham Maslow's 1943 essay on "The Authoritarian Character"[2] synthesizes clinical observations about verbal expressions—an approach that lends itself to analyzing other verbal expressions. The essay discusses two archetypal personality structures that have social, political, and rhetorical implications: authoritarian and democratic character structures.

Maslow's Authoritarian Character Structure

In the authoritarian character structure, everything revolves around authority. In the authoritarian worldview the world is a jungle that requires both strict hierarchical organization and the glorification of dominance and submission. The fundamental premise of the authoritarian worldview is that life is essentially threatening. Maslow explains:

> Like other psychologically insecure people, the authoritarian person lives in a world which may be conceived to be pictured by him as a sort of jungle in which every man's [woman's] hand is necessarily against every other man's [woman's], in which the whole world is conceived of as dangerous, threatening, or at least challenging, and in which humans are conceived of as primarily selfish or evil or stupid. . . . This jungle is peopled with animals who either eat or are eaten, who are either feared or despised. One's safety lies in one's own strength, and this strength consists primarily in the power to dominate. If one is not strong enough the only alternative is to find a strong protector.[3]

Because danger is all around, the protector-protected relationship predominates. Protectors demand total obedience; and because the protected need protectors, their submission is willing and sometimes ecstatic.

Authoritarian characters express contempt and hostility for those who fail to recognize the world's dangers because that contributes to the endangerment of protected parties. With danger lurking at every turn, Maslow's authoritarian characters know that each approaching creature must immediately be recognized and categorized either as superior (and thus to be feared, resented, bootlicked, and admired) or as inferior (and thus to be scorned, humiliated, and dominated). Each must be instantly ranked in a hierarchy from strongest to weakest. The authoritarian therefore struggles with diverse goals and measures, because speed and unity are essential for survival. All people, achievements, and events are measured on one scale—the scale of survival. Different authoritarians may stress different scales—such as strength, speed, or cunning—but Maslow argued that no authoritarian character could value diversity or tolerance because multiple scales confound superior-inferior ranking and thus compound the danger to all. A person judged superior is judged *universally superior;* inferiors are judged *universally inferior.* Judgments of superiority are made quickly. External characteristics that signal ranking on the superior-inferior scale include titles, physical stature and grooming, wealth, family name, race, gender, age, or behavior.

The authoritarian character structure regards any leader's kindness as weakness. Maslow wrote the following passage sixty years ago, so the language uses the masculine pronoun, but his assessment applies equally to male or female authoritarians.

> If he is in dominance status, he will tend to be cruel; if he is in subordinate status, he will tend to be masochistic. But because of the tendencies in himself, he will understand, and deep down within himself will agree with the cruelty of the superior person, even if he himself is the object of the cruelty. He will understand the bootlicker and the slave even if he himself is not the bootlicker or the slave. The same principles explain both the leader and the follower in an authoritarian group, both the slave owner and the slave.[4]

Significantly, authoritarian followers glory in their subservience to the leader. Among authoritarians there can be no negotiation of control because neither party finds negotiations valid or productive. Both realize that the worthless inferior is fortunate to have the dominating protector, and both realize that the protector feels little but contempt for the inferior.

Because the authoritarian character structure regards people as fundamentally selfish, evil, stupid, and dependent, the superior can use inferiors as the superior sees fit. Non-leaders may be seen as subhuman, characterized as "tools" or "pawns on a chessboard." This sadomasochistic tendency contributes to an authoritarian value system in which brutality, cruelty, selfishness, and hardness are exalted and in which sympathy, kindness, and generosity are reviled by leaders and followers alike.

Maslow lists other characteristics of authoritarianism that deserve attention. These include an "abyss between men and women" (men purportedly being able to survive better through strength), the soldier ideal, the importance of humiliation as a mechanism for establishing superiority, antagonism toward the education of inferiors, avoidance of responsibility for one's own fate, and the pursuit of security through order, discipline, and a variety of behaviors generally regarded as obsessive-compulsive. Pervading all of these characteristics is the impossibility of satisfaction. The best one can hope for in the jungle is temporary relief from constant danger; one must be most careful when the jungle seems safest.

Maslow's Democratic Character Structure

Maslow's democratic character sees the world as a basically friendly and supportive place, more greenhouse than jungle. Because there is little danger, there is little need for protection and, therefore, little need for submission, discipline, or obedience. Whereas the authoritarian character sees all differences between people in terms of superiority/inferiority, the democratic character views differences between people as largely independent of superiority and inferiority. When superiority-inferiority judgments must be made, the democratic character judges individuals in specific functional terms by appraising specific personal capabilities, functions, and performances. The democratic personality prefers to judge others, if they judge at all, on the basis of performance. As Maslow explained (again, in the gender-specific language of the time), the democratic character "customarily gives his permanent respect only to people who are worthy of respect for functional reasons. He doesn't give his respect automatically simply because he is supposed to, or because everybody else respects this person."[5] The democratic character examines functional characteristics, adjudicates them (as necessary) according to diverse values, and creates a leader-follower relationship (when necessary) for the attainment of a specific goal.

The democratic character views humans as colleagues or partners rather than rivals. The democratic structure does not use or manipulate people. It exhibits no tendency comparable to the sadomasochism of authoritarians. There is room for both selfishness and generosity, for hardness and compassion since different people value differently in different circumstances at different times. Democratic character types can be happier for longer periods of time because their basic needs have been satisfied. Danger is unusual, rather than normal, in everyday life.

Maslow observes that the authoritarian and democratic character types are constructions of internally consistent beliefs or tendencies, all of which revolve around the premise that the world is (or is not) an extremely threatening and dangerous place. They are frameworks for interpreting one's environment. Individuals interpret their worlds in ways that fit their psychological needs and enable them to coordinate their lives with others. The psychological makeup of both character structures suggests a tendency to find or create like-minded people. Theoretically, authoritarian leaders should be telling people about dangers, and authoritarian followers should be listening for good protectors. Democratic leaders ought to empower people, and democratic followers ought to develop functional relationships to work on problems. We find such tendencies in the discourse of the John Birch Society and the Gray Panthers.

TWO SOCIAL MOVEMENT ORGANIZATIONS

The John Birch Society and the Gray Panthers were begun by people who had found personal, professional, and financial satisfaction through institutions. Both organizations were comprised of people worried about trends they saw in U.S. society, but they engaged in very different kinds of rhetoric and attracted very different followers.

The John Birch Society

The John Birch Society was founded in 1958 as a secret, activist, anticommunist organization by Robert H. W. Welch, a retired candy company executive and former official of the National Association of Manufacturers.[6] Welch wanted a cadre of dedicated and disciplined patriots to help him take back the United States from the communists. Welch's central fear was communist domination. But unlike anticommunists with democratic character structures who watched the Kremlin and opposed communist expansion with foreign aid and military assistance, Welch maintained that most nations (including the United States) were ruled secretly by communists who had infiltrated and subverted their governments. He did not want a large organization because large organizations are difficult to discipline. He opposed the military programs that most anticommunists supported to oppose the Soviet Union, characterizing them as secret communist efforts to wreck the U.S. economy and to distract patriotic Americans from the "real" danger—communist subversion. For many years, he published an annual rating of the percentage of communist control over every nation in the world.

The John Birch Society was active and highly visible during the early 1960s with efforts to impeach Chief Justice Earl Warren, to prevent fluoridation of water supplies, and to "Get US out of the UN." Conventional wisdom holds that the John Birch Society disintegrated in the mid-1960s as a consequence of two phenomena. The first of these was the 1964 defeat of Senator Barry Goldwater—a presidential campaign in which the Birch Society was highly active and visible. The second was the belief dilemma posed for Birchers by the antiwar protests of the 1960s: Birchers opposed both the Vietnam war (as an effort by American communists to squander our national resources) and antiwar protestors of virtually all political stripes (as communist-inspired troublemakers).[7] As the Birch Society's visibility diminished, the public and scholars alike inferred that the Society had become insignificant.

But the John Birch Society did not disband in the mid-1960s; it simply evolved into a new phase. This was evident in the circulation of its two publications: *The John Birch Society Bulletin* (a monthly publication for members) and *American Opinion* (later *The New American*). The circulation of each periodical was virtually the same in 1979–1981 as it had been during the peak years of 1963–1965. Indeed, the mailed circulation of the members-only *Bulletin* was 50 percent greater in 1981 than any known previous estimate of the Society's membership.[8]

The John Birch Society might better have been called the Robert Welch Society, for Welch was its founder and autocratic leader until his death in 1985. The group's ideology was set forth in its manual, *The Blue Book of the John Birch Society*, which consisted of a series of lectures Welch delivered at the organization's founding in Indianapolis in 1958.[9] The Society's Web site (www.jbs.org) includes a heading called "Research." Clicking on "Books," followed by "The John Birch Society," brings you to "The Blue Book," which can be read online. Welch's picture appears in the "About Us" section more than 20 years after his death.

The Gray Panthers

The group that became known as the Gray Panthers began in March of 1970 at a New York City luncheon of six women approaching forced retirement from careers of public service. The luncheon was called by Margaret Kuhn, coordinator of programs in the United Presbyterian Church, Division of Church and Race, and associate secretary in the Office of Church and Society. Others included Eleanore French (director of the student division of the YWCA), Helen Smith (director of the Division of the Laity of the United Church of Christ), Polly Cuthberson (director of the American Friends Service Committee College Program), Ann Bennett (a religious educator and member of the Student Christian Peace Movement), and Helen Baker (a former editor of *Churchwomen* and a United Nations reporter). They decided that they would not let forced retirement keep them from improving social conditions.

The women continued to meet, and each used her large network of personal and professional acquaintances to find new members. Although their primary concern was ageism (discrimination on the basis of chronological age), their goals and priorities expanded to include "justice, freedom, and dignity for and with the oppressed" and "alternative lifestyles and opportunities for older and younger people which will eliminate paternalism, discrimination, segregation and oppression."[11] Their specific short-term goals included guaranteed employment for everyone wanting to work, a guaranteed annual income, greater participation in national decision making, radical tax reform to plug loopholes, and a drastic cut in military spending. Today the Gray Panthers Web site (www.graypanthers.org) indicates that they are active in health care reform and discrimination on the basis of age, race, and gender.

Maggie Kuhn emerged as the Gray Panthers' most visible leader until her death in 1995. Unlike Robert Welch, she was far from autocratic. On the third of August, the Panthers organization observes her birthday by celebrating "her tenacity, vision, and commitment to the Gray Panthers and to social and economic justice and peace."[12]

The Gray Panthers developed networks of local groups that stressed local autonomy and independent actions. Although relatively low in public visibility as a social movement organization, their Web site's issues page is tuned to current, pressing concerns. Health care tops their agenda, with specific calls for public action to "create and fund a single-payer, nonprofit and universal health care system; to regulate health maintenance organizations comprehensively, for the protection of patients and health care providers."[13] They also support scientifically-based sex education and legalized medical marijuana.

The Gray Panthers list a number of issues regarding what they call family security:

1. Oppose all efforts to limit or reduce Social Security programs

2. Prevent shortfalls to the Social Security system without destructive changes

3. Expand housing opportunities for low income persons

4. Undo the damage done by "welfare reform" and restore benefits to all in need . . .

7. Support utility subsidies for low-income persons[14]

The Gray Panthers react to the dangers of the world by seeking solutions rather than obedience. If we face increasing risk of illness, they reason, we need a way to provide affordable health care. If winters are cold and utilities are expensive, worry less about oil conspiracies and more about helping poor people pay their utility bills.

In short, the ideology and organizational style of the Gray Panthers reflect the characteristics of Maslow's democratic character structure. A person with the characteristics of Maslow's authoritarian character structure would have great difficulty with the Panthers' discourse. Certainly, people might want their Social Security benefits protected, but they would be frustrated by the lack of visible leadership and discipline, by the inattention to judging dangerous others, and by the faith in public policies.

THE AUTHORITARIAN CHARACTER OF JOHN BIRCH SOCIETY PERSUASION

The central arguments of the John Birch Society address all of the psychological needs of the authoritarian character while alienating those of the democratic character. By analyzing the core ideology expressed in *The Blue Book of the John Birch Society*[15] for evidence of authoritarianism and democratic character, we can see how the Society was built around its leader. This enabled Welch, as the protector, to reconcile belief dilemmas for his followers and to increase their dependence on him.

The Birch World as Jungle

The theme of the *Blue Book* was the danger of subversive communism. Welch claimed that if people were not aroused to that danger, they would soon be hanging from the same lamp posts while communist terror reigned. He told readers:

> The truth I bring you is simple, incontrovertible and deadly. It is that, unless we can reverse forces which now seem inexorable in their movement, you have only a few more years before the country in which you live will become separate provinces in a worldwide Communist dominion ruled by police-state methods from the Kremlin. (p. 1)

But unlike most other anticommunists, Welch regarded the danger as neither Soviet aggression nor nuclear war, but subversion. Lenin's strategy, he said:

> is taking us over by a process so gradual and insidious that Soviet rule is slipped over so far on the American people, before they ever realize it is happening, that they can no longer resist the Communist conspiracy as free citizens. This subversion comes from a gigantic conspiracy to enslave mankind; an increasingly successful conspiracy controlled by determined, cunning, and utterly ruthless gangsters, willing to go to any means to achieve its end. (p. 21)

These conspirators were "like an octopus so large that its tentacles now reach into all of the legislative halls, all of the union labor meetings, a majority of the religious gatherings, and most of the schools of the whole world" (p. 60). Welch continued: "The human race has never before faced any such monster of power which has determined to enslave it. There is certainly no reason for underrating its size, its efficiency, its determination, its power, or its menace" (p. 61). The John Birch Society's world was a dangerous place.

The worldview of the Society stressed constant, imminent, hidden, ruthless danger. It is difficult to read their material without experiencing a sense of duress, but each of us adapts to duress differently. The prototypical democratic character rejects the argument's central premise, perhaps rejecting valid arguments along with invalid ones. But the authoritarian character structure is inclined to recognize the fundamental theme and to read on. Having accepted the premise that an illusive, dangerous conspiracy is afoot, an authoritarian character must find a protector.

The Birch Tendency toward Autocracy

The authoritarian character of the John Birch Society's argument becomes more evident when we examine Welch's alternative to communist enslavement. The democratic character type would want to fight communist enslavement with a cooperative effort based on functional abilities, while the authoritarian would look for leadership and protection. Welch dismissed democracy as "merely a deceptive phrase, a weapon of demagoguery, and a perennial fraud" (p. 147). He observed that a republican form of government had "many attractions and advantages, under certain favorable circumstances . . . but it lends itself too readily to infiltration, distortion and disruption" (p. 146). That left autocracy: "The John Birch Society is to be a monolithic body [that] will operate under completely authoritative control at all levels" (pp. 146–147). This autocratic structure was necessary because "no collection of debating societies is ever going to stop the Communist conspiracy from taking us over" (p. 147).

Welch's autocratic structure did not tolerate negotiations over control. The Society, he said, "cannot stop for parliamentary procedures or a lot of arguments among ourselves" because "we are now being more and more divided and deceived, by accepting within our walls more and more Trojan horses" (p. 147). Therefore, "we are not going to have factions developing on the two-sides-to-every-question theme" (p. 149). Thus, Welch offered his readers the prototypical authoritarian solution for danger: a strict autocratic relationship.

But the Society's hierarchy was not simply Welch above the membership. He explained that the Society

> will function almost entirely through small local chapters, usually of from ten to twenty dedicated patriots. . . . Each will have a Chapter Leader appointed by headquarters . . . or appointed by officers in the field who have themselves been duly appointed by headquarters. (p. 51)

Welch's description of the John Birch Society's organizational structure emphasized the danger of the world, a need for a clearly ordered hierarchy in which all authority would flow down from the Belmont, Massachusetts, headquarters to the local chapters, and intolerance for dissension and democratic procedures. Even if a person with a democratic character structure wanted to heed Welch's alarm, such a person would be psychologically repelled from the Society by its rigid, monolithic, autocratic structure. But an alarmed authoritarian would seek precisely Welch's sort of autocracy for protection.

A second manifestation of the authoritarian tendency toward hierarchy was the Society's generalization of superiority from external characteristics. The reader of the *Blue Book* is introduced to all 26 members of the Council by their positions: they include a "Boston surgeon," a "worthy son of a famous 'free enterpriser' in the Northwest lumber industry," a "well-known and highly successful Texas businessman," and several corporate, religious, and military figures (p. 172). Not only did Welch fail to indicate the specific, functional relevance of their credentials to an understanding of communism or conspiracies for the benefit of any democratic characters in his audience, but he stated explicitly that the primary purpose of the Council was "to show [potential members] the stature and standing of the leadership of the Society" (p. 172). Stature and standing are important to the authoritarian, but not to the democratic character structure unless they are functionally relevant to the task at hand. Again, the rhetorical depiction of the Council could attract authoritarians but not democrats.

In addition to stature, the John Birch Society generalized superiority based on one's willingness to acknowledge the danger and the solution (in this case, Birchism). Others were judged by their agreement or disagreement with Welch. Historian Oswald Spengler's work fit "the known facts of history," while Arnold Toynbee was a "meretricious hack . . . who is one of the worst charlatans that ever lived" (p. 34). Presidents Roosevelt, Truman, and Eisenhower were all judged to have helped communism because Welch disagreed with them.[16] Among prominent conservatives of the time, Barry Goldwater and Ronald Reagan were applauded because they understood, while William F. Buckley and Russell Kirk were chastised because they did not.[17] Such pronouncements isolated members from the kind of two-sides-to every-question controversy that Welch disdained. Welch stressed safety through autocracy rather than safety through conservatism.

Birchist Sadomasochism

The *Blue Book* is replete with references to communists' sadistic treatment of their followers. We are told of the communists' "police state features" that imposed "brutal rule" and "slavery" upon "party members who are wholly subservient" (pp. 20, 17, 28, 60). This was important because communism "has been imposed and must always be imposed, from the top down, by trickery and terror; and then it must be maintained by terror" (p. 61). This terror was directed not only at the slaves but at recalcitrant party members themselves who "are shot in some dark alley or pushed off a subway platform in front of a moving train" (p. 162). Given this alarming picture of sadistic communist rule, the democratic character type might reasonably have expected Welch to offer an alternative of kindness rather than brutality, of cooperation rather than slavery, of participation rather than subservience, and of bottom-up rather than top-down organization.

But Welch's alternative to sadistic communist domination was the Birch Society's organizational structure that mirrored the communist monolith. The Society is ordered from the top down, with members obeying official directives and subject to removal for noncompliance. Indeed, Welch observed that:

> the biggest of all organizational mistakes is to set up a local group for some continuing purpose, exhort them to do a good job, and then leave them alone to do it. It is the leadership that is most demanding, most exacting of its followers, not the one which asks the least and is afraid to ask more, that achieves really dedicated support. (p. 72)

Contrast conservative-authoritarian Welch's organizational philosophy with that of conservative-democratic Ronald Reagan, who once said: "Surround yourself with the best people you can find, delegate authority, and don't interfere as long as the policy you've decided upon is being carried out."[18] The difference between Welch and Reagan stemmed less from differences in their conservatism than from their differing conceptions of authority. In true sadomasochistic fashion, Welch stressed the leader's responsibility to push his selfish, lazy, and stupid followers to their limits and the followers' ecstatic submission to that direction. It is important that Welch argued not only that such leadership was effective but that it encouraged "really dedicated support" rather than defection or mutiny. These tendencies are unlike anything in the democratic character structure.

Thus, the *Blue Book* suggested supplanting communist domination with Welch's domination until the quantity of government could be drastically reduced and a largely anarchistic polity created in which strength and protection would determine survival.[19] The Birch program functioned psychologically for those of authoritarian character and was dysfunctional for democratic character types, who preferred partnerships. The important point is that Welch's analysis paralleled the psychological continuum of authoritarianism rather than the political continuum running from freedom to control.

A second manifestation of the Birch Society's sadomasochism was the pattern of gratifications it afforded members for following Welch. Whereas democratic character types look for functional, practical benefits, the authoritarian character type seeks submission to a protector. In this regard, Welch announced:

> The men [women] who join the John Birch Society during the next few months or few years are going to be doing so primarily because they believe in me and in what I am doing. . . . And we are going to use that [personal loyalty], like every other resource, to the fullest advantage that we can. (p. 149)

Even the criterion for continued membership was loyal submission: "those members who cease to feel the necessary degree of loyalty can either resign or will be put out before they can build up any splintering following of their own inside the Society" (p. 149).

But on what basis was the potential Bircher expected to develop this deep personal loyalty to Welch? He explained his credentials as follows:

> With all my shortcomings, there wasn't anybody else on the horizon willing to give their whole lives to the job, with the determination and dedication I would put into it. . . . Whatever I have in me, of faith, dedication, energy, I intend to offer that leadership to all who are willing to help me. (pp. 114–115)

Put simply, others might have had better functional credentials for fighting communists, but one should attach oneself to Robert Welch (and only to him) because he alone was obsessed with this mission. The quantity of work and the obsessive-compulsive drive to spend himself thoroughly were regarded as more important than either the kind or quality of work, or the efficiency or prudence of the effort.

Welch's demand for personal loyalty on the basis of his obsession is all the more startling when we recognize that his practical, functional credentials were quite impressive. But the reader of the *Blue Book* learned neither that Welch had studied at the University of North Carolina, the U.S. Naval Academy, and Harvard Law School nor that he had written a primer on salesmanship and served in various official capacities for the National Association of Manufacturers. These seemingly pertinent facts were not divulged until a short postscript to the second printing of the *Blue Book*. The point is that Welch, a master salesman, could have sold his leadership to democratic characters by stressing his functional expertise. Instead, he emphasized (whether intentionally or not) his energy, his commitment, his constant reading of communist materials, and his willingness to exercise authority, dominance, and control—a package highly attractive to authoritarian character types.

Maslow explained that authoritarians revel in superior-inferior relationships. Inferiors know that they deserve to be controlled, while superiors find temporary satisfaction in the exercise of control. This theme pervaded *The Blue Book of the John Birch Society* as Welch condemned communist control and offered only his own control as the alternative. He sold the necessity for "dynamic, personal leadership" and personal loyalty based primarily on his compulsive-obsessive efforts and his readiness to punish those of dubious loyalty rather than on the basis of his notable, and apparently relevant, credentials. Potential members were asked to join the John Birch Society not because it would succeed, not because its tactics were well conceived, not because they could participate in it or shape its direction, but because they wanted to be personally loyal to Robert Welch.

Welch built the John Birch Society around members' personal loyalty to him, his dedication to identify and combat an illusive conspiracy with an autocratic style that would tolerate neither discussion nor parliamentary procedure, such that anyone quibbling with its leader, Welch, would be summarily expelled. How well did this work for them? One of the key voices of the Birch Society was Revilo Oliver, a classics professor at the University of Illinois. In 1966 Professor Oliver charged that Welch was controlled by "Jews" and that the entire Birch Society operation was an effort to distract real conservatives from the danger of International Zionism and Communism. Not surprisingly, Oliver was expelled from the Birch Society. But the Birch Society at that point began to talk about the conspiracy of "insiders" rather than mere communists. Later, John "Birdman" Bryant, a member of the Birch Society's more recent board, left the Society and his Web site renews Professor Oliver's charges against Welch. But the process of exposure need not stop there. Bryant charges that current Birch President John McManus is a Zionist and asks why the Birch Society continues to ignore the Jewish conspiracy. How did McManus respond? That is not entirely clear, because he was occupied writing a book alleging that the venerable William F. Buckley, Jr., was never really a conservative but, instead, a tool of Eastern Jewish liberals. And so it goes. The authoritarian character structure must be ever vigilant, for Welch's "principle of reversal" held that everything is the opposite of what it appears to be. The leader who rides this kind of premise is bound to be attacked by a string of followers who learn to use it themselves.

In summary, *The Blue Book of the John Birch Society* depicted a dangerous, threatening world in which ruthless conspirators were everywhere. Thus, the John Birch Society exemplified all three major characteristics of the authoritarian character structure: a view of the world as a threatening place, a tendency toward hierarchy, and a sadomasochistic tendency.

THE DEMOCRATIC CHARACTER OF GRAY PANTHER PERSUASION

As the ideology of the John Birch Society spoke to the needs of the authoritarian character structure, the ideology of the Gray Panthers spoke to the needs of the democratic character structure. Gray Panthers viewed the world not as a jungle but as an environment that people had created and could reshape if they tried. They advocated not a strict vertical hierarchy but a nearly flat organizational structure that valued local autonomy and independent action. Finally, the Gray Panthers opposed dominance and submission, which they regarded as paternalistic. Instead, their goal was to empower persons of all ages.[20]

The Gray Panthers' World as Rational but Misguided

The world described by Gray Panthers was not an especially threatening place, but it needed improvement. Potential members had lived in the world for six decades or more, and most of them had prospered sufficiently to devote their retirement years to social activism. The Gray Panthers originated in response to forced retirement:

> At this magic age of 65, the "golden ager," alias senior citizen, is expected to settle down into a benign twilight of small deeds and trivial sentiments, unhampered by any interests more profound than crocheting, trout fishing, and bingo games. . . . [The Gray Panthers were organized by six professional women, of whom none] was the least bit impressed by crocheting, trout fishing, or bingo. Their lives had been too active for them to willingly fade away. Each devoted the whole of her adult life to social service and social change; concern and commitment was part of them. (p. 3)

These women were not people who had lived in fear or under the protective custody of autocratic leaders. Instead, the women who founded the Gray Panthers had lived professional lives that had accustomed them to altering prevailing social conditions. Had they regarded the world as a jungle, they would have sought ways to lessen the dangers so that citizens could lead their lives without fear or shame. They viewed dangers and problems as challenges to be addressed, not as permanent environmental conditions to be feared.

Nevertheless, the world perceived by the Gray Panthers was far from perfect. Panthers were concerned most by the "societal illness" of ageism: "an arbitrary discrimination on the basis of chronological age, [that] permeates Western culture and our institutions. Such discrimination is harmful to all age groups" (p. 16). Because of ageism, older people had been made to feel ashamed of their appearance and the breadth of their experiences, and they were made to feel powerless and socially useless. Gray Panthers identified with other people who perceived themselves as powerless and sought to empower them all.

The world of the Gray Panthers also differed markedly from the world of the John Birchers because they regarded the world as amenable to change. Their 146-page *Manual* devoted nearly 70 pages to methods for effecting social change. Section V explained how to organize a Gray Panther network with tips on building a constituency, planning the first meeting, holding the first meeting, selecting local officers, developing leadership, fund-raising, projects, and programs. Section VI covered "organizing issues" with suggestions on setting an objective, identifying goals, examples of successes, and even a "social action checklist." Section VII explained organizational strategies, tools for action, and resources. It covered planning for action, legislative advocacy, lobbying, advocacy with respect to administrative agencies, litigation, public hearings, and public relations. All of these suggestions presumed that the legal and administrative system could be made to work more democratically. This was most apparent in the section that explained to local Gray Panthers how to secure funding from foundations, community development block grants, and such federal programs as revenue sharing. These suggestions implied a world very different from that of the John Birch Society.

Two issues during 2005 provided major rhetorical opportunities for the Gray Panthers. The first was President Bush's campaign to reform Social Security and Medicare. Their opposition to Social Security reform was:

> The phony hype about Social Security "going broke" is a myth being created by Wall Street profiteers who want to undermine the public's confidence in Social Security. They would like to convince young people that Social Security will "not be there for them." They would like us to believe that spending over $2 trillion to create a separate system to divert Social Security funds into the stock market (including giving a nearly $1 trillion windfall to the financial services industry to manage the new individual accounts) will "save" a system which hasn't missed a paycheck for 70 years. In 2004, the Congressional Budget Office projected that Social Security will be able to pay full benefits until the year 2052 and, after that, could continue to cover 81% of promised benefits. According to Social Security Commissioner Robert M. Ball, Social Security can be fixed with just a two percent increase in payroll funds. Gray Panthers believe that this gap can be largely closed by "lifting the cap" on income which is subject to Social Security taxes.[21]

Although the foregoing passage from the Panthers has elements of conspiracy argument, it nevertheless concludes with a pragmatic policy solution—a two percent increase in the payroll tax. But these dangers and solutions lack drama; for most people they fail to excite public fears or imagination.

Hurricane Katrina, much like the attacks of September 11, reached all Americans through the mass media. The images of destruction, despair, and inadequate responses provided grist for the mills of public discourse. For the Gray Panthers, Katrina provided visual evidence to support several of their key arguments. Katrina "destroyed any remaining illusions that somehow, everything that needs to be done will somehow be done, that adequacy of resources is not an issue." This was important for their worldview because it is "a common fallacy in every federal, state and local budget process wherein agency heads assure legislators that they can indeed 'do the job' with less than last year, less than is demonstrably necessary." From the Panther perspective, then, Katrina was an instance of our failure as a nation to meet our responsibilities because we failed to allocate our national resources properly. Was that, in their opinion, because of conspirators or policy choices? Their policy answer allows them to establish dichotomous value clusters—international security vs. domestic security, tax breaks for the wealthy vs. security and dignity for all Americans:

> Perhaps if our troops weren't fighting "pre-emptive" wars in Iraq and elsewhere, our National Guard could have responded more quickly to our domestic national disaster. Perhaps if politicians hadn't been pouring over a third of our federal budget into military related spending and expanding tax breaks for the wealthy, we would have had more resources to assure that the U.S. can provide true security and dignity for all Americans.[22]

In short, the Gray Panthers continue to view the world as essentially rational. In their world, it is possible to talk or reason with one's adversaries—something that makes no sense at all in the Birch jungle. In the rational world of the Gray Panthers, most of the bad things happen because people allow them to happen through misguided choices rather than through evil conspiracies.

Gray Panthers' Tendency toward Egalitarianism

Whereas Robert Welch stressed the need for a vertical organizational hierarchy, the Gray Panthers prescribed an egalitarian network of autonomous local groups. Contrast Welch's monolithic organization (local chapters with no room for debate and leaders appointed by him) with the following statement from *The Gray Panther Manual:*

> An organization is shaped and nurtured by knowledgeable and experienced, politically sophisticated, creative and concerned people. . . . We need a powerful and effective national organization. But to build it, we need pieces to put together, local pieces. These local pieces are the Networks, the grass roots Gray Panther groups and individuals around the country. (p. 1)

> All individual Gray Panthers and Gray Panther networks are not created from the same mold, nor are we forced to follow a strict format or role. Variation is the spice of life and we encourage local autonomy. Variation within the movement is an exciting and energizing force which we value. (pp. 15–16)

This passage valued many of the things that worried Welch. No authoritarian character type could be attracted to a group that talked about avoiding a strict format or mold because authoritarians *want* strict formats and roles. A true authoritarian personality would not want to be seen reading a manual that said, "Variation is the spice of life" (because variation is dangerous), "we encourage local autonomy" (because individual autonomy is reckless and suicidal), or that variation "is an exciting and energizing force" (because authoritarian character types perceive variation as a dangerous and debilitating force).

Another point of contrast can be found in the Gray Panthers' description of their organization. Did Maggie Kuhn appoint local leaders? Did they have stringent standards for membership? Did they dictate policy from national headquarters? The *Manual* was almost apologetic about the organization's decision to adopt Articles of Agreement in 1975, saying that "our hope was to develop minimal structure without violating the spirit of the movement" (p. 9). The *Manual* had this to say about becoming a member under the Articles:

> Our structure is still fairly loose and flexible. A person or a group may affiliate with the National Gray Panthers by stating in writing their agreement with and willingness to work toward the goals. However, we . . . encourage and support local network autonomy in choosing those issues of importance in their own communities. (pp. 15–16)

The Panthers' seriousness about local autonomy was perhaps most evident in their discussion of networks reporting to national headquarters. "Conveners can keep the national office informed in a number of ways, including an annual report, press clippings, task force reports, local newsletters and, for funding proposals, notification of the Project Fund." (pp. 32–33). Nowhere did the *Manual* suggest that the national office had any power to reject, amend, or review these reports. They were simply ways for the autonomous local networks to keep the national office and other local networks informed of their activities.

The Gray Panthers' Desire to Empower

Maslow said that the democratic character structure had no tendency comparable to the authoritarian character's sadomasochism, but he might have been impressed by the Gray Panthers' desire to empower people. Where authoritarians such as the Birchers demanded obedience and rejoiced in submission to their leader, the Gray Panthers tried to advance the frontiers of democracy by fighting against paternalism and by helping people overcome feelings of powerlessness.

The theme of empowerment pervaded the 1978 *Manual.* Their movement "reflects the new mood of outrage and protest against injustices felt by increasing numbers of powerless people" (p. 15). They fought ageism with an "intergenerational coalition" of persons who shared "our concern for the larger issues of social justice and empowerment" (p. 17). They saw themselves as a liberation movement: "We identify with these other liberation groups and collectively reflect the widespread nature of the status disadvantaged and call for a massive redistribution of opportunities and privileges as well as major ideological changes" (p. 18). The Gray Panthers' struggle against ageism helped them see that "many of the institutions and organizations that purport to serve people are afflicted with a deep, insidious paternalism, offering little or no voice to the recipients" (p. 18). Clearly, the Gray Panthers were committed to improving the quality of life for "those who consider themselves powerless" (p. 22).

The democratic character of the Gray Panthers was also evident in the *Manual*'s section on "Developing Leadership." The authoritarian character is unconcerned about developing leaders because real leaders are people high on the survival scale. But democratic leadership entails facilitation rather than command, and its skills can and should be learned by everyone as a means of empowerment. The Gray Panther leader's role was "to inspire the group" and "to point the way" (p. 42). A good leader, the *Manual* said, is interested, personal, encouraging, enthusiastic, sharing, supportive, praising, dependable, willing to assume responsibility, willing to work hard, able to grow, and has a sense of humor (pp. 42–47). The *Manual* failed to mention the qualities of toughness and exactness that were so important to Welch, just as Welch had put little stock in being encouraging, sharing, supportive, praising, or having a sense of humor. Different personalities require different styles of leadership and followership, and the differences between the democratic Gray Panthers and the autocratic John Birchers are stark.

In summary, *The Gray Panther Manual* exhibited all of the characteristics of the democratic character structure. Panthers saw the world as a misguided but relatively unthreatening place. They were egalitarian and constructed a flat organizational structure that maximized local autonomy. They identified with people who were made to feel powerless and sought to combat paternalistic practices in society, whether they affected older people or others. Their leaders were taught to be supportive facilitators who empowered their members.

Conclusions

This analysis of the ideological statements of the John Birch Society and the Gray Panthers suggests four conclusions. The first is that the John Birch Society's *Blue Book* depicted a threatening world and stressed the need for ecstatic submission to a dynamic, personal leader within an autocratic hierarchy—a depiction congruent with the archetypal authoritarian character structure and incompatible with the democratic character structure. In one rhetorical stroke Robert Welch recruited the ardent, dedicated followers he needed and wanted; alienated potentially troublesome democratic character types who valued variety and discussion; and consolidated his recruits into a band of loyalists who became more, not less, reliant on him during times of ideological dissonance.

In contrast, *The Gray Panther Manual* stressed the need to empower individuals and groups who perceived themselves as passive and powerless—a depiction congruent with the archetypal democratic character structure and incompatible with the authoritarian character structure. The Panthers in one rhetorical stroke recruited the diverse, talented people they needed; alienated potentially troublesome authoritarian character types; and consolidated a vast array of autonomous local protests into one national movement that became less, not more, dependent on particular national leaders who faced all of the risks and dangers of advancing age.

Second, the psychological gratifications Welch provided for authoritarian characters allowed him to present contradictory arguments: the protection of freedom through dictatorial leadership, the protection of capitalism through noncompetitive organization, and strength through submission. By creating a strong protector-protected relationship with protector-hungry followers, Welch reserved for himself the ability to resolve belief dilemmas. Indeed, belief dilemmas might well have led to ideological defections without a leader such as Welch to resolve them.

On the other hand, the psychological gratifications Gray Panthers provided to democratic character types enabled them to avoid the passivity they disliked. By grounding their fight against ageism in the struggle of oppressed peoples against paternalism, they invited the support of democratic personalities of all ages. And by empowering their members with local autonomy, they maximized their members' freedom to use their personal skills in the ways that they found most meaningful and rewarding.

These two cases demonstrate that it is possible for social movements to provide psychological, as well as political or philosophical, reasons for membership. Each organization discouraged the membership of persons most likely to disrupt it, while providing gratifications for those most able to advance its work. The arguments worked for members so members would work for the organizations.

Third, this chapter has demonstrated that persuasive functions do not necessarily bear a linear relationship to social movement messages. It is possible for a movement to recruit, confront, and consolidate, all in one message. Not all members of the John Birch Society fit precisely the description of the authoritarian character structure, but its message spoke to authoritarian tendencies. It created for its members an organization which was probably more authoritarian than most of its individual members because they were bound together by shared mistrust of the world and their need for protection against it. In contrast, the Gray Panthers created a movement that was probably more democratic in character than most of its members because it allowed its individual and collective affiliates to do as they pleased without the review or approval of either the national headquarters or other locals. They were able to combat ageism with an ideology that made membership attractive to democratic personality types of all ages.

Fourth, the persuasive discourse of the John Birch Society and the Gray Panthers provided psychological gratifications that were truthful and straightforward. Welch delivered what he promised: an authoritarian, anticommunist organization under his personal control. Never did he claim to offer anything else that might have broadened his appeal. The Gray Panthers provided local autonomy and minimal oversight, aspects of the organization that persuaded democratic personality types to join.

Notes

[1] For further information on authoritarianism and dogmatism, see T. W. Adorno, Else Frenkel Brunswik, Daniel J. Levinson, and R. Nevitt Sanford, *The Authoritarian Personality* (New York: Harper, 1950); Erich Fromm, *Escape from Freedom* (New York: Avon Library, 1965); and Milton Rokeach, *The Open- and Closed-Mind* (New York: Basic Books, 1960): 39–51.

[2] Abraham Maslow, "The Authoritarian Character Structure," *Journal of Social Psychology* 18 (1943): 401–411.

[3] Maslow, 402–403.

[4] Maslow, 408.

[5] Maslow, 406.

[6] Several sources (including *Who's Who*) have reported that Robert Welch served in important capacities with the National Association of Manufacturers during the 1950s. The N.A.M. insists that he was only one of two hundred honorary officials and never held a position of responsibility. This is from correspondence with Dr. Jane Work, Department of Legislative Planning, National Association of Manufacturers, April 15, 1983.

[7] Stephen Earl Bennett, "Modes of Resolution of a 'Belief Dilemma' in the Ideology of the John Birch Society," *Journal of Politics* 33 (1971): 735–772.

[8] Circulation data are published in accordance with federal statutes in the December issues of these publications. Circulation is the best index of Society membership, since their rolls remain secret and their primary activities are educational.

[9] See J. Allen Broyles, *The John Birch Society: Anatomy of a Protest* (Boston: Beacon Press, 1966); Gerald Schomp, *Birchism Was My Business* (New York: Macmillan, 1970); and two reports by the Anti-Defamation League of B'nai B'rith: Benjamin R. Epstein and Arnold Forster, *Report on the John Birch Society, 1966* (New York: Random House, 1966), and *The Radical Right: Report on the John Birch Society and Its Allies* (New York: Random House, 1967). Birch was a fundamentalist Baptist missionary in China and became involved in U.S. intelligence operations during World War II. He seems to have displayed too much bravado in an encounter with a Chinese officer, and Welch regards him as the first casualty in the final struggle against communism.

[10] http://www.jbs.org/node/22, accessed 7 August 2006.

[11] *The Gray Panther Manual*, Harriet L. Perretz, compiler (Philadelphia: The Gray Panthers, 1978), 3–4, 22.

[12] http://www.graypanthers.org/graypanthers/maggie.htm, accessed 7 August 2006.

[13] http://www.graypanthers.org, accessed 6 February 2006.

[14] http://www.graypanthers.org, accessed 6 February 2006.

[15] Unless otherwise noted, all quotations in this section are from Robert H. W. Welch, Jr., *The Blue Book of the John Birch Society* (Belmont, MA: Western Islands, 1961). The page numbers are noted in parentheticals at the end of each quotation.

[16] Robert Welch, *The Politician* (Belmont, MA: Belmont Publishing, 1963): 279.

[17] Welch strongly supported the Goldwater candidacy as early as the 1958 organizational session (see 109). Goldwater was not a Welch supporter. After reading *The Politician,* Goldwater wrote that "most of the John Birchers are patriotic, concerned, law-abiding, hardworking and productive. There are a few whom I call Robert Welchers, and these are the fanatics who regard everyone who doesn't totally agree with them as communist sympathizers." Barry Goldwater, *With No Apologies* (New York: William Morrow, 1979): 119.

[18] Ann Reilly Dowd, "What Managers Can Learn from Manager Reagan," *Fortune* (15 September 1986): 33–41. The same management philosophy was expressed during the first debate between Reagan and Mondale published in *The Weekly Compilation of Presidential Documents* 20 (7 October 1984): 1446.

[19] Welch's utopia is a highly individualistic society epitomized by his slogan, "Less Government and More Responsibility" (p. 117).

[20] Unless otherwise indicated, all references (i.e., page numbers in parentheses) to the ideology of the Gray Panthers or their manual refer to *The Gray Panther Manual.*

[21] http://www.graypanthers.org/nucleus/, accessed 7 August 2006.

[22] http://www.graypanthers.org, accessed 6 February 2006.

CHAPTER

7

Languaging Strategies and Tactics of Social Movements

Human language is the vehicle for political and social thought, debate, and action. It is a powerful tool and is far more than a collection of words and rules for proper usage. Charles Wilkerson writes that the term "languaging strategy" broadens the concept of language "to include the act as symbol as well as the symbol as act."[1] Language as symbol is the instrument and tool for human action and expression and the means of sharing social, political, and cultural values. Through language and social interaction, individuals and groups identify with a culture, a set of values, or political or social entities. As we assess our political and social environments, we *create* language that may structure, transform, or destroy the environment. Thus, the creation of language as symbol systems is essential to the development of societies and cultures. Language acts as the agent for social integration, the means of cultural socialization, the vehicle for social interaction, the channel for the transmission of values, and the glue that bonds people, ideas, and society.

Through language, social movements transform perceptions of social reality, alter self-perceptions of members, legitimize the movement, prescribe courses of action, and sustain the movement. Language is *political* in the sense that it is purposeful and consequently *persuasive* attempt to determine the way in which people relate to their larger, social environment. Social consciousness results from a largely symbolic interpretation of sociopolitical experience. Paul Corcoran argues that

> *all* language is political because every speech setting, however private and intimate, involves power relations, social roles, privileges, and contested meanings. It is not simply *difficult* to separate out the intermingling of politics and language. Rather, one *cannot* distinguish between politics and language because they do not occupy separate spheres of existence that merely "overlap." In a much stronger sense, language articulates and confirms all the things that we call political: the weak and strong, the valued and the rejected, the desired and the undesirable, "us" and "them."[2]

155

In this chapter, we provide an overview of the importance of human interaction in creating a social reality and identify language strategies and tactics used by social movements across history.

COMMUNICATION, SOCIETY, AND SOCIAL ORDER

At the heart of our perspective of social movements is the notion of interaction. Interaction is not so much a concept as an orientation for viewing human behavior and, ultimately, society. Through interaction, people continually undergo change and, consequently, so does society. Interaction is a process involving acting, perceiving, interpreting, and acting again. This interaction among people gives rise to reality, which is largely symbolic. Thus, symbolic interaction with others gives meaning to the world and creates the reality toward which persons act.

Interaction, as a concept, is not limited to spoken and written language. Objects exist in physical form but derive their meaning through social interaction. Depending on our social groups and frames of reference, specific objects may "communicate" success, status, and acceptance. The clothes we wear or our hairstyle can communicate group identity. For the peasant, a rake is a tool for survival but, in concert with others, it can also serve as a weapon for revolution. This transformation results from social interaction. Objects take on meaning for individuals as they interact with others. Societies, therefore, consist of people interacting. When people interact, they influence the behavior of one another, so behavior is created by interaction rather than simply a result of interaction.

Individuals interact within larger networks of individuals and groups, and although society's networks are far removed from individuals, the impact of such networks may be considerable. Social networks—formal or informal, social or political—provide a framework within which social action takes place. The networks are not determinants of action. Even structural aspects of society, such as social roles or class, should be viewed as setting *conditions* for behavior and interaction rather than as *causing* specific behavior or interaction. Human interaction, then, is at the core of human existence. It gives meaning to the self, symbols and languages, social networks and societies, worldviews, and social objects.

Symbols

It is impossible to talk of human interaction without addressing the symbolic nature of humans. Distinctively human behavior and interaction are carried on through the medium of symbols and their attached meanings. What distinguishes humans from lower animals is the ability to function in a symbolic environment. Humans alone can create, manipulate, and use symbols to control their behavior and the behavior of others. All animals communicate, but humans are uniquely symbolic.

George Herbert Mead defined symbols in terms of meaning. A system of symbols "is the means whereby individuals can indicate to one another what their responses to objects will be and hence what the meaning of objects are."[3] The human, as a cognitive creature, functions in a context of shared meanings that are communicated through language (which is shared meanings or symbols). Symbols, of course, are more than part of a language system. They may be objects or modes of conduct.

Virtually all human action is symbolic and the by-product of the stimulus of symbols. Before we can formulate a response to any situation, we must define and interpret the situation to ensure an appropriate response. Meanings for symbols derive from interaction in specific social contexts. New interaction experiences may result in new symbols or new meanings for old symbols that may change one's understanding or perception of the world. Our view of the world alters and changes as our symbol system is modified through interaction. This process suggests that our reality consists of symbolic systems.

Social Reality

Reality is a social product arising from interaction, and communication extends or limits *realities*. To discover our own reality or that of someone else, we must first understand the symbol system and then the meanings the symbols have for all concerned. Mutual understanding and subsequent action is accomplished through interaction. The construction of reality is an active process involving recognition, definition, interpretation, action, and validation through interaction. In sum, communication becomes the vehicle for the creation of society, culture, rules, regulations, and behavior. A complex and constantly changing matrix of individual and societal expectations grows from this chain of actions. This perspective recognizes the dynamic, ever-changing nature of society.

Society

Individuals constantly interact, develop, and shape society. People exist in action and must be viewed in terms of action. Society may be viewed as individuals in interaction; individuals acting in relation to each other; individuals engaging in cooperative action; and people communicating with self and others. New situations constantly arise requiring modification or reinforcement of existing societal rules. Even "old" joint action arises out of a background of previous actions of the participants.

Self-control is inseparable from social control. The notion of free will is restricted and limited by an individual's culture. The interrelationship between social control and self-control is the result of commitment to groups that produce self-fulfillment, self-expression, and self-identity. Social control is not a matter of formal government agencies, laws, rules, and regulations. Rather, it is a direct result of citizens identifying and internalizing the values of a group so that the values become essential to their self-esteem and actions in support of the social order. Adherence to the rules of society becomes a fair price to pay for membership in the society.

Thus, language and symbols may regulate behavior by creating expectations, producing negative bias, or subordinating other considerations by allowing one norm or value to supersede other symbols.[4] In addition to creating expectations of behavior, symbols create social sanctions (war as God's will) or function as master symbols (to die for freedom).

Social Symbols in Social Movements

Symbols and symbolic acts provide shared meanings, perceptions, and security within social movements and social movement organizations. Verbal symbols or language, according to Richard Weaver, constitute a "social and cultural creation functioning somehow within the psychic constitution of those who use it. . . . The question of stability in language cannot be considered apart from the psychic stability of the culture group."[5] The uses and styles of verbal symbols may signal conformity or rebellion in society.

Every desire and emotion is a valid reason to initiate symbolic exchange. Emotional responses may be bad reasons for acting, but they are valid when grounded in one's reality. Wayne Booth asserts:

> The real art lies always in the proper weighing—and what is proper is a matter finally of shared norms, discovered and applied in the experience of individuals whose very individuality is forged from other selves. Every protest implies an affirmative ground for protest; every affirmation implies many negations.[6]

Thus, emotional expressions through words and actions contribute to social movement cohesiveness or division by affecting relational patterns.

The intended and perceived meanings of social symbols—words, gestures, acts, signs, and signals—may be difficult to grasp, and their impact or stimulation may differ among individuals, groups, and organizations. Hugh Duncan emphasizes that "it is the ambiguity of symbols which makes them so useful in human society."[7] The meaning of the V sign with two fingers has ranged from victory during World War II to peace during the Vietnam War. The clenched fist symbol meant power, independence, pride, and self-determination to members of the black power movement in the civil rights struggle. From "new and fixed meanings," we think, we feel, and ultimately we act.

Robert Brooks demonstrated the ambiguity of symbols in his investigation of how three groups (black college students, white college students, and white police officers) interpreted the meaning of the phrase "black power."[8] He discovered three dominant dimensions: aggression, goals, and mystique. Whites (both students and police officers) perceived aggression, violence, confrontation, and racial domination inherent in the concept of black power. Blacks associated various political goals such as equal rights and equal opportunity with the phrase. Blacks also endowed black power with nonmaterial attributes such as self-identity, pride, and awareness. Uttering the phrase black power and raising a clenched fist serve as symbolic justifications for feelings and actions and provide a bridge or link to social action.

Because significant symbols often have standard meanings within groups and organizations, they serve both expressive and persuasive functions. Harold Laswell recognizes that influencing collective attitudes is possible by the manipulation of significant symbols such as slogans.[9] He believes that a verbal symbol might evoke a desired reaction or organize collective attitudes of *a people* toward a symbol. Murray Edelman writes, "to the political scientist patterning or consistency in the contexts in which specific groups of individuals use symbols is crucial, for only through such patterning do common political meanings and claims arise."[10] Thus, symbols such as "Red power!" the gray panther logo, American flag, burning cross, clenched fist, beards and long hair, turtle costumes, red roses, and swastika evoke specific responses, and these symbols provide us with an index of group beliefs, attitudes, values, and conceptual rationales for claims. James Andrews addresses the essential roles of symbols in the persuasive efforts of social movements to alter perceptions, prescribe courses of action, and mobilize followers:

> The exciting, and frustrating, characteristic of a social movement is that it moves and what makes it move, in large measure, is the way language is manipulated to control or interpret events. In this sense, rhetoric makes moving possible—moving in all directions, pushing, shoving, lurching forward, and falling backward as the movement encounters its environment. Growing out of the environment, intruding into the environment, reacting to the environment, and becoming a part of the environment, the social movement is simultaneously a rhetorical response and a rhetorical stimulus.[11]

LANGUAGING STRATEGIES OF SOCIAL MOVEMENTS

Languaging strategies are patterns or methods of language usage that attempt to achieve a specific purpose, goal, or objective. They state key movement messages, themes, and rationales for actions. The "effect" of the strategy may be intended, real, unintended, or all three. All communication is audience centered and purposeful. However, some messages heard by nontargeted audiences may generate different responses. For example, a literal interpretation and presentation of biblical scripture may be well received by an evangelical audience, but it could be perceived as insulting or even hostile to members of a more secular audience. This chapter explores three common language strategies: identification, polarization, and power.

Identification

Division permeates both our society and the social movements that would change or sustain the status quo, but communication can help societal elements articulate differences and relate to one another. Through communication we may "transcend" to higher plains of meaning that enable us to overcome differences. In communicating with one another, we seek similarity or common references, what Kenneth Burke calls "identification."[12] All people are different, but we have common factors in which we are "consubstantially" (substantially) the same—not identical but sharing important aspects of nature and substance.[13] The process of identification reduces ambiguity and, in so doing may encourage cooperation.

There is a very close relationship between *identification* and *persuasion*. Burke claims, for instance, that "you persuade a man [woman] only insofar as you can talk his [her] language by speech, gesture, tonality, order, image, attitude, idea, *identifying* your ways with his [hers]." He notes that

> we might well keep in mind that a speaker persuades an audience by the use of stylistic identifications; his [her] act of persuasion may be for the purpose of causing the audience to identify itself with the speaker's interests; and the speaker draws on identification of interests to establish rapport between himself [herself] and his [her] audience.[14]

Identification, however, is more than merely relating to others; it is an instrument of transformation. At some level, reality, an event, or a group makes sense (is rational) even though one person's rationalization may be a second person's factuality. Our responses and conclusions are the results of the process of transformation that originates from our awareness of division.

While persuaders may strive for a substantial sameness or similarity with audiences, division is ever present. For instance, Gregory Stephens writes about how Frederick Douglass' "multiracial abolitionism" infuriated the white Garrisonian and black nationalist elements of the antislavery movement. Douglass attempted to stake out the middle ground and work with other elements through a rhetoric of "antagonistic cooperation" and "redeemable ideals."[15] Like Douglass, we seek to balance our needs for "personal coherence" and "social coordination." The need for personal coherence underscores division from those who are different; the need for social coordination underscores identification because persons with whom we identify index our realities. Transformation occurs at various levels from the most obvious to the most subtle. Thus, when you "put identification and division ambiguously together, so that you cannot know for certain just where one ends and the other begins, you have the characteristic invitation to rhetoric."[16]

Levels of Identification

There are many levels of identification, with the most obvious being a persuader's attempt to establish common ground with an audience. Simple common ground may result from groups identifying according to gender, age, race, ethnic background, or sexual orientation. Women identify with other women, Chicanos with Chicanos, African Americans with African Americans and gays and lesbians with gays and lesbians. Protestors may feel common ground because of their work, education, religion, or social status. This happens, for instance, when United Farm Worker organizers emphasize that they are farm workers of Mexican background, attend Roman Catholic services, and advocate programs that will benefit farm workers. The early labor movement united around specific trades such as machinists, cigar makers, and masons and also around trades within trades such as locomotive engineers, firemen, brakemen, and conductors. Ironically, these superficial similarities may be all that participants have in common.

Nearly all social movement persuaders use the notion of *a people* to unify and to provide a means of identification for otherwise disparate groups. They claim to speak in the name of the people, for the will of the people, and in the "soul and spirit" of the people. Movements portray themselves as majority movements, people's or citizen's movements, and grassroots movements. Since the movement and the people become one, they share common interests, needs, values, and wisdom—common ground.

Through interaction and identification, we can become involved in many groups, causes, or movements; formulate or change allegiances; and vicariously share in the role of leader or spokesperson. There are many ways social movements may enhance or create a sense of identification with audiences.

Identification Tactics

The *implied we* is a subtle means of establishing a feeling of commonality or common ground. Persuaders use plural pronouns to imply identification and a common purpose and struggle. In an address to The Rockford Pro-Life Breakfast for Clergy and Lay Leaders, Allan Carlson included these statements in his closing remarks: "*We* are beginning to win the contest for family renewal," "I believe that the Holy Spirit is moving in *our* time toward some great end," "If *we* but open *our* eyes and ears, there are portents or signs all about *us* that a new Great Awakening is at work in this land," and "As always, *our* task now as Christians is to open *our* hearts to God" (emphasis added).[17] A barrage of simple plural pronouns such as we, our, and us in place of leader-centered and individualistic pronouns such as I, me, and mine invites a feeling of common ground—a common bond. Audiences sense active involvement *together* in a great moral struggle.

When people become *involved with groups or participate in group actions*, they may become more tolerant, if not sympathetic, of the views of other persuaders or groups. Individuals who are separated by loyalties to competing groups or organizations may unite around a single cause. In the 1880s, several trade unions united under the banner of the American Federation of Labor to present a united front in their individual struggles for better wages and working conditions. It was not until 1955, however, that the organization for unskilled factory workers (the Congress of Industrial Organizations) and the American Federation of Labor merged into the AFL-CIO, a single organization with which most union members could identify.

Social movement members and sympathizers may share significant aspects of *appearance*. United Farm Worker organizers tend to dress like farm workers while those of far right religious and political organizations such as the Christian Coalition and the John Birch Society are likely to dress in suits and ties.

Persuaders and movements may achieve identification by *adapting language* to audiences. Two of Stokely Carmichael's (the leader of SNCC) speeches on black power illustrate this method of identification.[18] Carmichael gave one speech to a predominantly black audience in Detroit on July 30, 1966, and a second to a predominantly white, university audience in Whitewater, Wisconsin, on February 6, 1967. The addresses were surprisingly similar in content and examples, but they differed significantly in style and persuasive appeals. For the black audience, Carmichael personified the ideology he was advancing—in delivery, style, and attitude, while for the white, academic audience, he dwelt mainly on an explanation of ideology and sounded scholarly. For the black audience, he interpreted the notion of black power in terms of pride, self-identity, and political mobilization, while for the white audience he interpreted the slogan in terms of mainstream American ideals, using such phrases as "social and political integration" and "pluralistic society." He advocated violent resistance in the Detroit speech, but in the Whitewater speech he used milder references to violence and addressed them in a context of self-defense. Carmichael's delivery to the black audience was "cool and very hip," while his delivery to the white audience was that of an intellectual or "politically enlightened leader." Clearly, Carmichael *identified* with each audience by carefully selecting and presenting language.

Protestors may identify with audiences through *content adaptation*. For example, they may use examples that listeners and readers easily understand to emphasize similarity between persuader and audience. Frederick Douglass, a free slave speaking before a white audience commemorating the Fourth of July in 1852, illustrated the similarity between "slaves" and "masters" in terms of abilities, jobs, and domestic roles:

> Is it not astonishing that, while we are plowing, planting, and reaping, using all kinds of mechanical tools, erecting houses, constructing bridges, building ships, working in metals of brass, iron, copper, silver, and gold; that, while we are reading, writing, and ciphering, acting as clerks, merchants, and secretaries, having among us lawyers, doctors, ministers, poets, authors, editors, orators, and teachers; that while we are engaged in all manner of enterprises common to other men, digging gold in California, capturing the whale in the Pacific, feeding sheep and cattle on the hillside, living, moving, acting, thinking, planning, living in families as husbands, wives, and children, and above all, confessing and worshipping the Christian's God, and looking hopefully for life and immortality beyond the grave, we are called upon to prove that we are men![19]

Persuaders reflect the audience's values, beliefs, and attitudes by *identifying with the moral symbols and revered documents* of society rather than attacking or disparaging them. The "Women's Declaration of Independence" adopted at the Seneca Falls convention in 1848 was modeled closely after the Declaration of Independence with such modifications as "We hold these truths to be self-evident, that all men *and women* are created equal." The National Labor Union used the same identification strategy when it adopted its "Platform of

Principles" in 1868: "We hold these truths to be self-evident, that all *people* are created equal." Movements for and against slavery, women's rights, temperance, and abortion have employed the Bible as their central source of ideological beliefs and evidence.

Social movements also *identify with the values, beliefs, and attitudes* of audiences by identifying with heroes and founders. For example, at a gathering of modern women's rights leaders in the 1960s, a large portrait of an earlier generation of women's rights leaders—Susan B. Anthony, Lucretia Mott, Elizabeth Cady Stanton, Lucy Stone, and Anna Howard Shaw—hung in front of each leader seated on a platform. The leaders and members of the contemporary women's liberation movement wanted to show they were the heirs of the societal norms, values, beliefs, traditions, and struggles of the founders of the women's rights struggle begun more than a century before.

A persuader may create identification by *referring to individuals unrelated to the movement* but whom the audience honors and respects. The announcer for the Christian Crusade radio broadcasts of Rev. Billy James Hargis always introduced him with these words: "Now speaking for Christ and against Communism—Dr. Billy James Hargis."[20] The Nation of Islam leader Louis Farrakhan addresses his controversial status in speeches by associating himself with Jesus Christ and Moses.[21]

Movements attempt to *link themselves with other social movements* active at the time that have already gained a degree of respect. Thus, the civil rights movement helped to legitimize the Native-American, women's liberation, and gay rights movements in the United States, the Free Quebecois movement in French-speaking Canada, and the Roman Catholic civil rights movement in Northern Ireland.

At the heart of the notion of identification, then, is the belief that symbols unite people. Language, as symbols, consists of vocabulary, rules, and enactment or presentation. It reveals the persuader's attitude about an issue or group, and the persuader can induce cooperation, or at least insure a fair hearing under most circumstances, by demonstrating similarities with the audience. But there is competition.

Polarization

To *unite* with one group, cause, or movement is to *separate* from some other group, cause, or social movement. As Burke claims, if there were no divisions, there would be no need for rhetoric. Perfect identification would require no further communication. "Since identification implies division, we find rhetoric involving us in matters of socialization and faction."[22] And since identification and unity inevitably result in separation and division, social movements also employ a rhetoric of polarization.

Andrew King and Floyd Anderson define polarization as "the process by which an extremely diversified public is coalesced into two or more highly contrasting, mutually exclusive groups sharing a high degree of internal solidarity in those beliefs which the persuader considers salient."[23] Social movements utilize a rhetoric of polarization to transform relationships by creating clear distinctions between the evil other and the virtuous self, a we-they dichotomy. Richard Lanigan writes that "polarization creates a lived perspective of reality based on values divisions that characterize one individual as 'good, right, lawful, rational, and the like,' while his neighbor becomes 'evil, wrong, unlawful, irrational, and so on."[24] Thus, people are either pro-union or pro-management, rich or poor, a have or a have not, a patriot or a traitor, a liberal or a conservative.

King and Anderson claim that persuaders create polarization through two primary strategies: affirmation and subversion:

> A strategy of affirmation is concerned with a judicious selection of those images that will promote a strong sense of group identity. A strategy of subversion is concerned with a careful selection of those images that will undermine the *ethos* of competing groups, ideologies, or institutions.[25]

These strategies contrast "us" with "them." The first represents the highest of values in a moral struggle. John Bowers, Donovan Ochs, and Richard Jensen identify the second as: "the exploitation of *flag issues* and *flag individuals* as the two major tactics protestors use to polarize. . . . Attacking such individuals help the agitating group receive media attention."[26] There is no middle ground. You are for peace or for war, for abortion or against abortion, for protecting the environment or for exploiting it, for globalization or for nationalism.

A rhetoric of polarization, then, divides in order to unite those who support a cause and to force commitment from those attempting to remain uncommitted. Lanigan claims that "the ideological presumption is that a confrontation of power blocs will force the uncommitted middle to rally to the 'just' side—theirs!"[27] The polar opposite for social movements includes all individuals and groups who do not openly support the social movement and thus are responsible directly through actions or indirectly through indifference or fear for allowing an intolerable situation to come into existence and to worsen day by day. Persuaders hold firmly to the adage that "if you are not with us, you are against us." There is no middle ground, no neutrals, in the struggle between good and evil. *We* include all the righteous, moral, self-sacrificing individuals and groups—the true believers—who are willing to stand up and say NO! to evil conditions, forces, actions, and trends. *They* include institutions, the so-called silent majority, the media, countermovements, competing social movements, competing organizations within social movements, and those for whom the movement is fighting (women, gays, Hispanics) but have yet to join or support the movement.

Power

Virtually all political and protest communication is about power, domination, or control. Kenneth Hacker identifies three dimensions of power.[28] The first is conflict over concrete political interests, revealed in policy preferences. In this case, language is objective and descriptive. For the gay community, "civil unions" would at least allow some prescribed rights relating to shared property, tax breaks, healthcare coverage, and survivor benefits. The second is control over how issues are defined, debated, and actions taken. Language is critical in framing issues and defining concepts. The debate over "civil unions" versus "same sex marriage" is a serious one. The words differ greatly in terms of rights, protections, and a "sacred sacrament." The third is control over agendas and decision making. Here language is more utilitarian.

A truism among social movement theorists and practitioners is that the *agent who controls language controls the world.* The language of symbols and symbolic acts that sanctifies actions and feelings, reinforces or transforms fixed meanings, sustains beliefs, and signifies proper, dubious, and improper means of expression is selected, reinforced, and maintained by social institutions such as schools, churches, courts, and legislative chambers. J. Vernon Jensen writes about how the British, including those who were sympathetic and antagonistic to the colonists, used the family metaphor when referring to and attempting to control colonists on the eve of the American Revolution. Members of Parliament called colonists "offspring," "children," and "sons" of the "mother country" and "homeland." They urged colonists to return to the "breast" or "bosom" of their mother, and chastised them as "recalcitrant children" for their "misconduct," "waywardness," and "mischief."[29] Philip Wander reveals how the pro-slavery movement in the South used the image of the "savage child" to argue that freeing adult slaves was dangerous both to society (to turn inferior, uneducated, and uncivilized savages loose in the states) and to the slaves themselves (to turn *children* loose who could not fend for themselves in any way without white, adult supervision and discipline).[30]

All social movements struggle to free themselves from symbols and symbolic acts (such as movie portrayals of Native Americans as bloodthirsty savages or the tomahawk chop at baseball games) that degrade and consign them to lower rungs in the hierarchy—to gain control of their worlds. When protestors insist on being called blacks or African Americans instead of Negroes or niggers, Native Americans instead of Indians or redskins, black men instead of boys, and women instead of girls, they are demanding far more than political correctness. They are seeking equality, dignity, legitimacy, and the right to name themselves rather than live under labels attached to them by slave owners, European colonists, and a male-dominated society. The gay rights movement of the 1990s struggled to replace sexual *preference* with sexual *orientation*, *special rights* with *civil rights*, and *agenda* with *goals*. Each change altered how individual Native Americans, African Americans, gays, and lesbians perceived themselves to be what people.

Thus, power in language is exhibited in many ways: arguments grounded in language that legitimize the rule of those who govern, appeals to moral authority, and narratives of preferred behavior, to name a few. It is also important to recognize that *how* something is said gives language power as much as *what* is said.

LANGUAGING TACTICS OF SOCIAL MOVEMENTS

A rhetorical tactic is a more narrow and specific use of language that aids the accomplishment of a larger strategy. Some tactics may be used in a single strategy or to perform a single persuasive function. Because of the variety of audiences protestors must address, ranging from dedicated members to hostile elements, they employ a variety of language tactics. A few seem to dominate across time and social movements.

Slogans

George Shankel defines a slogan as "some pointed term, phrase, or expression, fittingly worded, which suggests action, loyalty, or which causes people to decide on and to fight for the realization of some principle or decisive issue."[31] For centuries protestors have chanted, shouted, and sung slogans; printed them in leaflets, pamphlets, newsletters, and newspapers; worn them on buttons, tee shirts, jackets, and the seats of their pants; and have written, painted, or pasted them on billboards, posters, banners, automobile bumpers, buses, subways, sidewalks, walls, and the Internet.

Slogans are so pervasive in society that it is easy to underestimate their persuasive power. They have grown in significance because of television, the Internet, and the advertising industry which has made a science of sloganeering. Advertisers discovered long ago that it is easier to link product attributes to existing beliefs, ideas, goals, and desires of the consumer rather than try to change preferences. To say that a cookie tastes "homemade" does not tell us if the cookie is good or bad, hard or soft; it simply evokes fond memories of Mother's baking. Social movements have both informed and learned from the advertising industry. The few words of a slogan may communicate a key idea or theme one wants to associate with an issue, group, product, or event.

Slogans have a number of attributes that enhance their persuasive potential for social movements. They are unique and readily identifiable with a specific social movement or social movement organization. They are easy to say and to remember. Slogans are often fun because they contain active verbs and adjectives; they can be witty and rhyme—designed to be repeated or chanted. They release pent-up emotions and frustrations and act as a verbal surrogate for physical aggression. Finally, slogans may create a "blindering" effect by preventing audiences from considering alternative ways of thinking, feeling, and/or acting. They are definitive statements of the social movement's truths and rely on audience dispositions to achieve expected responses. By recognizing the symbols to which audiences have become conditioned to respond, social movement persuaders formulate slogans that have profound, persuasive, organizing effects.

Social movements use three types of slogans. *Spontaneous slogans* are original, impromptu creations of individual protestors improvised during demonstrations or gatherings. They are often short, rhythmical chants such as "Shut it down" (counterculture movement), "Freedom, freedom, freedom" (civil rights movement), "Bring the troops home" (antiwar movement), "Peace" (peace movement), and "Fur Is Dead" (animal rights). Other spontaneous slogans are longer and more issue oriented, such as "Housewives are unpaid slaves" (women's liberation movement) and "We have our Bible, we don't need your dirty books" (censorship movement).

Sanctioned slogans are official slogans of social movement organizations and are often placed on movement-produced materials. Examples are the civil rights slogan "Freedom Now" and pro-life's "Give to the unborn their first civil right—Life." Sanctioned slogans appear on mastheads of publications. The Native-American newspaper *Wassaji* uses "Let my people know." The Web site for the Religious Coalition for Reproductive Freedom uses the slogan "Pro-Faith, Pro-Family, Pro-Choice."

Advertising slogans are found most often on buttons, bumper stickers, and tee shirts. They tend to be short statements that emphasize a single demand or keep the social movement visible. Issue examples are "Recall Ralph Nader" (radical right groups), "Refuse to Choose" (pro-life), and "Solar employs, nuclear destroys" (antinuclear power). Organizational examples are "Gray Panthers" (senior power movement) and "Students Against Sweatshops" (worker rights).

The brevity of slogans limits their use in transforming perceptions of reality, but some encapsulate an intolerable situation in a few striking words, such as: "You can't hug your children with nuclear arms" (antinuclear movement); "Abortion: the American holocaust" (pro-life movement); "No more killing" (antiwar); or "Thanksgiving is Murder on Turkeys" (animal rights). Some attempt to redefine reality. The pro-life movement uses the slogan "Fetus is Latin for child." The movement against nuclear weapons asserts "Peace is more than the absence of war." And women's liberation claims "Porn is violence disguised." Others peer into a dark future. The antinuclear weapons movement used the slogan "Nuclear war is nuclear suicide," while the antinuclear power movement warned, "In case of nuclear accident kiss your children goodbye."

Protestors, particularly those in the pro-life, environmental, animal rights, and farm worker movements, include graphic pictures with slogans to enhance persuasiveness. For instance, the environmental movement's slogan "Ecology is for the birds" is accompanied by a picture of an oil-soaked duck. Pro-life slogans on bumper stickers and posters such as "Never to Laugh or Love" and "I Want to Live" portray a baby with a tear running down its cheek.

Slogans address self-perceptions, particularly in movements struggling for dignity and equality such as gay rights, the elderly, Native Americans, and women. For instance, some redefine selves, such as "Women are not chicks" (women's liberation); "Discover America with real Americans" (Native-American movement); and "God loves Gays" (gay rights). Others appeal to feelings of power and strength, such as the Gray Panther slogan "Panthers on the prowl." The simple but powerful slogan "Black power" generated a host of imitations: Brown power, Red power, White power, Gray power, Woman power, and Senior power. They enhance self-perceptions by expressing the social movement's ability and will to act. Slogans appeal to pride in self and the social movement and allow protestors to declare what people they are: "Say it loud, I'm black and I'm proud," "I am an Indian and I am pretty damn proud of it," and "I am lesbian and I am beautiful."

Slogans may polarize by identifying and challenging enemies. Anti-Vietnam War protestors chanted, "Hey, hey, LBJ, how many kids have you killed today?" The United Farm Workers used the slogan "Boycott Campbell's cream of exploitation soup." Protestors against the war in Iraq marched with posters reading, "Bush Anti-Christ in Training." Nearly all social movements employ slogans to show defiance that embolden members and challenge institutional legitimacy. They are fun and relatively safe ways to agitate and threaten the powers that be. Protestors shout threatening slogans such as "Tell him what to do with the broom" (women's liberation), "Hell no, we won't go" (anti-Vietnam War), "We will remember in November" (women's liberation), and "A Mouse that Roars Turns 25" (Catholics for a Free Choice).

Social movement slogans state demands in a few simple words. The brief slogan is an ideal means of calling attention to the key ideographs of movements such as equality, happiness, free speech, freedom, justice, rights, and peace. Samples include "Bring Them Home Now" (antiwar), "Stop Abortion Now" (pro-life), "Unchain Dissent" (antiwar), and "Freedom Now" (civil rights). Slogans apply direct or indirect pressure on other social movements, institutions, or institutional agents. Demands are phrased as an imperative statement and shouted or displayed in and around state legislatures, capitols, corporations, churches, courthouses, colleges, stores, beauty pageants, logging operations, abortion clinics, and nuclear power plants.

Slogans simplify complex issues, problems, solutions, and relationships. They bifurcate choices into "America—love it or leave it" (pro-Vietnam War) and "Abortion kills babies—choose life" (pro-life). Other slogans propose simple solutions, such as "No more nukes" (antinuclear power) and "Go vegetarian" (animal rights).

Slogans may create a strong personal identification with and commitment to a cause, particularly when protestors wear the slogans on buttons and tee shirts, place them on automobile bumpers, or carry them on placards such as "Nurses for Life" (pro-life), "I Am the Face of Pro Choice America" (pro-choice), and "Another Family for Peace" (antiwar). Such slogans provide both an opportunity for self-expression of beliefs and membership and a means of exhibiting commitment to a variety of audiences.

Songs

Songs have been a mainstay of social movements and institutions for centuries. Slaves on southern plantations before the Civil War used songs disguised as religious hymns to urge slaves to run away from plantations. In the early 1900s, the militant Industrial Workers of the World (known as the Wobblies) produced a little red book of *Songs of the Workers to Fan the Flames of Discontent*. Songs such as "We Shall Overcome" helped thousands of African Americans and their supporters confront institutional violence and hatred while carrying the civil rights struggle forward in the 1950s and 1960s. During the 1960s and 1970s, protest music became popular and commercially lucrative for the first time. Records by the Kingston Trio, the Chad Mitchell Trio, Simon and Garfunkel, and Bob Dylan sold in the millions.

Protest songs have a number of advantages over speeches, leaflets, editorials, and essays. For example, "Songs are created and designed for repetition, and they are often sung (perhaps with the addition of timely lyrics) throughout the life cycles of social movements."[32] They give persuaders a poetic license to challenge, exaggerate, and pretend in ways that audiences would find unacceptable, unbelievable, or ridiculous if spoken or written in prose. They have powerful nonverbal (voice, instruments, rhythm) as well as verbal (words, lyrics, repetition) components. Since protestors often sing songs *together* or *along with* a leader, they become active participants in the persuasive process rather than passive listeners to speeches or readers of printed or electronic messages. This active participation may enhance self-persuasion. Songs and prose messages work well together. For instance, Stephen Kosokoff and Carl Carmichael discovered that a combination of song and speech was more persuasive than either medium by itself.[33]

Protest songs attempt to transform perceptions of social reality by creating awareness of an urgent problem in the environment, often focusing on suffering and misery. Ralph Knupp discovered that "labor [song] portrays itself as unjustly excluded from its share of the pie of economic and social advantage" while "protest songs of the 1960s called into question the validity of the entire pie."[34] An aura of hope in labor songs ("There is power in a union") is replaced with despair in counterculture songs ("we're on the eve of destruction"). The verbal and nonverbal elements of protest music combine to transform perceptions of social reality. Instruments such as drums, trumpets, guitars, and harmonicas create forbidding and even apocalyptic moods. Rhythm may reduce inhibitions and defense mechanizations and make audiences more susceptible to rhetorical elements that portray an intolerable situation that warrants urgent attention and action. Cheryl Thomas argues rhythm can have a subliminal effect to "push the message more strongly."[35] Repetition, claimed by some to be the heart of persuasion, is a traditional characteristic of music that allows the persuader to reinforce again and again the miserable plight of the slave, laborer, woman, student, Hispanic, white male, or gay person.

Protest songs emanate mostly from self-directed social movements striving for personal freedom, equality, justice, and a fair share of the American dream. Songs polarize as members identify themselves—workers, African Americans, Hispanic Americans, women, gays, farmers—as innocent victims of circumstances and forces beyond their control.[36] The guilty others range from humans (white folks, husbands, bosses, preachers, landlords, rum sellers, and bankers) to things (idol gold, rum, and mushroom clouds), to an all encompassing "they." Songs challenge singers and listeners to separate themselves from evil others and to join the movement. As mentioned in chapter 3, a labor song of the 1930s and 1940s entitled "Which Side Are You On?" asks, "Will you be a lousy scab, or will you be a man?" The civil rights version of the same song asks, "Will you be an Uncle Tom, or will you be a man?"

Protest songs often attempt to energize audiences rather than to enhance feelings of self-identity or self-worth. The focus is on relational patterns, and they challenge singers and listeners to "show the world you're a man" (anti-civil rights) or "Dare to be a union man: Dare to stand alone" (labor 1865–1900). Some songs relate personal conversion experiences. The populist song "A Hayseed Like Me" begins the first verse with "I was once a tool of oppression" and the last verse with "But now I've roused up a little." The civil rights song "The Ballad of Bill Moore" relates the bravery of an assassinated civil rights protestor and notes, "he dared to walk there [Alabama] by himself, none of us here were walking with him." Songs call on audiences to act in some way: sing, march, demonstrate, picket, vote, organize, strike, talk, disrupt, agitate, and run away. A few challenge listeners to "stand up and be counted," "go tell it on the mountain," "give your hands to the struggle."

Labeling

Labeling is the process of naming, creating a specific "symbolic reality" of an action, event, person, or movement. Social movements employ verbal symbols to define good and bad and to identify with a set of social values or specific audience. Labeling is an act of judgment; it makes positive or negative associations. We act toward people, groups, and objects based on our understanding of them, and labels tell us what is important and what to expect.

Social movements label events to cast them in a light to engage supporters—that is, to control or to alter perceptions of reality or the environment. For instance, Samuel Adams labeled the shooting on the docks of Boston as the "Boston Massacre," transforming the perceptions of that event throughout the thirteen colonies and convincing many that revolution was the only answer to British despotism. When he addressed a largely black audience at the Cobo Auditorium in Detroit in 1966, Stokely Carmichael admonished listeners about what to call the violence that had taken place in several cities: "And don't you ever apologize for any black person who throws a Molotov cocktail. Don't you ever apologize. And don't you ever call those things riots, because they are rebellions! That's what they are."[37] Characterizing events as "insurrections" and "rebellions," rather than random violence and looting by out-of-control citizens, transformed them into uprisings of exploited victims who had grown sick and tired of their exploitation. The contemporary animal rights movement refers to trapped and ranched animals as "martyred victims" of "torture," of the "slaughter of the innocent" subjected to "sadistic" and "barbaric methods of capture and killing."

Social movements use negative epithets as labels to stigmatize those who do not join the cause. The animal rights movement calls members of the

National Rifle Association who hunt with electronic devices and dogs "thrill-seeking killers." The black rights movement used Uncle Tom and handker-chief head for "Negroes" who had sold out to the white establishment; they were "Oreos," black on the outside and white on the inside. Native-American activists called "Indians" Uncle Tomahawk and "apples," red on the outside and white on the inside.

Movements identify and label "devils." Burke claims that "men [women] who can unite on nothing else can unite on the basis of a common foe shared by all." He presents the ancient notion of a scapegoat, "the 'representative' or 'vessel' of certain unwanted evils, the sacrificial animal upon whose back the burden of these evils is ritualistically loaded."[38] The scapegoat, he writes, "is the 'essence' of evil."[39] And so it is that social movements inevitably identify one or more *devils* or *scapegoats*.

A devil may be as ambiguous as "they"—the opposite of the implied "we." A movement's devils may be more specific than "they" but as ill-defined as the rich, capitalists, bankers, foreigners, polluters, animal trappers, secular humanists, and internationalists. Devils may be individuals such as Henry Ford during the labor struggles of the 1920s and 1930s, President Johnson during the Vietnam War, Martin Luther King, Jr., for the anti-civil rights forces during the 1950s and 1960s, and George W. Bush during the War in Iraq. Devils may be *things* such as demon rum, nuclear power plants, cruise missiles, commercial developments, acid rain, pesticides, leghold traps, and guns.

The ideal devil according to Eric Hoffer is one omnipotent, omnipresent foreigner.[40] A *single* devil provides a clear rhetorical target for the social move-ment. An *omnipotent*, all-powerful devil requires a mass movement, self-defense, noninstitutional tactics, and total commitment. Individuals acting independently are powerless to bring about or resist change in confrontations with such a potent and vigorous evil force. An *omnipresent* devil is everywhere, involved in all that is evil, and thus requires constant vigilance and confronta-tion. And a *foreign* devil is unlike us in all matters of importance: anti-Ameri-can, anti-Christian, anti-God, anti-free enterprise, antifamily, anti-freedom. The notion of a single, an omnipotent, omnipresent, foreign devil creates iden-tification among movement members through antithesis by contrasting them with forces totally alien and without redeeming social value. Thus, virtually all social movements attempt to polarize struggles through vilification or name-calling that casts their target "in an exclusively negative light," "attributes dia-bolical motives to foes," and "magnifies the opponent's powers."[41]

Many social movements perceive that two or more devils are plotting—conspiring—in secret to do something evil, sinister, or unlawful. The conspir-acy is a kind of super devil because it combines evil forces into a single cause. Conspiracy can be powerful rhetoric for social movements because it appeals to Americans who have always been fearful of "foreign" plots to undermine our constitutional rights and way of life. Conspiracy is such an important appeal of social movements that the subject of chapter 12 is how movements use conspiracy appeals to make their cases for desperately needed change or resistance to change.

Ridicule

Movement persuaders heap abuse on devils through ridicule, negative associations, and metaphors that may dehumanize them into pigs, rats, vermin, parasites, vultures, scum, and feces. Ridicule is an effective means of polarizing the social movement and its opposition. Alinsky claims that "ridicule is man's [woman's] most potent weapon" because "it is almost impossible to counterattack ridicule. Also it infuriates the opposition, who then react to your advantage."[42] Ron Roberts and Robert Moss write that ridicule is a form of humor usually employed by social movements and countermovements "to demean the status of another individual or group." They claim "Ridicule has been used with some success in keeping people 'in their place.' "[43]

What, then, is this potent rhetorical tool? Dictionaries tell us that to ridicule is to make a person, group, place, thing, action, or idea an object of laughter and even of scorn. Ridicule attacks the basic worth and credibility of persons and ideas and thus challenges assigned or claimed legitimacy. Social movements and countermovements employ ridicule to make fun of a person, group, place, thing, action, or idea for being inconsistent, illogical, inept, silly, monstrous, or inhuman.

At one level of ridicule, protestors portray *inconsistencies* and *self-contradictions* in institutional or movement beliefs, claims, and actions. For example, cartoons highlight contradictions between pro-life's beliefs and the murder of physicians in Florida, New York, and elsewhere. One portrays a man holding a Bible in one hand and a gun in the other near a clinic; the caption reads "The right-to-lifers have spoken."[44] Ridicule at this level attacks beliefs, claims, and actions directly and persons or groups indirectly. The assault is more ideological than personal but reveals glaring inconsistencies and self-contradictions that challenge a movement's or institution's trustworthiness by mocking or making fun of its alleged sincerity, honesty, and fairness—important credibility traits in U.S. society.

At a second level, protestors get more personal while mocking a group's ideas, actions, and statements as *illogical, irrational,* or *unreasonable.* An anti-Vietnam War poster and bumper sticker reads, "Join the army; travel to exotic, distant lands; meet exciting, unusual people and kill them."[45] A Native-American cartoon printed at Thanksgiving portrays a colonist walking away from three Indian braves, one of whom is saying, "They've shot twenty-nine of our braves, polluted all the rivers, killed most of the game, and raped the chief's sister. Now he wants us to drop over next Thursday for turkey dinner will all the fixin's."[46] These exaggerated irrationalities of the army and colonists attack their competence by ridiculing their powers of reasoning, judgment, and fairness.

At a third level, protestors get increasingly personal as they make fun of the opposition as *inept* or *stupid.* A Friend of Animals advertisement in magazines shows pictures of a lynx, fox, and raccoon wearing female wigs; the caption reads, "You look just as stupid wearing theirs."[47] In contrast, an opposition cartoon portrays a bald, shirtless, and overweight animal rights activist holding a sign reading "Save the Gophers" and lying flat on his face after tripping over a gopher hole. The caption reads, "Embarrassing moments within the animal rights movement."[48] This level of ridicule brings into question a wide range of credibility traits: intelligent, knowledgeable, mentally alert, honest, and rational. Charges of ineptness and stupidity not only demean the opposition, but imply obvious superiority of the attacker.

At a fourth level, protestors attack the opposition as *silly, trivial,* or *comical.* Arlo Guthrie wrote and performed one of the most famous songs of the 1960s student and antiwar movements following his arrest in New England while he was a vacationing college student. His rambling "Alice's Restaurant Massacre" that runs more than twenty minutes portrays the police chief, police officers, a blind judge, military recruiters, and psychiatrists as silly, outrageous, and ridiculous. This level of ridicule attacks persons and their actions more than ideas and claims and depicts oppositions as unworthy of serious consideration because they are so trivial and comical.

At a fifth level, protestors attack the opposition as *monstrous, bizarre,* and *grotesque.* Opponents are not silly buffoons but ugly monsters. An anticapitalist cartoon depicts a gross and bloated male in a suit saying, "Starvation's God's way of punishing those who have little or no faith in capitalism."[49] An anti-pro-life cartoon portrays two ugly, "dirty old men" carrying protest signs reading "Outlaw Abortion" and "Keep 'Em Barefoot and Pregnant."[50] This level of ridicule shows oppositions not merely as inconsistent, illogical, inept, or silly but as vicious humans. They are dangerous to humanity because they are industrious and vigorous in their efforts to exploit and harm others.

At a sixth level, protestors attack oppositions as *inhuman* and *brutish.* Movements portray their targeted enemies or devils as animals, insects, and diseases. For example, males are "chauvinist pigs" and "rats" (women's liberation); liquor dealers are "rummies" (temperance movement); and American Nazis are "cancers" (anti-hate group movement). This level of ridicule dehumanizes the opposition by portraying it as animalistic or an inanimate object without the abilities to reason, know, make judgments, or act fairly.

An implied comparison is present in all instances of ridicule. If the opposition is irrational, the movement is rational; if the opposition is stupid, the movement is intelligent; and if the opposition is monstrous, the movement is natural and attractive. The act of ridicule gives persuaders feelings of power, control over their environment and lives, and superiority. Ridicule is both a common ground and a confrontational strategy.

Obscenity

The act of swearing has always been a part of human social interaction. Sigmund Freud writes that "the first human being who hurled a curse instead of a weapon against his adversary was the founder of civilization."[51] Obscenity is a form of swearing that uses indecent words and symbolic acts. Political scientist Harold Laswell refers to the use of obscenity as "the process by which the irrational bases of society are brought out into the open."[52]

Obscenity is a rough instrument because it is the ultimate form of symbolic conflict. It is a potentially powerful tool for social protestors. "Dissent," argue Ray Fabrizio, Edith Karas, and Ruth Menmuir, "has its own rhetoric, one that can be studied in its full range of tones—resentful or resigned, angry or agonized, irate or ironic, furious or downright funny."[53]

Protestors against the war in Vietnam and U.S. culture in the 1960s and 1970s used obscenities to express their rage, frustrations, and perceptions after traditional language strategies and forms failed to get attention, to gain access to the mass media, or to change established policies and practices. They claimed that obscene rhetoric was appropriate for describing and attacking an obscene society engaged in obscene actions.

Haig Bosmajian writes that "the dissenter wants to be heard, to be listened to, and if shouting obscenities is the only way he [she] can get people to listen to him [her], so be it."[54] An obscene word, phrase, or gesture can provide a summation of the group situation that lends emotion to the group's political and social interests and reifies and magnifies issues at hand. The use of obscenity, then, reflects a political reality of frustration with and separateness from institutions and the environment that protestors can no longer tolerate. The international peace organization Naked for Peace and affiliated groups such as Baring Witness have conducted demonstrations from Antarctica to Australia, Spain, England, San Francisco, and Champaign, Illinois, in which nude women and men spell out peace words and symbols such as: Vote, Peace, Make Love Not War, No War, the peace symbol, and a peace dove. An article on the Web site entitled "Making Their Bodies Figures of Speech" explains:

> Women from all ages and walks of life took off their clothes, not because they are exhibitionists but because they felt it was imperative to do so. They wanted to unveil the truth about the horrors of war, to commune in their nudity with the vulnerability of Iraqi innocents, and to shock a seemingly indifferent Bush administration into paying attention.[55]

No symbol is intrinsically or literally *dirty*. Obscenity, like beauty, is in the eye and mind of the beholder. Words become dirty or taboo because of social conventions, not logical bases of argument. Specific words, phrases, and gestures may be viewed as more or less obscene over time. The contextual elements of who and where are vital. For instance, sex, position, age, and status influence perceptions of taboo symbols. Obscenities by women, children, teenagers, and high-status individuals are more shocking than those used by middle-aged men or dockworkers. Police officers have reacted most angrily to obscenities uttered by young, female protestors. The outrageousness of obscenity, particularly when used in public or sacred places and by young people, women, and professionals jolts people into awareness that a significant number of people are disaffected enough with society to violate its fundamental rules of conduct and its value system.

Obscenity is metaphorical because it implies meanings and disengages the symbol from the thing signified. Verbal obscenity implies a link between a person, group, or object to some religious, sexual, or excretory reality. For instance, calling someone a "son of a bitch" or a "bastard" implies more than birth heritage because it attacks an individual by linking the person to a socially negative construct. The strength of obscenity, then, lies in the linking or comparative process.

Verbal and nonverbal obscenities violate societal norms and expectations and, the more obscene the word or gesture, the greater the violations and the potential impact on an audience. During the Vietnam War, antiwar protestors used obscenity to alter the way Americans viewed the military conflict and society. Jerry Rubin, a founder of the Yippies, argued that a new language of protest was critical because institutions controlled the old language and thus perceptions of the war and its opposition:

> When they control the words, they control everything, and they got the words controlled. They got "war" meaning "peace"; they got "fuck" being a "bad word"; they got "napalm" being a good word—they got decency that to me is indecent. The whole thing is like backwards, and we gotta turn it around.[56]

Protestors may attempt to enhance self-concept and self-esteem by employing obscenities to discredit and humiliate the opposition. The sexual mocking of authority figures may relieve the protestor of personal feelings of inadequacy and reduce authority figures below the protestor's own perceived social worth. Each obscenity gives the user the power to mock and challenge the most powerful of foes in relative safety. Obscenity may also demonstrate the user's "sexual, social, and political liberation" from a repressive, "parental establishment."[57] Radical gay rights groups such as Act-Up and Queer Nation appear half-naked and exhibit erotic lovemaking during demonstrations and marches. Such obscenity demonstrates social and political independence, and exhibits freedom over one's mouth and body.

Protestors use obscenity to challenge the legitimacy of institutions by heaping obscenities on their perceived devils to discredit and humiliate them. For example, students at Kent State University called National Guard members "fascist bastards," and students at Jackson State College called police "motherfuckers."[58] Such obscenities enable social movements to define and stereotype the opposition as vile, hypocritical, impotent, and stupid—literally as obscene.

Social movements use obscenity to goad institutions into exhibiting their true natures for all to see. Protestors in Chicago during the 1968 Democratic National Convention bombarded the police with nonstop verbal and nonverbal obscenities. These continual taunts eventually resulted in what *The Walker Report to the National Commission on the Causes and Prevention of Violence* called "unrestrained and indiscriminate police violence," a "police riot."[59] Police gassed, clubbed, kicked, and used motorcycles to run over innocent onlookers, pedestrians, residents, delegates to the Democratic Convention, photographers, and reporters as well as the protestors who provoked the hatred. They discredited and humiliated themselves because they lost control, an unforgivable sin for institutions and their agents.

Obscenity-laden strategies preclude meaningful courses of action or dialogue with institutions, but they do express an extreme contempt for society's standards and a burning desire for revolutionary change. "Civility," Dan Rothwell observes, "is an instrument of the status quo; verbal obscenity is a symbol of rebellion against the power structure. Agitators seek profound change, and profanity offers a profound change from the accepted style of dissent."[60]

Ugly, obscene, and sometimes violent confrontations and media exposure may produce important by-products. They make moderate social movement elements and critics within the system seem respectable. Thus, institutions may open dialogues with moderate movement elements because of fear or to counteract radical elements. Obscenity may enhance the credibility of movement leaders among members and sympathizers because they have the nerve to shout what others only feel. For instance, Rothwell notes "the Black Panthers' obscene vilification of police apparently expresses the private feelings of many black Americans. Although they may not approve of the Panther terminology, they may admire those who have the courage and audacity to insult policemen."[61] Group chanting of obscenities makes everyone equal, involves everyone in the protest, and both shares and reduces the risk involved. Obscenity allows movement members to release pent-up hostility and fear. Psychologist Chaytor Mason asserts that obscenity serves as a safety valve that helps society function without excessive frustration.[62] Verbal aggression is often a surrogate for physical aggression and, consequently, may have a therapeutic value for society by sparing it from bloodshed.

While obscenity may be an effective means of performing persuasive functions for some social movement organizations, it may have serious adverse effects. Although obscenity may capture the attention of the public and the media, it may draw attention to itself and away from the social movement's demands, and even this attention tends to be short-lived. When the shock of seeing and hearing obscenities wears off, there is nothing left. Obscenities may become so commonplace in society, such as the famous "F-word," they no longer have any effect for protestors. The social unacceptability of verbal and nonverbal obscenity relegates its use to minorities in both society and social movements. The repugnance for the public use of profanity denies to social movements the support of important legitimizers in and out of the movement. Obscenity may produce violent reactions that members do not anticipate. Shortly after noon on May 4, 1970, a group of approximately fifty protestors approached a line of Ohio National Guardsmen on the Kent State University campus. The protestors were shouting obscenities, and a photograph clearly shows several students making obscene gestures. The

Guard moved forward to dispel the students from the Commons. In the end, four students lay dead and nine were wounded.[63]

Nonverbal and Symbolic Acts

Social movements utilize symbolic acts ranging from the logo on the organization's letterhead or Web site to the unmistakable "flipping the bird" to law enforcement officials. Our goal is not to provide a laundry list of such acts, but to illustrate the importance, power, and effectiveness of nonverbal, symbolic acts. Such acts may provide the essence of the message intended or enhance the persuasiveness of the message.

Clothes and appearance may generate a sense of shared group identification. Hippies of the 1960s, while decrying societal pressures to impose stultifying conformity on one and all, adhered to an identifying code of dress and appearance that included granny glasses, long hair, beards, old clothing, bandannas, and sandals. The group most noted for its opposition to the hippies and support of the war in Vietnam, construction workers, were clearly identifiable with their crew cuts, clean shaven faces, work clothes, and hard hats. The North American anarchist movement was an important part of the working class movements of the late nineteenth century but was thought dead by the end of the twentieth century. However, in the 1999 protests in Seattle against the World Trade Organization, the anarchists made a noticeable comeback. They gained attention when using the "Black Bloc," a tactic where protesters dressed in black with their faces covered and engaged in destroying property and confronting police.[64]

Sacred emblems are prominent in movements striving to espouse and sustain traditional values, beliefs, and attitudes. American, Confederate, and Aztec flags, Christian crosses and crucifixes, Jewish Stars of David, and Nazi swastikas are worn on clothing, portrayed on banners, and carried in demonstrations. The United Farm Workers carry red flags emblazoned with the black Aztec eagle to identify with rich historical heritage shared by farm workers and other immigrants of Mexican descent.

Movements use symbols to enhance identification. Leaders, members, sympathizers, and legitimizers may display a movement's symbol on placards, buttons, lapel pins, articles of clothing, and armbands to identify with one another and the cause. The symbol for women, gray panther, black panther, red rose (pro-life), and rusty clothes hanger (pro-choice) are prominent in contemporary movements. Those wishing to indicate their concern for the AIDS epidemic (including some members of Congress) have worn red ribbons, a symbolic gesture that communicates sympathy and perhaps agreement with the gay rights movement.

Protest groups create and employ symbolic gestures that communicate similarity of feelings, experiences, or attitudes. The peace movement of the 1960s and 1970s used the V sign formed by the index and forefinger to signify unity and commitment in their opposition to the war in Vietnam. The militant phase of the civil rights movement introduced the clenched fist sign to signify unity and power. Other movements—women's rights, antiwar, student rights, Native-American rights—adopted this sign for similar purposes.

During the Abolition Movement, hundreds of thousands of primarily Northern, middle-class white women participated in antislavery petition drives. The petitions were presented to members of Congress. During the age when women could not vote, petition drives provided a form of public participation in the debate over slavery. Their signatures became emblems of their existence, symbols of their opinions, and marks of their identity.[65]

Historically, symbolic acts have ranged from the violent to the nonviolent, from the illegal to civil disobedience, from a single actor or gesture to mass protests. Symbolic acts have included strikes, sit-ins, walkouts, picketing, guerrilla theater, vigils, burning draft cards, parades, and boycotts. A common antiwar act is to carry caskets representing military casualties to demonstrations, often in front of the White House or the Capitol Building. Demonstrators may file by and fill the caskets with the names of casualties.

CONCLUSIONS

Languaging strategies and tactics are the means for sharing cultural, political, and social values. They are the vehicles for social interaction and integration. Through interaction, we come to know ourselves, others, "our" society, and the world. Social movements use language "purposefully" to transform perceptions of society, to alter self-perceptions of members, to legitimize the movement, to prescribe courses of action, and to sustain the movement.

A rhetoric of identification may overcome differences and demonstrate commonality in many ways from simple gestures to common ideas to common hopes, values, or goals. The opposite is true for a rhetoric of polarization. Movements use language to make clear distinctions between groups in terms of "good" and "bad" or "us" and "them." The rhetoric of power controls symbols and definitions and hence perceptions and interpretations. Slogans have always been a powerful rhetorical device to enhance identification, purpose, and actions of movements. Likewise, music popularizes issues, enhances self-perceptions, lists demands, and prescribes courses of action.

Rhetorical tactics are specific, more narrow techniques that help to accomplish a larger strategy. Labeling generates positive or negative associations by forcing people to make judgments and evaluations. Ridicule polarizes the movement and its opposition, reducing the opposition to an object of laughter or scorn. Obscenity is the ultimate form of symbolic conflict, and it demands attention, expresses intense emotion, and provokes response. Nonverbal and symbolic acts generate a sense of shared group identity, whether a simple logo, emblem, or gesture.

Movements, above all, desire to alter beliefs, attitudes, and values to impact some behavior or action. Languaging strategies and tactics are the means by which social movements come into existence and accomplish their goals.

Notes

[1] Charles Wilkerson, "A Rhetorical Definition of Movements," *Central States Speech Journal* 27 (Summer 1976): 91.

[2] Paul Corcoran, "Language and Politics," *New Directions in Political Communication: A Resource Book*, David Swanson and Dan Nimmo, eds. (Newbury Park, CA: Sage, 1990): 53.

[3] George Herbert Mead, *Mind, Self, and Society* (Chicago: University of Chicago Press, 1972): 122.

[4] Dan Faules and Dennis Alexander, *Communication and Social Behavior* (Boston: Addison-Wesley, 1979): 130.

[5] Richard Weaver, *Language as Sermonic* (Baton Rouge: Louisiana State University Press, 1970): 120–121.

[6] Wayne Booth, *Modern Dogma and the Rhetoric of Assent* (Chicago: University of Chicago Press, 1974): 164, 193.

[7] Hugh Duncan, *Symbols in Society* (New York: Oxford University Press, 1968): 8.

[8] Robert D. Brooks, "Black Power: The Dimensions of a Slogan," *Western Speech* 34 (Spring 1970): 108–114.

[9] Harold D. Laswell, "The Theory of Propaganda," *American Political Science Review* 21 (1927): 627.

[10] Murray Edelman, *The Symbolic Uses of Politics* (Urbana: University of Illinois Press, 1967): 115.

[11] James R. Andrews, "History and Theory in the Study of the Rhetoric of Social Movements," *Central States Speech Journal* 31 (Winter 1980): 274.

[12] Kenneth Burke, *A Rhetoric of Motives* (Berkeley: University of California Press, 1969): 21-45.

[13] Lawrence W. Rosenfield, "Set Theory: Key to Understanding Kenneth Burke's Use of the Term 'Identification,'" *Western Speech* 33 (Summer 1969): 176.

[14] Burke, 55, 46.

[15] Gregory Stephens, "Frederick Douglass' Multiracial Abolitionism: 'Antagonistic Cooperation' and 'Redeemable Ideals' in the July 5 Speech," *Communication Studies* 48 (Fall 1997): 175–194.

[16] Burke, 25.

[17] Allan Carlson, "Twenty-Five Years Into the Culture of Death," *Vital Speeches of the Day* (15 March 1998): 347–348.

[18] For speeches and excellent analysis, see "Stokely Carmichael: Two Speeches on Black Power," Wayne Brockriede and Robert Scott, *The Rhetoric of Black Power* (New York: Harper and Row, 1969): 481.

[19] Frederick Douglass, "An Ex-Slave Discusses Slavery, July 4, 1852," *A Treasury of the World's Great Speeches*, Houston Peterson, ed. (New York: Simon and Schuster, 1965): 481.

[20] March 12, 1963, from a tape recording.

[21] September 14, 1985, from a video recording.

[22] Burke, 45.

[23] Andrew A. King and Floyd Douglas Anderson, "Nixon, Agnew, and the 'Silent Majority': A Case Study in the Rhetoric of Polarization," *Western Speech* 35 (Fall 1971): 244.

[24] Richard L. Lanigan, "Urban Crisis: Polarization and Communication," *Central States Speech Journal* 21 (Summer 1970): 108.

[25] King and Anderson, 244.

[26] John W. Bowers, Donovan J. Ochs, and Richard J. Jensen, *The Rhetoric of Agitation and Control*, 2nd ed. (Long Grove, IL: Waveland Press, 1993): 34-35.

[27] Lanigan, 112.

[28] Kenneth Hacker, "Political Linguistic Discourse Analysis," *The Theory and Practice of Political Communication Research*, Mary Stuckey, ed. (Albany: University of New York Press, 1996): 29.

[29] J. Vernon Jensen, "British Voices on the Eve of the American Revolution: Trapped by the Family Metaphor," *Quarterly Journal of Speech* 63 (February 1977): 43–50.

[30] Philip C. Wander, "The Savage Child: The Image of the Negro in the Pro-Slavery Movement," *Southern Speech Communication Journal* 37 (Summer 1972): 335–360.

[31] George E. Shankel, *American Mottoes and Slogans* (New York: Wilson, 1941): 7.

[32] Stephen Kosokoff and Carl W. Carmichael, "The Rhetoric of Protest: Song, Speech, and Attitude Change," *Southern Speech Communication Journal* 35 (Summer 1970): 295–302.

[33] Kosokoff and Carmichael, 301.

[34] Ralph R. Knupp, "A Time for Every Purpose Under Heaven: Rhetorical Dimensions of Protest Music," *Southern Speech Communication Journal* 46 (Summer 1981): 383–384.

[35] Cheryl Irwin Thomas, "'Look What They've Done to My Song, Ma': The Persuasiveness of Song," *Southern Speech Communication Journal* 39 (Spring 1974): 261.

[36] Charles J. Stewart, "The Ego Function of Protest Songs: An Application of Gregg's Theory of Protest Rhetoric," *Communication Studies* 42 (Fall 1991): 241–243.

[37] Stokely Carmichael, "Black Power," speech delivered in Detroit, 30 July 1966, from a tape recording.

[38] Kenneth Burke, *The Philosophy of Literary Form* (Baton Rouge: Louisiana State University Press, 1941): 193; Burke, *The Philosophy of Literary Form* (University of California Press edition, 1973): 39–40.

[39] Kenneth Burke, *The Grammar of Motives* (Berkeley: University of California Press, 1969): 407.

[40] Eric Hoffer, *The True Believer* (New York: Mentor, 1951): 87.

[41] Marsha L. Vanderford, "Vilification and Social Movements: A Case Study of Pro-Life and Pro-Choice Rhetoric," *Quarterly Journal of Speech* 75 (May 1989): 166–167.

[42] Saul Alinsky, *Rules for Radicals: A Practical Primer for Realistic Radicals* (New York: Vintage, 1971): 128.

[43] Ron E. Roberts and Robert Marsh Kloss, *Social Movements: Between the Balcony and the Barricade* (St. Louis: C.V. Mosby, 1974): 154.

[44] Cartoon by Oliphant, *The Denver Post*, Los Angeles Times Syndicate.

[45] Poster by Rosner.

[46] Cartoon from *Playboy*, 1969.

[47] Friends of Animals (Darien, CT: n.d.).

[48] Cartoon by Leigh Rubin.

[49] Cartoon from *Sawyer Press.*

[50] Cartoon by Bill Mauldin, *Chicago Sun Times.*

[51] As reported in "A Good Word for Bad Words," *Time*, 14 December 1981, 77.

[52] Harold Laswell, *Psychology and Politics* (Englewood Cliffs, NJ: Prentice-Hall, 1960): 184.

[53] Ray Fabrizio, Edith Karas, and Ruth Menmuir, *The Rhetoric of No* (New York: Holt, Rinehart and Winston, 1970): vi.

[54] Haig A. Bosmajian, "Obscenity and Protest," *Dissent: Symbolic Behavior and Rhetorical Strategies* (Boston: Allyn & Bacon, 1972): 299.

[55] www.sfheart.com/naked_for_peace.html, accessed 19 January 2006.

[56] As reported in Theodore Windt, Jr., "The Diatribe: Last Resort for Protest," *Quarterly Journal of Speech* 58 (February 1972): 10.

[57] Bosmajian, 298.

[58] *The Report of the President's Commission on Campus Unrest* (Washington, DC: U.S. Government Printing Office, 1970): 266, 439.

[59] Daniel Walker, *Rights in Conflict: The Violent Confrontation of Demonstrators and Police in the Streets of Chicago During the Week of the Democratic National Convention* (New York: Bantam Books, 1968): 135, 146, 154.

[60] J. Dan Rothwell, "Verbal Obscenity: Time for Second Thoughts," *Western Speech* 35 (Fall 1971): 234.

[61] Rothwell, 236.

[62] J. Dan Rothwell, *Telling It Like It Isn't: Language Misuse and Malpractice* (Englewood Cliffs, NJ: Prentice-Hall, 1982): 106.

[63] *Report of the President's Commission,* 265–410.

[64] Lynn Owens and L. Kendall Palmer, "Making the News: Anarchist Counter-Public Relations on the World Wide Web," *Critical Studies in Media Communication* 20 (December 2003): 335.

[65] Susan Zaeske, "Signatures of Citizenship: The Rhetoric of Women's Antislavery Petitions," *Quarterly Journal of Speech* 88 (May 2002): 147–168.

CHAPTER

8

Political Argument
in Social Movements

Our discussion of social movement persuasion now turns in a new direction. Since defining social movements and describing the systems perspective in the first two chapters, we have focused on the communication processes that characterize the growth and decline of individual movements. Remember the part of the definition that stated a movement "promotes or opposes change in societal norms or values" and encounters "opposition in a moral struggle." We will now analyze conflicts as arguments between opposing points of view. This chapter explains the concept of "argument" as it is used in rhetorical studies in general and presents a typology of arguments—a set of recognizable "moves" that recur in social movement persuasion—so that we can better understand the ways that movements propose and oppose change.

THE NATURE OF ARGUMENT

"Argue" is a familiar verb. You might have an argument with the person you are dating. The news is full of arguments among politicians. In general conversation, "arguing" is often perceived as hostile, destructive, and unreasonable. Consequently, we avoid it whenever possible. But communication theories, such as the interpretive systems model, remind us that humans reason and that two individual humans cannot reason identically all the time. When two (or more) parties reason differently about a subject that concerns them both, the result is a conflict in reasoning—an argument. Viewed from this perspective, arguments can be hostile or friendly, destructive or constructive, unreasonable or reasonable. Those of us who study and teach about human communication in democratic societies cling to the belief that even serious differences in reasoning can often (although not always) be friendly, constructive, and reasonable. Even when one of the parties, frustrated by unsatisfying discussions and debates, feels it necessary to go beyond the normal means of discussion to demonstrate, threaten, or revolt it is wise to explore the underlying conflict in reasoning that caused the uproar.

We will use the term "argument" in two ways, both of which may be different from your understanding. First, an argument is a linking of ideas in support of an identifiable proposition.[1] Second, arguments involve a clash in reasoning between parties. In his essay, "Where Is Argument?", Wayne Brockriede observed that "human activity does not usefully constitute an argument until some person perceives what is happening as an argument."[2] Two people may disagree but not perceive themselves to be arguing, or they can be in basic agreement but perceive themselves as arguing (perhaps because they dislike one another or because each wants to assert dominance).

The connection between the uses of "argument" becomes clearer when we consider British social psychologist Michael Billig's idea that human thought is an internal argument:

> All too often, psychologists have ignored the essentially rhetorical and argumentative dimensions of thinking. Human thinking is not merely a matter of processing information or following cognitive rules. Thinking is to be observed in action in discussions, in the rhetorical cut-and-thrust of argumentation. To deliberate upon an issue is to argue with oneself, even to persuade oneself. It is no linguistic accident that to propose a reasoned justification is rightly called "offering an argument."[3]

Sometimes we make part of this internal conversation public by stating an argument—casting it out as bait on the waters of human interaction to see if we get a bite. Chaim Perelman directs our attention to the way this bait attracts "adherents."[4] If they swallow the argument and make it their own, the two arguers are thus joined by the argument, and they both then take it in search of new adherents.

We mull over all relevant thoughts and values in an internal conversation, anticipate differences between our reasoning and the reasoning of those likely to hear us, and then make a statement that links ideas to support our position and/or to oppose their position. Either through agreement or disagreement we position ourselves relative to the proposed/opposed change. Because social movements, by definition, propose or oppose changes, we will present a typology of arguments related to the kinds of changes sought by the arguers. A typology of political argument based on the theme of change enables us to study the types of argument that recur in various movements and in ordinary systemic political rhetoric. Much as the chemist looks for the combination of known elements, the rhetorical analyst can study the ways different social movements use and combine basic kinds of argument.

Traditional analysts have relied on the writings of Aristotle and his successors to describe recurrent rhetorical techniques. As Herbert Simons suggested, however, social movements and the people who carry their arguments can rarely afford to use the logic of polite discussion.[5] If we want to taste the distinctive flavor of a social movement's persuasion, we must approach it on its own terms by studying how the flavor derives from the unique blend of the arguments available to it. A typology of political arguments can help us understand the kinds of ingredients from which the movement's persuasion is blended.

Rossiter's Political Spectrum

Clinton Rossiter created a typology of seven political philosophies based on orientation toward change.[6] The first, *Revolutionary Radicalism,* sees societal institutions as "diseased and oppressive, traditional values dissembling and dishonest; and it proposes to supplant them with an infinitely more benign way of life." *Radicalism* is "dissatisfied with the existing order, committed to a blueprint for thoroughgoing change, and thus willing to initiate reform, but its patience and peacefulness set it off sharply from the revolutionary brand." *Liberalism* is generally satisfied with the existing order and believes that the status quo can be improved "substantially without betraying its ideals or wrecking its institutions." *Conservatism,* like liberalism, is satisfied with the existing order but is suspicious of change. "The Conservative," says Rossiter, "knows that change is the rule of life . . . but insists that it be sure-footed and respectful of the past. . . . [The Conservative's] natural preferences are for stability over change, continuity over experiment, the past over the future." *Standpattism* prefers today over either past or future; it opposes any change, no matter how respectful of the past, believing that "society can be made static." *Reaction* "sighs for the past and feels that a retreat back into it, piecemeal or large scale, is worth trying." Reaction differs from Standpattism in two ways: it is unwilling to accept the present, and it is amenable to changing the present state of society. Reaction, like radicalism, limits the means it will employ to effect that change. But *Revolutionary Reaction* is willing and anxious to use subversion and violence to overthrow established values and institutions and to restore the era it views as the "Golden Age."

Rossiter's typology has several important rhetorical implications. First, it reveals that "revolutionaries" have much in common, whether they seek a New Age or a return to a Golden Age. They are willing to subvert and to kill, and they disdain discussion and compromise. A second rhetorical implication is that philosophies adjacent to one another share enough fundamental assumptions that their disagreements are argued in roughly compatible worldviews. The believers in adjacent philosophies appear reasonable to one another in that each regards the other as a potential, if misguided, ally. They concur enough to converse but differ enough to argue.

The third rhetorical implication is that philosophies opposite one another share no common assumptions. Believers in opposite philosophies make little sense to one another. These partisans have great difficulty persuading one another because their fundamental differences preclude compromise and constrain their ability to adjust to the other's assumptions. Indeed, they are more likely to talk *about* one another than *with* one another.

The fourth rhetorical implication of Rossiter's spectrum is consistent with the social judgment approach to attitude change: we distort our comparative judgments when we are ego involved.[7] This is particularly important to the study of social movements where we find an abundance of ego-involved persons. When we are ego involved, we distance ourselves from all those with whom we disagree and lump them into one perceptual category, even if they disagree with one another. We presume that they must agree with one another if they disagree with us, and we exaggerate their agreement with people whose positions are close to their own.

Thus, people create, rediscover, and rehearse arguments in anticipation of a chance to voice them. As Billig noted, the process of thinking is itself argumentative.[8] Every argument faces in some direction and implies disagreement with at least one other position. This is not to say that all arguments are well chosen or supported; indeed, they may not be voiced. But the set of arguments heard from a social movement provides evidence of individual and collective thinking.

Adjusting Rossiter's Model

We can extend the usefulness of Rossiter's spectrum by shaping it into a circle so that revolutionary radicalism and revolutionary reaction are adjacent to one another (see figure 8.1). In the center of figure 8.2 is apathy, ambivalence, and/or indecision; the perimeter represents intense or vehement argument. This figure presents Rossiter's seven philosophical types as spokes on a wheel rather than points on a circle, with the pure philosophical

Figure 8.1   Rossiter's Political Spectrum

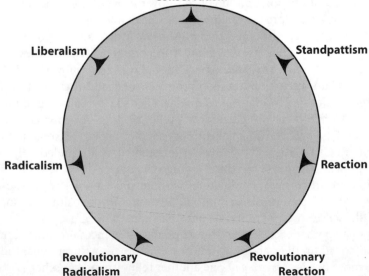

stances located on the rim and apathy at the hub. Imagine various arguments located along one of the spokes and across the wheel appears another philosophical position with its own continuum of arguments. The arguments of radical speeches and pamphlets would cluster toward the rim, while dispassionate academic discussions of social injustice might cluster toward the center. The arguers in each spoke agree about the nature of change, but disagree about the intensity of their beliefs or about the need for action.

THE TYPES OF POLITICAL ARGUMENT

The spokes of the wheel delineate seven additional types of political argument. An argument found between the spokes—for example, between Radical and Liberal positions, or between the Revolutionary Radical and Revolutionary Reaction positions—is an argument that reflects the arguer's anticipated differences with the audience's philosophical assumptions. These seven types of argument are Insurgent, Innovative, Progressive, Retentive, Reversive, Restorative, and Revolutionary (see figure 8.2).

Insurgent Argument

Insurgent argument falls between the Revolutionary Radical and Radical spokes of the model. It is typified by agreement on the corrupt, mendacious, and exploitative nature of societal norms, values, and institutions. The established order is vilified; specific individuals, institutions, and groups are held

---

Figure 8.2   Typology of Political Argument

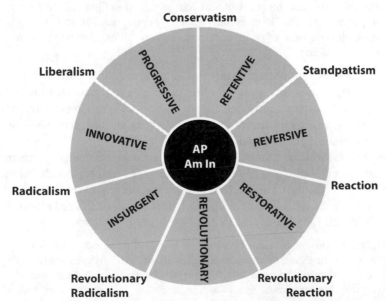

directly accountable for problems. The Industrial Workers of the World (IWW) blamed employers, as a group, for social conditions in the United States. The preamble to their Constitution of 1908 declared:

> The working class and the employing class have nothing in common. There can be no peace so long as hunger and want are found among the millions of working people and the few, who make up the employing class, have all the good things in life. Between these two classes a struggle must go on until the workers of the world organize as a class, take possession of the earth and the machinery of production, and abolish the wage system.[9]

The IWW's position that "there can be no peace" anticipates the call for patience or hope for incremental improvement in circumstances. Labor leader John Swinton was more specific in his denunciation of President Grover Cleveland for breaking the Pullman Strike of 1894:

> [President Cleveland] has this year stood out as a servile, mercenary and pusillanimous politician, the ally of money against manhood, fully ready to exercise his power, real and assumed, for the enslavement of the laborious masses who elected him to office.[10]

Roughly fifty years later, Black Muslim leader Malcolm X blamed the American government in its totality for the condition of Black America. He argued:

> You and I in America are faced not with a segregationist conspiracy, we're faced with a government conspiracy. Everyone who's filibustering is a senator—that's the government. Everyone who's finagling in Washington, D.C. is a congressman—that's the government. You don't have anyone putting blocks in your path but people who are part of the government. The same government that you go abroad to fight and die for is the government that is in a conspiracy to deprive you of your voting rights, deprive you of your economic opportunities, deprive you of decent education.[11]

The IWW, John Swinton, and Malcolm X all attributed blame for undesirable social conditions to a group or class of people, an important individual, or institution. Insurgent arguments imply that destroying the perpetrator can cure social ills, and they warn audiences to beware of outsiders who council cooperation, moderation, or patience.

Because radicalism is one boundary of the insurgent category, insurgent arguments rarely call explicitly for violent change. Indeed, much insurgent argument is antiviolent. These advocates are not willing to let the new order evolve slowly and naturally, but neither are they prepared to shed blood. Abolitionist William Lloyd Garrison in 1844 exhorted his followers:

> Up, then, with the banner of revolution! Not to shed blood, not to injure the person or estate of an oppressor, not by force of arms to resist any law, not to countenance a servile insurrection, not to wield any carnal weapons! No, ours must be a bloodless strife, . . . to overcome evil with

good. . . . Secede, then, from the government. Submit to its exactions, but pay it no allegiance, and give it no voluntary aid.[12]

Nevertheless, insurgent argument is not timid. In his 1934 proletariat play, *Waiting for Lefty*, Clifford Odets has a disillusioned wife tell her cabdriver husband how to fight the "bosses":

> JOE: One man can't . . .

> EDNA: I don't say one man! I say a hundred, a thousand, a whole million, I say. But start in your own union. Get those hack boys together! Sweep out those racketeers like a pile of dirt! Stand up like men and fight for the crying kids and wives. . . . Get brass toes on your shoes and know where to kick![13]

"Kicking" is arguably violent, but it is well short of terrorism or assassination. People for the Ethical Treatment of Animals (PETA) announced a campaign for the summer of 2000 to discourage children from fishing, a position that challenges the traditional image of Grandpa spending quality time with the kids, teaching them about wholesome fun:

> In a campaign aimed at getting kids to leave rods and reels behind as they leave for summer vacation, "Gill the Fish"—PETA's six-foot-tall "Save Our Schools" mascot—will distribute "Look Don't Hook" toy binoculars to students after school. . . . Why the flap over fishing? Fish feel pain—they have neurochemical systems like humans and sensitive nerve endings in their lips and mouths. They begin to die slowly of suffocation the moment they are pulled out of the water. And fishing hurts other animals, too, like birds and otters who swallow hooks and plastic bait or get tangled in lost fishing line. PETA is urging kids to give fish a break and, instead, learn about turtles, birds, and other wildlife by viewing them in nature.[14]

Mild as the insurgent message may be, the PETA campaign was a direct assault on some widely shared values and activities that shape summer vacations.

Insurgent argument may challenge recollections of what was or images of what could be. For example, many African Americans recall the effects of segregation at the hands of white officials, employers, and unions. The Web site for the United Automobile Aerospace and Agricultural Implement Workers (UAW), however, tells of the shared struggle for equity and justice and its association with Martin Luther King, Jr.

> UAW President Walter Reuther saw civil rights as a moral issue important to the continued success of American democracy and U.S. labor and civil rights leader Dr. Martin Luther King Jr. believed the support of labor unions would be an important factor in winning the fight minorities faced. As a result, their philosophies spawned a close friendship between the two. . . .

> Reuther marched alongside King many times during the 1960s, including the march in Birmingham, Ala., where police used dogs, fire hoses and other inhumane tactics before beating and arresting many of the march-

ers. King was among the religious leaders arrested that day. . . . It was his friend, Walter Reuther, who bailed King out of jail. . . .

> Organized labor continues to be a powerful force for social change. "I don't think you can separate civil rights and the rights of workers, for me it's one in the same" said Congressman John Lewis (D-Ga.).[15]

Rather than looking to their past, the United Farm Workers Union points out that union representatives in California's strawberry fields are better able to enforce pesticide laws than is the government:

> Strawberry workers in a union could act as marshals overseeing the use of pesticides more effectively than stretched and absent government agencies. They could do the same for issues of health, safety, child labor and wages. Moreover, union strawberry workers would work to take responsibility for their own condition, seeking better wages and benefits that would ripple through their communities. Union strawberry workers would bring sanity to the field hiring system. Willingness to provide sexual favors or not question conditions would no longer be a criteria [sic] for hiring. In addition to providing strawberry workers with the ability to speak up for themselves, their legitimate concern about their companies' success could bear fruit for the industry.[16]

Insurgent argument, then, is confrontational. It focuses on one or more social ills and blames them on persons, institutions, or values that are integral parts of institutions. Strategically, insurgent argument calls for strong action.

Innovative Argument

Innovative argument falls between the Radical and Liberal spokes of the Rossiter model and is characterized by a nagging dissatisfaction with the existing order and a preference for experimental change. There is an almost equal aversion to violence and to the status quo. Fundamental questions include: Is the political system part of the problem or part of the solution? Can normal channels produce sufficient change? Can actual practice be made to conform to traditional values?

Ralph Smith and Russell Windes suggest that it is advisable for social movement persuaders to identify discrepancies between traditional values and current practice and to argue that their innovation is, in fact, more traditional than the status quo.[17] This is a recurrent feature of innovative arguments. As mentioned in chapter 5, American Federation of Labor founder Samuel Gompers tied the goals and tactics of his movement to "Americanism." In a 1908 article, he explained:

> We American trade unionists want to work out our problems in the spirit of true Americanism—a spirit that embodies our broadest and highest ideals. If we do not succeed, it will be due to no fault of ours. We have been building the A. F. of L. in conformity with what we believe to be the original intent and purpose of America.[18]

Similarly, Martin Luther King's "I Have a Dream" speech grounded his call for integration in both Americanism and Christianity:

> I still have a dream. It is a dream deeply rooted in the American dream. It is a dream that one day this nation will rise up and live out the true meaning of its creed: "We hold these truths to be self-evident; that all men are created equal." I have a dream that one day every valley shall be exalted, every hill and mountain shall be made low, the rough places will be made plane and crooked places will be made straight, and the glory of the Lord shall be revealed, and all flesh shall see it together.[19]

A 1993 mailing from the Native American Rights Fund (NARF) identifies Chippewa values:

> Every Chippewa is taught from birth that these seven basic qualities must guide us as individuals and tribal members: honesty, respect, generosity, kindness, fairness, sharing and spirituality. Only by keeping this path can we meet our responsibilities to ourselves and to one another.[20]

The letter proceeds to argue that the Chippewa often stand alone with these values, despite the fact that most Americans would profess to hold similar values.

> Because my people are abused by a system of government that is not honest with us, is not respectful of our culture or our fundamental rights; a government that continues to degrade and abuse the land on which we all depend."[21]

The letter explains that the problem is that the practices of institutions are unfaithful to the fundamental values that are being upheld by the social movement.

> I ask you, can America continue to stand proud as a nation revered for its freedoms when its government allows religious freedom—the first freedom enunciated in the First Amendment—to be just a hollow promise to the *first* Americans?[22]

Of course, innovative arguments are frequently met by the response that their innovation is unwise or impractical. Many innovative arguments anticipate this response by differentiating the situation in question from similar situations in the past. Industrialist Henry Ford dismissed history as a standard by which to assess proposed innovation:

> What do we care what they did 500 or 1000 years ago? It means nothing to me. History is more or less bunk. It's tradition. We don't want tradition. We want to live in the present and the only history that is worth a tinker's damn is the history we make today.[23]

Yet sometimes "the history we make today" is an innovation based on the past.

Social movements seek to have the larger society commemorate their historic moments and leaders. The Martin Luther King, Jr., holiday and Labor Day are two examples. In 2000, after a two-year campaign, the United Farm Workers Union convinced California to declare March 31 a state holiday in honor of Cesar Chavez. His widow, Helen, issued the following statement:

During his lifetime, Cesar always tried to avoid personal recognition because he knew his work was really accomplished with the help of millions of decent people from all walks of life. So this bill is really a tribute to those who marched with him and sacrificed for farm workers and others who are less fortunate.

Therefore, we believe today's action is meaningful because, under the education and public service provisions of Sen. Polanco's bill, millions of school children will learn about Cesar's lessons on social justice, nonviolence and service to others.

With this unique legislation, Cesar's birthday won't be just another holiday. It will be a living tribute to this great man. It will be what Cesar was all about. He didn't just talk about helping the poorest and most powerless among us change their lives; he went out and did something about it.[24]

Stephen Browne has studied how Crispus Attucks, one of the casualties of the Boston Massacre, became memorialized in Boston through a determined campaign to transform him from "a figure virtually without identity into a major symbol of African-American resistance." He relates that

by 1860 Crispus Attucks had not only been retrieved from the oblivion of the Boston Massacre Orations; he had been inspirited and transformed into a living icon of a 'new' history, the telling of which had become the business of annual commemorations.[25]

Innovative argument, then, seeks substantial changes in the norms, values, or institutions of society without violent action. It grounds its proposals in the society's dominant creeds or values and rejects as irrelevant the suggestion that the innovation cannot or will not work. It is easy to see that innovative argument is safer than insurgent argument because innovators embrace rather than scorn the principles on which the society is founded, and they claim a moral advantage over both their insurgent and institutional adversaries. This enables innovators to confront the immediate but transient manifestations of the social order such as a corrupt official, a discriminatory law, or an unfair labor practice without confronting the order itself.

The danger of innovative argument is that the moderate elements of society often mistake innovative argument for insurgency because it seeks major change, sometimes through the use of "unpleasant" tactics. Just as King's dream contrasts with Malcolm X's indictment, so any innovative argument should be advanced as a reasonable alternative to insurgency. It argues that major changes are necessary for the established order to fulfill its own destiny. But when innovative arguments fail to present such a clear contrast, they are vulnerable to characterization as "subversive" or "revolutionary."

Progressive Argument

Progressive argument is a "systemic" approach to political argument. Unlike insurgent arguments that seek to replace the established means for reconciling differences or innovative arguments that believe in the underlying values but object to the ways that society acts on those values, progressive argument takes established procedures as givens. The philosophies of liberalism and conservatism agree that change of some sort is inevitable and that the institutional system for resolving disagreements should be used. Neither liberalism nor conservatism pursues change through "extra-systemic" or proscribed means such as subversion, violence, or illegal strikes. Progressive argument is therefore conducted within the "rules of the game." Robert Cathcart has described this as "managerial" rather than "confrontational" rhetoric.[26]

The United Farm Workers Union has often been confrontational, but in 1998 they used California's ballot initiative provision to work toward a new way to protect their jobs by protecting farmland from saltwater. Their Web site's discussion of the measure would do credit to any Washington public relations firm:

> Measure K, a United Farm Workers-sponsored initiative on the Nov. 3, 1998 ballot, was approved by voters in the Pajaro Valley Water Management Agency. It requires greater emphasis on conservation in solving serious salt-water intrusion in the coastal basin around Watsonville. More importantly, Measure K gives farm workers and other rural residents a greater voice in water use and acquisition.[27]

The ability to use progressive argument effectively is important when the social movement seeks to institutionalize the concessions won from the system. Lyndon Johnson's answer to critics who charged that "The System" was responsible for poverty, discrimination, and other social ills was a "War on Poverty." In his first State of the Union address, Johnson told Congress and the nation:

> We have in 1964 a unique opportunity and obligation—to prove the success of our system; to disprove those cynics at home and abroad who question our purpose and our competence. If we fail, if we fritter and fumble away our opportunity in needless, senseless quarrels between Democrats and Republicans, or between the House and the Senate, or between the South and North, or between the Congress and the administration, then history will rightfully judge us harshly.[28]

Johnson offered his audience an implicit choice: keep pride in your established system by making serious efforts to change socioeconomic conditions, or keep socioeconomic conditions as they are at the expense of proving the insurgents and innovators correct.

Progressive argument often attempts to stress the feasibility of patience and compromise with "the system." Johnson's 1968 State of the Union employed such an argument:

> A moment ago I spoke of despair and frustrated hopes in the cities where the fires of disorder burned last summer. We can—and in time we will—change that despair into confidence, and change those frustrations into achievements. But violence will never bring progress.[29]

In her stirring keynote address to the 1976 Democratic National Convention, African-American Congresswoman Barbara Jordan made it clear that she believed in the political system and the Democratic Party. She also distanced herself from the insurgent argument of Malcolm X and, more subtly, from the innovative argument of Martin Luther King:

> We cannot improve on the system of government handed down to us by the founders of the Republic, there is no way to improve upon that. But what we can do is to find new ways to implement that system and realize our destiny.[30]

But the rules of the game Johnson and Jordan supported were not static: the system Jordan praised in 1976 was not identical to the one faced by Dr. King in 1963 nor the one confronted by Malcolm X in 1965.

Labor unions today are usually able to resolve grievances through collective bargaining—the system for which they struggled prior to the New Deal. Detroit was an important center of union activity throughout the twentieth century. Consistent with that culture, the faculty of Wayne State University in Detroit unionized as members of the American Association of University Professors and the American Federation of Teachers (AAUP-AFT). This excerpt from the union local president's letter to the university president announced their intent to strike in terms far different from the labor tensions of the 1930s:

> Our fair-share proposal . . . will add newly hired faculty and academic staff to the union for a short time, giving us a fair opportunity to recruit them as long-term members. Perhaps more significantly, it will give an unmistakable signal to the administration, faculty, and staff of this university that the antiunion days are over. . . . All members of our bargaining unit want a fair compensation package. The offer your administration has put on the table does not meet that simple test. Our union recognizes that the university has many unmet needs. For over a decade, the leadership of our union has called for greater investment in technology and has warned of the university's dangerously heavy dependence on state appropriations for revenue. So we are not naive about the economics of the university, and we did not go into negotiations asking your administration to match the raises that faculties at some other state universities are receiving.[31]

The letter clearly positions the union and its members as insiders; they recognize that the university has unmet needs and imply that they share a commitment to the same code of fairness. Thus, yesterday's insurgency and innovation can become today's progressivism.

Institutions often refuse to listen to the arguments of insurgent and revolutionary persuaders. Because progressive argument follows established procedures, it more easily gains an audience. Progressive argument often refers to the threat of insurgency in order to press for moderate change.

Retentive Argument

Retentive argument revolves around conservative and standpat efforts to preserve important elements of the status quo. It bridges the distance between the standpatter who wants to maintain the status quo and the conservative who, although wary of change, recognizes its inevitability. The conservative prefers the present to the proposed future and attempts to insure that only necessary and practical changes are instituted. Retentive argument concerns cautious, minimal change, and it often seems trivial to radicals and reactionaries, both of whom want substantial changes.

Since retentive argument seeks to retain important procedures or qualities that are under attack, it often exhibits an ominous tone. In his memoirs, Senator Barry Goldwater reveals his hope that

> if what I have to say strikes a response in the hearts and minds of other Americans, perhaps they will enlist in the cause to keep our country strong and to restrain those who seek to diminish the importance and significance of the individual.[32]

Segregationists argued for retention of the old ways by wearing buttons that said simply, "NEVER!" and (as we will see in chapter 9) the New Right Movement coalesced around arguments to retain control over the Panama Canal.

Retentive argument is heard in presidential campaigns when we are warned about opponents. Gary Allen, who frequently wrote for the John Birch Society, warned in 1976:

> If even half of the Carter program is adopted, the average worker in America will face crippling new taxes, horrendous new regulations, and a spiraling rate of inflation that could wipe out any savings he hopes to have. It is a program for Big Government and "efficient Socialism." It is enough to make any sensible person wring his hands in horror.[33]

Jimmy Carter Democrats in 1980 and Walter Mondale Democrats in 1984 said comparable things about the anticipated effects of the Reagan programs on the poor, the elderly, and delicate foreign relations, and many Bush supporters in 1992 echoed Allen's critique of Carter in their campaign against Bill Clinton. All three campaigns lost, a sign that apocalyptic threats often reflect more fear than they generate.

Not all retentive argument is threatening. While governor of California, Ronald Reagan ridiculed criticism of socioeconomic conditions in the United States by comparing accomplishments here with the Soviet Union:

> I think if you put your minds to it you could match the Soviet Union's achievements. You would only have to cut all the paychecks 75 percent, send 69 million people back to the farm, tear down almost three-fourths of the houses in America, destroy 69 percent of the steel-making capacity, rip up fourteen of every fifteen miles of road, two-thirds of the railroad track, junk 85 percent of the autos, and tear out nine out of ten telephones.[34]

In this passage the politically conservative Reagan focused on retaining good things about American life. But we should not assume that only conservatives try to conserve.

Anarchists recently used retentive argument in relation to control of the Internet and biotechnology. The Black Ribbon Campaign stated that people value the Internet for its anarchistic character: the free exchange of information and ideas among people around the world, without the intervention of a governing body. Capitalists and other authoritarians would like to end this: they want nothing more than to attempt to carve up the Internet into an array of corporate/government fiefdoms, to make it just another commodity.[35]

The anarchists are similarly concerned that biotechnology companies seeking to alter the world's food production techniques are getting out of control:

> What right do these companies have to tinker with the DNA of these life forms for private gain, when the changes they make can (and do) have unforeseen consequences and will continue in perpetuity? Can the scientists-for-hire who do the gene tinkering for these firms see into the future and definitively say that no threat exists from biotechnologically-mutated life forms? They can't, of course, and they don't, if they wish to remain employed by the firm! You have the foundations for very poor decision making all there, a recipe for disaster.[36]

Retentive argument seeks to save or to preserve as much of the present as possible. It may range from Allen's alarm to Reagan's ridicule. In either case, retentive argument presents an unattractive picture of its adversaries, impugns their motives, and reduces progressive, innovative, and insurgent argument into one pattern that it characterizes as ill conceived, evil, and/or dangerous.

Reversive Argument

Reversive argument concerns efforts to return to a previous societal or political condition. Rather than stand pat and urge retention of "today," it uses the proposed "tomorrow" to argue that society has gone too far and that the tide must be reversed. In reversive argument, the standpatters are faced with the reactionary's call for major reversive change as well as the conservative's call for careful, respectful change.

One pamphlet urges its audience to reverse the precedent established by *Roe* v. *Wade* (legalization of abortion):

> The U.S. Supreme Court has excluded an entire group of humans from legal personhood and with it their right to life. . . . How long will it be before other groups of humans will be defined out of legal existence when it has been decided that they too have become socially burdensome? Senior citizens beware! Minority races beware! Crippled children beware! It did happen once before in this century you know. Remember Germany? Are you going to stand for this?[37]

William Rusher, publisher of the conservative *National Review,* painted a bleak picture of the future of the United States in 1975:

> If we succeed, we will have accomplished a mighty thing. We will have reversed . . . the whole downward-spiraling tide of the 20th century. There is no reason why this country's great experiment with freedom must end in failure. It was men and women who created the opportunity, and they who have botched it; and they can rescue it, even now, if they only will.[38]

In a similar vein, Jesse Helms, a former Senator from North Carolina, lamented:

> For forty years an unending barrage of "deals" . . . have regimented our
> people and our economy and federalized almost every human enterprise.
> This onslaught has installed a gigantic scheme for redistributing the
> wealth that rewards the indolent and penalizes the hard-working.[39]

But, said Helms, this onslaught can be reversed: "I believe we can halt the
long decline. There is nothing inevitable about it. There is a way back."

Reversive arguments are used by both sides of the political spectrum.
Several powerful pieces of reversive argument attack those on the right. Nelson Rockefeller, a liberal candidate for his party's presidential nomination,
addressed the 1964 Republican Convention to propose that the platform condemn extremism:

> There is no place in the Republican Party for such hawkers of hate, such
> purveyors of prejudice, such fabricators of fear, whether Communist, Ku
> Klux Klan, or Bircher. . . . These people have nothing in common with
> Republicanism. These people have nothing in common with American-
> ism. The Republican Party must repudiate these people.[40]

Rockefeller's call to reverse the trend toward extremism was drowned out by the
booing of an audience unworried by what it regarded as the right kind of extremism. The next evening the audience cheered as conservative presidential nominee Barry Goldwater exclaimed, "Extremism in defense of liberty is no vice!"

Contemporary anarchists object to the CIA's creation of a Web page for
children. Their language positions it as a "last straw" signaling that the CIA
and its supporters have gone over the brink:

> Isn't it pretty sick and twisted that the CIA has a Web page for kids? As if
> this murderous, secretive organization was some cuddly li'l agency you'd be
> happy to let near your kids? Sheesh. Basically, the page attempts to sanitize
> (and propagandize) the CIA, to get kids used to its existence and accepting
> of its mission—after all, they're the next generation of taxpayers![41]

Reversive argument may be near the middle of the typology, but it is
hardly moderate in tone. Indeed, it is frequently quite vehement as befits its
function of reversing societal direction. Reversive argument must direct its
audience to (1) see the current direction of society as dangerous, (2) see an
alternative direction as desirable, and (3) provide some vehicle for facilitating
the change in direction. It cannot rely on foot dragging, stubbornness, or apathy. The willingness of the people simply to "go along" with trends is part of
the problem. Reversive argument seeks action, and it can fail either because it
sounds too "radical" to standpatters and conservatives, or because it is insuf-
ficiently inspiring to accomplish its three objectives.

Restorative Argument

Restorative argument urges a full-scale return to a previous state of
affairs. The relative merits of that Golden Age are no longer debated: it is

clearly preferable to the existing order. Restorative argument centers on questions of when and why society went astray and how restoration can be accomplished. Reactionaries typically propose legislative or electoral solutions, a change in funding or enforcement of existing means, or a reconstitution of values to conform more closely to an earlier ideology. Revolutionary reactionaries urge more abrupt tactics for the overthrow of the existing order and restoration of the Ancient Regime.

Believing that our national problems stemmed from the intrusion of the federal government into unnecessary ventures, a campaign was advanced during the 1960s on behalf of "The Liberty Amendment" to the Constitution which would have prohibited government engagement in "any business, professional, commercial, financial, or industrial enterprise except as specified in the Constitution."[42] All such enterprises would be sold to private entrepreneurs, and the federal government's right to tax would be repealed. Supporters of the Amendment argued:

> We can renew the effectiveness of our Constitution. . . . We can restore the efficiency of our capitalist economy. The Liberty Amendment will accomplish both these purposes, by reducing the functions and powers of the Federal Government, and by restoring the abilities of people to take care of themselves, . . . and by curtailing destructive intervention in our free enterprise economy.[43]

No fan of taxes himself, Senator Jesse Helms argued that the critical turning point in our demise was the ban on prayer in public schools. He explains:

> It is hardly coincidence that the banishment of the Lord from the public schools has resulted in their being taken over by a totally secularist philosophy. Christianity has been driven out. In its place has been enshrined a permissiveness in which the drug culture has flourished, as have pornography, crime, and fornication. . . . I think there is no more pressing duty facing the Congress than to restore the true spirit of the First Amendment.[44]

And Robert Welch of the John Birch Society encouraged followers to work toward restoration of the nature of the United States in the latter half of the twentieth century.

> Push the Communists back, get out of the bed of a Europe that is dying with the cancer of collectivism, and breathe our own healthy air of opportunity, enterprise, and freedom. . . . And despite the bad scars and the loss of some muscles, this young, strong, great new nation, restored to vigor, courage, ambition, and self-confidence, can still go ahead to fulfill its great destiny, and to become an even more glorious example for all the earth than it ever was before.[45]

All three of these authors felt strongly the need to restore an earlier and better day, but disagreed as to whether to get there by cutting taxes, restoring prayer to the schools, or emphasizing individualism and laissez-faire capitalism.

Restorative argument, in short, alludes to an era or condition that was preferable to the present in one or more respects. Like reversive argument, it is characteristically immoderate; unlike reversive argument, it often presents a goal to be pursued.

Revolutionary Argument

Revolutionary argument urges total overthrow of the existing order but disagrees as to the form and/or nature of the new regime. While revolutionary radical and revolutionary reactionary groups frequently terrorize one another, they agree that the existing order is intolerable, corrupt, and burdensome. They also agree that its despicable nature justifies violent overthrow. Thus, some reactionaries migrate from radical to reactionary variants of revolutionary argument, and back again. It is possible to become a revolutionary radical from either direction: a frustrated radical or a disenchanted revolutionary reactionary. Revolutionary argument is the most confrontational form of political argument and relies heavily on brute force to destroy the persons and established institutions believed to be responsible for the problems of society.

For revolution to be considered, the prevailing regime must be seen as beyond redemption. Nineteenth-century anarchist Pierre Proudhon mastered this type of persuasion. In the following passage, Proudhon allows government no redeeming value:

> To be governed is to be watched, inspected, spied upon, directed, law-driven, numbered, regulated, enrolled, indoctrinated, preached at, controlled, checked, estimated, valued, censured, commanded, by creatures who have neither the right nor the wisdom nor the virtue to do so. To be governed is to be at every operation, at every transaction, noted, registered, counted, taxed, stamped, measured, numbered, assessed, licensed, authorized, admonished, prevented, forbidden, reformed, corrected, punished. It is, under pretext of public utility, and in the name of the general interest, to be placed under contribution, drilled, fleeced, exploited, monopolized, extorted from, squeezed, hoaxed, robbed; then, at the slightest resistance, the first word of complaint, to be repressed, fined, vilified, harassed, hunted down, abused, clubbed, disarmed, sacrificed, sold, betrayed, and, to crown all, mocked, ridiculed, derided, outraged, dishonored. That is government; that is its justice; that is its morality.[46]

Revolutionary argument depends on dramatic rhetorical depictions of its violent acts for effect. This is why several terrorist groups (often rivals) may claim responsibility for the same bombing—the destruction of property is generally less important than the symbolic mileage gained from it.

Socialist Eugene V. Debs proclaimed that

> the working class must get rid of the whole brood of masters and exploiters, and put themselves in possession and control of the means of production. . . . It is therefore a question not of reform, the mask of fraud, but of revolution."[47]

Clifford Odets concluded *Waiting for Lefty* with this speech by a tough cab driver:

AGATE: Christ, we're dyin' by inches! For what? For the debutantes to have their comin' out parties at the Ritz! . . . It's slow death or fight. It's war! . . . Hello America! We're storm birds of the working class. Workers of the world . . . our bones and our blood! And when we die they'll know what we did to make a new world![48]

Perhaps the most prominent advocate of revolutionary argument was the anarchist Johann Most. While others simply blew buildings to pieces, Most delighted in using language to describe violent acts. In a pamphlet on dynamite, he wrote:

Dynamite! Of all the good stuff, that is the stuff! . . . Place this in the immediate vicinity of a lot of rich loafers who live by the sweat of other people's brows, and light the fuse. A most cheerful and gratifying result will follow. In giving dynamite to the downtrodden millions . . . science has done its best work. . . . A pound of this stuff beats a bushel of ballots all hollow—and don't you forget it.[49]

In his famous speech, "The Beast of Property," Most proclaimed:

If the people do not crush them, they will crush the people, drown the revolution in the blood of the best, and rivet the chains of slavery more firmly than ever. Kill or be killed is the alternative. Therefore massacres of the people's enemies must be instituted.[50]

Dennis Kearney, a California labor leader during the 1870s, sought to rid California of people from Asia who constituted a source of cheap labor. But his violence was directed not only at the Asians, but also at his own union:

The first time you find a man in the ranks who is not true to the core take him by the nape of the neck and chuck him into the street and then take the bloody shrimps by the throat and tell them you will put big stones around their necks and throw them in the bay.[51]

Of course, exhorting people to violence entails risks to both the speaker and the audience. Anarchist Albert Parsons, a master of revolutionary argument, exhorted his audience:

If we would achieve our liberation from economic bondage and acquire our natural right to life and liberty, every man must lay by a part of his wages, buy a Colt's navy revolver, a Winchester rifle, and learn how to make and use dynamite. Then raise the flag of rebellion, the scarlet banner of liberty, fraternity, equality and strike down to the earth every tyrant that lives upon this globe.[52]

Lest his audience hesitate, Parsons reminded hearers that "until this is done you will continue to be robbed, to be plundered, to be at the mercy of the privileged few." Parsons was hanged in connection with the 1886 Haymarket Square bombing in Chicago. As Carl Smith, professor of American studies points out:

> It [the latter half of the nineteenth century] was a time of terrible cultural tension and anxiety, in which an appalling miscarriage of justice took place. . . . At the trial, the defense argued that although the defendants preached dynamite, there was no evidence to link them to this bomb. The trial was a travesty because the anarchists were convicted for their words, not their deeds.[53]

Revolutionary argument also offers praise to others for their violence. In May of 2000, a Pittsburgh lawyer went on a shooting rampage, killing and injuring a number of people. The Web site of the white supremacist Posse Comitatus organization said:

> Another White Male, Richard Scott Baumhammers, that couldn't take the darkening of Amerika takes ACTION in Pittsburg [sic], Pennsylvania! Kills 5 non-Whites including one jewess bastard! Ah, what's up Scott . . . couldn't find a queer? You ask, "what's wrong?" What's WRONG is that the jew bastards are destroying our once Great White Christian Republic and replacing it with a multicultural cesspool! Each of us must ask what we ARE contributing to STOP this rising MUD FLOOD? What are we doing to let the rest of our brethren know the plight of our RACE & NATION?[54]

Revolutionary argument recommends violent actions against the established order. It is possible for such terrorist rhetoric to be largely devoid of social or political ideology; such is the case today with the Irish Republican Army, the skinheads, and the neo-Nazis. While the threat of violence may pave the way for less extreme advocates, actual violence more often polarizes negotiations and renders reasoned, moderate argument exceedingly difficult. Of course, this is rarely important to the revolutionary, who sees moderation as part of the problem.

CONCLUSIONS

Seven types of argument—insurgent, innovative, progressive, retentive, reversive, restorative, and revolutionary—are found throughout political controversies. Many social movements have engaged in revolutionary, insurgent, and progressive arguments, while others have sought to preserve the status quo, reverse trends, or restore various Golden Ages. Each type of argument serves a different purpose, and each is a response to changing social relationships and rhetorical situations.

Insurgent argument addresses the corrupt, mendacious, and exploitative nature of societal norms, values, and institutions. It vilifies institutions, groups, and individuals accountable for problems. *Innovative argument* reveals dissatisfaction with the existing order and preference for experimental change. There is an aversion to both violence and the status quo. *Progressive argument* takes established procedures and values as givens but recognizes that change is inevitable through proper channels and means. *Retentive argument* addresses the importance of preserving significant elements of the status quo. Cautious, minimal change may be accepted grudgingly. *Reversive argument* proposes a return to a previous societal or political state. Society has gone too far and must reverse dangerous trends. *Restorative argument* urges a full-scale return to a previous, ideal state of existence. *Revolutionary argument* demands the complete overthrow of the existing order, by violent means if necessary. The preference is for either a glorious past or a glorious future totally different from the present.

Our examples show that each of the seven types of argument can be found in the discourse of almost any social movement. But when a social movement or a social movement organization relies disproportionately on one type of argument, we can detect rhetorical patterns that differentiate it from other movements or movement organizations.

Notes

[1] Roderick P. Hart, *Modern Rhetorical Criticism* (Glenview, IL: Scott Foresman, 1990): 117.

[2] Wayne Brockriede, "Where Is Argument?" *Perspectives on Argumentation: Essays in Honor of Wayne Brockriede*, Robert Trapp and Janice Schuetz, eds. (Long Grove, IL: Waveland Press, 1990): 4.

[3] Michael Billig, *Ideology and Opinions: Studies in Rhetorical Psychology* (Newbury Park, CA: Sage Publications, 1991): 17.

[4] See Chaim Perelman and L. Olbrechts- Tyteca, *The New Rhetoric: A Treatise on Argumentation,* John Wilkinson and Purcell Weaver, trans. (Notre Dame, IN: University of Notre Dame Press, 1969).

[5] Herbert W. Simons, "Persuasion in Social Conflicts: A Critique of Prevailing Conceptions and a Framework for Future Research," *Speech Monographs* 39 (November 1972): 227, 247.

[6] Unless otherwise noted, all references to Rossiter's typology refer to Clinton Rossiter, *Conservatism in America* (New York: Vintage Books, 1962): 11, 14.

[7] See Stephen W. Littlejohn and Karen Foss, *Theories of Human Communication,* 8th ed. (Belmont, CA: Wadsworth Publishing, 1992): 148–150, for a helpful summary of social judgment theory; or Muzafer Sherif and Carl Hovland, *Social Judgment: Assimilation and Contrast Effects in Communication and Attitude Change* (New Haven: Yale University Press, 1961).

[8] Billig, 17.

[9] "Preamble of the IWW Constitution as amended in 1908," *The American Labor Movement,* Leon Litwack, ed. (Englewood Cliffs, NJ: Prentice-Hall, 1962): 42.

[10] John Swinton, *Striking for Life: Labor's Side of the Question* (Westport, CT: Greenwood Press, 1970): 104, 110.

[11] Malcolm X, "The Ballot or the Bullet?" *Malcolm X Speaks,* George Breitman, ed. (New York: Ballantine Books, 1965): 31.

[12] William Lloyd Garrison, "No Union with Slaveholders," *William Lloyd Garrison,* George M. Frederickson, ed. (Englewood Cliffs, NJ: Prentice-Hall, 1968): 54.

[13] Clifford Odets, *Waiting for Lefty, Modern American Plays,* Frederick Cassidy, ed. (Freeport, NY: Books for Libraries Press, 1949): 195.

[14] "Gill the Fish Urges Kids to Boycott Fishing," http://www.peta.org/500gillbill.htm, accessed 10 May 2000.

[15] "Five Cents for Fairness," http://www.uaw.org/events/mlk/02/mlk02.html, accessed 8 August 2006.

[16] http://www.ufw.org/_board.php?mode=view&b_code=res_white&b_no=80&page=1&field= &key=&n=14#12, accessed 8 August 2006.

[17] Ralph Smith and Russell Windes, "The Innovational Movement: A Rhetorical Theory," *Quarterly Journal of Speech* 61 (April 1975): 143. Although we disagree with their conception of innovational movement, we find their characteristics of such movements useful for understanding innovational argument.

[18] Samuel Gompers, *Seventy Years of Life and Labor,* quoted in *Samuel Gompers Credo* (New York: American Federation of Labor Samuel Gompers Centennial Committee, 1950): 37.

[19] Martin Luther King, Jr., "I Have a Dream," *American Rhetorical Discourse,* 3rd ed., Ronald F. Reid and James F. Klumpp, eds. (Long Grove, IL: Waveland Press, Inc., 2005): 837–843.

[20] Quoted in John C. Echowak, letter (Boulder, CO: Native American Rights Fund, n.d.).

[21] Echowak, 1, 3.

[22] Echowak, 3.

[23] Henry Ford, "History Is More or Less Bunk," *Henry Ford,* John B. Rae, ed. (Englewood Cliffs, NJ: Prentice-Hall, 1969): 53.

[24] http://www.ufw.org/_board.php?mode=view&b_code=news_press&b_no=819, accessed 8 August 2006.

[25] Stephen H. Browne, "Remembering Crispus Attucks: Race, Rhetoric, and the Politics of Commemoration," *Quarterly Journal of Speech* 85 (May 1999): 171, 175.

[26] Robert S. Cathcart, "Movements: Confrontation as Rhetorical Form," *Southern Speech Communication Journal* 43 (Spring 1978): 237, 238.

[27] "Stop the Salt, Save Our Jobs," http://www.ufw.org/_board.php?mode=view&b_code=res_white&b_no=83&page=1&field=&key=&n=16, accessed 8 August 2006.

[28] Lyndon B. Johnson, "Annual Message to the Congress on the State of the Union," *Public Papers of the Presidents of the United States: Lyndon B. Johnson,* 1963, 1964, Book I (Washington, DC: U.S. Government Printing Office, 1965): 113.

[29] Lyndon B. Johnson, "Annual Message to the Congress on the State of the Union," *Public Papers of the Presidents of the United States, Lyndon B. Johnson* Book I (Washington, DC: U.S. Government Printing Office, 1970): 31.

[30] Barbara C. Jordan, "Democratic Convention Keynote Address," *Contemporary American Public Discourse,* 3rd ed., Halford R. Ryan, ed. (Long Grove, IL: Waveland Press, Inc., 1992): 274–278.

[31] Letter from AAUP-AFT President M. Marlyne Kilbey to WSU President Irvin D. Reid, home.msn.com/-mikemci/aaup/notice_letter, accessed 3 September 1999.

[32] Barry M. Goldwater, *With No Apologies* (New York: William Morrow, 1979): 14.

[33] Gary Allen, *Jimmy Carter, Jimmy Carter* (Seal Beach, CA: 76 Press, 1976): 68.

[34] Ronald Reagan, "Free Enterprise," *American Rhetoric from Roosevelt to Reagan,* Halford R. Ryan, ed. (Long Grove, IL: Waveland Press, Inc., 1983): 265–277.

[35] "The Anarchist Black Ribbon Campaign," http://a4a.mahost.org/black.html, accessed 8 August 2006.

[36] "Beware Biotechnology," http://a4a.mahost.org/biotech.html, accessed 8 August 2006.

[37] Dr. and Mrs. J. C. Willke, "The U.S. Supreme Court Has Ruled It's Legal to Kill a Baby. . ." (Cincinnati: Hayes Publishing, n.d.): 4.

[38] William A. Rusher, *The Making of the New Majority Party* (Ottawa, IL: Green Hill, 1975): 161, 162.

[39] Jesse Helms, *When Free Men Stand Tall* (Grand Rapids, MI: Zondervan, 1976): 11, 12.

[40] Nelson A. Rockefeller, "Address to the Third Session of the 1964 Republican National Convention in Moving Adoption of the Amendment to the Report of the Committee on Resolutions on the Subject of Extremism," Cow Palace, San Francisco, California, July 14, 1964. *Public Papers of Governor Nelson A. Rockefeller* (1964): 1330.

[41] "Random Hostile Thoughts," http://a4a.mahost.org/, accessed 8 August 2006.

[42] Lloyd G. Herbstreith and Gordan van B. King, *Action for Americans: The Liberty Amendment* (Los Angeles: Operation America, 1963): inside cover.

[43] Herbstreith and King, 105.

[44] Helms, 108.

[45] Robert H. W. Welch, *The Blue Book of the John Birch Society* (Boston: Western Islands, 1961): 39.

[46] Pierre Joseph Proudhon, *General Idea of the Revolution in the Nineteenth Century,* http://www.geocities.com/CapitolHill/5065/state.html, accessed 8 August 2006.

[47] Eugene V. Debs, "Outlook for Socialism in the United States," http://www.marxists.org/archive/debs/works/1900/outlook.htm, accessed 12 August 2006.

[48] Odets, 192.

[49] Quoted in Louis Adamic, *Dynamite: The Story of Class Violence in America* (New York: Chelsea House, 1958): 47.

[50] Johann Most, "The Beast of Property," reprinted in Charles W. Lomas, *The Agitator in American History* (Englewood Cliffs, NJ: Prentice-Hall, 1968): 39.

[51] Dennis Kearney, "The Chinese Must Go!" reprinted in Lomas, 29.

[52] Albert Parsons, "The Board of Trade: Legalized Theft," reprinted in Lomas, 44.

[53] Quoted in Robert Freed, "Making History," *Northwestern* (Fall 2000): 40.

[54] "Newsflash," www.posse-comitatus.org, accessed 12 May 2000.

CHAPTER 9

Argument from Narrative Vision in Social Movements

This chapter examines how people use narratives as frameworks for interpreting reality. It considers how some people construct stories to help other people see the world "properly." Two case studies demonstrate how a social movement can challenge an institution's narrative, how the interpretive frameworks and events are interdependent, and how a rhetorical form can become a political resource.

NARRATIVE AND RHETORICAL VISION

David Carr writes, "Human existence and action . . . consist not in overcoming time, not in escaping it or arresting its flow, but in shaping and forming it."[1] He maintains that each person lives in a remembered past and acts in expectation of a future that is a projection of past and present. We cast ourselves in an unfolding story and act it out. Because we choose the story and our role in it, we can switch stories at any time.

Howard Kamler explains that stories help us to "know" and to protect what we "know" from counterargument. Stories structure our lives by contextualizing otherwise ambiguous episodes, and they allow us to believe what we need to believe by defining what constitutes relevant evidence. Kamler also writes that we communicate by making our private stories public and public stories (such as myths) our own.[2] Moreover, storytelling invites audiences to agree for the sake of the story, whereas arguments invite disagreement and debate.

Earlier chapters discussed the importance of perceived environments and the need for social movements to transform perceptions. These functions are usually accomplished through narratives. Each narrative structures the past, projects a future, and prescribes a preferred course of conduct from a particular vantage point. Each narrative has an author, a narrator, a protagonist, and an audience; but it is the narrator's vantage point in time, intellect, wisdom, values, and character that positions the story for the audience. The reader-narrator identification is central. Readers who identify with the narrator step into the story, enact it, and retain the experience. Stories that facilitate these processes, in turn, foster identification. Readers can ignore an ill-defined or unconvincing narrator, and an audience repelled by the narrator may use the narrative to construct an opposing vision. The narrator's image and audience appeal are so important to the narrative that personal identification overpowers logical rigor.[3]

Carr theorizes that we organize our social relationships and communities through the telling and retelling of stories. Stories or myths link us to our contemporaries and to our predecessors and successors.[4] Storytelling engages people in a communicative relationship defined by the narrator-audience relationship. The narrator and listener create a "we" through their identification; "my story" becomes "our story" through co-creation. Interpretive communities coalesce around stories as each "we" acquires its own folklore and narrators. Narrators embellish the story by emphasizing different characters, motives, events, chronology, and plot lines. Carr distinguishes between stories that endure ("retentions") and those that can be remembered if necessary ("recollections").[5] Differences develop when one person's retention is another's mere recollection. Social movements often weave a variety of recollections into a new story to raise them to the level of retention.

If history is the creation of explanatory stories, and if communities form around their stories, then some of these narrative groups must inevitably conflict. Consider the historic conflicts among Christian denominations, all based on their varying interpretations of the story of Jesus of Nazareth. Likewise, most U.S. social movements offer conflicting narratives of the "meaning of America" and the essence of "the American Dream."

Fisher suggests that each narrative enacts a set of values and that these enacted values govern the narrative's audience appeal. Each narrative is judged by its narrative coherence (does the story work?) and by its narrative fidelity (does the story use the audience's beliefs and values?). He says that audiences look for *good* reasons, which they regard as stories that are consistent with what they know and value, appropriate to the pending decision, promising in effects for themselves, and consistent with what they regard as an ideal basis for conduct.[6] This view of persuasion hinges less on changing beliefs, attitudes, or values than on integrating beliefs and behaviors into a story regarded by the audience as coherent, relevant, compatible, promising, and proper.

The narrative position is largely compatible with the popular rhetorical perspective of symbolic convergence, sometimes known as "fantasy theme analysis." Ernest Bormann built upon Robert F. Bales' observation that individuals working together frequently dramatize or act out a "fantasy" (a recollection or an estimation of the future).[7] The verbalizing, expressing, or dramatizing of a fantasy orients listeners to the present by drawing on their pasts and futures. Some fantasies fall flat, but when listeners recognize a fantasy as one of their own, they respond emotionally as well as cognitively. They hitchhike on the original comment and extend the fantasy by polishing the image, adding examples, and extending it. Then a third person recognizes and joins the shared fantasy. Soon the individuals are drawing on their separate pasts and futures to create a shared present. Thus, they develop a common orientation to the present that binds them to one another by the shared vision and by the process of creating it. This process is called "chaining" (as in "they created an elaborate fantasy chain" or "the fantasy chained out to the entire group").

Bormann's primary contribution is his suggestion that fantasy-chaining transcends the small-group experience. If small groups create shared identities through group fantasizing, he reasons, so might large groups such as audiences, organizations, social movements, and societies. Bormann identifies rhetorical visions as "the composite dramas which catch up large groups of people in a symbolic reality."[8] They arise through communication and provide the themes, heroes, villains, values, and motivations that are invoked in later communication. Rhetorical visions are particularly pertinent where clear explanations are elusive.

> When the authentic record of events is clear and widely understood, the competing visions must take it into account. . . . [But] Whenever occasions are so chaotic and indiscriminate that the community has no clear observational impression of the facts, people are given free rein to fantasize within the assumptions of their rhetorical vision.[9]

Narrative and rhetorical vision are not identical frameworks. The narrative model is more perceptually grounded, more cognitive, and offers more analytical guidance. Fantasy theme analysis draws more heavily on imaginings than recollections, although most would agree that our fantasies and imaginings grow out of our experiences. But the connection between narrative and rhetorical vision should be apparent. Fantasies and rhetorical visions are narrative in form. Some fantasies stimulate recognition and empathy, thereby enhancing audience-narrator identification, inviting the audience to join in the creative process by participating in the story itself, fostering identification with like-minded auditors, and motivating listeners to remember the story. We will use the term "narrative vision" to encompass both Carr's sense of configured time and Bormann's collective imagining with respect to two social movement episodes.

First we examine the story told by the contemporary militia or patriot movement to see how a social movement situates itself, characterizes its legitimacy, and transforms the prevailing perceptions of reality. We will then explore the New Right's use of the Panama Canal controversy of the 1970s to mobilize a movement, gain control of the Republican Party, and to shape U.S. foreign policy in the 1980s.

PATRIOT MOVEMENT OR DOMESTIC TERRORISM?

Ruby Ridge, Waco, and Oklahoma City quickly became defining episodes in the stories of the militia or patriot movement. This section considers three elements of the militia narrative—claim to historic legitimacy, the sanctity of weapons, and characterizations of the 1995 Oklahoma City bombing—to understand better the interpretive stance of this contemporary social movement.

The Militia Movement as Historically Legitimate

The militia or patriot movement anchors itself in the Constitution, and the clash between the militias and the United States government results from their divergent interpretations of this document. There is little disagreement that colonists such as George Washington, John Adams, Benjamin Franklin, and Thomas Jefferson led a revolutionary movement to overthrow British rule and then established the United States of America to replace it. But the militia story portrays the federal government as an occupying force comparable to the British, with the militia themselves being heirs to the tradition of Washington and Jefferson. Their conflicting understandings of "true Americanism" during the 1990s framed strikingly divergent narratives of the "problem" and "solution."

The "Belligerent Claimant" Web site charged that "we have been living in occupied enemy territory for a very long time."[10] Dave Delany of Dave Delany's Freedom House writes about the historic roots of the militia.

> The militia is a "grass roots" tool of the people, designed to check the abuse of its own internal government, and to defend against the incursions of a foreign enemy. . . . We are now at odds with our history. . . . When the force directed against you is the army of the federal government or one of its fingers, you can hardly call upon the hand of the federal government to protect you! Do you somehow think that the commander in chief is immune from the abuse of power?[11]

In Delany's view the growth of a professional military is not a source of protection but a threat to all Americans: "Rather than replacing the local militia, the growth of the federal army requires the increase in the strength of the local militia. The local militia is the only defense against the tyranny of a standing army."[12] Thus, True Americans must be ever vigilant. Delany closes by quoting Benjamin Rush from 1787:

> "The American war is over, but this is far from being the case with the American revolution. On the contrary, nothing but the first act of the drama is closed." He was speaking then of the weakness of our nation. I am writing now of the weakness of our nation also. "Hear her proclaiming, in sighs and groans, in her governments, in her finances, in her trade, in her manufactures, in her morals and in her manners," (do you hear them?) "'The Revolution is not over.'" If we are to remain free, it never will be. God bless the militia.[13]

Delany grounds his position in the writings and addresses of John Hancock, Josiah Quincy, Joseph Warren, and Benjamin Rush, who helped found the United States and whom he views as wary of a professional military and supporters of a citizen militia to defend rights and property. Other militia voices have used patriotic uprising stories to develop their own "historical" lessons.

As discussed in chapter 5, *The Turner Diaries* is a novel about a 1991–93 American revolution by "The Organization" against the Zionist Occupied Government (ZOG). It is fiction presented as the diary of Earl Turner. Because it is fiction, the author has a free hand with the narrative. Because it looks like a diary, it invites a suspension of disbelief. Because it is the reminiscence of a "freedom fighter," it invites us to transfer the author's insights to our contemporary lives. The narrative persona of Earl Turner was created by Andrew Macdonald, the pen name of physicist William Pierce. Priscilla Meddaugh has pointed out that Pierce frequently identifies himself as "Dr. William Pierce" without explaining the relevance of his academic credentials in physics to his white supremacist argument.[14] Pierce used the Macdonald/Turner persona for a particular kind of discourse. "Dr. Pierce" is his voice for making the white supremacist case in logical, nonfictional terms while "Macdonald/Turner" is his voice for telling a story of revolution that invites identification and eschews logical argument.

Whereas Delany views the present from the perspective of the those who helped establish the United States, the voice of Macdonald/Turner looks at the United States from the post-revolutionary vantage point:

> All in all, it has been depressingly easy for the System to deceive and manipulate the American people—whether the relatively new "conservatives" or the spoiled and pseudo sophisticated "liberals." Even the libertarians, inherently hostile to all government, will be intimidated into going along.[15]

From his perspective in the fictional future, Turner can say that Americans deserved to lose their freedom because they failed to act when there was still time.

> Americans have lost their right to be free. Slavery is the just and proper state for a people who have grown as soft, self-indulgent, careless, credulous, and befuddled as we have. . . . Indeed, we are already slaves. We have allowed a diabolically clever, alien minority to put chains on our souls and our minds. These spiritual chains are a truer mark of slavery than the iron chains which are yet to come.[16]

Thus, Pierce recommends a course of action to his readers by moving them into a fictional future and then providing a flashback.

The Belligerent Claimant Web site extends that critique. In its view, the problem is not so much a matter of national weakness as an enemy occupation of America:

> The entirety of this Web site is to prove that we are AT WAR with the very government who calls us their chattel, and have been that way for over a century.

> Call it the United Nations, the United States, The New World Order, the Masons, the Jews, the Illuminatti [sic], the CFR [Council on Foreign Relations], the Trilateral Commission, or that furry thing from Star Wars. . . . We are at war with an Occupied Enemy.[17]

Who, then, is this occupying enemy?

> [They] have called themselves Yankees more often than not. If you believe in a strong and oppressive government, then you are a Yankee. If you believe in Life, Liberty and the pursuit of your own Happiness, then you are an American at heart. This is not about the Mason Dixon Line or where you were born. It has nothing to do with the northern or southern, eastern or western States, except that they are all under a government's control who could care less about the American people and our rights. . . .
>
> Now is the time to Call to Arms!
>
> We have waited far too long to act upon their aggression
>
> AMERICA IS AT WAR![18]

The voices of the contemporary militia movement therefore conceive of themselves as direct descendants of the citizen militias that overthrew the power of the Crown in the eighteenth century. They identify with George Washington less as a general and a president than as the landowner and slave owner who risked everything to stand up to the oppressive power of the State. Theirs is a worldview in which legitimacy comes not from the legal authority of executives, legislatures, police, and judges but from the inalienable rights each person possesses and loans—temporarily and grudgingly—to the government. Beyond the political beliefs expressed, note the language used. The tone of the language is blunt, aggressive, and uncompromising. It seems unlikely to appeal to happy people or to those who dislike confrontation. Thus, it invites identification with some people and alienates others.

The Inalienable Right to Bear Arms

As heirs to the citizen militias of the 1700s, today's activists believe, perhaps first and foremost, in the role of private gun ownership as the guarantor of freedom. They claim that the freedom fighters who wrote the Constitution did not write the Second Amendment to protect target shooters and deer hunters but to insure that an armed citizen militia could protect the security of their newly won independence and government. The institutional position is that circumstances have changed in two hundred years, and the armed forces and the police now perform the function originally assigned to the militia. Militia voices perceive any form of gun control as the government's effort to take away the most revered individual right.[19]

A statement posted on the Web captures the grandeur and the totality of the militia movement's causal link between gun ownership and freedom:

> The Soviet Union established gun control in 1929. From 1929 to 1953, 20 million political dissidents, unable to defend themselves, were rounded up and exterminated.

Turkey established gun control in 1911. From 1915 to 1917, 1.5 million Armenians, unable to defend themselves, were rounded up and exterminated.

China established gun control in 1935. From 1948 to 1976, 20 million Anti-Communists, Christians, political dissidents, and pro-reform groups, unable to defend themselves, were rounded up and exterminated.

Germany established gun control in 1938. From 1939 to 1945, 13 million Jews, Gypsies, mentally ill people and other "mongrelized peoples," unable to defend themselves, were rounded up and exterminated.

Guatemala established gun control in 1964. From 1964 to 1981, 100,000 Mayan Indians, unable to defend themselves, were rounded up and exterminated.

Uganda established gun control in 1970. From 1971 to 1979, 300,000 Christians, unable to defend themselves, were rounded up and exterminated.

Cambodia established gun control in 1956. From 1975 to 1977, 1 million "educated people," unable to defend themselves, were rounded up and exterminated.[20]

In short, seven countries instituted gun control and almost immediately rounded up and slaughtered almost 56 million innocent people. The posting dares the reader to call this a coincidence. The implied relationship is clearly causal: 56 million people would have lived if they had kept their guns.

The horror of gun control is prominent in the fictional *Turner Diaries*. Turner wonders:

> Why didn't we rise up three years ago when they started taking our guns away? Why didn't we rise up in righteous fury and drag these arrogant aliens into the streets and cut their throats then? Why didn't we roast them over bonfires at every street corner in America? Why didn't we make a final end to this obnoxious and eternally pushy clan, this pestilence from the sewers of the East, instead of meekly allowing ourselves to be disarmed?[21]

Turner's narrative attributes political legitimacy to individual citizens who are entitled to violate a gun control law. Far more importantly, his story invites readers to conclude that they are entitled to kill brutally those who support and enforce such laws.

The dominant militia theme is that citizens need to be able to use weapons to protect themselves. When the enemy has the upper hand, some militia voices urge premeditated or preemptive illegal acts. The Belligerent Claimant Web site, for example, offers tips to its readers:

> *TIP* #1: Visit your local auto dealership as a shopper and learn where they store the keys at night for the trucks on the lot. Do some research to locate any other important "bounty" required for self-defense when the time comes.

TIP #2: Research weaponry if you have no knowledge of the current firearms and ammunitions, etc. . . . If you do not have a modern gun, keep in
mind that captured weapons and guns from dead enemies (& compatri-
ots) work fine too.[22]

In short, the militia voices regard guns and other weapons as essential to protect basic rights, and they express no qualms about the means used to acquire
those weapons.

Although militia groups cherish their constitutional rights to bear arms
and to form a militia, the National Rifle Association has been careful to separate its own defense of gun ownership from the need for a militia. One militia member downloaded and shared with his colleagues the NRA' s position
on militias and guns:

the individual right to own firearms is guaranteed by the Constitution,
but the right to own firearms is not at all dependent upon the militia
clause. The militia clause of the Second Amendment merely adds to the
reason for the right, which is a common law right rooted in the right of
protection of self, family and community.

The Second Amendment guarantees an individual's right to arms;
participation in a citizen militia organization does not make that right
more valid nor any stronger.[23]

Militia Accounts of Violence: The Oklahoma City Bombing

We have seen that many militia voices characterize themselves as heirs to
the tradition of individual sovereignty and that they perceive the Second
Amendment's arms and militia protections as the only way to protect and/or
recover individual rights. This creates a rhetoric of virtual violence, as in *The
Turner Diaries*. But what does their rhetoric say about *actual* violence and
destruction, as in the 1995 bombing of the federal building in Oklahoma City?

Militia voices told four different stories to explain the 1995 bombing of
the federal building in Oklahoma City. The "Revolution: Ammo for Freedom
Fighters" Web site integrated the bombing into the violent narrative exemplified by *The Turner Diaries*. A reporter interviewed Ross Hullett, identified as
the "commander of the Oklahoma brigade," who said:

There are 20 militia members underground for every one in the open. . . .
There are four or five different groups in the shadows around here and
we're talking about dangerous people. I mean savage, vicious people. I
am one of them. . . . Our government has been lying to us for too long,
and Waco was the last damned straw. . . . Now we're telling them that
they'd better straighten out this government and they had better
straighten out Waco because, if they don't, it is going to get ugly. . . . You
think you've seen terror? You haven't seen shit yet."[24]

This militia spokesman's account characterized the Oklahoma City bombing
as a microcosm of the type and magnitude of terrorism that the militias will
produce. It is reminiscent of colonial propagandists such as Sam Adams who

did their best to maximize the movement's resources and resolve. This can help mobilization and confrontation, but it also invites institutional retaliation by admitting/claiming participation in a revolutionary act.

Other militia voices put a second, very different spin on the Oklahoma City bombing. Pierce's radio commentary turned the tables on government officials:

> I listened to the expressions of pious outrage by Bill Clinton and Janet Reno and the other government gangsters on television that evening, and I thought, "You hypocrites! What do you expect? You are the real terrorists. When a government engages in terrorism against its own citizens, it should not be surprised when some of those citizens strike back and engage in terrorism against the government. You are the ones responsible for this bombing, for the deaths of these children."[25]

Unlike the first example, Pierce's account distanced his followers from the bombing. He understands and justifies the hatred of government that could lead people to commit such acts, but he denounces the bombing and attributes ultimate blame for it to the president and the attorney general. There is no claim of militia strength or of any interest in flexing muscle through bombings.

The third view decried the bombings and focused on its perception of a government and media campaign to discredit the militias. One Internet posting stated:

> I am incapable of saying anything which would adequately express 1/100th of the disgust I feel for anyone who would do such a thing, or the sorrow I feel for the victims. However, the government, with massive help from the media, will use this opportunity to attack and murder more citizens and further restrict our rights—all in the name of "security"—all under the cloak of emotional hysteria.[26]

A fourth militia response to the bombing charged that the federal government itself destroyed the building. A *Stormfront* article by Eustace Mullins pulls no punches:

> J' accuse! This is the title of the French Novelist Emile Zola's trenchant work of the nineteenth century, which accused the government of France of brazen corruption. Today, in the United States, I accuse the federal government of planning and perpetrating the most horrible crimes, a series which culminated in the April 19, 1995 bombing of the federal building in Oklahoma City. This was a deliberate conspiracy by corrupt and treasonous elements in the federal agencies in Washington as part of a plan to provoke martial law, confiscate legal guns from American citizens, and to wipe out the citizens' militia of the several states.[27]

A video called *Cover-Up in Oklahoma* is sold on Amazon. "This video raises disturbing questions about the power of U.S. secret police agencies, shielded by corrupt politicians and the tightly controlled, mainstream press."[28] The product description includes:

Cover-Up in Oklahoma uses eyewitness accounts, expert testimony and extensive 'live' local newscast footage to prove the 'truck bomb' scenario promoted by the government and the mainstream media does not fit the facts." The video shows:

- The damage sustained by the Murrah federal building could not have been produced by a bomb on the street without additional charges placed on or near internal structural columns.

- The initial news coverage, supported by statements from state, federal, and local government officials, described the removal of multiple unexploded bombs from inside the Murrah federal building.

- Blast debris was blown out and away from the Murrah federal building, not into it, as would occur with a truck bomb on the street.

- The truck-bomb "crater," described in the national media, appears to have been an outright hoax.[29]

The description ends with this comment:

Viewers . . . will find a documentary that will force you to confront the probability that elements within our government and within the media are prepared to sacrifice both the truth and the lives of children to achieve their social and political objectives.[30]

All four militia versions of the Oklahoma City bombing underscore mistrust of government and encourage support for the militia itself.

In the aftermath of the bombing, it's important to examine our reasoning processes and emotions very carefully. We must remain vigilant of overzealous politicians, regulators, and federal agents. We must not be blinded by fear. A strong, nationwide emotional reaction is exactly what the administration (and its puppet-masters in the UN) need to grab what's left of our rights. The media will play their part because sensationalism always jacks up the ad rates. In both cases, it's all about money and control.[31]

Thus, the militia, like movement voices across the political spectrum, responded to the Oklahoma City bombing with four different stories: (1) the bombing shows that militia forces are stronger than previously thought and prepared to act, (2) the bombing was a regrettable but understandable reaction to government terrorism at Waco, (3) the bombing is regrettable but will be used by the government and the corporate media to attack the militia, and (4) the bombing was conducted by the government to warrant suppression of the militia.

Weaving the Story

How have the militia voices used language to tell their story? How has their story arrested the flow of time and shaped circumstances to reflect militia reality? And, finally, how has their story protected members of the militia movement from counterargument and attack?

The militia story connects members to the founders of the United States as patriots in an enemy-occupied territory. Their story is of a fight against a vile occupying force—be it British, New World Order, United Nations, or ZOG—that intrudes on the individual sovereignty at the heart of the American revolution. In this never-ending struggle over individual rights, the militia's central commitment must be to the sanctity of weapons, without which they will be overrun. They talk frequently of stockpiling guns and other weaponry to defend or to take back their rights and property from the occupying force, and they advertise training manuals so that they can be well prepared to use arms when the time comes. But their aggressive and uncompromising narrative often splinters in the face of real violence when their varied accounts fail to live up to the bravado of their call to arms.

Every social movement is large in scope, and it is the variety of stories and people who believe them that gives each movement its character. Most of these stories are shared by word of mouth, and the chaining-out process creates links among believers. This seems especially likely when the story is one of ideals betrayed, of heroism and martyrdom, and of "real truths" that corrupt institutions keep from us. Although such stories may not appeal to a large number of listeners, they do invite very intense feelings among those devoted to the cause who then propel and sustain a movement.

The centrality of weapons to the militia movement has important theoretical implications. The militia movement faces a strategic trilemma. Their first problem is that their divergent accounts of Oklahoma City undermined the credibility of their extreme rhetoric, while the pictures of bloodied children did little to win mainstream popularity. The second problem is that a full rhetorical retreat from Oklahoma City for public relations purposes invites several questions: If not Oklahoma City, then what sort of militia warfare would they support? After all, if the federal government has not infringed on their rights, then who has? And, therefore, if violence against the federal government is not in order, then against whom do they plan to use their arms? And if they do not plan to use their arms to protect and to reclaim their rights, then how are they like the founders of the country, and why are they acquiring their weapons and training? The third problem is that any attempts to resolve the first two problems with divergent accounts undermines the importance of narrative unity and discipline and thus undercuts the need for quasi-military operations from the outset.

This section has emphasized the militia narrative, but it is not realistic to consider any narrative in isolation because there are always an infinite number of stories available to the public, especially with the advent of Internet sites and chat rooms. As Bormann would remind us, it is the convergence of people around narratives and the divergence among narratives that lead to the rise and fall of social movements and to a movement's ability to win its struggle. We turn now to the comparison of two narratives that engaged one another in a struggle for dominance in the late 1970s.

THE PANAMA CANAL CONTROVERSY

Richard Viguerie boasted in 1981 that "no political issue in the last 25 years so clearly divided the American establishment from the American people as the Panama Canal treaties."[32] The proposed treaties were supported by the establishment: two Democratic and two Republican presidents, the Democratic leaders in both houses of Congress, the Joint Chiefs of Staff, "Big Labor, Big Business, Big Media, the big international banks, and just about every liberal political and cultural star you could name." Opposed to the treaties were "the American people—about 70 percent of them . . . probably 85 percent of registered Republicans" and a coterie of conservative spokespersons who would become known as the New Right: Senators Paul Laxalt, Jake Garn, and Bill Scott, Congressmen Philip Crane, Larry McDonald, and Mickey Edwards, and organizers Paul Weyrich, Howard Phillips, William Rhatican, Terry Dolan, and Viguerie himself. The treaties passed the Senate by a two-vote margin, a significant victory for President Carter. But many citizens remained deeply opposed to the treaties.[33]

The New Right movement used the proposed Panama Canal treaties to energize the conservative imagination. By advancing a narrative that made treaty ratification illogical, rather than arguing technicalities the New Right engaged less active conservatives in group fantasizing. To defeat the treaties and/or mobilize a new conservative majority, the New Right needed a rhetoric that would appeal to a variety of interpretive communities. Specifically, the New Right had four rhetorical tasks. First, they needed to incorporate the enduring symbols and beliefs of foreign policy conservatives, many of them Democrats, as the core of the anti-treaty coalition.Second, they needed to enhance U.S. recollections of the Panama Canal. Third, they needed to dramatize latent fantasies about a perilous world to keep Americans from trusting other nations. Fourth, and most delicately, they had to separate the Republican Party into two parts: linking the Ford-Kissinger-Rockefeller-Nixon wing with Carter and the Democrats while linking their own wing with treaty opposition, the New Right, and public opinion.

Ronald Reagan used the canal issue to win the 1976 North Carolina primary, and he continued to be a prominent anti-treaty voice. Unconvinced by a private briefing from the negotiators, Reagan told the Young Americans for Freedom that the treaties

> would eliminate the rights of sovereignty we acquired in the original treaty. . . . Without these rights we must ask what is to prevent a Panamanian regime one day from simply nationalizing the canal and demanding our immediate withdrawal. . . . Secrecy, of course, is no longer the issue. Security is.[34]

By using a narrative structure Reagan invited his young, unbriefed, conservative listeners to fantasize. Instead of telling them what he had learned from the negotiators, Reagan asked his audience to allay his fears. An anti-treaty letter in Reagan's name was sent out on Republican National Committee letterhead in late October. The letter advanced nine propositions:

1. In the process of giving up our canal, Mr. Carter has also surrendered our rights to build a new one if needed.

2. There's no guarantee our Naval Fleet will have the right of priority passage in time of war.

3. The U.S. does not have the right to intervene to defend the canal.

4. We must close down 10 of our military bases, Americans in the Zone will be under Panamanian rule, and we must pay [General Omar] Torrijos millions more each year for the canal.

5. These treaties could cost Americans hundreds of millions. . . . Plus we'll pay higher prices. . . . [Torrijos] maintains close ties with Fidel Castro and the Soviet Union.

6. [Torrijos] seized power by gunpoint . . . [and] controls the press, he's outlawed all political parties but the Marxist party and he controls the military.

7. Once we pull out, what's to stop Torrijos or his successor from nationalizing the canal and ordering us out at once?

8. Panama is one of the most unstable countries in Latin America.

9. From the beginning, Mr. Carter negotiated this treaty without consulting Congressional leaders.[35]

Five of the nine statements refer to President Carter; none mention that Republican Presidents Ford and Nixon agreed with him. Carter's victory over Ford in 1976 gave the Republican National Committee an incentive to send this letter, but by sending it and strongly opposing the treaties, the RNC significantly disadvantaged Republican treaty supporters such as Ford.

The Reagan letter was a major victory in the New Right movement's effort to persuade mainstream Republicans to oppose the Carter administration over the Treaty issue. The Republican leadership had significant political and organizational needs that provided incentives for them to oppose the treaties now advocated by the Democrats. Nevertheless, the Reagan letter was flawed because it was a propositional rather than a narrative argument. By detailing nine propositions, Reagan invited disagreement, which he received from many quarters because many Republican conservatives did not oppose the treaties.

The most trenchant response to Reagan came in a letter from actor John Wayne, an icon of patriotism and military heroism. Wayne's personal cover letter to "Ronnie" expressed his regrets:

> If you had given time and thought on this issue, your attitude would have gained you the image of leadership that I wished for you, rather than, in the long run, a realization by the public that you are merely making statements for political expediency.[36]

He told Reagan, "I'll show you point by God damn point in the Treaty where you are misinforming people."[37] Wayne then gave an important warning:

> If you continue these erroneous remarks, someone will publicize your letter to prove that you are not as thorough in your reviewing of the Treaty as you say or are damned obtuse when it comes to reading the English language.[38]

Attached to the cover letter was a four-page cut-and-paste summary of Reagan's nine points under the title "Scare Letter from the Honorable Ronald Reagan" along with Wayne's quite specific and technical responses. His responses were replete with phrases such as "the truth is," "completely misleading," "complete untruth," and "how dare you continue to make these statements." Wayne's conclusion spoke directly to Reagan's use of the canal as a vehicle for fund-raising.

> Quite obviously you are using . . . [the Panama Canal Treaty] as a teaser to attract contributions to our party. I know of our party's need for money; but if your attitude in order to get it is as untruthful and misleading as your letter, we haven't a chance."[39]

The tone of Wayne's letter may seem surprising in the post-Reagan era, but it must be read in the context of 1977 when the treaties had been supported by Nixon, Ford, and the Joint Chiefs of Staff. Senator Barry Goldwater also was moving toward support.

Wayne's letter highlights the rhetorical dilemmas facing the New Right in late 1977. Reagan was their best prospect for winning the presidency in 1980, and the Panama issue was their best chance for mobilizing support. But Reagan's arguments against the treaties could destroy his credibility. The rhetorical leadership of the anti-treaty forces passed from Reagan to Illinois Congressman Phillip Crane, a historian by profession, in January 1978.

Carter avoided a televised canal speech in 1977 even though speechwriter James Fallows feared this would leave "all the public argumentation to the other side . . . and by letting their crazy charges go unanswered for the moment we suggest that we don't have any answers."[40] Carter's advisors agreed that the basic problem was "the McGuffey Reader Complex":

> Since early this century . . . the myth that the Panama Canal and its surrounding territory was ours "in perpetuity" was taught as a truism in the classroom and in the grammar school textbooks. [The President must re-educate] the over 50, the grade school only, and Republican [audiences about manifest destiny, the Monroe Doctrine, and the "in perpetuity" clause].[41]

Herein lay Carter's rhetorical predicament. The New Right was constructing a coherent anti-treaty narrative out of the beliefs that older, conservative, Republican citizens acquired early in life. Even if that narrative were erroneous, it was nevertheless consistent with everything they had learned and retained about the canal. A narrative's persuasiveness hinges largely on its fidelity to its audience's experiences. The president was being urged to tell this audience that the facts they had learned in grade school (reinforced almost daily by the anti-treaty advocates) were wrong. Fallows recognized the predicament and its risks.[42] On January 25, 1978, Fallows outlined a Fireside Chat that was to be short, confident, positive, and simple. He outlined 28 points with discussions leading to 13 more.[43]

Contrasting pro- and anti-treaty narratives from 1974 to 1978 illustrate how the New Right used the canal issue to weave diverse public recollections and fantasies into a narrative vision that aroused and united conservatives and, ultimately, reoriented U.S. foreign policy. We will pay particular attention to the narratives of Crane (the movement's primary spokesman and legitimizer) and President Jimmy Carter (who spoke for the foreign policy establishment and the leadership of both parties).[44] Carter and Crane advanced comparable narratives. Each recounted our past, depicted our present situation, envisioned desirable and undesirable futures, dramatized and reconciled significant U.S. values and symbols, and espoused a preferred course of action consistent with the narrative and its values.

The Past: America's Claim to the Canal

President Carter's narrative found the original 1903 Hay-Bunau-Varilla Treaty to be out of step with a sense of fairness and morality because "no person from Panama ever saw that treaty before it was signed" or "was involved in the signing of that treaty."[45] The new treaties would reaffirm U.S. fairness because ratification "is what is right for us and what is fair to others."[46] Further, Carter argued that even the unfair treaty failed to grant the United States sovereignty over the canal.

Crane agreed that the original treaty was unfair, saying that it was advantageous to the United States and disadvantageous to Panama because it was a clever and legal treaty granting the United States sovereignty over the Canal Zone. The treaty epitomized shrewdness and opportunism, because "when any nation goes to the bargaining table it does so with the determination to act in its own best interests and to derive as many benefits as possible."[47]

Crane further maintained that the original treaty ceded all sovereignty over the Canal Zone to the United States. But the thrust of Carter's argument was that the treaty provided for Panamanian sovereignty and U.S. jurisdiction *as if we* had sovereignty. Crane cited several examples of acts usually associated with sovereignty, and he inferred that "the very yielding to Panama of certain small pieces of control proves that the United States has full control—de facto sovereignty—in the first place."[48] Carter's concern was the discrepancy between our *de facto* sovereignty and Panama's *de jure* sovereignty. His best handling of this issue came three months before Crane's book and four months before the Fireside Chat. Carter explained to a Denver audience:

> We have never owned the Panama Canal Zone. We've never had title to it. We've never had sovereignty over it . . . the Supreme Court has con-

firmed since then that this is Panamanian territory. People born in the
Panama Canal Zone are not American citizens. We've always paid them
an annual fee, since the first year of the Panama Canal Treaty that pres-
ently exists, for the use of their property. . . . People say we bought it; it's
ours; we ought not to give it away. We've never bought it. It's not been
ours. We are not giving it away.[49]

Crane never directly engaged these points.

Crane and Carter argued their positions differently. Crane's account
sidestepped the treaty's grant of control *as if* the United States held sovereignty despite reprinting the text of Article III of the 1903 treaty in his book.
It states that

the Republic of Panama grants to the United States all the rights, power
and authority within the zone . . . which the United States would possess
and exercise *if it* were the sovereign of the territory within which said
lands and waters are located [emphasis added].[50]

He focused instead on signs of sovereignty and exploited the fact that few
knew that the original treaty preserved Panamanian sovereignty in principle.
For his part, Carter too often summarized and asserted while Crane used
detailed extrinsic support such as testimony and court decisions. Carter's
claim that "the Supreme Court has confirmed since then that this is Panamanian territory," for example, seems to be refuted with Crane's specific references to *Wilson v. Shaw* (1907), *The United States v. Husband* (1972), and a
"veteran American diplomat and international law authority."[51]

Carter and Crane presented strikingly divergent histories that forced their
audiences to choose. If the United States held sovereign control over the
Canal Zone, then any sharing of that power would be surrender, retreat, or a
giveaway; but if Panama held sovereignty, there was nothing for the United
States to surrender. Fisher's first test for good reasons is the degree to which
the narrative is "true to and consistent with what we think we know and what
we value."[52] Crane's history met the first narrative test better than did
Carter's—even though it misused its own evidence—because it fit neatly with
the McGuffey Reader Complex and dramatized U.S. cleverness and power.

The Present: The Western Hemisphere Today

President Carter characterized Panama as one of our "historic allies and
friends" headed by a "stable government which has encouraged the development of free enterprise" and would hold democratic elections.[53] But Crane
described a "banana republic" dominated by "forty influential families"
where "poverty is abysmal" and in which General Omar Torrijos runs a "corrupt, vicious police state . . . built with the help of his Marxist allies" and kept
from bankruptcy only by "the New York banking community."[54] Carter
described legitimate disaffection in the hemisphere and depicted the canal as
"the last vestige of alleged American colonialism."[55] He eagerly anticipated
this "new partnership" and spoke of defending the canal with Panamanian

forces "joined with us as brothers."[56] In the Carter vision, the United States was a powerful, fair, generous neighbor ready and willing to demonstrate those admirable traits by sharing the canal with the Panamanians.

But Crane painted a future based on the proper places of property and generosity. Crane bluntly differentiated his world from Carter's:

> The world is not a Sunday school classroom in Plains, Georgia. It is a violent, conflict-ridden place where peace and freedom only survive when they are protected. . . . Peace comes only to the prepared and security only to the strong.[57]

Generosity among friends is noble; generosity in a jungle is foolish and cowardly. The Carter and Crane narratives dramatized divergent values. Carter told of a friendly, honest, rational, democratic, capitalist nation worthy of being our military and economic partner. Crane described a hostile, corrupt, childish, socialist nation unworthy of partnership with the United States. Accuracy aside, Crane's story built on his audience's belief in U.S. superiority and generosity but asked them to be suspicious and protective in this particular case. Carter's account played on his audience's perceptions of our traditions of fairness and military strength and asked his audience to demonstrate its trusting and generous nature.

The Future: The Kind of Power We Wish to Be

Carter and Crane agreed that the canal decision would demonstrate "the kind of great power we wish to be."[58] Carter claimed that Theodore Roosevelt "would join us in our pride for being a great and generous people, with the national strength and wisdom to do what is right for us and what is fair to others."[59] He said that ratification would be "a show of strength . . . national will . . . fairness and . . . confidence in ourselves." He explained that we need not "run over a little country. It's much better for us to show our strength and our ability by not being a bully and by saying to Panama, let's work in harmony."[60] Carter said that ratification would demonstrate that "we are able to deal fairly and honorably with a proud but smaller sovereign nation . . . [because] we believe in good will and fairness, as well as strength." He spoke of the "new partnership" as a "source of national pride and self-respect."[61]

But Crane saw ratification as "one more crucial American step in a descent into ignominy—to the end of America's credibility as a world power and a deterrent to aggression."[62] Crane's future envisioned neither friendship nor generosity but a reputation for cowardice and weakness. A "surrender in Panama would appear not as a noble act of magnanimity, but as the cowardly retreat of a tired, toothless paper tiger."[63]

The futures Carter and Crane envisioned diverged. Crane saw danger; Carter saw security. Crane wanted superiority; Carter promoted partnership. Crane implied force and punishment; Carter urged generosity and kindness. Crane found the United States weak; Carter thought us strong. Crane saw shame in "surrender"; Carter believed continued imperialism diminished our reputation. Each believed that the other side in the controversy indirectly helped U.S. enemies.

Outgrowth of the Narrative Debate

In the end, the treaties were ratified. But the New Right aroused public sentiment and developed a massive public relations machine, defined its identity, created a list of villains, and transformed treaty ratification into a rhetorical success. As Viguerie explained:

> Our campaign to save the canal gained conservative converts around the country, added more than 400,000 new names to our lists, encouraged many of the movement's leading figures . . . to run for public office, and produced significant liberal defeats. The New Right came out of the Panama Canal fight with no casualties, not even a scar. Because of Panama we are better organized. We developed a great deal of confidence in ourselves, and our opponents became weaker. That November [1978] the New Right really came of age.[64]

The New Right campaign accomplished four of the five functions of social movement persuasion despite losing the treaty vote. It enabled them to transform perceptions of reality, to transform perceptions of society, to prescribe courses of action, and to mobilize for action.

The Panama Canal controversy shows how a social movement can critique a bipartisan consensus and mobilize supporters by dramatizing their fears. The New Right's narrative enabled them to take over the rhetorical agenda of a Republican National Committee that hungered for a set of arguments with which to mobilize voters against Carter and the Democrats.

New Right organizers used the canal issue as a symbolic vehicle for energizing their movement. Because the debate was between narrative visions, defenders of the institutional narrative risked losing their entire policy framework. The New Right undermined public confidence in the assumptions underlying U.S. foreign policy and provided an alternative narrative framework through which subsequent events in Iran, Afghanistan, Nicaragua, Grenada, El Salvador, and the Persian Gulf would be interpreted.

Dramatic rhetorical narratives that excite the imagination are more persuasive than those that are more technical in nature. Both Crane and Carter claimed to have "the facts," and both established their authority and expertise. But Crane was better able than Carter to involve his audience in the process of collective fantasizing because his narrative provided themes that his audience interpreted as "good reasons."

Let us appraise the narratives with respect to Fisher's four criteria of narrative rationality. First, Crane's narrative dramatized U.S. heroism, strength, generosity, legality, and cleverness, while Carter's narrative required us to revise our sense of history and national character to admit that Teddy Roosevelt was a bully who tricked our neighbors. Crane's narrative was more consistent with what we "knew," "believed," and "valued" than Carter's. Ironically and importantly, the social movement used existing perceptions of history to build its case, while the institutional version sought to change perceptions.

Second, both narratives were appropriate to the ratification decision because they framed the issues and compelled a conclusion. Crane's account was self-supporting; his conflict with the defense establishment clouded the decision and made caution seem more prudent than trust. Carter, like Ford, tried to respond with administrative rhetoric, but this required him to allay the fears aroused by the movement. This left citizens with two questions: "After fourteen years of negotiating, what's the hurry?" and "If you are right, Mr. President, why is this convincing congressman so worried?"

Third, Crane's narrative was the more promising in its effects for his audience. It promised that the path of alleged cowardice and weakness would lead to friendship without respect, while resolve would lead to both power and respect. Carter's narrative promised that the choice of generosity and honor would lead to friendship, respect, and security while intransigence would lead to greater antagonism and vulnerability. Crane's account invites audience fantasizing because its stakes were so dramatic.

And fourth, Crane's narrative was the more internally consistent because of its simplicity. Carter's narrative presented several apparent inconsistencies. Why should we grant anything to people who are increasingly resentful? How are these resentful people developing this new sense of mutual purpose and trust with the United States? If Panama is friendly and stable, why need we worry about defending the canal? If we need to worry about defending the canal, why voluntarily relinquish any of our claim to it? Carter answered these questions reasonably well, but his answers were complex and evolved over several months. Crane's narrative provided few apparent inconsistencies. He did commit a critical logical error by arguing that the presence of all the signs of U.S. sovereignty over the canal proved sovereignty. But this inconsistency was buried deep in his argument, and it was obscured by his references to memoranda and court decisions on related points.

In short, President Carter advanced a technically sound argument for treaty ratification that did not meet the tests of good narrative. Crane's arguments against ratification, flawed as they were, met the narrative tests and involved audience members in the social movement. The treaty was ratified on administrative and technical grounds, but the social movement established its narrative framework as a viable alternative and used it a year later to frame events in Iran and Afghanistan and to overthrow the Ford-Carter-Kissinger "friendly giant" narrative.

CONCLUSIONS

A choice between narrative frameworks ultimately boils down to the question of believability, and believability hinges on the individual's personal inventory of words, meanings, experiences, associations, social influences, values, needs, and sense of causation. People believe what they need to believe to keep themselves afloat in the world. A narrative that embodies and dramatizes experiences and fantasies "makes sense" because it has coherence and fidelity. It excites us, and we wonder why no one noticed it before. We share our enthusiasm with our associates and create a sense of community in a shared vision through the act of collective fantasizing.

The militia movement adopted the story of the American Revolution and recast it with their members as the patriots and the federal government as the occupying force. Like the founders, contemporary militia talk about the need to resist gun control and stockpile arms so that they can resist the encroachment of the Yankees, ZOG, the United Nations, and the government of the United States. But the cohesive narrative fragmented with the Oklahoma City bombing; there was no consistent story to tell. They did it, or they didn't do it but they understood why it was done, or it was a despicable act by the government and media to discredit militias, or it was a horrific act of an unprincipled federal government. Without a consistent account of such a high profile incident, the movement was hard pressed to sustain itself.

The New Right transformed the controversy over the Panama Canal into a social movement versus establishment conflict. Crane's office legitimized his advocacy, and his reliance on old memoranda, court cases, testimony, and reprinted treaties created what Barnet Baskerville once called "the illusion of proof."[65] When Crane's narrative accounted for subsequent developments in Iran and Nicaragua, moderate Republicans such as Richard Nixon and Gerald Ford were perceptually exiled to the Carter position.

In a debate between narratives, the struggle over images, heroes, villains, values, and motives is central. These symbolic struggles determine how Americans, whether policy makers or ordinary citizens, will order the world around them and how they will perceive their policy alternatives. Narrative visions are the frameworks within which specific people, motives, and incidents are interpreted. As people recognize, share, and apply their vision, they recruit members and consolidate them into a working group.

This analysis of the militia and New Right movement narratives illustrates six important points about social movements and argument from narrative vision. First, activists coalesce around a narrative framework for interpreting political realities. Second, movements often ground their narratives in mainstream history. Third, an emerging social movement with a clear and convincing narrative can credibly challenge even a logical institutional narrative advanced by the president. Fourth, a narrative's unity or fragmentation can impact the movement's development. Fifth, the movement's narrative transcends its particular subject, and short-term losses can become long-term wins. Finally, because narratives help us to interpret events, and because events help us to validate our choice of narrative, political history is a series of struggles for narrative dominance.

Notes

[1] David Carr, *Time, Narrative, and History* (Bloomington: Indiana University Press, 1986): 89.

[2] Howard Kamler, *Communication: Sharing Our Stories of Experience* (Seattle: Psychological Press, 1983): 27–58.

[3] Walter R. Fisher, *Human Communication as Narration: Toward a Philosophy of Reason, Value and Action* (Columbia: University of South Carolina Press, 1987): 66–67.

[4] Carr, 1–113.

[5] Carr, 23.

[6] Fisher, 194.

[7] Ernest G. Bormann, "Fantasy and Rhetorical Vision: The Rhetorical Criticism of Social Reality," *Quarterly Journal of Speech* 58 (December 1972): 396–407; and "Fantasy and Rhetorical Vision: Ten Years Later," *Quarterly Journal of Speech* 68 (August 1982): 288–305. See also Dan Nimmo and James E. Combs, *Mediated Political Realities* (New York: Longman, 1983); and Murray Edelman, *Constructing the Political Spectacle* (Chicago: University of Chicago Press, 1988).

[8] Bormann, "Fantasy and Rhetorical Vision," 398.

[9] Bormann, "Fantasy and Rhetorical Vision," 405.

[10] "Belligerent 'Claimant' Page: A Call to Arms," http://www.geocities.com/Yosemite/Gorge/8270, accessed 19 July 2006.

[11] Dave Delany, "The Great Militia," http://users.mo-net.com/mlindste/mmmisu2.html, accessed 8 August 2006.

[12] Delany.

[13] Delany.

[14] Priscilla Marie Meddaugh, *The Other in Cyberspace Discourse on White Supremacy.* Unpublished doctoral dissertation. (Detroit: Wayne State University, 1999): 132.

[15] [William L. Pierce] Andrew Macdonald, *The Turner Diaries,* 2nd ed. (New York: Barricade Books, 1978).

[16] Macdonald, 33.

[17] "Belligerent 'Claimant' Page," accessed 19 July 2006.

[18] "Belligerent 'Claimant' Page," accessed 19 July 2006.

[19] Kenneth S. Stem, *A Force Upon the Plain* (Norman: University of Oklahoma, 1997): 108–118.

[20] http://www.wagoneers.com/pages/History/GunControl-the-proven-record.html, accessed 19 July 2006.

[21] Macdonald, 33–34.

[22] "Belligerent 'Claimant' Page," accessed 19 July 2006.

[23] http://www.firearmsandliberty.com/nra.militia.statement.html, accessed 19 July 2006.

[24] http://www.boogieonline.com/revolution/multi/terrorism/okc/militia.html, accessed 19 July 2006.

[25] http://www.stormfront.org/adv-okc.htm, accessed 19 July 2006.

[26] Ric Duncan. #0 @*176:200/36* via *176:40010* PRNet.

[27] http://www.stormfront.org/em-okc.htm, accessed 19 July 2006.

[28] *Cover-Up in Oklahoma*, http://www.amazon.com/gp/product/0966690702/qid=1153412770/sr=8-2/ref=sr_1_2/102-8266142-5585753?%5Fencoding=UTF8&v=glance&n=283155, accessed 19 July 2006.

[29] *Cover-Up in Oklahoma*, accessed 19-July 2006.

[30] *Cover-Up in Oklahoma*, accessed 19-July 2006.

[31] Duncan.

[32] Richard A. Viguerie, *The New Right: We're Ready to Lead* (Falls Church, VA: The Viguerie Company, 1981): 65–67.

[33] Although both Carter and Crane refer to 70–80 percent public opposition to the treaties, an August 1977 Gallup Poll reports only 47 percent opposition. See American Institute of Public Opinion, *The Gallup Poll: Public Opinion, 1972–1977,* Vol. 2 (Wilmington, DE: Scholarly Resources, 1978): 1181–1183. In his memoirs, *Keeping the Faith* (New York: Bantam Books, 1982), Carter calls his efforts to win support for the canal treaties his most difficult political battle.

[34] E. Pace, "Reagan Declares Canal Treaties Should Be Rejected by the Senate," *New York Times,* 26 August 1977, 1.

[35] John Wayne, "Scare Letter from the Honorable Ronald Reagan," November 11, 1977. Fireside Chat, 2-1-78, Box 17, Staff Office Files, Speechwriters' Chronological, Jimmy Carter Library.

[36] Wayne.

[37] Wayne.

[38] Wayne.

[39] Wayne.

[40] James Fallows, Memo to Hamilton Jordan, September 4, 1977. Fireside Chat, 2-1-78, Box 17, Staff Office Files, Speechwriters' Chronological, Jimmy Carter Library.

[41] Harlan J. Strauss, Letter to Jim Fallows, September 6, 1977. Staff Office Files, Speechwriters, James Fallows Files, Jimmy Carter Library.

[42] James Fallows, Letter to Harlan Strauss, September 19, 1977. Staff Office Files, Speech Writers, James Fallows Files, Jimmy Carter Library.

[43] James Fallows, Memorandum to Zbigniew Brzezinski, January 27, 1978 and Suggested Outline: Panama Canal Speech, 1-25-78. Fireside Chat, 2-1-78, Box 17, Staff Office Files, Speech writers' Chronological, Jimmy Carter Library.

[44] Phillip M. Crane, *Surrender in Panama: The Case Against the Treaty* (New York: Dale Books, 1978): 1–2; and Jimmy Carter, "Panama Canal Treaties," *Public Papers of the President of the United States: Jimmy Carter,* 1978 (Washington, DC: United States Government Printing Office, 1979): 259. About 100,000 copies of Crane's book were distributed in January 1978 by Richard Viguerie's associates.

[45] Jimmy Carter, "Radio-Television News Directors Association," *Public Papers of the Presidents: Jimmy Carter,* 1977 (Washington, DC: United States Government Printing Office, 1978): 1597 (referred to hereafter as 9-15-77).

[46] Carter, "Panama Canal Treaties," 262, 263.

[47] Crane, 41.

[48] Crane, 37.

[49] Jimmy Carter, "Denver, Colorado," *Public Papers of the Presidents: Jimmy Carter,* 1977 (Washington, DC: United States Government Printing Office, 1978): 1886 (referred to hereafter as 10-22-77).

[50] Quoted by Crane, 136.

[51] Crane, 36–37.

[52] Fisher, 194.

[53] Carter, "Panama Canal Treaties," 262.

[54] Crane, 56–57, 71, 66.

[55] Carter, "Panama Canal Treaties," 258, 261.

[56] Carter, "Panama Canal Treaties," 260, 262.

[57] Crane, 113–114.

[58] Carter, "Panama Canal Treaties," 262.

[59] Carter, "Panama Canal Treaties," 263, emphasis added.

[60] Carter, 10-22-77, 1890.

[61] Carter, "Panama Canal Treaties," 259, 262.

[62] Crane, 113.

[63] Crane, 1.

[64] Viguerie, 70–71.

[65] Barnet Baskerville, "The Illusion of Proof," *Western Journal of Communication* 25 (Fall 1961): 236–242.

CHAPTER

10

Argument from Transcendence in Social Movements

Theorists agree that confrontation is essential for the rise of a social movement. For instance, Robert Cathcart argues that confrontation is "the necessary ingredient" for a social movement to come into being and to proceed with its cause.[1] Kenneth Burke notes that "drama requires a conflict" and, building on Burke's writings, Leland Griffin claims, "The development of a countermovement is vital: for it 'is the bad side that produces the movement which makes history, by providing a struggle.' "[2]

As necessary as confrontation is for social movements, its results are a mixture of blessings and curses. On the one hand, confrontations with institutional forces and countermovements establish the social movement as a serious threat, contrast the collectives, reveal the ugly side of institutions and their collaborators, and create "doubts about the legitimacy and morality of the establishment."[3] On the other hand, resistance rhetoric threatens the social movement's existence by challenging its fragile claim of legitimacy, means and ends, norms and values, and credibility. The social movement must develop an effective rebuttal strategy to continue its momentum toward meaningful social change.

ARGUMENT FROM TRANSCENDENCE

Social movements may employ a *rhetoric of transcendence* to challenge institutions and to counter the persuasive efforts that threaten norms, values, and hierarchical relationships. In a rhetoric of transcendence, persuaders argue that a person, group, goal, thing, right, action, or proposal *surpasses*, is *superior* to, or was *prior* to its opposite. Karl Wallace writes, for example, that in considering relative merits "the point is, what is good and what is evil, and of good what is greater, and of evil what is the less."[4] Thus, a rhetoric of transcendence is an inherently comparative process.

When operating at the *highest level* of transcendence, persuaders claim that a goal, group, or right, for instance, is superior to or greater than *all* other options. The goal, group, or right has attained (through development, achievement, statute, discovery, or dogma) the *ultimate* state of perfection. When operating at the *lowest level* of transcendence, persuaders argue that a goal, group, or right is superior to or greater than *one* or *some* of its kind. Aristotle wrote centuries ago that

> the acquisition of a greater in place of a lesser good, or of a lesser in place of a greater evil, is also good, for in proportion as the greater exceeds the lesser there is acquisition of good or removal of evil.[5]

Thus, the goal, group, or right has not reached an ultimate state of perfection but is *more perfect* or *more preferable* than its opposite.

Burke describes transcendence as the building of a language "bridge whereby one realm is *transcended* by being viewed *in terms* of a realm 'beyond it.'"[6] Theorists from Cicero in ancient Rome to the twentieth century have identified four common points of comparison in establishing transcendence: quantity (more–less, large–small), quality (good–bad, excellent–poor), value (important–unimportant, desirable–undesirable), and hierarchy (high–low, above–below).[7]

Argument from Quantity

Arguments based on *quantity*, writes Burke, contend that one group is larger than a competing group or that one organization is more inclusive than one or more organizations with which it is identified.[8] For instance, PETA (People for the Ethical Treatment of Animals) and the International Fund for the welfare of animals claim to be the largest and fastest growing organizations within the animal rights movement. A person advocating censorship may claim that the right to speak for the *American people* transcends political parties, special interest groups, or liberals. Leaders of an industrial union open to all workers may claim that their organization transcends a *trade union* that represents only one trade (such as carpenters). For example, Terence Powderly compared the Knights of Labor to the steam locomotive of the day and the trade union with the "stage coach of half a century ago." Workers of "different trades and callings," he claimed,

> have had their eyes opened to the fact that the organization composed of but one trade or calling does not meet their wants, and must give way for a grander, mightier association, which recognizes the right of every honest man to come within its protecting folds.[9]

Thus, many protest groups struggle to become (or claim to be) the largest or most inclusive of all grassroots, people's, workers', professional, or reform organizations.

Argument from Quality

Persuaders who employ the comparative point of *quality* argue that one goal, proposal, or strategy, for instance, is good while a competing goal, proposal, or strategy is bad or evil. Truth is contrasted with falsehood, justice with injustice, freedom with slavery, equality with inequality, nonviolence with violence, prejudice with tolerance, moral development with moral underdevelopment. Michael Osborn points out that Martin Luther King, Jr., in his "Letter from Birmingham Jail" contrasted the "transcendent morality of the one group" (civil rights activists) "with the self-evident immorality of the other" (segregationists).[10]

Aristotle noted that when "people agree that two things are both useful but do not agree about which is the more so, the next step will be to treat of relative goodness and relative utility."[11] Thus, a persuader may contend that one proposal promises a *greater good* than a competing proposal or that one strategy is *less evil* than another strategy. Gary Selby writes that "radical abolitionists responded by appealing to what they claimed to be the transcendent principles of Christianity," ones that "transcended the details of biblical exegesis" slaveholders used to justify slavery.[12] Both were good, but the transcendent Christian principles were more fundamental than the Bible. Debaters, litigants, and legislators often argue about the "comparative advantages" or "comparative disadvantages" of supporting doctrine, resources, proposals, and actions. Persons warning of the potential catastrophic results of acid rain may recognize that solutions will cause economic hardships for some companies and workers, while persons arguing against using animals for medical research may admit that some research might be more difficult to perform without animals. But in each case, persuaders argue that the potential benefits outweigh the potential harms. For instance, animal rights advocates warn that demeaning animals demeans humans and that "this crime against nature and humanity" adversely affects "human health, world hunger, natural resources, and the environment."[13]

Argument from Value

Persuaders use the comparative point of *value* when arguing about what is more or less *important* or *significant* in society and social interactions. Although Frances Willard was an early and staunch leader in the struggle for suffrage for women, she came to argue that a "transformed world" was more important than "attaining the ballot."[14] In the same vein, Martin Luther King, Jr., wrote that "justice trumps peace as a value."[18] Some persuaders see meaningful change or movement progress as more important than ideological purity and consistency, while others see ideological principles as the heart and soul of a movement that transcend progress or expansion of the movement.

Persuaders may argue that a group's ends are so important that any means (vilification, dishonesty, disruption, violence) are justified or that the need to meet a crisis takes precedence over factional differences. For example, government agencies use "national security" to justify spying on U.S. citizens and the issuance of "disinformation." Political parties justify mudslinging and dirty campaign tricks by arguing that it is for "the good of the people." Militant elements of social movements use justice, freedom, equality, and independence to rationalize violence and terrorism. Attaining a goal or preventing a change, persuaders argue, is more important—is of greater value—than the means used, resulting factional differences, ideological disputes, or which movement leader or organization takes the lead or gets the credit.

Argument from Hierarchy

Persuaders use the comparative point of *hierarchy* when attempting to establish that one person, group, thing, act, right, or ideal exceeds another because it is of a higher order along a gradation or continuum: one race above another race, human above animal, spiritual over temporal, supernatural over natural, universal over the individual or local. Martha Watson writes that Martin Luther King, Jr.'s "Letter from Birmingham Jail" "moves the controversy" to a "higher level," "from the political to the moral realm."[16] In his study of transcendence as "dialectical confrontation," Robert Heath claims that Malcolm X, like King, sought "to lift the struggle 'above civil rights to the level of human rights.' Human rights transcend civil rights since the latter are given by man and the former are given by God."[17] "Transcendence, by moving upward" in the continuum "to the ultimate source of humanity, is a vital purifying dimension in the dialectical transformation of perspectives."

Persuaders may argue that humans, like causes, can be raised to a higher level on the hierarchy of worth. Watson argues that "in a sense, King offers his supporters a view of themselves as morally superior."[18] White supremacist groups have preached for centuries that white Europeans and their descendants are superior to other races. For instance, on a radio talk show, Charles Lynch, then leader of the Ku Klux Klan on the West Coast, declared the Klan was dedicated to preserving the white race, "a superior race intellectually, spiritually, and morally."[19] Medical scientists argue that it is ethical to experiment on animals because experiments eventually help save the lives of humans, a higher order of life. Animal rights activists, on the other hand, argue that the suffering and mutilation of animals is evil for what it does to living, feeling beings superior to inanimate objects and plants. Most movements claim they are *grassroots efforts*, stating or implying that grassroots collectives are more American, high-minded, and democratic and thus superior to others—institutional or uninstitutional.

The notion of *hierarchy* is a versatile argumentative tactic for social movements. For instance, if a member or leader does something to discredit the movement, a persuader might argue that the "power of truth" for which the movement is fighting "transcends the limitations of the personal agent who propounds it."[20] To counteract feelings of guilt or accusations of blame for the consequences of a movement's actions, a persuader might argue that the act was not an "inferior kind of crime" (breaking and entering, trespassing, petty theft, vandalism, killing in a drunken brawl) but a "transcendent kind of crime" actually "required by traditional values" or to further a just cause. Barry Brummett writes that "one may *avoid* guilt by engaging in *transcendence*. This avoidance of guilt puts the sin into a perspective which redefines it as 'not a sin,' as a virtue or as the requirement of some higher or nobler hierarchy."[21] All kinds of questionable actions are executed by institutions and social movements in the name of God.

The strategy of transcendence provides social movements with a variety of lines of argument for defending organizations, enhancing positions, countering other movements, and avoiding the necessity of denying the undeniable. It strengthens a movement's support among "the people" and important legitimizers because it refutes the opposition by identifying the movement symbolically (including its ideology, prescribed courses of action, mobilization efforts, and claims to legitimacy) with what is large, good, important, and of the highest order. It identifies the opposition with what is small, evil, unimportant, or of a lower order. Burke writes:

> Hence, to some degree, solution of conflict must always be done purely in the symbolic realm (by "transcendence") if it is to be done at all. Persons of moral and imaginative depth require great enterprise and resourcefulness in such purely "symbolic" solutions of conflict (by the formation of appropriate "attitudes").[22]

Comparison and contrast are inherent in all arguments from transcendence because something or someone must be shown as larger or smaller, better or worse, more important or less important, or higher or lower than something or someone else. What follows is a case study of the abortion controversy in which both sides utilize arguments from transcendence to accomplish a variety of persuasive goals.

THE ABORTION CONFLICT AS A CASE STUDY

The conflict over abortion is centuries old, but the current conflict in the United States began with the forming of pro-choice and pro-life organizations during the late 1960s to enhance and to resist increasing efforts to liberalize state laws governing abortion. On January 22, 1973, the United States Supreme Court dealt the fledgling pro-life resistance movement an "unqualified legal defeat."[23] In *Roe v. Wade*, the Supreme Court decided (1) that a woman's constitutional right of privacy precludes a state from prohibiting her from obtaining an abortion on demand during the first trimester of pregnancy, (2) that a state could regulate abortions during the second trimester only for the purpose of protecting the woman's life, and (3) that a state could regulate abortions during the third trimester to preserve the life of the child.[24] Thus, the Supreme Court viewed fetal life as a viable human only after the first six months of pregnancy. The pro-choice movement had apparently won the war over abortion.

Pro-life forces recovered quickly from the shock of the Supreme Court defeat and created a revivalistic social movement to make abortion unlawful under all circumstances and to reaffirm society's respect for all human life. Their solution during the early decades was a constitutional amendment defining human life as beginning at the moment of conception and prohibiting the termination of a "child's" life except in situations in which the "mother's" life is in grave danger. This amendment would overturn the Supreme Court decision and preclude further court and legislative actions (state and national) to liberalize abortion.

When the likelihood of a constitutional amendment passing both houses of Congress and being ratified by a sufficient number of states dwindled, the National Right to Life Committee and its affiliates in all fifty states, Baptists for Life, the American Life League, American Life Lobby, Catholic and evangelical churches, the Moral Majority, and allied groups mobilized massive political pressure from the grassroots level. Their goals were the passage of restrictive federal and state laws and denial of federal and state financial aid for abortions. They became involved in political campaigns at all levels to elect candidates who would support their positions through legislation, executive orders, and appointment of antiabortion justices to the Supreme Court to overturn *Roe v. Wade*.

More militant tactics became common in the mid-1980s, particularly Operation Rescue's efforts to blockade abortion clinics (designed to clog the jails by provoking police into brutality and massive arrests) and the Pro-Life Action League's use of "sidewalk counseling" (to discourage pregnant women from obtaining abortions). Groups pressured hospitals and physicians not to perform abortions, often by picketing homes and following family members to work and school. A few radical elements resorted to violence such as bombings, arson, vandalism, and shooting into clinics. The ultimate violence first occurred on March 10, 1993, when Dr. David Gunn was murdered by a pro-life militant in Pensacola, Florida.[25] Other assassinations of physicians and clinic workers followed in both the United States and Canada. Wanted posters featuring the faces of physicians who performed abortions and Web sites modeled after the Nuremberg Trials at the end of World War II informed antiabortion forces of the names, addresses, and phone numbers of "abortionists." When Dr. Barnett Slepian was gunned down in his kitchen by a sniper in 1998, his name was crossed off a national Web site list.

The pro-choice movement transformed itself into a resistance movement to counter the efforts of pro-life groups. Before *Roe v. Wade*, NARAL was the acronym for National Association for Repeal of Abortion Laws. After *Roe v. Wade*, it changed its name to the National Abortion Rights Action League and eventually to NARAL Pro-Choice America. It has worked closely with the Religious Coalition for Reproductive Choice, the National Organization for Women (NOW), and allied organizations to protect a woman's right to choose. Pro-choice became increasingly active as the pro-life movement pressured physicians and hospitals into refusing to perform abortions, achieved legislative successes, and seemed near victory with conservative, pro-life appointments to the Supreme Court. Organizations presented their cases through leaflets, mass mailings, Web sites, advertisements, and rallies in Washington, D.C., and other cities. They campaigned for pro-choice candidates, brought pressure on state legislatures and Congress, presented court cases, protected abortion clinics, and formed escorts for women trying to enter clinics.

Both pro-life and pro-choice have gained and lost from their relationships with institutional leaders. The administrations of Republican presidents Ronald Reagan and George H. W. Bush aided the pro-life movement through respect for life rhetoric and actions that denied federal funds for abortion procedures and limited international funds to countries that encouraged abortions. The election of Democratic president Bill Clinton in 1992 and the possibility of appointment of pro-choice justices to the Supreme Court tilted the conflict once more toward the pro-choice countermovement, spurring the pro-life movement into greater efforts to end legalized abortion. Rather than the struggle lessening, it entered a new and more militant phase. Within eight years the tide turned once again toward reining in *Roe v. Wade*. Both movements moved into high rhetorical gear with the election of Republican George W. Bush in 2000 and his reelection in 2004, Republican control of both houses of Congress, medical advances that enabled tiny, premature babies to survive and provided graphic images of fetuses in the womb, polls showing fewer Americans were in favor of unrestricted abortion, and the likelihood of pro-life justices joining the Supreme Court.

The raging conflict over legalized abortion in the United States provides an excellent case study of how movements and countermovements use argument from transcendence. Although the conflict has been punctuated with violence, disruptions, coercive tactics, terrorism, and murder, both movement and countermovement have relied primarily on symbols and symbolic actions to attain and maintain public support and to win victories in living rooms, voting booths, courtrooms, legislative chambers, and executive offices. An analysis of leaflets, pamphlets, mailings, Internet sites, books, newspaper essays, and advertisements reveals that, for nearly forty years, the pro-life and pro-choice movements have relied heavily on arguments from transcendence. These movements use the four points of comparison to define fundamental issues, present and defend cases, resolve dilemmas, enhance their credibility, attack one another, and refute charges made against their ideologies, tactics, organizations, and memberships. The remainder of this chapter focuses on how the pro-choice and pro-life movements have used arguments from transcendence in their clashes over personhood, rights, and reality.

THE CLASH OVER PERSONHOOD

The key premise on which all pro-life and pro-choice arguments from transcendence rest is the debate over when a *life* or a *person* comes into existence. Both social movements expend a great deal of rhetorical energy to establish the moment of *personhood* and to discount the other's claims. If a person exists at the moment of conception, abortion is murder. If a person does not exist until the moment of birth or viability, abortion is not murder but a medical procedure to terminate an unwanted pregnancy.

Pro-Life

Pro-life advocates argue that life begins at the moment of conception, that "human life is a continuous developmental process that begins at conception and ceases at death."[26] A "Voices of Women Who Mourn" feature on the Feminists for Life Web site has a former victim of abortion exclaim,

> In the seventies we were told a lie from the pit of hell (and it is still told today), that a pregnancy is just a blob of tissue in the uterus up until three months gestation. . . . I was pitiful in my ability to stand up against others' reasoning, no matter how powerful.[27]

In support of this claim, pro-life persuaders offer detailed chronologies with photographs of development from conception, through three weeks when the heart starts beating, to the moment of birth. They counter that, contrary to pro-choice claims and the Supreme Court decision that declared the unborn to be "not persons at all," scientists, medical authorities, every Protestant theologian since Calvin, the Catholic church, most Protestant denominations, and the Bible agree that life begins at conception, the moment the sperm and egg meet. For instance, National Right to Life claims, "Science tells us that the new life she carries is a complete and fully formed human being from the moment of fertilization."[28] Baptists for Life argues that

> every human embryo—from the earliest point, of the smallest size—has a full complement of chromosomes. Nothing needs to be added . . . . "Pre-embryo," "zygote," and "fetus" are terms that designate a stage of human life, much like "toddler," "teenager," and "adult."[29]

Web sites such as abort73.com provide links to the "biological" case against abortion that provide readers with medical testimony, prenatal development, abortion techniques, and photographic evidence that proves life begins at conception. Thus, the pro-life position is not merely *church* dogma or a *religious* or *philosophical* issue but a *scientific fact*, a basic human issue. This places the issue in the realms of "absolute truth" and "absolute standards of right and wrong" that transcend "moral relativism" that "continues to entrench itself more firmly in our society."[30]

If human life exists from the moment of conception, persuaders conclude, the fetus is a person, one of us, and not a "poorly functioning adult" but a "splendidly functioning baby."[31] The act of abortion, then, is not removing, as pro-choice claims, "a mass or blob of tissue," a "POC—product of conception," or a "clump of cells"; rather, it is the destruction, the "cold-blooded murder" of "a pre-born baby," "an innocent human life," and the "defenseless little child living in the mother's womb."[32] In the hierarchy of living beings, the fetus or baby is equal to its mother and transcends nonpersons. Because the fetus is both innocent and defenseless, it deserves special protection against its mother's (an equal but not superior) desire to kill it.

Pro-Choice

Pro-choice advocates counter pro-life's version of personhood by claiming that "no one knows when a fetus becomes a human being."[33] They assert that "medical, legal, and religious experts cannot, and will never, agree!" because the fetus has never been recognized legally, constitutionally, or historically as a *full-fledged person* but only as a *potential human being*.[34] The Religious Coalition for Reproductive Choice claims, "For centuries, theologians and scientists have argued the question of the beginning of life without reaching consensus. There is no single answer to this question."[35] Even the Bible declines to identify the fetus as a person. For instance, Exodus 21:22–23 regards the fetus not as a person but as belonging to the father; the killing of a woman but not of the fetus would warrant avenging. The New Testament does not address the issue. On the other hand, "The woman unquestionably fits the biblical portrayal of a person" because she is "a complex, many-sided creature with godlike abilities and moral responsibility to make" choices.[36] The Roman Catholic Church did not espouse the belief that the fetus was a person until the mid-nineteenth century, and even today "There is no Catholic teaching on when the fetus attains personhood, that is, becomes a human person with a soul."[37] The lack of agreement on personhood for the fetus "means determining when life begins—which no one knows—must ultimately rest on man-made definitions more arbitrary, philosophical and religious than scientific."[38] Contrary opinions are *theological* or *religious* beliefs held by the Roman Catholic Church and a few other denominations, not *biological* or *absolute facts* as pro-life advocates assert.

These claims place the opposition's belief of personhood at the moment of conception at the bottom of a hierarchy of beliefs: below scientific or biological facts, legal or constitutional statutes and decisions, biblical teachings, and prevailing theological beliefs. It is reduced in *importance* and in a *hierarchy* of beliefs to *merely* an arbitrary, man-made, religious issue among *religious denominations*. Thus, pro-choice persuaders conclude that antiabortion advocates give "a fertilized egg or a fetus legal standing equal to that of a pregnant woman" whose personhood is undisputed.[39] They argue that "a qualitative distinction must be made between its [the fetus] claims and the rights of a responsible person made in God's image who is living relationships with God and other human beings." To do otherwise would be "to dehumanize the woman, to consider her a mere 'thing' through which the fetus is passing."[40] "Existing life," the Religious Coalition for Reproductive Choice concludes, "is always sacred and takes precedence over a potential life."[41] The woman (a recognized person, literally "one who breathes") is clearly superior to (transcends) the fetus (a "cluster of cells" that "does not embody the qualities of personhood") she is carrying and thus deserves higher legal and constitutional standing.

THE CLASH OVER RIGHTS

The establishment of the personhood and hierarchical status of the woman or the fetus allows each movement to develop a case for which rights are most important and which are being violated or may be violated. Persuaders use the comparative points of value and hierarchy in their clashes over rights.

Pro-Life

Pro-life advocates argue that the fetus is a living human being and must be guaranteed the right to life—the "most basic value of our society," the "most fundamental right," the "paramount right," "the most basic human right bestowed on us by God"; it is "the one most fundamental right that no one can live without, the right to life."[42] In contrast to the right to life, a leaflet entitled *The Abortion Connection* claims, "There is NO 'constitutional' right to abortion. There is only a Supreme Court-created right from a split decision in *Roe v. Wade* on January 22, 1973."[43] This premise allows pro-life supporters to argue from the highest level of transcendence and to claim that "if all of our rights are to be protected, we must defend this first and most basic right— the right to life."[44]

Pro-life champions do not argue against women's rights, the freedom of choice, or religious liberty, but they place these values lower on the rights hierarchy and fundamentally dependent on the right to life. It is a matter, they claim, of competing rights. "On the one hand, you have the mother's right not to get pregnant. On the other hand, you have the baby's right not to be killed."[45] While the woman will, if she remains pregnant, experience "sickness, fatigue, reduced mobility, an enlarged body, and a new wardrobe," "abortion costs the unborn child his or her very life and it is a thoroughly permanent condition." The National Right to Life Committee acknowledges that "mothers have a right to be fully informed about the facts a few hours before making this life or death decision," but never "the right to kill her baby."[46] In a leaflet bearing a picture of an unborn but fully developed fetus, the author asks, "Does her [the woman's] rights include dealing out a death sentence to another human being who is completely defenseless?" and a Web site claims that "nothing short of anarchy can guarantee the perfect freedom of choice."[47] The point appears to be a reverse value argument: the end (preserving a woman's right of privacy and choice) does not justify the means (depriving the fetus of the right to life).

Pro-life persuaders use a combination value and hierarchy argument when they point to state and federal laws designed to protect the defenseless. For example, one writer notes that state laws guarantee "the right of inheritance, to damages received while yet unborn, to get a blood transfusion over the mother's objection, to have a guardian appointed, and other rights of citizenship" but not the "most basic right of all—the right to life."[48] Newspaper advertisements entitled "Eagles, Beagles, Babies and 'There Oughta Be a Law'" contain large pictures of a bald eagle, two beagle puppies, and a fetus. A caption reads, "Ours is a peculiar society. We have laws protecting wildlife and dogs, but not defenseless human beings."[49] The advertisements report that stealing one eagle egg may result in a $5,000 fine, one year in jail, or both and that both houses of Congress overwhelmingly approved a federal law prohibiting the use of dogs in tests of chemical, biological, and radioactive warfare materials. While these laws protect the life and rights of eagles and beagles, the advertisements note, "Last year . . . more than 1,000,000 unborn babies were 'terminated' through 'abortion on demand.' Terminated means killed. Killed without penalty. Unless someone got a parking ticket in front of an abortion mill." The lines of argument are clear. Although states and the federal government have laws to protect the rights of privacy and choice for the mother and the lives and well-being of animals, no laws guarantee the unborn child the human right to life—the right that transcends all others.

Pro-Choice

Pro-choice counters pro-life by claiming that "every woman in a free society" has the fundamental, constitutional right—a basic American right—guaranteed by the Supreme Court to a safe, legal abortion because it is crucial to her health and well-being. It is a matter of "reproductive freedom," a basic human right.[50] "The welfare of the mother," a universally recognized person, "must always be our primary concern," pro-choice advocates argue, and freedom of choice (reproductive freedom) is fundamental.[51] The president of Catholics for a Free Choice argued, "To grant absolute right to life to fetuses at all stages of development, from a single cell to viability, is to denigrate women's lives, health, and capacities."[52] Choice, free from unwarranted governmental intrusion into our private lives, is the "most precious of individual rights."[53]

Persuaders claim that the right to privacy, on which the Supreme Court based its decision in *Roe v. Wade* in 1973, is guaranteed by the First, Ninth, and Fourteenth Amendments to the Constitution. Any effort to limit this choice is a direct threat to religious liberty and the constitutional provision of separation of church and state.[54] The pro-choice slogan, "Not the church, not the state, women must decide their fate," sums up the movement's fundamental beliefs in freedom and privacy. Pro-choice advocates contend, then, that the value of a woman's health and well-being exceeds (transcends) that of a potential person, and the rights of privacy and freedom of choice are the most important of all human rights because they are essential to our religious liberty and reproductive freedom. All other rights are lower in the hierarchy and of less importance.

THE CLASH OVER REALITIES

The pro-life and pro-choice movements offer very different views of reality. The first portrays the present as the worst of times and the second portrays the present as the best of times, but each also takes a look backward and a look forward in presenting their cases for bringing about or resisting change. Dominant arguments are from quality and value.

Pro-Life

Pro-life rhetoric dwells little on the past and never claims there were few or no abortions prior to *Roe v. Wade* in 1973. A publication by Americans Against Abortion argues that 84 to 87 percent of so-called back-alley abortions of the past "were not done in back alleys at all" but by "reputable physicians" in medical facilities.[55] During the 2004 presidential campaign, Glen Stassen, professor of Christian Ethics at Fuller Theological Seminary, published a study in which he claimed that abortions increased in number during pro-life President George W. Bush's first administration because of his economic policies. The National Right to Life Committee issued two lengthy rebuttal essays on its Web site claiming that abortion had been declining since at least 1990, including Bush's first term.[56] The decline was attributed to the pro-life movement's crusade to end all abortions.

Pro-life persuaders dwell mostly on what has happened in the past when humans were labeled as nonpersons. They offer Nazi Germany and the extermination of six million Jews as indisputable evidence of what happens when some humans are judged to be inferior. Pictures and accounts of the Holocaust are often intermixed with pictures of aborted fetuses. A number of sources refer to the treatment of Native Americans as savages and of African Americans who, as nonpersons, could be bought, sold, or killed, particularly after the *Dred Scott* decision of 1857.[57] Thus, pro-life advocates imply that abortion and abortion-related deaths prior to 1973 were inconsequential and use historical accounts of Native Americans, slavery, and Nazi Germany as lead-ins to accounts of the current horrors. The past was obviously superior morally to the present, at least for the unborn and the women who carried them.

Pro-life rhetoric dwells on the present. It abounds with accounts and pictures of the cruel, barbarous slaughter of the unborn—a "national atrocity" and a "hidden slaughter similar to the Holocaust."[58] This evil is perpetrated for insignificant reasons compared to the right to life. Persuaders claim that 98 percent of abortions are for social and professional reasons, literally killing unborn humans "on a whim." Millions die every year because pregnancy is inconvenient or the mother wants to rid herself of an annoying problem.

Nurses and physicians tell stories about when they had to starve, smother, or bash in the head of an aborted fetus when it refused to die, and these stories are often accompanied by gory, full-color pictures of tiny bodies torn apart by a variety of abortion methods and dumped in buckets and trash cans. The most controversial effort to show life and death in the womb is a video entitled *The Silent Scream* that purports to show the struggle for life of a fetus being "murdered" by a vacuum aspirator. Joseph Scheidler, founder and director of the Pro-Life Action League, narrates this struggle: "She retreats frantically from the device. But it pulls her legs off. Then it disembowels her. She struggles violently with her arms. Her head falls back; her mouth opens in anguish."[59] A twenty-eight page reprint of an article entitled "Ex-Abortion Workers: Why They Quit" appears on a Web site sponsored by the Pro-Life Action League. It includes the gruesome personal stories of doctors, nurses, and clinic staff who had "religious conversions that helped—or demanded—their exit," accounts of fetuses born alive, a "little baby—that was making little sounds and moving and kicking," tiny body parts that had to be ground up in extra powerful disposals, and the smell of babies burning in the clinic crematorium.[60] Clearly, the fetus is an unborn child that far surpasses a blob or mass of tissue.

The prime battleground since the late 1990s has centered on late-term abortions, those in the third trimester of pregnancy. Pro-life champions have termed these procedures "partial-birth" abortions or "partial-birth infanticide" and described them in horrific detail. They offer clinical descriptions and firsthand testimony of nurses and physicians that portray the "heinous" or "gruesome" procedures performed on near-term fetuses who are often alive at the time of their "murder."[61] The Web site of the National Right to Life Committee provides links to facts and legislation, including partial-birth abortion, recent court decisions, and rebuttals to articles that claim fetuses don't feel pain.[62] After citing a step-by-step late-term abortion described in the *New York Times Magazine*, Tom Bethell, the Washington correspondent for *The American Spectator* exclaimed, "Murder, is what it was. The infant was within a few inches of drawing its first breath. Instead, it was stabbed in the back of the head by the attending 'doctor.'"[63] These doctors, he noted, "are the American successors to Mengele, who performed experiments in Nazi Germany." Bethell astutely noted that this procedure shifted the focus of the abortion debate from "'a woman's right to choose' to what is being chosen: infanticide." The implication is that, contrary to claims of medical authorities, late-term abortions are quite common, if not typical of abortions in the United States. The shift is from a right high on the good scale (free choice) to an act highest on the evil scale (murder and infanticide).

The pro-life movement's campaign against late-term abortions has attracted many supporters and met with considerable success. Some twenty-eight states had outlawed such procedures or stopped them temporarily by mid-1998. Congress passed legislation in the same year to ban all late-term abortions, but President Clinton vetoed it. The House of Representatives voted 296 to 132 to override the veto, and the Senate came within three votes of doing the same. Congress passed the Unborn Victims of Violence Act that prohibited late-term abortions in 2004, and President George W. Bush signed it into law on April 1. Pro-life has found a battle in the abortion war that resonates well with a sizable majority of American citizens (some estimates are 80 percent), including many nominal pro-choice supporters.

Pro-life advocates claim that all acts of abortion, not just partial-birth, are so heinous that pro-abortion forces have created euphemisms to mask reality. These include "terminating a pregnancy," "post-conceptual planning," "menstrual extraction," and "exercising a woman's right to choose." And they claim that the tragedies of the present, largely unreported and covered up, go beyond the unborn. Women who have been "exploited by abortion" suffer life-threatening complications and even death, serious mental and psychological problems, and increases in sterility, miscarriages, tubal pregnancies, and premature babies. Persuaders argue that abortion-on-demand has caused child abuse to increase by 500 percent. Joan Appleton, reportedly a former "dedicated feminist," activist in the National Organization for Women, and head nurse at an abortion clinic in Virginia, is quoted as saying she was tormented by questions such as why abortion "was such an emotional trauma for a woman . . . ? If it was right, why was it so difficult? . . . Why are they coming back to me months and years later—psychological wrecks?"[64] The conclusion is obvious: this is the worst of times. The past may not have been perfect, but it was far better than the present with its hidden tragedies for both the unborn and the mothers that kill them.

What about the future? Pro-life persuaders predict a chain reaction, a slippery slope, because, "Once we permit killing of the unborn child, there will be no stopping." The list of non-persons may grow to include anyone considered to be a burden because if the state can legalize murder of some, it can do so for the many. One leaflet warns:

> How long will it be before other groups of humans will be defined out of legal existence when it has been decided that they too have become socially burdensome?
>
> SENIOR CITIZENS BEWARE
>
> MINORITY RACES BEWARE
>
> CRIPPLED CHILDREN BEWARE
>
> Once the decision has been made that all human life is no longer an unalienable right, but that some can be killed because they are a social burden, then the senile, the weak, the physically and mentally inadequate and perhaps someday even the politically troublesome are in danger.[65]

The message is clear. The United States must return to a better past when morals and ethics reigned to stop the evils of the present and to avoid even greater evils of the future.

Pro-Choice

Pro-choice defenders trace abortion practices back to ancient Egypt and conclude that there have always been and always will be abortions. Early pro-choice leaflets contained police photographs of mutilated, dead women on bathroom floors from self-induced and "back-alley" abortions and abused or murdered unwanted babies, including the body of a deformed baby that had been thrown into a furnace. Later leaflets and mailings write of the "horror," "slaughter," and "butchery" of past abortions in which women had used knitting needles, coat hangers, Lysol, and soap suds to induce abortions, often in filthy conditions. NARAL claims that "history demonstrates that restricted access does not eliminate abortion; instead, women are forced to seek control over their reproductive lives in any way possible, often risking serious injury or death."[66] The only issue, advocates argue, is whether abortions will be legal and safe or illegal and brutal as in the past.

In a letter to pro-choice sympathizers, actress Joanne Woodward wrote of a haunting part she played in which a woman faced the evils of a back-alley abortion. Kate Michelman (former executive director of NARAL) relates her personal story about receiving an abortion. First, she was treated in the most demeaning fashion by medical and legal officials; second, she had to be declared an unfit mother even though she had three small children and; third, she had to receive her husband's permission even though he had abandoned the family and refused to pay child support.[67] In the past, persuaders claim, the wealthy could get hospital abortions because they could afford to travel long distances and pay large sums of money. The poor, on the other hand, had to turn to the butchery of the back alley even when they were the "innocent victims of rage and violence" such as child abuse, rape, and incest.[68]

The Religious Coalition for Reproductive Choice counters pro-life's claim that most abortions are for frivolous reasons, arguing that even today:

> There is nothing "convenient" about having an abortion. It is socially stigmatized and personally wrenching. Women who have abortions often do so because they care about others—they want to bring children into the world under positive circumstances. The decision to have an abortion often is made because of poverty, concern for the welfare of existing children, and lack of commitment and support by the prospective father.[69]

Contrasting itself with pro-life forces who do not believe women are capable of making informed, intelligent, selfless, moral choices, the National Coalition of Abortion Providers (NCAP) intersperses its motto ("We trust women") frequently in the margins of its Web site www.ncap.com. Catholics for a Free Choice declares that "we will continue, as an organization, to put ourselves on the line, to raise the moral and ethical dimensions of reproductive issues, and to insist that women be respected as their own moral agents."[70]

Pro-choice contrasts the horrors of the past with safe, legal abortions since 1973. "Almost overnight," NCAP notes, "the 'back-alley' abortionists gave way to a new group of doctors, nurses, administrators, and support staff determined to mainstream the provision of abortion services."[71] Today all women, including the poor, receive "safe and skilled treatment in hospitals and clinics," children are wanted and eagerly awaited, maternal and infant health has improved markedly, and countless women have been saved from injury and death.[72] Web sites include testimony from women who claim to have made the correct decision and not to have had any ill-effects from abortion procedures. Advocates claim that death from legal abortion is rare, that the abortion procedure is actually safer than childbirth, and that there has been no detectable increase in mental illness or psychological stress resulting from abortions. One Web site relates that by 1990 the risk of death from legal abortion was .03 per 100,000 procedures compared to child birth that is "ten times higher."[73] Clearly the *quality* of life for women and infants since *Roe v. Wade* transcends the past to which pro-life would have all Americans return.

Pro-choice advocates have increasingly warned audiences that the administrations of past and current presidents, Congress, and state governments, in support of the pro-life cause, have placed unwarranted and evil restrictions on abortion that jeopardize the woman's right to choose. They cite antichoice executive decisions, gag rules on counselors, parental and spouse consent laws, class discrimination against the poor who cannot get federal funds for abortion, and denial of abortions to institutionalized women, military wives and women, Peace Corps workers, and children pregnant from incest. Sources claim that since 1995, states have enacted more than 400 antichoice measures. "Such laws," NARAL warns, "would only force women to seek illegal and self-induced abortions, endangering their health and lives."[74] The National Abortion Federation quotes Bill and Karen Bell on the death of their daughter who was afraid to tell them she was pregnant: "Becky found someone operating outside the law who would help her. Becky had a back alley abortion. Indiana's parental involvement law ultimately led our daughter to her death."[75] Pro-choice warns of slipping slowly back to the butchery of the past.

Pro-choice has found it increasingly necessary to address the highly volatile "partial-birth" issue. One article describes the term "partial-birth abortion" as "a striking example of how language can be manipulated to suit a particular need . . . a political term created to incite and confuse."[76] Another notes that it is not a medical term found in any medical textbooks and does not refer to any specific medical procedure. The "term is concocted by antichoice extremists to propagate gross misrepresentations about what are, in reality, harmful bans that obstruct access to safe medical care."[77] The Abortion Access Project warns these bans could "prohibit safe and common abortion procedures performed throughout pregnancy . . . [and] gravely endanger women's health."[78] Those who use the "partial-birth" term and have sponsored state and federal laws that are designed to prevent it know full well that such procedures are extremely rare. "When women have third-trimester abortions, they do so because their fetuses have severe or fatal anomalies or because the pregnancy endangers their lives." According to the Alan Guttmacher Institute, of the 1.3 million abortions performed in 2000, 88 percent were performed during the first trimester and only 1 percent after 21 weeks. Pro-choice partisans cite pro-life leaders as admitting that the issue and proposed bans are "a scam being perpetrated by people on our side," "futile and worthless," and that such legislation "doesn't stop any abortions."[79] Randall Terry, founder of pro-life's Operation Rescue, is quoted as saying, "I don't think it will stop a single abortion."[80] Argument from transcendence enables pro-choice to claim the moral high ground in its struggle with those willing to manipulate language, arguments, and reality to achieve evil ends.

The pro-choice movement increasingly peers into the future, and declares, for example, that

> the fact is, the need for abortion will never go away until we, as a country, can achieve two of NARAL Pro-Choice America's goals: better access to more effective contraceptive options and better access to other kinds of reproductive health care and information.[81]

In spite of this fact, choice advocates warn, "this basic American right is seriously at risk," and describe the horrors that will take place if their resistance efforts fail. Since laws and constitutional amendments will not eliminate abortions, they claim, women will be "dragged back" to the untold suffering—the nightmare—of illegal abortions. Women would have to choose between compulsory pregnancy or death at the hands of quack abortionists. Extending the opposition's argument about protecting the rights of the fetus legally, persuaders describe the chaotic impact such laws might have on our "entire system of civil and criminal laws." The woman would have to register her fetus with a "fetus-protection agency," and if the fetus were to die from disease, be miscarried, or be killed in an auto or sporting accident, the woman could be charged with premeditated murder and be jailed for life or executed. Physicians could be convicted of homicide for performing an abortion and suffer the same fate.[82]

Pro-choice advocates warn that in addition to the horrors of criminalizing abortion, infant and maternal mortality would increase, intolerable governmental intrusion into the private lives of pregnant women would be legal, and religious liberty would diminish because "one particular theology would become civil law." On the other hand, Debi Jackson, executive director of Cincinnati Women's Services, imagines "a world where abortion is considered a private matter" to be "decided by the woman herself" and, if she chooses, her partner, family, and clergy. She would be reminded that "motherhood is a sacred honor," but if her pregnancy poses serious risks, she could have an abortion at any gynecologist's office, her religious and spiritual preferences would he honored, the "recovery period could be spent in a softly lit room in quiet, contemplative meditation."[83] Essentially, the rhetoric of the pro-choice movement attempts to do what a resistance movement must do— convince audiences that the present must be preserved at all cost because it is *far better* than, transcends, the past or the future for which the opposition is striving and in danger of achieving.

THE CLASH OVER COMPETING SOCIAL MOVEMENTS

The pro-life and pro-choice movements use a variety of arguments from transcendence to establish their size and stature and to justify their motives and methods while shrinking the opposition and painting it as evil. The transcendent points of quantity, quality, and hierarchy are common in these competing rhetorical efforts.

Pro-Life

Pro-life champions claim their movement is not a narrow, conservative, religious, and political movement but a "great people's movement," "the largest grassroots, citizens movement in recent history," a "majority movement" that transcends all religions and political parties. The American Life League claims that, with more than 300,000 members nationwide, it is "the largest grass-roots, pro-life educational organization in the United States."[84] The National Right to Life Committee reports that it "has grown to represent 3,000 chapters in all 50 states and the District of Columbia."[85] Persuaders argue that polls cited in pro-choice literature are highly misleading when, in fact, pro-life is the majority movement. They cite polls that show 56 percent of Americans (60 percent of 18–29 year olds) believe abortions should be performed only when the "mother's" life is in danger or in cases of rape and incest; that 49 percent compared to 45 percent consider themselves to be pro-life; that 65 percent believe abortion should not be permitted after fetal brainwaves are detected; and that 77 percent of Americans oppose abortion for social, non-medical reasons.[86] One writer notes that if the following question were asked, results would favor the pro-life position: "Should an innocent human being be killed for the crime of another?"[87]

Pro-life defenders contend their movement is not a small political/religious coalition, but a massive movement that represents the true beliefs of the United States, including most religious denominations. On the contrary, pro-choice seeks support from the Unitarian Fellowship, the Episcopal Church, and other small denominations. One leaflet argues that, since it is possible for only eleven people in the National Council of Churches to convey an "official stand" for thirty-three denominations with forty-two million members, the "religious" support for the pro-choice stance should be discounted.[88]

Pro-life partisans see their movement as socially superior. This "majority movement," they claim, is supported by "ordinary people," "people from all across the country and in every walk of life," "moms, dads, business people, retired people and children," as well as "some of the finest minds in the country," nurses, physicians, lawyers, courts, state and federal legislators of both parties, and former presidents Reagan and Bush.[89] Feminists for Life quotes actress Patricia Heaton as saying, "I wanted to find a group that had compassionate, intelligent, reasonable people who are fun loving and life-affirming."[90]

Pro-life lays claim to moral superiority. The American Life League declares it "is firmly established on moral and ethical principles based on the natural law (the moral law), the Word of God and the Magisterial teaching of the Catholic Church."[91] David Mall, in his book entitled *In Good Conscience: Abortion and Moral Necessity*, reviews the moral development principles and theories of philosopher Jean Piaget and psychologist Lawrence Kohlberg and contrasts the two movements. He asserts that pro-life advocates have reached a high level of moral development in which they struggle for the rights and welfare of others while pro-choice advocates never advance beyond an immature, self-centered stage of moral development and are willing to kill their unborn to achieve social and professional benefits.[92] This moral underdevelopment is revealed in the evil motives of abortionists. In a "VERY URGENT" action-gram to NRLC's members, Dr. John Willke declared that the NRLC's sole purpose was to stop the wholesale slaughter of unborn babies in their mother's wombs, while "Planned Parenthood, NARAL and the National Organization for Women exist to make sure that unborn babies don't live. That's a very sorry reason."[93]

Pro-life contrasts its unselfish crusade to save unborn lives with the abortionists' motive to maintain the abortion-on-demand industry for financial profit, alleging that pro-choice is only interested in the $700 million a year they get from killing babies and selling these bodies for soap and cosmetics.[94] The Web site abortionismurder.org opened for sometime with a video screen full of dollar signs and the exclamation, "the abortion industry grows rich off the spilt blood of unborn children." The opening page of the site told readers that, "Million dollar ad campaigns have schooled us in 'choice' but told us nothing of abortion itself. Day after day, year after year, it lurks in the shadows destroying, destroying, destroying."[95] The Pro-life Action League claims that "our pictures of aborted children," like those of Nazi concentration camps that "exposed the murderous truth of Nazi genocide," "lay bare the blatant lies and hypocrisy used by the abortionists to conceal the wholesale slaughter of unborn babies."[96]

Labels attached to pro-choice supporters such as "social engineering advocacy groups," tiny minorities, and the "abortion industry" lead to charges that a hidden goal of the "pro-abortion" movement is an amoral, antireligion society. STOPP International offers a 25-page, detailed plan for defeating Planned Parenthood that, it claims, has been led by secular humanists as far back as Margaret Sanger with the goal of "spreading the ideas and philosophies of the Humanist Manifestos to the community in general and to our children in particular."[97] Joseph Sobran of the American Life League claims the hidden agenda of the pro-choice movement is to subvert Christian morality in the United States. Proof lies in the partial-birth conflict:

> Now, in the current debate over "partial-birth abortions," the advocates of legal abortion have shown themselves willing to defend the most hideous abortions of all, in which nobody can doubt that a child is being killed and, moreover, dying in agony. They express moral indignation not against the "abortion providers" who perform such atrocities, but only against those who insist on describing these abortions in accurate detail.[98]

Perhaps the greatest rhetorical dilemma facing the pro-life movement is a growing militancy that has resulted in the killing of physicians who have performed abortions in the United States and Canada. Since the 1970s, there have been at least seven murders, sixteen attempted murders, more than 200 bombings and arsons, 750 death and bomb threats, and hundreds of acts of vandalism, stalking, and burglary. It may be risky for pro-life members and leaders to condemn violence unconditionally because they risk fragmenting the movement, but they must do so for moral and practical reasons. A *Newsweek* poll following the murder of Dr. Slepian revealed that 86 percent of Americans believed such killings hurt the pro-life movement.[99] Most pro-life groups condemn violence in very strong terms. For instance, the Pro-Lifers Against Clinic Violence Web site states

> We firmly believe that violence and abuse have no place in the pro-life movement. The misguided extremists who take part in clinic bombings and abortionist shootings are *not* supported by mainstream pro-lifers and do *not* speak for us. Violence is contrary to what the pro-life movement stands for and hurts our cause.[100]

Priests for Life proclaims,

> We first of all reject violence as a solution to any problem . . . . The only consistent and correct position is to reject both the violence of shooting and the violence of abortion . . . . To be silent would be irresponsible, and it is not an option.[101]

Although most pro-life movement leaders and followers condemn *violence*, they justify and espouse *militancy* for a higher law. Militants, they claim, defend these *higher principles* and do not act through self-interest. A writer in the *National Right to Life News* claims "the appeal of the pro-life movement is to those principles of justice and nondiscrimination which transcend self-seeking."[102] Monsignor Thomas C. Corrigan defended the "Cleveland Eleven" who were arrested for disrupting an abortion clinic by contending that, when "the laws of God (which say that abortion is wrong) are in opposition to the laws of man (which say abortion is legal), people are justified in siding with the Gospels and challenging man-made laws."[103] Pro-life claims that the *end* may *justify* or *transcend* the *means* used. During his trial for trespassing in an abortion clinic sit-in, Dabien Avila of Fort Wayne, Indiana, declared that "when life or property is in danger . . . a person does have a right to go in. He has a right to attempt in a reasonable manner to stop the destruction of life or property."[104]

Thus, pro-life condemns violent acts while defending militant tactics by developing three of the four points of comparison that establish transcendence: hierarchy (higher principles, higher law), quality (noble purposes, lesser crime or evil), and value (end over means, extraordinary circumstances, life over a building). These points allow persuaders to condemn violence and to praise militant actions and thereby to answer challenges from pro-choice and to avoid dividing the movement into factions over tactics.

Pro-Choice

Pro-choice advocates describe their movement as a "massive state-by-state grassroots campaign" and mobilization that has the "overwhelming support" of the "vast majority" of Americans. It is the majority movement. They claim that polls continually show that four out of five Americans, including the majority of Roman Catholics and almost all Protestant and Jewish groups, support the pro-choice position that "there are situations in which abortion may be a moral alternative."[105] They talk about the hundreds of thousands who have marched for pro-choice in Washington, D.C., the 38 religious organizations that belong to the Religious Coalition for Reproductive Freedom (originally the Religious Coalition for Abortion Rights), and the 8,000 members of Clergy for Choice "representing over 25 mainstream denominations." Catholics for a Free Choice have claimed that Catholics "reject the bishops' position that abortion should be illegal in all circumstances," citing surveys that show only 22 percent agree with the bishops and that "Catholic women in the United States are as likely as women in the general population to have an abortion, and 29 percent more likely than Protestant women."[106]

Advocates claim the pro-choice community is being heard and heeded in elections throughout the country because its motives, goals, and methods are virtuous (quality) and desirable (value). Pro-choice disputes claims that the movement advocates abortion. Some sources claim, we "don't know anyone" connected with the movement "who is 'pro-abortion.'"[107] Instead, the movement is pro-family, for reproductive freedom, for peace among nations, and an advocate of help for the poor, a sound educational system, and a clean environment while struggling against racism, classism, and sexism. Its methods are limited to electing pro-choice candidates and preserving abortion rights through the courts. As a result, the pro-choice position has received the endorsement of such highly credible groups as the American Medical Association, the American Bar Association, hundreds of doctors of obstetrics and gynecology, the President's Commission on Population Growth and the American Future, the National Conference of Commissioners on Uniform State Laws, the U.S. Commission on Civil Rights, and the National Academy of Scientists Institute on Medicine.

In contrast, pro-choice claims pro-life is an "antichoice minority," a "tiny, fanatical minority," a "vocal, powerful minority."[108] Compared to the pro-choice movement that represents most Americans and mainline religious groups, pro-life consists of a small group of religious zealots, religious sects, a few small Protestant denominations, Orthodox Jews, and the Roman Catholic hierarchy (not Catholics themselves) allied with the extreme right-wing, hate groups, spineless and pandering politicians, and arch conservatives such as former senator Jesse Helms of North Carolina and Senator Orin Hatch of Utah and the reverends Jerry Falwell and Jimmy Swaggart. The cover of one leaflet is the picture of weeping, pro-life advocate Rev. Jimmy Swaggart on television admitting to having consorted with prostitutes.[109] Pro-life advocates are dangerous extremists, ruthless fanatics, terrorists, and irrational, moral zealots who will stop at nothing until they achieve their evil, self-serving goals: return women to a position of subservience, force their religious dogma on the American people, foster class discrimination, end sex education in the schools, and outlaw all forms of birth control. In a press release entitled "Hypocrisy on the Hill," Nancy Keenan, president of NARAL, reported that members of Congress "illustrated the hypocrisy of antichoice lawmakers who oppose a woman's right to choose but then refuse to support initiatives to help women who carry their pregnancy to term."[110]

Pro-choice literature chronicles the ruthless guerrilla and terrorist tactics of so-called right-to-life groups who "have an iron disregard for life" and are often in "a frenzy amounting to hysteria."[111] These acts include death threats, claims of spreading deadly anthrax germs in clinics, threats to kidnap children, arson, bombings, shootings into clinics while patients and staff are inside, acid sprayed into clinics, hate campaigns, obscenity shouting, blockades of clinics, stalking of physicians and physicians' families, and threats to hospitals where abortions might take place. A letter from the Religious Coalition for Reproductive Choice charges that "in their violence toward women and their doctors, they are terrorists cut from the same cloth as KKK night riders who used terror to stop African-American citizens from exercising their right to vote."[112] After Dr. David Gunn was murdered by a pro-life advocate outside a clinic in Pensacola, Florida, in March 1993, pro-choice supporters said they had been expecting this to happen as terrorist tactics had escalated:

> Anyone who wants to check the fertile soil in which fanaticism grows has only to listen to the leaders' responses to the assassination of the 47-year-old doctor and father of two: "While Gunn's death is unfortunate," said Don Treshman of Rescue America, "it's also true that quite a number of babies' lives will be saved." While it is wrong to kill, said Randall Terry [leader of Operation Rescue], "we have to recognize that this doctor was a mass murderer." "Praise God," said a protestor at a clinic in Melbourne, Florida, "one of the (baby) killers is dead!"[113]

Following the murder of Dr. Barnett Slepian in 1998, the media quoted Rev. Donald Spitz, founder of Pro-Life Virginia, who called Slepian's killer a "hero" because, "We as Christians have a responsibility to protect the innocent from being murdered. Whoever shot the shot protected the children." Spitz claimed the killers of physicians were "being forced into it" because the government had limited other means of protest.[114] An editor of *The Progressive* concluded, "Religious fundamentalism is morphing into religious vigilantism before our very eyes."[115] In an article entitled "Opting Out of the War," NCAP asks readers of its Web site to contrast the two movements:

> So, what are the casualties—murders and attempted murders, on the antiabortion side? Zero. How many crisis pregnancy centers have been bombed? None. How many blockades, stalkings, incidents of vandalism of the right-to-life organizations? Zip. Even the number of "pranks" and

harassment perpetuated against the anti's is infinitesimal in comparison. . . . This is clearly one-sided violence, or to name it—terrorism.[116]

The article also stated, "The antiabortion movement has done almost nothing to put the brakes on this violence" while it is attracting "violent, muddle-headed misfits" who want to "commit an act of 'heroism' for a good cause."

Thus, the rhetoric of the pro-choice movement claims that it transcends the pro-life movement that destroys life in the name of protecting life. The pro-life movement is smaller (quantity), consists of and is supported by evil persons and groups (quality), and employs evil means to achieve evil and self-centered goals (quality).

CONCLUSIONS

Social movements argue from transcendence when they claim that an organization, group, goal, thing, right, act, or proposal surpasses, is superior to, or is prior to that of the opposition. It is a comparative argument based on quantity (more–less), quality (good–bad), value (important–unimportant), or hierarchy (high–low).

The pro-choice and pro-life movements rely on argument from transcendence to establish positions on fundamental issues, to attack one another, and to defend themselves. They employ the comparative points of value and hierarchy when establishing positions on personhood (the issue on which all subsequent arguments rest) and to attack opposition claims regarding personhood of the fetus or woman. They employ hierarchy and value points when arguing which rights are most basic (at the top of the rights hierarchy) and which are most important. They employ the points of value and quality when presenting versions of reality: the past, present, and future. Pro-choice, as a resistance social movement, claims that the present is the best of times while both the past and future have been or might be full of horrors. Pro-life, as a revivalistic social movement, implies that the past was the best of times while the present is full of horrors and the future is likely to be worse. They employ the points of quantity, quality, and hierarchy when establishing themselves (including size, motives, morals, and methods) as the superior movement in the abortion conflict.

Each movement's argument from transcendence is a fragile interdependent network of premises based on a single major premise: either the woman is a full-fledged person while the fetus is a potential person or the fetus is a person from the moment of conception and deserves special protection because of its innocence and vulnerability. Neither movement rests comfortably on the moral high ground to which it lays claim. True believers of each movement are extremists in the sense that they accept no compromises or exceptions to life or choice. Each fears that acceptance of any abortions (due to incest or rape, for instance) or any restrictions (late-term abortions, for instance) will lead to a plunge down a slippery slope on which they will lose their struggle for life or choice. Many people, including many of each movement's sympathizers, have reservations about and support exceptions to or qualifications of these premises. If the recipient of a pro-choice or pro-life message seriously questions or denies the central premise, the network of transcendent arguments crumbles. Thus, neither the woman nor the fetus has the inalienable rights claimed. The past, present, and future was not, is not, and will not be as bright or dark as portrayed.

Social movements have limited resources and find it difficult to prove that an institution, competing movement, norm, or value is utterly without value. Transcendence allows a movement to address *degrees* of size, importance, goodness, or risk. For instance, a social movement need not establish that it, its cause, or its methods are without flaw but only that it is larger than an institution or opposing movement claims, that it is more honorable than institutions or countermovements, that its plan is safer than current or proposed policies, or that its tactics are less evil than ones employed by institutions or countermovements.

Argument from transcendence allows a social movement, or a faction of a movement, to stress its superiority, explain its ideology, and justify its tactics without having to destroy other factions or antagonize institutions that might be potential allies. A social movement does not have to deny competing rights but only to claim that such rights are less important or lower on a hierarchy of rights. Thus, a movement may reduce the risk of fracturing the movement by antagonizing elements within or scaring away potential supporters.

This chapter has illustrated how the pro-choice and pro-life movements employ argument from transcendence in their continual conflict over legalized abortion. The four points of comparison—quality, quantity, value, and hierarchy—enable both movements to establish, attack, and defend positions on personhood, competing rights, visions of reality, and organization (including membership, motives, and tactics). It is difficult to imagine how social movements could carry forward their struggles and meet oppositions without relying upon this essential language bridge.

Notes

[1] Robert S. Cathcart, "Defining Social Movements by Their Rhetorical Form," *Central States Speech Journal* 31 (Winter 1980): 271.

[2] Kenneth Burke, "Catharsis—Second View," *Centennial Review* 5 (1961): 130; Leland M. Griffin, "A Dramatistic Theory of the Rhetoric of Movements," *Critical Responses to Kenneth Burke*, William Rueckert, ed. (Minneapolis: University of Minnesota Press, 1969): 464.

[3] Cathcart, 271.

[4] Karl R. Wallace, *Francis Bacon on Communication and Rhetoric* (Chapel Hill: University of North Carolina Press, 1943): 65.

[5] Aristotle, *The Rhetoric, Book I*, W. Rhys Roberts, trans. (New York: Modern Library, 1954); available at http://classics.mit.edu/Aristotle/rhetoric.1.i.html, accessed 16 August 2006.

[6] Kenneth Burke, *Language as Symbolic Action* (Berkeley: University of California Press, 1966): 187.

[7] Marcus Tullius Cicero, *Topics*, H. M. Hubbell, trans. (Cambridge: Harvard University Press, 1959): 433; Kenneth Burke, *A Rhetoric of Motives* (Berkeley: University of California Press, 1969): 231–279.

[8] Burke, *Rhetoric of Motives*, 11–12.

[9] Terence Powderly, "Address of the Grand Master Workman," Proceedings of the General Assembly of the Knights of Labor, 7 September 1880, 176.

[10] Michael Osborn, "Rhetorical Distance in 'Letter from Birmingham Jail,'" *Rhetoric & Public Affairs* 7 (Spring 2004): 33.

[11] Aristotle, *Book I.*

[12] Gary S. Selby, "Mocking the Sacred: Frederick Douglass's 'Slaveholders Sermon' and the Antebellum Debate Over Religion and Slavery," *Quarterly Journal of Speech* 88 (August 2002): 329, 336.

[13] Charles J. Stewart, "Championing the Rights of Others and Challenging Evil: The Ego Function in the Rhetoric of Other-Directed Social Movements," *Southern Communication Journal* 53 (Winter 1999): 101.

[14] Amy R. Slagell, "The Rhetorical Structure of Frances E. Willard's Campaign for Woman Suffrage, 1876–1896," *Rhetoric & Public Affairs* 4 (Spring 2001): 2.

[15] Martha Solomon Watson, "The Issue of Justice: Martin Luther King Jr.'s Response to the Birmingham Clergy," *Rhetoric & Public Affairs* 7 (Spring 2004): 3.

[16] Watson, 3, 15.

[17] Robert L. Heath, "Dialectical Confrontation: A Strategy of Black Radicalism," *Central States Speech Journal* 24 (Fall 1973): 171, 173.

[18] Watson, 18.

[19] From a recording of the "The Joe Pine Show," n.d.

[20] Burke, *Rhetoric of Motives*, 76.

[21] Barry Brummett, "Burkeian Scapegoating, Mortification, and Transcendence in Presidential Campaign Rhetoric," *Central States Speech Journal* 32 (Winter 1981): 256.

[22] Kenneth Burke, *The Philosophy of Literary Form* (Berkeley: University of California Press, 1973): 312.

[23] Richard D. Orlaski, "Abortion: Legal Questions and Legislative Alternatives," *America*, 10 August 1974, 50.

[24] *United States Supreme Court Reports*, vol. 35 (Rochester, NY: Lawyers Co-Operative Publishing Company, 1974): 147–149.

[25] "The Death of Doctor Gunn," *Newsweek*, 22 March 1993, 34–35.

[26] *Abortion: Questions and Answers* (Washington, DC: Committee for Pro-Life Activities, 1983): n.p.

[27] http://www.feministsforlife.org/voices/Voices%20from%20Winter02-03.pdf, accessed 20 August 2006.

[28] http://www.nrlc.org/abortion/facts/abortionresponses.html, accessed 20 August 2006.

[29] "Life Matters," http://www.bfl.org/Files/BaptistForLife/documents/LifeMatters11read.pdf, accessed 8 August 2006.

[30] "About Us," www.all.org/about/policy3.htm, accessed 19 August 2005.

[31] *Abortion: Questions and Answers*; *What Is the Key Question?* (Minneapolis: For LIFE, 1977)

[32] *The Hidden Holocaust* (Taylor, AZ: The Precious Feet People, n.d.): n.p.; mailing from Judie Brown, president, American Life Lobby, Stafford, VA, n.d., n.p.; "About Us," www.all.org, accessed 11 August 2005.

[33] "Where Does Life Begin?" http://www.rcrc.org/pdf/Words_of_Choice.pdf, accessed 11 August 2006.

[34] Mailing from the Religious Coalition for Abortion Rights, n.d., n.p.; *Saving Abortion* (New York: Association for the Study of Abortion, n.d.): 2; *Legal Abortion: Arguments Pro & Con* (New York: Westchester Coalition for Legal Abortion, 1978): n.p.

[35] http://www.rcrc.org/pdf/Words_of_Choice.pdf, accessed 11 August 2006.

[36] "Perspectives of Faith," http://www.rcrc.org/faith_choices/index.htm, accessed 11 August 2005.

[37] "Facts: Catholic Teaching on Abortion," http://www.cath4choice.org/new/howtotalk/Question18.asp, accessed 19 August 2005.

[38] *Saving Abortion*, 2–3; mailing from the Religious Coalition for Abortion Rights, n.d., n.p.

[39] *Sponsors & Members* (Washington, DC: Religious Coalition for Abortion Rights, 1978): n.p.; *What Is the RCAR?*, n.p.

40 *We Affirm: Excerpts from Statements about Abortion Rights as Expressed by National Religious Orga-nizations* (Washington, DC: Religious Coalition for Abortion Rights, 1978): n.p.; *Abortion: Why Religious Organizations in the United States Want to Keep It Legal*, n.d., n.p.

41 "Perspectives of Faith," accessed 11 August 2005.

42 *We Care, We Love, We Are Pro-Life*, n.p.; mailing from Judie Brown, 2–4; *Abortion: A Catholic Issue*, n.p.; "Philosophy," www.all.org/about/policy3.htm, accessed 11 August 2005; "Competing Rights," http://www.abort73.com/HTML/I-B-3-competing.html, accessed 12 August 2006.

43 *The Abortion Connection*, n.d., n.p.

44 *Why Vote Pro-Life*, n.p.; *Abortion: A Catholic Issue*, n.p.

45 "Competing Rights."

46 "What is the pro-life response to abortionists' arguments?" http://www.nrlc.org/abortion/facts/abortionresponses.html, accessed 11 August 2006.

47 *Is This Life Worth a Postage Stamp?* (n.d.): n.p.; "The 'Choice' Façade," http://abort73.com/HTML/I-B-2-choice.html, accessed 11 August 2006.

48 Ken Unger, *What You Don't Know Can Hurt You!* (Ashtabula, OH: Protestants Protesting Abortion (n.d.): n.p.

49 Advertisement, Lafayette, *Indiana Journal and Courier*, 11 May 1980, B-7.

50 http://www.prochoiceamerica.org/news/press-releases/2005/20050628.html, accessed 11 August 2006.

51 Mailing from Kenneth Edelin, Planned Parenthood Federation of America, n.d., 1; mailing 4 from Faye Wattleton, president, Planned Parenthood Federation of America, n.d., 1.

52 http://www.ms4c.org/update/400lead.htm, accessed 11 August 2006.

53 "Special Advisory Memorandum" from Kate Michelman, executive director, NARAL, April 19, 1988, 1–4.

54 http://www.rcrc.org/pdf/RCRC_EdSeries_Religious_Liberty.pdf, 11 August 2006.

55 *Americans Against Abortion*, Summer, 1986, 2.

56 http://www.nrlc.org/rko/index.html, accessed 11 August 2006.

57 *What Is the Key Question?*, n.p.; *Heartbeat*, September/ October 1991, 2–3; Paul Marx, *The Mercy Killers* (Palos Verdes Estates, CA: Right to Life, 1974): 1–11.

58 http://www.prolifeaction.org/truth/, accessed 11 August 2006; www.abortionismurder.org, accessed 11 August 2006.

59 "America's Abortion Dilemma," *Newsweek*, 14 January 1985, 25.

60 http://www.meehanreports.com/quit.html, accessed 11 August 2006.

61 Allan Carlson, "Twenty-Five Years Into The Culture of Death," *Vital Speeches of the Day*, 15 March 1998, 345.

62 www.nrlc.org, accessed 11 August 2006.

63 Tom Bethell, "A Heinous Procedure," *The American Spectator* (April 1998): 20.

64 http://www.meehanreports.com/quit.html, accessed 11 August 2006.

65 Dr. and Mrs. J. C. Willke, "The U.S. Supreme Court Has Ruled It's Legal to Kill a Baby. . ." (Cincinnati: Hayes Publishing, n.d.): n.p.

66 "The Safety of Legal Abortion and the Hazards of Illegal Abortion," http://www.prochoiceamerica.org/assets/files/Abortion-Access-to-Abortion-Science-Safety-of-Legal-Abortion.pdf, accessed 11 August 2006.

67 Mailing from Kate Michelman, executive director, NARAL, July 25, 1988, 1–2.

68 *What Is RCAR?*, n.p.; *Abortion: Why Religious Organizations in the United States Want to Keep It Legal*, n.p.

69 "Words of Choice: Countering Pro-Life Rhetoric," http://www.rcrc.org/pdf/Words_of_Choice.pdf, accessed 11 August 2006.

70 http://www.discoverthenetwork.org/individualProfile.asp?indid=1857, accessed 11 August 2006.

71 "The Need for a New Conversation on Abortion," http://www.ncap.com/promoting_conversation.html, accessed 11 August 2006.

72 *Abortion Q & A* (Washington, DC: NARAL, n.d.): n.p.; *Abortion Fact Sheet* (New York: NARAL, n.d.): n.p.; mailing from Edelin, 3–4.

[73] "Words of Choice: Countering Anti-choice Rhetoric," http://www.rcrc.org/pdf/Words_of_Choice.pdf, accessed 15 September 2006.

[74] "Choice: Defending a Fundamental American Freedom," www.prochoiceamerica.org/generation/faq.cfm, accessed 19 August 2005.

[75] "Parental   Involvement,"   http://www.prochoice.org/about_abortion/stories/parental_involvement.html, accessed 15 September 2006.

[76] "Words of Choice," accessed 15 September 2006.

[77] "The So-Called "Partial-Birth" Abortion Ban," http://www.abortionaccess.org/partial-birthabortion.htm, accessed 15 September 2006.

[78] "The So-Called "Partial-Birth" Abortion Ban"; see also http://www.aclu.org/reproductiverights/abortionbans/12669res20040326.html, accessed 15 September 2006.

[79] "Partial-Birth Abortion," http://www.ncap.com/promoting_ncap.html, accessed 11 August 2006.

[80] "So-Called," accessed 11 August 2006.

[81] "NARAL Pro-Choice America," www.prochoiceamerica.org/about/index.cfm, accessed 11 August 2005.

[82] Mailing 3 from Molly Yard, president, National Organization for Women, n.d., 2–3; *Saving Abortion*, 1–3; *Constitutional Aspects of the Right to Limit Childbearing*, n.p.

[83] "The World as I Would Create It," http://www.ncap.com/promoting_providers.html#The_World, accessed 11 August 2006.

[84] "What Is American Life League," http://www.all.org/about_faqs.php?PHPSESSID=b7895753f332f997fc77144de62f6fce#1, accessed 11 August 2006.

[85] "Mission Statement," http://www.nrlc.org/Missionstatement.htm, accessed 11 August 2006.

[86] http://www.nrlc.org/rko/stassenpart2.html, accessed 15 September 2006.

[87] *Abortion: Public Opinion*, n.p.; Brown, 1–3.

[88] *Abortion: Public Opinion*, n.p.; *Heartbeat*, 1–3; *Abortion: A Catholic Issue*, n.p.

[89] *The Communicator*, September 1978, 2; November/December 1977, 2; October/November, 1980, 3.

[90] www.feministsforlife.org, accessed 24 August 2005.

[91] "Does ALL have a religious affiliation?", http://www.all.org/about_faqs.php?PHPSESSID=b7895753f332f997fc77144de62f6fce accessed 11 August 2006.

[92] David Mall, *In Good Conscience: Abortion and Moral Necessity* (Libertyville. IL: Kairos Books, 1982): 41.

[93] John Willke, president, National Right to Life Committee, "Action-Gram," 9 February 1987, n.p.

[94] *Abortion: Death Before Life*, n.p.; *The Hidden Holocaust*, n.p.

[95] http://www.abortionismurder.org, accessed 30 August 2005.

[96] http://www.prolifeaction.org/truth/, accessed 11 August 2006.

[97] http://www.all.org/stopp/plan.htm, accessed 20 July 2006.

[98] Joseph Sobran, "The Tactics of Subversion," *The New American* 15 April 1996, 15.

[99] "The Abortion Wars Come Home," *Newsweek*, 9 November 1998, 35.

[100] http://lifepeace.tripod.com/, accessed 29 July 2006.

[101] http://www.priestsforlife.org/articles/wewillnotgoaway.html, accessed 20 July 2006.

[102] *Indiana Right to Life*, reprinted from *National Right to Life News*, Feb. 1980, n.p.

[103] Cleveland, Ohio *Catholic Universe Bulletin*, 17 September 1976, 2, col. 4.

[104] *The Communicator*, January 1978, 3.

[105] *Religious Freedom and the Abortion Controversy* (Washington, DC: RCAR, 1978): n.p.; Yard mailing 2, 2–4; letter from the Religious Coalition for Reproductive Freedom, n.d., n.p.

[106] http://www.cath4choice.org/new/howtotalk/Question17.asp, accessed 19 August 2005; http://www.cath4choice.org/new/howtotalk/Question5.asp, accessed 19 August 2005.

[107] *You Know Them as the Right to Life People. They Oppose Abortion. But Did You Know . . .* (Washington, DC: NARAL, n.d.): n.p.; *The Abortion Dilemma*, n.p.

[108] *Abortion Q & A*, n.p.; Wattleton mailing 4, 1–3.

[109] *Listen to the Anti-Choice Leaders. Then Help Us Stop Them Before It's Too Late* (New York: Planned Parenthood Federation of America, n.d.): n.p.

[110] http://www.prochoiceamerica.org/news/press-releases/2005/pr06092005_appropriations.html, accessed 20 July 2006.

[111] Mailing from Karen Mulhauser, executive director of NARAL, n.d., 2; mailing from Gloria Steinem, n.d., 1.

[112] Letter from the Religious Coalition for Reproductive Freedom.

[113] Ellen Goodman, "This Time, However, the Word 'Terrorism' Is Perhaps too Mild," Lafayette, Indiana *Journal and Courier*, 16 March 1993, A4.

[114] "Preachers of Hate," *The Progressive*, December 1998, 8; "The Abortion Wars Come Home," 34.

[115] "Preachers of Hate," 8.

[116] http://www.ncap.com/promoting_providers.html#Opting_Out_of_the_War, accessed 11 August 2006.

CHAPTER

11

Argument from Conspiracy in Social Movements

As human beings, we have an insatiable need for order, reason, and "explanations of all natural phenomena," so we have limited tolerance for explanations ranging from uncontrolled chaos and a world with no one in charge to coincidence, accident, mistake, bad luck, or stupidity.[1] Inevitably, some will argue that a conspiracy—a combination of two or more people plotting to do something illegal or to harm us in some way—is responsible for the phenomenon we find frightening, worrying, disconcerting, or confusing. For example, fear of a communist conspiracy drove much of U.S. political and religious rhetoric for nearly seventy years. In the 1990s, militias warned of a conspiracy by big government and big corporations to deprive Americans of their basic liberties. And today many Christian evangelicals fear a secular humanist conspiracy that is plotting to destroy our Christian foundations.

Conspiracy arguments become widely disseminated and accepted "when they explain an otherwise ambiguous evil" or "a pattern of anomalies."[2] A pattern or repetition of events intensifies the search for an explanation and increases the likelihood that people will suspect a conspiracy is at work.[3] Steven Goldzwig writes, for example, that "the ideological explanation" of conspiracy argument "restructures an ambiguous, inexplicable situation by explaining it in a plausible, unifying, and coherent way to its audiences."[4]

The past two centuries have witnessed an abundance of ambiguous evils and anomalies, including wars, economic crises, declines in traditional social morals and values, assassinations, natural and technological disasters, massacres, and a variety of threatening *isms*: socialism, communism, fascism, secularism, terrorism, racism, and feminism. Richard Hofstadter claims that persons who see conspiracies as explanations do not see events as "part of the stream of history" but as "the consequences of someone's will." With someone in charge, the world of conspiracy "is far more coherent than the real world, since it leaves no room for mistakes, failures, or ambiguities."[5] Dan Nimmo and James Combs address what attracts many to conspiracy theories in an uncertain and dangerous world:

To explain historical chaos as simply chaos does not appeal to dramatic
sensibilities. . . . History is much more understandable, interesting, and
exciting if it is a grand romantic melodrama, full of adventure, mystery,
peril and threat and wherein there is a moral to the story.[6]

It is little wonder, then, that argument from conspiracy, in Kenneth Burke's
words, is "as natural as breathing."[7]

A conspiracy may be real or imagined, but the fundamental process is
the same: a chain of apparently unrelated events, actions, and groups are
linked to reveal *orchestrated* actions designed to cause all sorts of social, economic, political, religious, and moral problems. Robert Welch, founder of the
John Birch Society, claimed that he "had unearthed the all-important linear
connection—an unbroken string of associations—among apparently disparate historical happenings to establish a master conspiracy."[8] As James Darsey
writes, "Conspiracy requires deliberate, conscious design, systematic and
deceptive intent; conspiracies are nothing if not purposive."[9] Thousands of
books, pamphlets, articles, and Web sites have attempted to prove or disprove, for example, that a conspiracy was behind the Oklahoma City bombing, the *Challenger* disaster, the assassinations of John Kennedy and Martin
Luther King, Jr., the downing of Korean Airline Flight 007 by Russian fighter
planes, and the dreadful events of 9/11. This literature provides examples of
how those who would have us believe that conspiracies are responsible for
unexplained or poorly explained phenomena argue their cases from cause-to-
effect, narrative, hypothesis, generalization, sign, and syllogism.

Rhetorical theorists have, with good reason, dismissed conspiracy arguments as loaded with argumentative fallacies and masses of irrelevant detail
designed to seduce paranoid, noncritical, and ignorant audiences. Marilyn
Young, Michael Launer, and Curtis Austin claim, for instance, that conspiracy theorists build their arguments on hypothetical premises and hypothetical
evidence.[10] It is easy to understand their criticism and skepticism if you read
publications that claim, for instance, that the Vatican plotted and carried out
the assassination of Lincoln; former representatives Phil Gramm and Newt
Gingrich created a contract to destroy America; former president Reagan and
Pope John Paul II ("a couple of ANTICHRIST DEVILS") conspired to commit genocide; and the government of the United States planned and carried
out the alleged "terrorist" attacks of September 11, 2001.[11]

In spite of outrageous claims and seemingly preposterous evidence presented in many conspiracy arguments, most are supported by impressive
amounts of proof, and there are *real* conspiracies. As the saying goes, "Even
paranoids have enemies." Darrin McMahon claims that "conspiracies have been
around for as long as there have been people to plot."[12] The Soviet Union did
conspire to take over eastern European countries; John Wilkes Booth and his
comrades did conspire to assassinate President Lincoln, Vice President Andrew
Johnson, and members of the cabinet; the CIA and other forces did conspire to
assassinate Cuban leader Fidel Castro; police forces in the United States did conspire to destroy the Black Panther Party; and there was a Watergate conspiracy

during the Nixon administration. Conspiracies to set prices among "competitors," to manipulate the stock market, to perpetrate fraud, and to commit murder are prosecuted in the United States every year. A U.S. government document entitled "Elements of Conspiracy Investigation" assists the Bureau of Alcohol, Tobacco and Firearms (ATF) and other agencies in prosecuting conspiracies by setting forth the history of conspiracy, the essential elements of the crimes, defenses, the process of prosecution, and the liability for substantive offences.[13]

While understanding argumentative forms and fallacies is helpful in critiquing specific conspiracy arguments, a deeper understanding of argument from conspiracy is possible if it is studied as a *process* in *relation* to competing argument. David Zarefsky claims that "conspiracy argument responds to this situation by asserting that things are not really what they seem" and "transforms the situation into one presenting a clear-cut choice of alternatives."[14] In most situations, conspiracy argument is developed after an official or institutional explanation of a phenomenon has been widely disseminated and generally accepted. Those dissatisfied with an official explanation, or lack of it, may develop a counter-rhetoric with conspiracy as its centerpiece. They "focus on what is *secret* as a basis for inducing polarization."[15] Thomas Goodnight and John Poulakos observe that "the struggle characteristically emerges between two parties: those who claim to be aware of a conspiracy . . . and those who argue these claims to be preposterous and malevolently inspired."[16]

A persuader intent on weaving an argument claiming that a conspiracy is the *cause* or the *best explanation* of an event or body of facts starts from a decidedly underdog position. "The initial odds of winning such a battle" are "stacked in favor of the challenged authority" who has a head start and both legitimacy and credibility that goes with institutional agents and their rhetoric.[17] Few audiences are truly paranoid or ignorant of events or facts disseminated in the press, and most people trust official or institutional explanations until someone proves otherwise. On the other hand, the mere accusation of a conspiracy may be enough to prove it for some; once underway, the *accusation* cannot be "easily dispelled" and may be "virtually impossible to disprove."[18] Zarefsky suggests that inferences may be more persuasive than documents.[19]

Those who would sell a conspiracy theory must create arguments with three essential persuasive ingredients. They must undermine trust in the institution's ability and willingness to locate and tell the *truth*, challenge the *believability* of the official explanation, and offer a *more believable* explanation.

SOWING DISTRUST

The persuader who would replace an official explanation of an event with one centered on the actions of a conspiracy must arouse *serious doubt* in the minds of targeted audiences. This may be the most essential ingredient in establishing a conspiracy theory. How can we trust an explanation if we cannot trust the institutional storyteller?

Capitalizing on Distrust

Persuaders may capitalize on a sense of distrust and suspicion that permeates our social interactions. Gary Wills cites Henry David Thoreau's famous statement, "That government is best which governs least." Wills writes:

> We are pious toward our history in order to be cynical toward our government. We keep summoning the founders to testify against what they founded. Our very liberty depends so heavily on distrust of government that the government itself, we are constantly told, was constructed to instill that distrust. . . . Since human nature cannot be trusted, power must be so insecurely seated that even slight opposition to it can stymie it.[20]

This mistrust is exacerbated during "times of social strain."[21] For example, in the early 1950s, "distrust, suspicion, and panic permeated all social interactions, and few Americans ventured to openly question the premise of domestic Communist subversion."[22] Hans Toch writes:

> Into this predisposing situation emerged Senator Joseph McCarthy and his Communist Conspiracy. McCarthy's "stab in the back" formula dealt directly with the events of the preceding half-decade, and provided an explanation for them which was not only *coherent* and *face-saving*, but also an obvious *depository for accumulated feelings.*[23]

This situation enabled the John Birch Society, Billy James Hargis' Christian Crusade, and Carl McIntire's Twentieth Century Reformation Hour to flourish in the 1950s and 1960s as forces dedicated to exposing and confronting the communist conspiracy that had allegedly taken over U.S. society, including mainline churches, education, entertainment, and the military.

In his studies of the "radical right," Dale Leathers claims that the dominant value of this rhetoric is "mistrust," and that its "startling contention" is that "all institutionalized voices in America are to be mistrusted."[24] Our increasingly global and complex society of the twenty-first century has fed an epidemic of distrust. According to Goldzwig:

> It is a basic and unyielding mistrust rather than perhaps an abiding paranoia that now holds sway in contemporary relations and this mistrust undermines our major social, technical, and public and private spheres. In short, we are wary of each other and our institutions because they have failed our expectations. . . . At base, both protagonist and antagonist share the secret of mutual mistrust. . . . Mistrust is at the center of the vortex and mistrust feeds the ongoing alternative characterizations of the transformed contemporary conspiracy myth.[25]

Conspiracy advocates appeal to the centuries-old fear in the United States that real threats to our republic and way of life will come from within. They portray secret and subtle "foreign" forces working everywhere among us—infiltrating the pulpit, the academy, the government, and the media. During the massive immigration of the mid-nineteenth century, particularly from Catholic Ireland, nativists claimed that "through its secret agents, Catholic immigrants, the Catholic hierarchy began to infiltrate the country with 'alien' notions such as sectarian *Bibles*, liberality of strong drink, and end of democratic government."[26]

If conspiracy advocates cannot tap into general distrust, they may use mistrust of institutional *agents* or *agencies* such as the ATF, FBI, and CIA. Thomas Metzger, founder of White Aryan Resistance (WAR), warns followers that they cannot trust the "*criminal* justice system" because "officers of the court will lie, cheat, and steal, etc. to serve their masters."[27] Darsey theorizes that the "combination of power and mystery" that surrounds so many of the decisions and actions that affect our lives in the new technical-scientific age practically invites suspicion. He observes that "increasingly, issues of public importance are decoded from shadowy traces and decided in darkened rooms by the technically initiated. Arenas for conspiratorial activity abound, and the opportunity for sinister conspiracies multiply."[28]

Persuaders may call an explanation into question by *associating* the official version of an event or situation with distrusted agencies such as the U.N., the CIA, or the IRS. Young and Launer write: "Association/disassociation is probably the most powerful tool of persuasiveness and the most basic human thought process."[29] For instance, Thomas Metzger tells readers of his Web site that "the 'new' FBI more closely resembles the old KGB" of the Soviet Union.[30] For Metzger, anything the "iron heel" (his epithet for the U.S. government) advocates or touches becomes part of the conspiracy to destroy the republic and its white, European heritage.

Persuaders enhance distrust by associating institutional explanations with distrusted or hated *groups* such as liberals, humanists, Zionists, internationalists, advocates of the New World Order, and communists. Bernard Duffy claims that the antihumanist rhetoric of the religious right attempts to make "the audience skeptical of all opposing claims, even those made by the most disinterested observers; they too may be humanists."[31] Bob Fletcher, a representative of the Montana Militia, exhibited such associative distrust at the 1995 Senate hearings on the militia movement called in response to the Oklahoma City bombing. He agreed with radical-right literature that claimed the FBI and IRS were headed by "lesbians, sex perverts, child molester advocates, Christian haters, and the most doctrinaire of communists."[32] George Lincoln Rockwell, founder of the American Nazi Party, told an audience at the University of Kansas how, as a Naval officer, he had become curious about Senator McCarthy and proceeded to read the complete transcripts of the Senate hearings.[33] Instead of the "louse" he expected to find in Senator McCarthy, he discovered a "sissy," a "super, easygoing nice guy" who was confronting "arrogant, and obnoxious, and vicious" witnesses and the media. As he investigated further, Rockwell determined that the "entire media of public information were lying," and that every group seemed to have those that were "pro-McCarthy" and those that were "con-McCarthy" except one—the violently anti-McCarthy American Jewish Committee.

Creating Distrust

Often persuaders must create distrust in institutional explanations of phenomena, and the key to undermining trust is the claim that an institution is attempting "to thwart the search for the truth."[34] Thomas Metzger, for example, told followers:

> President Bush now protects that criminal traitorous President Clinton by halting investigations of his Chinagate dealings. Why would President Bush do that, because he is part and parcel of the conspiracy to hand over America to the U.N. governing bodies.[35]

Institutions fuel such claims by classifying information as secret or top secret, by refusing to change secret classifications even after credible sources challenge their necessity or legality, and by refusing to reveal some or part of the classified information that might verify the official explanation or undermine a growing conspiracy theory. An institution may refuse to reveal sources or to explain how information was discovered that formed the basis for its case. Protestors ask, "What are they hiding anyway?"[36]

In the introduction to his book entitled *Others Unknown*, Timothy McVeigh's defense attorney, Stephen Jones, writes that "the real story" of the Oklahoma City bombing remains a mystery for

> many reasons, but perhaps the most important has been the U.S. government. And in the end, the Oklahoma City bombing conspiracy may not be merely the crime itself but also the systematic, deliberate attempt of our federal government to prevent all of us from finding out what exactly happened on that terrible morning."[37]

Jones relates that when he agreed to take over McVeigh's defense, Susan Otto, one of the original defense attorneys, commented to him, "When you know everything I know, and you will soon enough, you will never think of the United States of America again in the same way."[38] The obvious message is that institutions are untrustworthy, if not downright evil, and are attempting to hide something from the American people. Why else would an institution refuse to reveal sources, share documents, provide information, and explain its investigative methods? Jones relates again and again how the *government*, rarely identified as the *prosecution*, tried to hide vital information it was required by law to share with the defense. He continually turned to the judge to force the "government" to cooperate. His claims of obstruction and repeated use of the word "government" played upon a growing mistrust of the institution in the United States and lent credence to his counterconspiracy theories that one of two social movements with foreign roots, or perhaps both, was the true perpetrator of the horrible bombing in Oklahoma City.

Some persuaders cite historical examples of institutional deception to establish that U.S. institutions and agents are not always trustworthy. One Web site claims, for instance, that in the 1794 Jay Treaty, the United States agreed to pay 600,000 pounds sterling to King George even though the colonies had won the Revolutionary War.[39] The Senate ratified the treaty in "secret session" and ordered that it "not be published." Americans learned about this outrageous, secret agreement only because Benjamin Franklin's grandson ignored the order and published it. The "exposure" from this publication "and resulting public uproar so angered Congress that it passed the Alien and Sedition Acts (1798) so federal judges could prosecute editors and publishers for reporting the truth about the government." The same site reports that the Library of Congress has 349,402 uncatalogued books and 13.9 million uncatalogued rare manuscripts, and notes ominously, "There may be secrets buried in that mass of documents even more astonishing than a missing Constitutional Amendment." This report sounds sinister even when the explanation may be as simple and pragmatic as lack of funds or staff to catalogue this immense volume of books and manuscripts.

Persuaders report the discovery of previously denied or unrevealed documents as evidence that the institution cannot be trusted to tell the truth about an event under scrutiny. Ralph de Toledano, in an article entitled "Was *Challenger* Sabotaged?" asked,

> But are we being told everything that is so far known? I suggest that we
> are not. . . . This is not idle conjecture on my part but is based on infor-
> mation I have received from a source I consider reliable who has access to
> the intelligence community. And that information is very disturbing."[40]

Goodnight and Poulakos suggest that as "old evidence is seen as less conclusive" and inconsistent and old explanations are offered continually, suspicions grow in a search for truth and there is a hunger for conclusive proof.[41]

Conspiracy theorists also create doubts in the minds of audiences by describing aspects of events, institutional actions (or lack of them), and explanations as mysterious, curious, strange, suspicious, weird, and unexplainable. In his effort to prove that the Soviets sabotaged the shuttle *Challenger*, Kirk Kidwell writes of a Delta rocket "mysteriously" experiencing a "shut down," the "mysterious disappearance" of a top Air Force expert on rocket self-destruct procedures, and the "absolute mystery" why Soviet spy ships steamed at "flank speed" away from Cape Canaveral the morning of the *Challenger* disaster.[42] The repetition of such words as "mysterious," "suspicious," and "strange" sows mistrust and enhances suspicion.

Official silence and secrecy are used as proof of cover up, deception, or manipulation of the truth. Zarefsky writes that Abraham Lincoln used such reasoning to connect Stephen Douglas to the conspiracy to expand slavery into new states. Lincoln claimed that "although Douglas promised to investigate the matter, he has made no report. Since he would stand to gain by clearing himself, his silence is a sign that he is implicated."[43] Secret meetings (often in secret locations with outcomes and actions unknown except to *insiders*) feed the notion of a conspiracy and raise doubts about the truthfulness of official explanations. In his study of the theo-political conspiracy rhetoric in an ultraconservative Roman Catholic publication, Goldzwig identifies both mystery and secrecy as key elements:

> By working through the various connections between liberal bishops, seemingly handpicked advisers, and other mysteriously nefarious events in the implied network of intrigue, *The Wanderer* is able to dramatically establish the conspiratorial tone of the discourse. The idea that things are being hatched in "some quarter" by these church bureaucrats gives audiences reason to believe in "actual conspiracies" also "documented" in *The Wanderer* rhetoric.[44]

The Principle of Reversal

The creation of mistrust enables persuaders to employ one of their most effective tactics when presenting and defending conspiracy arguments, the *principle of reversal*. "To trust appearances is *naïveté*," they claim, because "everything is the opposite of what it appears to be."[45] When "confronted with potentially dissonant information," the persuader merely applies the principle of reversal "to arrive at a conclusion different from that of" one who believes or espouses the institutional version of events. There is no need to refute or distort evidence to reach or maintain conspiracy claims.[46] Denial of a conspiracy confirms its existence because whatever conspirators claim is not what they believe, and appearances are not real because they are "*always* and *without exception* the exact opposite of what they appear to be."[47] A John Birch Society leaflet employed the principle of reversal when attacking Senator J. William Fulbright's proposal for improving relations with the Soviet Union: "What Senator Fulbright calls myths are realities, and what he calls realities are myths. One of his realities is: 'The Soviet Union, though still a formidable adversary, has ceased to be totally hostile to the West.'"

Mistrust enables the persuader to employ the principle of reversal to address all sorts of unpleasant questions. If proof of a conspiracy is elusive, that shows how powerful the conspiracy is. If investigators cannot locate conspirators, that proves they are everywhere. If accused conspirators do not appear to be evil or part of a damnable plot, that proves how clever they are. Darsey cites Brian Keeley as suggesting that "conspiracy theories are the only theories for which evidence *against* them is actually construed as evidence *in favor* of them."[48] Like many interchangeable elements of conspiracy argument, advocates not only use the principle of reversal to verify a conspiracy but also to vilify the conspiracy by accusing it of using the principle. A pamphlet entitled *A Cross Section of the Truth* accuses the communist conspiracy of using the principle of reversal for devious reasons. They claim it is a "tactical thread which runs through all Communist strategy":

> But the basic tactic has many parallel or affiliated forms: In the midst of stealing something, be the first to cry "stop thief" at somebody else; always accuse your enemies, first and loudly, of the very crimes you are yourself committing; knock a rival down by some foul and hidden blow, then jump on him as a weakling for having fallen. . . . Variations of this theme are

countless and commonplace in the orchestration of the Conspiracy. And a great deal of the strategy which the *Insiders* have developed since 1800 can be more quickly understood if this principle of reversal is kept in mind.[49]

Similarly, Robert Welch, founder of the Birch Society, claimed that his keen knowledge of how communists worked enabled him to see through the façade of Martin Luther King, Jr.:

> The record clearly shows that Martin Luther King was an almost perfect example of the Communist principle of reversal—that is of claiming exactly the opposite of what they are really doing. While always acting under the pretense of advocating nonviolent measures, King was actually the leading promoter and instigator of racial violence in America. He was a key figure in the Communist plans to create so much turmoil and anarchy in our country as to enable a Communist-run central government to counter such confusion with the massive use of a national armed force—which is the forerunner of Communist tyranny.[50]

Mistrust allows the arguer to use the principle of reversal tactic as proof a conspiracy exists and as proof the conspiracy is diabolical. There is no acknowledgment of argumentative inconsistency in the two-sided use of this principle.

CHALLENGING PLAUSIBILITY

It is relatively easy to challenge the *plausibility* or *believability* of reports or stories once trust in sources and storytellers has eroded. Audiences are unlikely to believe accounts from sources whose honesty and truthfulness are highly questionable.

Implausible Labels

Persuaders attempt to make words such as "accident," "mishap," "coincidence," and "circumstantial" sound ridiculous or deceptive. For instance, the Indiana Citizens Volunteer Militia Web site began with five paragraphs attacking the actions of former president Clinton with the same declaration: "It is surely much more than coincidence, that . . . ."[51] Kidwell entitled his article on the *Challenger* disaster "What a Coincidence! The *Challenger* Fits a Pattern of 'Accidents.'" He reported eight unexplained disasters involving American and French launch vehicles considered among the most reliable in the world. To substitute a Soviet conspiracy to sabotage the shuttle *Challenger* for the government's "accident" or "malfunction" argument, he claims that "now, a number of experts, in and out of the government, are beginning to consider the possibility that the thread of sabotage is woven through all these disasters." Kidwell quotes one of his unnamed U.S. sources as stating, "Simple logic demands at least the possibility of foul play," and an unnamed French source as saying, "It requires more faith to believe these disasters were all coincidence than it does to believe they were caused deliberately."[52]

Failure to Consider Alternative Explanations and Evidence

Those who see conspiracy at work express dismay that institutions have failed to consider obvious explanations. Kidwell, for example, notes that in spite of the numerous rocket failures around the world, "At present, no official government agency is even investigating the possibility of sabotage."[53] De Toledano claimed he was "not asserting that the *Challenger* was sabotaged—only that this possibility should be given serious consideration and not brushed aside as an Ian Fleming fantasy."[54] He noted that it took only one "deliberately careless person" to cause such a tragedy "and NASA does not seem to be inquiring."

Other persuaders charge institutions with ignoring important evidence. Bob Fletcher of the Montana Militia claimed at Senate hearings that militia sources had located the famous John Doe #2 in the Oklahoma City bombing and were aware of his name and location, but "for some reason the FBI is steering away from this gentleman."[55] Timothy McVeigh's attorney repeatedly questions the lack of governmental interest in critical events, clues, or people related to the bombing. For instance, there was evidence of a call that came to the Justice Department in Washington reporting the bombing thirty minutes before it happened, but the FBI had not pursued it. Some "believed the caller had been McVeigh," Jones writes, "I had my doubts. But whether it had or hadn't been Tim, the FBI's lack of interest was—again—surprising. But the FBI's lack of interest in a lot of things continued to be surprising."[56] Conspiracy authors Jonathan Vankin and John Whalen identify eighteen links between the CIA and Jonestown prior to the massacre of hundreds of men, women, and children in Guyana—a great many by apparent suicide and others apparently shot. In spite of such information, they write, "The House Permanent Select Committee on Intelligence announced that there was 'No evidence' of CIA involvement at Jonestown."[57] The implication is obvious: government agencies would not ignore such vital, readily available evidence unless they were covering up or taking part in a conspiracy.

Simplicity of Explanations

Persuaders show the extreme simplicity, and therefore unbelievability, of the official version of an event. For instance, attorney Jones questioned the plausibility that two untrained loners with limited knowledge of how to make a bomb and no network to assist them in planning, carrying out, and escaping from the bombing could have carried out the worst act of domestic terrorism in U.S. history. He identifies seven deadly terrorist acts against U.S. troops and personnel around the world that always fit the same *pattern* and remained "unsolved and unprosecuted." "Given all this," he asks, "does it seem so far-fetched that what happened in Oklahoma City might not be as simple as the government said?"[58] No, he tells his readers,

> The real story of the bombing, as the McVeigh defense pursued it, is complex, shadowy, and sinister. It stretches weblike, from America's heart-

land to the nation's capital, the Far East, Europe, and the Middle East, and much of it remains a mystery.

Likewise, Bob Fletcher of the Montana Militia claimed to have a lengthy report from a former FBI agent that disputed the single fertilizer bomb in a rental truck theory for the Oklahoma City bombing. He stated that evidence showed there was more than one bomb inside the building, and the government's argument was "absolute baloney."[59]

Fundamental to most claims of complexity over simplicity are assertions that conspirators are omnipresent in all institutions, particularly the government, and that the causes of evil actions are rarely as simplistic as institutions would have us believe. For instance, Norman Olson of the Michigan Militia suggested the possibility of a more complex conspiracy explanation to replace the government's simplistic single bomber theory in the Oklahoma City tragedy: "It very well may be that there was a conspiracy at higher levels. People behind those people who we have been fed by the press to accept or believe that perhaps it was one angry individual."[60]

Persuaders tap into the distrust of government they have fostered to argue that simplicity and denial are merely parts of the effort to deceive. One Web site addresses a letter to an eight-year-old named Virginia (similar to the famous letter to Santa Claus) that offers a conspiratorial explanation for the war in Iraq:

> *Yes, Virginia, there are government conspiracies.* And the biggest government conspiracy of all is the claim that there are no government conspiracies. Because government conspiracies are creatures of the dark places. They function best when invisible and deniable. But not this time. This time the conspiracy is in the light for all to see. The lie is known, the tellers of that lie identified, their cooperation and collusion plain for the world to see. . . . Bush, Powell, Cheney, Blair, Rumsfeld, etc. et. al. have proved that reality before the world. And with that new awareness, every controversy that was ever dismissed solely on the claim that there are no government conspiracies can be, indeed must be, re-examined in the light of the knowledge that government conspiracies are a very real part of everyday life.[61]

Ironically, simplicity over complexity is the same argument institutions use to debunk most conspiracy arguments offered by social movements and skeptics.

OFFERING A BETTER STORY

If the conspiracy persuader can cause audiences to lose trust in institutional ability and willingness to be open and truthful and to raise doubts about the believability of official explanations, audiences may be willing to consider a competing story centered on a conspiracy. The persuader must create a competing argument that appears to be *more plausible* and based on *superior evidence* to that of the institutional explanation of a phenomenon.

A Coherent Pattern

The conspiracy argument ties together numerous bits of information or examples into a coherent pattern or mosaic, usually resulting in argument from hypothesis, example, sign, or cause to effect. Evidence and associations contained in conspiracy argument may be readily available to institutions and the public but are *selected* and *organized* to support a different claim—a claim that a conspiracy rather than an accident, mechanical failure, human error, stupidity, or coincidence best explains an event. Stephen Browne writes that the conspiracy narrative gives "the sense of being better able to account for the full sweep and complexity of events."[62] Similarly, Young, Launer, and Austin conclude that conspiracy argument "provides a worldview which is complete, capable of answering . . . all uncomfortable questions. Its apparent internal cohesiveness provides the narrative fidelity and probability which make it persuasive."[63]

Conspiracy argument, then, is an exercise in connecting the dots to lead an audience to a more reasonable explanation and, in doing so, to undermine the official explanation by offering a more plausible one. For example, in a follow-up article on the *Challenger* disaster entitled "The Question Persists: Was Shuttle Sabotaged?" De Toledano identified nine interconnected, serious effects of the tragedy, including destruction of 25 percent of shuttle capability, cessation of military research and missions, and damage to former president Reagan's antiballistic missile Strategic Defense Initiative program (dubbed the Star Wars program). "Putting it all together," he concluded, "it 'amounts to valid reasons' for Soviet sabotage."[64]

Overwhelming Proof

Rhetorical theorists note that a conspiracy "charge is also virtually impossible to disprove" and that "oftentimes the mere accusation of conspiracy is enough to 'prove' it."[65] This is a rhetorical tar baby effect. Whoever touches a conspiracy gets stuck to it; the more one struggles to get free, the more one is associated with it. Recall the principle of reversal. Regardless of this apparent "Got you" effect of conspiracy charges, a basic truism of argumentation—burden of proof—maintains that we must prove claims. Normally, we reject arguments that shift the burden of proof to others by challenging them to disprove an unsupported claim.

Conspiracy advocates attempt to fulfill rather than to shift the burden of proof. They are noted for carefully accumulating and arranging large amounts of evidence, some say "overwhelming proof," to establish claims. For instance, Robert Welch began the John Birch Society with a speech that detailed the communist conspiracy and the dangers of big government to his hand-picked audience of eleven businessmen. It became the 165-page *Blue Book of the John Birch Society.* Attorney Jones devoted forty-seven pages of his book to establishing two meticulously traced counterconspiracy theories for the Oklahoma City bombing. The first traced Terry Nichols' (McVeigh's alleged co-conspirator) connections and numerous contacts with Islamic radicals in the Philippines and the Middle East. The second traced a conspiracy of white supremacists in Arkansas with connections in Europe.[66] A pamphlet entitled *Why Don't You Believe What We Tell You?* contains thirty-seven pages of quotations from Jewish leaders and publications from 1883 to 1976 to prove that a Jewish, Zionist, communist conspiracy is attempting to create a new world order.[67] Those who detect a conspiracy may attempt to persuade the skeptical by out-proving or overwhelming the opposition.

The persuader who establishes a conspiracy argument must accept the burden of proof that requires *proving one case* and *disproving another*—the competing official or institutional explanation widely disseminated by the mass media. For example, in a lengthy Internet message entitled "The Attack on the Pentagon," Leonard Spencer attempts to establish that, contrary to official accounts, American Airlines Flight 77, a Boeing 757, did not crash into the Pentagon on September 11, 2001. He reviews the documented time line, seismic evidence, eyewitness reports, pictures, and accounts of the damage and debris, and the few CCTV frames released to the public and press. He concludes that Bush and

> his administration are mere puppets, acting out a script written and con- ceived by some higher power. But who is pulling the strings? . . . I do not know, but the attack on the Pentagon, the headquarters of the most pow- erful military machine the world has ever seen, was perhaps the sym- bolic confirmation of a secret coup d'etat that in reality took place some time ago.[68]

Thus, the official explanation "is tested over and over again for weaknesses," with the result that suspicion increases as the evidence for the conspiracy "becomes overwhelming."[69]

A study of evidence in paranoid (conspiracy) and non-paranoid dis- course found that the "paranoid" discourse contained significantly more ref- erences to general, specific, and documented others (extrinsic evidence) and significantly fewer non-attributed assertions (intrinsic evidence) than did "non-paranoid" discourse, that so-called paranoids were "not significantly more likely to distort evidence than 'non-pananoids,'" and that the principle of reversal makes it unnecessary for the paranoid to distort evidence. Because "the political 'paranoid's' conspiratorial worldview" leads them to distrust their audience, they "attempt to combat this perceived hostility with cold, hard facts—verifiable references to credible others.[70] Critics should look more to how evidence is selected and employed to support claims than to the quantity and quality of evidence offered.

Overwhelming support and a coherent narrative or pattern are insuffi- cient, however, to sell a conspiracy argument to replace an institutional explanation. The persuader must establish *motivation* and *evilness*.

Motivation

As Zarefsky notes, "Like many other argument patterns, conspiracy charges depend upon an analysis of motives. The argument will not be persuasive unless the alleged conspirator is shown to have a motive for participating in the plot."[71] In other words, the persuader who weaves a conspiracy argument must be able to answer the "why" question: Why would the Soviet Union want to sabotage the shuttle *Challenger*? Why would white supremacists, or extremists in the Philippine Islands, or (as some militia leaders claimed) the Japanese government want to blow up the federal building in Oklahoma City? Why would President Reagan and Pope John Paul II want to conspire to commit genocide? If there is no motive, there is no conspiracy. In contrast, the greater the motive, the greater the believability of the conspiracy argument.

Kidwell, for instance, claims a source reported to him, "There exists a very strong presumption among defense, aerospace, and intelligence experts that the Soviets are attempting to scuttle the SDI [Reagan's antimissile Strategic Defense Initiative] through active measures."[72] The Soviet inability to counter SDI technologically, militarily, and economically provided sufficient motive for sabotaging the *Challenger* and numerous other U.S. and European rockets. The net effect of these "mishaps," Kidwell concluded, was a great curtailment of SDI research and destruction of U.S. capability to launch crucial satellites to monitor Soviet troop movements and nuclear deployments. De Toledano claimed the "shuttle taxis" repeated successes had "driven Soviet scientists wild" and that "the USSR" was "driven by a desperate need to retard Mr. Reagan's Star Wars [SDI program]."[73] Thus, the Soviet Union had significant motivation to launch a conspiracy to destroy the *Challenger*.

When Iranian dissidents were attempting to overthrow the Shah in Iran, members of the Iranian Students Association in the United States were arrested during demonstrations and protests. They saw conspiracies between the Shah and Savak (the Shah's secret police) and the U.S. government, police, and CIA. Pamphlets and fliers distributed on college campuses cited the motives for this unlikely conspiracy. They centered on *control* (the CIA had created Savak in 1956 and did not want to lose control of its offspring), *security* (the U.S. depended on the Shah regime to counter rising revolutionary movements and increasing Soviet activities in the region and had supplied it with some of the most sophisticated military hardware in the U.S. arsenal), and *economy* (vast oil reserves essential for transportation, heating, and industry in the United States and billions of American dollars invested in and loaned to Iranian business and industry).

> The U.S. government and establishment are deeply concerned about the fate of the Shah and monarchy in Iran. Should the regime be toppled, the U.S. huge economic, political, and military interests would be in clear jeopardy. That is why the U.S. government is trying its utmost, though at the cost of massive bloodshed and all-out repression, to keep the puppet Shah in power.[74]

In each of these examples, persuaders identified numerous, plausible motives sufficient to lead organizations, leaders, agencies, and governments to enter into conspiracies. Too much was at stake for them not to take decisive and deadly action. In Darsey's words, each conspiracy theorist must provide a "credible purpose as the preeminent element of motive."[75]

Evilness

One essential question remains: Were the elements that entered into the alleged conspiracy capable of unspeakable evil? If audiences do not believe that an alleged conspirator was able and willing to carry out evil plots and deeds, they are unlikely to accept a conspiracy argument. A history of secretive, evil actions may lead to serious distrust of institutions. For example, a Web site explains why 9/11 conspiracy theories are believable for many:

> They've [the American people] seen 40 years of *CIA* wrongdoing, including ridiculously implausible plots like assassinating *Fidel Castro* with a cigar and the *Kennedy assassinations*. They've seen unlikely government conspiracies proven beyond a shadow of a doubt, plots like *Watergate* and the *MKULTRA mind control* experiments. For God's sake, the U.S. government has even confessed to feeding radioactive mush to retarded children—*just to see what would happen*. The real questions isn't "Why would you believe the U.S. Government was behind September 11?" Rather the question is "Why *wouldn't* you?"[76]

It may be easy for distrusting audiences to believe an institution has "done it again."

Some persuaders portray the evilness of the conspiracy without regard to specific events. For example, Robert Welch described the communist conspiracy as devious, brutal, bloodthirsty, and inhumane. Its leaders were "determined, cunning, and utterly ruthless gangsters" who had used "brutality, the countless tentacles of treason, and murder on a scale never before dreamed of in the world."[77]

Other persuaders tie the conspiracy to historical events and associate it with evil groups to establish the evil nature of the conspiracy. Tony Alamo, president and pastor of the Alamo Christian Church in Alma, Arkansas, claims that the Communist party, the Nazi party in Germany, Neo-Nazis, and many other terrorist groups are or were secret divisions of the Vatican.

> Remember, as I told you in my literature *The Pope's Secrets*, the Vatican and her agents always cover themselves to her advantage, especially when someone starts exposing her. For instance, she slaughtered six million Jews in WWII; then, when she saw that she was losing the war, she hid 1,000 Jews in Catholic convents and some in the Vatican. Then she said, "See how we love the Jews!!" And, of course, the Vatican media only showed the part about their hypocritically hidden 1,000 and shifted the blame from the Vatican to a nation of people (the Germans) knowing that no one would exterminate all Germans for such a crime.[78]

If readers believe these associations are the real cause and force behind the Holocaust, they are likely to believe the Vatican is capable of any evil, including a simple "smear campaign" against Rev. Alamo and efforts to stir up violence against Christians and Jews. Apparently insignificant motives may instigate great evil. An anti-Jewish Web site claims a Zionist conspiracy of "powerful bankers killed Lincoln merely to prevent him from creating a new type of money they could not use to bribe politicians in Washington, so they hired J. Wilkes Booth."[79]

Other persuaders tie the conspiracy to current events to establish evilness. Kidwell acknowledged that "some, perhaps, find it beyond belief that the Soviets would actually resort to such 'dirty tricks'" as sabotaging the *Challenger*, and then asked,

> But, given the opportunity, would the same Kremlin leaders who ordered the destruction of a civilian airliner with 269 innocent human beings on it [a reference to the shooting down of KAL Flight 007 by Soviet fighter planes in 1983] fail to order the sabotage of the U.S. space program?[80]

In a similar vein, Norman Olson of the Michigan Militia took issue with those who refuse to consider that the federal government could be capable of events so terrible as the bombing in Oklahoma City.

> I submit to you sir [Senator Specter of the Senate Judiciary Committee] that the Central Intelligence Agency has been in the business of killing Americans and killing people in the United States and around the world since 1946. I submit to you sir that the Central Intelligence Agency is probably the grandest conspirator behind all of this government.[81]

John Trochman, representing the Militia of Montana at the same hearings, explained why American citizens were angry and did not consider it farfetched to suspect the government that allows

> our military to label caring patriots as the enemy then turn their tanks loose on U.S. citizens to murder and destroy [referring to the Branch Davidians in Waco, Texas] or directs a sniper to shoot a mother in the face while holding her infant in her arms [referring to Ruby Ridge].[82]

When defiant Muslim protestors took to the streets on December 1, the first day of Moharram to commemorate the martyrdom of Muhammad's grandson in 682, Iranian troops were allegedly ordered to "shoot to kill." Handouts on U.S. campuses claimed the resulting bloodshed was a result of the conspiracy between the Shah and the United States:

> The U.S. government, which has been fully backing the Shah over the past 26 years, has thrown its all-out support behind the Shah. While endorsing the imposition of military rule in Iran, the U.S. government, and Jimmy Carter himself personally, have openly encouraged the Shah to take any steps necessary and to use whatever means possible to "restore authority and stability."

The persuaders in each of these illustrations claimed the alleged conspirators were ruthless enough to commit the evils for which they were being accused. In Hofstadter's words, the enemy "is the perfect model of malice, a kind of amoral superman: sinister, ubiquitous, powerful, cruel, sensual, and luxury-loving."[83] Thus, the conspiracy had both motive and capability to do unspeakable harm.

CONCLUSIONS

Conspiracy argument is common, interesting, complex, varied, and often outrageous. Many such arguments have withstood the test of time—the communist conspiracy, the secular humanist conspiracy, the Vatican or Papal conspiracy, international bankers. A growing number of scholars have attempted to understand conspiracy argument, reveal its complexities and weaknesses, and develop standards for judging its rationality or validity.

Conspiracy argument is understood best when viewed as a process in relation to competing argument. Conspiracy argument usually appears after an official or accepted explanation of a phenomenon has been widely disseminated in the media and has attained an aura of credibility and legitimacy. Some find the official explanation unsatisfactory and determine to set the record straight by revealing a sinister conspiracy as the driving force behind the phenomenon. In challenging an institutional or official explanation, the conspiracy persuader is at a distinct disadvantage, not only starting out after a competing argument has been disseminated but also rarely having the credibility, legitimacy, and resources available to institutional storytellers.

To make conspiracy arguments palatable to audiences beyond small numbers of true believers, persuaders must create arguments with three essential ingredients: they must undermine trust in an institution to locate and tell the truth; they must challenge the believability of the official explanation or story; and they must offer a more believable explanation that establishes both motive and evilness of the conspiracy.

Conspiracy persuaders capitalize on a sense of distrust that permeates societal interactions, or they associate the institutional explanation with agents, agencies, and/or societal groups that are not trusted. Even if there is an aura of distrust in society or distrust of agencies and groups, persuaders may find it necessary to create distrust of the explanation by claiming that the institution is attempting to stifle the search for truth rather than to encourage it. They label events and institutional acts as mysterious, curious, or suspicious, and they cite secrecy and silence as signs of a cover-up or manipulation of the truth.

Conspiracy persuaders challenge the believability of an official explanation by ridiculing the characterization of an event as an accident, mishap, or coincidence. They express surprise and dismay that the institution has failed to follow up on obvious explanations and evidence, and they attack the extreme simplicity of the official explanation—the same tactic institutions use to debunk conspiracy arguments.

Conspiracy theorists cannot succeed by merely attacking official explanations; they must offer more believable explanations. Thus, conspiracy arguments are carefully crafted mosaics of facts, examples, signs, causes, associations, and claims. The accumulation of large bodies of evidence meets the counterarguer's burden of proof and attempts to overwhelm the competing institutional argument. A coherent pattern and an abundance of evidence help to establish motive and the evilness of the alleged conspiracy. The persuader attempts to establish that the conspiracy had both substantial reason for and the capability of committing unspeakable evil.

Conspiracy argument, then, is more process than form. It counters an explanation or argument found wanting in significant ways with one constructed and supported by those who project themselves as having no motive other than locating and telling the truth. It is an effort to offer a more believable explanation and to overwhelm competing argument with an abundance of proof. Without a competing argument, the persuader has no evil target to discredit, no explanation to debunk, and little evidence from which to draw different premises and conclusions. In many ways, the institutional storyteller and narrative enhance the likelihood of a competing conspiracy argument. The institution's efforts to maintain control of the story enhance the conspiracy weaver's credibility and the believability of the conspiracy argument. Efforts to maintain secrecy, to revise the original story, to withhold vital information, to deny or attack the conspiracy theory and its proponents create doubts about the institution's version of the story and its commitment to locating and telling the truth.

Notes

[1] Marilyn Young and Michael K. Launer, "Evaluative Criteria for Conspiracy Arguments: The Case of KAL 007," *Warranting Assent: Case Studies in Argument Evaluation*, Edward Schiappa, ed. (Albany: State University of New York Press, 1995): 23.

[2] David Zarefsky, "Conspiracy Arguments in the Lincoln-Douglas Debates," *Journal of the American Forensic Association* 21 (Fall 1984): 71–72.

[3] G. Thomas Goodnight and John Poulakos, "Conspiracy Rhetoric: From Pragmatism to Fantasy in Public Discourse," *Western Journal of Speech Communication* 45 (Fall 1981): 305.

[4] Steven R. Goldzwig, "Theo-Political Conspiracy Rhetoric in *The Wanderer*," *The Journal of Communication and Religion* 14 (September 1991): 27.

[5] Richard Hofstadter, *The Paranoid Style in American Politics and Other Essays.* (New York: Alfred Knopf, 1954): 32, 36.

[6] Dan Nimmo and James E. Combs, "Devils and Demons: The Group Mediation of Conspiracy," *Mediated Political Realities* (New York: Longman, 1983): 211.

[7] Kenneth Burke, *The Rhetoric of Motives* (Berkeley: University of California Press, 1969): 166.

[8] Charles J. Stewart, "The Master Conspiracy of the John Birch Society: From Communism to the New World Order," *Western Journal of Communication* 66 (Fall 2002): 431.

[9] James Darsey, "A Conspiracy of Science," *Western Journal of Communication* 66 (Fall 2002): 482.

[10] Marilyn J. Young, Michael K. Launer, and Curtis C. Austin, "The Need for Evaluative Criteria: Conspiracy Argument Revisited," *Argumentation and Advocacy* 26 (Winter 1990): 100, 103.

[11] Justin D. Fulton, *Lincoln's Assassination* (Minneapolis: Osterhus, n.d.); *How the Conservative Revolution Crowd Plans to Destroy America* (Leesburg, VA: The New Federalist, 1995); Tony Alamo, *Genocide Treaty, FBI and the Neo-Nazis* (Alma, AR: Alamo Christian Church, n.d.); Leonard Spencer, "The Attack on the Pentagon," www.serendipity.li/wot/pentagon/spencer05.htm, accessed 23 September 2005.

[12] Darrin M. McMahon, "Conspiracies So Vast," www.boston.com/news/globe/ideas/articles/2004/02/01/conspiracies_so_vast?, accessed 21 September 2005.

[13] BATF P4510.5, *Elements of Conspiracy Investigation* (Washington, DC: Department of Treasury and Bureau of Alcohol, Tobacco and Firearms, 1993): 5.

[14] Zarefsky, 72

[15] Darsey, 472; Zarefsky, 72.

[16] Goodnight and Poulakos, 301.

[17] Young and Launer, 8; Goodnight and Poulakos, 309.

[18] Goldzwig, 17; Zarefsky, 72.

[19] Zarefsky, 74.

[20] Garry Wills, *A Necessary Evil: A History of American Distrust of Government.* (New York: Simon & Schuster, 1999): 16.

[21] Marouf Hasian, Jr., "Understanding the Power of Conspiratorial Rhetoric: A Case Study of *The Protocols of the Elders of Zion*," *Communication Studies* 48 (Fall 1997): 203.

[22] Hans Toch, *The Social Psychology of Social Movements* (New York: Bobbs-Merrill, 1965): 61.

[23] Toch, 62.

[24] Dale G. Leathers, "Fundamentalism of the Radical Right," *Southern Speech Journal* 33 (Winter 1968): 248, 255.

[25] Steven R. Goldzwig, "Conspiracy Rhetoric at the Dawn of the New Millennium: A Response," *Western Journal of Communication* 66 (Fall 2002): 496–497.

[26] A. Cheree Carlson, "The Rhetoric of the Know-Nothing Party: Nativism as a Response to the Rhetorical Situation," *Southern Communication Journal* 54 (Summer 1989): 373–374.

[27] http://www.resist.com/updates/aryanupdate11.28.99.htm, accessed 15 September 2006.

[28] Darsey, 472, 477.

[29] Young and Launer, 22.

[30] http://www.resist.com/updates/2003/3.2.03aryanupdate.htm, accessed 2 March 2003.

[31] Bernard K. Duffy, "The Anti-Humanist Rhetoric of the New Religious Right," *Southern Speech Communication Journal* 49 (Summer 1984): 359.

[32] "U.S. Militia Movement," Senate Judiciary Committee, 16 June 1995, recorded by C-SPAN.

[33] George Lincoln Rockwell, "Speech at the University of Kansas," 20 February 1964, from a tape recording.

[34] Goodnight and Poulakos, 303.

[35] http://www.resist.com/update/2001updates/10.28.01aryanupdate.htm, accessed 28 October 2001.

[36] Darsey, 472.

[37] Stephen Jones and Peter Israel, *Others Unknown: The Oklahoma City Bombing Case and Conspiracy* (New York: Public Affairs, 1998): xii–xiii.

[38] Jones and Israel, 313.

[39] http://www.let.rug.nl/usa/E/thirteen/thirt06.htm, accessed 21 July 2006.

[40] Ralph de Toledano, "Was *Challenger* Sabotaged?" *The New American*, 10 March 1986, 19.

[41] Goodnight and Poulakos, 303.

[42] Kirk Kidwell, "What a Coincidence! The *Challenger* Fits a Pattern of 'Accidents,'" *The New American*, 29 September 1986, 17.

[43] Zarefsky, 66.

[44] Goldzwig, "Theo-Political," 22.

[45] Leathers, 254; Craig Allen Smith, "The Hofstadter Hypothesis Revisited: The Nature of Evidence in Politically 'Paranoid' Discourse," *Southern Speech Communication Journal* 42 (Spring 1977): 287.

[46] Smith, 287.

[47] Charles J. G. Griffin, "Jedidiah Morse and the Bavarian Illuminati: An Essay in the Rhetoric of Conspiracy," *Central States Speech Journal* 39 (Fall/Winter 1988): 300; Dale G. Leathers, "Belief-Disbelief Systems: The Communicative Vacuum of the Radical Right," *Explorations in Rhetorical Criticism*, Gerald P. Mohrmann, Charles J. Stewart, and Donovan J. Ochs, eds. (University Park: Pennsylvania State University Press, 1973): 135.

[48] Darsey, 470.

[49] *A Cross Section of the Truth* (Belmont, MA: The Review of the News, 1968).

[50] Robert Welch, "Why Join the John Birch Society?" n.d., n.p.

[51] "Gun Registration vs. American Freedom," www.elkhartcvm.homestead.com/Declaration, accessed 16 April 2002. For an interesting narrative on what befalls some movement leaders, visit http://www.icvmmilitia.homestead.com/ and read the section about "If you are searching for the group that was known as ICVM, you'll be disappointed," accessed 21 July 2006.

[52] Kidwell, 17.

[53] Kidwell, 17.

[54] De Toledano, 19.

[55] "U.S. Militia Movement."

[56] Jones and Israel, 160.

[57] "The Jonestown Massacre: CIA Mind Control Run Amok?" excerpted on the Internet from Jonathan Vankin and John Whalen, *50 Greatest Conspiracies of All Time*, 1995.

[58] Jones and Israel, xii.

[59] "U.S. Militia Movement."

[60] "U.S. Militia Movement."

[61] http://www.whatreallyhappened.com/virginia.html, accessed 21 July 2006.

[62] Stephen H. Browne, *Edmund Burke and the Discourse of Virtue* (Tuscaloosa: University of Alabama Press, 1993): 19; Goldzwig, "Theo-Political," 19

[63] Young, Launer, and Austin, 106.

[64] Ralph de Toledano, "The Question Persists: Was Shuttle Sabotaged?" *The New American*, 30 June 1986, 24.

[65] Zarefsky, 73; Goldzwig, "Theo-Political," 17.

[66] Jones and Israel, 117–165.

[67] *Why Don't You Believe What We Tell You?* (Torrance, CA: The Noontide Press, 1982).

[68] http://www.serendipity.li/wot/pentagon/spencer05.htm#Piecing_It_All_Together, accessed 21 July 2006.

[69] Goodnight and Poulakos, 306.

[70] Smith, 286–287, 283.

[71] Zarefsky, 74.

[72] Kidwell, 17.

[73] De Toledano, "The Question Persists," 24.

[74] "Bloodbath in Iran," flier of the Organization of Iranian Moslem Students, n.d.

[75] Darsey, 486.

[76] http://bouncaround.blogspot.com/2005/11/september-11-conspiracies.html, accessed 24 July 2006.

[77] Robert Welch, *The Blue Book of the John Birch Society* (Boston: Western Islands, 1961): 21, 3.

[78] Alamo.

[79] Michael S. Waltman, "Stratagems and Heuristics in the Recruitment of Children into Communities of Hate: The Fabric of Our Future Nightmares," *Southern Communication Journal* 69 (Fall 2003): 28–29.

[80] Kidwell, 17.

[81] "U.S. Militia Movement."

[82] "U.S. Militia Movement."

[83] Hofstadter, 31–32.

CHAPTER

12

Justifying Violence through Good Reasons

Persuasion is the primary agency through which social movements attempt to bring about or resist change by satisfying essential functions. Violence is incidental in most social movements and is often perpetrated by institutional agents and opposition groups attempting to stifle the movement through physical assaults, bombings, and assassinations. The histories of the abolition, civil rights, labor, and pro-choice movements, for example, are replete with instances of institutional and oppositional violence against leaders, demonstrators, sympathizers, and facilities.[1] Martin Luther King, Jr., and Medgar Evers are only two of many civil rights leaders and workers who were murdered. Hundreds of abortion clinics have been targets of arson and bombs, and several physicians and support staff have been shot or killed in the United States and Canada.

In spite of such violence, most social movement leaders and members espouse nonviolent means to bring about or resist change for philosophical and pragmatic reasons. Philosophically, they have a profound respect for law and order and struggle with the notion of nonviolent civil disobedience, let alone violent acts. They cite the pacifist teachings and actions of the early Christians, Henry David Thoreau's essay on civil disobedience, and Mohandas Gandhi's concept of Satyagraha (see chapter 5). For instance, Thoreau wrote in 1849,

> Why has every man a conscience then? I think that we should be men first, and subjects afterward. It is not desirable to cultivate a respect for the law, so much as for the right. The only obligation which I have a right to assume, is to do at any time what I think right.

If a law "is of such a nature that it requires you to be the agent of injustice to another, then, I say, break the law. Let your life be a counter friction to stop the machine."[2]

Social movements are aware that a philosophy of nonviolence places them and their struggles on the moral high ground and challenges the legitimacy of reactionary institutions and opposition forces. In his 1963 address from the steps of the Lincoln Memorial, Martin Luther King, Jr., declared,

> We must forever conduct our struggle on the high plane of dignity and discipline. We must not allow our creative protest to degenerate into physical violence. Again and again, we must rise to the majestic heights of meeting physical force with soul force."[3]

Similarly, in a speech in Austin, Texas, United Farm Worker leader Cesar Chavez told his audience:

> We know that when human beings are concerned for one another, that the thing that all of us want when we're concerned for one another, is to build and not to destroy. And we're concerned really for the dignity of man.[4]

At the end of a twenty-four day fast in 1972, Chavez issued a statement in which he assured his followers: "So long as we are willing to sacrifice for that cause, so long as we persist in nonviolence and work to spread the message of our struggle, then millions of people around the world will respond with their hearts."[5] Nonviolent resistance captures the moral high ground and enables the movement to transcend the immoral stands and actions of institutions and their supporters.

Social movements also have pragmatic reasons for espousing nonviolence. For instance, Martin Luther King, Jr., reacted not only philosophically but pragmatically to the challenge of Black Power advocates who threatened to use violence to defend black Americans and to overthrow racist state and local governments. He wrote:

> They fail to see that no internal revolution has ever succeeded in overthrowing a government by violence unless the government had already lost the allegiance and effective control of its armed forces. Anyone in his right mind knows that this will not happen in the United States."[6]

Violence simply would not work, as racists in Little Rock, Arkansas, discovered in 1957 when President Eisenhower sent in federal troops to stop the violence that was preventing the integration of Central High School. Chavez argued that nonviolence was more powerful than violence because it provided "the opportunity to stay on the offensive, and that is of crucial importance to win any contest."[7] Like other leaders, he understood that movements must employ persuasive strategies that enable them to establish important links with social and institutional legitimizers and to sustain efforts over decades. Only nonviolent symbols and actions can take the movement through the long haul to ultimate success.

Chavez saw only two results from violent actions on behalf of a cause, neither of which furthered the cause. In an essay on Martin Luther King, Jr., in 1978, he wrote: "If we resort to violence then one of two things will happen: either the violence will be escalated and there will be many injuries and perhaps deaths on both sides, or there will be total demoralization of the workers."[8] Similarly, early twentieth-century anarchist Emma Goldman, who gained the epithet "Red Emma" for her outspoken agitation on behalf of women's rights and against the military draft during World I, opposed the armed revolution and violence advocated by anarchist Johann Most (see chapter 8) because "individuals were often the victims of violent revolution and she felt that individuals were 'the heart of society.'"[9] Her "philosophy of the sovereignty of the individual" did not allow her to "accept any method of social change that would violate or harm individual liberties."

While a rhetoric of nonviolence dominates the words and actions of social movements, nearly every social movement spawns extremist elements and individuals who resort to violence, including John Brown of the abolitionist movement, the Molly Maguires of the early labor movement, hatchet-wielding saloon wreckers in the temperance movement, the Ku Klux Klan in the white supremacist movement, the Weather Underground in the peace and counter-culture movements, and the Environmental Liberation Front (ELF) in the environmental movement. Extremists believe that violence is not only justified but is also the only available and effective means to further the cause they believe is literally a matter of life and death, whether it be ending British tyranny, slavery, starvation wages and living conditions, the "fatal appetite" for alcohol, destruction of the environment, war, or the threat to white supremacy. If, for instance, abortion is the murder of innocent, unborn children, violence is warranted to end a terrible evil that has existed for over thirty years. Violent acts attract widespread public and institutional attention and condemnation, and historians record violent acts out of proportion to their roles in social movements. While movements in general receive scant attention in historical accounts and the mass media, readers and viewers are well informed about violent acts through words and pictures. Examples include the Boston Tea Party, John Brown's raid at Harper's Ferry, the Homestead Strike, lynchings by the Ku Klux Klan, and arsons by the Environmental Liberation Front (ELF).

Most social movement leaders and sympathizers condemn violence as strongly as do institutions and the public and view it as morally reprehensible. The American Association of Pro Life Obstetricians and Gynecologists warned after the murder of Dr. David Gunn in Florida that "violence begets violence" and declared that "these actions should be deplored and condemned by all Pro-Lifers."[10] D. Michael McCarron of the Florida Catholic Conference wrote, "We condemn these killings in no uncertain terms. . . . The commandment 'Thou shalt not kill,' the basis of the pro-life movement, has been violated."[11] At Senate hearings following the Oklahoma City bombing, Ken Adams of a Michigan Militia exclaimed, "We are certainly totally against violence" and "we will be the first to expose them. We will be the first, if they are breaking the law, to turn them over to law enforcement agencies."[12]

Leaders worry that violent acts in the name of the movement will adversely affect the movement. Pro-life leaders feared "a rising tide of zealotry" would "force a schism in their movement," and Paige Cunningham, president of Americans United for Life, warned, "We cannot be linked with violence."[13] Perpetrators of violence are labeled "misguided extremists" who hurt the cause by embarrassing the movement and damaging its credibility.[14] Julie Lewin of the Fund for Animals and other animal rights activists were so concerned about negative effects on their movement by an attempted bombing of a surgical center that they suspected "it may have been instigated by an agent provocateur."[15]

The fears of leaders and members that violence may do more harm than good to the cause is amply justified by history. For instance, when members of the Weather Underground set off more than a ton of ammonium-nitrate fertilizer and fuel oil on the University of Wisconsin campus in 1972 that destroyed Sterling Hall and the Army Mathematics Research Center, severely damaged several other buildings, and killed a physics student named Robert Fassnacht, they expected it to "energize and radicalize the peace movement, bringing about a quick end to U.S. involvement in Vietnam."[16] Instead, it gave the moral advantage to President Richard Nixon, "reinforced hostility to students among the general public," and ended all peaceful antiwar demonstrations on campus. Erica Eisinger, an antiwar activist on campus at the time, later remarked, "The bombing was so extreme and unjustifiable and horrible, it stopped us in our tracks. . . . We identified with Fassnacht, not the bombers."[17]

Clearly, those who resort to violence in the name of a cause must be concerned about the inevitable backlash from within and without that may deny them legitimacy, support, sympathy, and influence while inviting institutional repression. Robert Francesconi writes that "legitimacy is an ongoing process of reason-giving" that "seeks an interpretation of a specific situation in such a way that the action will be perceived to be consistent with socially shared values."[18] They must employ persuasion that will, in Donald Bryant's words, succeed in "adjusting ideas to people and of people to ideas."[19] This is no easy task. People in the United States see themselves as peace-loving, nonviolent people, not like those in other countries who resort to violent and inhumane acts. Violence of any type immediately raises serious ethical, moral, humane, and legal questions. The most limited violence may cost human and nonhuman lives and millions of dollars in damage. No matter how limited the nature and intent of violent acts, they have the potential of entangling the movement, public, and institutions into ever-greater acts of violence and conflicts with police forces.

How, then, do social movement militants adjust the idea of violence to us and us to the idea of violence? If, as Karl Wallace claims, the "substance of rhetoric is good reasons," what good reasons do radical activists employ to make these essential adjustments?[20] Wallace identifies three "general categories of values that help us to decide whether our decisions and actions are good or bad, right or wrong . . . the desirable, the obligatory, and the admirable or praiseworthy, and their opposites." This chapter analyzes the messages of American radicals from the colonial period to the twenty-first century that have justified the use of violence by identifying, in Wallace's terms, "statements in whose predicates are the words, *is a desirable thing, is morally obligatory, is morally admirable or reprehensible, is a good thing, is praiseworthy,* and the like."[21]

THE MOVEMENT MUST ADDRESS SITUATIONAL DEMANDS

Lloyd Bitzer writes that "prior to the creation and presentation of discourse, there are three constituents of any rhetorical situation" and the "first is the *exigence*" that he defines as "an imperfection marked by urgency; it is a defect, an obstacle, something waiting to be done, a thing which is other than it should be."[22] Accordingly, messages that offer reasons for violence identify exigencies (what persuaders perceive to be grave social, political, and humane crises) that warrant violent acts.

An Unbearable Exigence

The labels activists attach to exigencies reveal both the severity and urgency of the situations: murder, atrocity, slaughter, holocaust, massacre, and extermination. On a scale of social defects or crises, these labels are at the top of the most extreme and morally reprehensible evils that are premeditated, planned, and carried out ruthlessly. Activists speak of enslaving millions, murdering the unborn, destroying innocent human life, torturing animals, committing genocide against horses, and conducting a reign of terror.[23] Anti-Vietnam War protestors in the 1960s and 1970s stressed the escalating casualties among U.S. soldiers and South Vietnamese civilians, the use of napalm, the bombing and burning of villages, and the killing of prisoners of war as an unbearable human burden in an immoral war.

Situations are portrayed as urgent—matters of life and death. Mark Rudd, a leader of the Weather Underground, stated that from 1965 to 1975 the fact that "our country was murdering millions of people" never left his mind. Action was "urgent and immediate."[24] Other militants focus on themselves or the people. For instance, environmentalists such as the Earth Liberation Front and Earth First! speak of fighting for our lives as "insane people . . . are consciously destroying our environment" and killing our earth.[25] The Web site of the Westboro Baptist Church in Topeka, Kansas, warns that "the modern militant homosexual movement," often referred to as "sodomites," poses

> a clear and present danger to the survival of America, exposing our nation to the wrath of God as in 1898 B.C. . . . When God has turned his back on a people, sodomites rule the land. America is on the cusp of that condition.[26]

Similarly, Samuel Adams, advocating independence from Great Britain before the Continental Congress, exclaimed, "Can you give the colonies any security that such a period [of equality] will ever come? No. *The period, countrymen, is already come!* The calamities were at our door. The rod of oppression was raised over us."[27] Stokely Carmichael of the Student Nonviolent Coordinating Committee (SNCC) warned his audience at the Oakland, California, Auditorium in 1972 that Armageddon was imminent:

> We are talking about the survival of black people—nothing else, nothing else, nothing else. And you must understand that. . . . Many of us feel—

many of our generation feel—they they're getting ready to commit genocide against us. Now many people say that's a horrible thing to say about
anybody, but if it's a horrible thing to say, then we should do as brother
Malcolm said, we should examine history.[28]

In his brief history of genocide, Carmichael related what white Europeans
had done to the red people in America, the helpless yellow people in
Hiroshima, the beautiful people in Vietnam, the Aztecs in South America,
and Africans turned into slaves. It was time to act with any means possible to
overcome unspeakable evil and to avoid disaster. As a member of the Weather
Underground stated, we must do whatever it takes, by any means necessary,
because "doing nothing in a period of repressive violence is itself a form of
violence."[29] The movement has a moral obligation to take action *now* on
behalf of innocent victims, often others rather than selves, before it is too late.

An Evil Force

Heinous evils require evil perpetrators who are lacking in morality, social
consciousness, and feeling. Although all social movements speak of terrible
evils and identify the devils responsible for perpetrating and prolonging them,
extremists see the devils as totally devoid of any socially redeeming value and
incapable of changing on their own or being converted through normal persuasive strategies.

Chapter 11 mentioned Thoreau's statement: "That government is best
which governs least." The statement is from his essay on "Resistance to Civil
Government," and in it he also declared: "That government is best which
governs not at all." While it is doubtful that many activists advocating violence have read Thoreau's essay, they would probably support his philosophy
about the lack of government enthusiastically.[30] Activists portray tyrannical,
corrupt, oppressive, monstrous government as the root cause of all that is evil
and threatening the nation's well-being. Samuel Adams labeled the colonial
government a "cruel and unforgiving despotism," while fellow colonialist
John Dickinson claimed Great Britain had an "inordinate passion for power"
with the goal of "enslaving the colonies."[31] Louis Beam, a white supremacist
who advocated the theories of guerrilla warfare in "Leaderless Resistance"
(1983), exclaimed: "Communism now represents a threat to no one in the
United States, while federal tyranny represents a threat to EVERYONE."[32]

Defenders of executed Oklahoma City bomber Timothy McVeigh portray a government and its agents "run amok" and "out of control" that must
be stopped at all cost.[33] Eric Rudolph, the convicted Atlanta bomber, wrote:
"When the regime in Washington legalized, sanctioned, and legitimized this
practice [abortion], they forfeited their legitimacy and moral authority to
govern."[34] He also stated: "The purpose of the attack [on Olympic Park] on
July 27th was to confound, anger, and embarrass the Washington Government in the eyes of the world for its abominable sanctioning of abortion on
demand." Force was necessary "to drag this monstrosity of a government
down to the dust."[35] For some activists, the government symbolizes all insti-

tutions. Members of the Weather Underground in the 1970s, for example, developed an overwhelming hatred of every institution, declared that none were innocent, and saw all of them—universities, churches, corporations, the military, and government—as legitimate targets for violence.

As technology has transformed the world into a global village, radicals have increasingly turned their attention to what the ELF calls "greedy earth-raping corporations" who care only about their bottom line.[36] After its multi-million dollar arson attack on an unfinished resort near Vail, Colorado, an e-mail from ELF warned, "We will be back if this greedy corporation continues to trespass into wild and unroaded areas."[37] The World Trade Organization and its annual meetings have become prized targets for activists who see it as the embodiment of "ruthless multinational corporations" that trample on human rights, destroy the environment, and exploit Asian workers. The WTO is a perfect target because it is secretive, suspicious, headquartered far away, and nobody knows who runs it.

When reading the writings and Web sites of extremists, it is difficult to determine whom they trust, let alone endorse. For example, Thomas Metzger's white supremacist White Aryan Resistance (WAR) Web site not only attacks all minorities derisively (particularly Jews, Hispanics, and African Americans), but the government (the Iron Heel) that is working feverishly to destroy the American way of life, the American people (sheeple), Democrats (the Niglet Party), Republicans (the Spiclet Party), "counterfeit Aryans," religious fundamentalists, and anyone who believes in "the great spook in the sky" (God).[38]

Inflammatory words to frame the exigence and its perpetrators are not unusual in the rhetoric of social movements. For instance, during the growing conflict over the war in Vietnam, Martin Luther King, Jr., was reported to have labeled it an "abominable, evil, and unjust war."[39] What is unusual in the rhetoric of violent extremists is the vehemence and inclusiveness with which the instigators are demonized. Moderate, nonviolent social movement elements believe they can and must convert legitimizers and those who control their destinies if they are to resolve exigencies. Trust remains a constant, even when strained. For example, following the horrendous bombing of Birmingham's Sixteenth Street Baptist Church in 1963 in which four young girls were killed, Martin Luther King, Jr., stated in his eulogy:

> These tragic deaths may lead our nation to substitute an aristocracy of character for an aristocracy of color. The spilt blood of these innocent children may cause the whole citizenry of Birmingham to transform the negative extremes of a dark past into the positive extremes of a bright future. Indeed, this tragic event may cause the whole South to come to terms with its conscience."[40]

It is difficult to imagine an extremist leader expressing such sentiments under any circumstances.

Radical social movement activists clearly establish an exigence that no socially conscious person can ignore. Activists meticulously craft an intolerably heinous situation perpetrated by unspeakably evil forces that, in Bitzer's words, "invites a response" but not "just any response." It invites, even demands, "a *fitting* response, a response that fits the situation."[41] How, then, do activists attempt to convince audiences that violence is a "fitting response" to the situation? As Stephen Browne writes

> The success of that struggle [for collective renewal] is dependent in large part on the ways violence gets represented, and we are becoming increasingly aware of just how complex and necessary are the rhetorical practices through which communities from Oklahoma to Beirut come to terms with human destruction.[42]

THE MOVEMENT IS MORALLY OBLIGATED TO RESPOND

Karl Wallace argues that "whether or not something is desirable depends on one's motives, goals or ends—upon that for the sake of which we act. We act to reduce certain painful or unpleasant tensions."[43] Radical activists claim they are morally obligated to counter the "tensions" of murder, atrocity, massacre, slavery, and torture, and their motive or goal is summed up in a single word, "justice."

A Classic Ideograph

Justice is a classic ideograph (see chapter 3).[44] The ideograph "is a high-order abstraction representing collective commitment to a particular but equivocal and ill-defined normative goal." What is most important for militants advocating violence to attain their goals is that the ideograph justice, a widely shared social value, "warrants the use of power, excuses behavior and belief which might otherwise be perceived as eccentric or antisocial, and guides behavior and belief into channels easily recognized by a community as acceptable and laudable."[45]

Justice appears in radical messages as a "high-order abstraction," as if no explanation or definition is required. In colonial America, for instance, Samuel Adams spoke of the "justice of our cause," and John Dickinson spoke of the obligation "to the rest of the world to make known the justice of our cause."[46] In an oration delivered on the Fourth of July, abolitionist William Lloyd Garrison demanded immediate emancipation of all slaves, and declared "That this demand is founded in justice, and is therefore irresistible."[47] Damon Hall, in his study of the ELF, writes that its "members are motivated by a moral duty to stop the culture of injustice and implement natural justice," a reference to the "historical dichotomy between positive [man-made] and natural law versions of justice."[48] As noted in chapter 8, Barry Goldwater created a political furor when he declared, "Extremism in defense of liberty is no vice, and moderation in the pursuit of justice is no virtue."[49]

Although the notion of justice may be quite abstract, its significance and impact for activists is not. Weather Underground member David Gilbert became convinced that he was "fighting for a just cause" and therefore "had to do something about what was going on."[50] That something was violence. Norman Olson of a Michigan militia warned that "when justice is removed from the equation, then the dynamic of revenge, retribution, and retaliation will take place."[51] Maintaining or achieving justice warrants any means necessary.

The context of the message reveals the motive of the persuader and provides a clearer meaning of justice. At his trial for the military-like raid on the federal arsenal at Harper's Ferry, radical abolitionist John Brown exclaimed:

> If it is deemed necessary that I should forfeit my life for the furtherance of the ends of justice, and mingle my blood further with the blood of my children and the blood of millions in this slave country whose rights are disregarded by wicked, cruel, and unjust enactments—I submit, so let it be done![52]

Elsie Lewis of the American Life League stated after the murder of Dr. Gunn in 1986:

> For the most part, when there is an unjust law, you obey it, and you try to change it. But when they are killing two million babies a year—it is so heinous an injustice. . . . Since 1973 a holocaust has been going on . . . I don't condemn those who did.[53]

We discover the activist's meaning of justice by learning what it is not—the denial or loss of liberty, freedom, equality, or life itself.

Militants see the pursuit of justice as a moral imperative (a moral obligation) that warrants any means necessary to achieve this end. A Web site defending the actions of Timothy McVeigh in Oklahoma City asks, "If the government is your enemy, then is killing the agents of the government morally wrong?" The answer is no because, "Patriots almost to a man and woman feel that both Ruby Ridge and the Branch Davidian Massacre were despotic acts of a government run amok, and acts which deserve punishment of the most severe nature."[54] Another Web site claims McVeigh and other like-minded people "felt the government had to pay for the Waco massacre."[55] Extremists in the pro-life movement argue that "if abortion is murder, then any means to prevent it—even murder—is morally justified."[56] For instance, the Army of God Web site claims that the killings of Dr. David Gunn, Dr. John Britton, and his "accomplices" were morally justified and legitimate: "We the undersigned, declare the justice of taking all godly action necessary, including the use of force, to defend innocent human life (born and unborn)."[57]

Karl Wallace writes: "The last class of good and values is that of the praiseworthy-blameworthy, the admirable-reprehensible."[58] Extremists employ this class of good and values by identifying and attacking the perpetrators of reprehensible evils and blaming them for the necessity of violent reactions and countermeasures. The violent actions of extremists thus become praiseworthy and admirable because they are punishing those who committed past evils; by doing so, they are mitigating future evil.

Transcendent Claims

Argument from transcendence provides radical activists with moral justifications for using violence. For instance, the ELF argues that natural law transcends positive or man-made law because it "recognizes not only the intrinsic worth but also the interconnectivity of all life, the fundamental principle of ecology." Therefore, the ELF has "a moral duty to stop the culture of injustice and implement natural justice."[59] This argument also enables the Animal Liberation Front (ALF) to argue that "it is quite reasonable to value the life of an innocent animal above the life of someone who goes around torturing helpless animals."[60] Innocent animals and the environment are protected by natural law, so it is imperative that the people "step outside of this societal law to enforce natural law."[61]

Argument from transcendence also enables persuaders to contrast greater and lesser evils or wrongs to justify violence. Animal rights activists argue that destroying buildings is lesser violence than burning animals with blowtorches and immersing them in scalding water. Similarly, Jan Carroll of the National Right to Life Committee offered no apologies for destruction of abortion clinics because the "violence that goes on inside the clinic is much more damaging to the moral fiber of this nation."[62] David Gilbert claimed the Weather Underground resorted to violence only "to stop the much greater violence that was going on" in Vietnam.[63] Others play a numbers game that contrasts greater and lesser evils. For example, Fr. David Trosch told the Mobile, Alabama, *Register* that "if 100 doctors need to die to save over 1 million babies a year, I see it as a fair trade."[64] These transcendent arguments from quality and quantity assert that while violence is evil, stopping a greater evil through violence is a comparative good and therefore advantageous.

A transcendent motive or purpose may justify violence. A pro-life advocate said attacks on clinics were like the riots of the civil rights movement, "equally wrong, but served a higher and nobler purpose in that they moved lethargic government leaders to act."[65] When John Brown addressed the jury at his trial, he claimed that if he had acted "in behalf of the rich, the powerful, the intelligent, the so-called great, . . . every man in this court would have deemed it an act worthy of reward rather than punishment." Instead, he had acted "in behalf of his [God's] despised poor," and it "was not wrong, but right" because he had acted for a higher and nobler purpose.[66] He had acted not out of self-interest or hatred but for the poorest of the poor who could not fight for themselves. For this higher, nobler purpose he was ready to die.

God's Will

Radical activists not only see violence as morally justified, the striving for a transcendent motive or cause, but also claim they are acting according to biblical injunctions and "exacting violence on behalf of God."[67] In his study of Nat Turner's *Confessions*, Stephen Browne writes that Turner's slave rebellion was transformed into a "moral drama" in which Turner was "literally dispossessed of individual will." His actions became "divine imperatives to act within his community in order to transform it," so "the revolt was not the work of corrupt man but of a very angry God."[68] Like Nat Turner, the Army of God manual declares that "Our Most Divine Sovereign Lord God requires that whosoever sheds man's blood, by man shall his blood be shed. Not out of hatred of you, but out of love for the persons you exterminate." The manual acknowledges that "vengeance belongs to God" but sees humans as His executioners. Activists portray themselves as God's humble instruments placed on earth to fulfill His grand design.[69] Michael Bray, editor of *Capital American Christian News*, writes that "abortion providers should be stoned to death" and that "with each blow . . . by the Grace of God, he may confess his sins and be saved before expiring."[70] The extremists are acting out of love and for the good of their victims, not out of hate or earthly vengeance—all on behalf of God.

History chronicles the slaughter of people once they are deemed to be other than human, and extremists add new chapters to these chronicles by using scripture to justify their actions. Pastor Fred Phelps of the Westboro Baptist Church declares "sodomites" are "worthy of death for their vile, depraved, unnatural sex practices" and cites Bible verses that call them "dogs because they are filthy, impudent and libidinous . . . natural brute beasts . . . sows wallowing in their own feces."[71] Sodomites' only hope is repentance and departing from their sin, but this is "not very likely, though, since God has given them up." Like Nat Turner, Phelps sees his mission as biblically sanctioned to end sodomy and to save the nation from ruin.

Violence is morally obligatory if the cause is just, the end justifies the means, the goal is transcendent, the motive is admirable and selfless, and the actor is obeying God. It becomes an admirable and praiseworthy act for which the actor is both blameless and honorable. Not to act would be dishonorable and unfaithful to God's word and assigned mission.

THE MOVEMENT TURNS TO VIOLENCE

John Bowers, Donovan Ochs, and Richard Jensen theorize that social movements must employ *petition* (see chapter 3), "all the normal discursive means of persuasion" through the courts, legislatures, boards of trustees, corporate and church hierarchies, before they resort to marches, demonstrations, and civil disobedience.[72] If activists do not first work through normal channels and means, more drastic strategies are unlikely to gain adherents. These admonitions echo those of Gandhi who discovered that "huge verbal output" was insufficient for achieving the great goals he proposed for India, but warned that "symbolic action must not be used as a substitute in place of words, but only as a supplement." He wrote:

> Since satyagraha is one of the most powerful methods of direct action, a *satyagrahi* exhausts all other means before he resorts to Satyagraha. He

will therefore constantly and continually approach the constituted authority, he will appeal to public opinion, educate public opinion, state his case
calmly and coolly before everyone who wants to listen to him, and only
after he has exhausted all these avenues will he resort to Satyagraha.[73]

If symbolic actions such as nonviolent civil disobedience must follow all normal means of persuasion, then violence must be chosen as the final strategy
to promote or resist change. It requires an offering of very good reasons
because most persons in and out of the movement do not accept it as warranted under any circumstances.

Although radical activists see themselves as fighting for a moral cause
that transcends all others and justifies all means necessary—including violence—they provide additional justifications for resorting to violence. Each
justification is based on the underlying premise that they were forced to use
violence; they had no other choice; and they were morally obligated to act
decisively and effectively.

The Last Resort

Extremists claim they tried all normal, peaceful, and legal means to
address a grave exigence marked by urgency and, only after remarkable
patience and restraint, did they turn to violence as a last resort. This is the
argument colonialist John Dickinson offered so eloquently in his 1775
address entitled "Declaration on Taking Up Arms:"

> We saw the misery to which such despotism would reduce us. We, for ten
> years, incessantly and ineffectually besieged the throne as supplicants; we
> reasoned, we remonstrated with Parliament in the most mild and decent
> language. . . . We have pursued every temperate, every respectful mea-
> sure. . . . Fruitless were all the entreaties, arguments, and eloquence of an
> illustrious band of the most distinguished peers and commoners, who
> nobly and strenuously asserted the justice of our cause.[74]

Dickinson and like-minded colonialists concluded that armed revolution was
the only means by which they could attain justice. Similarly, the Weather
Underground claimed that institutions had not only ignored nonviolent
efforts to end the war in Vietnam and bring about critical cultural changes but
had effectively eliminated all possibility of successful nonviolent protest.
Their position hardened after President Richard Nixon acknowledged that
there was continuing opposition to the Vietnam War on college campuses
and around the nation, and declared emphatically, "However, under no circumstances will I be affected whatever by it."[75]

Social movement leaders see denial of normal means to bring about
change as a cause, if not a justification, of violence. Martin Luther King, Jr., a
staunch advocate of nonviolence, quoted President John Kennedy's statement that "those who make peaceful revolutions impossible only make violent revolution inevitable."[76] On the opposite end of the scale, radical white
supremacist Matt Hale, founder of the World Church of the Creator, claimed

that "when free speech ends, violence often begins."[77] He felt vindicated in 1999 when the state of Illinois once again denied his application for a license to practice law and follower Benjamin Smith went on a two-state shooting rampage that left two dead and seven wounded. Militants argue that they have passed the point of petition and nonviolent civil disobedience and violence is the only viable option left to bring about or resist change. They are not to blame, institutions are.

Radicals ridicule and criticize the ineffective tactics of moderates. The Animal Liberation Front (ALF) relates that "M" (it never gives real or full names to avoid arrest and prosecution) always "felt stupid walking around in a circle, chanting a slogan, carrying a sign on a stick," actions that never seemed to accomplish anything.[78] It also tells the story of "Ramona" who was fed up with "all the bullshit you have to go through to bring about change." She wanted "to find a way to really *do* something. Now, she said, she'd decided. She wanted to join ALF" that freed animals and destroyed experimental laboratories. Although Malcolm X never took part in violence or called for it overtly, he, too, was fed up with the lack of action. He exclaimed to an audience in Detroit in 1964:

> As long as you got a sit-down philosophy, you will have a sit-down thought pattern. And as long as you think that old sit-down thought, you'll be in some kind of sit-down action. They'll have you sitting in everywhere. It's not so good to refer to what you're going to do as a sit-in. That right there castrates you. Right there it brings you down. What goes with it? Think of an example of someone sitting. An old woman can sit. An old man can sit. A chump can sit. A coward can sit. Anything can sit. Well, you and I have been sitting in long enough, and it's time today to start doing some standing and some fighting to back that up.[79]

The ELF criticizes the legal efforts of moderate environmental groups that do not challenge those responsible for environmental destruction. It warns that, unlike other environmental groups, it is "no longer adhering to a flawed, inconsistent 'nonviolent' ideology."[80]

Radicals claim that the exigence continues as moderates adhere to a philosophy of nonviolence. Eric Rudolph, in explaining why he bombed clinics, gay facilities, and the Atlanta Olympics, said that some claim the system works and will eventually reverse *Roe v. Wade*, "yet, in the meantime thousands [of babies] die everyday."[81] At the 1969 national convention of the Students for a Democratic Society (SDS), the Weathermen wrested control from moderates, claiming that years of protest had done little or nothing to stop the war. A member of the Weather Underground asserted that "the marches on Washington were up to 500,000, a million and they weren't really slowing down the United States effort [in Vietnam], it intensified."[82]

Extremists grow sick and tired of tactics that do not produce results; they are no longer willing to wait for gradual change. They form their own groups, or when possible take over others such as the SDS and SNCC, to conduct the struggle their way—which includes violence. They demand *real* change *now*, not in some promised time that never seems to come.

Producing Results

Radicals claim that nonviolent tactics—a rhetoric of petition—not only fail to alleviate exigencies but actually make matters worse. For instance, while protestors employ normal methods in unceasing efforts to win hearts and minds, government oppression increases, the destruction of the environment and life continues unabated, and the mass murder of children persists. Eric Rudolph, the Atlanta bomber, wrote, "I ask these peaceful Christian law-abiding Pro-Life citizens, is there any point at which all of the legal remedies will not suffice and you would fight to end the massacre of children?"[83]

Militants argue that institutions are not moved by patient and reasonable nonviolent protest; instead, they unleash soldiers and police, attack protestors, and imprison activists. Rev. Donald Spitz, head of Pro-Life Virginia, said, "The government is becoming more and more repressive of antiabortionists, silencing their free-speech rights" and forcing some to kill abortion doctors.[84] The results among members are feelings of alienation and despair, of being manipulated, and expecting to die for the cause without making a difference. They believe they have been coerced to employ violence to produce results; more talk and more words leads only to more persecution.

Unlike petition and civil disobedience that are ineffective, make matters worse, or take years to produce meaningful results, extremists contend that selective violence—called catastrophic events by the Weather Underground—gets attention and shows "the enemy that we are serious about defending what is sacred."[85] It generates results. The ELF argues, for instance, that "monkeywrenching" (primarily arson and destruction of logging and construction equipment) "in one night" can accomplish what years of political and legal battles could not do.[86]

Violence energizes social movements by demonstrating character and giving them "a sudden zest for fighting."[87] There is a strong sense of ego-enhancement in radical messages. Activists speak of the bravery exhibited by those who confront evil forces with all means necessary to further the cause. Colonialist Dickinson, for example, declared that "honor, justice, and humanity forbid us tamely to surrender that freedom which we received from our gallant ancestors."[88] The Weather Underground romanticized violence as a way of life by claiming that institutions were forcing them to be outlaws like Bonnie and Clyde and Butch Cassidy and the Sundance Kid[89] (all of whom died with guns blazing, never backing down to authority or overwhelming odds; they continue to be larger-than-life heroes in popular culture).

Dying for the cause may be the highest calling of the radical activist. The Eye on Hate Web site, for instance, relates that "to the end, McVeigh [the convicted and executed Oklahoma City bomber] never implicated the others," and "You might say that he 'consecrated' his life to the cause. And in death, martyrdom would be the overriding factor for McVeigh." He "died much as Earl Turner [the mythical hero in *The Turner Diaries*] died, believing that he had given the ultimate sacrifice and seeing in those who befriended and assisted him what Turner saw in his brethren of the 'order.'"[90] Above all, radicals such as McVeigh not only believe strongly but also act strongly. White supremacist leader Dennis Mahon exclaimed: "Timothy McVeigh is my hero. Wish we had a thousand more like him. He took action." Radical martyrs become mythical heroes for their causes. White Aryan Resistance celebrates James Earl Ray month each January to honor the "lone wolf" who brought down the hated Martin Luther King, Jr., with a single shot.[91] Under a column entitled "Hail Eric Rudolph," contributors to a Web site call him a "true hero" and ask, "Would it be a good idea to celebrate 'Eric Rudolph' Holiday on the same day when blacks have their Martin Luther King Day?"[92] Risking one's life for the cause in violent action is seen as more admirable and praiseworthy than taking part in ineffective nonviolent civil disobedience. The cult of the heroic lone figure who willingly stands up for justice, uses any means necessary, and risks life itself remains strong in American mythology.

THE MOVEMENT MUST DEFEND SELVES AND OTHERS

Karlyn Campbell writes that "it is necessary to distinguish between those who advocate aggressive violence and those who advocate violent self-defense or counterviolence."[93] Those who resort to counterviolence recognize, she writes, "that such means must be *justified* by particular circumstances" that usually involve prior violence by others—institutions or countermovements in the case of social movements. This justification is useful to social activists because it is likely to resonate with U.S. audiences. As Campbell notes, "Our national rhetoric has sought to legitimize counterviolence on numerous occasions so that a critical distinction is not without precedent." The Gulf of Tonkin incident that justified the escalation of U.S. military involvement in Vietnam, the invasion of Kuwait that justified the first Gulf War, and the terrorist attacks in New York and Washington, D.C., that justified the invasions of Afghanistan and Iraq come readily to mind in institutional rhetoric.

Counterviolence

A frequent claim of radical activists is that institutions resorted to violence first, forcing them to retaliate. In one line of argument, militants portray themselves as victims who merely respond to violence with violence. They have a legitimate, moral right to fight back. For example, Dickinson said Great Britain was attempting to enslave the colonies through violence and "thereby rendered it necessary for us" to abandon appeals and take up arms.[94] Environmentalists see themselves as being "compelled to fight back," while those defending McVeigh claim he was merely following the "ground rules" of a "despotic government."[95] One Web site says simply, "There is nothing wrong with violence. Our detractors use it every chance they get."[96] Retaliatory violence is warranted because social institutions have sanctioned violence as a legitimate means of bringing about or resisting change. What is legitimate or good for institutions must be legitimate or good for the social movement.

A second line of argument is that the horrific nature of violent acts instigated by institutional agents warrant equally violent responses. For instance, the Weather Underground said the murder of Black Panther leader Fred Hampton by police showed the government was willing to use violence in Chicago as well as in Vietnam, and "There's no way to be committed to nonviolence in the middle of the most violent society history has ever created."[97] Timothy McVeigh, white supremacist Dennis Mahon, and militia leaders claim the FBI's actions at Ruby Ridge and the ATF actions that led to the fiery death of seventy-five Branch Davidians at Waco, Texas, show that "any and all methods are legitimate when it comes to saving your nation."[98] Not only is violence justified, but activists are morally obligated to make the government pay for its violent acts.

Thus, extremists take on a moral responsibility for which they are not initially responsible. They serve as the executioner of institutional evil and violence, an obligation they did not choose and for which they cannot be blamed. Since institutions make counterviolence necessary, and God wills it, radical violence is justified and praiseworthy.

Self-Defense

Society recognizes the legitimacy and moral acceptability of self-defense when the circumstances warrant an extreme reaction to violence or threat of violence. As Campbell notes, "Conventionally, we do not think of self-defense as a form of violence," but it is typically a form of counterviolence.[99]

Militants most often threaten or reserve the right to use violent self-defense rather than resort to it, but the media and institutions portray threats as the real thing. Malcolm X and the Black Panthers, for instance, spoke of the "ballot or the bullet" and carried weapons, but neither were guilty of violence even though Malcolm X and many Black Panther leaders met violent deaths. Black Panther leader Fred Hampton was killed in a hail of police gunfire while he slept in his apartment. Police originally claimed he was firing at them from his window and they acted in self-defense, but subsequent investigations proved they were the instigators. Stokely Carmichael was branded a dangerous radical because of his black power philosophy and statements such as, "We have no alternative but to fight, whether we like it or not. On every level in this country black people have *got* to fight, *got* to fight, *got* to fight."[100] A more accurate characterization of Carmichael's threats comes when he quotes Black Panther leader Huey P. Newton's statement, "As the racist police escalate the war in our communities against black people, we reserve the right to self-defense and maximum retaliation." A reading of Carmichael's speeches reveals an emphasis on preparing, uniting, organizing, community-building, and creating a defense fund if retaliation becomes necessary "to fight for our humanity."

There are radical leaders and elements that encourage or carry out violent self-defense. In his Fourth of July oration, Garrison counseled slaves "not to fight for their freedom, both on account of the hopelessness of the effort, and because it is rendering evil for evil." Minutes later he compared the causes of the American Revolution, such as a three-penny tax on tea and impressments of American seamen, and asked "how much blood may be lawfully spilt in resisting the principle, that one human being has a right to the body and soul of another, on account of the color of his skin?"[101] When the ELF declares that "environmental protection is a matter of self-defense" and that "we will stand up and fight for our lives against this iniquitous civilization until its reign of terror is forced to end," its history of violent acts such as arson takes a position beyond the mere threat of retaliation.[102] The emphasis in its messages, however, is legitimate self-defense—acting only when acted upon. Its Web site gives this hypothetical situation that emphasizes self-defense:

> If someone is going to shoot you in the back six times, do you nicely, kindly ask him to shoot you only three or four times? No, you freakin' turn around and punch them in the face, grab the gun from them, and shove it up their ass![103]

Violent self-defense permeates our history and mythology and is portrayed as justifiable and praiseworthy. It is a theme in popular books, movies, and television series. Virtually every presidential speech that offers good reasons for military actions assures the public that such actions are self-defense; we act only after being acted upon. Self-defense is legal by statute and justifies shootings by police officers, shopkeepers, home owners, and others. Why, then, is violence not a legitimate option for those trying to eliminate a deadly societal evil when all other means have failed?

Justifiable Homicide

Justifiable homicide, like self-defense, is based on *circumstances* when it becomes a moral obligation to resist deadly force with equally deadly force to defend others. Theologians and ethicists, for instance, distinguish between just and unjust wars. Like self-defense, institutional agents, police officers, members of the military, and common folk justify violence by arguing that it was warranted to prevent harm to others.

When movement extremists use justifiable homicide as a reason for violence, they often set forth hypothetical circumstances that would warrant such actions. For instance, John Trochmann of the Militia of Montana commented: "When someone comes to destroy my family, I won't have a choice. If that were ever to happen, I would defend till the last drop of blood."[104] Fr. Trosch reasoned: "If a person with a shotgun happened upon the scene of massive butchering of innocent children, and failed to act with deadly force, as quickly as possible, he would be committing a grave offense against God."[105] Other pro-life extremists argue that homicide is justified because the unborn are being murdered. Rev. Spitz called the killer of Dr. Slepian in New York a hero because, "We as Christians have a responsibility to protect the innocent from being murdered. Whoever shot the shot protected the children."[106]

Institutions do not always accept justifiable homicide as grounds for violent acts committed by or in the name of social movements. When Fr. Trosch attempted to place an ad in newspapers describing the killing of abortion doctors as justifiable homicide, his bishop censured him and relieved him of his pastoral duties. At about the same time, the Army of God circulated petitions after the murders of Drs. Gunn and Britton arguing that the acts were justifiable homicide. A Florida judge rejected this argument, ruling that "the defense was not valid because it did not meet the standards of Florida homicide law, which is cited only in cases of self-defense or when a defendant killed a third person.[107]

It is difficult to make the claim of justifiable homicide when neither the perpetrator nor the people are threatened directly. Abortion is legal and does not affect any person once born. A Hummer may get poor gas mileage, immigrants may move into neighborhoods and do work many of us do not want to perform, and a resort may take the place of trees and change a mountain view, but they do not threaten the lives of extremists or others they are protecting.

A Just War

Allusions to and declarations of war are common in the rhetoric of social movements. Most often they are used metaphorically, expressing an implied comparison, likeness, or similarity to violent conflicts rather than actual violent confrontations. For instance, when Cesar Chavez exclaimed: "We're declaring war, war on the pesticides that are poisoning and killing our people," he was alluding to the nationwide grape boycott and normal persuasive efforts such as demonstrations, picketing, speeches, and a video entitled *The Wrath of Grapes* that was sold to churches and other socially conscious groups around the country.[108] Stephen Browne writes that abolitionist Angelina Grimke's "battle" was a "war of words, a *logomachia*, wherein good and evil vie for the convictions of the people."[109] Chavez, Grimke, and other social movement leaders use warlike terms such as critical battle, fight, battleground, enemy lines, and final assault to emphasize their dedication to a cause and its serious nature, but they do not use warlike tactics to bring about or resist change.

Such is not the case with extremist elements of social movements. They do not speak of war as a metaphor—a mere figure of speech—but espouse and practice the real thing when they declare a violent revolution or holy war against the persons and institutions they deem responsible for heinous evils. Following the violent confrontations with police during the 1968 Democratic National Convention in Chicago, members of the Weather Underground became convinced that "the radical movement was ready for revolution" and "prepared for a violent assault on the institutions of state power."[110] When they declared a state of war against the symbols and institutions of U.S. injustice and used the slogan "Bring the War Home!" they intended to "make the war [and its 'carnage'] visible in the United States." Small groups of Weathermen bombed hundreds of symbols and buildings, including the U.S. Senate, the Pentagon, the State Department, and Fort Dix. Extremist pro-lifers such as the Army of God justify attacks on abortion clinics and personnel by claiming that all other options expired following the imprisonment and suffering of its "God-fearing men and women" who tried passive resistance. The abortion industry responded to nonviolence by hardening its already "blackened, jaded hearts."[111]

Invoking the image of warfare justifies the taking of human lives in the name of a just cause. A Weather Underground member explained their bombings by stating, "We believed we were at war, and we weren't into symbolic acts of protest. We wanted to leave a crater. In a war somebody has to die."[112] Another Web site justifies violent "resistance to a despotic government" by citing Rush Limbaugh's statement that war is about "killing people and breaking things."[113] This site also notes that war has "rules about whom you kill, whom you target, what you do with innocents and noncombatants, what you do with prisoners of war." The Weather Underground tried to avoid harming innocent people by sending warnings to newspapers and other sources in time to evacuate areas. Unfortunately for Robert Fassnacht, the bomb at the University of Wisconsin went off prematurely before any warning could be given.

Indiscriminate killing is rarely warranted, but targeting the enemy is. Thus, the infamous "Nuremberg Files" Web site of pro-life extremists calls providers "baby butchers, lists names, photos, addresses, and license plate numbers, contains wanted posters, and crosses off names of those killed."[114] The day after the execution style murders of the husband and mother of Judge Joan Lefkow in Chicago in March 2005, some white supremacist Web sites praised the killings with the exclamation "Rahowa!" an acronym for "Holy War," and a Ku Klux Klan site said, "Too bad she [Judge Lefkow] wasn't home too!"[115]

When social movement organizations or so-called lone wolves determine that violence is the only means to bring about or resist change, there are no limits on the actions taken and the tragedies produced. Former Weatherman Brian Flanagan warned in an interview a few years ago that "if you think you have the moral high ground, you can do some pretty dreadful things."[116] If violence becomes widespread and is deemed a danger to society, institutions may label it "terrorism" to justify any means necessary to destroy the threat; there is likely to be little opposition from the public or moderate social movement organizations. If a social movement becomes committed to violence, the result may be a civil war or a revolution in which persuasion becomes a mere sideline to full-scale violence or guerrilla warfare. Unless institutions are ready to collapse or the movement receives significant outside help, such as during the American Revolution, the violence is unlikely to be successful. Recall Martin Luther King, Jr.'s warning that social movements sometimes "fail to see that no internal revolution has ever succeeded in overthrowing a government by violence unless the government has already lost the allegiance and effective control of its armed forces."[117]

CONCLUSIONS

This chapter analyzed the messages of U.S. extremists from the colonial period to the present to discover the "rhetoric of good reasons" created to justify the use of violence in the furtherance of what they believe is a just and moral cause. The defense for violent action is an unbearable exigence (murder, slavery, destruction of the environment, holocaust) perpetrated by an unreconcilable evil force (usually the government) that demands a fitting response. If the situation is a matter of life and death, literally the survival of self or others, how can any means be ruled out?

When extremists cross the line from verbal or symbolic violence to actual violence when humans are injured or killed and/or buildings and machinery are destroyed, they face a major rhetorical challenge. They must persuade audiences that they and their extreme methods offer legitimate means to bring about urgently needed change. They must be regarded as legitimate if they are to gain support, sympathy, and influence within the movement—and to avoid public backlash and institutional suppression. Extremists must adjust the idea of violence to people and people to the idea of violence. This is a tall rhetorical order.

Theoretically, extremists have three major audiences for their persuasive efforts: institutions, the public, and social movement members and sympathizers. However, if we accept Lloyd Bitzer's argument that "properly speaking, a rhetorical audience consists only of those persons who are capable of being influenced by discourse and of being mediators of change,"[118] extremists have only one audience, those who believe in and support the social movement's cause and ideology, and this audience is factionalized.

Institutions are often the targets of violent acts and can sustain their powers and legitimacy with the public only by showing that they are in control, will not surrender to threats and violence perpetrated by dangerous social radicals, and are capable of maintaining social order and tranquility. They are also assigned the task of preserving sacred doctrines and social structures. Violent acts break laws and threaten doctrine and structure, so suppression is the institution's "fitting response" to violent situations from whatever source. All extremist rhetoric is rejected out of hand.

History shows that the public not only accepts but also demands that institutions act with all means necessary to suppress dangerous extremists, particularly when they and their actions are branded as terrorists and terrorism. There was little outrage after any of the following events: when John

Brown went to the gallows; anarchists were executed and imprisoned after the Haymarket Riot; civil rights leaders and sympathizers were killed and black churches were bombed; protesting students were killed on the Kent State University Campus; and the Branch Davidian compound went up in flames with dozens of men, women, and children inside. The public was relieved when the FBI and police agencies captured members of the Weather Underground, Timothy McVeigh, and Eric Rudolph. Few people will attend or access, let alone be influenced by, radical speeches, writings, and Internet sites. Words and arguments cannot overcome the horrific nature of extremist violence that get widespread media attention because of fears of where such violence will lead.

Although extremists may be unable to persuade institutions and the public that violence is warranted, theorists agree that extremist rhetoric and violent acts often succeed in making moderate elements of movements more acceptable and may lead to changes that would not have taken place were radicals not active in the cause. William Lloyd Garrison seems reasonable and less a threat when compared to John Brown, or the American Federation of Labor when compared to the Molly Maguires, or Martin Luther King, Jr., when compared to Stokely Carmichael, or the SDS when compared to the Weather Underground.

Unlike their moderate counterparts who maintain faith in the system and their ability to persuade people and institutions to bring about urgently needed change, extremists have lost faith in the system and the potential of persuasion to bring about meaningful results in a worsening situation. Moderates are willing to wait because change is coming, even if painfully slow, but extremists are out of patience and want significant change now. While moderates condemn all forms of real violence (including war) on philosophical, moral, and pragmatic grounds, extremists believe that the exigence with its high degree of urgency warrants using all means necessary—murder, bombings, arson—to attain justice.

If extremists cannot convince movement moderates that violence is warranted, who are they addressing? The answer appears to be those who claim not to support violence but understand why some resort to it, those who accept violence under certain circumstances, other extremists, and themselves. Self-persuasion may be a primary function of offering "good reasons" for violence.

Extremists claim they have a moral obligation—a moral imperative—to respond with violence to achieve justice, a widely shared social value that warrants the use of power. This use of power is laudable when used for moral purposes and to punish evil doers. Arguments from transcendence compare man-made law to natural law, greater and lesser evils, greater and lesser goods, and transcendent motives. Extremists claim to have a higher and nobler purpose than ordinary and institutional uses of violence. They are acting according to God's will and biblical injunctions and out of love and concern for their victims, not revenge or personal gain.

Extremists claim they were forced to use violence. They had no choice after petition proved ineffective and counterproductive. Violence is a last resort entered into reluctantly when institutions deny the usual means of persuasion and respond to nonviolence with violence and suppression. Years of nonviolent civil disobedience have produced few meaningful results and were degrading. They can wait no longer to resolve the unbearable exigence. They argue that violence gets results, energizes the movement, counteracts despair and feelings of ineptitude, and produces heroes who are willing to suffer and die for the cause.

Extremists claim their violence is counterviolence because institutions employed violence first and committed horrific acts against people, animals, and the environment. Thus, they are morally obligated to retaliate, and this makes their actions admirable and praiseworthy. They are acting in self-defense that has a long history of legitimacy in our society and is protected by statutes. Similarly, they frame actions as justifiable homicide because acts are based on circumstances that warrant citizen action to stop evil. Some see counterviolence as a just war against evil forces and for a greater good. They not only talk the talk but also take up arms in a just cause to bring about revolutionary change.

Although extremist elements of social movements offer an impressive array of "good reasons" for their violent actions tied directly to shared social values, traditions, and myths, they rarely overcome the philosophic and pragmatic opposition of moderates and other nonviolent extremists. Some of the strongest condemnations of violent actions come from within the movement. Fundamentally, the movement sees violence as immoral and counterproductive because it replaces all normal means of persuasion and shuts off the possibility of dialogue with legitimizers and institutional agents. The good reasons offered so eloquently may be designed, consciously and unconsciously, to convince extremists themselves that their violent and sometimes deadly acts are warranted for the cause and worth the risks posed to their freedom and lives. Self-persuasion is essential if they are to sustain efforts they believe are essential to resolve exigencies and overcome evil forces.

Notes

[1] Richard J. Jensen and John C. Hammerback, eds., *The Words of Cesar Chavez* (College Station: Texas A & M University Press, 2002): 162–163.

[2] Henry D. Thoreau, "Resistance to Civil Government," *Walden and Resistance to Civil Government,* William Rossi, ed. (New York: W.W. Norton, 1992): 227, 233.

[3] Martin Luther King, Jr., *The Autobiography of Martin Luther King, Jr.,* Clayborne Carson, ed. (New York: Warner, 1998): 225.

[4] Jensen and Hammerback, 58.

[5] Jensen and Hammerback, 168.

[6] King, 330.

[7] Jensen and Hammerback, 96.

[8] Jensen and Hammerback, 96.

[9] Martha Solomon, "Ideology as Rhetorical Constraint: The Anarchist Agitation of 'Red Emma' Goldman," *Quarterly Journal of Speech* 74 (May 1988): 185.

[10] http://www.aaplog.org/newsviol.htm, accessed 15 September 2006.

[11] *The Sunday Visitor*, 7 August 1994, 1, 5.

[12] "U.S. Militia Movement," Senate Subcommittee on Terrorism, 16 June 1995, recorded by C-SPAN.

[13] John McCormick, "Rising Tide of Zealotry," *Newsweek*, 30 August 1993, 59.

[14] http://lifepeace.tripod.com/., accessed 25 July 2006.

[15] *Time*, 28 November 1988, 24.

[16] "The Fatal Bombing that Historians Ignore," *The Chronicle of Higher Education*, 17 August 2001, B24.

[17] "The Fatal Bombings that Historians Ignore," B7.

[18] Robert A. Francesconi, "James Hunt, the Wilmington 10, and Institutional Legitimacy," *Quarterly Journal of Speech* 68 (February 1982): 49–50.

[19] Donald C. Bryant, "Rhetoric: Its Functions and Its Scope," *Quarterly Journal of Speech* 39 (December 1953): 413.

[20] Karl R. Wallace, "The Substance of Rhetoric: Good Reasons," *Quarterly Journal of Speech* 49 (October 1963): 239–249.

[21] Wallace, 243

[22] Lloyd F. Bitzer, "The Rhetorical Situation," *Philosophy & Rhetoric* 1 (Winter 1968): 6.

[23] http:www.prochoice.org/about_naf/index.html; Hall Quinn, "Fighting to Free Animals," *Macleans*, 3 December 1984, 58.

[24] *The Weather Underground*, a documentary by Sam Green and Bill Siegel recorded from PBS television station WTTW (Chicago), 27 April 2004.

[25] Jennifer Foote, "Trying to Take Back the Planet," *Newsweek*, 5 February 1990, 24.

[26] http://www.godhatesfags.com/main/faq.html, accessed 26 July 2006.

[27] James Andrews and David Zarefsky, eds, *American Voices: Significant Speeches in American History 1640–1945* (New York: Longman, 1989): 74.

[28] Mitchell Goodman, ed., "Stokely Carmichael: A Declaration of War," *The Movement Toward a New America: The Beginnings of a Revolution* (Philadelphia: Pilgrim Press, 1970): 180.

[29] *The Weather Underground*.

[30] Thoreau, 226.

[31] Andrews and Zarefsky, 69, 61.

[32] http://www.louisbeam.com/leaderless.htm, accessed 27 July 2006.

[33] http://www.lizmichael.com/mcveigh.htm, accessed 15 September 2006; www.commondreams.org/cgi-bin/print.cgi?file=/headlines01/08it-04.htm, accessed 1 April 2005.

[34] http://www.crimelibrary.com/terrorists_spies/terrorists/eric_rudolph/10.html, accessed 26 July 2006.

[35] http://www.boston.com/news/globe/editorial_opinion/oped/articles/2005/04/15/eric_rudolphs_legacy/, accessed 26 July 2006.

[36] http://en.wikipedia.org/wiki/Timeline_of_Earth_Liberation_Front_actions, accessed 26 July 2006.

[37] http://www.factnet.org/cults/earth_liberation_front/vail_fire.html, accessed 26 July 2006.

[38] http://www.resist.com/updates/aryanupdate11.28.99.htm, accessed 26 July 2006; http://www.resist.com/updates/aryanupdate11.14.99.htm, accessed 26 July 2006; http://www.resist.com/positions/Government.html, accessed 26 July 2006.

[39] *Weather Underground*.

[40] King, 232.

[41] Bitzer, 10.

[42] Stephen H. Browne, "'This Unparalleled and Inhuman Massacre': The Gothic, the Sacred, and the Meaning of Nat Turner," *Rhetoric & Public Affairs* 3 (Fall 2000): 328.

[43] Wallace, 244.

[44] Michael Calvin McGee, "The 'Ideograph': A Link between Rhetoric and Ideology," *The Quarterly Journal of Speech* 66 (February 1980): 7.

[45] McGee, 15.

[46] Andrews and Zarefsky, 71, 61.

[47] William Lloyd Garrison, *Selections from the Writings and Speeches of William Lloyd Garrison* (New York: Negro Universities Press, 1968): 188.

[48] Damon M. Hall, "Linguistic Sabotage: The Earth Liberation Front and the Appropriation of Society's Key Terms," unpublished master's thesis, Purdue University, 2004, 78, 19.

[49] http://www.lizmichael.com/mcveigh.htm, accessed 26 July 2006. Goldwater's statement continues to be used by proponents of a number of causes, as on this Web site.

[50] *The Weather Underground.*

[51] "U.S. Militia Movement."

[52] Andrews and Zarefsky, 262.

[53] Judith Adler Hennessee, "Inside a Right-to-Life Mind," *Mademoiselle,* April 1986, 261.

[54] http://www.lizmichael.com/mcveigh.htm, accessed 26 July 2006.

[55] http://eyeonhate.com/mcveigh/mcveigh6/html, accessed 11 April 2005.

[56] David Van Biema, "Apologists for Murder," *Time,* 15 August, 1994, 39.

[57] http://www.armyofgod.com/defense.html, accessed 26 July 2006.

[58] Wallace, 245.

[59] Hall, 48, 78.

[60] Hal Quinn, "Fighting to Free Animals," *Macleans,* 3 December, 1984, 58.

[61] Earth Liberation Front, *FAQ's 6;* Hall, 52.

[62] Randy Frame, "Violence against Abortion Clinics Escalates Despite the Opposition of Pro-life Leaders," *Christianity Today,* 1 February 1985, 46.

[63] *The Weather Underground.*

[64] John McCormick, "Rising Tide of Zealotry," *Newsweek,* 30 August 1993, 59.

[65] *Christianity Today,* 1 February 1985, 46.

[66] Andrews and Zarefsky, 262–263.

[67] http://www.publiceye.org/rightist/rudolph.html, accessed 26 July 2006.

[68] Browne, 325–326; see http://www.pbs.org/wgbh/aia/part3/3h500t.html for the text of *The Confessions of Nat Turner,* accessed 21 August 2006.

[69] "Anti-abortion Extremists: The Army of God and Justifiable Homicide," http://www.prochoice.org/about_abortion/violence/army_god.html, accessed 11 August 2006.

[70] Van Biema, 39.

[71] www.godhatesfags.com, accessed 26 July 2006.

[72] John W. Bowers, Donovan J. Ochs, and Richard J. Jensen, *The Rhetoric of Agitation and Control,* 2nd ed. (Long Grove, IL: Waveland Press, 1993): 20.

[73] Allen H. Merriman, "Symbolic Action in India: Gandhi's Nonverbal Persuasion," *Quarterly Journal of Speech* 61 (October 1975): 291, 292.

[74] Andrews and Zarefsky, 62.

[75] *The Weather Underground.*

[76] King, 340.

[77] "Hate.com: Extremists on the Internet" (Princeton, NJ: Films of the Humanities and Sciences, 1998).

[78] "Human Bondage," *Rolling Stone,* 3 March 1988, 90–91.

[79] Malcolm X, "The Ballot or the Bullet," speech delivered in Detroit, April 3, 1964, from an audio recording.

[80] http://www.csmonitor.com/2002/0926/p01s01-ussc.html, accessed 27 July 2006.

[81] http://www.crimelibrary.com/terrorists_spies/terrorists/eric_rudolph/10.html, accessed 27 July 2006.

[82] *The Weather Underground.*

[83] http://www.crimelibrary.com/terrorists_spies/terrorists/eric_rudolph/10.html, accessed 27 July 2006.

[84] Kim Bolan, Mark Miller, and Sarah Van Boven, "Abortion Wars Come Home," *Newsweek* 9 November 1998, 34.

[85] *Weather Underground.*

[86] Hall, 60.

[87] *The Weather Underground.*

[88] Andrews and Zarefsky, 64.

[89] *Weather Underground.*

[90] http://www.eyeonhate.com/mcveigh/mcveigh6.html, accessed 27 July 2006.

[91] "Aryan Update," www.resist.com, accessed 30 January 2000.

[92] http://www.rightwingnews.com/crackpots/rudolph.php, accessed 27 July 2006.

[93] Karlyn Kohrs Campbell, "The Rhetoric of Radical Black Nationalism: A Case Study in Self-Conscious Criticism," *Central States Speech Journal* 22 (Fall 1971): 158.

[94] Andrews and Zarefsky, 61.

[95] http://www.lizmichael.com/mcveigh.htm, accessed 27 July 2006.

[96] http://www.rightwingnews.com/crackpots/rudolph.php, accessed 27 July 2006.

[97] *Weather Underground.*

[98] http://eyeonhate.com/mcveigh/mcveigh6/html, accessed 11 April 2005.

[99] Campbell, 158.

[100] Goodman, 181.

[101] Garrison, 189–190.

[102] http://www.splcenter.org/intel/intelreport/article.jsp?aid=82, accessed 27 July 2006; Hall, 49–50.

[103] www.earthliberationfront.com, accessed 21 December 2000.

[104] "U.S. Militia Movement."

[105] Van Biema, 39.

[106] "Preachers of Hate," *The Progressive*, June 1985, 8.

[107] http://www.prochoice.org/about_abortion/violence/army_god.html, accessed 28 July 2006.

[108] *The Wrath of Grapes*, United Farm Workers of America, AFL-CIO, 1986.

[109] Stephen Browne, "Encountering Angelina Grimke: Violence, Identity, and the Creation of Radical Community," *Quarterly Journal of Speech* 82 (February 1996): 65.

[110] Milton Viorst, *Fire in the Streets: America in the 1960s* (New York: Simon and Schuster, 1969): 468; *The Weather Underground.*

[111] http://www.prochoice.org/about_abortion/violence/army_god.html, accessed 28 July 2006.

[112] "The Fatal Bomb that Historians Ignore," B24.

[113] http://www.lizmichael.com/mcveigh.htm, accessed 27 July 2006.

[114] Rene Sanchez, "Jury: Anti-Abortion Web Site Threat to Doctors," Lafayette, Indiana *Journal and Courier,* 3 February 1999, A3.

[115] http://www.msnbc.msn.com/id/7129533, accessed 15 September 2006.

[116] *The Weather Underground.*

[117] King, 330.

[118] Bitzer, 8.

CHAPTER 13

The Use of Terrorism by Social Movements

Each edition of this book has been unique because social movements have persuaded in varying ways over the years. Early editions featured chapters on obscenity and songs of protest, but it is now more important to discuss the use of violence and terror by social movements. The Bush Administration took the position that 9/11 "changed everything" and required Americans to engage in a permanent war on terror that has to date included military operations in Afghanistan and Iraq. Moreover, the Palestinian group Hamas, long branded by the world as a terrorist organization, won a landslide electoral victory in January 2006 to topple the Fatah party from power after four decades and drastically altered the prospects for peace in the Middle East. It is prudent in today's world to understand more fully and completely how terrorist acts make sense to some people.

DEFINING "TERRORISM"

What is "terrorism" and why should it be covered in a book on social movements? Definitions abound, and each empowers some interests over others. Our purpose is neither to favor movements nor restrict them but rather to help you understand the complex persuasive interactions that play out again and again—with the "good guys" and "bad guys" sometimes showing up in unexpected places. If we are to achieve that purpose in our discussion of terrorism, we must avoid simplistic definitions that presume terrorism is any violence done by the "bad guys" or suggest that terrorism is nothing more than a label applied to violence for political advantage.

Political and legal communication scholar Joseph S. Tuman finds Alex P. Schmid's definition useful for studying terrorism as communication.[1] Schmid's definition is lengthy because it is based on his review of previous definitions and incorporates their components:

Terrorism is an anxiety-inspiring method of repeated violent action, employed by (semi-) clandestine individual, group or state actors, for idiosyncratic, criminal, or political reasons, whereby—in contrast to assassination—the targets of violence are not the main targets. The immediate human victims of violence are generally chosen randomly (targets of opportunity) or selectively (representative or symbolic targets) from a target population, and serve as message generators. Threat- and violence-based communication processes between terrorist (organization), (imperiled) victims, and main targets are used to manipulate the main target (audience), turning it into a target of terror, a target of demands, or a target of attention, depending on whether intimidation, coercion, or propaganda is primarily sought.[2]

Schmid's definition of terrorism works after two decades because it draws several important distinctions. First, it differentiates assassinations (the violent removal of opposition personnel) from terrorism that violently attacks a target audience to inspire anxiety intended to bring pressure on the opposition personnel. Second, it allows for both "terrorism from below" against the powerful and "terrorism from above" by the powerful to suppress opposition. Third, Schmid's definition of the terror strategy provides for choices by potential terrorists: the three kinds of actors provide for organizational choices, the three kinds of reasons provide choices of objectives, and the kinds of audience provide opportunities for audience analysis, selection, and adaptation. In short, Schmid's definition of terrorism meshes with Lloyd Bitzer's model of the rhetorical situation because anyone contemplating terrorism must make rhetorical decisions about the exigence, about the main audience capable of resolving it, and of the susceptibility of that audience to pressure from repeated violent acts against selected targets.

The experiences of the last two decades suggest some enhancements to Schmid's definition. "Anxiety-inspiring" seems inadequate to describe the aftermath from bombings of trains, planes, and automobiles. Such events inspire *fear*, which destabilizes our beliefs about safety and order. Chapter 6 discussed Abraham Maslow's democratic character structure (that perceives the world as generally safe) and his authoritarian character structure (that perceives the world as generally dangerous). Terrorist acts have the potential to affirm the authoritarian worldview, to destabilize the democratic worldview, and to discomfort those of mixed views—depending on the frame used to describe the terrorist acts by those in position to influence public opinion. When Schmid wrote in 1983, the 24-hour news cycle was an emerging concept, terrorist attacks occurred elsewhere, and "anxiety" was an adequate descriptor. Today, when one avian bird flu death in Turkey alarms countries on different continents and when a disturbed airline passenger reaching for his medicine is shot by security personnel, we suggest raising the definitional threshold to "fear-inspiring."

Second, although terrorists commit acts, the meaning of those acts is a cocreation of the terrorists, the mass media who report the actions, and the institutions who respond to them. Together they create the dialectic discussed in chapter 1, such that movement terrorists "encounter opposition in a moral struggle." This process differs in degree, but not in kind, from petitions, rallies, and other movement strategies. Saul Alinsky wrote of the importance of perceived threat: "It is only when the other party is concerned or feels threatened that he will listen—in the arena of action, a threat or a crisis becomes almost a precondition to communication."[3] Alinsky specialized in tactics that exposed his targets to pressure from constituencies they valued. For example, when a bank ignored unemployed steelworkers to protect their major investors, Alinsky had the workers store rotting fish in safe deposit boxes until the other box holders pressured the bank to negotiate a solution. The reaction of the other box holders to the actions of the steelworkers cocreated a situation to which the bank had to respond. Without that dialectic, the bank could have continued to ignore the steelworkers.

What, then, is the relationship between terrorism and social movements? Our concern is with terrorist acts that meet the standards of Schmid's definition (adjusted to "fear") that are undertaken in accordance with the characteristics of social movements discussed in chapter 1. Put differently, we are interested in fear-inspiring acts conducted by (semi-) clandestine, organized, uninstitutionalized collectivities against targets that are not their main audiences to promote or oppose changes in norms or values that encounter opposition in a moral struggle in which persuasion is pervasive.

Persuasion is hardly pervasive when one kills a primary audience. Thus, neither Pearl Harbor nor the assassination of Dr. King would qualify as terrorism by this definition. The 1969 Stonewall riot, in which gay patrons of the Stonewall Inn rioted following a police raid, was a defining moment for the movement, but it falls outside our definition of terrorism. Moreover, we will not argue that there are terrorist movements and non-terrorist movements, but that terrorism is a strategy occasionally used by some factions of movements to alter the configuration of the rhetorical situation in which they find themselves.

TUMAN'S MODEL OF TERRORISM AS A COMMUNICATION PROCESS

Joseph S. Tuman designed an informative model of terrorism as a communication process. The left side of figure 14.1 illustrates a terrorist committing an act against a target audience (TA1). The right side of the model highlights the reverberations from this action. Recalling the definition of terrorism as an action to induce fear and persuasive pressures among audiences other than those attacked, Tuman posits other target audiences (TA2, TA3, and TA4 in the diagram, although the potential number is unlimited). The attack on TA1 is interpreted by each of the other target audiences who learn about it through the mass media (MM) and political discourse from the president and other

Figure 14.1   Tuman's Model of Terrorism as Communication

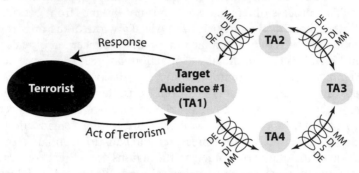

Joseph S. Tuman, *Communicating Terror: The Rhetorical Dimensions of Terrorism*, p. 29. Copyright 2003 by Sage Publications, Inc. Reprinted by permission.

leaders (DI), all of whom variously define and label the perpetrators, victims, and motives for the act (DE) and establish its symbolic significance (S).[4]

Terrorism and mass media (MM) have developed an important symbiotic relationship. Sandra Silberstein has written that "unfortunately, for those of us living in this electronic age, terrorism is an act made for television. . . . Terrorism feeds on television in a system of mutual survival."[5] Of course the terrorism of the Spanish Inquisition, the Ku Klux Klan, and others existed prior to the electronic mass media. The pre-television era's low visibility seemed to benefit "terrorism from above" (i.e., oppression) whereas today's omnipresent camera creates a potential platform for any enterprising terrorist with the willingness to engage the lens. Many experts on terrorism worry greatly about this "cocreation" of terrorism by terrorists and the media, but the alternative may be suppressing coverage, thereby failing to inform people. This is a classic instance of members of a social movement exploiting societal and institutional norms and values, thus posing a major *dilemma* for institutions attempting to reply to and stifle terrorism. In practice, the local and international media ordinarily report the attack, with the extent of coverage depending on factors such as the number of fatalities and injuries, the availability of visuals depicting the damage, and the immediacy of reactions to it—all of which are routine elements of any reporting. Callous as it may be, an explosion that injures no one, provides no pictures, and elicits no official reaction is unlikely to receive coverage.

Two years before the 9/11 attack, *Warp Speed* identified five characteristics of the contemporary news system that worried its authors, Bill Kovach and Tom Rosenstiel.[6] Central to their concern was the availability of new communication technologies that permit faster and faster transmission of news and a proliferation of news outlets. The first implication is the "never-ending news cycle" in which "the press is increasingly oriented toward ferrying allegations rather than first ferreting out the truth." The weekly news magazines have considerably more time to investigate and synthesize before reporting than do the 24-hour news channels. The second trend is that "sources are gaining power over journalists" by dictating the terms and time frames for the use of information. This partly results from the decline of effective gatekeepers because the proliferating news outlets have varying standards. Kovach and Rosenstiel asked, "What does the news organization that requires high levels of substantiation do with the reports of those with lesser levels of proof?" Frequently, they argued, "Argument is overwhelming reporting" as economics drives the need for cheap chatter to fill news time and space.[7]

Finally, they warned of a "Blockbuster Mentality" that provides cheaper and easier rewards for covering crises than for worldwide reporting of diverse stories. As audiences fragment, news organizations seek formulaic stories that reassemble, however temporarily, the old mass audience.[8] Put differently, we tend to become news independent when we feel that nothing important is happening and news dependent during a blockbuster crisis. If contemporary news media have incentives toward blockbuster stories, then terrorists have an increasingly ready audience for their symbolic acts. This poses a significant dilemma for Western institutions that place a high value on freedom of the press.

The symbolic importance of the target is extremely important. Contemporary terrorism has focused attention on kidnappings, beheadings, and bombings because the target symbol has been the ordinary, innocent person as victim (DE). Such attacks make at least two persuasive claims. The first is that no citizen of a representative democracy is "innocent" of the "crimes" of her or his government. The second is that no individual person is safe from the terrorists and that it would be prudent for individuals to urge their leaders to rethink their policies.

But ordinary individuals are not the only symbols (S) that can serve as currency for terrorist acts, as when antiwar demonstrators at Kent State University in 1970 burned the ROTC building. An unexploded bomb found in a Starbuck's coffee shop received coverage for several days in 2005, coverage that would probably not have attended a similar episode at Joe's Diner.

The final communication process at work in Tuman's model is the rhetorical discourse (DI) used to characterize the attacks. Dan Nimmo and James Combs explored the ways in which political experiences are mediated by stories and labeled the logic of television journalism a "melodramatic imperative": "Moral justice is at the heart of most melodrama. . . . Suspense is the key . . . anxiety reigns . . . and characters traits are clear cut: Good are good, bad are bad. Finally, happy endings are preferred but not essential . . . tragic endings suffice."[9] Terrorist acts fit neatly into this melodramatic logic. This is important not simply because it virtually insures coverage of the terrorist acts, but also because it assures *continuing* coverage of the act as part of a moral struggle between good and evil—precisely the formulation sought by social movements. The melodramatic imperative of journalism requires an embodiment of good in response to the act, and that role is invariably seized by, or thrust upon, institutionalized political leaders, most notably U.S. presidents.

Carol Winkler writes that presidents since World War II have tended to (re)define terrorism in terms of the threats they face. She found that Democratic presidents were more likely to frame terrorist attacks in narratives of *criminal* acts to be punished, while Republican presidents were more likely to discuss them in *war* narratives that require military response. She observes that the war narrative makes the commander-in-chief the key figure in combating terror and provides long term narrative coherence for the public. The crime narrative does neither, with the result that the war narrative has provided a more effective presidential rhetoric. On the other hand, Winkler notes that U.S. State Department statistics show significantly more average casualties per year from terrorism under Republican presidents (46) than under Democrats (11)—even after excluding 2001 from the count.[10] The significant difference in casualties may require more frequent and extensive rhetorical responses to explain and justify the losses. One who characterizes an attack as a crime contains it while one who characterizes it as part of a war expands and extends its impact. Moreover, the crime narrative imposes the standards and procedures of the rule of law which are largely inapplicable with respect to enemies during war. Legal actions, however, may be ineffective in deterring violent terrorist acts. Clearly, leaders who select either the criminal or the war narrative face serious *dilemmas*; neither is foolproof.

It is crucial to note that the extended target audiences are not necessarily within the same culture or society as the original target. When responding to international terrorism, the reactions of a wide variety of nations and cultures must be considered. Crucial to Tuman's model are the little squiggles between the various audiences, which signify communication between audiences. Because symbols are interpreted variously depending on the perspectives of audiences, presidential accounts (for example) mean different things to different audiences. The reaction of one audience is conveyed through media reports to other audiences, creating a ripple effect. From the terrorist's perspective, the model somewhat resembles a pinball game. The ball is set in motion by the terrorist act; it caroms off the objects it encounters setting off lights and buzzers, racking up points until it drops out of play.

This interpretation of Tuman's model suggests that the half-life of terrorist acts is an important rhetorical consideration. When the responses of the various audiences contain the impact of the act, they frustrate the terrorists—and they may contribute to the occurrence of another attack. Conversely, responses that keep the effects of a terrorist attack alive may stave off subsequent attacks but contribute to the terrorists' goal. It is another *dilemma* facing counterterrorists.

WHY TERRORIZE?

Most of us react to a terrorist act with shock and revulsion. We perceive of terrorists in the same types of terms that Robert Ivie found we once used with regard to the Soviet Union—animals, barbarians, a natural menace, unfeeling machines, mentally disturbed, satanic, fanatics, and ideologues.[11] When we use such images, we often overlook or dismiss the strategic purposes of terrorists. As military historian Thomas Mockaitis notes:

> Al Qaeda has definite goals. It needs the active support of a few states and the tacit support of many people who share its sense of grievance even if they do not applaud its methods. Despite appearances to the contrary, bin Laden uses terror in a calculated way to achieve a particular effect.[12]

If as students of persuasion we underestimate the strategic purposes, we leave ourselves ill-prepared to engage the actions of terrorists strategically.

There are three strategic purposes for terrorist acts. One is to inspire anxiety and fear. Is the world a safe or dangerous place? Your answer to this question may be influenced by having a cross burned in your yard, seeing people like you beaten on television, seeing skyscrapers collapse, seeing people flee from London Underground stations, and seeing "Elevated Threat" warnings scroll across a television screen. In short, a relatively small number of people may destabilize and reshape the fundamental beliefs millions of people have about their daily safety in the world and, therefore, about their dependence on, or independence from, authority figures.

A second purpose of terrorist acts is to induce secondary target audiences to pressure the main target audience. Christopher Hewitt concludes his study of terrorism in the United States with this observation: "The evidence suggests that terrorism is used by those who can see little chance of getting what they want through regular political channels. They turn to bullets because ballots do not work."[13] Tuman explains that the public audience and the victims are distinct from the government or institutional audience from whom the ultimate action is sought.[14] Terrorists' messages to governments normally claim credit for the act and offer justifications.[15] These messages frequently threaten additional acts if certain actions are not taken, such as releasing prisoners, withdrawing troops, ending alliances, or withholding support for nations or regimes.

Audiences may be governments of other countries. Tuman notes the importance of varying reactions from governments that are friendly, hostile, and neutral toward the nation attacked. Also important are the responses of peoples and cultures who are friendly, hostile, and neutral toward the perpetrators of the attack. Part of the terrorists' strategy may be to separate governments and their people or to divide national alliances on the bases of domestic politics.[16]

Bonnie Cordes studied messages from European terrorists aimed at three audiences. The first was the government. The second was the group's constituency ("the people," "the workers," or "the oppressed peoples of the Third World"). The purpose of communicating with this second audience was to express "their purpose, their courage, and their selflessness; to proclaim their love and sacrifice for this people they no longer see, to engender support amongst them, to draw sympathy and perhaps, to mobilize them." They communicated with "like-minded groups" to:

> transmit their worth to all others—acceptance into the "terrorist community" is not only essential to their national and/or international standing but also generates a pool of sympathizers and potential recruits. Proclamations of solidarity for other groups enhance their image and buy them matched salutes of solidarity, creating the effect of a larger and more powerful organization.

The third audience was the terrorists themselves. These messages sustained the movement and members' morale.

> The members of a [terrorist] group must feel good about themselves. Writing is the expression of the group's immediate feelings and an attempt to adjust them constantly upward. Thus, the *autopropaganda* effect of the communiqués is to applaud and glorify the terrorists, to justify and even to criticize their actions, as well as to motivate members for further activity.[17]

Alinsky addressed the need to communicate with the constituency: "Every move revolves around one central point: how many recruits will this bring into the organization."[18] Hewitt writes:

> Contact between extremists is most likely to occur when they are mobilized by organizations. Extremist organizations attract individuals with extreme opinions and disseminate extreme ideologies. Therefore, members of such organizations are likely to have their views reinforced, and to feel that violence is legitimate and encouraged. This has been noted for both left-wing and right-wing movements.[19]

A terrorist attack may be undertaken with the hope of winning recruits or sympathizers or for mobilizing sympathizers into the terrorist organization.

The third purpose of terrorist acts is to invite overreaction by the institutions they hope to change. At least since the days of the Boston Massacre, forces of order have shown a tendency to overplay their hand and to create martyrs, alienating the constituency they need to remain in power. John Bowers, Donovan Ochs, and Richard Jensen describe the agitation strategies of "escalation/confrontation" that invites institutional forces to overreact and look foolish or intolerant and "guerrilla and Gandhi" that couples nonviolent resistance with violent destruction. They also note:

> One principle governs the rhetorical stance taken by any establishment: *Decision makers must assume that the worst will happen in a given instance of agitation.* The corollary to this principle is equally important: *Decision makers must be prepared to repel any overt act on the establishment.*[20]

Terrorists understand and extend this principle by provoking overreactions that drive some neutrals to sympathize with them and some sympathizers to mobilize.

The problem for terrorists and counterterrorists alike is that ignoring or containing the acts encourages them to escalate their acts until they get the response they seek. Indeed, one school of thought is that terrorism occurs when people who feel intensely about something feel ignored.[21] To the extent that terrorists act on an intense desire to be heard, publicly ignoring them would seem to fuel their frustration and encourage another attack. Conversely, media, and government officials who respond and cocreate a climate of fear may provide the response the terrorists sought. Institutions are caught in a lose-lose dilemma, exactly where terrorists want them to be. Students of social movement terrorism should be attuned to the strategic purposes behind terrorist acts.

THE RHETORIC OF TERRORISM

Richard Leeman believes there is more to terrorism than the violent act.[22] The key is what he terms "bipolar exhortation," and he identifies two bipolar themes: opposition to an inhumane system and an absence of neutrality. The first element is the characterization of a bipolar world of good and evil in which the terrorists stand with the good that is oppressed by an institutionalized system of inhumane evil. Because the system and those supporting it are evil, they are deserving victims. Observers may recoil from the inhumanity of the terrorists' act, but the terrorists point to the greater, more fundamental evil they oppose. This is difficult to grasp in relation to defenses of the 9/11 attacks, but the logic is evident in Pat Buchanan's comment on the bombing of abortion clinics: "Well, those things are probably foolish and counterproductive [but] . . . when we get to the end of this thing, you've got 29 buildings bombed, and you've got 15 million unborn children."[23] The second theme is that the evil system makes neutrality impossible. One must either join with the terrorists or be considered enemies.

According to Leeman, exhortation has two intertwining themes: that action is primary and that any other form of communication is a diversion. In practice, however, the existence of these themes results in a rhetoric that features "action" as a god term. Self-evident truths are asserted and action is urged, but evidence and proofs are deemed wasteful—whether they support the asserted truth or the efficacy of the action.

Religious dogma is not an essential ingredient for a rhetoric of terrorism's bipolar exhortation, but it can be a catalyst. In his provocative book *The End of Faith*, Sam Harris writes:

> Our situation is this: most of the people in this world believe that the Creator of the universe has written a book. We have the misfortune of having many such books on hand, each making an exclusive claim as to its infallibility. People tend to organize themselves into factions according to which of these incompatible claims they accept. . . . . All are in perverse agreement on one point of fundamental importance, however: "respect"

for other faiths, or for the views of unbelievers, is not an attitude that [the Creator] endorses.[24]

Harris maintains that "the religious moderate is nothing more than a failed fundamentalist"[25] It is in this sense that religious dogmas provide the raw ingredients from which some people construct their themes of bipolarity: the impossibility of neutrality and the importance of asserted truths over rational proof and action.

THE ROLE OF PERSUASION IN COUNTERING TERRORISM

How can institutions counter terrorism as it has been discussed in this chapter, particularly with the many rhetorical dilemmas they face? Mockaitis asserts that while domestic security and military force are important, terrorists cannot be defeated without a "hearts and minds" campaign.[26] His approach emphasizes how counterterrorists should use persuasion with secondary audiences in combination with force to defeat terrorist movements, thus completing the process of "encountering opposition in a moral struggle in which persuasion is pervasive." Mockaitis advocates a three-pronged counterterrorism strategy of homeland security, offensive military action, and a hearts and minds campaign. Because this book is about social movement persuasion, we will focus on the tactical and strategic considerations of a hearts and minds campaign.

The first strategic consideration of a hearts and minds campaign is to do no harm.[27] As noted in chapter 12, Bitzer recommends that we judge a rhetorical act in terms of its "fitting response" to the demands of a rhetorical situation. Thus, Mockaitis would have us assess a counterterrorist response in terms of its fitting response to the terrorists' purposes for their assorted audiences. If the terrorists seek attention, the response should not maximize that attention. If the terrorists seek to incite a climate of fear, the response should not cocreate that climate. If the terrorists seek to divide allies, the response should not facilitate this split. If the terrorists seek to transform neutrals into sympathizers, the response should do nothing to make sympathizing with terrorists easier for neutrals.

The second strategy is to move toward a balanced policy, foreign policy in the case of international terrorism. "More balanced" does not mean giving in to terrorists or accepting their worldview. It can mean, for example, "balancing" policy so that it is more receptive to the interests of the neutrals (and potentially even some hostiles) who are important audiences for the terrorists. This balancing can provide neutrals with a vested interest in defeating terrorism.

The third strategy is nation building. Although then governor Bush campaigned against nation building, a changing world has led President Bush to see the symbolic potential of a liberated and rebuilt Afghanistan. Freed from the Taliban and its support for al Qaeda, a rebuilt Afghanistan has the potential to demonstrate the benefits of similar liberation for the rest of the Muslim world. The nations to be built or supported need not be those where the terrorists hold sway, but those that provide ready audiences for terrorist messages.

The fourth strategy is to cultivate friends and allies. Nations beset by terrorist attacks need more friends and allies and fewer enemies and adversaries. Alliances among Western democracies, unlike those among dictatorships, rest on the shifting sands of public opinion. "Domestic opinion in each member state must be persuaded not only as to the justness of the war on terrorism as a whole," writes Mockaitis, "but to the rightness of each action within it."[28] It is frequently prudent for nations to avoid a counterterrorist step they could reasonably take because of the toll it would take on their alliances. In this delicate chess game, a move not made may frustrate the terrorists more than a bold move that creates martyrs for their cause. Remember the principle, "Do no harm."

The fifth strategy is to win hearts and minds at home. This is difficult because, as Mockaitis writes, "The cumulative effect of small, unseen victories, most occurring in the sordid underworld of covert operations, will ultimately win the war. Such victories do not, however, generate popular support nor provide political capital."[29] Put differently, the things that win and sustain public support are unlikely to do very much to defeat the terrorists, while the tactics that work are either unseen or unlikely to enhance public support. This poses another *dilemma* for institutions, even very powerful ones. In 1777, George Washington and his half-starved Continental Army wintered in New Jersey, were branded as terrorists by Great Britain and loyalists in the colonies, and faced the most powerful army and navy in the world. But Washington understood the power and necessity of public opinion in support of a cause. Bruce Chadwick writes:

> He would fight a war of attrition. Unable to defeat the Americans, tired of losing men and equipment, and weary of the great cost of the American war and the criticism a long conflict would surely bring, Washington was certain England would simply quit.[30]

An indirect approach seems advisable. Counterterrorism requires domestic support, but it need not be the sole basis on which those hearts and minds are won.

Richard Neustadt was among the first to highlight the need for presidents to maximize their popular and professional influence in one area so they can expend it in another.[31] Given the inherent problems of maintaining support during a sustained war on terror, it might be prudent for a president to use domestic policies to win hearts and minds while moderating public attention to counterterrorism. The alternative would appear to be to lose crucial domestic support over divisive domestic problems while appearing to focus on a counterterrorist effort that saps public support.

In short, Mockaitis suggests combining domestic security and offensive military action against terrorists with a campaign for hearts and minds at home and around the world. Above all, institutions and their leaders should strive to make counterterrorist choices that avoid contributing to the terrorists' aims. Additionally the terrorists' secondary audiences must be addressed, triangulating the engagement by balancing policies, building nations, bolstering alliances, and building public support at home. This is not an easy rhetorical or political task when a nation is proclaimed to be "at war." Even metaphorical wars are costly.

CASE STUDY: AL QAEDA AND THE 9/11 ATTACKS

Let us use the material presented thus far to analyze the 9/11 terrorist attacks and institutional responses to them from a social movement's perspective. This is an exercise in understanding the terrorists' actions, and it is crucial that students of public discourse be able to study and discuss such acts without being (or being regarded as) disrespectful of the victims of the attack or of those who have tried their best to respond to them. Thoughtful readers will vary in their reactions to what follows, and that should produce some lively discussions.

The Fundamental Causes of 9/11

One explanation for the terrorists' actions emphasizes the clash of civilizations. This perspective foregrounds differences between Islam and the Judeo-Christian religions, differences between Western modernization and traditional societies, and the legacy of the Crusades. These sources of conflict are unquestionably important and provide important rhetorical resources, but they fail to answer a crucial question: Why now, after all these centuries?

To answer that question requires an understanding of the fundamentals of the Islamic worldview. While space dictates a cursory overview, we will highlight some key concepts. John L. Esposito, founding director of Georgetown University's Center for Muslim-Christian Understanding writes:

> Islamic law states that it is a Muslim's duty to wage war not only against those who attack Muslim territory, but also against . . . [those] who refuse Muslim rule. Muslims gave these people two choices: conversion or submission to Muslim rule with the right to retain their religion and pay a poll tax. . . . If they refused both these options they were subject to war. Muslim jurists saw jihad as a requirement in a world they saw divided between . . . the land of Islam and . . . a land of war. The Muslim community was required to expand the [land of Islam] throughout the world so that all of humankind would have the opportunity to live within a just political and social order.[32]

Islam is a "community of believers in a special covenant with God that transcended all other allegiances."[33]

The passage above points to four potential actions that could pose difficulties with the tenets of Islam. First, people might refuse Muslim rule. Second they could refuse both to convert to Islam and to pay the poll tax. It would be difficult for devout people to ignore their faith's commandments to struggle against such trespasses. Many therefore engage in struggles they regard as defensive of their faith and territory. But allies of their adversaries often intercede and attack Muslim territory, thereby creating a third grievance that inspires another defensive jihad. Ultimately, some believers move toward the fourth position—that they must expand the land of Islam through an offensive jihad to expand the rule of justice as they define it. The historical struggle over the creation of Israel and the demands for a Palestinian state pose obvious stimuli for defensive jihads. The State of Israel was carved out of Muslim territory, and Western powers frequently intervened to protect Israeli interests.

But more crucial than Israel for Osama bin Laden and al Qaeda were the Soviet invasion of Afghanistan, the Iraqi invasion of Kuwait, and the Saudi response to it. Bin Laden formed al Qaeda to defend Muslim Afghanistan from the 1979 Soviet invasion, and they prevailed. Meanwhile, political and oil interests were encouraging the governments of Saudi Arabia, Kuwait, Iraq, and the United States to align in opposition to the fundamentalist government of Iran, led by the Ayatollah Khomeini. When Saddam Hussein's Iraqi forces invaded Kuwait in August of 1990, bin Laden offered al Qaeda to the Saudi effort to defend Kuwait. The Saudi decision to seek American rather than Muslim assistance transformed the conflict. As Esposito writes:

> The admission and stationing of foreign non-Muslim troops in Islam's holy land and their permanent deployment after the Gulf War, bin Laden would later say, transformed his life completely, placing him on a collision course with the Saudi government and the West.[34]

At this point, al Qaeda faced two adversaries: the non-Muslim interests and their military forces stationed in Muslim lands and, arguably more important, the Muslim leaders who put interests and allegiances before their commitment to Islam. Westernized, secular governments in Muslim nations such as Saudi Arabia and Iraq caused bin Laden to initiate his jihad.

What do fundamentalist movements do when a major part of their problem is moderation? Traditionally, they strive to polarize people. Rohan Gunaratna writes that al Qaeda's first wave of attacks targeted "secular and moderate Muslim countries such as Egypt, Saudi Arabia, Jordan, and Pakistan," but the approach met harsh setbacks.[35]

Because Western governments perceived these struggles as linked to Muslims, they underestimated their own vulnerability. Al Qaeda seized the opportunity to strike at the more distant enemies who supported their Muslim enemies. Ayman Muhammed al-Zawahiri identified six Western target audiences that were key to the fight against Islam: "the United Nations, Muslim regimes that work with the West, multinational corporations, international communications and data exchange systems, international news agencies and satellite media channels, and international relief agencies."[36]

Bin Laden issued a Declaration of Holy War in August 1996. According to Esposito, the goals "were to drive U.S. forces out of the Arabian peninsula, overthrow the Saudi government, and liberate Islam's holy sites of Mecca and Medina, as well as support revolutionary groups around the world."[37] In 1998 he issued a decree to the effect that it was the duty of Muslims to kill Americans and their allies. During the late 1990s the White House became increasingly concerned about bin Laden and al Qaeda, but the 2000 election campaign centered on domestic issues, and the new administration had other foreign policy priorities.

The Terrorist Acts

On September 11th al Qaeda attacked the World Trade Center and the Pentagon by air. As illustrated in Tuman's model, the reverberations from these physical attacks were in a chain reaction of rhetorical, cultural, and behavioral choices that continue to transform the United States today. Did al Qaeda underestimate us by expecting us to do nothing, or did we respond as they anticipated when they planned the attack?

Pragmatically, the World Trade Center housed people from many nations who worked for an assortment of multinational corporations that furthered a global economy at odds with al Qaeda's vision of a desirable world. The destruction of the Twin Towers, therefore, inflicted serious damage on several of the target audiences identified by al-Zawahiri. Bin Laden's reaction to the strikes emphasized the immediate practical consequences, which he calculated to be a trillion dollars. He drew a striking comparison for his followers: "Losses on the Wall Street market reached 16 percent . . . $640 billion of losses from stocks, by Allah's grace. So this amount, for example, is the budget of Sudan for 640 years."[38]

Symbolically, it was the largest building in the skyline of the Western world's largest city, the media capital of the United States. Minoura Yamasaki designed each of the Twin Towers as a core covered with a tube. The bomb detonated by terrorists in 1993 had damaged, but did not topple, the Towers. When the airliners hit and exploded on 9/11, the intense heat transferred through the core and led to the collapse in a way that would not have occurred in many other structures.

The attack on the Pentagon, assuming it was an original target, was less pragmatic than symbolic. Although the Pentagon is the practical and symbolic hub of U.S. military power, its architecture isolates the damage from an attack by one airplane. Moreover, U.S. military power could not be eliminated simply by damaging this building. Although the attack had practical significance, the fact that the terrorists could breach its security had symbolic importance that could not be ignored.

Media Reaction to the Terrorist Acts

Much as the core and tube architectural structure of the Twin Towers magnified the force of the explosions and caused the Towers to collapse, the mass media and its extensive reach magnified the social and political effects of the attacks. The blockbuster spectacle, the melodramatic imperative, and presidential rhetoric all came into play quickly on 9/11.

The number of tourists in New York any weekday morning at 8:45 guaranteed that someone would videotape the attack on the towers, and New York's status as the media capital of the world assured immediate international media coverage. The 24-hour news cycle and the visual drama of attacks on large buildings of both functional and symbolic importance assured continuing saturation coverage of the attacks and their aftermath. The convergence of local and national news decision making in Manhattan and Washington guaranteed national coverage. We can only speculate as to whether attacks on Fort Knox or General Motors headquarters would have received comparable treatment. Television networks immediately began nonstop coverage, and nonstop coverage usually involves partially verified bits of information—such as inaccurate reports of the gunman on the grassy knoll in Dallas when President Kennedy was assassinated, inaccuracies about the attempted assassination of President Reagan, and false reports of Middle Eastern terrorists in Oklahoma City. The heart-pounding drama aired continuously and public attention was riveted on videos of planes crashing into the Twin Towers, bloodied victims, and bone-weary rescuers.

Blockbuster stories rekindle the melodramatic imperative of U.S. news, and coverage of 9/11 fit easily and swiftly into melodramatic logic. Tragedy, anxiety, fear, and suspense were palpable; they created an immediate but undefined and unfocused demand for justice against evil. Melodrama is an ongoing story of good versus evil, but in this case, the source of evil remained unclear. These attacks *looked* like the work of foreign terrorists. But Timothy McVeigh had planned the Oklahoma City bombing to look like a terrorist attack. The 9/11 attacks were similar and larger, and they enacted the final scene of *The Turner Diaries*.[39] Was this an attack by Middle-Eastern terrorists? Or was it militia retaliation for McVeigh's conviction for Oklahoma City? Or perhaps were Middle-Eastern terrorists returning the favor by emulating the right-wing militia's favorite novel? As the networks endlessly repeated their footage of the carnage from New York and Washington, the explosions reverberated through the echo chamber and viewers experienced the aftershocks again and again. The 24-hour blockbuster melodrama raised four major questions: What happened? Who was responsible for the acts? How will moral justice be achieved? Should Americans be fearful or reassured?

The news media took charge of telling the story first—what happened. Reporters in New York and Washington interviewed families and officials with story fragments to share. But all the hours of coverage provided only piecemeal understanding, partly because the demands of melodrama required that their coverage continue. The terrorists—whoever they were—were getting the extensive coverage of their act that they had sought and, undoubtedly, expected.

Institutional Responses to the Terrorist Acts

Clearly, the 9/11 attacks and their coverage created a national fear that required a presidential address. But how does a leader engage followers in a time of danger? Leaders may respond to danger and public fear with reassurance. The mantra for such a speechwriting team would have been President Franklin D. Roosevelt's "The only thing we have to fear is fear itself." The general rhetorical strategies would have been to fight terror with *reassurance*, blockbuster melodrama with *containment* of the story, and rage with *measured authoritative* responses that demonstrated how fully the terrorists had failed to destabilize the security of the United States and the world. The leader would approach the acts as *criminal*. General themes of a *reassurance narrative* might have been articulated something like this:

> Today a small band of fanatics attacked the World Trade Center and the Pentagon. All of the perpetrators died in the attacks, and the security and intelligence forces of all civilized nations are on the trail of their few surviving accomplices. Those responsible will be brought to justice and will pay for their despicable actions. We have all seen coverage of the terrible devastation and grief caused by the attacks. It is crucial for us to remember that these despicable people attacked three buildings and that the rest of the country was, and remains, safe and secure. From time to time the world has witnessed terrible acts by misguided people. Americans have confidence in the overriding goodness of the vast majority of the world's people, and we know that incidents like this are rare.
>
> We are a courageous people, and an attack like this tests our courage. Let those who would doubt us marvel at the heroism of those brave people who risked and gave their lives today to save people they did not know. Let us all dedicate ourselves to doing our jobs as they did and going on with our lives—mindful and aware of the risks, but courageously embracing those risks as our own indispensable contributions to the struggle for truth, justice, decency, and the American way.

As this hypothetical speech indicates, it was possible for the speechwriting team to reassure Americans that the *entire* nation was not in *imminent* danger. Indeed, this is generally how the British people responded to the London Underground bombings of July 2005. As with all rhetorical choices, however, there are downsides to this type of narrative. It may not prepare audiences adequately for the possibility of equal or worse terrorist acts; it may provoke further terrorist acts to make institutions and audiences take the terrorists and their cause more seriously; and the terrorist networks may be too distant, powerful, or entrenched in some nations for the criminal justice system to work effectively. Reassurance is critical but difficult to bring about when many unknowns remain and the terrorist acts are seemingly monumental.

A second approach to the situation is, by now, quite familiar. After two presidential statements referring to "the attacks," the third address transformed them into *war* rather than a *crime*.[40] Although the attackers remained nameless "others," the administration redefined their "attacks" into a war against this nation and proclaimed that "our responsibility to history is already clear: To answer these attacks and rid the world of evil."[41] Facing a daunting struggle between a decisive response and the need for clarity in defining the enemy, the speechwriters transcended known acts and agents and proclaimed retaliation against the enemies of evil and terror.[42] It was a response that a world economic, political, and military power might be expected to make. Indeed, many of today's leaders and younger generations see it as their "Pearl Harbor."

From the outset, the media and political institutions have portrayed the entire nation as endangered by the attacks in a way that inadvertently helped cocreate al Qaeda's message of terror. Rather than providing reassurance that the nation was safe unless proven to be further endangered, institutional rhetoric presumed us endangered—they prepared for the worst case scenario—until someone could produce evidence sufficient to prove that evil had been *forever* eliminated. A climate of fear, complete with color-coded terrorist levels, was firmly in place as the terrorists hoped it would be. Western political institutions have subsequently taken countless policy steps and actions to combat the "evildoers" in the name of the War on Terror. The result has been a series of terrorist produced *rhetorical dilemmas* that remain unresolved and exacerbated by deadly terrorist acts in Spain, England, Indonesia, and elsewhere.

First, Western institutional rhetoric has failed to appreciate adequately its significant successes. The U.S and its allies surprised al Qaeda by successfully invading Afghanistan and defeating the Taliban, destroying much of its infrastructure and causing a split between bin Laden and al-Zawahiri over the direction of their efforts.[43] But because institutional rhetoric focused on *capturing* bin Laden and *eliminating* terror and evil from the world, important accomplishments appear to have been undervalued by those who could claim credit for them while enabling bin Laden and other terrorists to taunt institutions and threaten grave future consequences through audio and videotapes broadcast throughout the world. Institutions would like to take these bombastic pronouncements and warnings with the proverbial "grain of salt," but they dare not do so because they must prepare for the worst and communicate this to their publics. To do so, however, is to enhance fears and to call attention to the terrorists whom they cannot afford to ignore, exactly the responses terrorists desperately need. In spite of military setbacks and loss of leaders, terrorists have succeeded in spreading fear, energizing sympathizers and followers alike, and appearing to be invulnerable to Western military might.

Second, Western institutions must continue to argue they are winning the war in Iraq as an essential component of the War on Terror. But the presence of non-Muslim troops in Muslim lands compounds bin Laden's original grievance and enhances his appeal to potential converts and sympathizers. Mockaitis, for example, regards the Iraq invasion as a classic case of a response doing more harm than good:

> The invasion of Iraq illustrates how some actions can do more harm than good. Launched ostensibly to remove Saddam Hussein so that he could not provide al Qaeda with weapons of mass destruction, Operation "Iraqi

Freedom" has definitely soured. Coalition forces may have come as libera-
tors, but they are now seen as conquerors. While few in the Arab world
had any love for Saddam, most resent the high-handed manner in which
the U.S. engineered his removal without international approval. They
rightly point out that Washington demanded Iraqi compliance with all
UN resolutions while winking at Israeli defiance of the same organization.
This resentment has inspired Mujahidin from all over the Middle East to
join their Iraqi brothers in the current guerrilla war against the coalition.[44]

Growing numbers of critics in the United States and its allies have questioned
the massive commitment to military actions in Iraq, required of any non-met-
aphorical war, while devoting far fewer resources to natural disasters and
security at home.

Third, the war in Iraq has confounded the "battle for hearts and minds"
portion of the counterterrorist response. It quickly separated the United
States from some of its oldest European allies. In this sense, the 9/11 attacks
provoked a fragmented Western response that has divided the target audiences al-Zawahiri had identified. Terrorists know that national interests are
likely to take precedence over coordinated, international responses. Moreover, the interplay between al Qaeda activities and Western institutional and
media responses have provided ample opportunities for Islamic political
groups to propagandize and thus radicalize and mobilize Muslim followers.[45] It is also difficult to win hearts and minds when the inevitable consequences of warfare (civilian casualties, mistaken bombing of sacred secular
and holy places, prisoner abuses, suffering among the populace) enable terrorists to condemn and recruit. The bombing of a wedding party can overshadow numerous good deeds and painstaking accomplishments. The British
forces in southern Iraq, for instance, had enjoyed a comparably quiet time
and Iraqi public support since early in the invasion until a video of British
troops beating protestors behind a wall infuriated the Iraqi populace and
played into the hands of terrorist elements.

Fourth, having repeatedly linked Iraq with the War on Terror, Western
leaders have found it exceedingly difficult to disentangle the two, even if they
wanted to do so. While arguing that we are winning the dual wars, leaders
must continue to argue that they are engaged in an unending war against
overwhelming terror and evil. But how are they to do this without contributing to the polarization sought by the Islamic fundamentalists—that there are
two worlds, one good and the other evil between which there must be a jihad?
Consider the following exhortations:

Believe, endure, outdo all others in endurance, be ready, and observe
your duty.[46]

We cannot yield at this point in time, that we must remain steadfast and
strong, that it's the intentions of the enemy to shake our will.[47]

If signs of relaxation and retreat start to show in the leadership . . . [we]
must find ways to straighten it out and not permit it to deviate.[48]

One of those statements is by President George W. Bush, one is from the Koran, and one is by Ayman Muhammed al-Zawahiri—but which is which? All three statements share a commitment to commitment, duty, and endurance. The first statement is from the Koran; the second is from the president; and the third is from al-Zawahiri. While all of these call for unyielding commitment, terrorists understand what George Washington understood about British institutions and public opinion two centuries ago. It is very difficult to sustain public and political commitment for military actions thousands of miles from home when casualties mount, costs escalate, mistakes are made, and victory seems elusive. There are increasing public demands in Western nations that their troops return home, away from harm. Terrorist hostages beg their governments to give in to terrorist demands, thus placing pressure on the terrorists' primary audiences. Victims of terrorist bombings and assassinations inevitably blame "foreign" institutions for the acts rather than the terrorist perpetrators with a simple logic: if you were not here, there would be no terrorists or violent acts.

The foregoing discussion is not meant to suggest that the world is not dangerous or that terrorists are not planning attacks. Neither is it intended as political second-guessing of institutional leaders who have faced decisions of unimaginable difficulty. Terrorists have known for centuries that they can pose no-win dilemmas for powerful institutions and achieve visibility, attention, and results that far exceed their numbers and means. The current set of terrorists are among the best in the acts they perform and their use of the mass media. By responding in culturally predictable ways to the 9/11 attacks, Western institutions may have unintentionally and inadvertently helped the masterminds of the attacks toward their goals.

Western institutions should be prudent about the dangers of terrorism. Dangers are rhetorically constructed for people out of events and implications either as the context in which everything else should be understood or as a piece within a frame of security. By making terror the overarching frame, the media and Western institutional rhetoric have participated unwittingly in the cocreation of al Qaeda's climate of terror and compounded bin Laden's original grievance—the presence of non-Muslim troops in Muslim lands.

Institutional responses engaged the terrorists in a moral struggle, much as any social movement would want. By waging war on terror and evil, Western institutions have achieved some important tactical goals in their campaign against terrorists. But by sending troops into Afghanistan and Iraq, the conduct of that struggle has complicated the "hearts and minds" dimension of the campaign against terrorism. Traditional allies have been alienated, many neutrals have been driven to sympathize with the terrorists, and the United States and Great Britain have been left to wage the war economically and militarily with few strong partners. As the terrorists might have planned on waging a protracted struggle, domestic support for the war has waned.

CONCLUSIONS

This chapter has discussed the use of terrorism by social movements and strategic considerations useful for people and institutions responding to such acts. It used a particular definition of terrorism so that we could navigate through the traps of considering all violent acts we dislike as terrorist or labeling all disorderly protests as terror. The key considerations are the use of a violent act by an uninstitutional collectivity against some target to inspire fear among selected audiences in the hope that they will in turn pressure the institutions who are the terrorists' main target. In this sense, terrorist acts are part of a persuasive process that includes the mass media, many secondary target audiences, and counterterrorist institutions.

Terrorists have several potential purposes and audiences, and they communicate differently with those various audiences. They pose nearly impossible dilemmas for institutions of all kinds. The melodramatic imperative of contemporary news and the blockbuster nature of crisis news create opportunities for exposure that terrorists readily exploit. Counterterrorism requires a careful combination of domestic security, offensive military actions, and a campaign for the hearts and minds of the secondary target audiences whom the terrorists seek to influence. If not handled with rhetorical skill, the counterterrorist efforts can cocreate the very conditions sought by the terrorists.

Notes

[1] Joseph S. Tuman, *Communicating Terror: The Rhetorical Dimensions of Terrorism* (Thousand Oaks, CA: Sage, 2003): 11.

[2] Alex P. Schmid, *Political Terrorism: A Research Guide to Concepts, Theories, Data Bases and Literature* (New Brunswick, NJ: Transaction Press, 1983): 70. Cited in Tuman, 13–14.

[3] Saul D. Alinsky, *Rules for Radicals: A Pragmatic Primer for Realistic Radicals* (New York: Vintage Books, 1971, 1989): 89.

[4] Tuman, 29.

[5] Sandra Silberstein, *War of Words: Language, Politics and 9/11* (New York: Routledge, 2004): 2.

[6] Bill Kovach and Tom Rosenstiel, *Warp Speed: America in the Age of Mixed Media* (New York: Century Foundation Press, 1999).

[7] Kovach and Rosenstiel, 7.

[8] Kovach and Rosenstiel, 6–7.

[9] Dan Nimmo and James E. Combs, *Mediated Political Realities* (New York: Longman, 1990): 16.

[10] Carol K. Winkler, *In the Name of Terrorism: Presidents on Political Violence in the Post-World War II Era* (Albany: State University of New York Press, 2006): 200–207.

[11] Robert L. Ivie, "Speaking 'Common Sense' about the Soviet Threat: Reagan's Rhetorical Stance," *Western Journal of Speech Communication* 48 (Winter 1984): 39–50.

[12] Thomas R. Mockaitis, "Winning Hearts and Minds in the 'War on Terrorism,'" *Grand Strategy in the War against Terrorism*, Paul B. Rich and Thomas R. Mockaitis, eds. (London: Frank Cass, 2003): 22, http://www.questia.com/PM.qst?action=openPageViewer&docId=108521486, accessed 4 August 2006.

[13] Christopher Hewitt, *Understanding Terrorism in America: From the Klan to al Qaeda* (New York: Routledge, 2002): 50

[14] Tuman, 20-23.

[15] Bonnie Cordes, "When Terrorists Do the Talking: Reflections on Terrorist Literature," *Inside Terrorist Organizations*, David C. Rapoport, ed. (New York: Columbia University Press, 1988): 150–171, http://www.questia.com/PM.qst?a=o&d=59648553, accessed 4 August, 2006.

[16] Tuman, 21–23.

[17] Cordes, 154.

[18] Alinsky, 113.

[19] Hewitt, 46.

[20] John W. Bowers, Donovan J. Ochs, and Richard J. Jensen, *The Rhetoric of Agitation and Control*, 2nd ed. (Long Grove, IL: Waveland Press, 1993): 42–43, 48.

[21] Hewitt, 23–24.

[22] Richard W. Leeman, *The Rhetoric of Terrorism and Counterterrorism* (New York: Greenwood Press, 1991).

[23] Quoted by Leeman, 3.

[24] Sam Harris, *The End of Faith: Religion, Terror, and the Future of Reason* (New York: WW. Norton, 2004): 13.

[25] Harris, 20.

[26] Mockaitis, 21–23.

[27] Mockaitis, 31.

[28] Mockaitis, 34.

[29] Mockaitis, 35.

[30] Bruce Chadwick, *George Washington's War* (Naperville, IL: Sourcebooks, 2005): 117.

[31] Richard E. Neustadt, *Presidential Power: The Politics of Leadership from FDR to Carter* (New York: John Wiley, 1960, 1980).

[32] John L. Esposito, *Unholy War: Terror in the Name of Islam* (New York: Oxford University Press, 2002): 34–35.

[33] Esposito, 39–40.

[34] Esposito, 12.

[35] Rohan Gunaratna, *Inside Al Qaeda: Global Network of Terror* (New York: Berkley Books, 2002): 308.

[36] Gunaratna, 300.

[37] Esposito, 21.

[38] Gunaratna, 300–301.

[39] [William Pierce] Andrew Macdonald, *The Turner Diaries*, 2nd ed. (New York: Barricade Books, 1978).

[40] George W. Bush, "Remarks at the 'National Day of Prayer and Remembrance Service,'" September 14, 2001, http://frwebgate4.access.gpo.gov/cgi-bin/waisgate.cgi?WAISdocID=2633422005+2+0+0&WAISaction=retrieve, accessed 22 August 2006.

[41] Bush.

[42] For an extended discussion of President Bush's response and his development of the "Evildoers" see Craig Allen Smith, "President Bush's Enthymeme of Evil: The Amalgamation of 9/11, Iraq, and Moral Values," *American Behavioral Scientist*, 49 (September 2005): 32–47.

[43] Gunaratna, 311–314.

[44] Mockaitis, 31.

[45] Gunaratna, 301.

[46] The Koran, quoted in Gunaratna, 298.

[47] George W. Bush, "The President's News Conference of April 13, 2004," *Weekly Compilation of Presidential Documents* Volume 40, Number 16 (19 April 2004): 587–588, http://frwebgate1.access.gpo.gov/cgi-bin/waisgate.cgi?WAISdocID=263534101493+1+0+0&WAISaction=retrieve, accessed 22 August 2006.

[48] Gunaratna, 298.

CHAPTER

14

Resisting Social Movements

If we are to understand why and how institutions react to and resist the persuasive efforts of social movements, we must first understand the purposes and powers institutions share with one another and non-institutional forces such as social movements. These relationships often determine the timing and nature of strategies appropriate in a given situation.

POWERS AND PURPOSES OF INSTITUTIONS

Each institution has a set of explicit and implicit purposes such as self-preservation, perpetuation, value maintenance, policy making, and enforcement.[1] Institutional members are elected, appointed, or hired to fulfill these purposes. They must protect territorial boundaries, cultural norms, and values from real and imagined threats and from enemies found both inside and outside the institution. Emblems of authority and rituals such as civic holidays, religious holy days, days of honoring founders, inaugurations, flags, memorials, insignia, and uniforms reinforce the status quo, authority, legitimacy, and allocation of power and influence. The arrival of Air Force One is a major event in cities around the world and exhibits presidential and U.S. power.[2] Elections are heralded as historic and peaceful exchanges of high office. The signing of important legislation garners media coverage and praise for addressing critical issues. A flag in the president's lapel and salute to the military guard as he exits the Marine helicopter on the White House lawn exhibits patriotism and military power.

As noted in chapter 3, when society confers legitimacy on institutions, it confers powers to perpetuate this grant. John Bowers, Donovan Ochs, and Richard Jensen discuss how French and Raven's "five social powers" (legitimate, coercive, reward, referent, and expert) are distributed between institutions and social movements. An institution always controls legitimate power (is perceived to have a charter, social contract, or assigned position through which it can exert influence) and normally is capable of exerting coercive power (is perceived as capable of influencing by threat of punishment). Institutions and social movements share reward power (the capability of conferring rewards), referent power (ability to identify with groups and individuals), and expert power (the image of having superior knowledge or skill in a particular area), although social movements "depend almost completely on referent power and expert power"[3] because they have few meaningful rewards to offer and are perceived as outsiders. Figure 13.1 indicates the ways social powers are controlled and shared in society.

Andrew King argues that powers are derived from a material resource base, psychosocial base, and organizational/syntactic base.[4] In early times, the *material resource* base was land, but in modern times it became money. Today the material resource is information or knowledge, and access to it confers power on groups and individuals. The *psychosocial* base provides group members with a sense of identity that binds them through common interests, habits, culture, and values. *Organizational/syntactic* bases of power include legislative rules, regulations, and norms of behavior. Power, then, is a multidimensional offensive and defensive weapon shared unequally by institutions and social movements because of the nature of social order.

According to Hugh Duncan, social order is always expressed in some kind of hierarchy.[5] Hierarchy differentiates people into ranks based on variables such as age, sex, race, skills, knowledge, position, and wealth. These rankings function as societal structures that enable institutions to maintain control. Forms of social drama create national symbols that unify and transcend local, isolated concerns. When enacted within situations, they provide legitimacy and the continuation of regimes in whose hands reside the power of social control.

Legitimacy is the most vulnerable point of attack for social movements because regimes must demonstrate competence, fairness, justice, and reasonableness to maintain public trust and support. Social control is usually viewed as the result of institutional influences such as laws, the courts, and policing agencies, but no institution can long survive solely on the threat of force. Public communication is a vital tool. Through it, institutions create and control images and relationships that legitimize their authority. The

Figure 13.1   Social Power Control

	Institution	Social Movement
Legitimate Power	Constitution, elected officials	
Coercive Power	Courts, police, military	
Reward Power	Contracts, tax incentives	Leadership, ego enhancement
Referent Power	Churches, founding fathers	Organizations, heroes and martyrs
Expert power	Universities, scientists	Authors, personal experience

growing influence of the mass media and the Internet has made it increasingly difficult for institutions to create and control images and to sustain authority. This was exhibited most clearly in the disintegration of the Soviet Union and its control over its eastern European satellite nations.[6]

People experience situations through symbols and describe similar situations in a variety of ways. Events do not simply exist; they are interpreted by those who experience them. Consequently, the *definitions* and *framing of situations* are valuable commodities that leaders of institutions and social movements compete to control. Public perceptions and impressions (of, for example, freedom, justice, or equality) are influenced by significant myths and symbols that are emotional, intense, and cultural in nature. Society is a dynamic, interacting entity consisting of many levels that act and compete simultaneously. The fight for legitimacy is a fight for public perceptions and acceptance. Patriotic, religious, and social myths and symbols are important weapons in this struggle. Sherry Shepler and Anne Mattina note: "Cultural myths, especially those engendered by a patriarchal structure, may inhibit and/or repress groups who try to challenge a long-standing myth, while championing other groups."[7]

Institutions are accustomed to framing situations. For instance, they define and interpret the war on terrorism, torture of prisoners, patriotism, family values, national security, and democracy. In spite of this definitional power, they may find it difficult to counteract opposing frameworks. For example, how might institutions respond to the following characterizations that challenge prevailing definitions of *situations, institutions, symbols,* and *acts of violence*?

- "The university administration provoked the confrontation with students."
- "Our legal system discriminates against Hispanic Americans."
- "The flag represents imperialism."
- "The FBI shot an unarmed mother in the face while she was holding her baby."

The philosophy of democracy and the Bill of Rights makes institutional responses to social movement challenges and activities troublesome. The Constitution denies the right of institutions to abridge the freedoms of speech and the press and the right of the people to assemble peaceably, while granting rights to the people to "petition the Government for a redress of grievances," "to keep and bear arms," and to privacy. At the same time, institutions are mandated to "establish Justice, insure domestic Tranquility, provide for the common defence," and "promote the general Welfare."[8]

DEMOCRACY AND RESISTANCE TO SOCIAL MOVEMENTS

There is probably no concept more important to the theory of democratic government than free speech. Historically, however, institutions have attempted to limit, control, or suppress freedom of expression by the press and individuals for the "good of the nation" and "national security." For instance, the Sedition Law of 1798 attempted to suppress newspapers that attacked the U.S. government for remaining neutral when the Republic of France declared war on England. This law forbade the publication of matter intended to defame the government or to bring its officers into disrepute. During the Pullman Strike in 1894, the courts forbade Eugene V. Debs to communicate with the membership of the American Railway Union. He was arrested when he refused to obey and was sentenced to six months in jail. The Espionage Acts of 1917 forbade anyone to cause or to attempt to cause insubordination, disloyalty, mutiny, or refusal of duty in the armed forces. It was unlawful to write or speak against U.S. involvement in World War I. When Debs, by then the leader of the Socialist Party, delivered an antiwar speech in Canton, Ohio, in 1918, he was arrested, tried, and convicted under the Espionage Act and received a ten-year sentence, entering a federal prison four months after the war had ended. During World War II, Congress established the U.S. Office of Censorship to monitor all actions and written materials that challenged the wisdom of a U.S. presence in Europe and Asia. Until recently, colleges and universities routinely restricted the speaking activities of politicians, activists, and unapproved student groups on their campuses.

During the 1960s and 1970s, demonstrators challenged laws restricting free expression and assemblage. The civil rights, students' rights, and anti-Vietnam War movements stimulated the consideration of free speech issues such as limits on expression, limits of criticism of public officials, citizen surveillance, the right to privacy, and the right to wear emblems such as peace symbols, flags, and black armbands. The courts provided important victories for protestors. For example, the Supreme Court broadened the definition of "speech" to include symbolic acts and the wearing of symbols such as armbands. Other decisions supported the right to speak against the government and to talk about its overthrow (as long as no action to overthrow is proposed), to resort to a rhetoric of the streets if other channels of redress are blocked, to carry a foreign or "enemy" flag as long as the carrier does not advocate the overthrow of the government, and to burn the American flag as a symbolic act.[9]

In response to the broadening of civil rights and rights of expression, institutions have sought to control access and dissemination of information as the principal means of shaping and guiding public understanding of social policy. The war over the freedom of expression has become the war over the freedom of information. Beginning with former president Lyndon Johnson, the press has had less access to government leaders and information. Official information from government agencies has become secret, classified, or selective, so it is increasingly difficult to distinguish fact from fiction, truth from propaganda.

Some presidents, vice presidents, and cabinet members have viewed the press as an enemy rather than as a partner in the democratic process; they attack the "liberal," "eastern establishment," and "biased" press. In his famous Des Moines, Iowa, address to the Midwest Regional Republican Committee meeting in 1969, then vice president Spiro Agnew declared,

> The purpose of my remarks tonight is to focus your attention on this little group of men [television news directors and anchors] who not only enjoy a right of instant rebuttal to every presidential address but, more importantly, wield a free hand in selecting, presenting, and interpreting the great issues of our nation.[10]

Agnew warned that this "tiny and closed fraternity of privileged men, elected by no one, and enjoying a monopoly" wielded immense power. For instance, "A raised eyebrow, an inflection of the voice, a caustic remark dropped in the middle of a broadcast can raise doubts in a million minds about the veracity of a public official or the wisdom of a government policy." The networks got the message and eliminated critical responses by network reporters and selected experts following presidential speeches.

Political institutions and agents are not the only entities who attempt to in control information and free speech. During the 1990s, the University of Wisconsin and other educational institutions created policies to guarantee "politically correct" speech and to eliminate "hate speech" such as racial, ethnic, and gender name-calling on their campuses. The courts have ruled against many of these policies as infringements on freedom of expression.

When resisting social movements, how much free expression should institutions tolerate? Are all opinions equal? Are there differences in the form and content of expression that are sufficient to limit some expressions rather than others? When is national security really at stake? When are we at war? These are difficult and important issues to ponder, especially for residents of a democracy. For instance, many groups who want to display nativity scenes on courthouse lawns or in public schools would be outraged if anti-Christian groups were allowed to erect their symbols in the same places. Ethnic, social, and religious groups who have fought for the rights to protest, hold demonstrations, and present their cases without interruption have attempted to deny those same rights to others.

A balance between rights is difficult to maintain. For example, communication scholars generally agree that speakers who appeal only to the emotions of audiences impede logical and critical thinking. Thus, many scholars have concluded that such appeals are unethical and undemocratic because they undermine the free, full, and rational discussion of issues. Wayne Flynt argues that during the 1963 civil rights disturbances in Birmingham, Alabama, prominent leaders took undemocratic stances, employed faulty logic, and appealed to white fear, frustration, and anger.[11] Is such rhetoric more or less ethical than that of protestors shouting insults and obscenities at clergy, public officials, and police officers?

A troublesome decision for institutions is the level of response. The national government may be most concerned with issues, policy, and movement leaders, while the local government may focus primarily on property, events, maintenance of order, and citizens' rights. Local police, for example, believe they are charged with maintaining law and order and view protestors as disrupters of the peace and commerce whose tactics may lead to anarchy.[12] Law enforcement officers are often ordered to react with restraint but also with force sufficient to control demonstrations in emotionally supercharged situations. These instructions are particularly difficult when the ideological views and actions of the protestors are contrary to the basic values and training of the police officers.

There are several problems inherent in institutional bureaucracies. First, there is little agreement on whether negotiations with social movements should take place and, if they do, which branch of government should deal with them (the executive, legislative, or judicial). Second, institutions are comprised of individuals with their own beliefs, attitudes, and values. Third, reaching consensus and implementing policy are not merely matters of issuing directives; there are differences between theory and practice, issues and policy, planned procedures and their implementation. Fourth, democracy is not an entity but a process of regulating human behavior, and this process is often slow, insensitive, and riddled with contradictory principles.

How does an institution balance the rights of society against those of individuals, the majority against the minority, the popular against the unpopular? For social movements, the cause is supreme; the resources are few; and the time to act is now. The urgency expressed in social movement rhetoric encounters a rhetoric of democratic government based on the premises that social change is evolutionary rather than revolutionary and that policies enacted are the will of the majority and policies rejected are favored by small minorities or special interests.

Thus, the philosophical principles as well as the operational structure of a democracy dictate not only the strategies and tactics of social movements but also the forms and types of institutional responses. Democracy makes resistance to social movements varied and complex. According to Theodore Windt, "administrative" rhetoric is characterized by a defensive posture that views all questions about policy as attacks on the authority and credibility of the institution.[13] In the same vein, Bowers, Ochs, and Jensen write that the principle that governs the rhetorical stance of decision makers is the assumption that the worst will happen as a result of outside agitation.[14] To maintain their power, credibility, and legitimacy within the hierarchy, institutional leaders must continually provide evidence of superiority, control, and willingness to respond quickly and decisively to all threats or attacks on the institution.

In summary, institutions view all challenges as questioning established authority, doctrines, myths, and symbols—often in circumstances threatening national security. On the other hand, social movements perceive their challenges to be questions of the acceptability of policies and actions in the time-honored American tradition of social protest. Obviously, these divergent views influence the nature and types of institutional response. This chapter focuses on four strategies institutions and their supporters employ when responding to challenges: evasion, counter-persuasion, coercive persuasion, and adjustment.

THE STRATEGY OF EVASION

Institutions usually select evasion as the first strategy. They may pretend that a social movement does not exist, see it as unworthy of institutional response, or feel it would be dangerous to their status or to society to grant the movement any *official* recognition. By ignoring the movement, they hope that it will go away or dissolve.

The Media

Although social movements must use the mass media to gain public visibility and legitimacy, nearly all media are controlled by corporations, and the electronic media are licensed by the government. There is little inclination to report on social agitators or to see them as newsworthy. Dieter Rucht writes that, while "most movements need the media, the media seldom need the movements" because social movements "seldom possess information that journalists desperately seek."[15] The media rarely cover social movements, so most Americans are unaware, for example, that a United Students against Sweatshops, the Rainforest Action Network, the Earth Liberation Front, and anarchist groups exist or that the temperance, Native-American, and militia movements are continuing their struggles. As a result, social movements remain out of sight and out of public mind.

Media invisibility is not the case with institutions and their leaders. For instance, when President George W. Bush and his administration came under increasing attacks in the fall of 2005 over the handling of the war in Iraq and reports of unlawful spying on U.S. citizens, networks covered a number of press conferences, broadcast a televised version of his Saturday radio show, and granted him full coverage for a primetime speech. Although a few Democratic and Republican critics were allowed brief responses, social movement spokespersons were nowhere to be seen or heard. The Sunday morning talk shows involve experts from government, science, industry, and academia in discussions of wide ranging issues from the war on terrorism to global warming, but these lineups rarely include representatives of social movements, regardless of their credentials.

Invisibility within Institutions

Invisible social movements and organizations are not consulted or represented on task forces dealing with major issues, do not appear on election ballots, and may be denied meeting places or parade permits because they are not recognized as legitimate groups. For example, during the Democratic Convention in Chicago in 1968, the mayor denied permits for the Yippies to use Soldier Field and members of the National Mobilization Committee to use Lincoln Park after curfew hours. Organizers of the annual Saint Patrick's Day parade in New York have attempted to deny permission for gay and lesbian Irish to take part.

Without a place to meet, particularly one that may enhance their credibility, social movement organizations and their sympathizers have difficulty attaining significant social standing in the eyes of the public. The American Civil Liberties Union (ACLU) antagonized the American Legion when it defended communists who killed four Legionnaires in 1919. It and its sympathizers were prevented from holding meetings in the World War Memorial in Indianapolis until an Indiana Supreme Court decision in 1973 ruled that the memorial was state property and not under the control of the American Legion.[16] It took fifty-four years for one institution to overrule another. A common practice today is for institutions to provide a space or location for protestors to meet, protest, and make speeches that is far removed from streets and entrances used by institutional members to attend meetings.

Institutional leaders avoid meeting with representatives of social movements because such meetings could be interpreted as a sign that the movements are worthy opponents and have something important to contribute. Bureaucratic procedures enable institutions to delay official responses, pass-the-buck, be unavailable for comment, and give movements the runaround. Institutions maintain the appearance of addressing issues by referring them to committees, special commissions, or task forces often populated with those who support the institutions or people who are, in fact, responsible for the very problems (such as water or air pollution, the price of oil, illegal immigration, and highway construction) the movements hope to correct. Postponement tactics slow or delay the decision-making process regarding a social movement's charges and demands. Issues, such as civil rights and women's rights, are tied up in the courts or Congress for years while little or no change takes place. Members of civil rights movements throughout most of the twentieth century faced jury trials with all-white juries.

Institutions may pay a price for this "head in the sand" approach. For instance, when violent protests erupted in Seattle in December 1999 during the World Trade Organization (WTO) meetings, reporters noted that city officials had not taken the situation seriously although many groups had been planning protests for months and had consulted regularly with city officials. There were warning signs that the protests could be violent. The same thing happened with the Native American Movement that resulted in the takeover of Alcatraz Island, the siege at Wounded Knee, South Dakota, and the trashing of the Bureau of Indian Affairs in Washington, D.C. Bowers, Ochs, and Jensen write: "The actions by the establishment may make agitators angry and actually energize them rather than causing them to give up their agitation as the establishment hopes."[17]

THE STRATEGY OF COUNTER-PERSUASION

Institutions employ a strategy of counter-persuasion when they can no longer avoid encounters with social movements. They challenge a social movement's version of reality and attempt to discredit its leaders, members, and demands.

Framing Issues

The secret to success is not to overreact but to characterize the social movement's ideas as ill-advised, poorly informed, and lacking merit. By manipulating the social context, institutions can expand, narrow, or selectively alter arguments and definitions of the situation. For instance, as the U.S. approached the invasion of Iraq in 2003, the goal seemingly shifted from eliminating weapons of mass destruction, disposing of a dangerous leader, defeating worldwide terrorism, and ensuring a steady supply of petroleum to liberating a captive nation. Eventually it became "the War on Terrorism." Members of the peace movement encountered a complex and seemingly ever-changing target for protest and had great difficulty trying to overcome repeated charges that they were unpatriotic and un-American. Institutions framed protestors as antimilitary, soft on terrorism, defeatist, unconcerned about the safety and security of Americans, and traitors whose revelations about secret spying on Americans and CIA-run prisons in various foreign countries were aiding the enemy.

Institutions are keepers of political, social, religious, and historical information. They argue that if movements had the information they have, the movements would not be making such wild charges or claims, all the while making every effort to prevent movements from getting more information. When forced, institutions release selected and edited bits of information.

While social movements may gain a modicum of legitimacy by challenging the accuracy and completeness of information as evidence of institutional deception and manipulation, they find it more difficult to attack information from neutral sources such as researchers and sympathetic theorists or those who were once part of the movement. Institutional converts pose unique problems for movements such as pro-choice, animal rights, Native American, and environmentalism. For instance, Patrick Moore (a Ph.D. in ecology) was a founder and full time activist with Greenpeace until he became disillusioned with its "sharp turn to the political left" and its abandonment of "science and logic in favor of emotion and sensationalism."[18] In 1991 he founded Greenspirit because he believed that "compromise and co-operation with the involvement of government, industry, academia, and the environmental movement is required to achieve sustainability." He has maintained the Web site www.greenspirit.com for nearly ten years to present scientific findings, to offer solutions for sustaining the environment, and to challenge extremists who, he claims, are antihuman, antiscience and technology, anti-trade, antibusiness, and anti-civilization. For instance, he writes that the environmental movement attempted to deny the nutritional advances of genetically enhanced food crops by "using 'Frankenfood' scare tactics and misinformation campaigns." It is difficult for the movement to attack or ignore a person so well versed in movement tactics and with verifiable environmental and scientific credentials.

Enhancing Fear Appeals

An effective means of resisting change is to appeal to fundamental *fears*. For example, institutional agents and agencies supporting slavery prior to the Civil War countered abolitionist messages with warnings of violent and deadly slave uprisings, often recalling Nat Turner's rebellion and John Brown's raid on the federal arsenal at Harper's Ferry. The Know-Nothing Party of the 1840s and 1850s played on Protestant fears of a seemingly massive Catholic immigration by warning of a papal conspiracy to take over the U.S. and force it to espouse Catholicism. Antilabor union forces created fears of anarchist revolutions and later the "red scare" when communism came on the scene. During the women's rights movement in the nineteenth century, the media warned that terrible things would happen if women gained the right to vote. Cartoonists portrayed female army officers reviewing all-female military units; women at political rallies while husbands were at home taking care of the children; and women smoking and drinking in saloons while husbands were doing the laundry. The alleged stripping of soldiers, workers, husbands, and fathers of their manhood has remained a rhetorical staple of those opposing women's rights and supporting the military for more than a century. Today, the warnings include allegations that environmentalists are endangering the U.S. economy by preventing oil independence and threatening the livelihoods of factory workers, loggers, and fishermen and women or gay rights advocates are immoral and pose grievous threats to the family and traditional way of life.

Institutional warnings play on fundamental, long-standing fears and the siege mentality Americans have harbored since before the Revolution. Evil forces are always striving to defeat us, so we must be ever vigilant against evil, foreign, and omnipresent evildoers.[19] Recently there have been repeated warnings that any restrictions on presidential authority and decisions in the global war on terrorism—literally a war against freedom—would result in another "9/11."

Revealing True Motives

An institution or its surrogates may challenge the *motives* of persuasive efforts by or seemingly on behalf of a social movement. In 1983, when ABC-TV was about to air its nuclear holocaust special entitled *The Day After*, Phyllis Schlafly (president of the Eagle Forum) sent leaflets to schools throughout the nation denouncing the video in advance as "virulently anti-American," "dishonest," and a "vicious smear of America" because it suggested that the United States might have started the war. To Schlafly *The Day After* was a thinly veiled "political" video created to support the pro-pacifist and antinuclear movements and "offensive to President Reagan and to religious people."[20] Following demonstrations in 1999 during the WTO meetings in Seattle, Fareed Zakaria wrote a column in *Newsweek* challenging the "plea for the downtrodden of the world" (a common plea in protest rhetoric). He argued:

> There's just one problem: the downtrodden beg to differ. Representatives of the developing nations at the meeting angrily pointed out that the demonstrators were seeking to protect the jobs and benefits of *Western* workers, who are rich and privileged by any standard. In fact, if the demonstrators' demands were met, the effect would be to crush the hopes of much poorer Third World workers—the original indigenous people.[21]

Cries of anarchy have often united the "silent majority" by identifying protestors as dangerous criminals and degenerates. Ralph Smith and Russell Windes note that antigay persuaders who identify themselves as "agents of the majority" describe their pro-gay antagonists as a "small but vocal minority" that "is about to impose its will on the silent and inactive majority" and as "a loud, militant, and over-influential minority."[22]

Opponents of social movements throughout U.S. history have found it easy to generate feelings of suspicion toward those who are "different" or "foreign" and to create fears about social movement motives and objectives. As mentioned in previous chapters, the day after Martin Luther King, Jr., had been arrested and placed in solitary confinement in Birmingham, Alabama, eight white clergymen (including four bishops and a rabbi) placed an open letter advertisement in the newspaper asking him to stop his "unwise and untimely" demonstrations in their city because it was doing more harm than good. They referred to King and his followers as outside agitators, extremists, law breakers, and anarchists.[23] The clergy were not alone in their attacks and characterizations. Local officials identified integration with despised external movements and threats such as communism. In their eyes, integration was a tool of the communist conspiracy that threatened Christian and democratic principles and values (which they viewed as fundamental social values). Pro-segregation forces believed King's call for brotherhood, freedom, justice, and equality was part of the communist line and that he was, in fact, a Soviet-trained communist agent.

Movement leaders must spend a great amount of rhetoric and energy explaining and justifying actions and ideology to sympathizers and the public. Although the violent actions of the true anarchists in Seattle during the WTO meeting resulted in thousands of dollars in damage and greatly embarrassed the city and the United States government, the anarchists' actions and threatening rhetoric enabled authorities to crack down on all protestors, violent and nonviolent, and to identify all as dangers to society.

Denigrating the Opposition

Moral outrage and righteous indignation over alleged evil motives justify counterattacks that employ labeling and name-calling. Lawrence Rosenfeld defines coercive semantics as attempts "to discourage real discussion of alternatives, and to render counterarguments meaningless by labeling the opponents as evil."[24]

Henry Gonzalez, elected to Congress in 1961 from Texas, led an aggressive counterattack against militant Chicanos. His charges followed three themes: (1) militants practiced reverse racism and preached hate based upon race; (2) militants displayed bad qualities and harmed the Mexican-American community; and (3) militant attacks on him were personal and unfair. Gonzalez's perspective was that the militants "have adopted the same positions, the same attitudes, the same tactics as those who have so long offended them."[25] Nearly identical charges were made in the 1980s and 1990s against Louis Farrakhan (leader of the Nation of Islam) for allegedly making anti-Semitic statements and against the Black Panthers in Indianapolis for urging African Americans to boycott stores in their neighborhoods that are owned by Korean Americans. S. I. Hayakawa (president of San Francisco State University in 1968 and later a U.S. senator) claimed that rebellious students were attempting to overthrow the government and were all drug addicts. He referred to students as "cowards who resort to violence, lies, and deceit."[26]

Martha Solomon, in examining the rhetorical strategies of the Stop ERA (Equal Rights Amendment) campaign, found that opponents of the women's movement ridiculed members as unattractive and lesbian. She concluded that "with sharp satire the group paints an unappealing picture of the feminists' physical appearance and nature, emphasizing their disregard for traditional standards of feminine attractiveness and sexuality."[27] Phyllis Schlafly proclaimed, "If man is targeted as the enemy, and the ultimate goal of women's liberation is independence from men and the avoidance of pregnancy and its consequences, then lesbianism is the highest form in the ritual of women's liberation."[28] Ridicule may weaken the self-confidence and self-esteem of protestors and challenge their efforts to attain legitimacy.

Counter-persuasion deals primarily with social movement leaders and members rather than the movement's issues and demands. Name-calling, labeling, and ridicule attack individuals directly. Perhaps the easiest way to discredit a movement is to discredit its leaders and most fervent followers. If the leaders and true believers are evil, then the motives, goals, and objectives of the movement must be evil. As noted in chapter 1, political cartoonists of the 1990s portrayed militia movement leaders and members as ignorant, marginally employed people whose motives and goals were laced with anti-Semitic and racist slurs. Sherry Shepler and Anne Mattina claim that when Jane Addams spoke out against entry by the United States into World War I (as noted in chapters 4 and 5), resistance forces framed "Addams as a less than credible source" to marginalize her concerns and make "them undeserving of response."[29]

THE STRATEGY OF COERCIVE PERSUASION

The strategy of coercive persuasion is persuasive if those who employ it *convince* target audiences (social movements, other institutions, and the public) that *force* will follow *noncompliance* because the persuader has both the *capability* and *intent* of using it for *legitimate* and *desirable* ends.[30] When avoidance and counter-persuasion fail to stifle a social movement and an institution commits itself to direct action and sustained conflict, coercive persuasion comes into play and involves tactics ranging from threats to harassment. Institutions have a war chest of potentially lethal threats.

Expulsion

Institutions may threaten to fire workers, expel students, deport the foreign born, excommunicate the true believer, or discharge members of the military. For instance, employers fought the labor movement for years with threats to blacklist union members by publicizing their names throughout the country so no one would hire them. Governments threaten exile or deportation, schools threaten suspension or expulsion, the military threatens to discharge gay members who violate the "don't ask, don't tell" policy. Religious organizations threaten to excommunicate members or to deny them important rites or sacraments. The Roman Catholic Church, for example, barred an eleven-year-old child from a Catholic school because she would not renounce her mother's pro-choice activism; denied sacraments to members of NOW in California because the organization was pro-choice; and threatened to deny sacraments to elected officials and political candidates in 2004 who espoused pro-choice views. University administrators and police photographed student demonstrators in the 1960s and 1970s to identify students for possible expulsion and for reporting to parents or draft boards. The mere presence of government agents with cameras led some demonstrators to disperse.

Restrictive Legislation and Policies

The passage and implementation of restrictive legislation and policies is an effective means of coercive persuasion. For example, the University of California at Berkeley in 1964 established a policy prohibiting individuals from soliciting funds and advocating political causes on campus. Several students were arrested for violating this policy. This undemocratic and unconstitutional policy suppressed student actions until protest organizations challenged it in court. Some cities used zoning laws during the 1960s and 1970s to eliminate underground presses that produced free newspapers and newsletters in private homes, contending that such presses were businesses and could not be operated in homes zoned as family dwellings. Challenging restrictive policies and legislation through legal channels takes time and money, assets that favor institutions rather than social movements.

During the red scare following World War I and the cold war that followed World War II, concern for national security led many states to require persons who would teach at state colleges or universities to sign loyalty oaths in front of notary publics who then affixed their seals to the documents. The oath in Indiana read:

> I solemnly swear (or affirm) that I will support the Constitution of the United States of America, the Constitution of the State of Indiana, and the laws of the United States and the State of Indiana, and will, by precept and example, promote respect for the flag and the institutions of the United States and the State of Indiana, reverence for law and order and undivided allegiance to the Government of the United States of America.

Any professor, instructor, or teacher who, in the judgment of the college or university, exhibited behavior inimical to this oath could be fired. Persons wishing to join the armed forces had to read a list of some three hundred organizations deemed by the attorney general of the United States to pose a danger to national security and to fill out a form swearing that they had never been members of or associated with members of any of the organizations listed. If they refused to answer the questions and sign their names, they could be denied admittance to any of the armed forces. If they answered falsely, they could be fined up to $10,000, imprisoned for up to five years, or both.

Harassment

Institutions employ harassment to intimidate and to show who has the real power in the confrontation with social movements. In an overt form of harassment during the Vietnam War, the head of the Selective Service System ordered the reclassification of leading student protestors. For example, Peter Wolff and Richard Shorn were classified II-S as full-time students at the University of Michigan. When they participated in a demonstration protesting U.S. involvement in Vietnam, the local Selective Service Board reclassified both as I-A, eligible for the draft. The board argued that by participating in the antiwar demonstration, Wolff and Shorn became "delinquents" and thus were in violation of Section 12(a) of the Universal Military Training and Service Act. They further argued that a student deferment was not a "right" but a "legislative grace."[31] Students who wished to remain in school got the message.

In a less obvious form of harassment, National Guardsmen were called out to "protect students" in a two-day march on the Pentagon in 1967. The large number of heavily armed troops restricted the movement of and access to the student marchers. It soon became clear that the troops were present to control rather than to protect the protestors; this institutional show of force cost the taxpayers more than one million dollars.

Harassment tactics may be covert. During the Johnson and Nixon Administrations, the FBI, the CIA, Army Intelligence, and the Treasury Department investigated antiwar demonstrators and student leaders for communist connections or sympathies on which the government might base administrative actions. The FBI launched its counterintelligence operation (COINTELPRO) in May 1968 to counteract the New Left. Until it ceased operation on April 28, 1971, COINTELPRO secretly photographed college students, created files and lists of suspected communist sympathizers, and sent letters (many allegedly from parents and concerned citizens) to boards of trustees to get leftist students expelled. It sent letters to school boards and superintendents suggesting that certain teachers be fired for leftist activities. For instance, a Washington, D.C., teacher's only dangerous activity was participation in the Young Socialist Alliance, the youth affiliate of the Socialist Workers. The FBI reported activities of students to parents, encouraging them to protest to the college for allowing leftist organizations to operate on campus. The secret file created while Bill Clinton was a college student and anti-Vietnam War protestor was used against him when he campaigned for the presidency in 1992. The file included details of a visit he had made to the Soviet Union while a Rhodes Scholar at Oxford University.

Use of Surrogates

Some institutions have tried to challenge social movement organizations with more cooperative ones. Corporations played the CIO and AFL against one another during the 1930s and 1940s. Grape growers in California signed contracts with the Teamsters Union to counteract the United Farm Workers Organizing Committee's efforts to unionize grape workers. Nine growers and right-wing organizations created, financed, and handpicked the leaders for a counter-organization called the AWFWA (Agricultural Workers Freedom to Work Association), allegedly a farm workers' organization. The courts outlawed the AWFWA as a flagrant violation of fair employment laws. When giant retailer Wal-Mart came under increasing attack from union, environmental, community, and consumer groups in 2005, it partially funded and formed "Working Families for Wal-Mart," composed of community leaders ranging from clergy to Latino activists to businesswomen "to speak up for the world's largest retailer and launch counterattacks when they sense criticism is unfair."[32]

Institutions often rely on surrogates to suppress social movements. Jerome Skolnick claims that counterdemonstrators have attacked many protestors with the knowledge and tacit approval of administrative and civil authorities:

> By far the greater portion of physical harm has been done to demonstrators and movement workers, in the form of bombings of homes and offices, crowd-control measures used by police, physical attacks on demonstrators by American Nazi party members, Hell's Angels and others, and random harassment such as the Port Chicago Vigil has endured.[33]

The Ku Klux Klan and White Citizens Councils were surrogates for southern state and community authorities during the civil rights struggles. Anti-environmental groups such as the Wise Use Movement and the Sahara Club have telephoned threats and warnings to environmental activists, recorded license plate numbers, and videotaped activists as a signal of future retaliation.[34] When threats proved ineffective, they resorted to coercion by picking fights with demonstrators, assaulting movement leaders, and setting fire to homes. The signal is clear—we know who you are and where we can find you.

Infiltration

Government agents and sympathizers routinely infiltrate social movement organizations and protest groups in the United States with the primary purpose of gathering information to inhibit their activities. During the cold war, a standing joke was that the membership of communist groups in the United States included more undercover FBI agents than communists. Years after Malcolm X's assassination it became known that his chief bodyguard was an undercover New York police officer. With easy access to social movement Web sites, institutions can routinely monitor messages and activities.

One purpose of infiltration is to instigate militant and violent acts to discredit social movements. Michael Stohl reports that "regimes and their agent provocateurs (both official and self-identified) have both encouraged insurgent groups to plan and execute terrorist actions not only to provide grounds for arrest but also to alienate potential supporters within the population."[35] Labor movement leaders have charged that corporations have routinely planted people within unions to instigate strikes and violent acts to discredit unions and justify repression. Terence Powderly charged that during the long and disruptive strike of the streetcar drivers in St. Louis in 1886, "men who were employed by detective agencies" hired by employers "stood up on the floor of that Assembly, made inflammatory speeches urging the men to deeds of violence, and urged that the property of the streetcar companies be destroyed." Although "the good sense of the men" in the union prevented violent actions by the Knights of Labor, "agents of a nefarious spy system induced some desperate men to blow up the cars on the streets."[36]

Arrests and Use of Courts

Arrest is a common form of coercive persuasion. It has been used in recent years against antinuclear power, environmental, antiapartheid policies of South Africa, pro-choice, pro-life, and gay rights activists. Some groups such as pro-life's Operation Rescue want to be arrested to clog the jails, but others see the possibility of being arrested as humiliating and embarrassing.

Arrests often have little to do with public security or any violation of laws. For instance, a student at the University of California at Berkeley was arrested for public obscenity because he carried a sign that read "Freedom Under Clark Kerr" (Kerr was president of the university). The first letter of each word was highlighted, but the arrest was aimed at removing a protestor rather than the rhetorical implication. As noted in chapter 1 the administration at Purdue University in 1986 arrested demonstrators who had constituted a mock shantytown on Memorial Mall to protest the apartheid policies of South Africa.

Multiple charges can tie up movement leaders for years with court appearances that drain a movement's finances and create harmful publicity. Bowers, Ochs, and Jensen write that the Black Panthers were involved in more than sixty criminal prosecutions requiring $300,000 in bail money in the first six months of 1967.[37]

While the courts have sometimes ruled in favor of protestors (for instance, expanding freedom of speech to symbolic speech, including symbols and symbolic actions), rulings often place severe limits on social movements. For instance, protestors may speak against the government, but they cannot advocate its overthrow, cannot put the American flag to "an ignoble use," cannot exceed the bounds of rational discourse, cannot invade the privacy of others, cannot place "undue strain" on a community's resources, and cannot "inconvenience" people not in the target audience. Institutions, of course, determine when protestors are advocating overthrow of the government and what is ignoble, irrational, invasive, or inconvenient.

Coercive persuasion offers several advantages to institutions. First, coercive persuasion may generate fear among a social movement's leaders, followers, and sympathizers. They may become hesitant to act; members may become hesitant to take part in demonstrations; and sympathizers may withdraw moral and financial support. Second, coercion isolates leaders from followers. Third, coercion enables institutions to portray social movement leaders as common criminals and dangerous social deviants.

THE STRATEGY OF ADJUSTMENT

Institutions employ a strategy of adjustment when they "adapt, modify, or alter their structures, their goals, and their personnel in response to an external ideological challenge."[38] This strategy involves making some concessions while not accepting the movement's demands or goals. It typically occurs after institutions have tried evasion, counter-persuasion, and coercive persuasion.

Institutions must approach accommodation and apparent concessions with caution because, as Tocqueville wrote two centuries ago, people grasp at opportunities, so "the most perilous moment for a bad government is one when it seeks to mend its ways."[39] Institutions do not want to appear weak or timid, but they also must not appear to be deceptive, cynical, or tyrannical. Adjustments must appear serious and well-meaning when they may be little more than tokens to appease public questions and social movement demands. An effective adjustment tactic gives the appearance of being responsive to movement concerns. Andrew King claims that accommodation is usually a short-term solution for the institution that buys time, saves face, and appears gracious.[40]

A danger is that a concession may rejuvenate a social movement by renewing hope of victory. If concessions do not appear to meet significant social movement demands or expectations, movements may replace moderate leaders, often incorporated into institutional positions, with radical elements and become a more serious threat to institutions. This happened in the civil rights movement with the rise of the Black Panthers and when radical leaders Stokely Carmichael and H. Rap Brown assumed leadership of SNCC and became highly visible and popular. It has happened in recent years with the rise of ELF in the environmental movement and ALF in the animal rights movement.

Short-Term Solutions and Agreements

The strategy of adaptation addresses superficial elements of conflict and seldom results in permanent solutions to social unrest and demands. As noted in chapter 1 Julia "Butterfly" Hill took residence on a tiny platform at the top of a redwood tree on December 10, 1997. She remained there until December 1999 when, according to an agreement filed at the Humboldt County Recorder's Office, "Hill and her supporters pledged to pay $50,000 to Pacific Lumber to make up for lost logging revenue. The company agreed to spare Hill's redwood and a 2.9 acre buffer zone around it."[41] Although Hill was out of the tree and the company agreed to a small, mainly symbolic, saving of one giant redwood tree, nothing was resolved. The struggle and logging continued.

Laws passed that seem to favor social movements often lack enforcement mechanisms to make them effective. Unsympathetic institutions do not willingly enforce laws that do not favor their interests. For example, the United Farm Workers were instrumental in passing agricultural laws in California that severely limited the use of certain deadly pesticides and required the posting of signs when fields had been sprayed with dangerous chemicals. When Governor George Deukmejian came into office in 1983, he refused to enforce the laws, including the paper signs he said were too expensive for the multi-billion dollar agricultural industry.

Court decisions often suffer the same fate. It took years, for instance, to make northern and southern states obey the 1954 Supreme Court decision (*Brown v. Board of Education*) that struck down the separate but equal doctrine that had allowed segregation of the races. The hope is that protestors will become discouraged and go away or that the issue will disappear. During the efforts to integrate public schools, a common strategy for white citizens was to close public schools or to create their own schools to avoid integration. In 1963 Rev. George Fisher, pastor of the Edgewater Baptist Church in Birmingham, Alabama, obtained 75,000 signatures on petitions endorsing the closing of schools rather than acquiescing to enforced integration. There was massive resistance to integrating schools in the late 1950s. Governor Thomas Stanley of Virginia urged that "consideration be given to the repeal of Section 129 of the state constitution, which mandated that the state maintain free public schools."[42] Many school districts delayed opening public schools, and Norfolk closed its public schools from September 1958 to February 1959.

When laws or decisions are made, some are framed so ambiguously or are so full of loopholes that institutional offenders can easily circumvent them. For instance, when the Supreme Court handed down a decision on abortion in the late 1990s, newspaper headlines exemplified the ambiguity of what the Court had decided:[43]

> *The Miami Herald*: "Court Affirms Abortion Rights"
>
> *The Orlando Sentinel*: "Court Weakens Abortion Rights"
>
> *The Oakland Tribune*: "Roe Reaffirmed"
>
> *USA Today*: "High Court Reins in Roe"
>
> *San Francisco Chronicle*: "Court Upholds Right to Abortion"
>
> *Chicago Tribune*: "Ruling Weakens Abortion Right"
>
> *Minneapolis Star*: "Abortion Ruling Lands in the Middle"

Ambiguity enables institutions to frame issues to avoid making serious changes or to admit that the status quo has been seriously altered. Indeed, the framing can extend to interpreting various decisions as strengthening current policy.

Symbolic Gestures

Adjustment tactics include symbolic actions such as issuing press releases that promise investigation of problems or the naming of special committees and commissions to study the issues the social movement has raised. These gestures provide a visible response and show of concern while reducing the sense of urgency of social movement demands, which buys time for the institution. Presidents, governors, and political candidates address concerns such as equal rights, the environment, animal rights, ethics, and the needs of senior citizens and then go about business as usual when elected. Although this adjustment strategy is similar to bureaucratic delays, it involves a public acknowledgment of the movement's demands.

Sacrificing personnel is a common institutional tactic. University deans and presidents, police chiefs and officers, and mid-level executives often are dismissed or "resign" from their positions when they become targets of social movements, are portrayed as unresponsive to citizen or group needs, or become convenient and expendable symbols of institutional "responsiveness." This tactic is particularly effective when a social movement focuses its agitation and anger on a single individual or unit. Elimination of the individual or unit leaves the movement without a target. Public sympathy for an institution may increase when sacrificed individuals are seen as tragic victims of *radical* protestors.

Cooperation and Co-optation

A subtle adjustment tactic is cooperation with protestors and organizations by providing protection, access to facilities, or material support. Open and publicized cooperation frustrates social movements by making institutions less of an enemy and target of outrage. Cooperation may defuse a movement's energy, momentum, and recruiting efforts, buy time for counterefforts, encourage attitudes of neutrality among citizens, and generate favorable press.

Cooperation may lead to outright co-optation of the cause in which institutions seemingly take on the cause as their own. Congress, for example, seemed to take on the civil rights cause in the years following the assassination of John F. Kennedy by passing civil rights and voting laws and creating an equal employment opportunity commission. Institutional groups, including corporations, literally took over the ecology or environmental movement in the 1970s. Advertising Council ads featured a tearful Native American looking at a trashed America from his canoe or a hilltop overlooking a freeway.

Admission to Institutional Circles

Incorporation of movement leaders and sympathizers within institutional bodies is a common adjustment tactic. During the 1960s and 1970s, students, blacks, and women became appointees, often as tokens, to committees, boards, and study commissions. Governmental agencies, schools, religious groups, and corporations began to hire a few minorities and to appoint them to serve in a variety of nonauthoritative—and therefore nonthreatening—positions. For example, U.S. colleges and universities appointed students to serve on boards of trustees, grievance committees, grade-appeal committees, and curriculum committees. Representation, however, did not mean power to influence policy decisions. At the start of the twenty-first century, the phrase "glass ceiling" still has significance for women and minorities who lag far behind white males in salaries and leadership positions.

CONCLUSIONS

Institutions must confront challenges and threats to their existence, even though complete annihilation of existing institutions seldom occurs in today's world. For an institution, any concession to dissenters may be costly. Negotiations often create strains and an atmosphere of risk in a win/lose situation. Institutions tend to employ a combination of four strategies in meeting the threats posed by social movements: evasion, counter-persuasion, coercive persuasion, and adjustment. The combination depends on the relationship of institutions to the social movement, the environment within which it is operating, and the acceptability of any potential change.

When using the strategy of *evasion*, institutions attempt to ignore a social movement, pretending that it does not exist or is not worthy of response. They try to avoid direct contacts with movement leaders to reinforce a symbolic invisibility. When an institution can no longer ignore a social movement, it may use *counter-persuasion* to challenge the movement's version of reality and to discredit its leaders, members, or demands. Institutional persuasion appeals to fundamental fears among the public. It warns of dire results, even anarchy, if the movement is successful. It may challenge the nature and motives of the movement and question the accuracy or veracity of the movement's persuasive efforts. Institutions use *coercive persuasion* when the strategies of evasion and counter-persuasion seem ineffective in stifling a movement. Coercive persuasion includes tactics ranging from threats to harassment. It may be overt through police actions, telephoned threats, and arrests or covert through secret files on protestors, sending letters under the guise of concerned parents or citizens, and infiltration of movement organizations. Institutions use a strategy of *adjustment* to give the appearance of being responsive to "legitimate concerns" by pledging funds to address elements of a problem, creating special study commissions, and sacrificing personnel the movement finds offensive.

Over time, bits and pieces of social movement ideologies find their way into institutional policies regardless of the strategies employed to stifle them. Social security, farm supports, unemployment benefits, the eight-hour day, civil rights, equal opportunity, voting rights, collective bargaining, and fair housing were social movement demands long before established political parties enacted them into law. The task for institutions is to allow (perhaps even to encourage) dissent without threatening social, political, economic, or religious orders. Institutions have many more resources than social movements, and responses may emanate from individuals, organized resistance groups, local leaders, statewide organizations, and national authorities that may include the whole federal government. The trick for an institution is to use the best strategy for the situation and to avoid the appearance of overreacting or abusing the powers the people have granted to it to provide for the security and maintenance of social structure.

Notes

[1] See John W. Bowers, Donovan J. Ochs, and Richard J. Jensen, *The Rhetoric of Agitation and Control*, 2nd ed. (Long Grove, IL: Waveland Press, 1993): 11–12.

[2] Kenneth T. Walsh, *Air Force One: A History of the Presidents and Their Planes* (New York: Hyperion, 2003).

[3] Bowers, Ochs, and Jensen, 13–15.

[4] Andrew King, *Power and Communication* (Long Grove, IL: Waveland Press, 1987): 48–53.

[5] Hugh Dalziel Duncan, *Symbols in Reality* (New York: Oxford University Press, 1968): 78–92.

[6] Sidney Tarrow, *Power in Movement: Social Movements and Contentious Politics* (Cambridge: Cambridge University Press, 1998): 73–76.

[7] Sherry R. Shepler and Anne F. Mattina, "'The Revolt Against War': Jane Addams' Rhetorical Challenge to the Patriarchy," *Communication Quarterly* 47 (Spring 1999): 152.

[8] Thomas James Norton, *The Constitution of the United States: Its Sources and Its Applications* (New York: America's Future, 1949): 4–5, 206.

[9] Haig A. Bosmajian, ed. *Dissent: Symbolic Behavior and Rhetorical Strategies* (Boston: Allyn & Bacon, 1972).

[10] Spiro T. Agnew, "Des Moines, Iowa Address to the Midwest Republican Committee," November 13, 1969, from a tape recording.

[11] Wayne Flynt, "The Ethics of Democratic Persuasion and the Birmingham Crisis," *Southern Speech Communication Journal* 35 (Fall 1969): 45.

[12] For a discussion of police response to protestors, see Irving Horowitz, *The Struggle Is the Message* (Berkeley, CA: The Glendessary Press, 1970): 48–58.

[13] Theodore Windt, "Administrative Rhetoric: An Undemocratic Response to Protest," *Communication Quarterly* 30 (Summer, 1982): 247.

[14] See Bowers, Ochs, and Jensen, 48–64.

[15] Dieter Rucht, "The Quadruple 'A': Media Strategies of Protest Movements since the 1960s," Wim van de Donk, Brian D. Loader, Paul G. Nixon, and Dieter Rucht, eds., *Cyberprotest: New Media, Citizens and Social Movements* (London: Routledge, 2004): 32, 33, 35.

[16] Michael D. Murray, "To Hire a Hall: 'An Argument in Indianapolis,'" *Central States Speech Journal* 26 (Spring 1975): 12–20.

[17] Bowers, Ochs, and Jensen, 50.

[18] http://www.greenspirit.com/logbook.cfm?msid=83, accessed 31 July 2006.

[19] Peter Knight, ed. *Conspiracy Nation: The Politics of Paranoia in Postwar America* (New York: New York University Press, 2002); Richard O. Curry and Thomas M. Brown, *Conspiracy: The Fear of Subversion in American History* (New York: Holt, Rinehart, and Winston, 1972).

[20] ABC Film *The Day After*, Eagle Forum, November 1983.

[21] Fareed Zakaria, "After the Storm Passes," *Newsweek*, 13 December 1999, 40.

[22] Ralph R. Smith and Russell R. Windes, "The Pro-gay and Antigay Issue Culture: Interpretation, Influence and Dissent," *Quarterly Journal of Speech* 83 (February 1997): 31, 38.

[23] Martin Luther King, Jr., *The Autobiography of Martin Luther King, Jr.*, Clayborne Carson, ed. (New York: Warner, 1998): 187–204.

[24] Lawrence Rosenfeld, "The Confrontation Policies of S. I. Hayakawa: A Case Study in Coercive Semantics," *Today's Speech* 18 (Spring 1970): 18.

[25] John Hammerback, Richard Jensen, and Jose Gutierrer, *A War of Words* (Westport, CT: Greenwood Press, 1985): 104.

[26] Rosenfeld, 20.

[27] Martha Solomon, "The Rhetoric of Stop ERA: Fatalistic Reaffirmation," *Southern Speech Communication Journal* 44 (Fall 1978): 47.

[28] Solomon, 47.

[29] Shepler and Mattina, 163.

[30] Herbert W. Simons, "Persuasion and Social Conflicts: A Critique of Prevailing Conceptions and a Framework for Future Research," *Speech Monographs* 39 (November 1972): 232. See also Parke G. Burgess, "Crisis Rhetoric: Coercion vs. Force," *Quarterly Journal of Speech* 59 (February 1973): 69.

[31] Harold Medina, "Students Have Rights Too," *Free Speech and Political Protest*, Marvin Summers, ed. (Lexington, MA: D. C. Heath, 1967): 102.

[32] Associated Press, "Pro-Wal-Mart Group Created," Lafayette, Indiana *Journal and Courier*, 20 December 2005, B5.

[33] Jerome Skolnick, "The Politics of Protest," *Dissent: Symbolic Behavior and Rhetorical Strategies*, Haig Bosmajian, ed. (Boston: Allyn & Bacon, 1972): 156.

[34] CBS, *60 Minutes*, 6 June 1993.

[35] Michael Stohl, ed., *The Politics of Terrorism* (New York: Dekker, 1983): 5.

[36] "Report of the General Master Workman," *Proceedings of the General Assembly of the Knights of Labor*, 6 October 1886, 38.

[37] Bowers, Ochs, and Jensen, 55.

[38] Bowers, Ochs, and Jensen, 60.

[39] Tarrow, 74.

[40] King, 27.

[41] "Tree's Best Pal Returns to Earth," Lafayette, Indiana *Journal and Courier* 19 December 1999, A3.

[42] Alexander S. Leidholdt, *Standing Before the Shouting Mob: Lenoir Chambers and Virginia's Massive Resistance to Public-School Integration* (Tuscaloosa: The University of Alabama Press, 1997): 67.

[43] These headlines were compiled by Al Neuharth, retired CEO of the Gannett Company and founder of *USA Today*.

Selected Bibliography

ARTICLES AND CHAPTERS

"An Interview with Bert Carona," *Western Journal of Speech Communication* 44 (Summer 1980): 214–220.

"An Interview with Jose Angel Gutierrez," *Western Journal of Speech Communication* 44 (Summer 1980): 202–213.

Andrews, James R. "The Ethos of Pacifism: The Problem of Image in the Early British Peace Movement," *Quarterly Journal of Speech* 53 (February 1967): 28–33.

———. "Piety and Pragmatism: Rhetorical Aspects of the Early British Peace Movement," *Speech Monographs* 34 (November 1967): 423–436.

———. "Confrontation at Columbia: A Case Study in Coercive Rhetoric," *Quarterly Journal of Speech* 55 (February 1969): 9–16.

———. "The Rhetoric of Coercion and Persuasion: The Reform Bill of *1832*," *Quarterly Journal of Speech* 56 (April 1970): 187–195.

———. "The Passionate Negation: The Chartist Movement in Rhetorical Perspective," *Quarterly Journal of Speech* 59 (April 1973): 196–208.

———. "Spindles vs. Acres: Rhetorical Perceptions on the British Free Trade Movement," *Western Speech* 38 (Winter 1974): 41–52.

———. "History and Theory in the Study of the Rhetoric of Social Movements," *Central States Speech Journal* 31 (Winter 1980): 274–281.

———. "An Historical Perspective on the Study of Social Movements," *Central States Speech Journal* 34 (Spring 1983): 67–69.

Armada, Bernard J. "Memorial Agon: An Interpretive Tour of the National Civil Rights Museum," *Southern Communication Journal* 63 (Spring 1998): 235–243.

Appel, Edward C. "The Rhetoric of Dr. Martin Luther King, Jr.: Comedy and Context in Tragic Collision," *Western Journal of Communication* 61 (Fall 1997): 376–402.

Bacon, Jacqueline. "Taking Liberty, Taking Literacy: Signifying the Rhetoric of African-American Abolitionists," *Southern Communication Journal* 64 (Summer 1999): 271–287.

Baskerville, Barnet. "The Cross and the Flag: Evangelists of the Far Right," *Western Speech* 27 (Fall 1963): 197–206.

Benson, Thomas W. "Rhetoric and Autobiography: The Case of Malcolm X," *Quarterly Journal of Speech* 60 (February 1974): 1–13.

Benson, Thomas W. and Bonnie Johnson. "The Rhetoric of Resistance: Confrontation with the Warmakers, Washington, DC, October 1967," *Today's Speech* 16 (September 1968): 35–42.

Berry, Edward. "Doing Time: King's 'Letter from Birmingham Jail,'" *Rhetoric & Public Affairs* 8 (Spring 2005): 109–132.

Bezayiff, David. "Legal Oratory of John Adams: An Early Instrument of Protest," *Western Journal of Speech Communication* 40 (Winter 1976): 63–71.

Black, Jason Edward. "Extending the Rights of Personhood, Voice, and Life to Sensate Others: A Homology of Right to Life and Animal Rights Rhetoric," *Communication Quarterly* 51 (Summer 2003): 312–331.

Borda, Jennifer L. "The Woman Suffrage Parades of 1910–1913: Possibilities and Limitations of an Early Feminist Rhetorical Strategy," *Western Journal of Communication* 66 (Winter 2002): 25–52.

Bormann, Ernest G. "Fantasy and Rhetorical Vision: The Rhetorical Criticism of Social Reality," *Quarterly Journal of Speech* 58 (December 1972): 396–407.

———. "Some Random Thoughts on the Unity or Diversity of the Rhetoric of Abolition," *Southern Communication Journal* 60 (Spring 1995): 266–274.

Bosmajian, Haig A. "The Nazi Speaker's Rhetoric," *Quarterly Journal of Speech* 46 (December 1960): 365–371.

———. "Nazi Meetings: The *Sprechabend,* the *Versaamlung,* the *Kundgebung,* the *Feierstunde,*" *Southern Speech Journal* 31 (Summer 1966): 324–337.

———. "Obscenity and Protest," *Today's Speech* 18 (Winter 1970): 9–14.

———. "Freedom of Speech and the Heckler," *Western Speech* 36 (Fall 1972): 218–232.

———. "Defining the 'American Indian': A Case Study in the Language of Suppression," *Speech Teacher* 22 (March 1973): 89–99.

———. "The Abrogation of the Suffragists' First Amendment Rights," *Western Speech* 38 (Fall 1974): 218–232.

———. "Freedom of Speech and the Language of Oppression," *Western Journal of Speech Communication* 42 (Fall 1978): 209–221.

Bostdorff, Denise M. "The Internet Rhetoric of the Ku Klux Klan: A Case Study in Web Site Community Building Run Amok," *Communication Studies* 55 (Summer 2004): 340–361.

Bowen, Harry W. "A Realistic View of Non-Violent Assumptions," *Today's Speech* 15 (September 1967): 9–10.

Branham, Robert James. "Speaking Itself: Susan Sontag's Town Hall Address," *Quarterly Journal of Speech* 75 (August 1989): 259–276.

———. "The Role of the Convert in *Eclipse of Reason* and *The Silent Scream,*" *Quarterly Journal of Speech* 77 (November 1991): 407–426.

Branham, Robert James and Sharon Howell. "The Evolution of the PLO: A Rhetoric of Terrorism," *Central States Speech Journal* 39 (Fall/Winter, 1988): 281–292.

Brockriede, Wayne E. and Robert L. Scott. "Stokely Carmichael: Two Speeches on Black Power," *Central States Speech Journal* 19 (Spring 1968): 3–13.

Brommel, Bernard J. "The Pacifist Speechmaking of Eugene V. Debs," *Quarterly Journal of Speech* 52 (April 1966): 146–154.

———. "Eugene V. Debs: The Agitator as Speaker," *Central States Speech Journal* 20 (Fall 1969): 202–214.

Brooks, Robert D. "Black Power: The Dimensions of a Slogan," *Western Speech* 34 (Spring 1970): 108–114.

Brown, William J. "The Persuasive Appeal of Mediated Terrorism: The Case of the TWA Flight 847 Hijacking," *Western Journal of Speech Communication* 54 (Spring 1990): 219–236.

Browne, Stephen H. "Encountering Angelina Grimke: Violence, Identity, and the Creation of Radical Community," *Quarterly Journal of Speech* 82 (February 1996): 55–73.

———. "Textual Style and Radical Critique in William Lloyd Garrison's *Thoughts on African Colonization*," *Communication Studies* 47 (Fall 1996): 177–190.

———. "Remembering Crispus Attucks: Race, Rhetoric, and the Politics of Commemoration," *Quarterly Journal of Speech* 85 (May 1999): 169–187.

———. "'This Unparalleled and Inhuman Massacre': The Gothic, the Sacred, and the Meaning of Nat Turner," *Rhetoric & Public Affairs* 3 (Fall 2000): 309–332.

Burgchardt, Carl R. "Two Faces of American Communism: Pamphlet Rhetoric of the Third Period and the Popular Front," *Quarterly Journal of Speech* 66 (December 1980): 375–391.

Burgess, Parke G. "The Rhetoric of Black Power: A Moral Demand," *Quarterly Journal of Speech* 54 (April 1968): 122–133.

———. "The Rhetoric of Moral Conflict: Two Critical Dimensions," *The Quarterly Journal of Speech* 56 (April 1970): 120–130.

———. "Crisis Rhetoric: Coercion vs. Force, *Quarterly Journal of Speech* 59 (February 1973): 61–73.

Burkholder, Thomas R. "Kansas Populism, Woman Suffrage, and the Agrarian Myth: A Case Study in the Limits of Mythic Transcendence," *Communication Studies* 40 (Winter 1989): 292–307.

Campbell, Finley C. "Voices of Thunder, Voices of Rage: A Symbolic Analysis of a Selection from Malcolm X's Speech 'Message to the Grass Roots,'" *Speech Teacher* 19 (March 1970): 101–110.

Campbell, Karlyn Kohrs. "The Rhetoric of Radical Black Nationalism: A Case Study in Self-Conscious Criticism," *Central States Speech Journal* 22 (Fall 1971): 151–160.

———. "The Rhetoric of Women's Liberation: An Oxymoron," *Quarterly Journal of Speech* 59 (February 1973): 74–86.

———. "Femininity and Feminism: To Be or Not To Be a Woman," *Communication Quarterly* 31 (Spring 1983): 101–108.

———. "Style and Content in the Rhetoric of Early Afro-American Feminists," *Quarterly Journal of Speech* 72 (November 1986): 434–445.

———. "'The Rhetoric of Women's Liberation: An Oxymoron' Revisited," *Communication Studies* 50 (Summer 1999): 138–142.

Carlson, A. Cheree. "Gandhi and the Comic Frame: 'Ad Bellum Purificandum,'" *Quarterly Journal of Speech* 72 (November 1986): 446–455.

———. "The Rhetoric of the Know-Nothing Party: Nativism as a Response to the Rhetorical Situation," *Southern Communication Journal* 54 (Summer 1989): 364–383.

———. "Creative Casuistry and Feminist Consciousness: A Rhetoric of Moral Reform," *Quarterly Journal of Speech* 78 (February 1992): 16–32.

———. "Defining Womanhood: Lucretia Coffin Mott and the Transforming of Femininity," *Western Journal of Communication* 58 (Spring 1994): 85–97.

Carter, David A. "The Industrial Workers of the World and the Rhetoric of Song," *Quarterly Journal of Speech* 66 (December 1980): 365–374.

Cathcart, Robert S. "New Approaches to the Study of Movements: Defining Movements Rhetorically," *Western Speech* 36 (Spring 1972): 82–88.

————. "Movements: Confrontation as Rhetorical Form," *Southern Speech Communication Journal* 43 (Spring 1978): 233–247.

————. "Defining Social Movements by Their Rhetorical Form," *Central States Speech Journal* 31 (Winter 1980): 267–273.

————. "A Confrontation Perspective on the Study of Social Movements," *Central States Speech Journal* 34 (Spring 1983): 69–74.

Chapel, Cage William. "Christian Science and the Nineteenth Century Woman's Movement," *Central States Speech Journal* 26 (Summer 1975): 142–149.

Charland, Maurice. "Constitutive Rhetoric: The Case of the *Peuple Quebecois*," *Quarterly Journal of Speech* 73 (May 1987): 133–150.

Chesebro, James W. "Rhetorical Strategies of the Radical Revolutionary," *Today's Speech* 20 (Winter 1972): 37–48.

Chesebro, James W., John F. Cragan, and Patricia McCullough. "The Small Group Technique of the Radical Revolutionary: A Synthetic Study of Consciousness Raising," *Speech Monographs* 40 (June 1973): 136–146.

Christiansen, Adrienne E. and Jeremy J. Hanson, "Comedy as Cure for Tragedy: ACT UP and the Rhetoric of AIDS," *Quarterly Journal of Speech* 82 (May 1996): 157–170.

Clark, Thomas D. "Rhetorical Image-Making: A Case Study of the Thomas Paine–William Smith Propaganda Debates," *Southern Speech Communication Journal* 40 (Spring 1975): 248–261.

Cloud, Dana L. "The Null Persona: Race and the Rhetoric of Silence in the Uprising of '34," *Rhetoric and Public Affairs* 2 (Summer 1999): 177–210.

Condit, Celeste Michelle. "The Functions of Epideictic: The Boston Massacre Orations as Exemplar," *Communication Quarterly* 33 (Fall 1985): 284–299.

————. "Crafting Virtue: The Rhetorical Construction of Public Morality," *Quarterly Journal of Speech* 73 (February 1987): 79–97.

————. "Democracy and Civil Rights: The Universalizing Influence of Public Argumentation," *Communication Monographs* 54 (March 1987): 1–18.

Condit, Celeste Michelle and John Louis Lucaites, "The Rhetoric of Equality and the Expatriation of African-Americans, 1776–1826," *Communication Studies* 42 (Spring 1991): 1–21.

Conrad, Charles. "The Transformation of the 'Old Feminist' Movement," *Quarterly Journal of Speech* 67 (August 1981): 284–297.

————. "The Rhetoric of the Moral Majority: An Analysis of Romantic Form," *Quarterly Journal of Speech* 69 (May 1983): 159–170.

Coughlin, Elizabeth M. and Charles E. Coughlin. "Convention in Petticoats: The Seneca Falls Declaration of Women's Rights," *Today's Speech* 21 (Fall 1973): 17–23.

Cox, J. Robert. "The Rhetoric of Child Labor Reform: An Efficacy-Utility Analysis," *Quarterly Journal of Speech* 60 (October 1974): 359–370.

————. "Perspectives on Rhetorical Criticism of Movements: Antiwar Dissent, 1964–1970," *Western Speech* 38 (Fall 1974): 254–268.

Crandell, S. Judson. "The Beginnings of a Methodology for Social Control Studies in Public Address," *Quarterly Journal of Speech* 33 (February 1947): 36–39.

Crocker, James W. "A Rhetoric of Encounter Following the May 4th, 1970, Disturbances at Kent State University," *Communication Quarterly* 25 (Fall 1977): 47–56.

Cuklanz, Lisa M. "'Shrill Squawk' or Strategic Innovation: A Rhetorical Reassessment of Margaret Sanger's *Woman Rebel*," *Communication Quarterly* 43 (Winter 1995): 1–19.

Darsey, James. "The Legend of Eugene V. Debs: Prophetic *Ethos* as Radical Argument," *Quarterly Journal of Speech* 74 (November 1988): 434–452.

———. "From 'Gay Is Good' to the Scourge of AIDS: The Evolution of Gay Liberation Rhetoric, 1977–1990," *Communication Studies* 42 (Spring 1991): 43–66.

———. "A Conspiracy of Science," *Western Journal of Communication* 66 (Fall 2002): 469–491.

Dees, Diane. "Bernadette Devlin's Maiden Speech: A Rhetoric of Sacrifice," *Southern Speech Communication Journal* 38 (Summer 1973): 326–339.

Delgado, Fernando Pedro, "Chicano Movement Rhetoric: An Ideological Interpretation," *Communication Quarterly* 43 (Fall 1995): 446–455.

———. "Chicano Ideology Revisited: Rap Music and the (Re)articulation of Chicanismo," *Western Journal of Communication* 62 (Spring 1998): 95–113.

———. "When the Silenced Speak: The Textualization and Complications of Latino Identity," *Western Journal of Communication* 62 (Fall 1998): 420–438.

DeLuca, Kevin Michael, "Trains in the Wilderness: The Corporate Roots of Environmentalism," *Rhetoric & Public Affairs* 4 (Winter 2001): 633–652.

Denton, Robert E. "The Rhetorical Functions of Slogans: Classifications and Characteristics," *Communication Quarterly* 28 (Spring 1980): 10–18.

Dick, Robert C. "Negro Oratory in the Anti-Slavery Societies: 1830–1860," *Western Speech* 28 (Winter 1964): 5–14.

Dionisopoulos, George N.; Victoria J. Gallagher; Steven R. Goldzwig; and David Zarefsky. "Martin Luther King, the American Dream and Vietnam: A Collision of Rhetorical Trajectories," *Western Journal of Communication* 56 (Spring 1992): 91–107.

Doolittle, Robert J. "Riots as Symbolic: A Criticism and Approach," *Central States Speech Journal* 27 (Winter 1976): 310–317.

Dow, Bonnie J. "The 'Womanhood' Rationale in the Woman Suffrage Rhetoric of Frances E. Willard," *Southern Communication Journal* 56 (Summer 1991): 298–307.

———. "AIDS, Perspective by Incongruity, and Gay Identity in Larry Kramer's '1112 and Counting,'" *Communication Studies* 45 (Fall-Winter 1994): 225–240.

———. "Spectacle, Spectatorship, and Gender Anxiety in Television Coverage of the 1970 Women's Strike for Equality," *Communication Studies* 50 (Summer 1999): 143–157.

———. "Fixing Feminism: Women's Liberation and the Rhetoric of Televised Documentary," *Quarterly Journal of Speech* 90 (February 2004): 53–80.

Duffy, Bernard K. "The Anti-Humanist Rhetoric of the New Religious Right," *Southern Speech Communication Journal* 49 (Summer 1984): 339–360.

Duffy, Margaret E. "Web of Hate: A Fantasy Theme Analysis of the Rhetorical Vision of Hate Groups Online," *Journal of Communication Inquiry* 27 (July 2003): 291–312.

Eich, Ritch K. and Donald Goldmann. "Communication, Confrontation, and Coercion: Agitation at Michigan," *Central States Speech Journal* 27 (Summer 1976): 120–128.

Erickson, Keith V. "Black Messiah: The Father Divine Peace Mission Movement," *Quarterly Journal of Speech* 63 (December 1977): 428–438.

Erlich, Howard S. "Populist Rhetoric Reassessed: A Paradox," *Quarterly Journal of Speech* 63 (April 1977): 140–151.

Ferris, Maxine Schnitzer. "The Speaking of Roy Wilkins," *Central States Speech Journal* 16 (May 1965): 91–98.

Fishman, Donald. "Reform Judaism and the Anti-Zionist Persuasive Campaign, 1897–1915," *Communication Quarterly* (Fall 1998): 375–395.

Flores, Lisa A. "Creative Discursive Space through a Rhetoric of Difference: Chicana Feminists Craft a Homeland," *Quarterly Journal of Speech* 82 (May 1996): 142–156.

Flores, Lisa A. and Dreama G. Moon, "Rethinking Race, Revealing Dilemmas: Imagining a New Racial Subject in *Race Traitor*," *Western Journal of Communication* 66 (Spring 2002): 181–207.

Flynt, Wayne. "The Ethics of Democratic Persuasion and the Birmingham Crisis," *Southern Speech Journal* 35 (Fall 1969): 40–53.

Flynt, Wayne and William Warren Rogers. "Reform Oratory in Alabama, 1890–1896," *Southern Speech Journal* 29 (Winter 1963): 94–106.

Foss, Karen A. "Out from Underground: The Discourse of Emerging Fugitives," *Western Journal of Communication* 56 (Spring 1992): 125–142.

Karen A. Foss and Kathy L. Domenici. "Haunting Argentina: Synechdoche in the Protests of the Mothers of the Plaza de Mayo," *Quarterly Journal of Speech* 87 (August 2001): 237–258.

Frank, David A. "*Shalem Achschav* Rituals of the Israeli Peace Movement," *Communication Monographs* 48 (September 1981): 165–182.

Freeman, Sally A; Stephen Littlejohn; and W. Barnett Pearce. "Communication and Moral Conflict," *Western Journal of Communication* 56 (Fall 1992): 311–329.

Fulkerson, Gerald. "Exile as Emergence: Frederick Douglass in Great Britain, 1845–1847," *Quarterly Journal of Speech* 60 (February 1974): 69–82.

Fulkerson, Richard P. "The Public Letter as a Rhetorical Form: Structure, Logic, and Style in King's 'Letter from Birmingham Jail,'" *Quarterly Journal of Speech* 65 (April 1979): 121–136.

Gallagher, Victoria J. "Memory and Reconciliation in the Birmingham Civil Rights Institute," *Rhetoric and Public Affairs* 2 (Summer 1999): 303–320.

———. "Black Power in Berkeley: Postmodern Constructions in the Rhetoric of Stokely Carmichael," *Quarterly Journal of Speech* 87 (May 2001): 144–157.

Gallagher, Victoria J. and Kenneth S. Zagacki. "Visibility and Rhetoric: The Power of Visual Images in Norman Rockwell's Depictions of Civil Rights," *Quarterly Journal of Speech* 91 (May 2005): 175–200.

Ganesh, Shiv, Heather Zoller, and George Cheney. "Transforming Resistance, Broadening Our Boundaries: Critical Organizational Communication Meets Globalization from Below," *Communication Monographs* 72 (June 2005): 169–191.

Gilder, Eric. "The Process of Political *Praxis:* Efforts of the Gay Community to Transform the Social Significance of AIDS," *Communication Quarterly* 37 (Winter 1989): 27–38.

Gillespie, Patti P. "Feminist Theatre: A Rhetorical Phenomenon," *Quarterly Journal of Speech* 64 (October 1978): 284–294.

Goldzwig, Steven R. "A Rhetoric of Public Theology: The Religious Rhetor and Public Policy," *Southern Speech Communication Journal* 52 (Winter 1987): 128–150.

———. "A Social Movement Perspective on Demagoguery: Achieving Symbolic Realignment," *Communication Studies* 40 (Fall 1989): 202–228.

Goldzwig, Steven R. and Patricia A. Sullivan. "Narrative and Counternarrative in Print-Mediated Coverage of Milwaukee Alderman Michael McGee," *Quarterly Journal of Speech* 86 (May 2000): 215–231.

———. "Conspiracy Rhetoric at the Dawn of the New Millennium," *Western Journal of Communication* 66 (Fall 2002): 492–506.

Goodnight, G. Thomas and John Poluakos. "Conspiracy Rhetoric: From Pragmatism to Fantasy in Public Discourse," *Western Journal of Speech Communication* 45 (Fall 1981): 299–316.

Grano, Daniel J. "Spiritual-Material Identification in the Deep Ecology Movement," *Southern Communication Journal* 68 (Fall 2002): 27–39.

Gravlee, G. Jack and James R. Irvine. "Watts' Dissenting Rhetoric of Prayer," *Quarterly Journal of Speech* 59 (December 1973): 463–473.

Gregg, Richard B. "The Ego-Function of the Rhetoric of Protest," *Philosophy and Rhetoric* 4 (Spring 1971): 71–91.

Gregg, Richard B. and A. Jackson McCormack. "'Whitey' Goes to the Ghetto: A Personal Chronicle of a Communication Experience with Black Youths," *Today's Speech* 16 (September 1968): 25–30.

Gregg, Richard B., A. Jackson McCormack, and Douglas J. Pederson. "The Rhetoric of Black Power: A Street-Level Interpretation," *Quarterly Journal of Speech* 55 (April 1969): 151–160.

Griffin, Charles J. G. "Jedidiah Morse and the Bavarian Illuminati: An Essay in the Rhetoric of Conspiracy," *Central States Speech Journal* 39 (Fall/Winter, 1988): 293–303.

———. "'Movement as Motive': Self Definition and Social Advocacy in Social Movement Autobiographies," *Western Journal of Communication* 64 (Spring 2000): 148–164.

———. "The 'Washingtonian Revival': Narrative and the Moral Transformation of Temperance Reform in Antebellum America," *Southern Communication Journal* 66 (Fall 2000): 67–78.

———. "Movement as Memory: Significant Form in *Eyes on the Prize*," *Communication Studies* 54 (Summer 2003): 196–210.

Griffin, Cindy L. "A Web of Reasons: Mary Wollstonecraft's *A Vindication of the Rights of Woman* and the Re-Weaving of Form," *Communication Studies* 47 (Winter 1996): 272–288.

Griffin, Leland M. "The Rhetoric of Historical Movements," *Quarterly Journal of Speech* 38 (April 1951): 184–188.

———. "The Rhetorical Structure of the Antimasonic Movement," *The Rhetorical Idiom,* Donald Bryant, ed. Ithaca, NY: Cornell University Press, 1958.

———. "The Rhetorical Structure of the 'New Left' Movement: Part I," *Quarterly Journal of Speech* 50 (April 1964): 113–135.

———. "A Dramatistic Theory of the Rhetoric of Movements," *Critical Responses to Kenneth Burke,* William Rueckert, ed. Minneapolis: University of Minnesota Press, 1969.

———. "On Studying Social Movements," *Central States Speech Journal* 31 (Winter 1980), 225–32.

Gring-Pemble, Lisa M. "Writing Themselves into Consciousness: Creating a Rhetorical Bridge between the Public and Private Spheres," *Quarterly Journal of Speech* 84 (February 1998): 44–61.

Gronbeck, Bruce E. "The Rhetoric of Social-Institutional Change: Black Action at Michigan," *Explorations in Rhetorical Criticism,* Gerald Mohrmann, Charles Stewart, and Donovan Ochs, eds. University Park: Pennsylvania State University Press, 1973.

Gunter, Mary F. and James S. Taylor. "Loyalist Propaganda in the Sermons of Charles Inglis, 1717–1780," *Western Speech* 37 (Winter 1973): 47–55.

Gustainis, J. Justin and Dan F. Hahn, "While the Whole World Watched: Rhetorical Failures of Anti-War Protest," *Communication Quarterly* 36 (Summer 1988): 203–216.

Hagan, Martha. "The Antisuffragists' Rhetorical Dilemma: Reconciling the Private and Public Spheres," *Communication Reports* 5 (Summer 1992): 73–81.

Hagen, Michael R. *"Roe vs. Wade*: The Rhetoric of Fetal Life," *Central States Speech Journal* 27 (Fall 1976): 192–199.

Hahn, Dan F. "Social Movement Theory: A Dead End," *Communication Quarterly* 28 (Winter 1980): 60–64.

Hahn, Dan F. and Ruth M. Gonchar, "Studying Social Movements: A Rhetorical Methodology," *Speech Teacher* 20 (January 1971): 44–52.

Haiman, Franklyn S. "The Rhetoric of the Streets: Some Legal and Ethical Considerations," *Quarterly Journal of Speech* 53 (April 1967): 99–114.

———. "Nonverbal Communication and the First Amendment: The Rhetoric of the Streets Revisited," *Quarterly Journal of Speech* 68 (November 1982): 371–383.

Hammerback, John C. "The Rhetoric of Righteous Reform: George Washington Julian's 1852 Campaign against Slavery," *Central States Speech Journal* 22 (Summer 1971): 85–93.

———. "George W. Julian's Antislavery Campaign," *Western Speech* 37 (Summer 1973): 157–165.

———. "Jose Antonio's Rhetoric of Fascism," *Southern Communication Journal* 59 (Spring 1994): 181–195.

Hammerback, John C. and Richard J. Jensen. "The Rhetorical Worlds of Cesar Chavez and Reis Tijerina," *Western Journal of Speech Communication* 44 (Summer 1980): 166–176.

———. "Ethnic Heritage as Rhetorical Legacy: The Plan and Delano," *Quarterly Journal of Speech* 80 (February 1994): 53–70.

Hancock, Brenda Robinson. "Affirmation by Negation in the Women's Liberation Movement," *Quarterly Journal of Speech* 58 (October 1972): 264–271.

Hansen, Andrew C. "Rhetorical Indiscretions: Charles Dickens as Abolitionist," *Western Journal of Communication* 65 (Winter 2001): 26–44.

Harold, Christine L. and Kevin Michael DeLuca, "Behold the Corpse: Violent Images and the Case of Emmett Till," *Rhetoric & Public Affairs* 8 (Summer 2005): 263–286.

Hasian, Marouf, Jr. "Understanding the Power of Conspiratorial Rhetoric: A Case Study of *The Protocols of the Elders of Zion*," *Communication Studies* 48 (Fall 1997): 195–214.

———. "Jurisprudence as Performance: John Brown's Enactment of Natural Law at Harper's Ferry," *Quarterly Journal of Speech* 86 (May 2000): 190–214.

Hasian, Marouf, Jr. and Geoffrey D. Klinger, "Sarah Roberts and the Early History of the 'Separate But Equal' Doctrine: A Study in Rhetoric, Law, and Social Change," *Communication Studies* 53 (Fall 2002): 269–283.

Hayden, Sara. "Reversing the Discourse of Sexology: Margaret Higgins Sanger's *What Every Girl Should Know*," *Southern Communication Journal* 64 (Summer 1999): 288–306.

———. "Negotiating Feminity and Power in the Early Twentieth Century West: Domestic Ideology and Feminine Style in Jeannette Rankin's Suffrage Rhetoric," *Communication Studies* 50 (Summer 1999): 83–102.

Heath, Robert L. "Dialectical Confrontation: A Strategy of Black Radicalism," *Central States Speech Journal* 24 (Fall 1973): 168–177.

———. "Black Rhetoric: An Example of the Poverty of Values," *Southern Speech Communication Journal* 39 (Winter 1973): 145–160.

Heider, Carmen. "Suffrage, Self-Determination, and the Women's Christian Temperance Union, 1879–1882," *Rhetoric & Public Affairs* 8 (Spring 2005): 85–108.

Heisey, D. Ray and J. David Trebing. "A Comparison of the Rhetorical Visions and Strategies of the Shah's White Revolution and the Ayatollah's Islamic Revolution," *Communication Monographs* 50 (June 1983): 158–174.

———. "Authority and Legitimacy: A Rhetorical Case Study of the Iranian Revolution," *Communication Monographs* 53 (December 1986): 295–310.

Henry, David. "Recalling the 1960s: The New Left and Social Movement Criticism," *Quarterly Journal of Speech* 75 (February 1989): 97–128.

Henry, David and Richard J. Jensen. "Social Movement Criticism and the Renaissance of Public Address," *Communication Studies* 42 (Spring 1991): 83–93.

Hensley, Carl Wayne. "Rhetorical Vision and the Persuasion of a Historical Movement: The Disciples of Christ in Nineteenth Century American Culture," *Quarterly Journal of Speech* 61 (October 1975): 250–264.

Hogan, J. Michael and L. Glen Williams. "Defining 'the Enemy' in Revolutionary America: From the Rhetoric of Protest to the Rhetoric of War," *Southern Communication Journal* 61 (Summer 1996): 277–288.

———. "Republican Charisma and the American Revolution: The Textual Persona of Thomas Paine's *Common Sense*," *Quarterly Journal of Speech* 86 (February 2000): 1–18.

Hogan, Lisa S. and J. Michael Hogan, "Feminine Virtue and Practical Wisdom: Elizabeth Cady Stanton's 'Our Boys,'" *Rhetoric & Public Affairs* 6 (Fall 2003): 415–436.

Hong, Nathaniel. "Constructing the Anarchist Beast in American Periodical Literature, 1880–1903," *Critical Studies of Mass Communication* 9 (March 1992): 110–130.

Hope, Diana Schaich. "Redefinition of Self: A Comparison of the Rhetoric of the Women's Liberation and the Black Liberation Movements," *Today's Speech* 23 (Winter 1975): 17–25.

Houck, Davis W. "'By Any Means Necessary': Re-Reading Malcolm X's Mecca Conversion," *Communication Studies* 44 (Fall 1993): 285–298.

———. "Killing Emmett," *Rhetoric & Public Affairs* 8 (Summer 2005): 225–262.

Howe, Roger J. "The Rhetoric of the Death of God Theology," *Southern Speech Communication Journal* 37 (Winter 1971): 150–162.

Hunsaker, David M. "The Rhetoric of *Brown v. Board of Education*: Paradigm for Contemporary Social Protest," *Southern Speech Communication Journal* 43 (Winter 1978): 91–109.

Huxman, Susan Schultz. "Mary Wollstonecraft, Margaret Fuller, and Angelina Grimke: Symbolic Convergence and a Nascent Rhetorical Vision," *Communication Quarterly* 44 (Winter 1996): 16–28.

Hynes, Sandra S. "Dramatic Propaganda: Mercy Otis Warren's 'The Defeat,' 1773," *Today's Speech* 23 (Fall 1975): 21–27.

Ilkka, Richard J. "Rhetorical Dramatization in the Development of American Communism," *Quarterly Journal of Speech* 63 (December 1977): 413–427.

Jabusch, David M. "The Rhetoric of Civil Rights," *Western Speech* 30 (Summer 1966): 176–183.

Japp, Phyllis M. "Esther or Isaiah?: The Abolitionist-Feminist Rhetoric of Angelina Grimke," *Quarterly Journal of Speech* 71 (August 1985): 335–348.

Jefferson, Pat. "The Magnificent Barbarian in Nashville," *Southern Speech Journal* 33 (Winter 1967): 77–87.

———. "Stokely's 'Cool': Style," *Today's Speech* 16 (September 1968): 19–24.

Jensen, J. Vernon. "British Voices on the Eve of the American Revolution: Trapped by the Family Metaphor," *Quarterly Journal of Speech* 63 (February 1977): 43–50.

Jensen, Richard J. and John C. Hammerback. "'No Revolutions without Poets': The Rhetoric of Rodolfo 'Corky' Gonzales," *Western Journal of Speech Communication* 46 (Winter 1982): 72–91.

———. "Radical Nationalism Among Chicanos: The Rhetoric of Jose Gutierrez," *Western Journal of Speech Communication* 44 (Summer 1980): 191–202.

———. "Feminists of Faith: Sonia Johnson and the Mormons for ERA," *Central States Speech Journal* 36 (Fall 1985): 123–137.

———. "From Muslim to Mormon: Eldridge Cleaver's Rhetorical Crusade," *Communication Quarterly* 34 (Winter 1986): 24–40.

———. "'Your Tools Are Really the People': The Rhetoric of Robert Parris Moses," *Communication Monographs* 65 (June 1998): 126–140.

Jensen, Richard J. and Cara J. Abeyta. "The Minority in the Middle: Asian-American Dissent in the 1960s and 1970s," *Western Journal of Speech Communication* 51 (Fall 1987): 402–416.

Jensen, Richard J. and Allen Lichtenstein. "From Yippie to Yuppie: Jerry Rubin as Rhetorical Icon," *Southern Communication Journal* 60 (Summer 1995): 332–346.

Jensen, Richard J., Thomas R. Burkholder, and John C. Hammerback. "Martyrs for a Just Cause: The Eulogies of Cesar Chavez," *Western Journal of Communication* 67 (Fall 2003): 335–356.

Johnson, Davi. "The Rhetoric of Huey P. Newton," *Southern Communication Journal* 70 (Fall 2004): 15–30.

Jorgensen-Earp, Cheryl R. "'Toys of Desperation': Suicide as Protest Rhetoric," *Southern Speech Communication Journal* 53 (Fall 1987): 80–96.

Jurma, William E. "Moderate Movement Leadership and the Vietnam Moratorium Committee," *Quarterly Journal of Speech* 68 (August 1982): 262–272.

Kendall, Kathleen E. and Jeanne Y. Fisher. "Frances Wright on Women's Rights: Eloquence versus Ethos," *Quarterly Journal of Speech* 60 (February 1974): 58–68.

Kennicott, Patrick C. "Black Persuaders in the Antislavery Movement," *Speech Monographs* 37 (March 1970): 15–24.

Kennicott, Patrick C. and Wayne E. Page. "H. Rap Brown: The Cambridge Incident," *Quarterly Journal of Speech* 57 (October 1971): 325–334.

Killingsworth, M. Jimmie and Jacqueline S. Palmer. "The Discourse of Environmentalist Hysteria," *Quarterly Journal of Speech* 81 (February 1995): 1–19.

King, Andrew A. "The Rhetorical Legacy of the Black Church," *Central States Speech Journal* 22 (Fall 1971): 179–185.

———. "The Rhetoric of Power Maintenance: Elites at the Precipice," *Quarterly Journal of Speech* 62 (April 1976): 127–134.

King, Andrew A. and Kenneth Petress. "Universal Public Argument and the Failure of Nuclear Freeze," *Southern Communication Journal* 55 (Winter 1990): 162–174.

Klumpp, James F. "Challenge of Radical Rhetoric: Radicalism at Columbia," *Western Speech* 37 (Summer 1973): 146–156.

Knupp, Ralph E. "A Time for Every Purpose Under Heaven: Rhetorical Dimensions of Protest Music," *Southern Speech Communication Journal* 46 (Summer 1981): 377–389.

Kosokoff, Stephen and Carl W. Carmichael. "The Rhetoric of Protest: Song, Speech, and Attitude Change," *Southern Speech Journal* 35 (Summer 1970): 295–302.

Kroll, Becky Swanson. "From Small Group to Public View: Mainstreaming the Women's Movement," *Communication Quarterly* 31 (Spring 1983): 139–147.

Kuypers, Jim A. "From Science, Moral-Poetics: Dr. James Dobson's Response to the Fetal Tissue Research Initiative," *Quarterly Journal of Speech* 86 (May 2000): 146–167.

Lake, Randall A. "Enacting Red Power: The Consummatory Function in Native American Protest Rhetoric," *Quarterly Journal of Speech* 69 (May 1983): 127–142.

———. "Order and Disorder in Anti-Abortion Rhetoric: A Logological View," *Quarterly Journal of Speech* 70 (November 1984): 425–443.

Lange, Jonathan I. "Refusal to Compromise: The Case of Earth First!" *Western Journal of Speech Communication* 54 (Fall 1990): 473–494.

———. "The Logic of Competing Information Campaigns: Conflict Over Old Growth and the Spotted Owl," *Communication Monographs* 60 (September 1993): 239–257.

Larson, Barbara A. "Samuel Davies and the Rhetoric of the New Light," *Speech Monographs* 38 (August 1971): 207–216.

Larson, Charles U. "The Trust Establishing Function of the Rhetoric of Black Power," *Central States Speech Journal* 21 (Spring 1970): 52–56.

Lawton, Cynthia Whalen. "Thoreau and the Rhetoric of Dissent," *Today's Speech* 16 (April 1968): 23–25.

Leathers, Dale G. "Fundamentalism of the Radical Right," *Southern Speech Journal* 33 (Summer 1968): 245–258.

———. "Belief-Disbelief Systems: The Communicative Vacuum of the Radical Right," *Explorations in Rhetorical Criticism,* Gerald Mohrmann, Charles Stewart, Donovan Ochs, eds. University Park: Pennsylvania State University Press, 1973.

Lee, Ronald. "The Rhetorical Construction of Time in Martin Luther King, Jr.'s 'Letter From Birmingham Jail,'" *Southern Speech Communication Journal* 56 (Summer 1991): 279–288.

Lee, Ronald. and James R. Andrews. "A Story of Rhetorical-Ideological Transformation: Eugene V. Debs as Liberal Hero," *Quarterly Journal of Speech* 77 (February 1991): 20–37.

Leff, Michael and Ebony A. Utley, "Instrumental and Constitutive Rhetoric in Martin Luther King Jr.'s 'Letter from Birmingham Jail,'" *Rhetoric & Public Affairs* 7 (Spring 2004): 37–52.

Linkugel, Wil A. "The Speech Style of Anna Howard Shaw," *Central States Speech Journal* 13 (Spring 1962): 171–178.

———. "The Woman Suffrage Argument of Anna Howard Shaw," *Quarterly Journal of Speech* 49 (April 1963): 165–174.

———. "The Rhetoric of American Feminism: A Social Movement Course," *Speech Teacher* 23 (March 1974): 121–130.

Lippman, Monroe. "Uncle Tom and His Poor Relations: American Slavery Plays," *Southern Speech Journal* 28 (Spring 1963): 183–197.

Logue, Cal M. and Eugene E. Miller. "Communicative Interaction and Rhetorical Status in Harriet Ann Jacobs' Slave Narrative," *Southern Communication Journal* 63 (Spring 1998): 182–198.

Lomas, Charles W. "The Agitator in American Society," *Western Speech* 24 (Spring 1960): 76–83.

———. "Agitator in a Cassock," *Western Speech* 27 (Winter 1963): 16–24.

Lucaites, John L. and Celeste Michelle Condit. "Reconstructing Equality: Culture-typal and Counter-Cultural Rhetorics in the Martyred Black Vision," *Communication Monographs* 57 (March 1990): 4–24.

Lucas, Stephen E. "Coming to Terms with Movement Studies," *Central States Speech Journal* 31 (Winter 1981): 255–266.

Maddux, Kristy. "When Patriots Protest: The Anti-Suffrage Discursive Transformation of 1917," *Rhetoric & Public Affairs* 7 (Fall 2004): 283–310.

Mandziuk, Roseann M. "Commemorating Sojourner Truth: Negotiating the Politics of Race and Gender in the Spaces of Public Memory," *Western Journal of Communication* 67 (Summer 2003): 271–291.

Mann, Kenneth Eugene. "Nineteenth Century Black Militant: Henry Highland Garnet's Address to the Slaves," *Southern Speech Journal* 36 (Fall 1970): 11–21.

Mansfield, Dorothy M. "Abigail S. Duniway: Suffragette with Not-so-common Sense," *Western Speech* 35 (Winter 1971): 24–29.

Martin, Howard H. "The Rhetoric of Academic Protest," *Central States Speech Journal* 17 (November 1966): 244–250.

Martin, Kathryn. "The Relationship of Theatre of Revolution and Theology of Revolution to the Black Experience," *Today's Speech* 19 (Spring 1971): 35–41.

Mattina, Anna F. "'Rights as Well as Duties': The Rhetoric of Leonora O'Reilly," *Communication Quarterly* 42 (Spring 1994): 196–205.

McClearey, Kevin E. "'A Tremendous Awakening': Margaret H. Sanger's Speech at Fabian Hall," *Western Journal of Communication* 58 (Summer 1994): 182–200.

McClure, Kevin R. "Frederick Douglass' Use of Comparison in His Fourth of July Oration: A Textual Critique," *Western Journal of Communication* 64 (Fall 2000): 425–444.

McDorman, Todd F. "Challenging Constitutional Authority: African American Responses to *Scott v. Sandford*," *Quarterly Journal of Speech* 83 (May 1997): 192–209.

McEdwards, Mary G. "Agitative Rhetoric: Its Nature and Effect," *Western Speech* 32 (Winter 1968): 36–43.

McGee, Brian R. "Speaking About the Other: W.E.B. DuBois Responds to the Klan," *Southern Communication Journal* 63 (Spring 1998): 208–219.

———. "Thomas Dixon's The Clansman: Radicals, Reactionaries, and the Anticipated Utopia," *Southern Communication Journal* 65 (Summer 2000): 300–317.

McGee, Michael C. "In Search of 'The People': A Rhetorical Alternative," *Quarterly Journal of Speech* 61 (October 1975): 235–249.

———. "'Social Movement': Phenomenon or Meaning," *Central States Speech Journal* 31 (Winter 1980): 233–244.

McGuire, Michael. "Mythic Rhetoric in *Mein Kampf*: A Structuralist Critique," *Quarterly Journal of Speech* 63 (February 1977): 1–13.

McKerrow, Raymie E. "Antimasonic Rhetoric: The Strategy of Excommunication," *Communication Quarterly* 37 (Fall 1989): 276–290.

McPhail, Mark Lawrence. "Passionate Intensity: Louis Farrakhan and the Fallacies of Racial Reasoning," *Quarterly Journal of Speech* 84 (November 1998): 416–429.

McPherson, Louise. "Communication Techniques of the Women's Liberation Front," *Today's Speech* 21 (Spring 1973): 33–38.

Mechling, Elizabeth W. and Gale Auletta. "Beyond War: A Socio-Rhetorical Analysis of a New Class Revitalization Movement," *Western Journal of Speech Communication* 50 (Fall 1986): 388–404.

Mechling, Elizabeth W. and Jay Mechling. "Hot Pacifism and Cold War: The American Friends Service Committee's Witness for Peace in 1950s America," *Quarterly Journal of Speech* 78 (May 1992): 173–196.

———. "The Jung and the Restless: The Mythopoetic Men's Movement," *Southern Communication Journal* 59 (Winter 1994): 97–111.

Medhurst, Martin J. "The Sword of Division: A Reply to Brummett and Warnick," *Western Journal of Speech Communication* 46 (Fall 1982): 383–390.

———. "The First Amendment vs. Human Rights: A Case Study in Human Sentiment and Argument from Definition," *Western Journal of Speech Communication* 46 (Winter 1982): 1–19.

———. "Resistance, Conservatism, and Theory Building: A Cautionary Note," *Western Journal of Speech Communication* 49 (Spring 1985): 103–115.

Merriam, Allen H. "Symbolic Action in India: Gandhi's Nonverbal Persuasion," *Quarterly Journal of Speech* 61 (October 1975): 290–306.

Miller, Jackson B. "'Indians,' 'Braves,' and 'Redskins': A Performative Struggle for Control of an Image," *Quarterly Journal of Speech* 85 (May 1999): 188–202.

Miller, Keith D. and Kevin Quashie. "Slave Mutiny as Argument, Argument as Fiction, Fiction as America: The Case of Frederick Douglass's *The Hero Slave*," *Southern Communication Journal* 63 (Spring 1998): 199–207.

Mixon, Harold D. "Boston's Artillery Election Sermons and the American Revolution," *Speech Monographs* 34 (March 1967): 43–50.

Monsma, John W., Jr. "John Brown: The Two Edged Sword of Abolition," *Central States Speech Journal* 13 (Autumn 1961): 22–29.

Morris, Richard. "Educating Savages," *Quarterly Journal of Speech* 83 (May 1997): 152–171.

Morris, Richard and Philip Wander. "Native American Rhetoric: Dancing in the Shadows of the Ghost Dance," *Quarterly Journal of Speech* 76 (May 1990): 164–191.

Murphy, John M. "Domesticating Dissent: The Kennedys and the Freedom Rides," *Communication Monographs* 59 (March 1992): 61–78.

———. "Epideictic and Deliberative Strategies in Opposition to War: The Paradox of Honor and Expediency," *Communication Studies* 43 (Summer 1992): 65–78.

Nelson, Elizabeth, Jean. "'Nothing Ever Goes Well Enough': Mussolini and the Rhetoric of Perpetual Struggle," *Communication Studies* 42 (Spring, 1991): 22–42.

Nelson, Jeffrey and Mary Ann Flannery. "The Sanctuary Movement: A Study in Religious Confrontation," *Southern Communication Journal* 55 (Summer 1990): 372–387.

Newsom, Lionel and William Gorden. "A Stormy Rally in Atlanta," *Today's Speech* 11 (April 1963): 18–21.

Nimmo, Dan and James E. Combs. "Devils and Demons: The Group Mediation of Conspiracy," *Mediated Political Realities*. New York: Longman, 1983.

O'Brien, Harold J. "Slavery Sentiments that Led to War," *Today's Speech* 9 (November 1961): 5–7.

Olson, Kathryn M. and G. Thomas Goodnight. "Entanglements of Consumption, Cruelty, Privacy, and Fashion: The Social Controversy over Fur," *Quarterly Journal of Speech* 80 (August 1994): 249–276.

Orban, Donald K. "Billy James Hargis: Auctioneer of Political Evangelism," *Central States Speech Journal* 20 (Summer 1969): 83–91.

Osborn, Michael and John Bakke. "The Melodrama of Memphis: Contending Narratives During the Sanitation Strike of 1968," *Southern Communication Journal* 63 (Spring 1998): 220–234.

Osborn, Michael. "Rhetorical Distance in 'Letter from Birmingham Jail,'" *Rhetoric & Public Affairs* 7 (Spring 2004): 23–36.

Panetta, Edward M. and Marouf Hasian, Jr. "Anti-Rhetoric as Rhetoric: The Law and Economics Movement," *Communication Quarterly* 42 (Winter 1994): 57–74.

Patton, John H. "Rhetoric at Catonsville: Daniel Berrigan, Conscience and Image Alteration," *Today's Speech* 23 (Winter 1975): 3–12.

————. "A Transforming Response: Martin Luther King Jr.'s 'Letter from Birmingham Jail,'" *Rhetoric & Public Affairs* 7 (Spring 2004): 53–65.

Pauley, Garth E. "John Lewis's 'Serious Revolution': Rhetoric, Resistance, and Revision at the March on Washington," *Quarterly Journal of Speech* 84 (August 1998): 320–340.

Pearce, Kimber Charles. "The Radical Feminist Manifesto as Generic Appropriation: Gender, Genre, and the Second Wave Resistance," *Southern Communication Journal* 64 (Summer 1999): 307–315.

Pearce, W. Barnett, Stephen W. Littlejohn, and Alison Alexander. "The New Christian Right and the Humanist Response: Reciprocated Diatribe," *Communication Quarterly* 35 (Spring 1987): 171–192.

Pearson, Kyra. "Mapping Rhetorical Interventions in 'National' Feminist Histories: Second Wave Feminism and *Ain't I a Woman*," *Communication Studies* 50 (Summer 1999): 158–173.

Perkins, Sally J. "The Rhetoric of Androgyny as Revealed in *The Feminine Mystique*," *Communication Studies* 40 (Summer 1989): 69–80.

Perse, Elizabeth M., Douglas M. McLeod, Nancy Signorielli, and Juliet Dee. "News Coverage of Abortion Between *Roe* and *Webster*: Public Opinion and Real World Events," *Communication Research Reports* 14 (Winter 1997): 97–105.

Pezzullo, Phaedra C. "Performing Critical Interruptions: Stories, Rhetorical Invention, and the Environmental Justice Issue," *Western Journal of Communication* 65 (Winter 2001): 1–25.

Phifer, Elizabeth F. and Dencil R. Taylor. "Carmichael in Tallahassee," *Southern Speech Journal* 33 (Winter 1967): 88–92.

Pollock, Arthur. "Stokely Carmichael's New Black Rhetoric," *Southern Speech Journal* 37 (Fall 1971): 92–94.

Powell, Kimberly A. "The Association of Southern Women for Prevention of Lynching: Strategies of a Movement in the Comic Frame," *Communication Quarterly* 43 (Winter 1995): 86–99.

Powers, Lloyd D. "Chicano Rhetoric: Some Basic Concepts," *Southern Speech Journal* 38 (Summer 1973): 340–346.

Press, Andrea L. "The Impact of Television on Modes of Reasoning about Abortion," *Critical Studies of Mass Communication* 8 (December 1991): 421–441.

Railsback, Celeste Condit. "The Contemporary American Abortion Controversy: Stages in the Argument," *Quarterly Journal of Speech* 70 (November 1984): 410–424.

Ramsey, E. Michele. "Inventing Citizens During World War I: Suffrage Cartoons in *The Woman Citizen*," *Western Journal of Communication* 64 (Spring 2000): 113–147.

Reed, Robert Michael. "The Case of Missionary Smith: A Crucial Incident in the Rhetoric of the British Anti-Slavery Movement," *Central States Speech Journal* 29 (Spring 1978): 61–71.

Reynolds, Beatrice K. "Mao Tse-Tung: Rhetoric of a Revolutionary," *Central States Speech Journal* 27 (Fall 1976): 212–217.

Riach, W. A. D. "'Telling It Like It Is': An Examination of Black Theatre as Rhetoric," *Quarterly Journal of Speech* 56 (April 1970): 179–186.

Rice, George P., Jr. "Freedom of Speech and the 'New Left,'" *Central States Speech Journal* 21 (Fall 1970): 139–145.

Richardson, Larry S. "Stokely Carmichael: Jazz Artist," *Western Speech* 34 (Summer 1970): 212–218.

Riches, Suzanne V. and Malcolm O. Sillars. "The Status of Movement Criticism, " *Western Journal of Speech Communication* 44 (Fall 1980): 275–287.

Ritchie, Gladys. "The Sit-In: A Rhetoric of Human Action," *Today's Speech* 18 (Winter 1970): 22–25.

Ritter, Ellen M. "Elizabeth Morgan: Pioneer Female Labor Agitator," *Central States Speech Journal* 22 (Winter 1971): 242–251.

Ritter, Kurt W. "Confrontation as Moral Drama: The Boston Massacre in Rhetorical Perspective," *Southern Speech Communication Journal* 42 (Winter 1977): 114–136.

Rogers, Richard S. "The Rhetoric of Militant Deism," *Quarterly Journal of Speech* 54 (October 1968): 247–251.

Rosenwasser, Marie J. "Rhetoric and the Progress of the Women's Liberation Movement," *Today's Speech* 20 (Summer 1972): 45–56.

Rossiter, Charles M. and Ruth McGaffey. "Freedom of Speech and the 'New Left': A Response," *Central States Speech Journal* 22 (Spring 1971): 5–10.

Rostek, Thomas. "Narrative in Martin Luther King's *I've Been to the Mountain Top*," *Southern Communication Journal* 58 (Fall 1992): 22–31.

Rothman, Richard. "On the Speaking of John L. Lewis," *Central States Speech Journal* 14 (August 1963): 177–185.

Rothwell, J. Dan. "Verbal Obscenity: Time for Second Thoughts," *Western Speech* 35 (Fall 1971): 231–242.

Roy, Abhik and Robert C. Rowland. "The Rhetoric of Hindu Nationalism: A Narrative of Mythic Redefinition," *Western Journal of Communication* 67 (Summer 2003): 225–248.

Rude, Leslie G. "The Rhetoric of Farmer Labor Agitators," *Central States Speech Journal* 20 (Winter 1969): 280–285.

Salvador, Michael. "The Rhetorical Subversion of Cultural Boundaries: The National Consumer's League," *Southern Communication Journal* 59 (Summer 1994): 318–332.

Sanchez, John and Mary E. Stuckey. "Communicating Culture Through Leadership: One View from Indian Country," *Communication Studies* 50 (Summer 1999): 103–115.

Sanger, Kerran L. "Slave Resistance and Rhetorical Self-Definition: Spirituals as a Strategy," *Western Journal of Communication* 59 (Summer 1995): 177–192.

Scott, Robert L. "Justifying Violence—The Rhetoric of Militant Black Power," *Central States Speech Journal* 19 (Summer 1968): 96–104.

———. "The Conservative Voice in Radical Rhetoric: A Common Response to Division," *Speech Monographs* 40 (June 1973): 123–135.

Scott, Robert L. and Donald K. Smith. "The Rhetoric of Confrontation," *Quarterly Journal of Speech* 55 (February 1969): 1–8.

Sedano, Michael Victor. "Chicanismo: A Rhetorical Analysis of Themes and Images of Selected Poetry from the Chicano Movement," *Western Journal of Speech Communication* 44 (Summer 1980): 177–190.

Seibold, David. "Jewish Defense League: The Rhetoric of Resistance," *Today's Speech* 21 (Fall 1973): 39–48.

Selby, Gary. "The Limits of Accommodation: Frederick Douglass and the Garrisonian Abolitionists," *Southern Communication Journal* 66 (Fall 2000): 52–66.

———. "Mocking the Sacred: Frederick Douglass's 'Slaveholders Sermon' and the Antebellum Debate Over Religion and Slavery," *Quarterly Journal of Speech* 88 (August 2002): 326–341.

———. "Scoffing at the Enemy: The Burlesque Frame in the Rhetoric of Ralph David Abernathy," *Southern Communication Journal* 70 (Winter 2005): 134–145.

Shafer, George. "The Dramaturgy of Fact: The Treatment of History in Two Anti-War Plays," *Central States Speech Journal* 29 (Spring 1978): 25–35.

Shepler, Sherry R. and Anne F. Mattina, "'The Revolt Against War': Jane Addams' Rhetorical Challenge to the Patriarchy," *Communication Quarterly* 47 (Spring 1999): 151–165.

Short, Brant. "Earth First! and the Rhetoric of Moral Confrontation," *Communication Studies* 42 (Summer 1991): 172–188.

Sillars, Malcolm O. "The Rhetoric of the Petition in Boots," *Speech Monographs* 39 (June 1972): 92–104.

_____. "Defining Movement Rhetorically: Casting the Widest Net," *Southern Speech Communication Journal* 46 (Fall 1980): 17–32.

Silvestri, Vito N. "Emma Goldman, Enduring Voice of Anarchism," *Today's Speech* 17 (September 1969): 20–25.

Simons, Herbert W. "Patterns of Persuasion in the Civil Rights Movement," *Today's Speech* 15 (February 1967): 25–27.

———. "Requirements, Problems, and Strategies: A Theory of Persuasion for Social Movements," *Quarterly Journal of Speech* 56 (February 1970): 1–11.

———. "Persuasion in Social Conflicts: A Critique of Prevailing Conceptions and a Framework for Future Research," *Speech Monographs* 39 (November 1972): 227–247.

———. "Changing Notions about Social Movements," *Quarterly Journal of Speech* 62 (December 1976), 425–430.

———. "On Terms, Definitions and Theoretical Distinctiveness: Comments on Papers by McGee and Zarefsky," *Central States Speech Journal* 31 (Winter 1980): 306–315.

———. "Genres, Rules, and Collective Rhetorics: Applying the Requirements-Problems Strategies Approach," *Communication Quarterly* 30 (Summer 1982): 181–188.

———. "On the Rhetoric of Social Movements, Historical Movements, and 'Top Down' Movements: A Commentary," *Communication Studies* 42 (Spring 1991): 94–101.

Simons, Herbert W. and Elizabeth W. Mechling. "The Rhetoric of Political Movements," *Handbook of Political Communication,* Dan Nimmo and Keith Sanders, eds. Beverly Hills, CA: Sage, 1981.

Simons, Herbert W., Elizabeth Mechling, and Howard Schreier. "Functions of Communication in Mobilizing for Action from the Bottom Up: The Rhetoric of Social Movements, *Handbook on Rhetorical and Communication Theory,* Carroll C. Arnold and John W. Bowers, eds. Boston: Allyn & Bacon, 1984.

Simpson, Tessa and Stephen King. "The Sanctuary Movement: Criminal Trials and Religious Dissent," *Journal of Communication and Religion* 15 (March 1992): 15–28.

Slagell, Amy R. "The Rhetorical Structure of Frances E. Willard's Campaign for Woman Suffrage, 1976–1896," *Rhetoric & Public Affairs* 4 (Spring 2001): 1–23.

Smiley, Sam. "Peace on Earth: Four Anti-War Dramas of the Thirties," *Central States Speech Journal* 21 (Spring 1970): 30–39.

Smith, Arthur L. "Henry Highland Garnet: Black Revolutionary in Sheep's Vestments," *Central States Speech Journal* 21 (Summer 1970): 93–98.

Smith, Craig Allen. "The Hofstadter Hypothesis Revisited: The Nature of Evidence in Politically 'Paranoid' Discourse," *Southern Speech Communication Journal* 42 (Spring 1977): 274–289.

———. "An Organic Systems Analysis of Persuasion and Social Movement: The John Birch Society, 1958–1966," *Southern Speech Communication Journal* 59 (Winter 1984): 155–176.

Smith, Donald H. "Social Protest . . . and the Oratory of Human Rights," *Today's Speech* 15 (September 1967): 2–8.

———. "Martin Luther King, Jr.: In the Beginning at Montgomery," *Southern Speech Journal* 34 (Fall 1968): 8–17.

Smith, Ralph R. "The Historical Criticism of Social Movements," *Central States Speech Journal* 31 (Winter 1980): 290–297.

Smith, Ralph R. and Russell Windes. "The Innovational Movement: A Rhetorical Theory," *Quarterly Journal of Speech* 61 (April 1975): 140–153.

———. "The Rhetoric of Mobilization: Implications for the Study of Movements," *Southern Speech Communication Journal* 42 (Fall 1976): 1–19.

———. "Collective Action and the Single Text," *Southern Speech Communication Journal* 43 (Winter 1978): 110–128.

———. "Symbolic Convergence and Abolitionism: A Terministic Reinterpretation," *Southern Communication Journal* 59 (Fall 1993): 45–59.

———. "The Interpretation of Abolitionist Rhetoric: Historiography, Rhetorical Method, and History," *Southern Communication Journal* 60 (Summer 1995): 303–311.

———. "The Progay and Antigay Issue Culture: Interpretation, Influence and Dissent," *Quarterly Journal of Speech* 83 (February 1997): 28–48.

Snider, Christy Jo. "Patriots and Pacifists: The Rhetorical Debate about Peace, Patriotism, and Internationalism, 1914–1930," *Rhetoric & Public Affairs* 8 (Spring 2005): 59–84.

Snow, Malinda. "Martin Luther King's 'Letter from Birmingham Jail' as Pauline Epistle," *Quarterly Journal of Speech* 71 (August 1985): 318–334.

Solomon, Martha. "The Rhetoric of STOP ERA: Fatalistic Reaffirmation," *Southern Speech Communication Journal* 44 (Fall 1978): 42–59.

———. "Stopping ERA: A Pyrrhic Victory," *Communication Quarterly* 31 (Spring 1983): 109–117.

———. "Ideology as Rhetorical Constraint: The Anarchist Agitation of 'Red Emma' Goldman," *Quarterly Journal of Speech* 74 (May 1988): 184–200.

———. "Autobiographies as Rhetorical Narratives: Elizabeth Cady Stanton and Anna Howard Shaw as 'New Women,'" *Communication Studies* 42 (Winter 1991): 354–370.

Sowards, Stacey K. and Valerie Renegar. "The Rhetorical Functions of Consciousness-Raising in Third Wave Feminism," *Communication Studies* 55 (Winter 2004); 535–552.

Sproule, J. Michael. "An Emerging Rationale for Revolution: Argument from Circumstance and Definition in Polemics Against the Stamp Act, 1765–1766," *Today's Speech* 23 (Spring 1975): 17–23.

Stephens, Gregory. "Frederick Douglass' Multiracial Abolitionism: 'Antagonistic Cooperation' and 'Redeemable Ideals' in the July 5 Speech," *Communication Studies* 48 (Fall 1997): 175–194.

Stewart, Charles J. "Labor Agitation in America: 1865–1915," *America in Controversy: History of American Public Address,* DeWitte T. Holland, ed. Dubuque, IA: Brown, 1973.

———. "A Functional Approach to the Rhetoric of Social Movements," *Central States Speech Journal* 31 (Winter 1980): 298–305.

———. "A Functional Perspective on the Study of Social Movements," *Central States Speech Journal* 34 (Spring 1983): 77–80.

———. "The Internal Rhetoric of the Knights of Labor," *Communication Studies* 42 (Spring 1991): 67–82.

———. "The Ego Function of Protest Songs: An Application of Gregg's Theory of Protest Rhetoric," *Communication Studies* 42 (Fall 1991): 240–253.

———. "The Evolution of a Revolution: Stokely Carmichael and the Rhetoric of Black Power," *Quarterly Journal of Speech* 83 (November 1997): 429–446.

————. "Championing the Rights of Others and Challenging Evil: The Ego Function in the Rhetoric of Other-Directed Social Movements," *Southern Communication Journal* 64 (Winter 1999): 91–105.

————. "The Master Conspiracy of the John Birch Society: From Communism to the New World Order," *Western Journal of Communication* 66 (Fall 2002): 424–447.

Stitzel, James A. "Inflammatory Speaking in the Victor, Colorado, Mass Meeting, June 6, 1904," *Western Speech* 32 (Winter 1968): 11–18.

Stokes, Ashli Quesinberry. "Constituting Southern Feminists: Women's Liberation Newsletters in the South," *Southern Communication Journal* 70 (Winter 2005): 91–108.

Strange, Lisa. "Dress Reform and the Feminine Ideal: Elizabeth Cady Stanton and the 'Coming Girl,'" *Southern Communication Journal* 68 (Fall 2002): 1–13.

Strother, David B. "Polemics and the Reversal of the 'Separate but Equal' Doctrine," *Quarterly Journal of Speech* 49 (February 1963): 50–56.

Tedesco, John L. "The White Character in Black Drama, 1955–1970: Description and Rhetorical Function," *Communication Monographs* 45 (March 1978): 64–74.

Terrill, Robert E. "Colonizing the Borderlands: Shifting Circumference in the Rhetoric of Malcolm X," *Quarterly Journal of Speech* 86 (February 2000): 67–85.

————. "Protest, Prophecy, and Prudence in the Rhetoric of Malcolm X," *Rhetoric & Public Affairs* 4 (Spring 2001): 25–54.

————. "Irony, Silence, and Time: Frederick Douglas on the Fifth of July," *Quarterly Journal of Speech* 89 (August 2003): 216–234.

Thomas, Cheryl Irwin. "'Look What They've Done to My Song, Ma': The Persuasiveness of Song," *Southern Speech Communication Journal* 39 (Spring 1974): 260–268.

Thomas, Gordon L. "John Brown's Courtroom Speech," *Quarterly Journal of Speech* 48 (October 1962): 291–296.

Thurber, John H. and John L. Petelle. "The Negro Pulpit and Civil Rights," *Central States Speech Journal* 19 (Winter 1968): 273–278.

Tonn, Marie Boor. "Militant Motherhood: Labor's Mary Harris 'Mother' Jones," *Quarterly Journal of Speech* 82 (February 1996): 1–21.

————. "Donning Sackcloth and Ashes: *Webster v. Productive Health Services* and Moral Agony in Abortion Rights Rhetoric," *Communication Quarterly* 44 (Summer 1996): 265–279.

Van Graber, Marilyn. "Functional Criticism: A Rhetoric of Black Power," *Explorations in Rhetorical Criticism,* Gerald Mohrmann, Charles Stewart, and Donovan Ochs, eds. University Park,: Pennsylvania State University Press, 1973.

Vonnegut, Kristin S. "Poison or Panacea?" Sarah Moore Grimke's Use of the Public Letter," *Communication Studies* 46 (Spring 1995): 73–88.

Wagner, Gerard A. "Sojourner Truth: God's Appointed Apostle of Reform," *Southern Speech Journal* 28 (Winter 1962): 123–130.

Walsh, James F., Jr. "An Approach to Dyadic Communication in Historical Social Movements: Dyadic Communication in Maoist Insurgent Mobilization," *Communication Monographs* 53 (March 1986): 1–15.

————. "An Approach to Group Communication in Historical Social Movements: Group Communication in Maoist Insurgent Mobilization," *Southern Speech Communication Journal* 51 (Spring 1986): 229–255.

————. "Paying Attention to Channels: Differential Images of Recruitment in Students for a Democratic Society, 1960–1965," *Communication Studies* 44 (Spring 1993): 71–86.

Waltman, Michael S. "Strategies and Heuristics in the Recruitment of Children into Communities of Hate: The Fabric of Our Future Nightmares," *Southern Communication Journal* 69 (Fall 2003): 22–36.

Wander, Philip C. "Salvation Through Separation: The Image of the Negro in the American Colonization Society," *Quarterly Journal of Speech* 57 (February 1971): 57–67.

———. "The John Birch and Martin Luther King Symbols in the Radical Right," *Western Speech* 35 (Winter 1971): 4–14.

———. "The Savage Child: The Image of the Negro in the Pro-Slavery Movement," *Southern Speech Communication Journal* 37 (Summer 1972): 335–360.

Ware, B. L. and Wil A. Linkugel. "The Rhetorical *Persona:* Marcus Garvey as Black Moses," *Communication Monographs* 49 (March 1982): 50–62.

Warnick, Barbara. "The Rhetoric of Conservative Resistance," *Southern Speech Communication Journal* 42 (Spring 1977): 256–273.

———. "Conservative Resistance Revisited," *Western Journal of Speech Communication* 46 (Fall 1982): 373–378.

Watson, Martha Solomon. "The Issue of Justice: Martin Luther King Jr.'s Response to the Birmingham Clergy," *Rhetoric & Public Affairs* 7 (Spring 2004): 1–22.

Watts, Eric King. "Cultivating a Black Public Voice: W.E.B. DuBois and the 'Criteria of Negro Art,'" *Rhetoric & Public Affairs* 4 (Summer 2001): 181–202.

———. "'Voice' and 'Voicelessness' in Rhetorical Studies," *Quarterly Journal of Speech* 87 (May 2001): 179–196.

Weaver, Richard L., II. "The Negro Issue: Agitation in the Michigan Lyceum," *Central States Speech Journal* 22 (Fall 1971): 196–201.

Weisman, Martha. "Ambivalence Toward War in Anti-War Plays," *Today's Speech* 17 (September 1969): 9–14.

Weitzel, Al. "King's 'I Have a Dream' Speech: A Case Study of Incorporating Orality in Rhetorical Criticism," *Communication Reports* 7 (Winter 1994): 50–56.

Whedbee, Karen. "Perspective by Incongruity in Norman Thomas's 'Some Wrong Roads To Peace,'" *Western Journal of Communication* 65 (Winter 2001): 45–64.

Whitfield, George. "Frederick Douglass: Negro Abolitionist," *Today's Speech* 11 (February 1963): 6–8, 24.

Wilkie, Richard W. "The Self-Taught Agitator: Hitler 1907–1920," *Quarterly Journal of Speech* 52 (December 1966): 371–377.

———. "The Marxian Rhetoric of Angelica Balabanoff," *Quarterly Journal of Speech* 60 (December 1974): 450–458.

Wilkinson, Charles A. "A Rhetorical Definition of Movements," *Central States Speech Journal* 27 (Summer 1976): 88–94.

Williams, David E. "The Drive for Prohibition: A Transition from Social Reform to Legislative Reform," *Southern Communication Journal* 61 (Spring 1996): 185–197.

Williams, Donald E. "Protest Under the Cross: The Ku Klux Klan Presents Its Case to the People," *Southern Speech Journal* 27 (Fall 1961): 43–55.

Wilson, Kirt H. "The Contested Space of Prudence in the 1874–1875 Civil Rights Debate," *Quarterly Journal of Speech* 84 (May 1998): 131–149.

———. "Interpreting the Discursive Field of the Montgomery Bus Boycott: Martin Luther King Jr.'s Holt Street Address," *Rhetoric & Public Affairs* 8 (Summer 2005): 299–326.

Windt, Theodore O. "The Diatribe: Last Resort for Protest," *Quarterly Journal of Speech* 58 (February 1972): 1–14.

————. "Administrative Rhetoric: An Undemocratic Response to Protest," *Communication Quarterly* 30 (Summer 1982): 245–250.

Woodward, Gary C. "Mystifications in the Rhetoric of Cultural Dominance and Colonial Control," *Central States Speech Journal* 26 (Winter 1975): 298–303.

Wurthman, Leonard B. "The Militant-Moderate Agitator: Daniel O'Connell and Catholic Emancipation in Ireland," *Communication Quarterly* 30 (Summer 1982): 225–231.

Yoder, Jess. "The Protest of the American Clergy in Opposition to the War in Vietnam," *Today's Speech* 17 (September 1969): 51–59.

Yousman, Bill. "Who Owns Identity? Malcolm X, Representation, and the Struggle Over Meaning," *Communication Quarterly* 49 (Winter 2001): 1–18.

Zacharis, John C. "Emmeline Pankhurst: An English Suffragette Influences America," *Speech Monographs* 38 (August 1971): 198–206.

Zaeske, Susan. "The 'Promiscuous Audience' Controversy and the Emergence of the Early Woman's Rights Movement," *Quarterly Journal of Speech* 81 (May 1995): 191–207.

————. "Signatures of Citizenship: The Rhetoric of Women's Antislavery Petitions," *Quarterly Journal of Speech* 88 (May 2002): 147–168.

Zarefsky, David. "President Johnson's War on Poverty: The Rhetoric of Three 'Establishment' Movements," *Communication Monographs* 44 (November 1977), 352–373.

————. "A Skeptical View of Movement Studies," *Central States Speech Journal* 31 (Winter 1980): 245–254.

BOOKS

Boase, Paul H. *The Rhetoric of Christian Socialism.* New York: Random House, 1969.

————, ed. The Rhetoric of Protest and Reform: 1878–1898. Athens: Ohio University Press, 1980.

Bormann, Ernest G. *Forerunners of Black Power: The Rhetoric of Abolition.* Englewood Cliffs, NJ: Prentice-Hall, 1971.

Bosmajian, Haig A., ed. *Dissent: Symbolic Behavior and Rhetorical Strategies.* Boston: Allyn & Bacon, 1972.

Bosmajian, Haig A. and Hamida Bosmajian. *The Rhetoric of the Civil Rights Movement.* New York: Random House, 1969.

Bowers, John W.; Donovan J. Ochs; and Richard J. Jensen. *The Rhetoric of Agitation and Control, 2/E.* Long Grove, IL: Waveland Press, 1993.

Brandes, Paul D. *The Rhetoric of Revolt.* Englewood Cliffs, NJ: Prentice-Hall, 1971.

Browne, Stephen H. *Angelina Grimke: Rhetoric, Identity, and the Radical Imagination.* East Lansing: Michigan State University Press, 1999.

Campbell, Karlyn Kohrs. *Man Cannot Speak for Her: A Critical Study of Early Feminist Rhetoric.* New York: Greenwood Press, 1989.

Carpenter, Ronald H. *Father Charles E. Coughlin: Surrogate Spokesman for the Disaffected.* Westport, CT: Greenwood, 1998.

Chesebro, James W., ed. *Gayspeak: Gay Male and Lesbian Communication.* New York: Pilgrim Press, 1981.

Chesebrough, David B. *Frederick Douglass: Oratory from Slavery.* Westport, CT: Greenwood, 1998.

Condit, Celeste Michelle. *Decoding Abortion Rhetoric: Communicating Social Change.* Urbana: University of Illinois Press, 1990.

Darsey, James. *The Prophetic Tradition and Radical Rhetoric in America.* New York: New York University Press 1997.

Dow, Bonnie J. *Prime-Time Feminism: Television, Media, Culture, and the Women's Movement Since 1970.* Philadelphia: University of Pennsylvania Press, 1996.

Fisher, Randall M. *Rhetoric and American Democracy: Black Protest Through Vietnam Dissent.* Lanham, MD: University Press of America, 1985.

Hammerback, John C., R. J. Jensen, and J. A. Gutierrez. *A War of Words: Protest in the1960s and 1970s.* Westport, CT: Greenwood, 1985.

Hammerback, John C. and Richard J. Jensen. *The Rhetorical Career of Cesar Chavez.* College Station: Texas A & M University Press, 1998.

Hampton, Wayne. *Guerrilla Minstrels: John Lennon, Joe Hill, Woody Guthrie, and Bob Dylan.* Knoxville: University of Tennessee Press, 1986.

Harre, Rom, Jens Brockmeier, and Peter Muhlhausler. *Greenspeak: A Study of Environmental Discourse.* Thousand Oaks, CA: Sage, 1998.

Hill, Roy L. *The Rhetoric of Radical Revolt.* Denver: Bell Press, 1964.

Hribar, Paul A. *The Social Fasts of Cesar Chavez: Critical Study of Nonverbal Communication, Nonviolence, and Public Opinion.* Los Angeles: University of Southern California, 1978.

Jorgensen-Earp, Cheryl R. *"The Transfiguring Sword": The Just War of the Women's Social and Political Union.* Tuscaloosa: University of Alabama Press, 1997.

Lampe, Gregory P. *Frederick Douglass: Freedom's Voice, 1818–1845.* East Lansing: Michigan State University Press, 1998.

Leeman, Richard W. *The Rhetoric of Terrorism and Counterterrorism.* Westport, CT: Greenwood Press, 1991.

————. (ed) *African-American Orators: A Bio-Critical Sourcebook.* Westport, CT: Greenwood, 1996.

Linkugel, Wil A. and Martha Solomon. *Anna Howard Shaw: Suffrage Orator and Social Reformer.* Westport, CT: Greenwood Press, 1991.

Lomas, Charles W. *The Agitator in American Society.* Englewood Cliffs, NJ: Prentice-Hall, 1968.

Pearce, W. Barnett and Stephen W. Littlejohn. *Moral Conflict: When Social Worlds Collide.* Thousand Oaks, CA: Sage, 1997.

Phillips, Donald E. *Student Protest, 1960–1970: An Analysis the Speeches and Issue.* Lanham, MD: University Press of America, 1985.

Scott, Robert L. and Wayne E. Brockriede. *The Rhetoric of Black Power.* New York: Harper and Row, 1969.

Smith, Arthur L. *Rhetoric of Black Revolution.* Boston: Allyn & Bacon, 1969.

Smith, Arthur L. and Stephen Robb. *The Voice of Black Rhetoric.* Boston: Allyn & Bacon, 1971.

Smith, Ralph R. and Russell R. Windes. *Progay/Antigay: The Rhetorical War over Sexuality.* Thousand Oaks, CA: Sage Publications, 2000.

Windt, Theodore Otto. *Presidents and Protestors: Political Rhetoric in the 1960s.* Tuscaloosa: University of Alabama Press, 1990.

Index